AND BOOK TRAINING PACKAGE AVAILABLE

ExamSim

Experience realistic, simulated exams on your own computer with interactive ExamSim software. This computer-based test engine offers knowledge and scenario-based questions like those found on the real exam and review tools that can show you where you went wrong on the questions you missed and why. ExamSim allows you to mark unanswered questions for further review and provides a score report that shows your overall performance on the exam.

Knowledge-based questions present challenging material in a multiple-choice format. Answer treatments not only explain why the correct options are right, they also tell you why the incorrect answers are wrong.

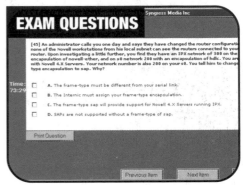

Additional CD-ROM Features

Complete hyperlinked **e-book** for easy information access and self-paced study.

DriveTime audio tracks offer concise review of key exam topics for in the car or on the go!

Applied **scenario-based questions** challenge your ability to analyze and address complex, real-world case studies.

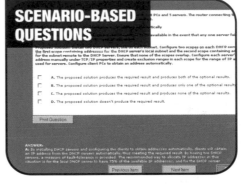

The **Score Report** provides an overall assessment of your exam performance as well as performance history.

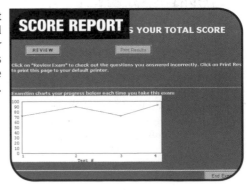

System Requirements:

A PC running Microsoft® Internet Explorer version 5 or higher

RHCE™ Red Hat® Certified Engineer Linux Study Guide

Second Edition

Syngress Media, Inc.

Osborne McGraw-Hill

New York   Chicago   San Francisco   Lisbon   London   Madrid
Mexico City   Milan   New Delhi   San Juan   Seoul   Singapore   Sydney   Toronto

Osborne/**McGraw-Hill**
2600 Tenth Street
Berkeley, California 94710
U.S.A.

To arrange bulk purchase discounts for sales promotions, premiums, or fund-raisers, please contact Osborne/**McGraw-Hill** at the above address. For information on translations or book distributors outside the U.S.A., please see the International Contact Information page immediately following the index of this book.

RHCE™ Red Hat® Certified Engineer Linux Study Guide, Second Edition

1234567890 AGM AGM 019876543210

Book p/n 0-07-213147-0 and CD p/n 0-07-213148-9
parts of ISBN 0-07-213149-7

Publisher Brandon A. Nordin	**Acquisitions Coordinator** Jessica Wilson	**Production and Editorial** Apollo Publishing Services
Vice President & **Associate Publisher** Scott Rogers	**Project Manager** Jenn Tust	**Series Design** Roberta Steele
Editorial Director Gareth Hancock	**VP, Worldwide Business** **Development** **Global Knowledge** Richard Kristof	**Cover Design** Greg Scott
Associate Acquisitions Editor Timothy Green	**Technical Editor** Paul Tibbitts	**Editorial Management** Syngress Media, Inc.

This book was published with Corel VENTURA™ Publisher.

From Global Knowledge

At Global Knowledge we strive to support the multiplicity of learning styles required by our students to achieve success as technical professionals. In this book, it is our intention to offer the reader a valuable tool for successful completion of the Red Hat Certified Engineer Certification Exam.

As the world's largest IT training company, Global Knowledge is uniquely positioned to offer these books. The expertise gained each year from providing instructor-led training to hundreds of thousands of students worldwide has been captured in book form to enhance your learning experience. We hope that the quality of these books demonstrates our commitment to your lifelong learning success. Whether you choose to learn through the written word, computer-based training, Web delivery, or instructor-led training, Global Knowledge is committed to providing you the very best in each of those categories. For those of you who know Global Knowledge, or those of you who have just found us for the first time, our goal is to be your lifelong competency partner.

Thank you for the opportunity to serve you. We look forward to serving your needs again in the future.

Warmest regards,

Duncan Anderson
President and Chief Executive Officer, Global Knowledge

ACKNOWLEDGMENTS

We would like to thank the following people:

- Richard Kristof of Global Knowledge for championing the series and providing us access to some great people and information.
- All the incredibly hard-working folks at Osborne/McGraw-Hill: Brandon Nordin, Scott Rogers, Timothy Green, Gareth Hancock, and Jessica Wilson.

The Global Knowledge Advantage

Global Knowledge has a global delivery system for its products and services. The company has 28 subsidiaries, and offers its programs through a total of 60+ locations. No other vendor can provide consistent services across a geographic area this large. Global Knowledge is the largest independent information technology education provider, offering programs on a variety of platforms. This enables our multi-platform and multi-national customers to obtain all of their programs from a single vendor. The company has developed the unique Competus™ Framework software tool and methodology which can quickly reconfigure courseware to the proficiency level of a student on an interactive basis. Combined with self-paced and on-line programs, this technology can reduce the time required for training by prescribing content in only the deficient skills areas. The company has fully automated every aspect of the education process, from registration and follow-up, to "just-in-time" production of courseware. Global Knowledge Network through its Enterprise Services Consultancy, can customize programs and products to suit the needs of an individual customer.

Global Knowledge Classroom Education Programs

The backbone of our delivery options is classroom-based education. Our modern, well-equipped facilities staffed with the finest instructors offer programs in a wide variety of information technology topics, many of which lead to professional certifications.

Custom Learning Solutions

This delivery option has been created for companies and governments that value customized learning solutions. For them, our consultancy-based approach of developing targeted education solutions is most effective at helping them meet specific objectives.

Self-Paced and Multimedia Products

This delivery option offers self-paced program titles in interactive CD-ROM, videotape and audio tape programs. In addition, we offer custom development of interactive multimedia courseware to customers and partners. Call us at 1-888-427-4228.

Electronic Delivery of Training

Our network-based training service delivers efficient competency-based, interactive training via the World Wide Web and organizational intranets. This leading-edge delivery option provides a custom learning path and "just-in-time" training for maximum convenience to students.

ARG

American Research Group (ARG), a wholly-owned subsidiary of Global Knowledge, one of the largest worldwide training partners of Cisco Systems, offers a wide range of internetworking, LAN/WAN, Bay Networks, FORE Systems, IBM, and UNIX courses. ARG offers hands on network training in both instructor-led classes and self-paced PC-based training.

Global Knowledge Courses Available

Network Fundamentals

- Understanding Computer Networks
- Telecommunications Fundamentals I
- Telecommunications Fundamentals II
- Understanding Networking Fundamentals
- Implementing Computer Telephony Integration
- Introduction to Voice Over IP
- Introduction to Wide Area Networking
- Cabling Voice and Data Networks
- Introduction to LAN/WAN protocols
- Virtual Private Networks
- ATM Essentials

Network Security & Management

- Troubleshooting TCP/IP Networks
- Network Management
- Network Troubleshooting
- IP Address Management
- Network Security Administration
- Web Security
- Implementing UNIX Security
- Managing Cisco Network Security
- Windows NT 4.0 Security

IT Professional Skills

- Project Management for IT Professionals
- Advanced Project Management for IT Professionals
- Survival Skills for the New IT Manager
- Making IT Teams Work

LAN/WAN Internetworking

- Frame Relay Internetworking
- Implementing T1/T3 Services
- Understanding Digital Subscriber Line (xDSL)
- Internetworking with Routers and Switches
- Advanced Routing and Switching
- Multi-Layer Switching and Wire-Speed Routing
- Internetworking with TCP/IP
- ATM Internetworking
- OSPF Design and Configuration
- Border Gateway Protocol (BGP) Configuration

Authorized Vendor Training

Cisco Systems

- Introduction to Cisco Router Configuration
- Advanced Cisco Router Configuration
- Installation and Maintenance of Cisco Routers
- Cisco Internetwork Troubleshooting
- Cisco Internetwork Design
- Cisco Routers and LAN Switches
- Catalyst 5000 Series Configuration
- Cisco LAN Switch Configuration
- Managing Cisco Switched Internetworks
- Configuring, Monitoring, and Troubleshooting Dial-Up Services
- Cisco AS5200 Installation and Configuration
- Cisco Campus ATM Solutions

Bay Networks

- Bay Networks Accelerated Router Configuration
- Bay Networks Advanced IP Routing
- Bay Networks Hub Connectivity
- Bay Networks Accelar 1xxx Installation and Basic Configuration
- Bay Networks Centillion Switching

FORE Systems

- FORE ATM Enterprise Core Products
- FORE ATM Enterprise Edge Products
- FORE ATM Theory
- FORE LAN Certification

Operating Systems & Programming

Microsoft

- Introduction to Windows NT
- Microsoft Networking Essentials
- Windows NT 4.0 Workstation
- Windows NT 4.0 Server
- Advanced Windows NT 4.0 Server
- Windows NT Networking with TCP/IP
- Introduction to Microsoft Web Tools
- Windows NT Troubleshooting
- Windows Registry Configuration

UNIX

- UNIX Level I
- UNIX Level II
- Essentials of UNIX and NT Integration

Programming

- Introduction to JavaScript
- Java Programming
- PERL Programming
- Advanced PERL with CGI for the Web

Web Site Management & Development

- Building a Web Site
- Web Site Management and Performance
- Web Development Fundamentals

High Speed Networking

- Essentials of Wide Area Networking
- Integrating ISDN
- Fiber Optic Network Design
- Fiber Optic Network Installation
- Migrating to High Performance Ethernet

DIGITAL UNIX

- UNIX Utilities and Commands
- DIGITAL UNIX v4.0 System Administration
- DIGITAL UNIX v4.0 (TCP/IP) Network Management
- AdvFS, LSM, and RAID Configuration and Management
- DIGITAL UNIX TruCluster Software Configuration and Management
- UNIX Shell Programming Featuring Kornshell
- DIGITAL UNIX v4.0 Security Management
- DIGITAL UNIX v4.0 Performance Management
- DIGITAL UNIX v4.0 Intervals Overview

DIGITAL OpenVMS

- OpenVMS Skills for Users
- OpenVMS System and Network Node Management I
- OpenVMS System and Network Node Management II
- OpenVMS System and Network Node Management III
- OpenVMS System and Network Node Operations
- OpenVMS for Programmers
- OpenVMS System Troubleshooting for Systems Managers
- Configuring and Managing Complex VMScluster Systems
- Utilizing OpenVMS Features from C
- OpenVMS Performance Management
- Managing DEC TCP/IP Services for OpenVMS
- Programming in C

Hardware Courses

- AlphaServer 1000/1000A Installation, Configuration and Maintenance
- AlphaServer 2100 Server Maintenance
- AlphaServer 4100, Troubleshooting Techniques and Problem Solving

About Syngress Media

Syngress Media creates books and software for Information Technology professionals seeking skill enhancement and career advancement. Its products are designed to comply with vendor and industry standard course curricula, and are optimized for certification exam preparation. You can contact Syngress via the Web at www.syngress.com.

Authors

David Egan (P. Eng., BASc Engineering U of T 78, MCT, RHCE, RHCX) has lived and worked in several countries and has worked with computers since the early days of the Apple and IBM type PC's. David's first "hobby-turned-job" was as a Z80 Assembler and C Language programmer for five years. David transitioned into a VMS/UNIX/NT/PC Systems Integration Consultant and Technology Instructor—An Edutainer—during the past 15 years. David is still consulting and writing the occasional book, but mostly contracting as a Course Director and Course Writer of UNIX-, NT- and Linux-based courses for Global Knowledge Inc. of Cary, NC (www.globalknowledge.com).

When not on the road—preaching the virtues of Linux and NT from his stage or showing the plan—he resides near Vancouver, B.C. with his lovely wife Deborah, daughter Vanessa, and son Callen.

Larry Karnis (RHCE, HP Certified IT Professional, SCO/Caldera Master Advanced Certified Engineer in UNIXWare 2, UNIXWare 7 and OpenServer 5, Learning Tree UNIX Programming and Systems Professional) is a Senior Consultant for Application Enhancements, a UNIX, Linux, and Internet consulting firm located in Toronto. Larry has over 20 years of UNIX experience, starting with UNIX Version 2.6.

Larry holds a bachelor's degree in Computer Science and Mathematics as well as 8 other professional and technical certifications. An avid Linux enthusiast since 1994, he routinely deploys and manages Linux based desktop, server, firewall, and routing solutions.

Contributors

Henry Maine (RHCE, RHCX, MCSE, MCT, B.S. in Computer Science) is a principal consultant for Maine Consulting Inc. In addition to providing consulting services for a number of corporate clients in the Charlotte, North Carolina region, he also travels the country offering Linux training as well as training in other subjects. Henry has a B.S. degree in Computer Science from Tennessee Technological University and over 10 years of systems administration and network management experience with various flavors of UNIX as well as OpenVMS and Windows NT. He has been an advocate of Linux for the past several years.

Kirk Rafferty is the Director of Operations at Fairplay Communications, a small ISP he started in 1999. He has been a Unix Systems Administrator for 11 years and a rabid Linux fan since 1993. Kirk lives and works in Denver, CO and enjoys spending time with his wife and three children, gaming, paintball, and "recreational hacking." He was a (minor) contributor to O'Reilly and Associates "Stopping Spam" book.

Chris Rogers has been configuring Linux servers since 1994. To give an idea how long that is in terms of the computing industry, the Web browser was Mosaic, Netscape 0.9 had just hit the FTP sites, and the Slackware distribution without X-windows could still fit on only 3 3.5" diskettes. Chris now owns an ISP catering to the Web needs of small businesses that runs exclusively on Red Hat Linux. He also is the Webmaster for a Fortune 500 financial company. Many thanks must go out to the Washington DC and Northern Virginia Linux Users' Groups (www.tux.org).

Craig Smith (Novell Administrator, Networking Essentials, NT Workstation, NT Server, NT Enterprise Server) currently works for Cincinnati State College as Network Analyst. He is also an outside consultant specializing in Linux server installations and custom programming. Craig started using Linux in 1994 and has since then used many different distributions of Linux. He installs and configures around 75 Red Hat systems a year. He has written and released several OpenSource applications for the Linux community. Currently, Craig possesses the SAIR GNU Linux certifications for installation, configurations, and administration of Linux systems.

Christopher Wedman works full time as a LAN Administrator for the University of Alberta and also does some freelance computer and network consulting. He is an experienced Web administrator and is well versed in developing customized scripts for Web sites. He has been using Linux since 1995 and advocates the use of Linux for custom business solutions.

Technical Editor

Paul Tibbitts has worked with Unix for 20 years as a System Administrator, Programmer, and Instructor. He has delivered over 300 classes covering basic and advanced user skills, system administration, and C programming. Paul holds B.S. degrees in Computer Science and Business from the State University of New York and is an HP Certified IT Professional.

Series Editor

David Egan (P. Eng., BASc Engineering U of T 78, MCT, RHCE, RHCX) has lived and worked in several countries and has worked with computers since the early days of the Apple and IBM type PC's. David's first "hobby-turned-job" was as a Z80 Assembler and C Language programmer for five years. David transitioned into a VMS/UNIX/NT/PC Systems Integration Consultant and Technology Instructor—"An Edutainer"—during the past 15 years. David is still consulting and writing the occasional book, but mostly contracting as a Course Director and Course Writer of UNIX-, NT-, and Linux-based courses for Global Knowledge Inc., of Cary, NC (www.globalknowledge.com).

When not on the road—preaching the virtues of Linux and NT from his stage or showing the plan—he resides near Vancouver, B.C. with his lovely wife Deborah, daughter Vanessa, and son Callen.

CONTENTS

10 Systems Administration and Security 603

This book's primary objective is to help you prepare for and pass the required Red Hat Certified Engineer written exam so you can begin to reap the career benefits of certification. We believe that the only way to do this is to help you increase your knowledge and build your skills. After completing this book, you should feel confident that you have thoroughly reviewed all of the objectives that Red Hat has established for the exam.

In This Book

This book is organized around the actual structure of the Red Hat written exam. Red Hat has let us know all the topics we need to cover for the exam. We've followed their list carefully, so you can be assured you're not missing anything.

In Every Chapter

- Each chapter begins with the **Certification Objectives**—what you need to know in order to pass the section on the exam dealing with the chapter topic. The Certification Objective headings identify the objectives within the chapter, so you'll always know an objective when you see it!

- **Certification Exercises** are interspersed throughout the chapters. These are step-by-step exercises. They help you master skills that are likely to be an area of focus on the exam. Don't just read through the exercises; they are hands-on procedures that you should be comfortable completing. Learning by doing is an effective way to increase your competency with the language and concepts presented.

- **Exam Watch Notes** call attention to information about, and potential pitfalls in, the exam. These helpful hints are written by authors who have taken the exams and received their certification; who better to tell you what to worry about? They know what you're about to go through!

- **S & S** sections lay out specific scenario questions and solutions in a quick and easy-to-read format.

SCENARIO & SOLUTION

What causes GPFs?	GPFs occur when an application tries to perform an activity that would compromise the data or integrity of another application, such as trying to take over its memory space
How do Illegal Operations affect the system?	They are typically limited to a single application. However, they may cause the gradual degradation of the system after the offending program has been closed.
What should I do if an application keeps causing errors, even after I have reinstalled it?	There may be a problem (bug) in the application itself. Check with the manufacturer for known errors and patches.

- The **Certification Summary** is a succinct review of the chapter and a re-statement of salient points regarding the exam.

- The **Two-Minute Drill** at the end of every chapter is a checklist of the main points of the chapter. It can be used for last-minute review.

- The **Self Test** offers questions similar to those found on the certification exam. The answers to these questions, as well as explanations of the answers, can be found in Appendix A. By taking the Self Test after completing each chapter, you'll reinforce what you've learned from that chapter, while becoming familiar with the structure of the exam questions.

Some Pointers

Once you've finished reading this book, set aside some time to do a thorough review. You might want to return to the book several times and make use of all the methods it offers for reviewing the material:

1. *Re-read all the Two-Minute Drills*, or have someone quiz you. You also can use the drills as a way to do a quick cram before the exam.

2. *Re-take the Self Tests.* Taking the tests right after you've read the chapter is a good idea, because it helps reinforce what you've just learned. However, it's an even better idea to go back later and do all the questions in the book in one sitting. Pretend you're taking the exam. (For this reason, you should

mark your answers on a separate piece of paper when you go through the questions the first time.)

4. *Complete the exercises.* Did you do the exercises when you read through each chapter? If not, do them! These exercises are designed to cover exam topics, and there's no better way to get to know this material than by practicing.

6. *Check out the Web site.* Global Knowledge invites you to become an active member of the Access Global Web site. This site is an online mall and an information repository that you'll find invaluable. You can access many types of products to assist you in your preparation for the exams, and you'll be able to participate in forums, on-line discussions, and threaded discussions. No other book brings you unlimited access to such a resource. You'll find more information about this site in Appendix B.

Red Hat Certified Engineer Certification

Although you've obviously picked up this book to study for a specific exam, we'd like to spend some time covering what you need in order to attain Red Hat Certified Engineer certification status. Because this information can be found on the Red Hat Web site, www.redhat.com, we've repeated only some of the more important information in the Introduction of this book, "How to Take the Red Hat Certification Exam." Read ahead to the introduction.

The CD-ROM Resource

This book comes with a CD-ROM that includes test preparation software and provides you with another method for studying. You will find more information on the testing software in Appendix A.

Why So Much Preparation for the Red Hat Linux Certification Examination

by David W. Egan, P. Eng, MCT, RHCE, RHCX

This article covers the reasons for pursuing industry-recognized certification, the importance of your RHCE certification, and prepares you for taking the actual examination. It gives you a few pointers on how to prepare, what to expect, and what to do on exam day.

Leaping Ahead of the Competition!

Congratulations on your pursuit of Red Hat Linux certification! Industrial certification has become a de facto standard in almost all networking and operating systems. The list of highly coveted certifications includes Cisco, Microsoft, Novell, SCO, and many more that are industry standard, industry and peer accepted, in demand, and an established mark of knowledge.

With the explosion in the Internet and intranet requirements of the last few years, and now the emergence of the "other" PC-based operating system called Linux, there is a huge need for skilled professionals with a proven "test" of knowledge and skill. This is what the Red Hat Certified Engineer examination provides.

This exam is not just a series of written exams. There are three parts to the exam:

- **Part 1** A 2.5-hour troubleshooting section; worth one third of the score.
- **Part 2** A 1-hour written part; worth one third of the final score.
- **Part 3** A 2.5-hour hands-on covering installation and configuration.

Each section requires a minimum score of 75 percent, with an overall average of 80 percent or more for all three parts to pass the examination.

Why a Grueling Day Examination?

The main reason for the certification exam is to provide a proven measurement of knowledge and competence. With the highly competitive nature of the computer industry today and the rapid evolution of the technologies, there is still a need for skilled professionals who are thoroughly grounded in the basics.

The basics for any operating system are installation, setup, management, and troubleshooting of the running or failed system. Although operating systems all provide the same generic services, each has peculiarities of how to troubleshoot and set up. There will always be a need for skilled networking and administrative people. The demand has been growing continuously as the computer revolution of the 1990s has exceeded all predictions. The boom has just begun in many experts' eyes. This means there are not enough people with "certified" skills available. This is where the Red Hat Certification is needed and accepted, the requirements provide proof of skill and knowledge.

Many networking and operating system companies started certification early in their product development life, such as Cisco, Novell, Microsoft, Sun, and SCO, to name a few. The reason was simple; in general, they provided a measured level of knowledge and skill. The exact levels varied between certifications, but the industry understood and accepted them as validation. The rest was left to the individual. The certifications progressed with the current developments and forced the students to prove they could keep up with technology.

The emergence of Linux as another "major" force in the operating systems wars of the late 1990s has provided a new skill shortage. The demand for Linux has skyrocketed as of late because it provides a rock-solid foundation with a plethora of industry-standard tools. Although Linux historically was an "erector set" design with no corporate support, Red Hat has changed that by providing support and customer service, making Red Hat Linux a viable alternative operating system to host networking services.

The certification test is a measurement of achievement in both skills and knowledge. But like any test, there must be a high level of knowledge tested. The failure rate has been documented at about 40 percent, and this may be low; first-time test takers may see 50 to 60 percent failure rates. There are quite a few third-party exam preparation books or courses currently available for RHCE because it is becoming an industry accepted standard in just the few short years it has been around (since 1999). It has been modeled after the Cisco exams, requiring the student to personally solve problems, install, administer, and set up the operating system and many of the standard component packages.

This exam is very Red Hat Linux specific. Knowledge of System V or BSD-based UNIX is certainly helpful ,as well as experience with file, print and network services like Apache, Samba, NFS, DNS, IPChains and DHCP, especially under Red Hat specifically. Experience with previous versions of Red Hat is always helpful. Real-life practice in setting up any of these previous versions, or clone versions of Red Hat Linux, is most important, next is memorizing the numbers and details. This information can be very helpful when you need to determine which areas of the exam will be most challenging for you as you study for the subsequent test.

How Should You Prepare for This Certification Exam?

Essentially, you need to work with the product extensively, daily if you can, and by doing so, you want to make all the basic concepts of operation and the tools of administration as second nature as possible, no manual needed. The only way to do get that familiar with Red Hat Linux is with LOTS and LOTS of experience installing, configuring and fixing. The only way to get experience is to do it yourself, do every example in this book, answer every question, no matter how mundane, then do them again and again, such that you can answer the exercises and questions without having to look anything up! Then you are ready, the exam is closed book, it is just you and the computer.

There is a LOT of material to cover in this book. Take one small section at a time and become familiar with it. Obviously, installation is a key first step. After that, start with the basics of administration and work up to the tough stuff, networking and security. Most important is to do it again and again. Typically, to learn to ride a bicycle takes more than a one attempt on more than one day, followed by many days of practice. This will be no different. Start practicing soon.

Why One Linux Vendor Certification?

Over the years, vendors of other operating systems and network hardware operating systems have created their own certification programs because of industry demand for a proven knowledge base. When the marketplace needs skilled professionals for any product that is the leading or cutting edge, certification is an easy way to identify them. Vendor certification benefits both the skilled professionals and the purchasers; it shows the products are in demand and the people skilled in their products are in demand. Employers benefit because it helps them identify specifically qualified individuals.

Universities and colleges are changing their focus to provide more specifically skilled graduates for the growing computer-related industries. The corporation itself provides a more direct route for those who are not in the university and college stream, and is targeted for those who are already in the position of needing the skill now, this week, not in a few years.

With the steadily changing technology industries forging ahead, only the vendors can provide not only immediate, definable standards of certification, but maintain the evolutionary pace of their products and services within these certification standards. While most certifications are very specific to one vendor, they provide a solid measurement of essential skills and knowledge that is very much tuned to their products.

Corporate Recognition

Corporate America and the rest of the world have come to appreciate and stand by these vendor certification programs for the value, measured achievement, and recognition they provide. Employers also recognize that certifications do not guarantee an absolute level of knowledge, experience, or performance; rather, they establish a meaningful baseline for the comparison of development and professional achievement levels. By seeking to hire vendor-certified employees, a company can assure itself that, not only has it found a person skilled in the specific operating system or networking system, but it has also hired a person who has demonstrated a measured level of skill with the specific products the employer uses.

Professional Recognition

Just as university degrees and diplomas indicate a measured level of achievement in a given field of study, certification provides a recognized measurement of skill and knowledge in a specific product such as Red Hat Linux. The pursuit of these recognition levels has always been seen by peers and employers as incrementally more valuable, now and in future endeavors.

In today's "skills needed now" marketplace, certification becomes a foot in the door and an indication that this professional understands that development of leading-edge skills will lead to career and personal advancement and satisfaction.

RHCE Sign-up

Red Hat provides convenient Web-based registration systems for the courses and test. To sign up for any of the Red Hat courses leading to certification and the RHCE exam, access http://www.redhat.com and register for the Red Hat Certification path. After the registration online, you will be e-mailed or telephoned to confirm that your request has been accepted.

RHCE Pretest

After registering, a pretest of questions requiring written answers and multiple choice is sent to each student to prequalify him or her for the course. If you have problems with any areas of this pretest, you should spend time studying them before going to the class to solidify the concept in your mind.

Red Hat Linux Certification Program

Red Hat offers one certification exam that provides RHCE, Red Hat Certified Engineer, status. There are three official Red Hat Linux courses that can be used to slowly (over a period of a few weeks to a few months) prepare a student for the exam. Each of these courses is either four to five days in length. The exam itself is a one-day, closed-book, individualized set of problems, questions, and an installation to perform in a time-limited environment.

The certification is dependent upon a candidate passing all three sections of the exam with at least 50 percent in any one and an overall average of 80 percent or greater. With the right amount of all-around experience and study materials, this exam can be passed without taking the associated classes.

RHCE Tip

There are three courses that cover the gambit of what is required to pass the Red Hat exam for those who may not have enough personal experience. There is also an accelerated four-day course that screams through all the material contained in the last two courses, the first course is assumed to be fully understood. The accelerated course, RH300 Rapid Track, starts on a Monday, continues until Thursday, and is immediately followed by the exam on Friday. For those individuals who are basically familiar with most but not all aspects of Red Hat Linux, then this is probably the best option currently. This is exam requires experience at installation and troubleshooting. Nothing prepares you better for this exam than having covered the material immediately before taking the exam itself ,without the distractions of life and work to slow you down.

Table 1 shows the available hands-on, instructor-led courses that are optional but desirable prerequisites to the Red Hat Certified Engineer examination.

Why 4 RHCE Oriented Courses?

For someone just starting out, there is an introductory course, RH033 that covers the basic command line and process management from the GUI interface. If you need to take this course because you know very little about UNIX or Linux, you are months away from being prepared to take the exam.

The second course is the RH133, Basic System Administration. All of this course must be second nature for you to be close to ready for the exam.

The third course in the series is RH253, geared to Networking and Security features of Red Hat Linux. This is where most students very close to being ready for the exam get the last bits of training they need on areas that they may not be that familiar with. After this course you are very close to ready if not ready. A little more practice with any new topics would be best.

If these first 3 courses are material that you are generally already familiar with, then the forth course might be all you need, RH300 Rapid Track. The Rapid Track races through the major topics that are not all that day to day in nature (configuration details that are usually done once and left to run) but are required for the exam.

The exam is typically available on the next day after the Rapid Track (Monday to Thursday is the course, Friday is the Exam).

| TABLE FM-1 | Red Hat Courses and Certification |

Course	Description
RH033	Introduction to Red Hat Linux (the fundamentals of the OS)
RH133	Red Hat Linux Systems Administration (basic network and user management)
RH253	Red Hat Linux Network and Security Administration
RH300	Rapid Track Certification (four days combining RH133 and RH253 plus some supplemental material not found in either of the RH133 or RH253)
RHCE	The one-day, three-part certification examination (Fridays and Mondays)

Each of these courses is a hands-on, intense, 4 or 5 day, week of learning. The first 3 are the slow ramp up to the RHCE Examination. It is not recommended that you take them back to back as you would most likely be overwhelmed. Practicing what you learned in each course for at least a week, preferably a month, will greatly improve your knowledge level and your readiness for the next course. Only for someone very familiar with Red Hat Linux would the Rapid Track be the right starting point. The Rapid Track course is very intense and very fast paced.

Exam Only

The training is just an option for anyone who may not have the breadth and depth of knowledge required to pass the RHCE Exam. But if you do already have all the experience and knowledge, you can challenge the exam without any training at any time. The choice is yours.

This book is meant to provide you with all the details you should need for the exam, all you have to add is the experience.

Computer Simulated Testing

In a past experience, a three-day written, oral, and physical candidate evaluation set were used to determine the one candidate out of 10 who would be accepted for a position at a prestigious international company. Many tests were one on one, some were one on many, a few were psychological, and all were timed. Very few of the tests were of the easy "day-to-day" stuff; most were related to the ability to handle situations and problems that might arise in various areas related to the job. The candidate needed to be "well suited" for the position, and all it entailed, within the company, as seen now and foreseen in the future by the company. Now that was an evaluation!

Measurement of anything always provides for variance. By measuring multiple levels of both skill and experience under pressure, like any good job would, the Red Hat Certification Exam is designed to cull out those with weaknesses in specific skill areas. Prepare until it becomes second nature, and then relax. Good Luck!

1

Planning

R ed Hat Linux is a modern, flexible, and mature operating system. Although it started life on the Intel platform, it has since been ported to many other platforms such as Amiga, DEC Alpha, Apple PowerPC, Sun workstations, and others. Linux boasts many other features:

- **Multitasking** Linux is a true preemptive multitasking operating system. All processes run independently of each other and leave processor management to the kernel.

- **Symmetrical multiprocessing** Linux currently scales up to 16 processors but only 8 on Intel-based systems.

- **Networking** Linux supports a multitude of networking protocols.

- **Interoperability** Linux can interoperate with Windows 9x/NT/NT 2000, Novell, Mac, and most other versions of UNIX.

- **Multiuser** Linux can handle multiple users simultaneously logged on to one machine.

- **Advanced memory management** Traditional UNIX systems used swapping to manage memory, where the entire memory structure of a program was written to disk when the system began running low on memory. Linux uses paging, a method that intelligently allocates memory when system memory is running low by prioritizing memory tasks. Linux currently supports up to 64GB of RAM.

- **POSIX support** POSIX defines a minimum interface for UNIX-type operating systems. Linux currently supports POSIX 1003.1. This ensures that POSIX-compliant UNIX programs will port easily to Linux.

- **Multiple file systems** Linux must be installed on Extended 2 Linux-formatted partitions, but if certain other OS file systems already exist on the same host, Linux will support several of these file system formats as well, including DOS/Windows, OS/2, and Novell. This is just another interoperability feature provided by Linux.

CERTIFICATION OBJECTIVE 1.01

Open Source and Free Software

All Linux distributions are based on the same idea: Take the Linux kernel and surround it with freely available software to create a usable operating system. Red Hat Linux 7.0 used Linux kernel 2.2, while version 7.1 uses kernel 2.4. Red Hat Software continuously evolves their distribution by using the most current, stable kernel, as well as the latest available software for each of its distributions.

History

Although Linux came into being in 1991, it can trace its lineage back much further. In 1969, a Bell Labs programmer named Ken Thompson invented the UNIX operating system. Around the same time, another programmer, Dennis Ritchie, was working on a new computer language called C. By 1974, the two had rewritten UNIX in the C language, and ported it to several different machines. It is this combination of UNIX and C that Linux owes much of its heritage to.

UNIX and C are at the heart of Linux and the Open Source movement. While languages such as Perl, Python, Java, and others make the headlines today, far more lines of open source code have been written than any other single language.

Though many of these programs have been ported to other operating systems, such as Windows NT, UNIX and UNIX-like operating systems have benefited from Open Source software the most.

Linux

In 1991, a student at Helsinki University in Finland posted this message to the Usenet group comp.os.minix:

```
From: torvalds@klaava.Helsinki.FI (Linus Benedict Torvalds)
Newsgroups: comp.os.minix
Subject: Gcc-1.40 and a posix-question
Message-ID: <1991Jul3.100050.9886@klaava.Helsinki.FI>
Date: 3 Jul 91 10:00:50 GMT
Hello netlanders,
Due to a project I'm working on (in minix), I'm interested in the posix
standard definition. Could somebody please point me to a (preferably)
```

```
machine-readable format of the latest posix rules? Ftp-sites would be
nice.
```

It was followed up a few months later with this post:

```
From: torvalds@klaava.Helsinki.FI (Linus Benedict Torvalds)
Newsgroups: comp.os.minix
Subject: What would you like to see most in minix?
Summary: small poll for my new operating system
Message-ID: <1991Aug25.205708.9541@klaava.Helsinki.FI>
Date: 25 Aug 91 20:57:08 GMT
Organization: University of Helsinki


Hello everybody out there using minix -
I'm doing a (free) operating system (just a hobby, won't be big and
professional like gnu) for 386(486) AT clones. This has been brewing
since april, and is starting to get ready. I'd like any feedback on
things people like/dislike in minix, as my OS resembles it somewhat
(same physical layout of the file-system (due to practical reasons)
among other things).
I've currently ported bash(1.08) and gcc(1.40), and things seem to work.
This implies that I'll get something practical within a few months, and
I'd like to know what features most people would want. Any suggestions
are welcome, but I won't promise I'll implement them :-)
Linus (torvalds@kruuna.helsinki.fi)
PS. Yes - it's free of any minix code, and it has a multi-threaded fs.
It is NOT portable (uses 386 task switching etc), and it probably never
will support anything other than AT-harddisks, as that's all I have :-(.
```

The student, of course, was Linus Torvalds. Linus had just purchased a (then) state-of-the-art 386 PC, and wanted, among other things, to learn how it worked. The MS-DOS operating system was too limiting, and immediately discounted. At the time, he had been using another UNIX-like operating system called Minix, a microkernel-based teaching operating system. Minix had many limitations, however, so Linus set about writing a new operating system that did not suffer the limitations of MS-DOS and Minix.

Linus was by no means the first person to come up with the idea of a free UNIX-like operating system. Several years earlier The Free Software Foundation, headed by Richard M. Stallman, announced a kernel called The HURD. Unfortunately, efforts on this new kernel faltered, and it wasn't until 1996 that a stable version of The HURD was available. William and Lynne Jolitz in 1991 were also busy porting Berkeley UNIX, BSD, to the Intel platform.

But Linux was quickly propelled to the front of the pack by the large army of programmers from all across the world, who all pitched in their expertise for the Linux kernel. Instead of the project becoming chaotic and unmanageable, Linux actually benefited from the large number of coders and testers, and nearly instant feedback every time a new kernel was released, which was often. At times, several versions of Linux were released in a single day. A few years after development had begun on Linux, it was a full-featured, stable operating system.

Today, the Linux kernel is developed the same as it was in the beginning. Programmers across the globe collaborate on discussion groups and e-mail lists to work on the Linux kernel. Most are not paid for their efforts, doing it instead from a sense of community that binds Linux developers.

CERTIFICATION OBJECTIVE 1.02

GPL and Open Source Licenses

The terms "Free" and "Open Source" software are commonly used to mean the same thing. While the differences are subtle, they are very important.

Free Software

Free software is the term typically used to refer to software that has been released under the GNU Public License, or GPL. The GPL (also called Copyleft) was designed with the philosophy that all software should be free. Not free as in zero price, but free as in open, as the Free Software Foundation's Richard Stallman puts it in his essay "The GNU Operating System and the Free Software Movement."

The term "Free software" is sometimes misunderstood—it has nothing to do with price. It is about freedom. To clear up some of the confusion, the following is the definition of Free software. A program is Free software for users if:

- *You have the freedom to run the program, for any purpose.*

- *You have the freedom to modify the program to suit your needs. (To make this freedom effective in practice, you must have access to the source code, since making changes in a program without having the source code is exceedingly difficult.)*

■ *You have the freedom to redistribute copies, either gratis or for a fee.*

■ *You have the freedom to distribute modified versions of the program, so the community can benefit from your improvements.*

Since "free" refers to freedom, not to price, there is no contradiction between selling copies and Free software. In fact, the freedom to sell copies is crucial: collections of Free software sold on CD-ROMs are important for the community, and selling them is an important way to raise funds for Free software development. Therefore, a program that people are not free to include on these collections is not Free software.

The idea of Free software is not new. In fact, back when mainframes ruled the data centers and universities, most software was free, and end users were free to modify it to suit their needs. In the same essay, Richard Stallman describes the situation at MIT in 1971:

"We did not call our software 'free software,' because that term did not yet exist, but that is what it was. Whenever people from another university or a company wanted to port and use a program, we gladly let them. If you saw someone using an unfamiliar and interesting program, you could always ask to see the source code, so that you could read it, change it, or cannibalize parts of it to make a new program."

In the 1980s, the trend reversed, and most new software was becoming proprietary. The idea that software should be shared soon turned into a criminal idea. Groups such as the "Software Publishers Association" sprang up, encouraging people to turn in colleagues and corporations who they suspected of violating software copyrights.

In 1984, Richard Stallman, began work on the GNU project. GNU stands for "GNUs Not UNIX," a self-recursive definition meant to imply that GNU software, unlike UNIX software, is open and free. Today, much of the software and utilities used in most Linux distributions, including Red Hat, are GNU utilities.

Here is the most recent version of the GNU Public License, of which most Red Hat Linux software falls under. It can be found at http://www.gnu.org:

GNU GENERAL PUBLIC LICENSE
Version 2, June 1991
Copyright (C) 1989, 1991 Free Software Foundation, Inc.
59 Temple Place - Suite 330, Boston, MA 02111-1307, USA

Everyone is permitted to copy and distribute verbatim copies of this license document, but changing it is not allowed:

PREAMBLE

The licenses for most software are designed to take away your freedom to share and change it. By contrast, the GNU General Public License is intended to guarantee your freedom to share and change free software—to make sure the software is free for all its users. This General Public License applies to most of the Free Software Foundation's software and to any other program whose authors commit to using it. (Some other Free Software Foundation software is covered by the GNU Library General Public License instead.) You can apply it to your programs, too.

When we speak of free software, we are referring to freedom, not price. Our General Public Licenses are designed to make sure that you have the freedom to distribute copies of free software (and charge for this service if you wish), that you receive source code or can get it if you want it, that you can change the software or use pieces of it in new free programs, and that you know you can do these things.

To protect your rights, we need to make restrictions that forbid anyone to deny you these rights or to ask you to surrender the rights. These restrictions translate to certain responsibilities for you if you distribute copies of the software, or if you modify it.

For example, if you distribute copies of such a program, whether gratis or for a fee, you must give the recipients all the rights that you have. You must make sure that they, too, receive or can get the source code. And you must show them these terms so they know their rights.

We protect your rights with two steps: (1) copyright the software, and (2) offer you this license which gives you legal permission to copy, distribute and/or modify the software.

Also, for each author's protection and ours, we want to make certain that everyone understands that there is no warranty for this free software. If the software is modified by someone else and passed on, we want its recipients to know that what they have is not the original, so that any problems introduced by others will not reflect on the original authors' reputations.

Finally, any free program is threatened constantly by software patents. We wish to avoid the danger that redistributors of a free program will individually obtain patent licenses, in effect making the program proprietary. To prevent this, we have made it clear that any patent must be licensed for everyone's free use or not licensed at all.

The precise terms and conditions for copying, distribution and modification follow:

TERMS AND CONDITIONS FOR COPYING, DISTRIBUTION AND MODIFICATION

0. This License applies to any program or other work which contains a notice placed by the copyright holder saying it may be distributed under the terms of this General Public License. The "Program" below refers to any such program or work, and a "work based on the Program" means either the Program or any derivative work under copyright law: that is to say, a work containing the Program or a portion of it, either verbatim or with modifications and/or translated into another language. (Hereinafter, translation is included without limitation in the term "modification.") Each licensee is addressed as "you."

    Activities other than copying, distribution, and modification are not covered by this License; they are outside its scope. The act of running the Program is not restricted, and the output from the Program is covered only if its contents constitute a work based on the Program (independent of having been made by running the Program). Whether that is true depends on what the Program does.

1. You may copy and distribute verbatim copies of the Program's source code as you receive it, in any medium, provided that you conspicuously and appropriately publish on each copy an appropriate copyright notice and disclaimer of warranty; keep intact all the notices that refer to this License and to the absence of any warranty; and give any other recipients of the Program a copy of this License along with the Program.

    You may charge a fee for the physical act of transferring a copy, and you may, at your option, offer warranty protection in exchange for a fee.

2. You may modify your copy or copies of the Program or any portion of it, thus forming a work based on the Program, and copy and distribute such modifications or work under the terms of Section 1 above, provided that you also meet all of these conditions:

    a) You must cause the modified files to carry prominent notices stating that you changed the files and the date of any change.

    b) You must cause any work that you distribute or publish, that in whole or in part contains or is derived from the Program or any part thereof, to be licensed as a whole at no charge to all third parties under the terms of this License.

c) If the modified program normally reads commands interactively when run, you must cause it, when started running for such interactive use in the most ordinary way, to print or display an announcement including an appropriate copyright notice and a notice that there is no warranty (or else, saying that you provide a warranty) and that users may redistribute the program under these conditions, and telling the user how to view a copy of this License. (Exception: if the Program itself is interactive but does not normally print such an announcement, your work based on the Program is not required to print an announcement.)

These requirements apply to the modified work as a whole. If identifiable sections of that work are not derived from the Program, and can be reasonably considered independent and separate works in themselves, then this License, and its terms, do not apply to those sections when you distribute them as separate works. But when you distribute the same sections as part of a whole which is a work based on the Program, the distribution of the whole must be on the terms of this License, whose permissions for other licensees extend to the entire whole, and thus to each and every part regardless of who wrote it.

Thus, it is not the intent of this section to claim rights or contest your rights to work written entirely by you; rather, the intent is to exercise the right to control the distribution of derivative or collective works based on the Program.

In addition, mere aggregation of another work not based on the Program with the Program (or with a work based on the Program) on a volume of a storage or distribution medium does not bring the other work under the scope of this License.

3. You may copy and distribute the Program (or a work based on it, under Section 2) in object code or executable form under the terms of Sections 1 and 2 above provided that you also do one of the following:

a) Accompany it with the complete corresponding machine-readable source code, which must be distributed under the terms of Sections 1 and 2 above on a medium customarily used for software interchange; or,

b) Accompany it with a written offer, valid for at least three years, to give any third party, for a charge no more than your cost of physically performing source distribution, a complete machine-readable copy of the corresponding source code, to be distributed under the terms of Sections 1 and 2 above on a medium customarily used for software interchange; or,

c) Accompany it with the information you received as to the offer to distribute corresponding source code. (This alternative is allowed only for noncommercial distribution and only if you received the program in object code or executable form with such an offer, in accord with Subsection b above.)

The source code for a work means the preferred form of the work for making modifications to it. For an executable work, complete source code means all the source code for all modules it contains, plus any associated interface definition files, plus the scripts used to control compilation and installation of the executable. However, as a special exception, the source code distributed need not include anything that is normally distributed (in either source or binary form) with the major components (compiler, kernel, and so on) of the operating system on which the executable runs, unless that component itself accompanies the executable.

If distribution of executable or object code is made by offering access to copy from a designated place, then offering equivalent access to copy the source code from the same place counts as distribution of the source code, even though third parties are not compelled to copy the source along with the object code.

4. You may not copy, modify, sublicense, or distribute the Program except as expressly provided under this License. Any attempt otherwise to copy, modify, sublicense or distribute the Program is void, and will automatically terminate your rights under this License. However, parties who have received copies, or rights, from you under this License will not have their licenses terminated so long as such parties remain in full compliance.

5. You are not required to accept this License, since you have not signed it. However, nothing else grants you permission to modify or distribute the Program or its derivative works. These actions are prohibited by law if you do not accept this License. Therefore, by modifying or distributing the Program (or any work based on the Program), you indicate your acceptance of this License to do so, and all its terms and conditions for copying, distributing or modifying the Program or works based on it.

6. Each time you redistribute the Program (or any work based on the Program), the recipient automatically receives a license from the original licensor to copy, distribute or modify the Program subject to these terms and conditions. You may not impose any further restrictions on the recipients' exercise of the rights granted herein. You are not responsible for enforcing compliance by third parties to this License.

7. If, as a consequence of a court judgment or allegation of patent infringement or for any other reason (not limited to patent issues), conditions are imposed on you (whether by court order, agreement or otherwise) that contradict the conditions of this License, they do not excuse you from the conditions of this License. If you cannot distribute so as to satisfy simultaneously your obligations under this License and any other pertinent obligations, then as a consequence you may not distribute the Program at all. For example, if a patent license would not permit royalty-free redistribution of the Program by all those who receive copies directly or indirectly through you, then the only way you could satisfy both it and this License would be to refrain entirely from distribution of the Program.

   If any portion of this section is held invalid or unenforceable under any particular circumstance, the balance of the section is intended to apply and the section as a whole is intended to apply in other circumstances.

   It is not the purpose of this section to induce you to infringe any patents or other property right claims or to contest validity of any such claims; this section has the sole purpose of protecting the integrity of the free software distribution system, which is implemented by public license practices. Many people have made generous contributions to the wide range of software distributed through that system in reliance on consistent application of that system; it is up to the author/donor to decide if he or she is willing to distribute software through any other system and a licensee cannot impose that choice.

   This section is intended to make thoroughly clear what is believed to be a consequence of the rest of this License.

8. If the distribution and/or use of the Program is restricted in certain countries either by patents or by copyrighted interfaces, the original copyright holder who places the Program under this License may add an explicit geographical distribution limitation excluding those countries, so that distribution is

permitted only in or among countries not thus excluded. In such case, this License incorporates the limitation as if written in the body of this License.

9. The Free Software Foundation may publish revised and/or new versions of the General Public License from time to time. Such new versions will be similar in spirit to the present version, but may differ in detail to address new problems or concerns.

   Each version is given a distinguishing version number. If the Program specifies a version number of this License which applies to it and "any later version," you have the option of following the terms and conditions either of that version or of any later version published by the Free Software Foundation. If the Program does not specify a version number of this License, you may choose any version ever published by the Free Software Foundation.

10. If you wish to incorporate parts of the Program into other free programs whose distribution conditions are different, write to the author to ask for permission. For software which is copyrighted by the Free Software Foundation, write to the Free Software Foundation; we sometimes make exceptions for this. Our decision will be guided by the two goals of preserving the free status of all derivatives of our free software and of promoting the sharing and reuse of software generally.

NO WARRANTY

11. BECAUSE THE PROGRAM IS LICENSED FREE OF CHARGE, THERE IS NO WARRANTY FOR THE PROGRAM, TO THE EXTENT PERMITTED BY APPLICABLE LAW. EXCEPT WHEN OTHERWISE STATED IN WRITING THE COPYRIGHT HOLDERS AND/OR OTHER PARTIES PROVIDE THE PROGRAM "AS IS" WITHOUT WARRANTY OF ANY KIND, EITHER EXPRESSED OR IMPLIED, INCLUDING, BUT NOT LIMITED TO, THE IMPLIED WARRANTIES OF MERCHANTABILITY AND FITNESS FOR A PARTICULAR PURPOSE. THE ENTIRE RISK AS TO THE QUALITY AND PERFORMANCE OF THE PROGRAM IS WITH YOU. SHOULD THE PROGRAM PROVE DEFECTIVE, YOU ASSUME THE COST OF ALL NECESSARY SERVICING, REPAIR OR CORRECTION.

12. IN NO EVENT UNLESS REQUIRED BY APPLICABLE LAW OR AGREED TO IN WRITING WILL ANY COPYRIGHT HOLDER, OR

ANY OTHER PARTY WHO MAY MODIFY AND/OR REDISTRIBUTE THE PROGRAM AS PERMITTED ABOVE, BE LIABLE TO YOU FOR DAMAGES, INCLUDING ANY GENERAL, SPECIAL, INCIDENTAL OR CONSEQUENTIAL DAMAGES ARISING OUT OF THE USE OR INABILITY TO USE THE PROGRAM (INCLUDING BUT NOT LIMITED TO LOSS OF DATA OR DATA BEING RENDERED INACCURATE OR LOSSES SUSTAINED BY YOU OR THIRD PARTIES OR A FAILURE OF THE PROGRAM TO OPERATE WITH ANY OTHER PROGRAMS), EVEN IF SUCH HOLDER OR OTHER PARTY HAS BEEN ADVISED OF THE POSSIBILITY OF SUCH DAMAGES.

END OF TERMS AND CONDITIONS

It is important to note that the Linux kernel, which is distributed under the GPL, contains the following preamble:

NOTE! This copyright does *not* cover user programs that use kernel services by normal system calls—this is merely considered normal use of the kernel, and does *not* fall under the heading of "derived work." Also note that the GPL below is copyrighted by the Free Software Foundation, but the instance of code that it refers to (the Linux kernel) is copyrighted by me and others who actually wrote it.

—Linus Torvalds

Open Source Software

Open Source software, like Free software, requires that software source code be provided and readable. What Open Source does not promote, however, are the philosophical reasons behind free software. Where the GPL makes freedom a central point, Open Source sidesteps the philosophy and sets only the guidelines for software to fit the Open Source definition. Richard M. Stallman in his essay, "Why Free Software Is Better than Open Source," states that:

The obvious meaning for "open source software" is "You can look at the source code." This is a much weaker criterion than "free software"; it includes free software, but also includes semi-free programs such as xv, and even some proprietary programs, including qt, under its former license.

That obvious meaning for "open source" is not the meaning that its advocates intend. (Their "official" definition is much closer to "free software.") The result is that people often misunderstand them. Of course, this can be addressed by publishing a precise definition for the term. The people using "open source software" have done this, just as we have done for "free software." However, this approach is only partially effective in either case. For free software, we have to teach people that we intend one meaning rather than another that fits the words equally well. For open source, we would have to teach them to use a meaning which does not really fit at all.

Here is the most recent version of "The Open Source Definition," which can be found at http://www.opensource.org:

Open source doesn't just mean access to the source code. The distribution terms of an open-source program must comply with the following criteria:

1. Free Redistribution
   The license may not restrict any party from selling or giving away the software as a component of an aggregate software distribution containing programs from several different sources. The license may not require a royalty or other fee for such sale.

2. Source Code
   The program must include source code, and must allow distribution in source code as well as compiled form. Where some form of a product is not distributed with source code, there must be a well-publicized means of downloading the source code, without charge, via the Internet. The source code must be the preferred form in which a programmer would modify the program. Deliberately obfuscated source code is not allowed. Intermediate forms such as the output of a preprocessor or translator are not allowed.

3. Derived Works
   The license must allow modifications and derived works, and must allow them to be distributed under the same terms as the license of the original software. (rationale)

4. Integrity of the Author's Source Code
   The license must not discriminate against any person or group of persons. (rationale)

5. No Discrimination Against Fields of Endeavor
   The license must not restrict anyone from making use of the program in a specific field of endeavor. For example, it may not restrict the program from being used in a business, or from being used for genetic research. (rationale)

6. Distribution of License
The rights attached to the program must apply to all to whom the program is redistributed without the need for execution of an additional license by those parties. (rationale)

7. License Must Not Be Specific to a Product
The rights attached to the program must not depend on the program's being part of a particular software distribution. If the program is extracted from that distribution and used or distributed within the terms of the program's license, all parties to whom the program is redistributed should have the same rights as those that are granted in conjunction with the original software distribution. (rationale)

8. License Must Not Contaminate Other Software
The license must not place restrictions on other software that is distributed along with the licensed software. For example, the license must not insist that all other programs distributed on the same medium must be open-source software. (rationale)

9. Example Licenses
The GNU GPL, BSD, X Consortium, and Artistic licenses are examples of licenses that we consider conformant to the Open Source Definition. So is the MPL.

Bruce Perens wrote the first draft of this document as "The Debian Free Software Guidelines," and refined it using the comments of the Debian developers in a month-long e-mail conference in June, 1997. He removed the Debian-specific references from the document to create the "Open Source Definition."

Services and Applications

If you think that Free and Open Source software is a new or niche idea, it may surprise you to learn that most of the Internet runs on Free or Open Source software. Most of your e-mail is passed across the Internet using Sendmail, a free program written by Eric Allman in 1979. A survey done by Netcraft in June 2001 showed that over 65 percent of Web sites on the Internet are using the Apache Web Server, or Apache derivatives. (The survey can be found at http://www.netcraft.com/survey/.) And every time you type a Web address into your browser, there's a good chance it resolves the location of that Web address against a server running BIND, a free implementation of the Domain Name System that runs the Internet. The free news server innd handles much of the Usenet traffic, and many people read that news using free newsreaders such as rn, tin, and mutt. One of the most popular (and powerful) editors, GNU/Emacs, is used to compose documents and source code, read e-mail, news, and even program in LISP.

In the development space, languages such as C, C++, Perl, Python, Tcl/Tk, Pascal, Cobol, Fortran, and many others are freely available, and, if you're curious as to how these compilers are built, the source code is available for every one of them.

CERTIFICATION OBJECTIVE 1.03

About Linux

You hear people talking about Linux all the time, but you also probably hear about the "Red Hat" Linux distribution, and names like SuSE, Caldera, Debian, Slackware, and others. Are they all Linux?

Recall that Linux is the operating system kernel. That is, Linux is the very heart of the operating system. However, like all operating systems, to be useful, Linux has to have utilities and programs to do the actual work. This is where distributions come in. All of the Linux distributions run the Linux kernel, but after that, the distributions vary from each other to some degree. For example, the Slackware distribution looks and feels much like Berkeley UNIX, whereas the SuSE distribution is much more System V'ish. Red Hat Linux tends to fall somewhere in between but is leaning toward System V more and more with each new release.

Current Support for Networking Services

Linux was built from the start to be a network operating system. This may seem obvious now, but consider that in 1991 nobody knew how important networking and the Internet would be to modern-day computing. This gives Linux a big edge in terms of network stability and integration.

Today, Linux supports the networking protocols contained in Table 1-1.

Flexibility of Open Source Software

Much ado has been made about Free and Open Source software, but what do you really get that you can't get from closed operating systems such as Microsoft Windows?

TABLE 1-1	Protocol	Description
Networking Protocols Supported by Linux	TCP/IP	This is the protocol used by the Internet and on most local networks.
	IP Version 6	This is the protocol that will eventually replace IP version 4 on the Internet.
	AppleTalk	The protocol used for Apple computers to communicate with each other.
	CCITT X.25 Packet Layer	The X.25 networking protocol.
	Acorn Econet/AUN	An older protocol, used by Acorn computers to access file and print servers.
	IPX	The Novell networking protocol, used to access Novell file and print servers.

- **Stability**   When a version of an open source program is released on the Internet, there is a large peer review of the source code. With so many people looking at the code, there's a much better chance somebody will see a bug, and even offer a correction. This type of peer review just isn't possible in the closed source world.

- **Modifications**   In a closed source environment, you're at the mercy of the vendor. If you want or need a feature, you can submit a request for features, and only hope the vendor will agree with you. If not, you're stuck. With open source, you have the source code, and you can add the features yourself, if need be, or you can hire a programmer to make the changes for you. Many times, you can post a message to the appropriate Usenet newsgroup saying "Gee, it sure would be nice if program Foo could do this." Sometimes somebody will have a patch written within a couple days that does just what you want.

- **Support**   There are literally thousands of open source advocates out there on newsgroups and e-mail lists who can answer your questions when you need help. Best of all, it's free. Contrast this with the big money you throw to the closed source vendors, who may or may not be able to help you. If you really feel the need to pay for support, there are several companies out there now providing 24/7 technical support for Linux.

■ **Freedom**   With proprietary software, the primary goal is to make money. That the software may be useful to you is only a secondary concern. Keep in mind, too, that software never truly belongs to you, but is instead licensed for your use. The software vendor has all the advantages; you have none of them. However, Free and Open Source software gives you the freedom to view, modify, and share the code with others.

R&D Processes and Practices

The traditional development process of software has always gone something like this: Software company decides to create a package. Specifications are drawn up, some prototyping is done, software designers write, rewrite, and refine it. It goes back and forth for review and bug testing. Finally, the decision is made to release the product; it gets stamped onto media, and shrink-wrapped. Only when the consumer unpacks the box does the software truly ever see the light of day, because throughout the entire lifecycle of the development process, the software was tested and developed only by the software company. Even in a beta testing program, the number of participants is nowhere near the masses of people who will finally use the software.

The Free and Open Source model differs significantly. Usually the process begins because a programmer has an "itch" that needs to be scratched. In other words, the programmer thinks it would be a fun project to, say, write a mail client, or perhaps she's been reading Usenet, hearing people lament how they wish X mail client had these features. In any case, the programmer whips out some code and posts it to the Internet, asking for participants, peer reviewers, or just comments. Perhaps a few people join in, and add features to this code. A new revision is posted for others to see. As people become more interested, the project takes on a life larger than perhaps the original author intended. A programmer in Colorado might be working on the user interface, while programmers in Spain and Iceland collaborate on some other area of code.

In May of 1997, Eric S. Raymond presented his paper, "The Cathedral and the Bazaar" at the 1997 Linux Kongress. You can find this essay at http://www.tuxedo.org/~esr/writings. Raymond likened traditional software companies to cathedral builders, skilled artisans who worked meticulously on their software projects within the hallowed walls of the giant software companies:

"I had been preaching the UNIX gospel of small tools, rapid prototyping, and evolutionary programming for years. But I also believed there was a certain critical complexity above which a more centralized, *a priori* approach was required. I believed that the most important software (operating systems and really large tools like Emacs) needed to be built like cathedrals, carefully crafted by individual wizards or small bands of mages working in splendid isolation, with no beta to be released before its time."

But Linux showed another type of development model, which Raymond calls "the Bazaar." This is an environment where anybody with a computer, a compiler, and the desire to write software, can join in. Raymond writes:

"Linus Torvalds' style of development—release early and often, delegate everything you can, be open to the point of promiscuity—came as a surprise. No quiet, reverent cathedral-building here—rather, the Linux community seemed to resemble a great babbling bazaar of differing agendas and approaches (aptly symbolized by the Linux archive sites, who'd take submissions from anyone) out of which a coherent and stable system could seemingly emerge only by a succession of miracles."

However, Linux has succeeded, and continues to do so using the same Bazaar-style development process it began with in 1991.

Future Development

The future of Linux is lined with uncertainty and excitement. Uncertainty because it's hard to predict just where the course of the Internet and technology will run. Exciting because Linux will be right there when it happens.

Even now, exciting things are happening in the Linux world. Kernel development continues at a brisk pace, and companies like Red Hat Software are showing that the world is taking Linux seriously. On the day of its Initial Public Offering, the price of Red Hat Software stock tripled. Entire companies make their livings on Free and Open Source software, such as Cygnus, SuSE, VA Research, and others.

Starting Out

Compared to previous versions of Linux, Red Hat Linux 7.x is pretty straightforward as far as operating system installs go. Still, you'll want to make sure you're prepared beforehand. Before installing Red Hat Linux 7.x make sure that:

- **You have documentation**   You'll want installation documentation and post-install documentation, so you'll know how to use your new system.

- **You have the correct hardware**   While Red Hat Linux supports more and more hardware with each release, you still need to check to make sure your components are supported.

- **You know your hardware's specifications**   You should know what interrupt your network card, for instance, operates on. If you're using SCSI peripherals, make sure you know all their SCSI IDs.

- **You know what installation method you will be using**   You should know what installation method you will be using: Upgrade, Server, Workstation, Laptop, or Custom.

- **You know how you will be laying your file systems out**

- **Optionally**   You should have the latest patches for the version of Red Hat you'll be installing.

Needs

What is the difference between a workstation and a server in the Linux world? Simply put, it is the selection of software packages to be installed. The workstation and laptop installation selects packages that are user-oriented, such as X and games, whereas the server installation preferentially installs network, file, and print services, but does not install X and most of the games. A custom installation lets you decide on everything.

Before you begin a Red Hat Linux installation, you need to know what the purpose of the machine will be. Will it be a development workstation? An FTP? A Web server? Or will it be a database server? Each of these examples requires a different configuration.

Workstation Installation

If you're new to Linux, or just need a basic workstation, Red Hat makes it easy to get started. During the installation, you are given four choices:

- Workstation
- Server
- Laptop
- Custom

Selecting "Workstation" (the "Laptop" install is much the same) will give you an easy and fast way (with some loss of flexibility in configuration) to get started. The Workstation install does the following:

- It removes any preexisting Linux and Linux swap partitions, but does not remove DOS partitions.
- It uses all free space on the primary drive.

The following partitions are created:

- A 64MB swap partition.
- On Intel systems, a 16MB partition (mounted as /boot) is created. The kernel and associated files reside here.
- On Alpha systems, a 2MB partition (mounted as /dos) is created, where the MILO boot loader will reside.
- The rest of the disk is mounted as /, where all other files are placed.
- If a DOS/Windows partition exists, Red Hat Linux will automatically configure your system to dual-boot.

At least 1.2 GB for just one X Desktop and 1.5GB, for both Gnome and KDE with games, of free disk space is required for a Workstation install. Remember that performing a Workstation install will automatically overwrite all of the existing Linux and Linux swap partitions on the disk.

Server Installation

The Server installation will give you a fast and easy way (with some loss of flexibility in configuration) to set up a Web, FTP, or other type of server class system. When presented with the three types of installs, select "Server." The Server install does the following:

- It removes all preexisting partitions (even DOS partitions).
- It uses all space on the primary drive.

The following partitions are created:

- A 256MB swap partition.
- On Intel systems, a 16MB partition (mounted as /boot) is created. The kernel and associated files reside here.
- On Alpha systems, a 2MB partition (mounted as /dos) is created, where the MILO boot loader will reside.
- A 256MB partition (mounted as /).
- A 512MB (or more) partition mounted as /usr.
- A 512MB (or more) partition mounted as /home.
- A 256MB partition mounted as /var.
- A hard disk of at least 1.9GB in size is required for a Server install.

on the
job

If you read the official Red Hat installation guide, it suggests you only need 650MB of disk for a minimal Server class install, less than for a workstation. If you add up the partitions actually created according to the docs, you get closer to the 1.9GB number. So, assuming the worst, you really need 1.9GB at the minimum.

Remember that performing a Server install will automatically overwrite all of the partitions on the disk, including DOS/Windows partitions.

on the
job

Note that a Server installation, unlike a Workstation installation, will remove all existing partitions on the primary hard drive, even DOS partitions.

Custom Installation

The Custom install gives you the most flexibility to choose how you want your system installed, but at some loss of ease and speed. You determine how the disk is laid out, what size each partition is, and which packages will be installed. The Custom install is recommended for veteran Linux users only.

CERTIFICATION OBJECTIVE 1.05

Hardware

Although Red Hat offers Linux for Intel, Sparc, and Alpha platforms, we will concentrate on the most common platform, Intel.

Intel and Clones

Installing on most Intel-based computers is pretty straightforward, but you'll save yourself a lot of time and frustration by knowing exactly what hardware you have. You should be familiar with the following information about your system:

- **Drives**   Check to see if you are using SCSI or IDE drives. You should know the manufacturer, model number, and capacity of the drive. If it's a SCSI drive, make sure you know its SCSI ID.

- **Hard drive controller**   You should know the manufacturer and model number of the drive controller. Oftentimes, this information is hard to obtain, so at the very least try to identify the chipset of the controller.

- **CD-ROM**   If you're using a SCSI or IDE CD-ROM, you probably won't have to worry about what type it is. However, if you are using a CD-ROM with a proprietary interface (common with older models), you should know the manufacturer, as well as the model number of the drive and controller. Also, for proprietary interfaces, you should note what IRQ it uses.

- **Mouse**   You should know what type of mouse interface you are using— PS/2, serial, or some other type.

- **Display adaptor**   If you will be running X, you will need the manufacturer, model number, and how much memory is on the adaptor.

- **Sound, video, and game adaptors**   If you want to set up sound on your system, you should know the manufacturer and model number of the sound card. You should also know what IRQ it uses, if any.

- **Network adaptors**   If you'll be networking your Linux system, you should know the manufacturer and model number of the network adaptor. You should also know what IRQ it uses, if any.

- **Monitor**   If you will be running X, you will need the manufacturer, model number, resolutions, and frequencies of the monitor.

Not all hardware will work with Linux. After you've collected information about your system, you should consult the Intel Hardware Compatibility List (HCL) in the next section to determine if your components are compatible with Red Hat Linux 7.*x.*

Intel Hardware Compatibility List

The current Hardware Compatibility List is available at http://hardware.redhat.com. Another source, for compatibility concerns, although somewhat dated, is on the Red Hat Linux CD-ROM. You can also check in /usr/doc/HOWTO/Hardware-HOWTO on an installed Red Hat Linux 6.x system (on the last CD-ROM of RH 7.x), or online at http://sunsite.unc.edu/pub/Linux/docs/HOWTO/Hardware-HOWTO.

```
sr d
r n 3 P/)fhi hof
Linux Hardware Compatibility HOWTO  —
Patrick Reijnen, <antispam.hardware_howto@antispam.reij-
nen.nl.com (remove both "antispam.")>
v99.3, 28 September 1999

This document lists most of the hardware supported by Linux and helps
you locate any necessary drivers.
```

```
Table of Contents


1. Introduction

1.1 Welcome
1.2 Copyright
```

1.3 System architectures

2. Computers/Motherboards/BIOS

2.1 Specific system/motherboard/BIOS
2.2 Unsupported

3. Laptops

3.1 Specific laptops
3.2 PCMCIA

4. CPU/FPU

5. Memory

6. Video cards

6.1 Diamond video cards
6.2 SVGALIB (graphics for console)
6.3 XFree86 3.3.2
6.3.1 Accelerated
6.3.2 Unaccelerated
6.3.3 Monochrome
6.3.4 Alpha, Beta drivers
6.4 S.u.S.E. X-Server
6.5 Commercial X servers
6.5.1 Xi Graphics, Inc
6.5.2 Metro-X 4.3.0

7. Controllers (hard drive)

7.1 Alpha, Beta drivers

8. Controllers (hard drive RAID)

9. Controllers (SCSI)

9.1 Supported
9.2 Alpha, Beta drivers
9.3 Unsupported

10. Controllers (I/O)

11. Controllers (multiport)

11.1 Non-intelligent cards
11.1.1 Supported
11.2 Intelligent cards

```
11.2.1 Supported
11.2.2 Alpha, Beta drivers

12. Network adapters

12.1 Supported
12.1.1 Ethernet
12.1.2 ISDN
12.1.3 Frame Relay
12.1.4 Wireless
12.1.5 X25
12.1.6 Pocket and portable adapters
12.1.7 Slotless
12.1.8 ARCnet
12.1.9 TokenRing Take a look at the token ring web site
12.1.10 FDDI
12.1.11 Amateur radio (AX.25)
12.1.12 PCMCIA cards
12.2 Alpha, Beta drivers
12.2.1 Ethernet
12.2.2 ISDN
12.2.3 ATM
12.2.4 Frame Relay
12.2.5 Wireless
12.3 Unsupported

13. Sound cards

13.1 Supported
13.2 Alpha, Beta drivers
13.3 Unsupported

14. Hard drives

14.1 Unsupported

15. Tape drives

15.1 Supported
15.2 Alpha, Beta drivers
15.3 Unsupported

16. CD-ROM drives

16.1 Supported
16.2 Alpha, Beta drivers
16.3 Notes

17. CD-Writers
```

---

1. Introduction

NOTE: USB is not yet supported by Linux.
(Actually, as of RedHat 7.x, USB is supported)

1.1. Welcome

Welcome to the Linux Hardware Compatibility HOWTO. This document lists
most of the hardware components (not computers with components built
in) supported by Linux, so reading through this document you can
choose the components for your own Linux computer. As the list of
components supported by Linux is growing rapidly, this document will

never be complete. So, when components are not mentioned in this HOWTO, the only reason will be that I don't know they are supported. I simply have not found support for the component and/or nobody has told me about support.

Subsections titled 'Alpha, Beta drivers' list hardware with alpha or beta drivers in varying degrees of usability. Note that some drivers only exist in alpha kernels, so if you see something listed as supported but it isn't in your version of the Linux kernel, upgrade.

Some devices are supported by binary-only modules; avoid these when you can. Binary-only modules are modules which are compiled for ONE kernel version. The source code for these modules has NOT been released. This may prevent you from upgrading or maintaining your system.
Linus Torvalds says "I allow binary-only modules, but I want people to know that they are *only* ever expected to work on the one version of the kernel that they were compiled for"
See <http://www.kt.opensrc.org/kt19990211_5.html#10> for information on source code availability of components.

The latest version of this document can be found on <http://users.bart.nl/~patrickr/hardware-howto/Hardware-HOWTO.html>, SunSite and all the usual mirror sites. Translations of this and other Linux HOWTO's can be found at <http://metalab.unc.edu/pub/Linux/docs/HOWTO/translations> and <ftp://metalab.unc.edu/pub/Linux/docs/HOWTO/translations>.

If you know of any Linux hardware (in)compatibilities not listed here, please let me know. Just send mail.

Still need some help selecting components after reading this document? Check the "Build Your Own PC" site at <http://www.verinet.com/pc/>.

Want to have a preconfigured Linux system? Have a look at <http://www.linuxresources.com/web/>.

1.2. Copyright

Copyright 1997, 1998, 1999 Patrick Reijnen

This HOWTO is free documentation; you can redistribute it and/or modify it under the terms of the GNU General Public License as published by the Free software Foundation; either version 2 of the license, or (at your option) any later version.

This document is distributed in the hope that it will be useful, but without any warranty; without even the implied warranty of

merchantability or fitness for a particular purpose. See the GNU
General Public License for more details. You can obtain a copy of
the GNU General Public License by writing to the Free Software
Foundation, Inc., 675 Mass Ave, Cambridge, MA 02139, USA.

If you use this or any other Linux HOWTO's in a commercial
distribution, it would be nice to send the authors a complimentary
copy of your product.

1.3. System architectures

This document only deals with Linux for Intel platforms. For other
Platforms, check the following:

o   ARM Linux
<http://www.arm.uk.linux.org/>

o   Linux/68k
<http://www.clark.net/pub/lawrencc/linux/index.html>

o   Linux/8086 (The Embeddable Linux Kernel Subset)
<http://www.linux.org.uk/ELKS-Home/index.html>

o   Linux/Alpha
<http://www.azstarnet.com/~axplinux/>

o   Linux/MIPS
<http://www.linux.sgi.com>

o   Linux/PowerPC
<http://www.linuxppc.org/>

o   Linux for Acorn
<http://www.ph.kcl.ac.uk/~amb/linux.html>

o   Linux for PowerMac
<http://ftp.sunet.se/pub/os/Linux/mklinux/mkarchive/info/index.html>

(The rest has been omitted for brevity)

What to Avoid

If you are going out specifically to purchase hardware for a Linux system, there are a
few things to keep in mind:

■   Avoid proprietary products, such as non-SCSI or non-IDE CD-ROM drives.

- Avoid hardware that says on the package, "Requires Windows."

- Winmodems are modems that handle processing on the system through proprietary interfaces. Because these interfaces are generally not published, Linux has little or no support for these devices.

- Avoid hardware not listed on the Hardware Compatibility List (HCL). Although some hardware not specifically mentioned on the HCL will work with Linux, you should research before you buy. Ask the manufacturer or others running Linux.

Reference Sources

One of the oft-cited reasons to use Linux is its incredible support base. If you're having problems, want to ask if a certain piece of hardware is supported, or just need Linux information, here are some resources.

- **The man pages**   Using the *man* command at a Linux prompt will give you help with Linux commands and libraries. For example, to get usage on the *ls* command, type **man ls** at a command prompt. For help using the *man* command, type **man man**.

- **Package documentation**   Many Red Hat Linux packages store their documentation in /usr/doc/*packagename.*

- **HOWTOs and FAQs**   These are located in /usr/doc/HOWTO and /usr/doc/FAQ, respectively.

- **The *info* command**   This will give hypertext information regarding many commands on your system.

- **The Linux Documentation Project** (LDP)   Located on the Web at http://www.linuxdoc.org.

- **The Red Hat Knowledge Base**   Located at http://www.redhat.com/knowledgebase.

- **Red Hat mailing lists**   Found at http://www.redhat.com/community/list_subscribe.html.

- **The Free Software Foundation**   Located at http://www.gnu.org.

- **The Open Source Community**   Located at http://www.opensource.org.

CERTIFICATION SUMMARY

This chapter outlined the differences and similarities between Open Source and Free software, which make up most Linux distributions. We covered the traits that make Linux a viable operating environment, such as preemptive multitasking and memory management. We also covered the history behind UNIX, and the community that has driven it. The two major licenses, the General Public License and the Open Source Definition, were discussed and compared.

Also covered were networking support and hardware compatibility. Finally, we outlined the different types of Red Hat Linux installations, as well as the advantages and disadvantages of each.

TWO-MINUTE DRILL

Here are some of the key points from the certification objective in Chapter 1.

Open Source and Free Software

❑ All Linux distributions are based on the same idea: Take the Linux kernel and surround it with freely available software to create a usable operating system.

❑ UNIX and C are at the heart of Linux and the Open Source movement.

❑ The Linux kernel is still developed today as it was in the beginning. Programmers across the globe collaborate on discussion groups and e-mail lists to work on the Linux kernel. Most are not paid for their efforts, but do it out of a sense of community that binds Linux developers.

❑ GPL and Open Source licenses' "Free software" is the term typically used to refer to software that has been released under the GNU Public License, or GPL. The GPL (also called Copyleft) was designed with the philosophy that all software should be free. Not free as in zero price, but free as in open.

❑ Since "free" refers to freedom, not price, there is no contradiction inherent in selling copies of Free software.

❑ The idea of Free software is not new. In fact, back when mainframes ruled data centers and universities, most software was free, and end users were free to modify it to suit their needs.

About Linux

❑ All of the Linux distributions run the Linux kernel. After that, the different distributions vary to some degree.

❑ From the start, Linux was built to be a network operating system

❑ The future of Linux is lined with uncertainty and excitement. Uncertainty because it's hard to predict just where the course of the Internet and technology will run. Excitement because Linux will be right there when it happens.

Starting Out

❑ Compared to previous versions of Linux, Red Hat Linux 7.*x* is pretty straightforward in regards to operating system installs.

❑ The Workstation and Laptop installations select packages that are user-oriented, such as X and games, whereas the server installation preferentially installs network, file, and print services and does not install X and most of the games.

❑ A custom installation lets you decide on everything you install.

Hardware

❑ Installing on most Intel-based computers is pretty straightforward, but you'll save yourself much time and frustration by knowing exactly what hardware you have.

❑ If you are using a CD-ROM with a proprietary interface (common with older models), you should know the manufacturer, and model number of the drive, and the controller. Also, for proprietary interfaces, you should know what IRQ it uses.

SELF TEST

The following questions will help you measure your understanding of the material presented in this chapter. Read all the choices carefully, as there may be more than one correct answer. Choose all correct answers for each question.

Hardware

1. Although originally intended to run on the Intel platform, Linux has been ported to which other platform?

   A. Sparc

   B. Alpha

   C. PowerPC

   D. All of the above

2. Currently, Linux scales up to how many processors?

   A. 2

   B. 8

   C. 16

   D. 32

3. The memory management system Linux uses is

   A. Swapping

   B. Paging

   C. Preemptive multitasking

   D. Byte-swapping

Open Source and Free Software

4. Although Linux is a direct descendent of UNIX, it was originally modeled around what operating system?

   A. MS-DOS

   B. Minix

   C. POSIX

   D. OSF/1

5. When using kernel components, such as drivers, the Red Hat version of Linux can use what type(s) of architecture?

   A. Static

   B. Microkernel

   C. Modular

   D. Monolithic

6. Linux was the first real free operating system, and spawned further free efforts such as the HURD kernel and BSD ports.

   A. True

   B. False

GPL and Open Source Licenses

7. The term "Free software" implies that

   A. The software is free of cost.

   B. The distributor cannot charge you for the software.

   C. The software is freely modifiable and distributable.

   D. Only the software's author can charge a fee for using it.

8. Most of the software and utilities in distributions such as Red Hat Linux are

   A. GNU utilities

   B. Red Hat RPMs

   C. Proprietary

   D. Linux kernel utilities

9. Most e-mail on the Internet passes through what Free/Open Source mail transport software?

   A. Microsoft Exchange

   B. Netscape

   C. Open Mail

   D. Sendmail

About Linux

10. Although there are many Linux distributions, the term "Linux" refers to

   A. Red Hat Linux

   B. The Linux kernel

   C. Linus Torvalds

   D. Free operating systems

11. The protocol used by the Internet is

   A. TCP/IP

   B. Ethernet

   C. IPX

   D. AppleTalk

12. Potential advantages of Free/Open Source software are

   A. Stability

   B. Support

   C. Freedom

   D. All of the above

Starting Out

13. A Workstation installation of Red Hat Linux gives you

   A. An easy and fast install with maximum flexibility in configuration

   B. A somewhat more complicated install with maximum flexibility in configuration

   C. An easy and fast install with minimum flexibility in configuration

   D. A somewhat more complicated install with minimum flexibility in configuration

14. DOS partitions are removed on what type(s) of Red Hat Linux installations? (Choose all that apply.)

   A. Workstation

   B. Server

   C. Workstation and Server

   D. None of the above

15. What type of install gives you the most flexibility in configuration?

   A. Workstation

   B. Server

   C. Custom

   D. Server and Custom

16. Approximately how much disk space is needed for a Red Hat Linux Workstation install that includes both Gnome and KDE desktop environments and X Games?

   A. 250MB

   B. 1500MB

   C. 900MB

   D. 1900MB

17. The kernel and associated files reside on which partition after a Workstation, Laptop, or Server type installation?

   A. /boot

   B. /etc

   C. /usr

   D. /var

18. In his paper, "The Cathedral and The Bazaar," Eric S. Raymond likened traditional software companies to

   A. Linux kernel developers

   B. A bazaar

   C. Cathedral builders

   D. UNIX developers

19. Which type(s) of hardware should you avoid using with Linux?

   A. SCSI drives

   B. Intel 486 systems

   C. IDE CD-ROMs

   D. Winmodems

20. When selecting disk drives for a Linux install, the following information should be documented:

A. Capacity

B. Drive type (SCSI or IDE)

C. Manufacturer

D. All of the above

SELF TEST ANSWERS

Hardware

1. ☑ **D.** All of the above. Linux has been ported to the Sparc, Alpha, and PowerPC platforms, as well as many others.

    ☒ **A**, **B**, and **C** are incomplete answers.

2. ☑ **C.** 16. Linux currently scales up to 16 processors (although for Intel, the maximum is now 8). There are plans for more processors, especially in the RISC environment where there are currently some 64 CPU systems (from Sun Microsystems, for example).

    ☒ **A**, **B**, and **D** are the incorrect number of processors.

3. ☑ **B.** Paging. Linux uses paging, a method that intelligently allocates memory when system memory is running low by prioritizing memory tasks.

    ☒ **A** is incorrect because swapping is used by NT and VMS. Swapping moves entire working sets of memory for processes that are not very busy out to disk and back when needed. **C** is incorrect because preemptive multitasking is how the system, with only one CPU, can appear to run many tasks simultaneously. Essentially, a schedule manager provides a restricted length time slice to each process and interrupts if that process is not finished. **D** is incorrect because byte swapping occurs when data is transferred between little endian CPU architectures (Intel, Motorola, Cyrix, AMD) and big endian CPU architectures (most RISC chips). The little or big endian refers to the order of the bytes in words and long words. Either the low order byte is first (little endian), or it is last (big endian).

Open Source and Free Software

4. ☑ **B.** Minix. Linux was originally modeled after the Minix operating system.

    ☒ **A** is incorrect because Linux was to be used instead of MS-DOS, which lacked networking, extended file system support, multitasking, and 32-bit memory management. DOS only had 20-bit memory management which was very limiting. **C** is incorrect because POSIX is the Portable Operating System Information exchange specification of the U.S. Government and is related to their decision in the mid 1980s to standardize on one OS. Unfortunately, POSIX was restricted to the AT&T and Sun OS versions of UNIX initially. The rest of the UNIX suppliers (DEC, HP, SGI, SCO, and so on) banded together to make their own Open Software Foundation version, OSF/1, that was to meet all POSIX requirements. **D** is incorrect because DEC was the only one to ever offer an OSF/1 version.

5. ☑   **C.** Modular. The Linux kernel uses a modular kernel architecture.
    ☒   **A** and **D** are incorrect because a static, or monolithic, architecture is one where all possible drivers are compiled into the kernel, whether needed all the time or not. **B** is incorrect because a microkernel is just another term given to some OS version kernels to make them sound modular, whether they are or not. A great marketing ploy.

6. ☑   **B.** False. The HURD kernel was being developed at the same time as Linux, and BSD was being actively ported to the Intel architecture.

GPL and Open Source Licenses

7. ☑   **C.** The software is freely modifiable and distributable.
    ☒   **A, B,** and **D** are incorrect because free software isn't about cost, but about freedom. It might be free, but you can be charged for it if there is value added, like documentation and additional tools (as Red Hat, Debian, TurboLinux, and Corel Linux do if you buy their product at any store). Unless specifically stated in the software distribution, the author is not the only one who can charge a fee if their software is bundled with other software as "value added."

8. ☑   **A.** GNU utilities make up the majority of software included in most Linux distributions today.
    ☒   **B, C,** and **D** are incorrect because most of these packages are kept in an easy to install RPM format. While GNU is a company, it releases the source code for all its programs and, as such, is not considered proprietary. Linux kernel utilities are a very small contingent, and are used for development purposes. Related to Linux, they are also freely available.

9. ☑   **D.** Most e-mail on the Internet passes through Sendmail, a free mail transport agent written by Eric Allman.
    ☒   **A** and **B** are incorrect because Microsoft obviously wrote Exchange, which also does mail services in the MS world, while Netscape creates HTTP servers as well as a freely available browser. **C** is incorrect because OpenMail (from HP) was designed as an enterprise e-mail forwarding and storage solution to support large numbers of users on a scalable server platform. It supports MAPI clients, POP3-based clients, SMTP, and X.400 connectivity as well as X.500 directories.

About Linux

10. ☑   **B.** The Linux kernel. All Linux distributions are built around the Linux kernel.
    ☒   **A, C,** and **D** are incorrect. Linus Torvalds is the architect of the Linux kernel and copyright

holder of the name Linux which he freely allows anyone to use. There are lots of other types of free operating systems, like FreeBSD, that use their own kernel design unrelated to the Linux kernel (at least not directly). Red Hat is one company that sells a Linux distribution and offers support and training services related to its products.

11. ☑   **A.** TCP/IP. Linux was built from the ground up to support TCP/IP and many other networking protocols.
     ☒   **B, C,** and **D** are incorrect. IPX is a proprietary protocol used by Novell systems, while AppleTalk is a proprietary protocol used by Apple Macintosh machines. All three of these network protocols (different "courier" methods) use Ethernet-based cabling and hardware, the media utilized for packet transfer (the "highway system").

12. ☑   **D.** All of the above. Free/Open Source software gives end users stability, support, freedom, and the ability to make modifications to the source code.
     ☒   There are no incorrect answer choices.

Starting Out

13. ☑   **C.** An easy and fast install with minimum flexibility in configuration. (You are not given any option to partition drives or select software.) This, however, sacrifices flexibility in configuration.
     ☒   **A, B,** and **D** are incorrect. The Custom installation provides a more complicated install with maximum flexibility in configuration. The Server installation, meanwhile, is a more complicated install with minimum flexibility in configuration (again, partitions and software are preselected). No option is easy, fast, and provides maximum flexibility.

14. ☑   **B.** DOS partitions are removed on Server installs only. You may remove them on Custom installs.
     ☒   **A, C,** and **D** are incorrect. Workstation installs only remove any existing Linux-type partitions.

15. ☑   **C.** The Custom install gives you the most flexibility in configuration.
     ☒   **A, B,** and **D** are incorrect because both Workstation and Server have predefined the partitions and software to install.

16. ☑   **B.** Approximately 1500MB of free disk space is needed for a Red Hat Linux Workstation install with Gnome, KDE, and X Games.
     ☒   **A, C,** and **D** are incorrect. In a barebones Custom installation, you might be able to use 250MB, definitely be able to use 900MB, and could almost install everything with 1900MB.

17. ☑ **A.** The kernel and associated files reside on the /boot partition.

☒ **B** is incorrect because the /etc directory is not usually on a separate partition. **C** and **D** are incorrect because /usr and /var are created as separate partitions on the server installation.

18. ☑ **C.** Eric S. Raymond likened traditional software companies to cathedral builders: small, disconnected groups of skilled artisans who work meticulously on isolated projects, their efforts eventually contributing to the larger project as a whole.

☒ **A, B, and D** are incorrect. The term Bazaar refers to the Linux community (made up of many groups, including the Linux kernel developers), which independently develops various pieces and then has another group (the distribution company) put it all together for the final product. Some of these groups may have come from previous UNIX developer groups, since Linux is closely related to UNIX in most underlying designs.

19. ☑ **D.** You should avoid attempting to use Winmodems with Linux.

☒ **A, B, and C** are incorrect. Linux plays well with most modern PC-oriented equipment, such as IDE CD-ROMS, Intel 486 systems (the few that are still around), and SCSI drives.

20. ☑ **D.** All of the above. Capacity, drive type, and manufacturer should be documented when selecting a hard drive for a Linux install.

☒ There are no incorrect answer choices.

RED HAT CERTIFIED ENGINEER

2

Installation Preparation

O ne of the strong points of Red Hat Linux is its easy installation. There are several different methods of installation, and each of them is automated to a considerable degree. However, before the actual installation, some preparation is necessary.

Planning the Installation

Before any software can be installed, the computer has to be able to recognize the hardware it will be using. The installation process will ask you about your hardware, so have this data ready before you start.

You should know the make and model number for each of the following pieces of hardware, if you have them:

- SCSI controllers
- Network interface cards (NIC)
- Video cards
- Sound cards

You might also need other information, such as the base I/O address and interrupt that each piece of hardware uses. Later in this chapter, we'll discuss hardware compatibility for Linux.

Packages to Be Installed

Red Hat Linux comes conveniently bundled with an array of preconfigured software packages. Most likely, you will not need to install all of these packages, and for security reasons (or office policy) it is a good idea not to. Your boss might not appreciate the office network being used to serve personal Web pages from each employee's installation of an Apache Web server. Also, every computer on your network doesn't need to run the innd network news service.

Limit the packages you install to only the ones you need. If other packages are required later, they can be installed easily enough with the rpm tool.

Partitioning the Drive

It is recommended that you make several partitions when preparing your hard drive to install Linux. This is a good idea for various reasons. First, Red Hat Linux runs two filesystems: a Linux native filesystem, and a Linux swap space. Second, if you want to install Red Hat Linux and another operating system on the same computer, you will have to create separate partitions for each.

The following section discusses more advantages of making partitions.

Stability and Security

The Linux native filesystem is usually divided among many hard drive partitions. The recommended configuration is a separate partition for each of these directories: /, /usr, /tmp, /var, and /home as well as separate partitions for corporate data, database services, and even the Web and FTP sites if they are expected to be large.

Partitioning the hard drive in this manner keeps system, application, and user files isolated from each other. This aids in protecting the file space that the Linux kernel and the rest of your applications use. Files cannot grow across partitions. Therefore, an application that uses huge amounts of disk space, such as a newsgroup server, will not be able to use up all of the disk space needed by the Linux kernel. Another advantage is that if a bad spot develops on the hard drive, it will be easier to restore a single partition than the entire system. Stability is improved.

Security, also, is improved. Multiple partitions give you the ability to mount some filesystems as read-only. For example, if there is no reason for any user (even root) to write to the /usr directory, mounting that partition as read-only will help protect those files from being tampered with.

While there are many incentives to partitioning your disk space, it might not be desirable for you. For single-user systems, or where disk space is scarce, a simpler filesystem layout would be called for. For example, if the /var directory is on its own partition of 300MB, only 100MB might be used. That makes 200MB of wasted disk space. As of RH 7.x, both the web and ftp document roots have been added to /var. These may add additional disk space requirements for /var.

Currently, there is no easy way to resize Linux partitions. Therefore, a lot of careful consideration should be put into whether you want to partition your disk space, and how to do it.

How Much Space Is Required?

You should size your Linux partitions according to your needs and the function of the computer. For example, a mail server will require more space for the /var directory because the mail spool resides in /var/spool/mail. You may even want to create a separate partition just to accommodate /var/spool/mail. As of RH 7.*x*, both the web and ftp document roots have been added to /var. These may add additional disk space requirements for /var. Generally, the root partition is a relatively modest size, and the rest is split up depending on system use.

Example: File Server   If the Linux system you are installing is to be a file server, then your filesystem could look something like Table 2-1.

The /usr filesystem is large enough to have Samba installed, as well as X11, if that is desired. Most of the disk space has been allocated to /var, for the log files, FTP and HTTPD services, to /home, for users' own files, and to /home/shared, for common files. Of course, this is only an example. The amount of disk space you allocate for file sharing will depend on factors such as the number of users and the type of files they work on.

Linux Swap Space

Normally, Linux can use a maximum 4GB of swap space. This 4GB can be spread over a maximum of eight partitions. Note that each swap partition is restricted to a maximum of 2GB.

There is no authoritative formula for deciding how much swap space should be made, but you can make an estimate based on the typical UNIX rule of thumb, swap space should be two to three times the amount of RAM. Disk space is very cheap compared to RAM.

TABLE 2-1	Filesystem	Size (MB)	Mounted on
Example Disk Partition Scheme for a Linux File Server	/dev/sda1	400	/
	/dev/sda5	2000	/var
	/dev/sda6	300	/usr
	/dev/sda7	60	Swap space
	/dev/sda8	1000	/home
	/dev/sda9	3000	/home/shared

The maximum amount of memory your system will use is the sum of all of the memory requirements of every program that you will ever run at once. You probably have no idea how much memory you absolutely need. You should buy as much memory as you can afford. The price of memory is CHEAP compared to your time in the long run trying to tune an underpowered system. Linux will comfortably run in 32MB of RAM; 64MB is better, while 128MB of RAM and above are magical!

Linux was able to address 1GB of RAM for systems running with Pentium 1 and below CPUs. Linux kernel 2.2 was able to address 4GB of RAM (using the Enterprise kernel) with newer Pentium II and higher systems. With the new 2.4 kernel in Red Hat 7.1, Linux has extended its memory capabilities on Pentium II and higher systems to 64GB of RAM.

The total amount of addressable space for any one program to use is the sum of available RAM and swap space. In general, Linux utilities are usually small, except for something like a database service, which can load huge tables into memory and might possibly use all the available memory while doing so. The same goes for video productions and high-end graphics applications that create cartoons and GIS systems to name a few.

You must have some swap space, as suggested earlier; two to three times the amount of RAM is common. Linux actively uses swap as additional RAM space for programs —and not just when physical memory is full. Pages of memory that haven't been used for a significant amount of time will be swapped out in an attempt to utilize as much physical memory as possible.

Essentially, you do NOT want your system to be using swap consistently. You should add more RAM if swapping is being used heavily. Swap space is on disk, which runs five to six orders of magnitude slower than RAM, so it is a significant performance hit. That said, you still must have swap space for those unexpected events when the system needs more memory space. Keep in mind, too, the installation will attempt to put the swap partition close to the front of the disk for whatever speed improvement it can get.

Another way to speed up swapping is to place swap partitions strategically. You aren't limited to having one swap partition in one place. This is especially useful if you are using more than one hard disk on more than one controller. You could put some swap space on a hard disk on each controller. If one controller is busy, then another can be used for swapping. Also, where you put the swap space on the hard disk can affect performance. If the data being used most often is at the beginning of the disk, but your swap space exists at the end, the drive has to work harder to move between the data and swap space. Keeping your swap space close to your "busy" data will result in more efficient use of your hard drive.

BIOS Limits

Be aware that some computers, built before 1998, may have a BIOS (Basic Input/Output System) that, at bootup (under DOS), limits access to hard disks beyond their 1024 cylinder. A common effect of this problem is your computer's inability to see any partitions past the first 512MB of disk space at boot time. If this limitation affects your computer, do not place any bootable partitions after this barrier, or the BIOS will not be able to access them and, your Linux operating system will not be able to load.

Partitioning Utilities

There are many disk-partitioning utilities for Linux—even utilities that do not run under Linux. Two of the main utilities that come packaged with Red Hat 7.*x* are fdisk/cfdisk and (during the installation steps only) Disk Druid. (Note: cfdisk is similar to fdisk, but with a full screen interface). They all work towards the same end, but Red Hat recommends you use Disk Druid during the installation. It is safer to use than fdisk, and it has a graphical interface that makes its use easier. Both fdisk and cfdisk are available once Linux is installed.

Partitioning Naming Conventions

UNIX is notorious for creating weird file names for hardware, and no one standard has been used by all the UNIX versions. Linux, meanwhile, has been using a simple standard for disk drives: disk device names have three letters, then a number. The first letter identifies the controller type (h is for IDE/EIDE, s is for SCSI). The second letter is d for disk, the third letter is for the sequential disk controller starting with "a." This means the first IDE drive would be hda, the next would be hdb, then hdc and hdd. The partitions are numbered starting from 1, but due to the DOS world, they may not be sequential, depending on how they were created. Under this rule, the partitions would be /dev/hda1, /dev/hda2, /dev/hda3. . ./dev/hda16 for the first IDE drive, then /dev/hdb1. . ./dev/hda16 for the second drive, and so on.

For SCSI drives, the name is sda for the first disk on the first controller. The partitions are /dev/sda1, /dev/sda2. . ./dev/sda15 (only 15 maximum partitions with SCSI, whereas IDE can have 16). The second disk on the same SCSI controller would be sdaa{1,2,...15}, and so on. The second controller would have sdb{1–15} for the first disk, then sdba{1–15} for the second disk on the second controller, and so on. In RH 7.*x,* there are 2048 configured SCSI devices. The number of disks and partitions already configured depends on the version and distribution of Linux.

EXERCISE 2-1

Partitioning Exercise

Although you probably have never had to do this on a basic MS Windows-oriented computer, for a real server system, one that's Windows- or UNIX-oriented, you should preplan your disk usage and partitions very carefully.

1. On a piece of paper, draw a rectangle to represent each hard drive on your computer.

2. Label them in order just as Linux would (e.g., Hard Drive 1: /dev/hda, Hard Drive 2: /dev/sda, Hard Drive 3: /dev/sdb).

3. Use this diagram to plan your Linux partitions visually.

Using this method, you can organize your data, keeping system or users' files together, as well as strategically plan where to place your swap partition(s).

CERTIFICATION OBJECTIVE 2.02

Intel CPU Hardware Selection and Configuration

You have to be very careful not to choose any hardware that Linux does not yet support. Unfortunately for Linux, hardware manufacturers are still targeting the Microsoft Windows market. In order for hardware drivers to come available for Linux, either the manufacturers have to recognize the Linux market and produce drivers, or a third party has to do it. The latter brings up one of Linux's strong points. There is a vast community of Linux users, many of whom produce drivers for Linux and distribute them freely on the Internet. If a certain piece of hardware is popular, you can be certain that Linux support for that piece of hardware will pop up somewhere on the Internet and will be incorporated into Linux distributions, such as Red Hat Linux.

Be careful when purchasing a new computer to use with Linux. Though Linux has come a long way the last few years, and you should have little problem installing it on most modern PCs,. you shouldn't assume Linux will run on *any* PC, especially if it is a laptop or some new state-of-the-art machine. The latest and greatest existing technology may not be supported under Linux (not yet, anyway). The hardware may also be targeted for specific operating systems and configurations. Winmodems and Winprinters are examples of hardware that will not work with Linux because they are targeted for MS Windows. Integrated hardware (e.g., video chips that share system RAM) and parallel port devices (other than printers) are other pieces of hardware you should be wary of. While there may be ways to make these types of hardware work, the process of actually making them work may cause more frustration than they're worth. Last years' model is an ideal choice; it is cheap and more likely to be supported. When it comes to laptops, your chances are best with brand names.

Unless it has been proven that Linux will run on a newer machine, choosing an older model might be a better choice. Linux will run very well on lower-end computers. This is one of Linux's strong points over other operating systems, such as Microsoft's Windows NT. Linux runs fine on 32MB of RAM, although more is always better, especially if you want to run any applications.

Hardware Compatibility

You are not left without help or resources when choosing the right hardware for Linux. There are many places you can turn to for help, including mailing lists and newsgroups. Perhaps the best places to look are the LDP (Linux Documentation Project) or the Red Hat Hardware List. The LDP is a global effort to produce reliable documentation for all aspects of the Linux operating system, including hardware compatibility. Within the LDP, you can find the Linux Hardware HOWTO.

Linux Hardware HOWTO

The Linux Hardware HOWTO is a document listing most of the hardware components supported by Linux. It's updated irregularly with added hardware support, so it is a relatively up-to-date source of information. The latest version of the Linux Hardware HOWTO is supplied on the 3rd CD-ROM of RH 7.*x* in PDF format and in various languages. The location is /HOWTO/Hardware-HOWTO. A more current listing can be found on the Red Hat Web site under "Support —> Hardware." It may also be found at http://users.bart.nl/~patrickr/hardware-howto/Hardware-HOWTO.html, within the LDP, which can be found at Sun Microsystems' Sunsite at http://metalab.unc.edu/LDP/HOWTO/Hardware-HOWTO.html or any mirror sites of Sunsite.

The Red Hat Hardware List

The Red Hat Hardware List specifies name brand hardware that has been tested with Red Hat Linux. Red Hat will provide installation support for any hardware listed as "supported." There is also an "unsupported" list. This list does not necessarily mean the specified hardware will not run Linux; it simply means Red Hat will not provide installation support for that hardware. There is a list for Intel, Alpha, and Sparc architectures.

Like the LDP, the Red Hat Hardware List is kept up to date by volunteers. If you want to check if any of the "latest" hardware (such as USB) will run on your Linux system, it's probably best to consult the Red Hat support site first, then maybe LDP's Linux Hardware HOWTO. However, if you want the option of being able to contact Red Hat for support, you should stay within the "supported" list of the Red Hat Hardware List.

EXERCISE 2-2

Hardware Compatibility

1. On the Web, visit http:// www.ibiblio.org/Linux. Once there, find the Linux Hardware Compatibility HOWTO. Take note of its date (it should be posted near the top). How current is it?

2. Research the topology of the network you are on and try to find a mirror of the Linux Documentation Project closest to you on the Internet.

RAM Sizing and Cache Issues

Accessing a disk is relatively slow when compared to accessing memory. To optimize the use of memory, the Linux kernel keeps track of files that have already been loaded. Should a request for one of these loaded files be received, the operating system will use the cached copy rather than going to the disk. For example, when a command such as ls is executed, the binary image for that command is copied into memory. If ls is called again, then the binary is retrieved from memory instead of performing another "slow" disk read.

Write-Through versus Write-Back Buffer Cache

There are two types of buffer caches. One type is *write-through*. With write-through buffer cache, any changes to blocks of data in the cache are written to disk at once. Early MS-DOS OS versions used this immediate writing of data to disk style of memory management. The second type is *write-back* buffer cache and is used by most multiuser operating systems such as Linux, UNIX, NT, and VMS to name a few. This second type is also referred to as "lazy write." The system maintains the file changes in memory and when there are some free CPU cycles, writes all file changes to the disk. The actual writes to the disk are done at a later time, usually in the background, so as not to slow down other programs. While write-through cache is less efficient in terms of CPU cycles, write-back cache is more susceptible to errors. If the operating system is trashed, or power is suddenly cut and any changes to the write-back buffer cache have not been written back to disk, the data changes stored in this buffer cache are lost. Whenever this happens, Linux automatically performs a file system check during bootup. As long as a proper shutdown procedure is followed to allow Linux to sync buffer cache to disk, Linux takes care of the cache automatically.

Buffer Cache Size and Available Memory

Linux automatically uses all free memory as cache and dynamically resizes the buffer cache as processes are started or stopped in memory. The system daemon bdflush is used to flush any dirty buffers (buffers where data has changed) back to disk. At any time, you can force all unwritten data to be written to disk by using the sync command (usually invoked at least three times to ensure that buffers are clean. Typically this is done during rescue mode when a minimal Linux is in memory and you want to ensure that any file changes you have made are absolutely written to disk; hence the "three times" rule.) When Linux boots, a daemon named update is started in the background. Update runs bdflush and performs a sync command every 30 seconds.

Disk Subsystems (IDE, EIDE, and SCSI)

These systems are set up and initialized before the operating system is loaded. After Linux has loaded, the settings for the disk subsystems can be modified or dealt with through software. However, in order for Linux to be loaded in the first place, the computer's BIOS has to be able to recognize the hardware that makes up these subsystems.

IDE and EIDE

IDE stands for Integrated Drive Electronics. It is on the IBM PC ISA 16-bit bus standard, and was adopted as a standard by ANSI in 1990 as an Advanced Technology Attachment (ATA). A setback to IDE was that it could only access 504MB of disk space. To work around this, Enhanced IDE (EIDE) was created. As well as being able to support hard disks larger that 504MB, EIDE also improved access speeds to hard drives. Support was added for additional hard disks, Direct Memory Access (DMA), and ATA Packet Interface devices (ATAPI), such as CD-ROMs and tape drives. ANSI adopted EIDE as a standard in 1994 as Advanced Technology Attachment-2 (ATA-2 or Fast ATA).

Another issue with Intel systems is that BIOS reports only 1024 cylinders on a disk no matter how many actual cylinders there are, which can affect both IDE or SCSI. This is a limitation inherent in older BIOS systems. In this case, you must put your /boot file system within the first 1024 cylinders, or the boot loader will be unable to boot your system because BIOS will not be able to supply the correct cylinder count. Most modern PCs manufactured after 1995 have a built-in fix called Logical Block Addressing, or LBA. A system that can report LBA, will adjust the cylinder, head, and sector numbers such that the entire disk is available using these logical addresses. In general, only on relatively old machines would this ever occur.

exam
ⓦatch

Problems due to hardware limitations are common and difficult to troubleshoot if you don't know about them. Familiarize yourself with as many hardware limitations as you can, including the 1024 cylinder limit inherent in some older PC models.

SCSI

The Small Computer System Interface (SCSI), developed by Apple Computer, allows your computer to interface to disk drives, CD-ROMs, tape drives, printers, and scanners. SCSI is faster and more flexible than EIDE, with support for 7, 15 or even 32 devices, depending on the SCSI bus width. Data transfer speeds for SCSI range from 5 to 160 or 320 MB per second. SCSI controllers are not common on most modern-day desktop PCs as SCSI disks are usually more expensive. The major PC vendors, however, will almost always provide SCSI disks and controllers for their high-end server products as the larger number of devices and faster bus speeds make them a better choice.

Disk or Partition?

A disk drive requires a partition table. The partition is a logical sequence of cylinders on the disk, while a cylinder represents all the sectors that can be read by all heads with one movement of the arm that contains all these heads. You can create one partition with all the cylinders, or you can create up to 16 total partitions on an IDE drive where only 15 are usable, making for a total of 15 partitions for SCSI with all 15 usable. The extended partition on an IDE-type drive cannot be used as a regular partition because it maintains the list of logical partitions within it only.

exam
ⓦatch

Only 15 of the 16 IDE partitions are usable; all 15 SCSI partitions are usable.

Primary, Extended, and Logical Partitions

You are limited to making only four primary partitions on each hard disk. To work around this, the extended partition was developed. Within an extended partition, logical partitions can be created. IDE disks can have up to 16 total partitions (3 primary and 1 extended, containing up to 12 logical partitions), whereas SCSI disks are limited to 15. Unfortunately, with the Intel PC, partition-naming conventions are neither simple nor straightforward. All logical partitions created within the extended partition have device names that range from 5 to 16 (or 15 for SCSI) no matter how many primary partitions are configured. If, for instance, you have one IDE disk and you create a single primary partition, it would be device hda1. If you then created an extended partition, technically it would be hda2 and unusable as a file system. Within this extended partition, hda2, you must create at least one logical partition, the name of which would be hda5. Names are not sequential for these devices.

Even worse is when you create a primary partition, then create an extended partition into which you generate one logical partition. If you then created a second primary partition from some free space, the IDE drive would renumber the partitions and your bootup process would fail entirely, as it would be pointed to the wrong partition due to the internal name change.

You should know the names of the devices, as well as the starting name and number of any logical partitions created on any basic disk drive. Also be aware of the idiosyncrasies when creating partitions on IDE type drives.

Cylinder/Head/Sector Geometry and Remapping

The size of a hard drive is determined by its geometry. The geometry includes the number of cylinders, heads, and sectors available on the hard disk. Together, these numbers make up an address on the hard disk. Normally, the geometry your BIOS will support is limited to 1024 cylinders, 256 heads, and 63 sectors. All modern-day disk drives use 512 bytes per sector. So 1024 cylinders times 256 heads times 63 sectors times 512 bytes equals about 8GB (gigabytes) or 8000MB. If your hard disk is larger than 504MB, and you have an old BIOS that reports this disk has just 1024 cylinders, your computer will not be able to address the entire hard disk. Most modern-day PCs bypass this problem by using Logical Block Addressing (LBA) for your hard disks.

Since SCSI devices have their own BIOS, this limitation does not affect SCSI hard disks.

Logical Block Addressing (LBA)

If your computer was manufactured after 1994, then you will likely be able to select LBA mode for your hard disks in your computer's CMOS. LBA involves a special way of addressing sectors. Instead of referring to a cylinder, head, and sector for a location on the hard disk, each sector is assigned a unique number from 0 to $N-1$, where N is the number of sectors on the disk. LBA mode allows geometry translation, which means that the BIOS can be fooled into believing the hard disk's geometry is acceptable.

Example   A hard disk with 2048 cylinders, 16 heads, and 63 sectors is installed in a machine. Without using LBA, the 1024 cylinder limit has been exceeded, so the

DOS-based boot loader will not be able to address any cylinders past 1024 on this hard disk. By using LBA mode, the BIOS reports to DOS that the hard disk has 32 heads instead of 16. This changes the geometry to 1024 cylinders, 32 heads, and 63 sectors—within the BIOS limits. The new geometry has the same storage capacity as before, and it can be accessed entirely through LBA mode translation.

Multiple Controllers

It is possible and desirable to use more than one disk controller interface card at the same time on the same PC. This is a common method to increase throughput on your system by reducing your read/write bottlenecks to the only disk.

You can use both SCSI and EIDE controllers in the same machine, but there are a few snags you should be aware of. The BIOS can only access the first two EIDE hard drives at boot time. Also, SCSI disks may not be accessible if EIDE drives are installed. The BIOS might have a setting to allow you to boot from SCSI hard disks. Make sure you understand which drives the BIOS will be able to access at boot time, because if you install the boot sector to a drive that cannot be accessed, Linux will not be able to boot.

When your computer boots, the BIOS assigns a number to each drive letter it sees. The order in which the BIOS assigns them might not be the same order that Linux does. This can confuse LILO and cause it to fail.

Example   Your computer is set up to boot Linux from a SCSI disk, and the BIOS assigns the number 0x80 to /dev/sda (the SCSI disk) and 0x81 to /dev/hda (the first EIDE drive). Linux, however, assigns 0x80 to /dev/hda, 0x81 to /dev/hdb (the second EIDE disk), and 0x82 to the SCSI disk. There is a disagreement between the BIOS and LILO. LILO will not find the boot sector on /dev/sda and, therefore, will not be able to boot Linux. When you run /sbin/lilo in Linux, you will get the message "BIOS-Drive 0x82 may not be accessible." (See the section on configuring LILO in Chapter 4 for more information. Look up the bios= option for /etc/lilo.conf.)

RAID and MD Systems

RAID (Redundant Array of Independent (or Inexpensive) Disks) can be set up in Linux using either hardware or software. The tradeoffs between them are performance versus price. Hardware implementations are more expensive than software implementations, but typically provide higher performance.

The hardware implementation of RAID uses a RAID controller connected to an array of several hard disks. A driver must be installed to be able to use the controller. Linux, meanwhile, offers a software solution to RAID with the md kernel patch. You should use Linux kernel 2.0.36 or a recent 2.2.*x* version. Once RAID is configured on your system, Linux can use it just as it would any other block device.

RAID can be set up with many different configurations, called *levels*. The following are a few basic RAID levels that RAID patches for Linux support:

RAID0   Reads and writes to the hard disks are done in parallel, increasing performance, but filling up all hard drives equally. Since there is no redundancy at this level, a failure of any one of the drives will result in total data loss. This level is used for speed increases. The limit to the speed of a RAID0 system is the bus speed that connects to the disks.

RAID0 is also called "Striping without parity," providing access to 100 percent of all disks used, while offering better performance with no recovery.

RAID1   This level mirrors information to two or more other disks. If one disk is damaged/removed, all data will still be intact and accessible from the other disk(s) available. Also, if any spare disks exist in the system, they can be used as another mirror to replace a missing or damaged drive. While performance may actually be decreased in this level (writes), reliability is greatly increased. RAID level 1 provides the least usable space, as all disks participating in the mirror contain a complete copy of the data. However, recovery is very good as is read performance.

RAID4   This level requires three or more disks. Like RAID0, data reads and writes are done in parallel to all disks. One of the disks in the set maintains only parity information on all the data. If one drive fails, then the parity information can be used to reconstruct the data. Reliability is improved, but since parity information is updated with every write operation, the parity disk can be a bottleneck on the system.

RAID5   RAID5 works on three or more disks, with optional spare disks. With this level, several disks can be combined with both performance and reliability increases. Unlike RAID4, parity information is striped across all the disks. Instead of dedicating one disk to store the parity information, it is distributed evenly across all disks. If one disk fails, the data can be reconstructed onto a spare disk or from the parity information. In either case, there is no stoppage of the RAID system; all data is still available even with one disk failed. RAID level 5 is the preferred choice in most cases: the performance is good, the recovery is high, and the cost is second best. You lose one disk out of the set essentially to parity, so with 5 disks in RAID level 5, you get 80 percent utilization for data, and 20 percent for parity (recovery) information. With 32 disks, you get 31 of 32 disks for about 96 percent utilization.

on the
Ü o b

The RAID system should be designed as "hot-swappable." This means that if a disk were to fail, the local administrator could just pull that bad disk out of the drive enclosure while everything is still running, replace it with a new drive, and the system would automatically rebuild the data onto the new disk. This is a very powerful, but relatively expensive, capability.

Linear Mode   Linear mode is combining one or more disks to work as one larger device. There is no redundancy in linear mode—the disks are simply filled up in the order they appear (e.g., disk 1, disk 2, and so on). The only performance gain linear mode will experience is when several users access data residing on different disks.

exam
Ⓦatch

The exam may use examples from any level of RAID, including a combination of several different levels into one solution.

IRQ Settings

An interrupt request (IRQ) is a signal that is sent by a peripheral device (NIC, Video, Mouse, Modem, Serial Port, or other) to the CPU to request some processing time. Each device you attach to a computer may need its own IRQ value. This value is unique to each device (except for possibly PCI devices; to be explained later) so as not to confuse the computer. The Intel architecture is limited to using only 16 IRQs (0–15) of which usually IRQs 5, 7, 9, 10, 11, and 12 are available with a bare bones system. Typically sound cards use 5; a printer uses 7; video cards, bus mouses, and network cards each need 1—leaving a total of 1. (Maybe!)

Planning the IRQ Layout-Standard IRQs

Some IRQs are reserved by the motherboard to control devices such as the hard disk controller and real-time clock. Do not use these interrupts, or there will be conflicts! In Linux, you can check /proc/interrupts to see which interrupts are being used. Any interrupt that is not assigned is a valid candidate for a new device to use. However, there is a standard IRQ layout you can follow (shown in Table 2-2).

TABLE 2-2	IRQ	Assigned to
Standard IRQ Layout for PCs	0	Nonmaskable interrupt (NMI)—detects parity errors
	1	System timer
	2	Cascade for controller 2
	3	Serial port 2, 4
	4	Serial port 1, 3
	5	Parallel port 2
	6	Floppy diskette controller
	7	Parallel port 1
	8	Real-time clock
	9	Redirected to IRQ2
	10	Not assigned (usually used for a network card)
	11	Not assigned
	12	PS/2 mouse, if installed
	13	Coprocessor
	14	Hard disk controller 1
	15	Hard disk controller 2

IRQs and the PCI Architecture

A common problem with PCs today is having more devices than available interrupts. PCI devices can get around this predicament by sharing an IRQ, accomplished using the PCI bus. The PCI bus is independent of the processor, so PCI devices can have their own internal interrupts that determine which device will send an IRQ to the processor. However, your BIOS must support PCI sharing for it to work. If it does, you should be able to turn it on through your computer's CMOS. Most modern PCs manufactured after 1998 contain PCI buses.

Plug-and-Play

With Plug-and-Play devices, computer users do not have to tell the computer the device is there. The operating system should be able to recognize the device and set it up automatically. Plug-and-Play has been available for Macintosh computers for quite some time, and has been incorporated into Microsoft's Windows operating systems. Linux is a little behind on this technology, though it is able to configure both ISA PnP devices (isapnp utility) and PCI PnP (Plug-and-Play). The kudzu utility looks for any hardware changes at bootup and allows you to configure them. Most PnP technology is driven by non-UNIX operating systems (Microsoft Windows and MacOS), and Linux is starting to play along with them.

Plug-and-Play Support in Linux

The unfortunate truth is that Linux doesn't handle Plug-and-Play very well. The main problem lies with Plug-and-Play support for devices that run on an ISA bus. ISA is an old technology from older IBM PCs, created without Plug-and-Play in mind, so support for it is very complicated. Red Hat includes some utilities to help handle ISA Plug-and-Play devices. These utilities (e.g., isapnp and pnpdump) are kept in a package named isapnptools. You should be able to find this package in rpm format with your Red Hat installation.

The newer, faster bus technology, PCI, is a different story. As Linux loads, device drivers can easily find their devices if they are PCI. This makes Plug-and-Play much easier for hardware that runs on a PCI bus. However, there still may be conflicts with the ISA bus. Support for PnP devices is improving, so the outlook is hopeful. Just keep in mind that you will probably have more trouble configuring an ISA device than a PCI.

Handling Jumperless Cards

Some cards have no jumpers; instead, information regarding which port, IRQ, and I/O address it uses is stored in a ROM chip on the card. With these cards is usually shipped a program that will allow you to change the settings. Alas, it is a Microsoft world, and these utilities usually need DOS to run. If you have a card that works like this, you'll need a DOS boot disk or partition to be able to configure them.

If you are not licensed to use MS-DOS or Windows, there are some possible alternatives. The FreeDOS Project (http://freedos.org) is an effort to create a free version of DOS that is compatible with MS-DOS. Within Linux, there is an MS Windows Emulator called WINE that is capable of running some Windows programs with varying degrees of success.

All in all, a better solution is to try to use hardware that does not need to be configured this way.

IRQs and Standard Serial Ports

The standard serial ports in Linux are /dev/ttyS0, /dev/ttyS1, /dev/ttyS2, and /dev/ttyS3 (COM1 through COM4, respectively). In your BIOS settings, the serial ports are normally set as ttyS0 and ttyS2 to IRQ 4, and ttyS1 and ttyS3 at IRQ 3. With Linux kernel 2.2 and above, there is the ability to share these interrupts. For kernel versions earlier than 2.2, you will need to assign unique IRQs to each serial port you use. This can be done at boot time by using the setserial utility and modifying the /etc/rc.d/rc.serial file similar to the following (assuming, of course, that all these interrupts are available):

```
/sbin/setserial  /dev/ttyS0  irq 3  # dumb terminal
/sbin/setserial  /dev/ttyS1  irq 4  # serial mouse
/sbin/setserial  /dev/ttyS2  irq 5  # first modem
/sbin/setserial  /dev/ttyS3  irq 9  # second modem
```

Serial and Other Interface Mice

For your mouse to work, you will need to know what interface and protocol it uses. Serial mice interface to a serial port, while PS/2 mice have a port and IRQ set aside. There is also another type of interface called a *busmouse*. Linux supports three standard busmouse-oriented protocols: Inport (Microsoft), Logitech, and ATI-XL. In order for a PS/2 mouse to work, support has to be compiled into the Linux kernel or compiled as a module.

Serial Mice

To use a serial mouse, you might need to assign it an IRQ if you are using more than three serial devices. Otherwise, it's just a matter of selecting the correct protocol for the mouse to use. Common protocols are Microsoft for Microsoft mice and Logitech for Logitech mice. The connector for a serial mouse is rectangular with 9 or 25 pins, and plugs into a serial post. The device file for serial mice is a linked file from /dev/mouse to whatever serial port it is using (e.g., /dev/ttyS0).

PS/2 Mice

A PS/2 mouse (used on newer PCs and most laptops) has its own port and uses IRQ 12. A PS/2 mouse uses a 6-pin mini DIN connector and communicates using the PS/2 protocol. The device file for PS/2 mice is /dev/psaux.

Busmouse

You can usually identify a busmouse from its round 9-pin connector. The mice usually plug into a card, which might have jumper settings or software (for DOS) to set IRQs and base I/O addresses. While most busmice use the BusMouse protocol, some older mice use other protocols, such as MouseSystems or Logitech. The device files for Inport, Logitech, and ATI-XL busmice are /dev/inportbm, /dev/logibm, and /dev/atibm, respectively.

The Red Hat installation process will ask you for information about your mouse. Know what kind of mouse you have! Later, you can modify your mouse settings by using the XF86Setup tool for X11 or the mouseconfig tool for using the mouse in console mode.

EXERCISE 2-3

Your Computer's CMOS Settings

Look through your computer's CMOS settings. To get into the CMOS settings, you normally have to press a key soon after you power on your computer. This key is commonly the DELETE or F1 key on your keyboard. Browse through the menus and try to locate the areas where the following information is kept:

- Your hard drive information: Take note of the "translation mode" your hard drive is using (e.g., CHS, Large, or LBA).

- Locate the IRQ settings that your motherboard assigns to your serial and parallel ports, real-time clock, and hard disk controllers. Can you change any of these settings? (Be careful that you don't save your changes!)

- Find out if your CMOS supports PCI sharing (for IRQs). If it does, is it turned on or off on your computer?

PC Card (PCMCIA)

Linux has one package that deals exclusively with PC cards called "Card Services." This package includes all the kernel modules you'll need to manage PCMCIA cards and a set of drivers for specific cards. The package also includes a daemon that handles the hot-swapping of most card types.

While development of the Card Services package is ongoing, there is often a period where there is no support for new technologies. For this reason, the latest laptop on the market is often not a good choice for a Linux installation. Support for Linux on most name brand laptops is now common. In fact, several name brand PC manufacturers offer some distribution of Linux as an optional configuration.

Supported Chip Sets

This list is frequently updated. A current list of supported chip sets can be obtained from the LDP's PCMCIA-HOWTO.

Supported Cards

The Card Services package comes bundled with a file named SUPPORTED.CARDS. Also, you can check the LDP's PCMCIA-HOWTO or the Red Hat Hardware Compatibility List for supported cards.

on the *During your career as a computer professional, there will be times you'll be asked
job to research a specific product or technology. To get an idea of how hard or easy this can be, call a local or international computer reseller or manufacturer and inquire about their latest laptop. Ask them if it supports Linux. What kind of answer do you get? Ask them if they have any earlier models that will. Do you believe the answers you receive are reliable? Check out the company's Web page, if you can, and find out if they provide any information about the product on the Internet. Doing this kind of research can be very trying, with or without success. Before deciding what kind of hardware you want to install Linux on, you should have a good understanding of what will and will not work. Start early and build a good base of reliable references you can use to find out new computer information. There are Web sites, such as Sunsite's Metalab (and mirrors), as well as magazines like Sys Admin Magazine and PC Magazine, to help you stay informed.*

Now that you have a better idea of your computer's settings, refer to the following Scenario & Solution.

SCENARIO & SOLUTION

You are using Linux and Apache to run a Web server on a LAN for a small office. Several of the employees who work in that office are responsible for updating various parts of the Web site. However, all of these people are Windows users, and are not experienced in using shell accounts. What package could you install to give these employees the easiest access to the files they need on the Web server?	One possibility is to install an ftp daemon, but for Windows connectivity, the Samba package would make the employees' work easier and more transparent. Users do not have to know how to use a shell account (and an editor such as emacs or vi) or an ftp client. The directories that contain the files they need could be mounted directly to their Windows desktop or separate drive letter.
You have run out of disk space for your /home directory! What are the steps you should take to move this data to the new hard drive you just installed?	First, you will have to prepare the new drive to accommodate the new /home filesystem. Use fdisk to create a partition with enough space for your /home directory. Use mke2fs to create the filesystem and then mount the partition somewhere temporarily (e.g., /mnt/tmp). Copy all your data from /home to the new partition (e.g., cp -a /home/* /mnt/tmp). Unmount both filesystems; then remount /home to the new partition. Edit /etc/fstab to reflect the new /home location as well.

CERTIFICATION SUMMARY

Planning your Linux installation makes the process an easier one. You can imagine how frustrating it would be to begin the installation and then discover something wrong; for example, a piece of hardware isn't supported, or you installed LILO in the wrong place and now Linux will not boot. Being prepared for this will help lessen your grief.

You should now know enough to be able to decide which hardware will fit your needs. Moreover, you should be able to find resources that help you make well-informed decisions about what hardware will work with Linux. Organization is the key to experiencing success with Linux, and it makes you look good.

TWO-MINUTE DRILL

Here are some of the key points from the certification objectives in Chapter 2.

Planning the Installation

❑ You should know the make and model number for each of the following pieces of hardware if you have them: SCSI controllers, network interface cards (NICs), video cards, and sound cards.

❑ You might also need other information, such as the base I/O address and interrupt each piece of hardware uses.

❑ Install only necessary software packages.

❑ The recommended configuration uses a separate partition for each of these directories: /, /usr, /tmp, /var, and /home.

❑ There should also be separate partitions for corporate data, database services, even Web and ftp sites, if they are expected to be large.

❑ Multiple partitions give you the ability to mount some filesystems as read-only. For example, mounting the partition for the /usr directory as read-only will help protect the files in that filesystem from being tampered with.

❑ A mail service requires more space for /var directory because the mail spool resides in /var/spool/mail. You may even want to create a separate partition just to accommodate /var/spool/mail.

❑ As of RH 7.x, both the web and ftp document roots have been added to /var. If these will be important services, you might want to put them on separate partitions for ease of management and security.

❑ Currently, there is no easy way to resize Linux partitions. Therefore, careful consideration should be put into whether you want to partition your disk space and how to do it.

❑ Generally, the root partition begins at a relatively modest size, but grows with kernel development and documentation needs. These can also be on separate partitions.

❑ Based on the typical UNIX rule of thumb, swap space should be two to three times the amount of RAM. Disk space is very cheap compared to RAM.

❑ Linux can use a maximum 4GB of swap space, which can be spread over a maximum of 8 partitions. Note that each swap partition is restricted to a maximum of 2GB.

❑ Essentially, you do NOT want your system to be using swap consistently. You should add more RAM if swapping is being used heavily.

❑ With the new 2.4 kernel in Red Hat 7.1, Linux has extended its memory capabilities on Pentium II and higher systems to 64GB of RAM.

❑ Be aware that some computers, built before 1998, may have a BIOS (Basic Input/Output System) that, at bootup (under DOS), limits access to hard disks beyond their 1024 cylinder.

❑ The first IDE drive would be hda and the next hdb, then hdc and hdd.

Intel CPU Hardware Selection and Configuration

❑ Unfortunately for Linux, hardware manufacturers are still targeting the Microsoft Windows market.

❑ Linux has come a long way the last few years and you should have little problem installing it on most modern PCs.

❑ You should still not assume Linux will run on any PC, however. Especially if it is a laptop or a new state-of-the-art machine.

❑ Winmodems and Winprinters are examples of hardware that will not work with Linux because they are targeted for MS Windows.

❑ The best places to look for acceptable are the LDP (Linux Documentation Project) or the Red Hat Hardware Compatibility List.

❑ The Small Computer System Interface (SCSI), developed by Apple Computer, allows your computer to interface to disk drives, CD-ROMs, tape drives, printers, and scanners. SCSI is faster and more flexible than EIDE, with support for up to 7, 15, or even 32 devices, depending on the SCSI bus width. Data transfer speeds for SCSI range from 5 to 160 or 320 Mbps.

❑ A disk drive requires a partition table. The partition is a logical sequence of cylinders on the disk, where a cylinder represents all the sectors that can be read by all heads with one movement of the arm containing all these heads.

❑ You can create one partition with all the cylinders.

❑ You can create up to 16 total partitions on an IDE drive of which only 15 are usable.

❑ You can create a total of 15 partitions for SCSI with all 15 usable.

❑ The extended partition on an IDE-type drive cannot be used as a regular partition, because it maintains the list of logical partitions within it only.

❑ It is possible and desirable to use more than one disk controller interface card at the same time on the same PC. This is a common method to increase throughput on your system by reducing your read/write bottlenecks to the only disk.

❑ RAID (Redundant Array of Independent (or Inexpensive) Disks) can be set up in Linux using either hardware or software.

❑ Linux offers a software solution to RAID with the md kernel patch. Once RAID is configured on your system, Linux can use it just as it would any other block device.

❑ RAID0 is also called "Striping without parity," providing access to 100 percent of all disks used, and offering better performance with no recovery.

❑ RAID level 1 mirrors information to two or more other disks but provides the least usable space as all disks participating in the mirror contain a complete copy of the data. However, recovery is very good, as is read.

❑ RAID5 works on three or more disks, with optional spare disks and parity information distributed evenly across all disks. If one disk fails, the data can be reconstructed onto a spare disk or from the parity, where all data is still available.

❑ RAID level 5 is the preferred choice in most cases, the performance is good, the recovery is high and the cost is second best. You lose one disk out of the set essentially to parity so with 5 disks in RAID level 5, you get 80 percent utilization for data, and 20 percent for parity (recovery) information. With 32 disks, you get 31 of 32 disks, or about 96 percent utilization.

❑ The Intel architecture is limited to using only 16 IRQs (0–15), of which usually IRQs 5, 7, 9, 10, 11, 12 are available with a bare bones system. Typically sound cards use 5; a printer uses 7; video cards, bus mouses, and network cards each need 1—leaving a total of 1. (Maybe!)

❑ Most modern PCs manufactured after 1998 contain PCI buses.

❑ Linux is able to configure both ISA PnP devices (isapnp utility) and PCI PnP (Plug-n-Play). The kudzu utility looks for any hardware changes at bootup and allows you to configure them

❑ Linux has one package that deals exclusively with PC cards called "Card Services." This package includes all the kernel modules you'll need to manage PCMCIA cards, as well as a set of drivers for specific cards. The package also includes a daemon that handles hot-swapping of most card types.

SELF TEST

The following questions will help you measure your understanding of the material presented in this chapter. Read all the choices carefully, as there may be more than one correct answer. Choose all correct answers for each question.

Planning the Installation

1. You install Linux onto a laptop and discover there are two PCMCIA cards, an Ethernet card, and a modem. What do you need to do in order to get these cards working?

   A. Recompile the Linux kernel to support Ethernet. Setting up the modem should be as easy as configuring the serial port it uses.

   B. Install the Card Services package (if it is not already installed) to get the needed kernel modules and utilities to manage PCMCIA.

   C. Run the ifconfig and route utilities to configure the cards.

   D. Edit the file /proc/devices to reflect the new hardware, then configure the files in /etc/sysconfig to get them up and running.

2. A coworker bought a brand new mouse to use on his Linux workstation. He tells you that the person he bought it from said it would work, but he is very frustrated because it doesn't even plug in correctly. The old mouse had a rectangular 9-pin connector, and the new mouse has a round 6-pin mini DIN connector. What is the most likely reason your coworker's new mouse doesn't work?

   A. The person who sold him the mouse sold him the wrong type. Your coworker should take it back and get a refund.

   B. The new mouse needs an adapter to change the round 6-pin mini DIN connector to the rectangular 9-pin connector.

   C. Your coworker's Linux workstation isn't set up to use a PS/2 mouse.

   D. Your coworker's Linux workstation isn't configured to use a busmouse.

3. What do you need to do in order to be able to use a third or fourth serial port in Linux? (Choose all that apply.)

   A. Obtain and install a hardware card that has more ports.

   B. Nothing. Linux kernel 2.2 and later already handles this for you.

   C. Add a new entry to the file /etc/serial.conf.

   D. Use the setserial utility to assign resources to the new serial port.

4. After installing an ISA Plug-and-Play device into a computer running Linux, what needs to be done in order to get the card working?

   A. Install and configure the isapnptools package for Linux.

   B. Nothing. Since it's a Plug-and-Play card, Linux will be able to install the device drivers and kernel modules automatically.

   C. The card will not work. Plug-and-Play ISA cards are not supported in Linux.

   D. Run the pnpprobe utility to set the resources the card should use.

5. You installed a printer onto a Linux workstation. After changing the IRQ and I/O address, you're finally able to get it working. Now the sound card has stopped working, however. What has most likely gone wrong?

   A. The sound card was probably a Plug-and-Play device, so the printer is now conflicting with either the IRQ or I/O address setting you selected.

   B. There is an IRQ conflict between the printer and the sound card.

   C. The sound card and printer are using the same device file in the /dev directory. You need to create a new link to use both devices.

   D. None of the above.

6. Which of the following RAID levels provides both redundancy and performance increases?

   A. RAID5

   B. RAID4

   C. RAID1

   D. RAID0

7. What problems might you come across when using systems that mix EIDE and SCSI technologies?

   A. You can't mix them together.

   B. There are potential IRQ conflicts between the controllers for each device.

   C. The computer's BIOS may not be able to access SCSI devices.

   D. SCSI disks cannot use LBA translations like EIDE devices can.

Intel CPU Hardware Selection and Configuration

8. Of the following hardware, which would be the easiest to install Red Hat Linux on?

A. The latest Dell laptop

B. An IBM PC XT

C. A 486DX/100 IBM Clone

D. A PowerMac G3

9. What downside is there to extensive partitioning?

A. Slower disk access.

B. There is no downside.

C. Data fragmentation.

D. The root partition might not be able to be accessed at boot time.

10. You attempt to install Linux on an old 80386 computer. You manage to scavenge an 800MB hard drive to use. However, when you boot the computer, it reports the hard drive to be only 504MB. Why?

A. The BIOS can access only the first partition, which must be 504MB.

B. The hard drive must have bad sectors.

C. The BIOS only supports IDE, not EIDE.

D. An 80386 CPU can only address 504MB of data.

11. What do you need to do in order to get past the 504MB barrier with an EIDE hard disk controller?

A. Add a SCSI controller.

B. Upgrade to an ATA-2 controller.

C. Set jumpers on the hard disks to support EIDE.

D. Set the hard drive translation mode to LBA in the BIOS.

12. A coworker transports some files via floppy disk from one Linux workstation to another. When she uses the disk in the second machine, the file she was trying to copy doesn't exist. What probably happened?

A. Your coworker doesn't have the correct permissions to use the disk on the second machine.

B. She probably did not properly unmount the disk from the first machine.

C. The floppy disk was probably full.

D. This is a security precaution that Linux uses to prevent the spread of computer viruses.

13. You get a phone call from a frustrated user who just bought a new modem. The modem is a Lucent 56K Winmodem, and the user is having trouble making it work in Linux. Which of the following is most likely the source of his trouble?

   A. An IRQ conflict is preventing Linux from using the modem.

   B. Winmodems are specific to Windows operating systems, and Linux cannot use them.

   C. The modem is a Plug-and-Play device, and the user does not have the isapnptools package installed/configured.

   D. Linux does not support 56K modems.

14. When planning your Red Hat Linux installation, which of the following information is the least important to take note of?

   A. The speed of your CD-ROM

   B. What type of mouse you will be using

   C. The frequency specifications of your monitor

   D. The model of your network card

15. RAID is an acronym for

   A. Redundant Array of Independent Disks

   B. Redundant Array of Inexpensive Disks

   C. Reliable Array of Independent Disks

   D. Redundant Assortment of Inexpensive Disks

16. What is the maximum number of partitions you can create for EIDE and SCSI disks?

   A. There is no maximum.

   B. 16 for EIDE and 15 for SCSI.

   C. 64 for EIDE and 16 for SCSI.

   D. Linux only supports a total of 64 partitions of all disks together.

17. What must be installed on laptops when peripheral cards are inserted into the PCMCIA/PC card slots?

   A. Nothing special is required.

   B. PC Card Services should be loaded automatically.

    C. PCMCIA.o must be inserted into memory using insmod.

    D. PC Card Services should load automatically, but not all devices and buses are probed properly.

18. One of your users insists on running their DOS contact manager program. What are your options?

    A. There's nothing you can do.

    B. This presents no problem. Just install the MS Windows Interface.

    C. You might be able to get WINE to run it.

    D. You run terminal emulation software from NT and have it display on Linux.

LAB QUESTION

You are interested in further researching RAID on your new Linux server, but you cannot find any help in the man pages. You need to load up the Documentation CD-ROM and then find the HOWTO on RAID, as well as the RAID information in the Linux Reference Guide. How do you do this?

SELF TEST ANSWERS

Planning the Installation

1. ☑ **B.** The Card Services package is needed in order for any PCMCIA device to work. Current versions of Red Hat Linux automatically detect and install card services during installation, so laptop installations are very simple now. However, you should verify the installation by thoroughly testing PCMCIA functionality. For example, to make sure no problems occur, you might swap cards between slots during system operation.

   ☒ **A** is incorrect, since Ethernet is the cabling standard handled by the network card. **C** refers to network setup utilities, while **D** indicates a file in memory (/proc is direct access to system memory) and is not where you would want to make these changes.

2. ☑ **A, B,** and **C.** The new mouse is a PS/2 mouse. Therefore, the Linux workstation will have to be configured to use a PS/2 mouse with the PS/2 protocol, and an adapter will be needed. The mouse could then be configured to use the PS/2 protocol using the XF86Setup or mouseconfig tool. If the store is close, however, taking it back and getting the right interface would be the best idea. There may actually be adapters to translate between serial ports and PS/2, but it is better just to get the right mouse.

   ☒ The new mouse is not a busmouse as suggested in **D.**

3. ☑ **A, B,** and **D.** You normally only get two serial ports at most. For serial ports, you would need to add an additional card. Use the setserial utility for Linux kernels earlier than 2.2.*x*. To configure the serial ports at boot time, edit the /etc/rc.d/rc.serial file to run the setserial command for each serial port you use. With kernel version 2.2.*x*, you don't need to assign unique IRQs for each serial port.

   ☒ **C** is incorrect because there is no /etc/serial.conf file.

4. ☑ **A.** Current support for older ISA Plug-and-Play devices is very good in Linux. The isapnptools package contains utilities that can be used to get the cards working if this package is not already installed. Try **man isapnp** in Linux for more information.

   ☒ **B** might be correct if the isapnptools had already been installed because on an existing PnP card during installation. Neither **C** nor **D** is correct, however, as Linux does support PnP, and the utility is not called pnpprobe, but isapnp.

5. ☑ **A** and **B.** The default IRQ for a parallel port (what the printer is using) is 5 or maybe 7. You probably configured the printer to use the same settings as the sound card. Try running **cat /proc/interrupts** to see what IRQs are being used, then choose a free one to assign to the sound card.

☒ **D** and **C** are incorrect, as this is a hardware problem, not a filename problem in Linux.

6. ☑ **C.** RAID1 provides both.

☒ **A, B,** and **D** are incorrect. There is no redundancy in RAID0, and performance can actually be decreased in levels 4 and 5.

7. ☑ **C.** Depending on the computer's BIOS, SCSI disks may not be accessible to the computer's BIOS, which can cause troubles when trying to boot Linux. This means you might not be able to boot from a SCSI disk, or that your BIOS will assign a different order to your hard disks than Linux will, confusing Linux as to which disk is which.

☒ **B** might be true, but only if you installed incorrect hardware settings. **A** and **D** are incorrect because you *can* mix these technologies in the same machine, and SCSI disks *do* use LBA when needed.

Intel CPU Hardware Selection and Configuration

8. ☑ **A, B, C, D.** It is very likely the laptop will not have problems with the current version of Linux. Although underpowered somewhat, the 486DX/100 will probably install with no problems as well. You might be able to get the XT to install but it would not be worth it. Get a small diskette version of Linux for the XT instead (and you can make it a firewall or router!). Chances are, there is probably a Linux distribution specifically for the MAC G3. Most distributions commercially sold are for Intel platforms, so you would have to find it somewhere on the Internet; try: http://sunsite.unc.edu.

☒ There are no incorrect answer choices.

9. ☑ **B.** There is no downside. In fact, it is recommended you separate specific file systems that are user-writeable for security reasons and for ease of management.

☒ **C** is only partially correct, as the partitions that are not written to often remain defragmented while the data partitions get heavily fragmented with time. **A,** too, is somewhat true but with the many advancements in drive technology, disk access is probably not a major issue. **D** is incorrect as the root partition is not accessed in DOS mode during bootup; it is accessed after the kernel has initialized.

10. ☑ **C.** The IDE (or ATA) standard does not support hard disks larger than 504MB. The 80386 computer was most likely manufactured before support for large drives was added with EIDE (ATA-s, or Fast-ATA).

☒ This is not a partition issue as indicated in **A,** nor does it involve bad sectors, as proposed by **B,** since it can see some of the drive. **D** is incorrect because the 80386 was a 32-bit system and with Linux can "see" more than 1024 cylinders. It just can't during DOS bootup.

11. ☑ **D.** EIDE controllers support hard disks larger than 504MB, but your computer's BIOS may not be able to access the entire drive unless LBA translation is used.

☒ A SCSI controller would not help (**A**), you would have to replace the motherboard to upgrade to ATA-2 (**B**) and EIDE is controller-specific, not disk-specific (**C**).

12. ☑ **B.** Linux uses disk buffering rather than floppies for speed reasons. If your coworker did not properly unmount the floppy, then the disk buffer was probably not written back to the disk. Therefore, the file would not be there.

☒ **A** might be true being that file permissions are important on a Linux disk, but only if they are using DOS diskettes (which you can do in Linux; check the man page on the mtools package). **C** and **D** are incorrect because Linux would report back a full disk, and there is no security precaution for viruses on floppies within Linux.

13. ☑ **B.** Winmodems are generally not supported under Linux. They are hardware devices that are incomplete when it comes to hardware design. This is made up for by way of software programming. However, in the case of Winmodems, the software only works for Windows operating systems.

☒ **A** may be correct too, but that is another issue. **C** is incorrect, as this is not a fully compliant type of PnP device, only Windows OSs would be able to recognize the device. Linux does support 56K modems.

14. ☑ **A.** The only thing the speed of your CD-ROM will affect is the amount of time the install will take if you are installing from a CD-ROM.

☒ **B, C,** and **D** are all important when planning your installation.

15. ☑ **A** or **B.** Independent or Inexpensive have both been acceptable for the "I" in RAID.

☒ **C** and **D** are not correct.

16. ☑ **B.** 16 for EIDE and 15 for SCSI. Of course, you need to use extended and logical partitions (for EIDE) to reach these limits.

☒ No devices support 64 partitions, as suggested in **C**, and Linux has no partition limits for all disks, as proposed in **A** and **D**.

17. ☑ **D.** Unfortunately, with each release, the laptop PC Card Services both improve and degrade. More cards are supported, but many laptops use new proprietary PC Card technology that may not work.

☒ **A** and **B** may be correct if all goes well as with most brand name laptops. **C** is incorrect as this is not a required file.

18. ☑ **C** and **D.** If you are lucky, it will run under the latest WINE version. As a desperate measure, you could run it remotely and have Linux display it in an X window.

☒ Though incorrect at present, **B** may soon be true, as there are some MS Windows emulation interfaces being developed. **A** may be true, too, if all this fails!

LAB ANSWER

Most of the help you need will be on the Documentation CD as follows:

```
# man raid
no manual entry for raid
(stick the Documentation CD into the drive, then)
# mount /dev/hdd /mnt/cdrom # assuming hdd is your CD Drive
# cd /mnt/cdrom/HOWTOs/
# ls *RAID*
Software-RAID-HOWTO
Root-RAID-HOWTO
# less Software-RAID-Howto
# xpdf  /mnt/cdrom/docs/pdf-en/rhl71rg*.pdf
# xpdf /mnt/cdrom/docs/pdf-en/rhl71ig*.pdf
```

RED HAT CERTIFIED ENGINEER

3

Installation

There is a perception that a workstation and server are two distinct systems. In the Linux environment, this categorization is more an optimization for usage than a type of platform. Both Workstation and Server installations use the exact same installation disk, the difference being the particular software sets, also called *packages*, loaded by each option.

The Workstation installation is designed mainly for inbound traffic to the host, where the workstation uses network services from the network servers. The workstation usage concept itself is one in which the user sits at the machine and performs day-to-day activities.

The Server installation includes all the common network services like Web, FTP, NFS, Samba, and many more. You can add any combination of these network services to any machine. At any time, you can upgrade a workstation to server status by installing these services. A server designation conceptually is a machine, centrally located and managed, that offers network services to many other hosts, usually workstations.

All installations now include the choice of configuring a firewall, and since the Workstation and Server designations are oriented more for perceived use, there are no actual limitations as in some operating systems.

The next section is an overview of the installation program, pointing out various aspects of the installation you need to be aware of. Overall, the chapter is designed to provide a bigger picture of the more difficult concepts.

The first preinstallation topic is the disk partitions, their layout, and what is needed for various installation options. Since unlimited possibilities abound when installing an operating system, you are introduced to various scenarios, such as what to do when the target system is new, and what's the best course of action when it has an operating system you may or may not want to keep.

There are many details related to concepts and design information that are useful to know, but if you wanted to get started immediately, you simply need to have some unallocated and unformatted free disk space. You can get this by simply adding a new disk drive to your system. The mechanics of adding a drive and changing your CMOS settings (so your CD-ROM is a bootable device) are beyond the scope of this book, but neither operation is complicated. Once the new drive is installed and your system is configured to boot from the CD-ROM drive, just stick the first CD-ROM from the Official Red Hat set into the CD drive and reboot! Take the defaults for a Workstation installation and see what happens; it will probably just install, dual-boot automatically, and voilà! You are ready to play!

Note: Some commercially available unofficial copies of Red Hat Linux may not be bootable. In such cases, you will need to create a floppy disk using the BOOT.IMG file on the first CD-ROM in the IMAGES directory to start your installation. Details on creating this diskette will appear later in this section.

CERTIFICATION OBJECTIVE 3.01

Disk Partitioning Strategies for Server and Workstation Installations

By the very nature of the usage, the Workstation installation is typically much simpler than the Server installation. Usually, Workstation installs are optimized for local user applications that are centered around the X-Window system and utilize services from the network.

The server system needs to be designed for optimal management and flexibility of use. This normally means the server has many more distinct partitions that make up the file system, allowing for more selective management of these individual partitions. For example, it is very common to have a separate partition for the user home directories. By separating the user home directories to one partition, disk quotas can be maintained on just that file system, and backups and restores are more specific. With the smaller file systems, failures are easier to rebuild, and expansion of any one-file system is made easier.

The Red Hat installation program has preconfigured options that build both a generic workstation and server, as well as a laptop workstation. Although these are not perfect, they are excellent starting points for new systems. The Custom option allows you to create any combination of partitions and software services for either, a workstation or server usage. The Custom option can be used to create any installation design, including a server or workstation type of installation.

CERTIFICATION OBJECTIVE 3.02

Choosing an Installation Class: Workstation, Laptop, Server, or Custom

This section will introduce you to the various installation options you will encounter during installation and try to demystify the reasons behind why there are many partitions, explain differences between the installation choices, and why you should choose one over the other.

Installation Options

Figure 3-1 details the different installation types found in Red Hat 7.1.

Laptop-Class Installation

A laptop-class installation provides a workstation-class installation that has some packages removed to save space and some packages added specifically for the laptop type of hardware. The Laptop installation allows you to select either GNOME or

FIGURE 3-1

Red Hat
installation types

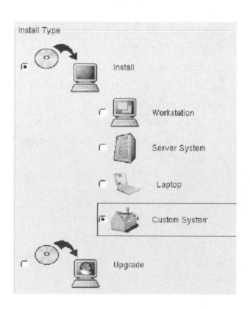

KDE desktop environments or both, plus Games, and is basically a Workstation installation.

For general installation details, follow the Workstation installation. The Laptop installation specifics are not covered in this section.

Upgrade Installation

For any version of Red Hat Linux starting with 3.0.3 or later, you can quickly update to the latest packages and kernel version by using this upgrade option.

Creating a Server or Workstation Using the Custom Installation Option

There is a Custom option that allows selection of any combination of software, and there are three other installation options—server, workstation, or laptop—each with preconfigured software package sets. All four options are presented during an interactive installation, as illustrated in Figure 3-1.

The Custom option can actually be used to create either a Server or Workstation installation but offers the added benefit that you can make changes to the default package sets.

The Custom installation requires that you be aware of how to configure disk drives and their partitions, what the swap partition is, how to create a swap partition, how to create separate file systems for important directory structures, and why you need to plan this all beforehand.

If you wanted to change the default partition layout or preserve an already installed operating system of any type, you would need to use the Custom Installation option. To use the Custom Installation for either a server or workstation installation would require that you know exactly what packages represent the workstation or server installation options.

Base Packages Installed

On the Red Hat CD-ROM in the /RedHat/base/ directory, there is a text file that lists all the packages associated with each group, as well as the specific sets of packages installed for the Workstation and Server installations. This package configuration file is called comps. This file can be viewed with any text-oriented editor, like Notepad on Windows or gNotepad on Linux. Figure 3-2 shows the GUI installation representation of the first few groups of packages.

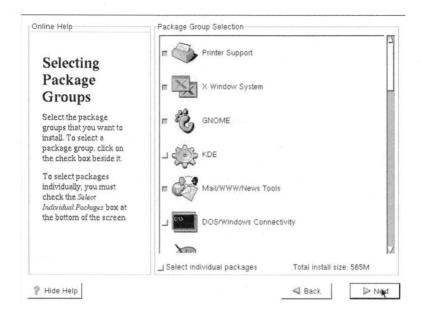

FIGURE 3-2

GUI installation
of the first few
package groups

A *package* is just one set of files related to a given application. For example, there is a Perl (programming language) package named perl-5.00503-2.i386.rpm. This Perl package, at about 4.3MB, is in the /RedHat/RPMS directory on the CD-ROM and contains all the required executables, libraries, help files, and installation requirements. You can install this package, or any other, on any Red Hat Linux host whenever necessary using the rpm (Red Hat Package Manager) utility, which will be discussed later.

A group of packages, such as the DOS/Windows Connectivity group includes a preconfigured set of these packages, as detailed in the following comps text file:

```
0 DOS/Windows Connectivity {
  dosfstools
  dos2unix
  unix2dos
  mtools
  zip
  tcsh
  samba-common
  samba-client
  perl
  unzip
}
```

You could customize the groups associated with any installation group or create new ones and add them to the comps file and then either provide the revised Red Hat directory via a network share or create a custom CD-ROM, in order to have customized workstation and server installations that anyone can use (such as remote offices wanting to stick to a standard installation for all corporate-wide machines).

Workstation and Laptop Installation Details

The following lists the minimum recommended disk space requirements for a basic workstation installation.

- Workstation with GNOME: 1.2GB
- Workstation with KDE: 1.2GB
- Workstation with both GNOME and KDE, and Games group: 1.5GB

This is just the minimum disk space, you will require more for actual data files such as documents, downloads, source files and e-mail to name a few. The more disk space, the better. If you are testing Linux for the first time, you should have at least a few hundred more megabytes of space to play with.

Behind the Scenes—The Partition Layout for Workstation

The Workstation installation option first deletes all ext2 (Linux) partitions. Then the Workstation installation uses *all* the remaining free space, whether it was ext2 type before or not, and creates three partitions as follows:

- 64MB swap partition
- 16MB /boot partition for all Intel platforms (a 2MB partition mounted as /dos and used for the Milo boot loader for an Alpha platform)
- A variable-sized partition for the root, denoted as "/", that consumes all available remaining free space

Dual-Boot with Previous OS

Any previous operating system that existed on the machine is left intact. This can be good or bad. It is good if this is a test or development system and you want to be able to boot into any one of the operating systems on the machine. It is bad if this machine will only be running Linux. The other operating systems will take up space that may never be available to the Linux operating system for use. You must decide whether you want to keep the previous operating system, before doing your installation.

exam
ⓦatch

The Apache Web Server package is NOT installed with a Workstation installation. You can add this package at any time using the rpm utility.

The Laptop installation allows you to select either the GNOME or KDE desktop environments or both, plus Games, and is basically a Workstation installation.

The Simplest Partition Strategy for a Workstation or Server

The simplest partition setup for a basic workstation is to create a single swap partition and then a single root partition. This is not a very well designed system for security or maintenance purposes, but it will work. This is NOT recommended for anything but a development system. A production server should maintain certain portions of the file system tree as separate partitions. More details are provided later on this topic.

If you do choose to install with only a single root partition, you can add additional partitions later, provided you have additional available disk space. Thus, your system can easily expand to meet the needs of its users.

Workstation Option Packages Installed

The list of file packages installed by a default Workstation installation is listed on the CD-ROM in /RedHat/base/comps. This list contains references, either directly or indirectly through the use of group names, to the hundreds of packages installed. Each package contains at least one file, and usually several of them. Hundreds of files are installed during an installation, and this is only the beginning.

```
0 --hide Workstation Common {
  @ Printer Support
  @ X Window System
  @ Mail/WWW/News Tools
  @ DOS/Windows Connectivity
  @ Utilities
  @ Graphics Manipulation
  @ Multimedia Support
  @ Networked Workstation
  @ Dialup Workstation
  @ Authoring/Publishing
```

```
@ Emacs
@ Development
```

Notice that the workstation contains ten groups (referenced by the @ symbol preceding the group name) of software packages. The comps syntax allows for packages or groups to be tested as selected and optionally to load more package groups if the selected package or group has been chosen, as in this next example:

```
0 Emacs {
  ? X-Window System {
    emacs-X11
  }
  ? Authoring/Publishing {
    psgml
  }
  emacs
  emacs-nox
}
```

The "? X Window System" indicates test if the X-Window System group has been selected already. If true (i.e., the X-Window System group has been selected), this test will include everything between the curly brackets (in this example { emacs-X11 }).

In both of the previous code listings, the group names, Workstation Common and Emacs, are preceded by a zero (0), indicating they are not part of the default selection group should the user select the Custom Installation option. Additionally, the "--hide" option provides a mechanism to hide this option during the Custom installation screen display of groups available.

Server Installation Details

If you are intending to run this machine as a server of common network services and do not wish to hunt through the selection of packages during the installation, then the Server Installation option is your best choice.

This installation will remove all partitions on all disks.

If you already have an operating system on this machine, it will be overwritten, with no opportunity given to back up anything during the installation. This installation assumes you are creating a full-time server and that any other operating system would just waste disk space.

Server Partitions

You need at least 2400MB, or 2.4GB, of total disk space. There are six partitions created, four with a fixed size and two that share the remainder of the disk or disks. The four fixed-size partitions created are a 256MB swap partition, a root partition of 256MB, a /boot partition of 16MB, and a /var partition of 256MB. The two variable-sized partitions created are a /usr partition of at least 512MB and a /home partition of at least 512MB.

The following list provides an overview of the partitions created automatically by a Server installation:

- 256MB swap partition
- 16MB /boot partition for all Intel platforms (a 2MB partition mounted as /dos and used for the Milo boot loader for an Alpha platform)
- A root (/) partition of 256MB
- A /var partition of 256MB
- A /home partition of at least 512MB
- A /usr partition of at least 512MB

exam
ⓦatch

The variable-sized partitions, /home and /usr, split the remainder of space and hence consume the rest of up to two additional disks if needed. If more than three disks are present, some of the disks will not be used.

Server Option Network Packages Installed

Table 3-1 is a sublist of the application packages loaded by the Server installation that are network related: (The order matches the sequence in the /RedHat/base/comps installation file.)

The Custom Installation Option

This Custom Installation option provides the most flexibility for an experienced Linux or UNIX administrator. During this installation option, you can select more or fewer groups and even individual packages within each group, configuring the partitions to suit your needs more explicitly.

TABLE 3-1	autofs	bind-utils	finger	ftp
Network-Related Packages Specific to Server Installation	whois	indexhtml	iptables	nfs-utils
	ncftp	ipchains	iputils	wget
	m4	nscd	nss_ldap	openldap-clients
	openssl	openssh	openssh-clients	krbafs
	pam_krb5	pidentd	portmap	gmp
	python	rdate	rhn_register	up2date
	rpm-python	python-xmlrpc	gnupg	rmt
	rsh	rusers	rwho	sendmail-cf
	stunnel	make	talk	tcp_wrappers
	telnet	traceroute	yp-tools	ypbind
	openssh-server	sysstat	xinetd	talk-server
	telnet-server	rusers-server	rwall-server	finger-server
	rsh-server	make	ypserv	

Selecting Packaged Sets

Of the many package sets available, each has a list of associated modules. In many cases, these module names are required for more than one group and hence appear duplicated in many of the package options. This ensures that all required dependencies are installed if only one or two optional packages are picked.

After all package group options have been selected, the system checks for duplicate name requests, and then installs all required packages just once. For full details on these package sets, see the /RedHat/base/comps text file.

Figures 3-3, 3-4, 3-5, and 3-6 show the various package set names available during a Custom installation in the GUI interface. Some packages will already be selected for you and will have either an asterisk (*) in the text interface selection box or will be a dark box to the left of the option, as depicted in Figure 3-3. These four figures contain all the package sets. During installation, only the first few names on the list can be seen, but there are actually more packages than can fit on one screen. To view them during installation, in the text interface you use the arrow keys to scroll up and down and in the GUI interface you click on the right side scroll bar, and you can press the SPACEBAR to toggle the selection on or off in either text or GUI mode.

Package set
names, first
screen

An asterisk means "selected." The base Linux system set of files is included automatically with any combination of packages you pick.

Note: Selected groups have dark boxes preceding them, whereas unselected options have light boxes beside them.

Package set
names, screen
two

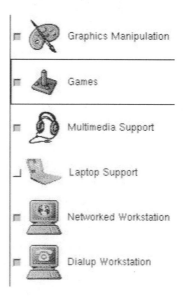

FIGURE 3-5

Package set
names, screen
three

FIGURE 3-6

Package set
names, screen
four

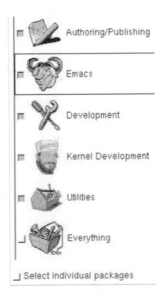

If you were doing a text-based install (an option in every installation), you would see a text-based set of choices as depicted in the following code:

```
[ ]     Printer Support
[*]     X-Window System
[*]     GNOME
[ ]     KDE
[*]     Mail/WWW/News Tools
[ ]     DOS/Windows Connectivity
[*]     File Managers
[ ]     Graphics Manipulation
[ ]     Console Games
[ ]     X Games
[*]     Console Multimedia
[*]     X multimedia support
[*]     Networked Workstation
[*]     Dialup Workstation
[ ]     News Server
[ ]     NFS Server
[ ]     SMB (Samba) Connectivity
[ ]     IPX/Netware(tm) Connectivity
[ ]     Anonymous FTP Server
[ ]     Web Server
[ ]     DNS Name Server
[ ]     Postgres(SQL) Server
[ ]     Network Management Workstation
[ ]     TeX Document Formatting
[ ]     Emacs
[ ]     Emacs with X-Window
[ ]     C Development
[ ]     Development Libraries
[ ]     C++ Development
[ ]     X Development
[ ]     GNOME Development
[ ]     Kernel Development
[ ]     Extra Documentation
[ ]     Everything

[ ] Select Individual Packages
```

In the preceding code, the choices are many and the combinations numerous. Pick only the packages you need. For instance, if you want to write C language programs, you would want the C Development packages and possibly the C Development

Libraries. The Extra Documentation package is usually a good idea for at least one machine in your network.

Disk Space Required for Installation Options

Most new computers come with very large disks, easily exceeding the 2.4GB (2400MB) needed for a full installation of Red Hat Linux. If you do not have this much space available, you should find out what space requirement is necessary for each installation.

Workstation-Class Space Requirements

A workstation-class installation (choosing to install GNOME or KDE) requires at least 1.2GB of free space. Choosing both GNOME and KDE, as well as the Games, requires at least 1.5GB of free disk space.

Server-Class Space Requirements

A server-class installation requires 2.1GB (2100MB) of disk space. If you were to use the Custom installation and decide which server packages to install, this installation would require 650MB for a minimal installation and at least 2.1GB of free space if every package is selected.

Laptop-Class Space Requirements

A Laptop-class installation (when choosing to install GNOME or KDE) requires at least 1.2GB of free space. If you choose both GNOME and KDE, as well as the Games you will need at least 1.5GB of free disk space.

Custom-Class Space Requirements

A Custom-class installation requires 300MB for a minimal installation and at least 2.4GB of free space if every package is selected.

on the
Job

The Everything option includes more packages than just selecting all the named groups, and thus requires more disk space overall. To use automatic partitioning, you must have enough free disk space available (1.2GB or more). If you do not have enough free disk space, this option will not appear during your installation, and you will be required to partition the disk.

How Much More Space Is Needed?

The question of disk space needed over and above operating system needs is always relevant. You will require as much as it takes, and probably more. The absolute minimum for a Red Hat Linux OS is around 300MB of disk space, if you install Linux with few server services and without X. With 500MB, you could probably sneak in X, but you still wouldn't have enough room for a few server services and games. You still need a minimum of 100MB or more to work with. 1.2GB for a Workstation installation is merely a starting point; you'll likely need lots of additional space for user data. As of early 2001, you probably cannot buy a new PC with less than 6000MB (6GB) of disk space. For a single-user workstation, this may be sufficient. For a server, it may be too small. If it is too small, you will know soon enough. However, it is easy to add disks to Linux and expand your file system at any time, so this should not be a big concern. Get the biggest disk you can afford as your starting point. Then, if you are new to Linux, select either Workstation for a single dedicated user or the Server option for Web, FTP, File and Print, DNS, and NFS services. If you have some Linux or UNIX experience, you will probably want to use the Custom Installation option for additional flexibility.

on the
()ob *All servers managed by the author have at least two disks containing between 6 and 10GB of disk space. You will probably find that if you are connected to the Internet and start creating Web and FTP content, by downloading applications, support material, new kernels, new games, and other amusements, you will very quickly use up the disk space. So go big! Get lots of disk space. It's cheap. Additionally, get a CD-R or CD-RW device to make backups, since single-write CD-ROMs have become very inexpensive lately, just like rewriteable CD-RW disks. Remember, the true cost of disk space is the cost of the disk space itself plus the cost of the backup media and associated backup hardware!*

CERTIFICATION OBJECTIVE 3.03

The Installation Process

There are many interrelated questions you need to answer during installation, just as there are many ways to access installation files, and many options on how to install the operating system. The following installation outline is designed to get you through it in as simple a fashion as possible, with just enough detail to keep you going.

Preinstallation Preparation

Red Hat Linux has been specifically crafted to work on almost any "old" PC hardware (built within the last five years or so). It can also be installed on Alpha and PowerPC-based computers, to name a few. Today, many manufacturers currently provide Linux driver support, and the list is growing quickly. You are probably better off with two- to three-year-old hardware rather than the most recent, since Linux drivers may not be available for them yet.

on the
Job

When the author got a new desktop PC without a network card, he stopped by the local computer shop to see what they could offer. Surprisingly, a number of network cards clearly stated "Linux Drivers Included." When purchased, the network card came with a Linux directory on the diskette containing the ".o" object file that needed to be put into the module library along with detailed instructions

Linux hardware support is gradually improving. Several of the major manufacturers, such as Compaq, Dell, and HP, offer their hardware preinstalled with Red Hat Linux. This is one way to get the latest hardware, with all the correct drivers, direct from the manufacturer. Check the hardware manufacturer's Web site for driver information.

on the
Job

The author has personally installed Linux on Toshiba, Dell, Compaq, and HP laptops without any problems. The biggest issue is usually the monitor settings, but with the current state of the probing by Linux, this has not been a problem since RH 6.0. Other potential problem areas are PC cards and the audio subsystem. Particularly in the case of PC cards, check that your computer's BIOS settings are compatible with Linux. In a completely contrary experience, another of the authors installed Linux on two different generations of Toshiba laptops—mid-1998 to mid-1999, which should be the "sweet spot" for being compatible—and yet both locked up while loading the Pcmciadd.img-based diskette, whether the BIOS was set for pcic compatibility or cardbus mode. Just goes to show that you never know.

You can check the Red Hat Web site at http://www.RedHat.com/hardware for current hardware drivers and pointers to other resources at any time.

PreInstalling Hardware Information

There is certain hardware configuration information about your system you should know before beginning:

- Hard drive(s): their geometry and size (and SCSI ID if using SCSI)
- Physical RAM (Random Access Memory) of the machine
- CD-ROM and its interface type: IDE or SCSI
- Mouse type and the port it is attached to
- NIC (Network Interface Card) make, model, and parameters
- SCSI adapter and settings if one is present

If you plan on installing the X-Window system, you'll also need:

- The video adapter card type and local video RAM memory size
- The monitor brand name or its specifications (horizontal and vertical refresh rates)
- Whether you plan on keeping your old operating system or not
- Primary use of this machine: workstation for a user or network server

Booting the First CD-ROM

Most current Intel-based PC hardware systems support booting from the CD-ROM drive directly. If you have purchased an official copy of Red Hat Linux 6.*x*/7.*x*, the first binary CD is designed to boot directly into the installation program.

Figure 3-7 shows the Red Hat 7.1 bootup screen that appears, whether you use the CD-ROM alone or start with the BOOT.IMG bootup diskette.

Creating Your Own Bootable CD-ROMs

You can download the .iso image files for every current Red Hat distribution, as well as many of Linux versions, from various sites around the Internet (such as ftp://sunsite.unc.edu/pub/Linux/distributions).

FIGURE 3-7

The Bootup
screen for Red
Hat Linux 7.1

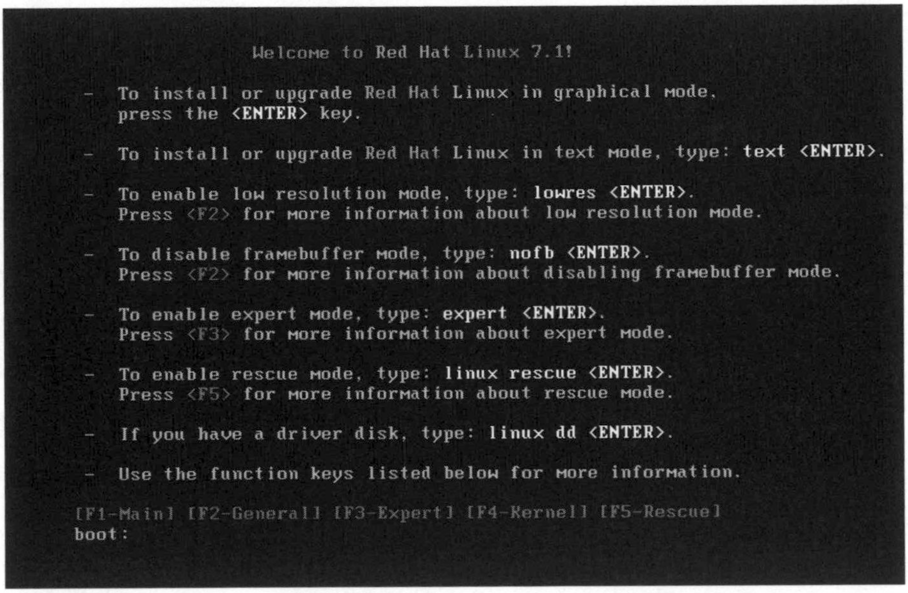

```
                    Welcome to Red Hat Linux 7.1!

    -   To install or upgrade Red Hat Linux in graphical mode,
        press the <ENTER> key.

    -   To install or upgrade Red Hat Linux in text mode, type: text <ENTER>.

    -   To enable low resolution mode, type: lowres <ENTER>.
        Press <F2> for more information about low resolution mode.

    -   To disable framebuffer mode, type: nofb <ENTER>.
        Press <F2> for more information about disabling framebuffer mode.

    -   To enable expert mode, type: expert <ENTER>.
        Press <F3> for more information about expert mode.

    -   To enable rescue mode, type: linux rescue <ENTER>.
        Press <F5> for more information about rescue mode.

    -   If you have a driver disk, type: linux dd <ENTER>.

    -   Use the function keys listed below for more information.

[F1-Main] [F2-General] [F3-Expert] [F4-Kernel] [F5-Rescue]
boot:
```

For example, the Red Hat 7.1 images are called: seawolf-i386-disc1.iso and seawolf-i386-disc2.iso. There are two additional files as well that you might find to download, as depicted in Figure 3-8: the source RPMs and the PowerTools disks. Each are about 650MB in size, so be prepared for a long wait on cable modem and DSL connections.

Many software packages that write CDs are aware of the .iso type file (ISO9660 is the standard CD-ROM format). The complete list of ISO images for Red Hat is depicted in Figure 3-9.

Another alternative is to download the entire distribution onto a single partition and install from that partition. This is a valid option during any installation. When

FIGURE 3-8

Downloading the
ISO image from
Sunsite.unc.edu

File transfer

Server: sunsite.unc.edu
File: /pub/Linux/distributions/redhat/7.1/emea/iso/i386/sea
Size: 668551168

Transferred: 48922624 bytes   1102 kbps   [Cancel]

FIGURE 3-9

The four ISO images available for Red Hat 7.1

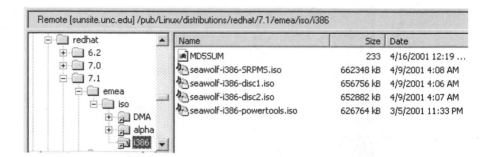

choosing the location of the files, you would indicate the type of file system and the partition ID.

The assumption throughout this book is that you have an official standard copy of the Red Hat software that contains all the necessary files for installation.

Installation Diskette(s) May Be Needed

In cases where your hardware does not boot from the CD-ROM, you will need to create a DOS-based boot disk, or disks, from the image files supplied with the CD-ROM set (or from those you downloaded from Internet sites).

You will need to create the installation diskette(s) as indicated next. There are a few options to consider here, depending on where the installation files will be retrieved from.

You need at least one of these three images on a diskette:

■ **boot.img** Installations using the local hard disk or CD-ROM

■ **bootnet.img** Installations using HTTP, FTP, or NFS primarily

■ **pcmcia.img** Installations on laptops that need to start the PC card manager service, originally known as the PCMCIA manager service

Depending on your hardware, you may also need one of the following:

■ **pcmciadd.img** Additional support for PCMCIA adapters

■ **drivers.img** Additional drivers for special hardware

These are secondary support disks (only asked for if needed):

■ **rescue.img** RH 6.0 used a single diskette for recovery of a failed system. You could always keep one handy for emergency purposes. It will boot the system with a minimal Linux kernel and its file system in a virtual RAM drive. This allows you to run various programs from the diskette and any mountable partition.

on the
Job

You can download the image files (boot.img and rescue.img) from a distribution of Red Hat 6.0 from the Internet to create these diskettes, which should work on any machine. Otherwise, the newer rescue mode needs to be booted directly from the CD-ROM or from the BOOT.IMG diskette.

To Use rescue.img

You must boot your machine with either the CD-ROM directly or via the Boot.img diskette and then the CD-ROM. When you get to the first screen prompt showing LILO, type **linux rescue**, and press ENTER. The boot disk will continue to load if using the CD-ROM, or you will eventually be asked for the next disk (PCMCIA if on a laptop). You must have the CD-ROM available in the local CD-ROM drive for rescue mode to install itself.

Essentially, the rescue installation loads a Linux kernel and a virtual file system into memory and includes a few very basic but essential binary files (utilities like fdisk, e2fsck, pico, mount, umount, mknod, and more) for you to try to recover your system with. You get a simple bash command shell with a simplified file system and some of the standard Linux system administration utilities.

When you start rescue mode, you are prompted for the keyboard and language modules, then are informed that the system has preloaded your entire file system set under the /mnt/sysimage directory.

on the
Job

For Red Hat 7.0 ONLY, you need to create the device files for any partitions you want to mount, as they are no longer supplied on the rescue disk virtual file system. Use the mknod command along with each device name. You have to issue a separate command for each to create all the device filenames you might need. For instance:

```
# mknod  /dev/hda; mknod  /dev/hda5; mknod  /dev/hda7
# would create 3 device files for the first IDE disk.
```

Remember, for RH 7.0 you need the unnumbered device file, /dev/hda, with fdisk. Within this bash shell, you can mount any partitions onto any directories that exist, or you can create the directories as needed before performing the mount to access any files on them. If the file system is corrupt on any partition, you can run the File System Check program, e2fsck, to repair the disk. You can edit files that need to be changed (such as fstab, lilo.conf, or any other configuration files), rebuild the LILO boot block, or do whatever you need to fix the system in this mode and then reboot.

The following is an illustration of how to boot into rescue mode:

```
Lilo:   linux rescue <ENTER>
? (installation of kernel and processes proceed)
```

Be aware that rescue mode will appear to be doing a complete installation, as indicated by some of the prompts you'll see. However, you'll soon be presented with the familiar bash shell command-line prompt after being prompted for language and keyboard and informed that your local file systems have already been mounted on /mnt/sysimage for you, if they were not corrupt (RH 7.1).

Creating Diskette Images

These boot diskette image files are supplied on the first CD-ROM of RH6*x*/RH 7.*x* and can be created in two ways:

- From any DOS-based system by using the supplied RAWRITE.COM utility (in \DOSUTILS on the first binary installation CD-ROM). (This does NOT work from within a DOS prompt of any Windows 9*x* system, but should work from the CMD.EXE prompt on NT.)

- Assuming your CD-ROM was drive E: on your DOS machine, you could simply enter: **E:> \dosutils\rawrite**

The RAWRITE program will next ask you for the name of the file to write to the diskette, then prompt you for the target (Enter **A:** at the second prompt).

You should supply the full path to the filename as shown next.

- **E:\images\boot.img**   (All versions of Red Hat)

- **E:\images\bootnet.img**   (All versions of Red Hat)

- **E:\images\pcmcia.img**   (All versions of Red Hat)

- **E:\images\pcmciadd.img**   (Red Hat 7.*x*)

- **E:\images\drivers.img**   (Red Hat 7.*x*)

You can view the files on this boot.img diskette as they are all DOS-oriented. You also must repeat this entire RAWRITE process for each image file you wish to create, as illustrated in Figure 3-10.

The contents of the BOOT.IMG file (after transferring to the diskette) are in DOS format (depicted in Figure 3-11).

Creating Diskette Images with Any UNIX/Linux System

You can also create diskette images by using the dd command from any running UNIX or Linux computer, along with the image files on the CD-ROM.

The supplied IMG (image) files on the diskette can be used from any UNIX/Linux system as well. The dd command to use would be for a typical Linux system (assuming the CD-ROM device is already in /etc/fstab):

```
[root]# mount /mnt/CD-ROM
[root]# cp /mnt/CD-ROM/images/*.img  /tmp
```

You can copy them all over, shown here, or use them directly off the CD-ROM:

```
[root]# dd  if=/tmp/boot.img  of=/dev/fd0
```

NOTE: You need a new diskette for each file.

You would need to repeat this for each image file you need, as previously stated. A list of these image names is presented in Figure 3-12.

Almost Ready to Install

With your system configured to either boot from the CD-ROM directly or from one of the boot image disks (BOOT.IMG, BOOTNET.IMG, or PCMCIA.IMG in the floppy drive and your Red Hat Linux 7.1 CD-ROM (marked with the number 1) in the CD-ROM drive, reboot or power cycle your machine.

FIGURE 3-10

Usage of the RAWRITE utility

```
F:\>\dosutils\rawrite
Enter disk image source file name: \images\boot.img
Enter target diskette drive: a:
Please insert a formatted diskette into drive A: and press -ENTER- :

F:\>\dosutils\rawrite
Enter disk image source file name: \images\drivers.img
Enter target diskette drive: A
Please insert a formatted diskette into drive A: and press -ENTER- :
```

FIGURE 3-11

The files
(BOOT.IMG) on
diskette

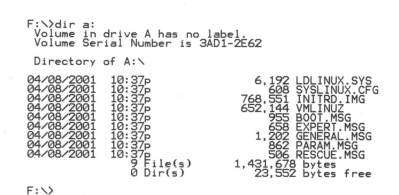

```
F:\>dir a:
 Volume in drive A has no label.
 Volume Serial Number is 3AD1-2E62

 Directory of A:\

04/08/2001  10:37p               6,192 LDLINUX.SYS
04/08/2001  10:37p                 608 SYSLINUX.CFG
04/08/2001  10:37p             768,551 INITRD.IMG
04/08/2001  10:37p             652,144 VMLINUZ
04/08/2001  10:37p                 955 BOOT.MSG
04/08/2001  10:37p                 658 EXPERT.MSG
04/08/2001  10:37p               1,202 GENERAL.MSG
04/08/2001  10:37p                 862 PARAM.MSG
04/08/2001  10:37p                 506 RESCUE.MSG
               9 File(s)      1,431,678 bytes
               0 Dir(s)          23,552 bytes free

 F:\>
```

Laptop Reboot

If you have a laptop that doesn't really power down, you will need to use the Shut
Down and Restart option of that operating system.

on the
job
*This inability to really shut down is a huge frustration for laptop users. You
might want to set the hardware to power down by using the Power button (if
this is configurable, that is—check the laptop manual). If the laptop does not
do this and power management doesn't work, you may have trouble turning
off the computer (especially if you have removed Windows entirely from the
laptop.)*

on the
job
*The author has had many laptops, most of which had a tiny reset button hidden
somewhere that you could use to force a reboot. You need to find out if your
laptop has one just in case. Most newer laptop models also have the "hold the
power button down for 6 seconds or more" option to force a power down.
Check your user manual for details on the Power button. Also, be aware that
some power saving modes won't operate without special disk partitions—
partitions that Linux cannot create. It may be necessary to download
software from the computer manufacturer to provide relatively complete
power management capabilities.*

FIGURE 3-12

List of IMG
(image) files
available with
RH7.*x*

boot.img   bootnet.img   drivers.img   oldcdrom.img   pcmcia.img   pcmciadd.img

Win9x/NT Reboot Procedure

For Windows 9x/NT, select Start and click the first option above Start: Shut Down. An option box should appear. Select the Restart option if it is not already selected and click OK. You may have to wait a few moments before the screen goes blank and the system BIOS starts rebooting.

Bootable CD-ROM

Most newer systems can be booted from the CD-ROM, which is probably the easiest way to accomplish an installation. Alternatively, you could boot your system from the Linux boot floppies, described earlier. Most systems have a BIOS setting that controls the boot search order, so you should consult your computer manufacturer's documentation for details.

Booting from DOS and Win9x; Not NT

If you already have MS-DOS 6.22, simply boot the machine until you get to a command prompt. If you have Win9x on your machine, reboot the machine into command mode. You cannot do this from NT, as it only works from a purely DOS-like command prompt, not from within the DOS PROMPT window of any MS Windows operating system.

Once in command mode, assuming you have access to your CD-ROM drive via an installed driver in the config.sys setup, you can run the file E:\DOSUTILS\ AUTOBOOT.BAT ((assuming your CD-ROM drive is E:). This will get you to the Installation program.

CD-ROM or Boot Diskette Starts Installation

After the hardware tests, the PC should boot from the CD-ROM or the floppy, whichever you have selected. After a few files are opened and decompressed, a Welcome To Red Hat Linux screen should appear.

You are finally at the first stage of the installation. This is a good time to point out a few things you'll need to know before moving on.

Necessary Information

The installation program uses either a full X-Window Graphical Interface (if it can load X), or it will default to an "almost graphical" text interface. Example figures from both the GUI and text-based interfaces are included in this section. Although the mouse does not work in the text interface specifically, you can move the cursor around using the UP and DOWN ARROW KEYS, the TAB key, and special function keys, as described next. It's not like a real GUI interface, but it's better than just a text command line. If you choose to attempt the graphical install and encounter problems, particularly display-oriented problems, restart the boot process and try the text interface.

Screen Cursor Movement, Selection, and Text Entry

The screens or windows that appear during the installation will have a standardized look and feel. The first screen offers an option to display help. Press the ENTER key to continue to the next screen. Some keys allow you to move through these screens the way a cursor would. In fact, in this situation, the "cursor" appears as a blinking underline or as a reverse-colored box over an item.

Figure 3-13 is just one of the many screens that appear during installation. Not all screens require cursor movement or force you to select multiple options. This screen shows all these features and is used to illustrate how to move around and select or deselect an option.

By pressing the ARROW KEYS, you can move up or down through the option selections at the top; in this case, the various mouse types. To get to the next field, press TAB to go forward to the next selection (in this case, Emulate 3 Buttons); then choose OK, followed by Cancel, and finally Help. If you TAB again, you will find

FIGURE 3-13

An Install screen example

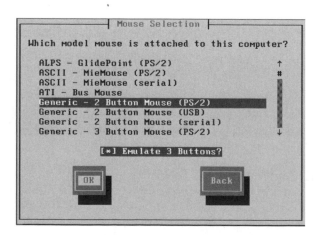

yourself back in the list of mouse devices. When not in a field of multiple selections, you can use the UP and DOWN ARROW KEYS to jump from one field to the next.

The keys shown in Table 3-2 can be used for navigation.

Assuming you are at the screen depicted in Figure 3-13, and your cursor is on the same option, if you press TAB, the cursor will move to the line "[ ] Emulate 3 Buttons?". You could toggle this selection on with the SPACEBAR, and off if pressed again. If you press TAB again, the cursor will move to the OK box.

At this point, you could use the arrow keys to move from OK to CANCEL to HELP to the *<mouse option>*. Once at the *<mouse option>*, the cursor keys select another *<mouse option>* line. Using ALT-TAB reverses the direction of the cursor movement. If you press ENTER or F12 at any time, it defaults to the OK option (unless you selected Cancel), along with all currently selected options.

Quick Overview of Installation

The installation starts after the initial bootup screen.

Part 1: Basic Workstation Installation Steps

For ease of installation, let the install program create the disk partitions as needed and select Continue. HOWEVER, if you do select Manually Partition, the screen in Figure 3-14 appears.

The Disk Druid utility is the best choice for beginners. (The fdisk tool will be explained later in this section.) The next screen shows the Disk Druid interface. Essentially, you can add if there is free space. This graphic only shows 2000MB free, which could be assigned to a partition. You can edit any partition and change the mount point if all other parameters are already set. If you wanted to change the partition layout, you need to delete unwanted partitions. Simply select the partition with your mouse and click Delete. You are prompted to confirm; select OK.

TABLE 3-2	Key	Function
Navigation Keys	TAB	Go to next element
	UP and DOWN ARROW KEYS	Move up/down through selections or menu items
	SPACEBAR	Toggle a selection ON or OFF
	F12, ENTER	Accept entries on current screen

FIGURE 3-14

Partitioning with
the Disk Druid
utility during
installation

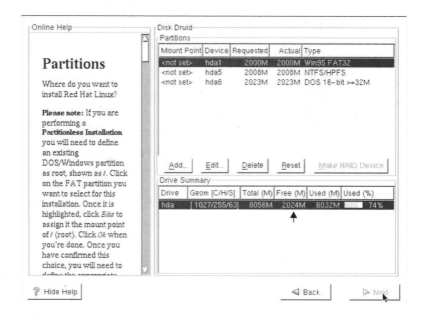

Assuming there is available space, as illustrated in Figure 3-14, you could add new
partitions by selecting Add (shown in Figure 3-15).

FIGURE 3-15

Adding a new
partition

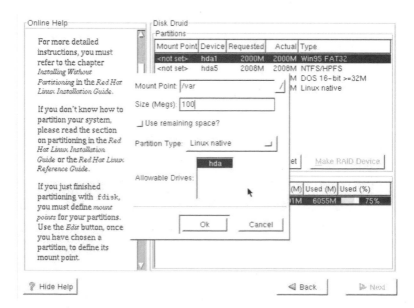

Once completed, as depicted in Figure 3-16, you can continue by clicking the Next button at the bottom of the screen.

At this point, you have only guessed at the sizes of each partition, and if you have been generous and made them big enough, your installation will work fine. If you were tight for space and guessed wrong for any partition size (for example the /usr partition needs lots of space, 512 is not enough for any of these installations), then your installation will fail and you will NOT be able to go back to redo the partitions. As a result, you will be forced to start your installation over and delete the old partitions, changing their sizes as needed. So, plan your partitions carefully and then add more space just in case!

Next, you should select all newly created partitions but skip any data partitions you have saved from a previous Linux installation, such as /home. Figure 3-17 shows all the Linux-oriented partitions you created and that already existed, assuming that you want to format them all. If you were saving the contents of a previous installations' /home directory, you would deselect that partition here so it would not get reformatted during this installation.

You are next presented with the LILO Configuration screen of options shown in Figure 3-18. If you are doing a text-based installation instead of a GUI interface, there are three separate screens provided for the information presented here.

It is always a good idea to create a boot diskette. This boot diskette will contain an MBR and all the files required to boot your system should you install your primary MBR onto the main disk (C:) and it fails for any reason. Additionally, if there were any options needed to be passed to the kernel at bootup, you can include them here.

FIGURE 3-16

Finished adding partitions with Disk Druid

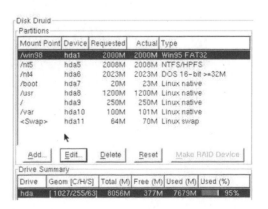

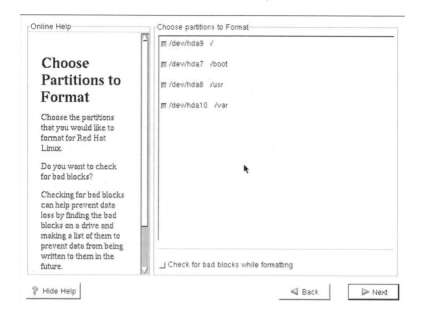

FIGURE 3-17

Formatting Linux Native partitions

The final section within Figure 3-18 contains the setup of where to put the boot record. If you already have a Windows installation, as depicted in Figure 3-18, then the

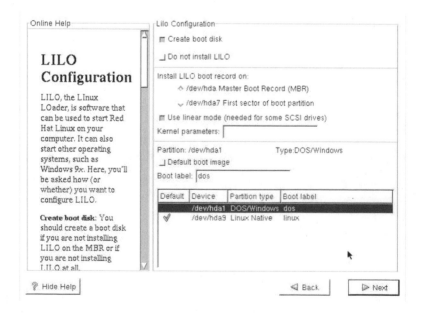

FIGURE 3-18

The LILO options screen includes Bootdisk, Kernel, and MBR setup options.

installer defaults to the Linux partition and will boot the Windows partition via the label name "dos." You could make the dos bootup option the default by selecting it and then choosing the Default Boot Image option, if desired. By default, the system will boot Linux after five seconds, or you can select the dos option to boot the previous Windows OS.

At this point, unless you really want to boot dos/Windows/NT as the default, you would simply select the OK button, and your system will be configured to boot Linux by default after five seconds (the timeout is not configurable at this point; once Linux is booted, you could change the timeout value by updating the text file /ctc/lilo.conf and running LILO)

The next step is the assignment of the network information (as in Figure 3-19). You can either use DHCP, if DHCP is available on your network, or provide the unique IP address and associated network mask values as a minimum to get started, along with the host name. Optional information includes the DNS server IP address and the Gateway IP address, also shown in Figure 3-19.

After network and host name configuration information, the Firewall Configuration option appears as depicted in Figure 3-20. It defaults to medium security, but if you are paranoid like most superusers should be, select the High option and click Next to continue.

FIGURE 3-19

Network configuration and host name setup

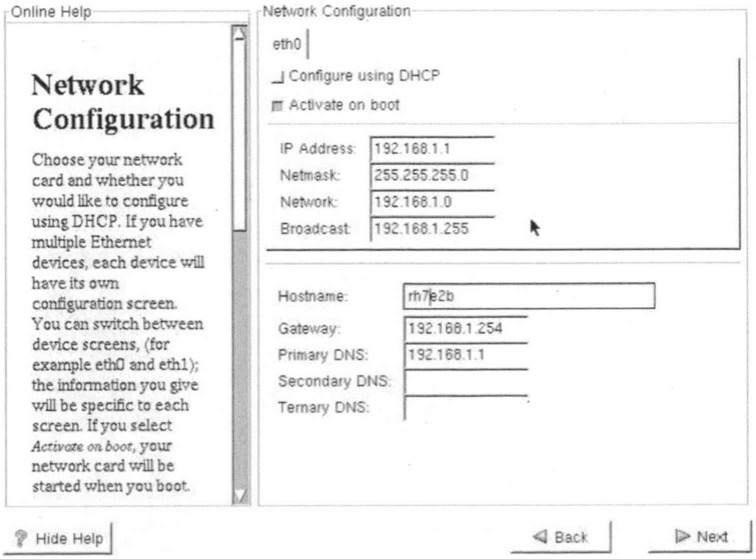

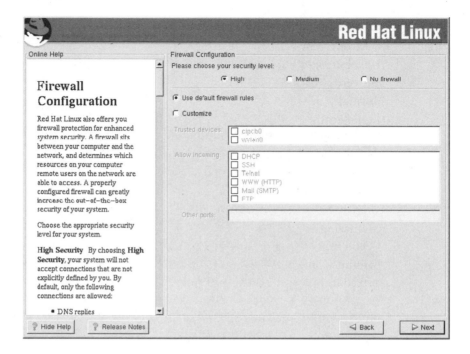

If you select the Customize option, assuming you already understand the network services listed, you can then select which services to allow in and which to block (as shown in Figure 3-21).

Both Telnet and FTP are considered insecure and should NOT be allowed through a firewall defense. Figure 3-21 shows them as not selected, while all the others are. You should configure the SSH (Secure Shell) service instead of FTP and Telnet. (This will be covered in a later chapter.)

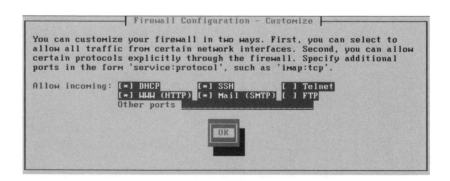

The next screen provides the mouse selection, as shown in Figure 3-22.

Most PC mice are two-button, but Linux/UNIX assumes you have a three-button device, so you must change the selection to the two-button option and verify that the box marked Emulate 3 Buttons (at the bottom) is selected. Normally, it will automatically select the Emulate 3 Buttons for you, which you should accept.

Technically, you can support multiple languages, if so desired. The default is simply USA English. Figure 3-23 shows you the many options available. Be aware that each additional language requires a significant amount of disk space.

The time configuration (shown in Figure 3-24) has plenty of bizarre locations you may never have heard of, so check it out, especially the GUI interface. It is quite an amazing application for just one little screen.

You must put in a valid password for the root account. Figure 3-25 shows the Account Configuration screen. The password itself is not echoed back to the screen. Instead, the asterisk character appears for each character typed in. A combination of letters, numbers, and shifted non-alphanumeric characters is the best choice. You must use at least eight characters as well.

FIGURE 3-22

Mouse
configuration

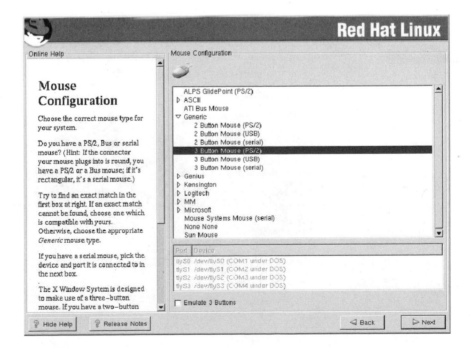

FIGURE 3-23

Language support selection

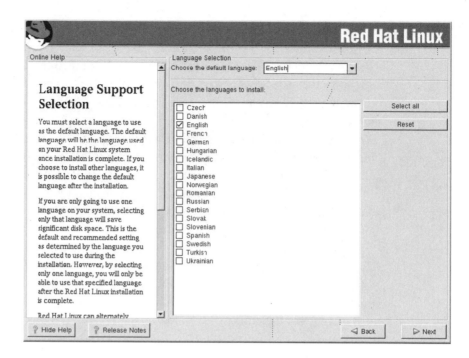

FIGURE 3-24

Time zone configuration

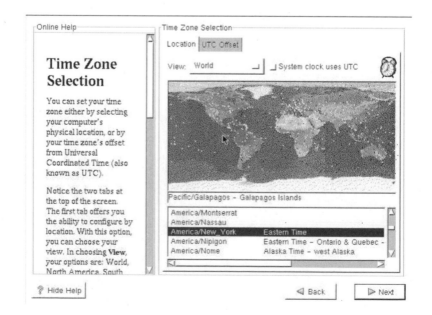

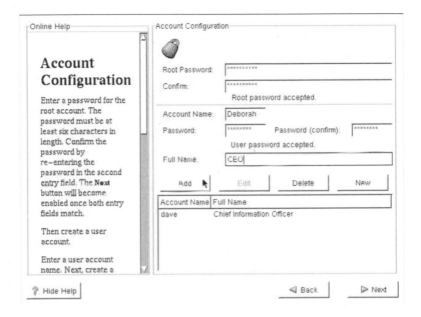

The lower half of Figure 3-25 allows you to add additional user accounts. All workstations should have one user account that is unprivileged. The root account should be left for administrative duties only.

This first screen requires that you add at least one user. You can add more than one user, as depicted with the next screen.

The next screen provides Authentication Configuration and encryption standards. All these services are explained in other sections and not discussed here. Simply accept the defaults for now.

The next screen lets you choose package groups to be installed. All of these groups are displayed at the beginning of the chapter, in Figures 3-6, 3-7, 3-8, and 3-9. A few package groups have been already picked for you by default. You can unselect them if desired. Notice the system keeps track of the size of the packages you have picked; add 50 percent to this size after decompression for what you probably need in real disk space. Unfortunately, the size shown does not indicate which directory structures (and hence, which file systems) require free space. This makes for a lot of trial and error when you are tight on space.

The final option on the package screen (depicted in Figure 3-9) is an option to select Individual Packages. This allows you to select specific packages out of any group, for a much finer customization level. This should not be done by beginners and is typically used when space is very limited and package selection is critical.

With this finely tuned package selection option afforded by Individual Package selection comes the requirement that you know exactly what packages require what other packages. If you don't, you may get an error indicating you missed a needed package (like that displayed in Figure 3-26).

If a package group you have selected has a dependency that cannot be resolved with already selected packages, an error occurs (as shown in Figure 3-26). Simply go back, select the necessary package, and continue until no further complaints appear. You have now completed the software package selection requirements of the installation. The next few screens depict the installation of the X-Window system.

At this point, you are informed that a log file of your installation will be kept in /tmp/install.log. Note also that this is the last point in which you can abort without actually changing your disks in any way. Up to this point, everything is memory resident. When you click Next (as depicted in Figure 3-27), you will have committed the disk partition changes, and you will see the formatting of the new partitions and then the installation of the packages.

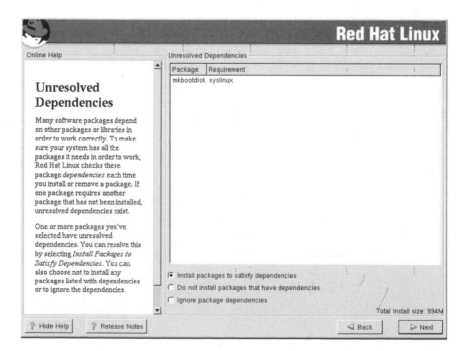

FIGURE 3-26

Unresolved dependencies in package groups

FIGURE 3-27

Ready to install

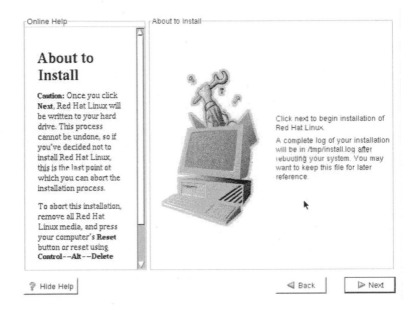

All selections and question are being recorded to an installation log that is put into the /tmp directory for your perusal after the installation. A few quick screens go by, formatting, copying the image to the disk, and then the actual package installation starts.

Ignore the estimated time required until at least a dozen or more packages have been installed as the estimated time will not be very accurate.

If you're installing from a CD-ROM, the required files are spread over two CD-ROM disks. You will be prompted when it's necessary to change disks.

When all packages are installed, a post-install procedure is completed that includes any package post-install procedures.

The final step is to create a boot diskette (as shown in Figure 3-28).

Creating a custom boot disk will allow you to boot the system, even if the traditional Linux boot loader, LILO, becomes corrupt or misconfigured. This is highly recommended! After this is complete, you're ready to reboot because you're done!

Caveat Emptor on Installation   Do not worry if you make a mistake the first time on a test machine. Just redo the installation; it will be significantly faster and easier than trying to correct a problem. There are so many options and possibilities in the overview just presented that it is not possible to name them all or take them all into account. In most cases, the default is sufficient if you do not understand the

FIGURE 3-28

Create a boot disk

question posed. Move on and get it installed; then read the FAQs, HOWTOs, and other related docs once you are up and running. You can always reinstall; the second and third installs are actually a very good thing considering you need to know this very well for the RHCE Exam.

Although you have finished the installation and have worked the concepts of partitioning (and possibly multiple operating system boots), there are still a few more details to note, such as LILO errors, BIOS issues, and others, all described in the following sections.

CERTIFICATION OBJECTIVE 3.04

The LILO Boot Process and Intel Hardware/BIOS Issues

The original Intel motherboard design provided a mechanism to start any operating system. It would load a bootup program, located in the first sector of the available disks starting with A: and followed by C:. This bootup program is located in an area most often called the master boot record, or MBR. This is the first program loaded by the BIOS. This program then loads the real operating system boot control program(s), which, in turn, starts the operating system.

The main issue with this bootup is that the MBR has to be found in the first 1024 cylinders of any disk. This is because the BIOS programs stored on the motherboard would not be able to "see" any value over 1024, a limitation of the original BIOS design. With newer motherboards, they use a mechanism called Logical Block Addressing, or LBA mode, on disks to alleviate this problem. The disk LBA mode reports back "logical" values for the cylinder, head, and sector so that the BIOS can then "see" a larger disk drive. Internally, the drive uses the LBA values to find the real cylinder, head, and sector. One way or another, you must ensure that the boot block for Linux is not past this magical boundary, or the boot will fail.

on the **job**

Usually, Linux opts for the /boot partition if it does not rewrite the MBR. You can put it on any partition available. The MBR is just the most convenient; the system can cascade to any previous OS. My laptop has LILO cascade to NT, which cascades to Win95. I can choose Linux first, or NT second, if I want, or just let it cascade to Win95.

Boot Control of Your System

Linux uses a set of files to boot your system, referred to collectively as LILO, which is short for Linux Loader. During or after installation, you have two options:

■ Create a boot disk

■ Update a local disk partition with the LILO MBR

The boot disk is an excellent way to hide the Linux system for other users. For development or help desk systems with multiple operating systems, you can create a boot disk that specifically boots just Linux when inserted into the floppy drive.

One major danger with a floppy is the chance of damaging that boot disk. You may want to make multiple copies to minimize possible problems. You can use the dd command to make multiple copies of the disk. Here is an example of the commands needed to create a copy of the original diskette to a local file and how to create duplicates from this local file:

```
$ dd  if=/dev/fd0    of=diskettebootup.img # stores a copy of diskette
$ dd  if=/diskettebootup.img   of=/dev/fd0  # makes the copy
```

There is a utility supplied with Linux that will create a bootup diskette from your running system with the required root and /boot partitions called mkbootdisk. You need to know the name of the running kernel, but you can have the system generate that for you and substitute it onto the command line as follows:

```
$ # to create a boot disk for the 'current kernel number'
$ mkbootdisk /dev/fd0 `uname -r`
```

Updating /dev/hda MBR

The old MBR, if there was a previous operating system, is moved to a new location, and Linux installs its own MBR. This is only the first part of the loading operation required to get Linux started. The second part of the bootup process is contained within the /boot directory structure.

/etc/lilo.conf

You can update or change your bootup options with the lilo configuration file, /etc/lilo.conf, and with the boot loader install utility, /sbin/lilo.

The first part of the loading operation provides a prompt allowing you to enter any valid listed boot option, along with any command options for that boot option. All LILO control is maintained by the system file, /etc/lilo.conf. The following listing shows the details of deciphering /etc/lilo.conf.

```
========================================================
[root@linux6 /root]# cat /etc/lilo.conf
boot=/dev/hda
map=/boot/map
install=/boot/boot.b
prompt
timeout=50
default=Win95
image=/boot/vmlinuz-2.2.5-15
        label=linux
        root=/dev/hda8
        initrd=/boot/initrd-2.2.5-15.img
        read-only
other=/dev/hda1
        label=Win95
        table=/dev/hda
[root@linux6 /root]#
========================================================
```

```
boot=/dev/hda
map=/boot/map
```

This is where the system is to look for the bootup and map info: the first hard disk.

```
install=/boot/boot.b
```

This is the location for the second part of the LILO program startup routine.

```
prompt
```

This forces the lilo: prompt to appear on the console.

```
timeout=50
```

This is the default five seconds before the boot process continues automatically.

```
default=Win95
```

Normally, the first boot listing (next section) is default. This line supercedes the default action and selects any boot choice via the identifying label.

```
image=/boot/vmlinuz 2.2.5-15
```

This is the actual virtual memory compressed kernel (version 2.2.5, with the -15 representing the Red Hat revision number) of Linux.

```
label=linux
```

This identifies the "boot option" label that appears if you press TAB at the LILO prompt.

```
root=/dev/hda8
```

This shows the location of the root, /, directory file system partition.

```
initrd=/boot/initrd-2.2.5-15.img
```

This reveals the location of the second stage (RAM disk) load.

```
read-only
```

During installation, the RAM disk file system is started in read-only mode. After the second stage is finished with a few tests, the RAM disk is unloaded from memory, and the real root partition is mounted from the file system in read/write mode.

The next section is another boot option—in this case, to boot Windows 95 on the first partition, known as C: to users of DOS/Windows 9*x* (known as /dev/hda1 to Linux).

```
other=/dev/hda1
        label=Win95
        table=/dev/hda
```

The table is the location of the partition table to be used—in this case, the first physical IDE type disk on the system.

What to Do When You See LILO

When you restart the system, after the internal POST (Power On Self Test), the LILO boot block, MBR, is loaded.

You then see a big picture of the Red Hat logo on the left, and all your boot options appear in the column on the right.

By default, you have five seconds to enter something; otherwise, the system will automatically continue with the first labeled boot (default) option.

By simply pressing ENTER, the default entry is selected, typically, the one known as Linux. If you wanted to select the other option, typically dos but could be anything like Win95 or NT, you would cursor to it and press ENTER. If you were at a command prompt, you could enter the specific label name (case should not matter) as shown below for an option called Win95.

```
lilo: win95<ENTER>
```

LILO Parameters

To pass a parameter to LILO, type the parameter after the label name. For example, if you wanted to start your system in rescue mode, you would type **rescue** at the prompt when booting with the Boot.img or Bootnet.img diskette. If you wanted to start your system in single-user mode, either of the two following commands would provide the same result:

```
lilo: linux  single<ENTER>
lilo: linux  1<ENTER>
```

Single-User Mode

A common kernel option is the word "single," or alternatively, the number 1. Both of these options change the default behavior of the startup such that the system boots into runlevel 1, also known as single-user mode.

Many more parameters can be added, including how much memory to use, and what device to load as the root device in the case of a broken mirror set. All of these are documented on the CD-ROM in the /usr/doc/LILO subdirectory.

Single-user mode is the most commonly used option. This is the system maintenance mode for experienced Linux administrators. In single-user mode, no file systems other than the root file system are loaded. You are then able to do clean backups and restores to any partitions in this mode. You also have the ability to run administration commands, recover or repair passwd and shadow password files, run file system checks, and so forth.

In some cases, to get out of single-user mode you just have to type **exit** and your system will go into multiuser mode. Alternately, if you have made changes or repairs to any partitions, you should reboot the machine. Press CTRL-ALT-DEL to reboot from within single-user mode.

LILO Errors

The LILO first stage will also indicate some common and not so common problems:

```
(nothing)      did not get to lilo at all
L          first stage loaded and started
LI          second stage loaded from /boot
LILO         all of lilo is loaded correctly
```

Occasionally, there may be an error due to partition table changes, bad blocks, and so forth. On these rare occurrences, you will only get partial LILO prompts:

```
LIL          second stage boot loader is started
LIL?          Second stage loaded at an incorrect address
LIL-          the descriptor table is corrupt
```

What to Do If /etc/lilo.conf Changes

If /etc/lilo.conf changes, you will first need to log in as root. If you want to add additional kernel options, use a text editor such as vi, pico, or joe to modify the /etc/lilo.conf file. Once modified, the changes must be added to the LILO boot process. This is done by running the /sbin/lilo utility at the prompt. This forces the update of the boot record to include the changed options.

exam ✦ ***Watch***

If you have a dual boot system, you may want to change the default to another operating system for a short period of time. You update the /etc/lilo.conf file and then must run /sbin/lilo to force the changes at bootup. This may also need to be done in some rescue situations, in which you will need to rebuild the boot record. In the case of a rescue, you should be aware that this boot record uses a relative offset to point to the files to be loaded. Make sure you mount any extra file systems, after the root file system, in similar locations to normal.

CERTIFICATION OBJECTIVE 3.05

Using Syslinux and loadlin

Although Red Hat Linux uses the LILO boot loader program to manage the initial bootup process, there are alternatives that other distributions of Linux use.

During installation, you will see another loader called Syslinux.n.m-x. This is an MS-DOS-based loader and is used on all the installation images because it is small enough to fit on a floppy and boot a basic Linux kernel. You can get more information about Syslinux from http://metalab.unc.edu/pub/Linux/system/boot/loaders/.

Another popular option is called loadlin. The loadlin program is also MS-DOS-based and requires a copy of the Linux kernel, and possibly an initial RAM disk if your drives are SCSI types, to be MS-DOS available. You can read the HOWTO and FAQs on loadlin if you want to use it instead of LILO. You can find out more about loadlin at http://metalab.unc.edu/pub/Linux/system/boot/dualboot/.

Essentially, the loadlin program relies on MS-DOS instead of your system BIOS to load Linux. The advantage is that loadlin can load a kernel beyond the 1024 cylinder boundary, from any file system that is accessible to MS-DOS. Note that loadlin cannot be used from any Win9x or NT DOS PROMPT environment; you must boot into MS-DOS mode.

There are also some commercial boot loaders available, like System Commander, that can create a table of optional boots for almost any other operating system you can install on an Intel-based PC. Some of these commercial products can update the NT boot loader system and provide a direct boot option to Linux from the NT boot prompt. More information on System Commander can be found at http://www.systemcommander.com/products/products.html.

There is a mini-HOWTO document for loadlin being used with Win95 on the documentation CD-ROM at HOWTOS/mini/Loadlin+Win95-98-ME, if further details are needed.

CERTIFICATION OBJECTIVE 3.06

Additional Installation Details

Now that the basic screens from the install have been explained, we can delve into greater detail regarding the more important aspects of Linux you should know before attempting an installation.

Partition Concepts

With either fdisk or Disk Druid utility, you must understand basic partitioning concepts. In Figure 3-29, 16 partitions are displayed. Though 16 partitions are possible, unless you needed them, you would probably not break a disk into this many sections. It is totally up to you, however. Keep in mind, though, that you can only use 15 of the partitions to actually hold any type of file system.

On a SCSI disk, there is no extended disk option, but you can still create 15 usable partitions. In this case, the naming scheme would be sca instead of hda for the first drive, then scb, scc, and so on.

FIGURE 3-29	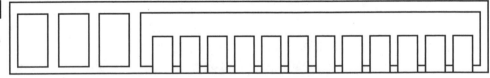
A maximum of 16 devices are possible for any one IDE disk, 15 of which are usable	

Preparation Details Before fdisk or Disk Druid

You will be introduced to the use of fdisk in full detail in the next section. There have been a few references during the installation about using fdisk and Disk Druid to create partitions, but you still need to know what all these partitions are actually for as there is no one particular answer.

You must decide what to do with your disk space before you begin partitioning it. This is the first, and probably most important, preinstall detail to know. So, what partitions will you need to create? If you have a new machine, you can let the Workstation or Server Installation options do it for you. If you plan to use the Custom option, you must first have a clear idea of your partition scheme.

Getting Started: The Sample Partition Table

As a preliminary step to getting started, you need to have a clear idea of how to separate your file system onto various disks. Table 3-3 can be used as a starting guide to decide how to create your partition scheme.

Improved Performance: Spreading the Load   Performance improvements can be obtained for any system in two simple ways:

- With increased memory
- By spreading the load of read and write operations across multiple disks, or even better, across multiple controllers

Keep this performance enhancement in mind when deciding what directory structure to put on which partition on each disk. You should try to keep the system files separate from the data files, and preferably on separate disks and controllers.

Another way to "spread the load" is to use software or hardware solutions that use various forms of RAID. On a big server, RAID can be an excellent way to provide better performance and better reliability. Hardware solutions are more expensive and provide better service than software-based RAID solutions should disasters occur. How to set up RAID is discussed in Chapter 5, or you can check the HOWTO documents for more information.

Table 3-3 lists some of the commonly separated file system directories in the left column, and in the right column contains comments regarding size and why to separate it. You can then fill in the second, third, and fourth columns with the actual information for your system and post it on the machine for easy reference.

TABLE 3-3	Use	Disk	Partition	Size (MB)	Comments
The Installation Worksheet	Swap	hda / hdb / hdc / ?			Required. Have to have at least one; two to three times memory is typical (can split swap space across multiple disks and controllers for better performance). 64MB defaults.
	/boot				Must be within first 1024 "seeable" cylinders on any disk. 16MB default.
	/ (root)				Contains system; typically provides access to all other partitions (required) No default; 600+ workstations; 256MB server. Note: recommended 1000+MB if no other partitions.
	(unusable as a file system)	hda / hdb /hdc / hdd			IDE—Extended container partition for the logical drives (max 12).
	/var				Variable area for system logs, spooling, e-mail, and so on. 256MB default server.
	/usr				Usually for "user" stuff: binaries, data, games, and so on. 512+MB default server.
	/home				Home directories, good idea to separate for backup and quota management. 512+MB default server.
	/var/ftp (RH7.x)				Separate if large FTP site.
	/yourdata				Your specific needs.
	/opt				Many third-party and commercial software packages install to here.

CERTIFICATION OBJECTIVE 3.07

Creating Partitions: Details

Now that you have the partition layout for your system, you need to actually create them. For this, you will probably use the fdisk utility, either from a boot diskette or from the running system. The next section details exactly how to use fdisk to create your system partitions.

Why Separate File Systems?

The UNIX, and hence Linux, file system has been historically split up into smaller, more manageable pieces for various reasons: everything started on small disks, small partitions are easier to dump and restore, partition limits can be used to restrict or control disk usage, and so on.

The Linux file system can also be broken up into smaller pieces or left as one large unit, if so desired. When would you use one big partition? When you have a large RAID5 disk farm providing your file system or when you are creating a small test system.

Linux File Systems: /tmp /boot /usr/local /var /home

The historical separations have been blurred over time, but the following are the Red Hat Linux recommended file system breakouts for the base system of any server:

/tmp	Used by everyone; no need to back up; gets very fragmented; usually has a crontab entry for "cleanup."
/boot	Represents second-stage extras for LILO; must be within first 1024 "seeable" cylinders.
/var	The variable area gets written to by memory; often used for mail and spooling; system memory data becomes very fragmented.
/home	Home directories of all users; good idea to keep them separate from system files if using quotas; restricts quota management "area."
/usr/local	Specific binaries, data, and setup files for this particular machine.

Additional file systems can be created to meet additional or specific needs of related groups of users (for example, /development, /dbms, /financials, /inventory, and so forth).

Possible Target File Systems for Separate File System Placement

Your Linux host may also be supporting a very specific set of applications (such as Web and FTP hosting), any one of the many file and print sharing services (like NFS, Samba, NetWare, and Macintosh), or a third-party application (database management system, financials, Geographical Information System, video, software development, and so forth).

In many cases, you probably want to break up these files into separate, manageable units, perhaps spread over many partitions if they are very large. This disperses the load across the file system, provides better disk management, backup, and recovery options, and allows for a more flexible overall system design.

Swap Space Partition Sizing and Placement

The total memory available to any and all programs is the sum of all RAM and swap space. Linux uses a linear memory model.

Although there is no hard-and-fast format, a good rule of thumb is to create your swap partition so it's two to three times that of small memory systems. This was typical in the early days of UNIX when RAM was very expensive and disk space was cheap. Current systems can easily have large amounts of memory. Is there an upper limit? Not really, especially when you consider it is 64GB for the Enterprise kernel alone. Still, you could have a smaller swap space if you had a huge amount of RAM.

One recommendation is to use two to three times the memory for any system with less than 512MB of RAM. After this point, it might seem wasteful to create a 1GB swapfile that is almost never used on a system with 512MB of RAM. You might opt for a 512MB or even as low as 256MB swap partition.

The swapfile is used sparingly for some system information, but is used heavily to page out user processes when more memory is needed. In essence, you *never* want to swap user processes. Keep in mind, RAM is in nanoseconds of speed, whereas disk is in milliseconds of speed—a million-fold difference. The swap is just there in case you have a sporadic need for lots more virtual memory. If your machine constantly uses swap space, this action will slow it down significantly. In such cases, You should get more RAM for your system or reduce the workload.

Technically speaking, you can have up to eight swap partitions, totaling a maximum of 4GB. Any single swap partition can be up to 2GB maximum. Swap partitions are only used for virtual memory, acting like additional RAM to your system, and use a different file system than the other partitions. Some high-end RDMS database systems have their own format and file system for partitions, like Oracle, to contain their data, as opposed to an ext2fs.

Supported File System Types

Linux natively supports many other file systems, such as DOS, HPFS, FAT, VFAT, and NTFS. So if you have OS/2, Windows 9x, or a DOS operating system using other partitions on the same machine Linux is installed on, you can access them. The system will be able to "see" the native files.

The most popular Linux file system is called Second Extended File System, denoted by ext2fs or just ext2. Most associated utilities will start with or contain e2, like e2fsck, dumpe2fs, mke2fs, and so on.

In the following code, the first command, df, displays the total, used, and available free space on all currently mounted file systems. The second command, mount, shows the type of file system. In this case, the device /dev/hda1 is mounted using VFAT as /DosC and represents direct access to what would be the C: drive of the Windows operating system on this first partition. Linux can directly access many other native file systems.

```
==================================================================
[root@linux6 /root]# df
Filesystem            1k-blocks      Used Available Use% Mounted on
/dev/hda8              932833    502478    382162  57% /
/dev/hda7               23300      2588     19509  12% /boot
/dev/hda1             1052064    914784    137280  87% /dosC
/dev/hda6             1052064    111648    940416  11% /dosE
/dev/hdb              556054     556054         0 100% /mnt/cdrom
[root@linux6 /root]# mount
/dev/hda8 on /          type ext2   (rw)
none      on /proc      type proc   (rw)
/dev/hda7 on /boot      type ext2   (rw)
/dev/hda1 on /dosC      type vfat   (rw)
/dev/hda6 on /dosE      type vfat   (rw)
none      on /dev/pts   type devpts (rw,mode=0622)
/dev/hdb  on /mnt/cdrom type iso9660 (ro)
[root@linux6 /root]# ls /dosC
CDsetup.bat      boot.ini      detlog.old    io.sys       sbide.sys
Exchange         bootlog.prv   detlog.txt    mscdex.exe   scandisk.log
My Documents     bootlog.txt   digipix       msdos.--     setuplog.old
```

```
Program Files     bootsect.dos   drvspace.bin   msdos.bak      setuplog.txt
RescuedDoc1.txt   ca_appsw       dswin          msdos.dos      suhdlog.—-
RescuedDoc.txt    command.com    ffastun.ffa    msdos.sys      suhdlog.dat
acess             command.dos    ffastun.ffl    mskids         system.1st
autoexec.bat      config.dos     ffastun.ffo    netlog.txt     temp
autoexec.dos      config.sys     ffastun0.ffx   ntdetect.com   w95undo.dat
autoexec.old      config.win     himem.sys      ntldr          w95undo.ini
boot.—-           dblspace.bin   io.dos         recycled       win95
[root@linux6 /root]#
================================================================
```

This listing shows a typical Workstation installation with two additional mount points for the C: and E: drives used by the Win9x and NT operating systems also resident on this machine. Why would you bother to do this: Test machine, help desk machine, development, only have one machine and need to practice, in a classroom, and many more possible scenarios. You would not do this for a typical single-user production machine.

One of the benefits is that you can move and copy files between the Linux partitions and the DOS partitions using standard Linux commands. You cannot, however, run any Windows applications within Linux unless you run a DOS or Windows Emulation package.

The fdisk Utility

The fdisk utility is universally available and should be one of the first tools you get acquainted with. There are many commands, even an expert mode, but you only need to know a few as discussed here.

Though you can modify the physical disk partition layout using many programs, we will be discussing the Linux implementation of fdisk. FDISK.EXE from DOS has the same name, and is also used for creating partitions, but doesn't incorporate any Linux-compatible features. A simple rule to follow is to use whichever fdisk is supplied with an operating system when creating partitions for that operating system.

Using fdisk: Starting, Getting Help, and Quitting   The following screen output shows how to start the fdisk program, how to get help, and how to quit the program.

```
====================================================
#  fdisk /dev/hda


Command (m for help): m
```

```
Command action
   a   toggle a bootable flag
   b   edit bsd disklabel
   c   toggle the dos compatibility flag
   d   delete a partition
   l   list known partition types
   m   print this menu
   n   add a new partition
   o   create a new empty DOS partition table
   p   print the partition table
   q   quit without saving changes
   s   create a new empty Sun disklabel
   t   change a partition's system id
   u   change display/entry units
   v   verify the partition table
   w   write table to disk and exit
   x   extra functionality (experts only)

Command (m for help): q


======================================================
```

The fdisk utility is all text-based and, as such, displays hard drive parameters at startup.

Using fdisk: In a Nutshell   You should print to screen (p) the current partition table entries. You then create a new (n) partition, either primary (p) or logical (l), partition number (1–4 for primary, 5–16 for logical), starting one number after whatever is the current last-used cylinder number. The size of the partition will depend on disk geometry; do not worry about exact size here. Normally, fdisk defaults to creating a Linux Native type (82) partition. For the swap partition, the partition type has to be toggled (t) to type 82, swap. Repeat these general steps for each required partition. Note that all other partitions should be type 83, Linux Native. Please note that fdisk is memory resident and makes all these changes in memory. You need to write (w) these changes to the disk as the last step, otherwise no changes will be made.

Using fdisk: Deleting and Creating Partitions   In the following screen output sample, you will remove the only partition. The sample output screen first starts fdisk. Then you print (p) the current partition table, delete (d) the partition by number (1 in this case), write (w) the changes to the disk, and quit (q) from the program.

Last chance to change your mind before deleting the current partition.

```
=========================================================
#fdisk /dev/hdb


Command (m for help): p
Disk /dev/hdb: 255 heads, 63 sectors, 525 cylinders
Units = cylinders of 16065 * 512 bytes

Device    Boot    Start    End    Blocks   Id  System
/dev/hdb1   *        1      525   4217031   6  FAT16
Command (m for help): d
Partition number (1-1): 1

Command (m for help): w


=========================================================
```

You did it! Now you can create the partitions you need.

Using fdisk: A New PC with No Partitions

After installing Linux on a new PC, you'll want to use fdisk to configure additional physical disks attached to the system. Create a new partition, type **Primary** for the first three, and then **Extended** for the rest of the disk as partition 4 before creating logical drives 5–16 within the extended partition. There is no need to create an extended partition unless you require more than four partitions on the new disk.

Using fdisk: Creating Partitions

The following screen output sample shows the steps used to create (n) the first (/boot) partition, make it bootable (a), and then finally write (w) the partition information to the disk. (Note: Although you may ask for a 16MB partition, the geometry of the disk may not allow that size, as in the example.)

```
=========================================================
# fdisk /dev hdb


Command (m for help): n
Command action
   l   logical (5 or over)
   p   primary partition (1-4)
p
First cylinder (1-256, default 1): 1
```

```
Last cylinder or +size or +sizeM or +sizeK (2-256,def 256): 2

Command (m for help): p
Disk /dev/hdb: 255 heads, 63 sectors, 256 cylinders
Units = cylinders of 16065 * 512 bytes
   Device Boot    Start      End    Blocks  Id  System
/dev/hdb1             1        2     16044  83  Linux
```

==

Repeat the commands to create the rest of the partitions. After all are created, you should end up with the final design as illustrated in the following output screen sample:

```
====================================================
Command (m for help): p

Disk /dev/hdb: 255 heads, 63 sectors, 256 cylinders
Units = cylinders of 16065 * 512 bytes
   Device Boot    Start      End    Blocks  Id  System
/dev/hdb1             1        2     16044  83  Linux
/dev/hdb2             3       18     64176  82  swap
/dev/hdb3            19      169   1203300  83  Linux
/dev/hdb4           170      250    649782   5  Extended
/dev/hdb5           170      201    248682  83  Linux
/dev/hdb6           202      257    449232  83  Linux

Command (m for help): w

====================================================
```

The fdisk Write Option   The last option used in the preceding listing, the w option, is actually the most important! Up to this point, you have been changing things in program memory and have not actually made any changes to the physical disk table at all. The write option, w, actually updates the disk's internal partition table information. This always requires a reboot, as significant changes were just made. The alternative to this option is q, which quits without saving these changes.

Disk Druid

One of the excellent additional programs supplied with the Red Hat Linux installation is the graphical Disk Druid program, which provides a more intuitive interface. The actions are similar, but the interface hides the need to know about the partition ID (it just uses a text name ID) and has an option called Growable. This option allows the system to determine how much disk space a partition will take based on available free space. However, Disk Druid is available only at initial installation time.

on the Job

This Growable option is very beneficial in the kickstart scripts (automated installation scripts), where the target hardware may have varying sized disks. All partition space can be allocated by allowing it to "Grow" to fill the disk during installation. This is something fdisk cannot do.

Hardware Installation Scenarios

You may be given machines with operating systems that use all the available disk space, or machines with operating systems that can be completely replaced.

One Operating System Only

If you do not want to save the old OS, you can delete all earlier partitions and start with no partitions on the disk. If the machine will only be used for one operating system, Linux, this is the best option. You then only need to decide whether the workstation or server options will meet your needs. If they do not meet your needs, you can use the Custom Installation option to modify either the workstation or server design to better suit your needs.

Already Have Windows x.xx

If you purchased a basic PC, chances are it was preconfigured with an MS Windows-based operating system. Most likely, the entire disk has been formatted as one big partition, known as the C: drive. This is an unfortunate design for you at this point. If you want to keep the current operating system as is, you can find some software that will shrink the partition down for you. There are commercial versions, such as Partition Magic from PowerQuest Inc. (http://www.powerquest.com), and free versions, such as the FIPS utility supplied on the installation images.

Note: Due to the variance of hardware and software available, neither of these products are guaranteed by Red Hat or the author to be without peril. You need to read the documentation and back up everything twice to be sure; then try this with the assumption that something may go wrong, and if so, you can always rebuild (assuming you know how to do this). Many before you have successfully used these utilities, including the author, but things can still go wrong, so be prepared for the worst.

If you use FIPS, it will create a second partition out of the available space you retrieved from any other partition. You should delete this new empty partition before starting the Linux installation. This will allow the installation script to create the workstation, or server, required partitions from the available space, or allow you to create the partition scheme yourself in the Custom installation.

Real-World Applications—Using Partition Magic   A preconfigured laptop came with 1.5GB of disk space on one IDE disk drive, which was allocated as one Primary partition, and had Windows 95 as the operating system. The first step was to make sure the current set of files on the disk drive was reduced to less than the 1GB boundary. Unnecessary software and files were archived and removed so there was only 800MB of used space on this primary disk. Using DEFRAG.EXE, the files were shifted to ensure they were within the first 800MB of the disk, then using Partition Magic Software, the first primary partition end cylinder value was changed so it ended at 1.0GB. This freed up 500MB for the second OS to be loaded. All of this was done through the Partition Magic Software, as well as with FIPS on a second equivalent PC. Both finished without loss of the original Windows 95 OS.

Changing a Partition Size

You can magically move the partition table boundary without loss of data by using the supplied FIPS program or a commercial product, such as Partition Magic.

You start with a disk that has only one partition, as shown next.

0   (cylinder count)   n

All cylinders are used by the single partition table entry. Assuming the actual files on this partition do not use all the disk space, or you can remove some to make unused space available, then you can shrink back the end cylinder for this first partition without affecting the files already contained on the disk.

The following listing shows what the disk might look like after you have changed the end wall of the first partition.

0   a a+1   n

Using the FIPS program, you can shrink the first partition and make the extra space available for one or more partitions. You can then use fdisk to add additional partitions, as illustrated in the following:

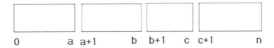

Primary and Extended Partitions

A partition on a disk is a logical set of cylinders that represent all or part of the entire disk. Each disk can be one big partition or separated into many portions. Due to a design in the early stages of the PC and the DOS operating system, you are restricted to a maximum of four primary partitions, one of which can be a special type of primary partition called an *extended* partition. Each of the other three primary partitions can represent one logical drive. The extended partition, though, is a special case that allows you to break it up into a maximum of 12 more "logical" partitions. This gives a total of 16 partitions, of which only 15 are usable on an IDE computer.

exam
Ⓦatch

A SCSI type disk is also capable of 15 partitions total, as there is no such thing as an extended partition.

Partition Filenames

All device files are located in the /dev directory. Linux has a standard naming convention for the different hard drive types (IDE or SCSI), the drive ID, and for each partition.

The IDE Partition Filename Convention   With IDE, a PC can have a maximum of four devices, two on both the first and second controllers. The first controller would be denoted as hda, hard disk "a" or first controller ID. Then the partition number follows as in hda1 for the first partition on the first drive on the first controller. The listing that follows shows a sample of a disk partition table with three partitions on a single disk.

The second drive, first partition would be hdb1, where the full path name is /dev/hdb1.

The third drive, first partition would be hdc1, where the full path name is /dev/hdc1.

SCSI Devices

SCSI is another type of interface for disk drives. It has more devices per controller: seven additional for early SCSI, and 15 for new SCSI implementations. SCSI is generally somewhat more expensive, but can provide a higher data throughput.

For SCSI devices, filenames begin with the letters sda, for SCSI disk on first controller. The partitions on this first drive are sda1, sda2, sda3, and so forth. The second drive partitions are sdb1, sdb2, and so on, and partitions on the sixth drive are sdf1, sdf2, sdf3, and so on. The listing that follows shows the names of the partitions for the third SCSI drive:

```
┌─────────┐   ┌─────────┐   ┌─────────┐
│         │   │         │   │         │
│         │   │         │   │         │
└─────────┘   └─────────┘   └─────────┘
   sdc1          sdc2          sdc3
```

Hard Disk Installation

Rather than install from a CD-ROM, you can chose to copy the CD-ROM image to a hard drive and install from the hard drive. To accomplish this, you must obtain the ISO (CD-ROM) images for the distribution CDs. Rather than burn those images onto CDs, you'd simply place the ISO files into a directory of your choice and provide that directory name when prompted.

Source Files on the CD-ROM

By far the easiest, this installation assumes that a standard ATAPI-type CD-ROM is locally attached. The CD-ROM installation can be selected from a standard Boot.img installation startup disk.

Source Files from Network Installations

Before you can get to any network source files, you need to configure your network card to be a part of the network. You will need to input a valid, unused IP address, the local network mask, the default gateway IP address (if network resource is on another network segment), and optionally, the primary DNS IP, the Domain Name, and the host name to use for this machine.

You are presented with three options during installation for setting up your machine on the network:

Static IP Address	You fill it in; you know the numbers.

BOOTP	Dynamically sent to you from a BOOTP server.
DHCP	Dynamically sent to you from a DHCP server.

The last two options are the easiest. Your machine sends out a BOOTP or DHCP request and these network type services send back all the IP information your machine needs to get on the network. However, they require an existing server on the network, already configured to reply to these requests.

The first option allows you to enter the information directly. If you are on a local network, an IP address and the associated Network Mask is enough information to get you on to your local network with access to a local server. If your network was 206.195.1.0, and your host was number 222, you could use the following information:

IP Address	206.195.1.222
Network Mask	255.255.255.0

You may also need or want to use advanced host name resolution so you don't have to remember the IP address of the servers. DNS can provide this service if it is already configured on your network. DNS is what the Internet uses for host name resolution. If DNS is not configured, you have to use the IP address of any network hosts you wish to get access to. DNS is just a convenience when there are many hosts, considering their names are usually easier to remember than their IP address.

IP Address	206.195.1.222
Network Mask	255.255.255.0
Default Gateway	206.195.1.254
Primary Name Server	192.168.15.1
Domain Name	vaddac.com
Host Name	linux56.vaddac.com

The Default Gateway IP is the portal to the rest of the network. In the preceding scenario, the DNS server is on another network somewhere and you will need the Gateway IP address to access it.

Source Files from FTP and HTTP

An FTP or HTTP server can be a convenient source of installation files.

To use either an FTP or HTTP server, you need to know the IP address and the name of the directory structure that contains the /RedHat directory tree.

IP Address	206.195.1.1	Or use the full domain name
Directory	/pub/I386	Directory containing RedHat/

Source Files from NFS

This installation option allows an NFS server on the network configured as an export server to provide the Red Hat subtree files via a network connection.

This assumes you have NFS running on another host accessible via a network connection on the target machine and that you have the installation files exported from that host. You will be asked for the NFS server IP address and the name of the exported directory.

NFS Address	206.195.1.1	Or use the full domain name
NFS export	/exports/I386	Directory containing /RedHat/

Creating an NFS Export Service

To create an NFS install server, you should copy the installation tree from the CD-ROM to a hard drive on the NFS server.

Copying Files and Exporting Local File Systems   The following output sample shows how to make a directory to hold the Red Hat file tree.

```
================================================================
# mkdir -p /nfs/exports
#
# mkdir /mnt/cdrom
#        # copy to a local file system
# cp -a /mnt/cdrom/RedHat   /nfs/exports
#        # add the export request
# echo '/nfs/exports  (ro)' >> /etc/exports
#        # stop and start the nfs service
# /etc/init.d/rc.d/nfs  stop
# /etc/init.d/rc.d/nfs  start
================================================================
```

At the Client You need to know the IP address of your NFS server as well as the name of the NFS export service and enter these when prompted. At an NT server, you can use the IPCONFIG /ALL command at a command prompt to see the IP information. At the UNIX or Linux NFS server, to display the IP information for your host, use the ifconfig command as root user (illustrated in the following screen output sample).

```
============================================================
[root@linux6 /root]# ifconfig
eth0 Link encap:Ethernet  HWaddr 00:00:C0:A8:16:BA
     inet addr:206.195.1.222  Bcast:206.195.1.255  Mask:255.255.255.0
     UP BROADCAST RUNNING MULTICAST  MTU:1500  Metric:1
...
[root@linux6 /root]#
============================================================
```

Source Files from Samba

Red Hat 6.0 is not able to use Samba services for installation. Red Hat 7.*x* can, however. Samba services represent the native Windows 9*x* and NT file-sharing protocol, SMB (Server Message Block). In previous incarnations and the latest versions, you can share the /RedHat directory from any Win9*x* or NT host as a local SMB share and access it through the network by knowing the name of the server and the share name.

An example share from the server identified as NT4PDCNYC having a share named REDHAT (representing the CD-ROM /RedHat directory) would use the following reference to connect to this resource:

```
\\\\NT4PDCNYC\\REDHAT
```

The Installation Log File

During every installation, a copy of the installation options and the related files is written to an installation log file called /tmp/install.log. This information is duplicated to the various console displays during the installation. Be sure to copy this file to a backup before you, or the system, inadvertently delete the file. You can view most of the information about your installation on one of the other virtual terminals maintained during the installation.

CERTIFICATION OBJECTIVE 3.08

Viewing Boot Time Information

There are actually many processes running and many parts to the installation. The system logs everything to an installation log file and separates related information between four of the five virtual console screens supported during the installation.

The Console Installation Output Screens

When you start the installation, you are on the first virtual console, which can be accessed using ALT-F1. A bash shell is on the second, the installation message log is on the third, kernel messages are on the fourth, and the output of mke2fs on each file system is displayed. If you want to see the other screens, you can press the following key sequences in any order at any time:

ALT-F1	Installation display (this is what you normally see, all others are FYI)
ALT-F2	Bash shell gives you access to limited system information
ALT-F3	The Installation message log is displayed
ALT-F4	Displays all kernel messages
ALT-F5	Installation displays partition formatting

Note: The partition formatting display includes the alternate superblocks. In an emergency situation in which a file system disk is corrupt and cannot be repaired by /sbin/fsck, the check program may want to try an alternate superblock. These are usually a multiple of some block size, like 8K. Block 8192 ends the first 8K, so 8193 is the next block and is a duplicate copy of the primary superblock. This ALT-F5 virtual terminal will provide the list of alternate superblock numbers. Superblocks contain the inode information and used bit block map, among other things. You can also get a listing of the internal file system information using the dumpefs program, as illustrated in the following sample screen output. The first command line lists the file system characteristics of the hda5 partition:

```
===========================================================
[root@rh6laptop /root]# dumpe2fs /dev/hda5 | head -5
```

```
dumpe2fs 1.14, 9-Jan-1999 for EXT2 FS 0.5b, 95/08/09
Filesystem volume name:    <none>
Last mounted on:           <not available>
Filesystem UUID:           57a1b50a-6f62-11d3-9656-c2da53691d05
Filesystem magic number:   0xEF53
[root@rh6laptop /root]#
================================================================
```

Using *PG UP/PG DOWN* at the Virtual Consoles

Another nice feature of Linux virtual terminals is that you can go back and forth through previous pages that have scrolled off the screen by using SHIFT-PGUP and SHIFT-PGDN. Although only a few more lines are available, the added feature is still very useful and is available at any time during system operation.

CERTIFICATION OBJECTIVE 3.09

The Bootup Messages in dmesg

The file /var/log/dmesg contains boot messages duplicated from the console output as seen during each bootup. These messages contain hardware information, process initialization, and sequencing information to name a few:

```
================================================================
[root@linux6 /root]# head -17 /var/log/dmesg
Linux version 2.2.5-15(root@porky.devel.redhat.com)(gcc version egcs-2.91.66 1
9990314/Linux (egcs-1.1.2 release)) #1 Mon Apr 19 22:21:09 EDT 1999
Detected 199964089 Hz processor.
Console: colour VGA+ 80x25
Calibrating delay loop... 398.95 BogoMIPS
Memory:62836k/65536kavailable(996k kernel code,412k reserved,928k data,60k init)
VFS: Diskquotas version dquot_6.4.0 initialized
CPU: Intel Pentium MMX stepping 03
?
autorun ...
... autorun DONE.
VFS: Mounted root (ext2 filesystem) readonly.
change_root: old root has d_count=1
Trying to unmount old root ... okay
Freeing unused kernel memory: 60k freed
Adding Swap: 72256k swap-space (priority -1)
[root@linux6 /root]#
================================================================
```

CERTIFICATION OBJECTIVE 3.10

Validating the Installation

After the installation is done, the installation script shuts down and reboots the machine. At this point, if a Workstation, Laptop, or Custom installation with X-Window was performed, the system defaults to start in runlevel 5, which is the X-Window login screen. A server installation, meanwhile, defaults to runlevel 3, which does not start X by default.

on the **Job**

If your X-Window server is not configured properly, you can press CTRL-ALT-FI to go back to a text-based login screen.

You must log in to the system as root. Then you can force the system to reinitialize back to runlevel 3, the text-based login level, where you can fix the X configuration and then go back to runlevel 5. All three steps are shown in the following screen output sample:

```
==============================================================
[root@linux6 /root]# init 3     # goes back to multiuser mode, no X

[root@linux6 /root]# Xconfigurator        # 'wizard' to set up X,
# NOTE: need video card type, memory and display type

[root@linux6 /root]# init 5            # multiuser mode with X on screen

[root@linux6 /root]#
==============================================================
```

Your runlevel 5 initial screen will show the Red Hat logo and a login screen. Once you have validated your login with a password, the GNOME system will initialize the desktop environment and display a screen something like Figure 3-30.

Alternatively, you might have selected the KDE Desktop, which would give you a display similar to Figure 3-31.

FIGURE 3-30

The X-Window system GNOME desktop

FIGURE 3-31

The Kool desktop environment for Red Hat Linux

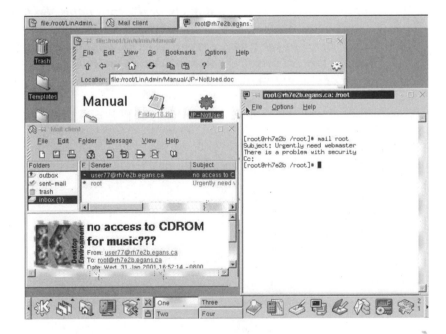

CERTIFICATION OBJECTIVE 3.11

Logging In as root

In any runlevel, you can log in using the default superuser account known as root. This is the only privileged account on the system after installation and has full privileges to do anything to the system. This account should only be used for system administration, and you should create alternative accounts for users to log in with. Some installations require one alternate account be created.

Part of the installation script includes the setting of the root password. The root user is the normal system administrator or superuser account within Linux and most UNIX systems. There is nothing special about this name; you can change it to anything. Changing it, in fact, is a good security idea. A more devious security idea is to assign the root account a useless UID and GID, like 65535/65535, which has access to nothing. This provides hackers with hours of fun trying to break into a useless login account. Having a backdoor account is also a good idea. This is an alternate root type account with a hard to guess name and password combination.

on the
Job

Changing the root account name or the root home directory location may break some applications, administration scripts, or future installation scripts. This is part of the price of security: more work on your part to maintain a higher level of security. You must decide which is more important: security or ease of management.

During installation, you can see a copy of the messages going into the dmesg file on the third console. Press ALT-F3 to access this terminal session. You can only look at the output. Use SHIFT-PGUP and SHIFT-PGDN to page up and down through the text (This has a limited number of retained lines, so you may not be able to see everything).

CERTIFICATION OBJECTIVE 3.12

How Do You Know Whether Your Hardware Is Supported?

Chances are, your hardware is supported, somewhere, somehow. Assume it is, and if in doubt, try some of the generic options for the device. A generic option might be a US Robotics or Hayes compatible modem, generic VGA or SVGA video card, a general multisync monitor, and so forth.

When your hardware is not supported directly from the Red Hat CD-ROM, you have a couple of options. You can search the Internet for information or get different hardware. Rarely does general hardware fail to work, since Linux runs on almost every known CPU and on almost all hardware six months older than the release date of the software. Brand new technology is unlikely to be supported, and non-name brand laptops are usually a nightmare.

This should not be a surprise. Most major brand name machines are directly supported, and most of their models from the last year or two should work. The operative word is *should*. Nothing is guaranteed. However, the many laptops that have Red Hat Linux installed attest to the high probability of it working with your hardware. If you want to see if it has already been tested, check the Red Hat Web site for the latest list of tested hardware.

http://www.RedHat.com/hardware	Keeps an up-to-date compatibility list

Laptops are notoriously full of proprietary hardware. There is a special Web site that keeps track of X-Window setups for all kinds of laptops, both new and old, including top brands, and some not-so-well-known name brands as well.

http://www.XFree86.org/cardlist.html	Has more complete X information

With all that said, there are a few other locations on the Internet where you can dig up installation and distribution information for funny, new, rare, and noncommercial hardware. There is even a special version of Linux for a Palm Pilot. You just have to do a little hunting on the Internet to find what you need.

Installation Complete

The information in this chapter is all you really need to know to get started. There's not much to know really, unless you have some bizarre equipment, want to customize the installation in funky ways, or have never partitioned a disk before. But if you get through all that, congratulations, you are well on your way to being a guru!

CERTIFICATION OBJECTIVE 3.13

Sample Installation Exercises

The following exercises are meant to provide you with a step-by-step set of progressively more complex installation exercises that cover everything from basic workstations to very specific and advanced server installations.

You should do these exercises on test machines only.

Introduction to Installation Exercises

All these exercises assume you have a basic PC available at your disposal to work with as a learning station. You do not need a network connection, nor do you need to know how to configure X for these exercises—you can simply select the default answers in most cases.

These exercises are designed to provide progressive development to help further your knowledge about installing Linux. A Workstation and Server installation will do all the disk partitioning for you. In these exercises, you will be asked to configure the installation for a specific usage and customize the disk partition table to meet the needs of the intended usage. This will require that you do a Custom installation in all but one of the exercises.

These exercises also assume your machine boots from the floppy during a normal reboot, that there is no pertinent information on these test machines, and that you realize all data will be overwritten on these machines.

EXERCISE 3-1

Disk Partitioning Strategies for a Workstation Installation

A typical workstation installation uses only available unused disk space. In this exercise, you will remove all current partitions and install this sample host strictly as a Linux OS workstation. You will need to create the partitions on a 2GB or larger hard disk (see Table 3-4).

1. Create a BOOT.IMG diskette; then reboot the system with this disk in the floppy drive.

2. Press ENTER to move through the first few screens.

3. Choose Custom Installation when presented with Installation Options.

4. Continue pressing ENTER until you are presented with the Partitioning Options.

5. Select Disk Druid (easiest, graphical) or fdisk, whichever you are familiar with.

6. Delete all partitions.

7. Create the first partition with all but about 100MB of disk space.

8. Use the remaining disk space for swap; make sure the partition is Linux Swap (Disk Druid) or ID 0x83 (fdisk).

9. When asked to select packages, leave the default choices.

10. Select a root account password (e.g., RedHat7 or Linux7.1).

11. Finish the Workstation installation normally (skip any network or X installation).

12. Reboot the machine when prompted.

13. Log in as root with your selected password.

on the job

For a more robust workstation, you could create the same partitions as per the workstation or server installation and just modify their size, to match your needs.

TABLE 3-4	Custom Installation as a Workstation (No Other OS) 200MHz Pentium, 2GB single disk, 64MB memory

Customized Workstation Installation

Partition	Size	Use	Comment
hda1	1900MB	/	Plenty of room for the base; can still add lots more, such as Web and print services
hda2	100MB	swap	More than adequate

EXERCISE 3-2

Advanced Workstation Installation

In this exercise, you will distribute your file system over more than just one partition. You will need to create the partitions on a 2GB or larger hard disk (see Table 3-5).

1. Create a BOOT.IMG diskette; then reboot the system.

2. Choose Custom Installation.

3. Use Disk Druid to reconfigure the partition table.

4. Delete all partitions.

5. Create the first partition with 16MB of disk space, Linux Native, and assign to /boot.

6. Create the next primary partition, hda2, as Linux Swap, and assign to ID 0x83.

7. Create a third partition with about 1200MB of disk space, Linux Native, and assign it to / (root).

8. Create an extended partition containing all the rest of the disk space.

9. Create the first logical partition, fifth in number, with about 250MB, and assign it to /var.

10. Create the next logical partition, hda6, with remainder (about 450MB) from Linux Native, and assign it to /home.

11. When asked to select packages, leave the default choices in place.

12. Enter a root password, such as "password" or "system."

TABLE 3-5

Advanced
Workstation
Configuration

Custom Installation as a Workstation (No Other OS)
200MHz Pentium, 2GB single disk, 64MB memory

Partition	Size	Use	Comment
hda1	16MB	/boot	Maintains bootup files
hda2	64MB	swap	Plenty of space
hda3	1200MB	/	The base with NFS, plus Web and print services
hda4	700MB	Extended partition	CANNOT be used for any file system; can only contain logical partitions within it
hda5	250MB (of 900 in hda4)	/var	Separate the spooling used by print services
hda6	450MB (rest of hda4)	/home	Web services

13. Finish the Workstation installation normally; do not configure the network or X.

14. Reboot the machine and log in as root.

EXERCISE 3-3

Disk Partitioning a Server Installation

In this exercise, you will use a Custom Installation option to create a basic server. You will need to create the partitions on a 2GB or larger hard disk (see Table 3-6).

1. Create a BOOT.IMG diskette; then reboot the system.

2. Choose Custom installation.

3. When prompted, select Disk Druid to edit partitions.

4. Delete all partitions.

Custom Installation as a Workstation (No Other OS)
200MHz Pentium II, 2GB single disk, 128MB memory

Partition	Size	Use	Comment
hda1	16MB	/boot	Maintains bootup files
hda2	64MB	swap	Probably plenty of space
hda3	320MB	/	The base with NFS, plus Web and print services
hda4	1600MB	Extended partition	CANNOT be used for any file system, can only contain logical partitions within it
hda5	350/1600MB	/var	Separate the spooling used by print services
hda6	500/1600MB	/home	Web services
hda7	50/1600MB	/home	No interactive users
hda8	700/1600MB	/usr	Additional network services such as DHCP, DNS, nw_mars. . .

5. Create the first partition with 16MB of disk space as Linux Native, and assign it to /boot.

6. Create the next primary partition, hda2 as Linux Swap and assign it to ID 0x83.

7. Create third partition with about 320MB disk space, Linux Native, and assign to / (root).

8. Create an extended partition containing all the rest of the disk space, 1600MB.

9. Create the first logical partition, hda5, with about 350MB, and assign to /var.

10. Create the next logical partition, hda6, with remainder (about 500MB) of Linux Native, and assign it to /home.

11. Create the next logical partition, hda7, with remainder (about 50MB) of Linux Native, and assign it to /home.

12. Create the next logical partition, hda8, with remainder of about 700MB Linux Native, and assign to /usr.

13. When asked to select packages, include Apache Web service, Novell service, DHCP service, and DNS service.

14. Enter a root password.

15. Finish the installation normally.

16. Reboot when prompted and log in as root.

Disk Partitioning Strategy for Database Server Installation

In this exercise, you will use a Custom Installation option and configure the partitions for an imaginary database server. You will need to create the partitions on a 2GB or larger hard disk (see Table 3-7).

1. Create a BOOT.IMG diskette; then reboot the system.

2. Choose Custom installation.

3. Select Disk Druid to make partition changes.

4. Delete all partitions.

5. Create the first partition with 16MB of disk space, Linux Native, and assign it to /boot.

6. Create the next primary partition, hda2, as Linux Swap, and assign it to ID 0x83.

7. Create third partition with about 320MB disk space, Linux Native, and assign to / (root).

8. Create an extended partition containing all the rest of the disk space, 1600MB.

9. Create the first logical partition, hda5, with about 350MB, and assign it to /var.

10. Create the next logical partition, hda6, with remainder, about 750MB Linux Native, and assign it to /opt.

11. Create the next logical partition, hda7, with remainder, about 500MB Linux Native, and assign it to /usr.

TABLE 3-7	Custom Installation as a Server (No Other OS)
	200MHz Pentium II, 2GB single disk, 128MB memory
Custom Database Server Installation	Main use is as database, file and print server, few interactive users

Partition	Size	Use	Comment
hda1	16MB	/boot	Maintains bootup files
hda2	64MB	swap	Probably plenty of space
hda3	320MB	/	The base with NFS, plus Web and print services, few users
hda4	1600MB	Extended partition	CANNOT be used for any file system, can only contain logical partitions within it
hda5	350/1600MB	/var	Separate the spooling used by print services
hda6	750/1600MB	/opt	Database system
hda7	500/1600MB	/usr	File services

12. When asked to select packages, include Ingres Database services.

13. Enter a root password.

14. Finish the installation normally.

15. Reboot and log in as root.

EXERCISE 3-5

Disk Partitioning Strategy for Custom Web Server Installation

In this exercise, you will configure a server that is primarily used as a Web service, using a Custom installation. You will need to create the following partitions on a 2GB or larger hard disk (see Table 3-8).

1. Create a BOOT.IMG diskette; then reboot the system.

2. Choose Custom installation.

3. Select Disk Druid to make partition changes.

4. Delete all partitions.

5. Create the first partition with 16MB of disk space, Linux Native, and assign it to /boot.

6. Create the next primary partition, hda2, as Linux Swap, and assign it to ID 0x83.

7. Create the third partition with about 1200MB disk space Linux Native, and assign to / (root).

8. Create an extended partition containing all the rest of the disk space, 700MB.

9. Create the first logical partition, hda5, with about 250MB, and assign it to /var.

10. Create the next logical partition, hda6, with remainder (about 450MB) of Linux Native, and assign it to /home.

11. When asked to select packages, include Apache Web Service.

12. Enter a password for the root account.

13. Finish the installation normally.

14. Reboot and log in as root.

TABLE 3-8	**Custom Installation as a Workstation (No Other OS)**

Custom Web Server Configuration

200MHz Pentium, 2GB single disk, 64MB memory
Web server mainly, few users

Partition	Size	Use	Comment
hda1	16MB	/boot	Maintains bootup files
hda2	64MB	swap	Plenty of space
hda3	1200MB	/	The base with NFS, plus Web and print services
hda4	700MB	Extended partition	CANNOT be used for any file system, can only contain logical partitions within it
hda5	250MB (of 900 in hda4)	/var	Separate the spooling used by print services

With all this new-found knowledge and practice in regard to installing Linux, here are some questions about a few real-world scenarios, along with their answers.

SCENARIO & SOLUTION

On your current PC with a CD-ROM, sound card, and 2MB SVGA S3 video card, you have an unused 1100MB partition on the first drive and 850MB on the second drive that you can use for a development and test platform of the X-Window system. What installation options are available to you?	**Workstation install** Chosen if you want a simple system. **Server install** Gives you all the basic networking functions. **Custom install** Allows you to customize it any way you want.
There is an older 90MHz Pentium PC that will be retired soon with 32MB of RAM and two hard disks of 800MB and 1200MB, respectively. What are your installation options? Why can't you choose any others?	There is enough space for any installation option. You may not want to use X on such a slow system, but you could run this as an interoffice Web, FTP, NFS, Samba, and/or print server even with a small amount of memory. **Workstation install** Chosen if you want a simple system. **Server install** Gives you all the basic networking functions. **Custom install** Allows you to customize the install any way you want.
You want to dual-boot the help desk machines (all five of them) so Linux is available as an option during reboot. You have a little money to spend on a hardware upgrade, but not enough to replace all the machines. You will want to run X and some network services to connect to the main server for file and print services. What are your installation options? Why can't you choose any others?	Add a new disk to each machine and maybe add RAM if there is less then 48MB. Adding a new 2+GB disk and upgrading all machines to at least 64MB of RAM will make the systems run better for all OSs, and the added disk space can be shared with the other operating systems, providing enough to do a full install of Linux. **Workstation install** (recommended) Chosen if you want a simple system. **Custom install** Allows you to customize the install any way you want. You cannot use a Server install, because it does not create a dual boot.

SCENARIO & SOLUTION

You already have Red Hat Linux 5.2 installed on your machine in five partitions that cover 2GB. None of the information is absolutely critical. What are your installation options? Why can't you choose any others?	This is a scenario that allows you to be lazy and use either the Workstation or Server install, depending on use. If you want to save some of the information, you can use the Custom option and just reformat the main system partitions. **Workstation Install** Chosen if you want a simple system. Wipes out all you old data. **Server Install** (recommended) Wipes out all your data. Gives you all the basic networking functions **Custom Install** Allows you to customize the install any way you want. You can also preserve the data on some or all of the partition.
You already have Red Hat Linux 5.2 installed on your machine in five partitions that cover 2GB. Two of the partitions are absolutely critical. What are your installation options? Why can't you choose any of the others?	Use the Custom installation. You cannot use the Server install. It blows away all other partitions. The Workstation install will delete all old Linux partitions and require the backup and restore of critical partition information.

CERTIFICATION SUMMARY

Installation is a very important aspect of the certification process. This chapter has dealt with the decisions necessary when installing Red Hat Linux on either a brand new machine or one with an existing OS.

Partitioning the disk into usefully assigned partitions is very important. The Custom Installation option provides the most flexible choice for the experienced installer. You can manage and create any number of partitions and install any package combination you want. For a user with little experience installing operating systems, the other two options—the Workstation and Server installation options—may fit your needs perfectly.

The Workstation installation creates three partitions from all scavenged Linux partition space, plus any unused disk space such as /boot, swap, and the / (root). It installs a preconfigured set of mostly user application-type packages, and then sets up your machine to dual-boot between the old OS and Linux.

The Server installation option deletes all old partitions, creates six partitions for the various system file structure, installs all the network services software packages, and installs the LILO boot loader to load this installation only.

The Custom installation option provides the most flexibility, but also requires the most knowledge concerning the details of installations.

✓ TWO-MINUTE DRILL

The following are some of the key points from the certification objectives in Chapter 3.

Disk Partitioning Strategies for Server and Workstation Installations

❑ If you have a relatively new PC, you should be able to install Linux without much grief.

❑ The Workstation installation is usually much simpler in design than the Server installation.

❑ The Custom option allows you to create any combination of partitions and software services for either workstation or server usage.

Choosing an Installation Class: Workstation, Server, Laptop, or Custom

❑ The Laptop installation allows you to select GNOME or KDE desktop environments or both, as well as Games, and is basically a Workstation installation.

❑ The Custom option can actually be used to create either a Server or Workstation installation but offers the added benefit of being able to make changes to the default package sets.

❑ If you wanted to change the default partition layout or preserve an already installed operating system of a certain type, you would need to use the Custom Installation option.

❑ A workstation-class installation, choosing to install GNOME or KDE, requires at least 1.2GB of free space. Choosing both GNOME and KDE plus the Games requires at least 1.5GB of free disk space.

❑ A server-class installation requires 2.1GB (2100 MB) of disk space.

❑ If you were to use the Custom installation and decide on the server packages to install, it would require 650MB for a minimal installation and at least 2.1GB of free space if every package was selected.

The Installation Process

❑ Red Hat Linux has been specifically crafted to work on almost any "old" PC hardware (built within the last five years or so).

❑ It can also be installed to Alpha- and PowerPC-based computers, to name a few.

❑ There is certain hardware configuration information about your system you should know before beginning:
The hard drive(s), their geometry and size (and SCSI ID if using SCSI)
The physical RAM (random access memory) of the machine
The CD-ROM and its interface type: IDE or SCSI
The mouse type and the port it is attached to
The NIC (Network Interface Card) make, model, and parameters
The SCSI adapter and settings if one is present

❑ If you plan on installing the X-Window system, you will also need to know:
The video adapter card type and local video RAM memory size
The monitor brand name or its specifications (horizontal and vertical refresh rates)
Whether you plan on keeping your old operating system or not

❑ You can install Linux in separate partitions and retain your previous OS, whether it was a Windows or Linux OS.

❑ You need to create some free, unpartitioned disk space either by adding a new disk or by removing/shrinking current partitions.

❑ You can use commercial partition adjusting products like Partition Magic or the freely available FIPS program supplied with the Linux distribution.

The LILO Boot Process and Intel Hardware/BIOS Issues

❑ The original Intel motherboard design provided a mechanism to start any operating system. It would load a bootup program, located in the first sector of the first disk starting with A: and followed by C:.

❑ This bootup program is located in an area most often called the master boot record, or MBR.

❑ The main issue with this bootup is that the MBR has to be found in the first 1024 cylinders of any disk.

❑ Newer motherboards use a mechanism called Logical Block Addressing, or LBA mode.

❑ When booting your system, Linux uses a set of files referred to collectively as LILO, which is short for Linux Loader.

❑ You can update or change your bootup options with the LILO configuration file, /etc/lilo.conf, and with the boot loader install utility, /sbin/lilo.

❑ To pass a parameter to LILO, type the parameter after the label name.

❑ A common kernel option is the word "single," or alternatively, the number 1.

❑ Single-user mode is the most commonly used option. This is the system maintenance mode for experienced Linux administrators. In single-user mode, no file systems other than the root file system are loaded.

Using loadlin

❑ Essentially, the loadlin program relies on MS-DOS instead of your system BIOS to load Linux.

❑ The advantage is that loadlin can install a kernel beyond the 1024 cylinder boundary from any file system accessible to MS-DOS.

❑ Note that loadlin cannot be used from any Win9x or NT DOS PROMPT environment; you must boot into MS-DOS mode.

Additional Installation Details

❑ With either fdisk or the Disk Druid utility, you must understand basic partitioning concepts.

❑ You can only use 15 of the partitions on IDE drives, and all 15 partitions on SCSI.

❑ It is recommended to spread the load out across as many disks and controllers as available to improve performance.

Creating Partitions: Details

❏ The UNIX, and hence Linux, file system has been historically split up into smaller, more manageable pieces for various reasons: everything started on small disks, small partitions are easier to dump and restore, partition limits can be used to restrict or control disk usage, and others.

❏ The Linux file system can also be broken up into smaller pieces or left as one large unit if so desired. When would you use one big partition? When you have a large RAID5 disk farm providing your file system or when you are creating a small test system.

❏ The total memory available to any and all programs is the sum of all RAM and swap space. Linux uses a linear memory model.

❏ Although there is no hard-and-fast format, a good rule of thumb is to create your swap partition so it's two to three times that of small memory systems.

❏ Linux natively supports many other file systems, such as DOS, HPFS, FAT, VFAT, and NTFS. So if you have OS/2, Windows 9x, or a DOS operating system using other partitions installed on the same machine as Linux, you can access them. This way, the system will be able to "see" the native files.

❏ The fdisk utility is universally available and should be one of the first tools you get acquainted with.

Viewing Boot Time Information

❏ When you start the installation, you are on the first virtual console. This console is accessed with ALT-F1. A bash shell is on the second, installation message log is on the third, kernel messages are on the fourth, and the output of mke2fs on each file system is displayed. If you want to see other screens, press the following key sequences at any time:

ALT-F1   Installation display (this is what you normally see, all others are FYI)
ALT-F2   The bash shell gives you access to limited system information
ALT-F3   The Installation message log is displayed
ALT-F4   Displays all kernel messages
ALT-F5   The installation displays partition formatting

The Bootup Messages in dmesg

❑ The file /var/log/dmesg contains boot messages duplicated from the console output, as seen during each bootup.

❑ These messages contain hardware information, process initialization, and sequencing information to name but a few.

❑ There are many files placed in the /boot directory after installation. They represent the compressed starting virtual memory kernel, vmlinuz-*x.x.x*, the loadable modules section, system map if needed, and more.

Validating the Installation

❑ After the installation is done, the installation script shuts down and reboots the machine.

❑ At this point, if a Workstation, Laptop, or Custom installation with X-Window is performed, the system defaults to start in runlevel 5, which is the X-Window login screen.

❑ A Server installation defaults to runlevel 3, which does not start X by default.

❑ You must log in to the system as root. Then you can force the system to reinitialize back to runlevel 3, the text-based login level, where you can fix the X configuration and then go back to runlevel 5.

Logging In as root

❑ This account should only be used for system administration.

❑ This is the only privileged account on the system after installation and has full privileges to do anything.

❑ In any runlevel, you can log in using the default superuser account known as root.

❑ Installations require that one alternative account be created.

How Do You Know When Your Hardware Is Not Supported

❑ Chances are, your hardware is supported somewhere, somehow. Assume it is, and if in doubt, try some of the generic options for the device.

❏ Rarely does most general hardware fail to work, since Linux runs on almost every known CPU and with almost all hardware that's at least six months older than the release date of the software.

❏ When your hardware is not supported directly from the Red Hat CD-ROM, you have a couple of options. You can search the Internet for information or purchase different hardware.

❏ A generic option might be a US Robotics or Hayes compatible modem, generic VGA or SVGA video card, a general multisync monitor, and so on.

SELF TEST

The following questions will help you measure your understanding of the material presented in this chapter. Read all the choices carefully, as there may be more than one correct answer. Choose all correct answers for each question.

Disk Partitioning Strategies for Server and Workstation Installations

1. Your main Linux Web server has been diagnosed as having to use swap on a regular basis. You notice there is only one big swap file on the same physical disk as the root file system. There are three other disks with space available. How many swap partitions can be utilized? What is the maximum size for any one? And what is the maximum overall swap space allowed per system?

    A. Eight partitions, max of 2GB for any one, 4GB total

    B. Six partitions, max of 3GB for any one, 4GB total

    C. Four partitions, max of 4GB for any one, 8GB total

    D. Two partitions, max of 5GB for any one, 8GB total

Choosing an Installation Class: Workstation, Server, or Custom

2. If you already have a PC with a previous version of Linux on it that you don't want to keep, which installation option will automatically delete only the Linux partitions and install a basic network and X-Window-ready Linux system?

    A. Workstation

    B. Server

    C. Custom

    D. Laptop

3. What program is used to manage a dual boot between Linux and Win98?

    A. LILO

    B. Syslinux

    C. bootp

    D. fdisk

The Installation Process

4. You have installed different versions of Linux before. During the installation, you are given a second option to create disk partitions, but are only familiar with the text-based disk partition management program called what?

   A. fixdisk

   B. rdisk

   C. fdisk

   D. druidisk

5. The previous user of your workstation could not get Windows to run so she ran the DOS FDISK.EXE with /MBR to put the boot sector back in place. Now you cannot run Linux. You boot up with the emergency startup disk you created. You need to update the MBR with the Linux Loader program which is located where?

   A. /etc/lilo.conf

   B. /bin/configlilo

   C. /sbin/lilo

   D. /bin/sys/liloconf

6. After you update the MBR, it only indicates one entry. You need to fix the setup file to include both options. What system file is used to set and create boot entries?

   A. /bin/sys/liloconf

   B. /sbin/liloconf

   C. /etc/lilo.conf

   D. /usr/sys/liloconf

The LILO Boot Process and Intel Hardware/BIOS Issues

7. When you try to boot your newly created installation with a root, /boot, and swap partition, the system complains that there is no active boot drive. What should you do?

   A. Reboot with the installation diskette and redo the installation.

   B. Reboot with a DOS boot diskette and run FDISK /MBR.

   C. Reboot with the installation diskette and run fdisk to activate the proper boot partition.

   D. Reboot with the bootup diskette created during installation. Use fdisk to fix the problem.

8. After completing your installation, the following appears on the console during bootup:

```
LI
```

Afterward, the system seems to hang. What is the most likely problem?

A. The system cannot find the second part of boot loader. /boot may be beyond the 1024 cylinder.

B. Another operating system boot loader is interfering with LILO.

C. You did not configure an active (boot) partition.

D. The system is waiting for special options to the command line.

Using loadlin

9. Your MIS manager has heard there is another boot loader capable of loading many different operating systems. Which of the following is an alternative boot loader that's available for Linux?

A. Syslinuz

B. bootfs

C. loadlin

D. pmagic

10. You have a PC that already contains a different version of Linux. During the installation, you are asked where to put the boot loader for LILO. You know there is already another loader called loadlin installed. Where should you put LILO?

A. In any partition except /boot

B. In any partition except /

C. In the partition /boot

D. You do not need to install the LILO boot loader

Additional Installation Details

11. During the installation, the authentication screen provides three options. You remember what shadow password is and MD5, but forget exactly what the third option NIS is, as well as what it does. Which of the following is the correct third option and its accompanying definition?

A. Network Inode Slave—Provides shared disk resources

B. Network Information Service—Provides centralized authentication

    C. New Internet Standard—Provides centralized authentication of shared access

    D. Newton Interrupt Sequence—File sharing protocol

12. A new product you are adding to the server asks you to go into single-user mode to run a system check on the file system. How do you start your system in single-user mode?

    A. lilo : boot 1

    B. lilo : init 1

    C. lilo : single user

    D. lilo : linux single

13. The MIS manager wants a further explanation of the drive table on the server; specifically, the type of partition that can contain logical partitions, known as what?

    A. ext2fs

    B. nfs

    C. primary

    D. extended

14. A Windows administrator is puzzled by the amount of swap space configured and wants to know what is recommended for Linux.

    A. The same as RAM memory.

    B. 40–90MB.

    C. The same as the server uses.

    D. Two to three times the RAM.

    E. There is no recommended amount of swap space.

Creating Partitions: Details

15. You are told to check the Web server drive table after installation. There are eight partitions. Your MIS manager asks how that can be. Her DOS OS machine can only create one primary and one extended partition. How many (E)IDE primary partitions can any one disk drive contain?

    A. 4 primary, 1 of which is an extended partition, making for 16 total partitions

    B. 3 primary, 2 are extended, making for a total of 12 partitions

    C. 12 primary, with 1 an extended partition

    D. 16 extended partitions

16. You are asked to install on a machine that has several versions of UNIX on it. There are many different partitions. You only want to use the same type of partitions Linux already uses. What is the native file system format used by Linux?

A. ufs

B. ext2fs

C. dos

D. fat

17. During the installation, you are asked to configure your network card to access the installation source files from an NFS server. Assuming you have already input the IP address and netmask for this host, you need to have what?

A. DNS Server IP, BOOTP Server IP, NFS export name

B. DNS export name, BOOTP Server IP, NFS Server IP

C. DHCP Server IP, DHCP name, NFS export name

D. NFS export name, NFS Server IP

18. Your MIS manager has asked you to put Linux on a laptop for a CEO. The laptop has about 1GB of free disk space, but there is one partition with all available space allocated to it. What free utility is supplied with the installation that allows you to resize a partition?

A. fdisk

B. FIPS

C. bootp

D. Syslinux

19. During installation, you create the first six partitions and allocate the file system directory to them sequentially, but there is one partition you CANNOT assign as a file system given the following partitions and their current setup design. Which one of the following is it?

A. hda4 is an extended partition.

B. hda1 is a primary partition.

C. hda5 is a logical partition.

D. hda2 is a primary partition.

20. You are in a rush to install a workstation with the minimum number of partitions. What partitions are absolutely required?

A. /boot, swap, /system

B. root(/), swap

C. swap, /boot, /usr

D. /boot, /root

LAB QUESTION

You need to test Red Hat 7.1 as a replacement for your current RH 6.2 installed Web Server. BUT, you do not want to lose the current 6.2 Web setup just yet. You just want to test 7.1 using the Web pages and CGI scripts to see if they will work. What can you do?

SELF TEST ANSWERS

Disk Partitioning Strategies for Server and Workstation Installations

1. ☑ **A.** Up to eight partitions, max of 2GB for any one, and 4GB for all swap space total.
   ☒ **B, C,** and **D** are all incorrect combinations.

2. ☑ **A** and **D.** This is the main benefit of the Workstation and Laptop options: little user interaction. The system creates the partitions from unused or previous Linux type partitions, and everything installs for a basic network-ready system.
   ☒ The server option (**B**) would wipe out all other OS versions, and a Custom installation (**C**) requires you answer a plethora of questions.

3. ☑ **A.** LILO. The Linux Loader program.
   ☒ **B, C,** and **D** are incorrect. Syslinux (**B**) is a DOS-oriented Linux kernel loader. bootp (**C**) is a network protocol, and fdisk (**D**) is the partitioning program.

The Installation Process

4. ☑ **C.** During an installation, there is Disk Druid from Red Hat and the universal fdisk utility (NOT the DOS-based utility).
   ☒ Although names can be almost anything in Linux and UNIX, druidisk, rdisk, and fixdisk are not known utilities, hence **A, B,** and **D** are all wrong.

5. ☑ **C.** /sbin/lilo resets the MBR for Linux, depending on /etc/lilo.conf, which is the configuration file for LILO and does not actually update the MBR—only the program /sbin/lilo can do that.
   ☒ The lilo.conf file (**A**) would contain an entry for both Linux and the other OS and can be used to provide access to the other operating system. **B** and **D** are both bogus files.

6. ☑ **C.** /etc/lilo.conf contains all boot entries, the timeout, and which labeled entry is chosen by default.
   ☒ All other choices are nonexistent files.

The LILO Boot Process and Intel Hardware/BIOS Issues

7. ☑ **D.** You need to boot into your installed Linux and use the fdisk utility to fix this problem. Although during an Installation, you can use the Linux-supplied fdisk utility (NOT the DOS-based utility fdisk) to mark the active (where boot block is located) partition. Use option p to print the current partition table, then a, and select the appropriate partition, usually hda1.

☒ If you did not do this during the installation, you cannot just redo the installation up to that point and fix it, so **C** is wrong. The DOS fdisk utility is not capable of fixing this for Linux, so **B** is wrong, and **A** is a little drastic but might be your only answer if you failed to make the recommended bootup disk at the end of the installation process.

8. ☑ **A.** /boot is beyond the 1024 cylinder count as seen by the DOS-level loader at this point in the bootup. You will need to use the emergency boot diskette created during the installation (assuming you created it) or reinstall the system again.

☒ If you see LI, then LILO is the boot loader, meaning no other OS loader is relevant (**B**), and that since it did boot there is obviously an active boot partition (**C**). All options are supplied at the "lilo:" prompt, which has not come up, so **D** is also wrong.

Using loadlin

9. ☑ **C.** loadlin can boot many different operating systems.

☒ Syslinux, not Syslinuz (**A**), is used only during installation by the install image disks. **B** and **D** are not programs.

10. ☑ **A, B,** and **C.** Since loadlin is probably already in hda1, the first partition, you should put LILO preferably in /boot, but any partition except root is usually fine AS LONG AS that partition is within the 1024 cylinder count which /boot usually is. Afterward, update loadlin to point to it.

☒ You do need to install LILO somewhere, so **D** is wrong.

Additional Installation Details

11. ☑ **B.** NIS, Network Information Service, is a standard centralized master copy of the authentication files distributed to all other hosts in a trusted network.

☒ **C, D,** and **E** are bogus.

12. ☑ **D.** lilo: linux single.

☒ You could use "init 1" if your system was running, but not at the LILO prompt (**B**). Neither "single user" nor "boot 1" are valid LILO options (**C** and **A**).

13. ☑ **D.** The first three partitions are referred to as Primary, the fourth is called an Extended partition and can contain up to 12 logical partitions on IDE type drives. This was a standard set in the early 80's and has survived the evolution of PCs.

☒ **A** refers to the e2fs (Extended 2 File System) format on the Linux drives. **B** refers to the

Network File System (NFS), a file-sharing service. **C** refers to the other type of partition available on IDE type disks.

14. ☑ **D.** It is recommended you have two to three times the amount of RAM, but there is no absolute here. The total amount of memory available to all programs is the sum of RAM and swap. Get as much RAM as you can. If you need more RAM but cannot afford it, your system will use swap space. However, this comes with a major hit on performance due to the slow speed of disks. If you do use swap space regularly, then you need more RAM for the system.
☒ Technically speaking, all the other answers are right, but **D** is the rule of thumb most commonly used.

Creating Partitions: Details

15. ☑ **A.** 4 total, 3 that are called primary and one that is considered a primary category but is designated as an extended type that can contain 12 logical partitions at most for a total of 16 named partitions.
☒ **B, C,** and **D** are all incorrect configurations.

16. ☑ **B.** Although the system usually denotes it as Linux Native, the conventional name is the Extended 2 File System, ext2fs or ext2, denoted with an ID of 0x83 (swap is ID 0x82).
☒ As of RH 7.*x*, you can install onto a DOS partition but it is needed for the exam. FAT is the MS-DOS file system format (**D**). It is not called DOS. That is the OS name (**C**). Some UNIX versions might use UFS, UNIX File System, format, but not Linux (**A**).

17. ☑ **D.** The IP address of the NFS server and the export directory name. You must already have an IP address and netmask (as well as an optional gateway IP if the services are on another network), or be using DHCP or BOOTP to obtain it, for the install host.
☒ A BOOTP server provides a special UNIX diskless workstation bootup service (DNS is not used during installations). Hence **A, B,** and **C** are all incorrect configurations.

18. ☑ **B.** FIPS is on the installation disk, but you need to read the documentation carefully.
☒ **A, C,** and **D** are incorrect. fdisk is used to delete or add partitions, but cannot resize an existing partition without loss of data. bootp is a network protocol, and Syslinux is a DOS-oriented Linux kernel loader.

19. ☑ **A.** hda4 is the extended partition name (on an IDE type drive) and cannot contain a file system, just logical drives.
☒ Partitions **B, C,** and **D** should be usable for file systems.

20. ☑ **B.** The minimum partition set is a swap and a root(/) partition.

☒ There is no /system partition, and you have to have at least a root (/) partition so **A, C,** and **D** are incorrect.

LAB ANSWER

Scenario 1: Buy a new disk and add it to the system. Then do a custom install to create a new installation of RH 7.1 to partitions on the new disk, adding an entry to /etc/lilo.conf to provide a boot option to both versions of Linux.

Scenario 2: If you can find about 500MB of free space on any current disk, you can do a custom installation and prune the packages down to just the minimum needed for the OS and Apache. You could use FIPS to repartition the 500MB (assuming you had not already created 16 partitions on IDE or 15 on SCSI) and use that as your sole root (/) partition, reusing the current swap partition. You could then update LILO with access to both versions by creating entries for both in /etc/lilo.conf.

Scenario 3: No space on server. Hmm. . .you've got to get creative and either find a test machine you can do the test install on OR back up everything on the main server after taking it off line. Do a quick 7.1 upgrade to the current 6.2 and see how it works. If it fails, you restore everything back to the way it was. Note: Test your backups first before proceeding!!!!

4

Basic
Configuration
and
Administration

A fter installation is complete on your Red Hat Linux system, you still have some work to do to make the system functional. User accounts need to be set up, file systems configured, and some packages may need to be added or removed.

This chapter will get you started with the basics that every Red Hat Linux administrator should know about their system. At the end of this chapter, you should know how to manage user accounts and environments, configure and mount file systems, use RPM to manage packages, configure PCMCIA, manage system daemons, and configure virtual consoles, keyboards, and mice.

CERTIFICATION OBJECTIVE 4.01

Adding, Deleting, and Modifying User Accounts

After installation, your system has only a single login account along with the root account. For some installations, you'll want to create more accounts. Even if you're going to be the only user on the system, it's a good idea to create a single, nonprivileged account to do your day-to-day work and use the root account only for administering the system. Accounts can be added to Red Hat Linux systems using various utilities like vi (manual method), useradd (command line oriented) and the *linuxconf* utility (text or graphical interface).

linuxconf

linuxconf can be run in graphical or character mode. If you have already configured X and are running a graphical desktop, llinuxconf will start in graphical mode. Otherwise, it will start in character mode. In either mode, the instructions are the same. Figure 4-1 shows linuxconf in graphical mode.

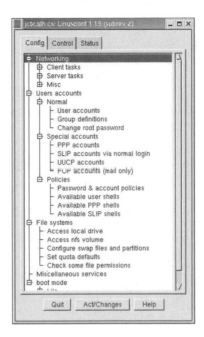

FIGURE 4-1

The linuxconf
main screen

EXERCISE 4-1

Adding a User with linuxconf

To add a user with linuxconf:

1. Run /bin/linuxconf.

2. Open Config | User Accounts | Normal | User Accounts. (This notation indicates you should open the Config tab, followed by the User Accounts tab, the Normal tab, and finally, the User Accounts tab. This will open the User Accounts form, as shown in Figure 4-2.) If you have more than 15 accounts on the system, linuxconf will present a Filter control screen. You can use this screen to select a smaller range of accounts to view or just click Accept to view all accounts.

3. Select the Add button.

4. Complete the form (Figure 4-3) and click the Accept button. The only required field is Login Name, but you will most likely want to specify more information for each account. Table 4-1 describes each field.

FIGURE 4-2

The User
Accounts form

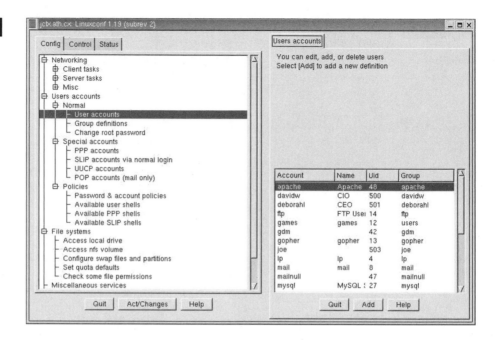

FIGURE 4-3

User account
creation

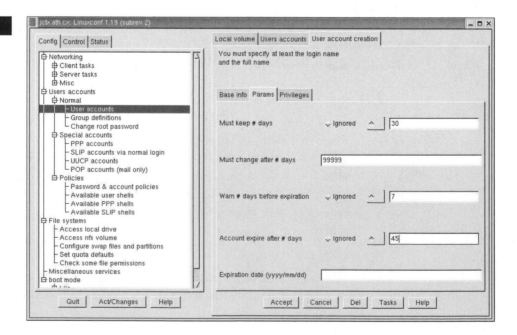

	Field	Instructions
TABLE 4-1 User Fields	The Account Is Enabled	Make sure this is checked if you want the user to be able to log in. If you're creating an administrative account that won't be used to log in, (some app needs it to run) uncheck this box.
	Login Name	The user logs in with this name. The login name should only contain alphanumeric characters, and the - and _ characters. In almost all cases, the Login name should not contain uppercase letters. Although a login name can be up to 256 characters, you typically want to keep it to 10 or less, for ease of account maintenance. Examples: nickS, DGcatherine, heatherR, willr.
	Full Name	The full name of the user. Example: Dana Gordon.
	Group (opt)	The numeric group ID (GID) the user will belong to. By default, Red Hat Linux creates a new group for every new user. If you want all your users to be in the Users group, enter **users** here.
	Supplementary Groups	Enter any additional groups you want this user to be a member of.
	Home Directory (opt)	By default, Red Hat Linux places new home directories in /home/username.
	Command Interpreter (opt)	Enter the name of the shell program this user will use. Red Hat Linux defaults to the Bourne Again Shell (bash).
	User ID (opt)	The user will be assigned the next available User ID (UID), if left blank. In most cases, it's best to leave this blank.
	Must Keep # Days	If set to a positive number, the user must keep new passwords this many days before being allowed to change it.
	Must Change After # Days	If set to a positive number, the user must change their password after this many days.
	Warn # Days Before Expiration	If set to a positive number, the user will be warned when logging on this many days before their password expires.
	Account Expire After # Days	If set to a positive number, the account will be locked after this many days. This is a good setting for temporary logins.

5. You will be prompted to enter the user's password. The password should be at least six characters (you'll get an error message if it's less than six characters, but linuxconf will allow you to use the password anyway) and

should contain a mix of upper- and lowercase letters, numbers, and symbols to keep it from being easily guessed. Enter the password in the Confirmation field to ensure you haven't misspelled it, then choose Accept.

6. When you have finished adding users, click Quit to exit linuxconf.

on the
①ob

Although creating user accounts may seem to be a straightforward process, there are a few things to watch out for:

- *linuxconf will let you get away with using invalid characters in usernames, such as %, &, *, and !. However, many Linux programs will fail to function with usernames that contain these characters.*

- *If your installation doesn't require each user to have their own unique group ID (GID), assign your users to the Users group. There's rarely a need for each user to have an individual GID, and having most users assigned to the Users group makes system administration easier. However, the reason for the individual group ID system is for security purposes. By default, everyone in the same group will likely have access to each other's files. With every user having a separate GID, file security is heightened. Each user will have to explicitly provide access to their files.*

- *Ask your users to use passwords that are difficult to guess. Spouses' and dogs' names make bad passwords. Several words strung together with numbers or symbols make better passwords, such as "toy+jobs" or "rule%key." These are easy to remember, yet difficult to guess.*

- *Discourage the use of shared accounts, where several people use a single account. Shared accounts are almost always unnecessary and are easily compromised.*

- *If you'll be using Network File System (NFS), make sure users maintain the same UID across systems. NFS can provide a centralized management of all user accounts across all participating machines. This greatly simplifies account maintenance at the expense of adding both administrative and additional network overhead.*

Deleting a User Account with linuxconf

Removing user accounts is as straightforward as adding them, with a few exceptions. When you remove a user from your system, you'll have to make some choices about how (or if) you will save the files in the user's home directory. linuxconf gives you several choices regarding this decision.

EXERCISE 4-2

Deleting a User Account with linuxconf

1. Run /bin/linuxconf.

2. Select Config | User Accounts | Normal | User Accounts. This will open the User accounts form. If you have more than 15 accounts on the system, linuxconf will present a Filter control screen. You can use this screen to select a smaller range of accounts to view or just choose Accept to view all accounts.

3. Select the account to be deleted.

4. Press the DEL button.

5. Select the appropriate option for the account data (see Table 4-2).

6. Choose the Accept button.

TABLE 4-2	Deleting Account Data Option	Action
Delete Account Options	Archive The Account's Data	Data stored in the user's home directory is archived in /home/oldaccounts, under the filename *username-yyyy-mm-dd-pid*.tar.gz, (where *username* is the name of the deleted user; *yyyy, mm,* and *dd* are, respectively, the year, month, and day the account was deleted. *pid* is the process ID of the linuxconf process that created this file; and .tar.gz indicates this file was tar'd and gzip'd. The user's home directory is then removed.
	Delete The Account's Data	The user's home directory and all its contents are removed.
	Leave The Account's Data In Place	Nothing is done to the user's home directory and its contents.

It is important to note that only files in the deleted user's home directory are processed. Any files owned by the deleted user stored outside the home directory still exist under the UID of the deleted user. If a new user is created with the old user's UID, the new user owns those files.

EXERCISE 4-3

Modifying a User Account Using linuxconf

1. Run /sbin/linuxconf.

2. Select Config | User Accounts | Normal | User Accounts. This will open the User Accounts form. If you have more than 15 accounts on the system, linuxconf will present a Filter control screen. You can use this screen to select a smaller range of accounts to view or just choose Accept to view all accounts.

3. Select the account to be modified.

4. Make the desired modifications to the account.

5. Choose Accept.

CERTIFICATION OBJECTIVE 4.02

The Basic User Environment

Each user on your Red Hat Linux system has an *environment* when logged on to the system. The environment defines where a user looks for programs to be executed, what the login prompt looks like, what terminal type is being used, and more. This section explains how default environments are set up.

Home Directories and /etc/skel

Red Hat Linux makes it easy to run a set of standard templates to propagate to new users' home directories via /etc/skel.

Home Directories

The home directory is the initial directory in which users are placed when they first log on to a Red Hat Linux system. For most normal users, this will be /home/*username*, where *username* is the user's login name. Users typically have write permission in their own home directory, so they're free to read and write their own files there. In Chapter 5, you'll learn how to configure disk quotas, so users don't allocate more than their fair share of disk space.

/etc/skel

The /etc/skel directory contains default environment files for new accounts. linuxconf copies these files to the home directory when a new account is created. Depending on the software installed, the files included in /etc/skel and their purposes are listed in Table 4-3.

As the system administrator, you can edit these files, or place your own files in /etc/skel. When new users are created, these files will be propagated to the new users' home directories. Additional entries are placed there by various programs during installation, such as emacs and secure shell.

TABLE 4-3	Files	Purpose
Files in /etc/skel and Their Purposes	.Xdefaultsscreenrc	Contains default settings for a few common X applications, if X is installed
	.bashrc	The individual per-interactive-shell startup file
	.bash_logout	Source the commands in this file upon logout
	.bash_profile	The personal initialization file, executed for login shells
	.kde, .kderc	The KDE desktop environment customization, if installed
	Desktop	The GNOME desktop environment customization, if installed

Window Manager Configuration File Locations

Red Hat Linux comes with several window managers. You will at some point want to configure one or more of them for use on your system. Window manager configuration files are stored in /etc/X11/*<windowmanager>*, where *<windowmanager>* is the name of the window manager. Within the window manager subdirectory, there is usually a file named system.*<windowmanager>*, which contains default behavior for the window manager.

CERTIFICATION OBJECTIVE 4.03

File System Configuration

There are as many, if not more, file system types as there are operating systems. Red Hat Linux can understand many of these formats.

File System Types

At the heart of every Red Hat Linux installation are the file systems on which it relies. Linux supports a rich set of different file system types (see Table 4-4).

on the **job**

If you have the kernel source RPMs loaded on your system, you can see which file systems any version or distribution of Linux currently supports. Look at the file /usr/src/linux/fs/file systems.c.

The File System Table

Information about your local and remotely mounted file systems is stored in /etc/fstab. Each file system is described on a separate line. Each line is composed of multiple fields, each separated by spaces or tabs. When your system boots, it processes each file system in the order listed.

TABLE 4-4	Linux File System Types

File System Type	Description
ADFS	The Acorn Disc Filing System. The standard file system of the Acorn's RISC-PC systems and the Archimedes line of machines. Currently, Linux supports ADFS as read-only.
Amiga FFS	The Fast File System is used by Amiga Systems computers.
Apple HFS	The Hierarchical File System used by the Apple Mac Plus and all later Macintosh computers.
MS-DOS, VFAT, and UMSDOS	These file systems allow you to read MS-DOS-formatted file systems. MS-DOS lets you read pre-Windows 95 partitions. VFAT lets you read Windows 95 partitions, and UMSDOS allows you to run Linux from a DOS partition (not currently supported by Red Hat). Note that it is possible to read a Windows 95 partition with only MS-DOS support enabled, but you will not be able to see the long filenames generated by Windows 95.
ISO 9660 CDROM	The standard file system used on CD-ROMs. It is also known as the High Sierra file system, or HSFS on other UNIX systems.
Minix	The standard file system for the Minix operating system. This is the original default Linux file system, although the ext2 file system has since superceded it.
NTFS	NTFS is the file system for Microsoft Windows NT. Currently it is only supported as read-only.
OS/2 HPFS	The standard file system for IBM's OS/2 operating system. Currently it is only supported as read-only.
/proc	The /proc file system is the Linux *virtual* file system. *Virtual* means that it doesn't occupy real disk space. Instead, files are created on the fly when you access them. /proc is used to provide information on kernel configuration and device status.
/dev/pts	The /dev/pts file system is the Linux implementation of the Open Group's Unix98 PTY support.
QNX	The standard file system for the QNX 4 operating system.
ROM	The ROM file system is a read-only file system, intended primarily for initial RAM disks.
Second Extended (ext2)	The standard file system for the Linux operating system.
System V and Coherent	The standard file system for Coherent, SCO, and Xenix.
UFS	The standard file system for BSD and BSD derivatives, SunOS, and NeXTstep.

| TABLE 4-4 | Linux File System Types *(continued)* |

File System Type	Description
Coda	Coda is a networked file system similar to NFS. Currently Linux supports Coda clients only.
NFS	The Network file system. This is the networked file system most commonly used among Linux and UNIX computers.
SMB	Server Message Block (SMB) is a protocol used by Windows for Workgroups, Windows 95, Windows NT, and OS/2 LAN Manager to share printers and files remotely.
NCP	Netware Core Protocol (NCP) is the network file system used by Novell, over the IPX protocol. NCP allows Linux to use NCP as a client.

A sample /etc/fstab might look like the following:

```
/dev/hda1      /            ext2      defaults          1   1
/dev/hda2      swap         swap      defaults          0   0
/dev/hda5      /usr         ext2      defaults          1   2
/dev/hda7      /tmp         ext2      defaults          1   2
/dev/hda8      /var         ext2      defaults          1   2
/dev/hda9      /home        ext2      defaults          1   2
/dev/hdc       /cdrom       iso9660   ro,noauto,user    0   0
none           /proc        proc      defaults          0   0
```

Table 4-5 provides a description of each field.

(NOTE: throughout this book, you may see references to *utility*(*#*). This indicates the *utility* name and which man page this utility can be found in. You do not need the (*#*) part to use the utility. For example, fsck(8) means you could read the manual page for the command using **man 8 fsck**.)

Mount Options

Although most file systems in /etc/fstab are given the mount option of Default, there are other options you can use. Options are listed in /etc/fstab, and are separated by commas (no spaces or tabs). The standard mount options are listed in Table 4-6.

Some file system types supported by Red Hat Linux have additional options. If you are using non-ext2 file systems on your system, consult the mount(8) man page for more information regarding special mount options for your file system types.

You can also access file system information via linuxconf.

	Field Name	Description
TABLE 4-5 Field Functions	fs_spec	Describes the block device or remote file system to be mounted.
	fs_file	Describes the mount point (the directory the file system will be mounted as). For swap partitions, this should be None.
	fs_vfstype	Describes the file system type. Valid file system types are minix, ext, ext2, xiafs, msdos, hpfs, iso9660, nfs, and swap. This field can also be set to Ignore, which will cause the system to ignore the entry. Ignoring an entry is useful for marking unused partitions.
	fs_mntops	Mount options. Specifies mounting options. Mount options are covered later in this section.
	fs_freq	Used by the dump(8) command to determine which file systems need to be dumped. A value of 0 indicates that the file system does not need to be dumped.
	fs_passno	Used by the fsck(8) program to determine the order in which file systems are checked upon boot. The root file system should have an fs_passno setting of 1, and other local file systems should have an fs_passno of 2. Remote file systems should have an fs_passno of 0, which indicates they should not be checked on boot.

EXERCISE 4-4

Run /sbin/linuxconf

Open Config | File systems | Access local drive. This opens the Local Volume display similar to Figure 4-4.

	Mount Option	Description
TABLE 4-6 Mount Options	async	I/O is done asynchronously to this file system.
	atime	Timestamps for each inode are updated when accessed.
	auto	Can be mounted with the -a option of the mount(8) command.
	defaults	Use the default mount options: rw, suid, dev, exec, auto, nouser, and async.
	dev	Interpret character or block special devices on the file system.
	exec	Allow binaries (programs) to be executed on this file system.

TABLE 4-6

Mount Options
(continued)

Mount Option	Description
noatime	Timestamps for each inode are not updated when accessed.
noauto	Cannot be mounted with the -a option of the mount(8) command (it must be mounted explicitly).
nodev	Do not interpret character or block special devices on the file system.
noexec	Do not allow binaries (programs) to be executed on this file system.
nosuid	Do not allow setuid or setgid permissions on programs to take effect.
nouser	Do not allow nonroot users to mount this file system.
remount	Attempt to remount a file system that has already been mounted. This is typically used to change mount options, and is only used by the mount(8) command (never used in /etc/mnttab).
ro	Mount the file system as read-only.
rw	Mount the file system as read-write.
suid	Allow setuid or setgid permissions on programs to take effect.
sync	I/O is done synchronously to this file system.
user	Allow nonroot users to mount this file system. This option also sets the noexec, nosuid, and nodev options, unless overridden.

CERTIFICATION OBJECTIVE 4.04

Using the Red Hat Package Manager

One of the mundane, yet necessary, duties a Systems Administrator faces is software management. Applications and patches come and go. After months or years of adding, upgrading, and removing software applications, it's hard to tell just what's on a system, what version a software package is, and what other applications it depends on. Outdated files often wind up laying around because nobody's quite sure what they belong to. Worse, you may install a new software package only to find it has overwritten a crucial file from a currently installed package. The Red Hat Package Manager (RPM) was designed to eliminate these problems. With RPM, software is managed in discrete "packages," a collection of the files that make up the software, and instructions for adding, removing, and upgrading those files. RPM also makes sure you never lose

FIGURE 4-4

File system
information in
linuxconf

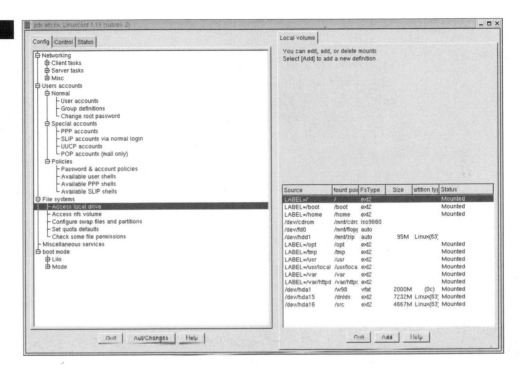

configuration files by backing up existing ones before overwriting. RPM also tracks
which version of an application is currently installed on your system.

A key feature of RPM is that filenames can be specified in Uniform Resource
Locator (URL) format. For example, if you know that the package foo.rpm is on the
FTP server ftp.rpmdownloads.com, in the /pub directory, you can specify that
filename as ftp://ftp.rpmdownloads.com/pub/fee.rpm. RPM is smart enough to log on
to the FTP server anonymously and pull down the file. You can also use the format
ftp://*<username>*:*<password>*@*hostname*:*<port>*/*path*/*to*/*remote*/*package*/*file*.rpm,
where *<username>* and *<password>* are the username and password you need to log
on to this system non-anonymously, and *<port>* specifies a nonstandard port used on the
remote machine. You may use these formats anywhere a filename is called for in RPM.

What Is a Package?

In the generic sense, a package is a container. It includes the files needed to accomplish
a certain task, such as the binaries, configuration, and documentation files in a software
application. It also includes instructions on how and where these files should be

installed and how the installation should be accomplished. A package also includes instructions on how to uninstall itself. RPM packages are often identified by filenames that usually consist of the package name, the version, the release, and the architecture for which they were built. For example, the package penguin-3.26.i386.rpm indicates this is the (fictional) Penguin Utilities package, version 3, release 26. i386 indicates it has been compiled for the Intel architecture. Note that although this is the conventional method of naming RPM packages, the actual package name, version, and architecture information are read from the contents of the file by RPM, not the filename. You could rename the file blag.rpm, but it would still install as penguin-3.26.i386.rpm.

What Is RPM?

At the heart of RPM is the RPM database. This database tracks where each file in a package is located, its version, and much more. The RPM also maintains an MD5 checksum of each file. Checksums are used to determine whether a file has been modified, which comes in handy if you need to verify the integrity of one or more packages. The RPM database makes adding, removing, and upgrading packages easy, because RPM knows which files to handle, and where to put them. RPM also takes care of conflicts between packages. For example, if package X, which has already been installed, has a configuration file called /etc/someconfig, and you attempt to install a new package, Y, which wants to install the same file, RPM will manage this conflict by backing up your previous configuration file before the new file is written. The workhorse of the RPM system is the program rpm. rpm is the "driver" responsible for maintaining the RPM databases. Of rpm's 10 modes of operation, we will cover the four most common: query, install, upgrade, and remove.

Validating a Package Signature

RPM has two methods of checking the integrity of a package: MD5 checksum and GPG signature. MD5 alone is adequate for verifying that the file is intact (no data was lost or corrupted while copying or downloading the file). GPG is used to establish the authenticity of the file; it can be used to confirm, for example, that an RPM file is indeed an official Red Hat RPM. Red Hat provides a GPG public key for its RPM files; the key is located in the RPM-GPG-KEY file on your distribution CD or can be downloaded from www.redhat.com/about/contact.html.

To authenticate your RPMs using GPG, import the key file using the command (assuming it's a CD-based keyfile):

```
# gpg --import RPM_GPG_KEY
```

You can then verify both the integrity and authenticity of an RPM with a command like this:

```
# rpm --checksig pkg-0.0.0-0.rpm
```

If you don't want to use GPG, you can check the integrity of the package only using this:

```
# rpm --checksig --nogpg pkg-0.0.0-0.rpm
```

To Add and Remove Components

RPM makes it easy to add and remove software packages to your system. It keeps a database regarding the proper way to add, upgrade, and remove packages, making it as simple as running a single command to add and remove software.

Install Mode

The Install mode, as its name suggests, is used to install RPM packages on your system. Installing a package is accomplished with the -i option.

```
# rpm -i penguin-3.26.i386.rpm
```

If the package was stored on a remote FTP server, you could use this:

```
# rpm -i ftp://ftp.rpmdownloads.com/pub/penguin-3.26.i386.rpm
```

Before installing the package, RPM performs several checks. First, it makes sure the package you're trying to install isn't already installed—RPM won't let you install a package on top of itself. It also checks to make sure you aren't installing an older version of the package. Next, RPM does a dependency check. Some packages depend on other packages being installed first. In this example, you've just downloaded the latest RPM version of Penguin utilities, and now want to install it.

```
# rpm -i penguin-3.26.i386.rpm
failed dependencies:
iceberg >= 7.1 is needed by penguin-3.26.i386.rpm
```

This error indicates that the Penguin package failed to install because it requires the Iceberg package, version 7.1 or later. You'll have to find and install the Iceberg package, and any packages Iceberg may require.

Finally, RPM checks to see if any configuration files would be overwritten by the installation of this package. RPM tries to make intelligent decisions about what to do with conflicts. If RPM replaces an existing configuration file with one from the new package, a warning will appear on the screen.

```
# rpm -i penguin-3.26.i386.rpm
warning: /etc/someconfig saved as /etc/someconfig.rpmsave
```

It's up to you to look at both files and determine what, if any, modifications need to be made.

Upgrade Mode

The -u switch is used to upgrade existing packages. For example, if Penguin utilities, version 3.25, is already installed, issuing the command:

```
# rpm -u penguin-3.26.i386.rpm
```

will replace the old version of the package with the new one. In fact, one of the quirks of RPM's Upgrade mode is that the older package doesn't even have to exist. -u works identically to -i in this case.

Remove Mode

The rpm -e command removes a package from your system. Like the Install mode, RPM does some housekeeping before it will let you remove a package. First, it does a dependency check to make sure no other packages depend on the package you are removing. If you have modified any of the configuration files, RPM makes a copy of the file, appends .rpmsave to the end of it, and then erases the original. Finally, after removing all files from your system and the RPM database, it removes the package name from the database.

NOTE: Be very careful about which packages you remove from your system. Like most Linux utilities, RPM assumes omniscience, and will silently let you shoot yourself in the foot. Removing the passwd or kernel package would be devastating.

Adding Updates, Security Fixes, and Other Items

Red Hat Linux is constantly being updated. As bugs or security problems are found, they are posted to Red Hat's Errata Web page, located at http://www.redhat.com/support/docs/errata.html. You should check this page regularly to ensure your system is up to date.

EXERCISE 4-5

Updating from the Red Hat Errata Page

Here's a good checklist to follow whenever you check the errata page:

1. Go to http://www.redhat.com/support/docs/errata.html. Select the Red Hat Linux General Errata link.

2. Scroll down to the Overview section. Go through the lists, selecting each package listed.

3. If you have an affected package loaded on your system, consider upgrading it with the recommended replacement.

4. Before replacing an affected package, consider the ramifications. You may need to bring the system down to single-user or perform a reboot.

5. When performing the upgrade, watch for configuration file warnings. If your local configuration files are replaced with new files, you may need to change the new configuration files to reflect your current settings.

6. Thoroughly test the new package. Make sure you have it configured correctly.

7. If a package is listed in the errata but not installed on your system, chances are there's no reason to put it on your system now. Read the detailed errata entry for that package carefully, and only install it if needed.

Red Hat has now included an RH Network Software Manager service that you can configure to check for revised packages, new packages, errata, and other information. You may obtain a free trial subscription to the service by registering at www.redhat.com/network; thereafter, a charge for the service is applied.

Verifying One or More Packages

Verifying an installed package compares information about that package with information from the RPM database on your system, or the original package. Verify does a check against the size, MD5 checksum, permissions, type, owner, and group of each file in the package. Here are a few verify examples:

- Verify all packages

  ```
  # rpm --verify -a
  ```

- Verify all files within a package against an RPM file

  ```
  # rpm --verify -p fileutils-4.0-1.i386.rpm
  ```

- Verify a file belonging to a particular package

  ```
  # rpm --verify --file /bin/ls
  ```

If the files or packages you were verifying checked out okay, you will see no output; otherwise, you'll see what checks failed. The output will be a string of eight characters, possibly with a "c" denoting configuration file, followed by the filename that failed. Each character in the eight-character field contains the result of a particular test. A "." (period) indicates that test passed. The following example shows /bin/vi with an incorrect group ID assigned to it:

```
# rpm --Verify --file /bin/vi
......G.   /bin/vi
```

Table 4-7 lists the failure codes and their meanings.

Seeing What Packages Are Installed

Without RPM, you'd need to search around your file systems to figure out whether a particular software package is installed. RPM makes it easy for you to figure out what RPM packages are installed and get information about those packages.

Query Mode

One of the strengths of RPM is that, ideally, every package or application file on your system is accounted for. Using RPM's query mode, you can determine which packages are installed on your system or what file belongs to a particular package.

TABLE 4-7	Failure Code	Meaning
	5	MD5 checksum
Failure Codes	S	File size
	L	Symbolic link
	T	File modification time
	D	Device
	U	User
	G	Group
	M	Mode

This can be a big help if you want to locate a file that belongs to a certain package. Query mode can also be used to identify what files are in an RPM file before you install it. This lets you see what files are going to be installed on your system before they're actually written.

The -q switch is used to query packages. By itself, -q will give you the version of a specified package. If you want to see which version of the tin newsreader you have on your system, you would issue the following command:

```
# rpm -q tin
tin-1.4.4-2
```

If you want to see which installed package owns a file, use the -f modifier. Here we want to see which package owns /etc/passwd.

```
# rpm -q -f /etc/passwd
setup-2.3.4-1
```

Likewise, if you want to generate a list of files belonging to a certain package, use the -l modifier.

```
# rpm -q -l tin
/etc/X11/applnk/Internet/tin.desktop
/usr/bin/rtin
/usr/bin/tin
/usr/share/doc/tin-1.4.4
/usr/share/doc/tin-1.4.4/README
/usr/share/doc/tin-1.4.4/doc
/usr/share/doc/tin-1.4.4/doc/CHANGES
/usr/share/doc/tin-1.4.4/doc/CHANGES.old
```

```
/usr/share/doc/tin-1.4.4/doc/DEBUG_REFS
/usr/share/doc/tin-1.4.4/doc/INSTALL
/usr/share/doc/tin-1.4.4/doc/TODO
/usr/share/doc/tin-1.4.4/doc/WHATSNEW
/usr/share/doc/tin-1.4.4/doc/auth.txt
/usr/share/doc/tin-1.4.4/doc/filtering
/usr/share/doc/tin-1.4.4/doc/good-netkeeping-seal
/usr/share/doc/tin-1.4.4/doc/internals.txt
/usr/share/doc/tin-1.4.4/doc/iso2asc.txt
/usr/share/doc/tin-1.4.4/doc/pgp.txt
/usr/share/doc/tin-1.4.4/doc/rcvars.txt
/usr/share/doc/tin-1.4.4/doc/reading-mail.txt
/usr/share/doc/tin-1.4.4/doc/tin.1
/usr/share/doc/tin-1.4.4/doc/tin.defaults
/usr/share/doc/tin-1.4.4/doc/umlaute.txt
/usr/share/doc/tin-1.4.4/doc/umlauts.txt
/usr/share/man/man1/tin.1.gz
```

One of the most common modifiers to -q is -a, query all packages on your system. A default Workstation system has over 350 packages installed. Here's a truncated output:

```
# rpm -q -a
chkconfig-1.2.16-1
sed-3.02-8
psmisc-19-4
XFree86-libs-4.0.1-1
glib-1.2.8-4
...
wmconfig-0.9.9-3
xfig-3.2.3c-3
xtoolwait-1.2-5
```

For even more information about a package, use the -i (information) modifier.

```
# rpm -q -i passwd
Name        : passwd             Relocations: (not relocateable)
Version     : 0.64.1             Vendor: Red Hat, Inc.
Release     : 4                  Build Date: Wed 12 Jul 2000 04:56:03 AM PDT
Install date: Thu 15 Feb 2001 07:03:11 AM PST    Build Host: porky.devel.redhat.com
Group       : System Environment/Base    Source RPM: passwd-0.64.1-
4.src.rpm
Size        : 17004              License: BSD
Packager    : Red Hat, Inc. <http://bugzilla.redhat.com/bugzilla>
Summary     : The passwd utility for setting/changing passwords using PAM.
Description :
The passwd package contains a system utility (passwd) which sets
```

```
and/or changes passwords, using PAM (Pluggable Authentication
Modules).

To use passwd, you should have PAM installed on your system.
#
```

Table 4-8 lists some of the most important entries:

Typically, the filename will indicate what's inside the package, but not always. You may receive a package simply named glibc.rpm, which isn't really helpful. You can use the -p modifier to find out what version and release this RPM contains (and perhaps rename it appropriately).

```
# rpm -q -p glibc.rpm
glibc-2.0.7-29
```

Creating and Using Custom RPMs

Source RPMs are, as the name indicates, the source codes used to build architecture-specific packages. Source RPMs are identified with the string "src" appearing where the architecture indicator normally appears, such as this:

```
polarbear-2.07-2.src.rpm
```

Binary RPMs are built from source RPMs. The source RPM contains the source code and specifications necessary to create the binary RPM.

TABLE 4-8	Tag	Description
Important Entries	Name	The name of the package.
	Version	The version of the package.
	Release	The number of times this package has been released using the same version of the software.
	Install Date	When this package was installed on your system.
	Group	Your RPM database is divided into groups, which describes the functionality of the software. Every time you install a package, it will be grouped accordingly.
	Size	The total size in bytes of all the files in the package.
	License	The license the original software has been released under.

Installing Source RPMs

Like normal RPMs, a source RPM (SRPM) is installed using the -i option. This will place the contents of the SRPM within the /usr/src/redhat directory structure.

The /usr/src/redhat/ Directory Structure

There are five subdirectories within the /usr/src/redhat directory structure (see Table 4-9).

When you build an SRPM, you will build it within this structure. If you install an SRPM, it will be extracted into this structure.

Changing Compile Options for a Source RPM

While most precompiled RPMs will serve your needs, there are times when you will want to modify the source code or compile options in the corresponding SRPMs.

The Spec File   To change the compile options in an SRPM, you must understand spec files. The spec file is stored in /usr/src/redhat/SPECS/<*packagename*>.spec. The spec file controls the way a package is built, and what actions are performed when it is installed or removed from a system. There are eight different sections in a spec file (see Table 4-10).

You would change the compile-time options for a package in the build section of the spec file. Here's a sample build section in a spec file:

```
%build
rm -rf $RPM_BUILD_ROOT
mkdir -p $RPM_BUILD_ROOT/usr/bin $RPM_BUILD_ROOT/etc
./configure --prefix=/usr --exec-prefix=/
make CFLAGS="$RPM_OPT_FLAGS" LDFLAGS=-s
```

TABLE 4-9	Directory	Purpose
Subdirectories with the /usr/src/redhat Directory Structure	/usr/src/redhat/SOURCES	Contains the original program source code.
	/usr/src/redhat/SPECS	Contains spec files, which control the RPM build process.
	/usr/src/redhat/BUILD	Source code is unpacked and built here.
	/usr/src/redhat/RPMS	Contains the resulting binary RPM.
	/usr/src/redhat/SRPMS	Contains the SRPM created by the build process.

TABLE 4-10	Section	Description
Spec File Sections	Preamble	Describes what information a user sees when he or she requests information about this package. It also contains a description of the package's function and the version, as well as information about the sources and patches used. It may also contain an icon to be used if the package is manipulated with a graphical RPM manager.
	Prep	If work needs to be done to the source code before actually building it, it's described here. At a minimum, this usually means unpacking the source code. The contents of this section are a shell script.
	Build	Commands to actually compile the spec file and build the sources are in a shell script here.
	Install	Commands to install the software on a system.
	Install and uninstall scripts	This section contains scripts that will be run on the end user's system to install or remove the software. RPM can execute a script before the package is installed, after the package is installed, before the package is removed, and after the package is removed.
	Verify	Although RPM takes care of most verification tasks, a script can be inserted here to take care of extra tasks the package builder may want to do.
	Clean	A script can be specified here to perform any necessary cleanup tasks.
	File list	This is a list of files in the package.

This section, a shell script, begins with some housekeeping. The fourth line runs the configure script in the software package, followed by a "make." You could, for example, modify the make command line to include another definition after LDFLAGS. The compile time options being passed in $RPM_OPT_FLAGS are defaults, set by RPM.

Building Custom Source and Binary RPMs

By now, you should understand how to modify an SRPM spec file to change compile-time options in the Build section. However, there's much more to building customized RPMs. Once you have modified the spec file, you need to tell RPM to build a new RPM and SRPM.

Starting a Build

You build an RPM with the build option of RPM, -b. You will normally modify the -b option with an "a," which means all steps of the build operation must be performed. The RPM build operation is directed at a spec file. For example, the command

```
# rpm -ba foo-2.2.spec
```

directs RPM to create a binary and source RPM from this spec file.

Building an RPM from a Tar Archive

Now that you understand the basics of building an RPM from an SRPM, it's relatively easy to build an SRPM and RPM from a tar archive.

Obtain the Source Files

You'll need to obtain the source code for the package you want to create. You'll need to locate the FTP or Web site for the software you want, obtain the latest version (or whatever version you want to use), and download it. Once you have a copy, put it in the SOURCES directory.

Create the Spec File

Here's where you get to brew a spec file from scratch. Depending on how complicated your source software is, you may wind up with a rather complex spec file. However, for this run, we're going to just cover the basics you'll need to get a spec file running.

The Preamble   You'll need to fire up your favorite text editor and start working on the spec file. Let's start with the preamble section. Here's the preamble (abridged) from fileutils-3.16.spec:

```
Summary: GNU File Utilities
Name: fileutils
Version: 3.16
Release: 10
Copyright: GPL
Group: Utilities/File
Source0: ftp://prep.ai.mit.edu/pub/gnu/fileutils-3.16.tar.gz
Source1: DIR_COLORS
Patch: fileutils-3.16-mktime.patch
Patch1: fileutils-3.16-glibc21.patch
Buildroot: /var/tmp/fileutils-root
```

```
Summary(de): GNU-Datei-Utilities
Summary(fr): Utilitaires fichier de GNU
Summary(tr): GNU dosya iþlemleri yardýmcý yazýlýmlarý
Prereq: /sbin/install-info
%description
These are the GNU file management utilities.  It includes programs
to copy, move, list, etc, files.
The ls program in this package now incorporates color ls!
```

Preamble entries consist of a tag, followed by a colon, followed by information. Some entries are language-specific; these are denoted by a two-letter country code in parentheses just before the colon. The order of the lines is unimportant. Table 4-11 lists entries that may be included in the preamble.

TABLE 4-11	Tag	Description
Preamble Entries	Name	The name of the package.
	Version	The version of the software being packaged.
	Release	The number of times this software has been packaged. This will become part of the package label and filename.
	Buildroot	The directory this package was built in.
	Copyright	Contains the software's copyright information.
	Group	Which RPM group this software should be packaged in.
	Patch	Patches applied to the software.
	Source	There are two entries for this tag. The first indicates where the packaged software's source may be found. The second gives the name of the source file in the SOURCES subdirectory.
	Summary	A short, one-line description of the software being packaged.
	URL	This tag, if present, usually indicates the home page, or where documentation for the software can be found.
	Distribution	The product line this package was created for. This is normally used by Linux distribution companies such as Red Hat Software to indicate which release this package was part of.
	Vendor	The group or organization that distributes the software being packaged.
	Packager	The group or organization that packaged this software.
	Description	This entry may take up more than one line. It is a detailed description of the packaged software.

The Prep Section   The prep section prepares the source files for packaging. Usually the prep section starts by removing the leftovers from any previous builds, and unarchives the source files. A sample prep section might look like this:

```
%prep
/bin/rm -rf $RPM_BUILD_DIR/foo-2.2
/bin/tar xzf $RPM_SOURCE_DIR/foo-2.2.tar.gz
```

Note that the prep section is nothing more than a shell script. The environment variables RPM_BUILD_DIR and RPM_SOURCE_DIR are preset by RPM. They expand to /usr/src/redhat/BUILD and /usr/src/redhat/SOURCE, respectively. This prep script extracts the contents of foo-2.2.tar.gz into the SOURCE directory. If we needed to do any patching to the sources, it would be done here.

There is, by the way, a predefined macro that will handle both of the steps we coded in the previous example. The %setup macro removes any files left over from a previous build, and then extracts the contents of the source file. Now, our prep script becomes

```
%prep
%setup
```

The Build Section   Like the prep section, the build section is also a shell script. This script will handle building binary programs out of the source code. Depending on the software, this step may be very easy, or quite involved. A sample build script might be:

```
%build
make clean
./configure -prefix=/usr -exec-prefix=/
make
```

These commands run "make clean" to ensure that any old object and configuration files are removed. Then the software's configure script (with some additional options) is run, which configures the software for the platform you're compiling on. The make command with no arguments is then run to compile the software.

The Install Section   Yet another shell script, the install section, allows you to build install targets within the source distribution. For uncomplicated software, this may be as simple as this:

```
%install
make install
```

The Files Section   This is a list of files that will become part of the package. Any files you want to distribute in the package must be listed here.

You may specify a %doc directive on a line, which indicates the file listed on this line is documentation. That file will be placed in the /usr/doc/<*package*> subdirectory when the end user installs this package on the system. Here's an example of a files section from our fictional package foo-2.2:

```
%files
%doc README
%doc FAQ
/usr/bin/foo
/usr/man/man1/foo.1
```

The preceding example shows that the files README and FAQ will be placed in the /usr/doc/foo-2.2 subdirectory.

Building the RPM and SRPM

At this point, it's just a matter of running

```
# rpm -ba foo-2.2.spec
```

to build your RPM and SRPM. Some other modifiers that are handy to run with the -b option are listed in Table 4-12.

Testing Your RPM

It's important you test your RPM thoroughly before releasing it for general distribution. Install it, uninstall it, run the program through its paces. Make sure the documentation

	Option	Description
TABLE 4-12	-bp	Execute only the prep section.
	-bl	Check the files section to make sure all the files exist.
Modifiers	-bc	Execute only the build section.
	-bi	Execute only the install section.
	-bs	Build only the SRPM.
	--test	Do not execute any build stages. (Useful for testing the syntax of your spec file.)

and man pages were installed correctly and that configuration files are present and have sane defaults.

exam
ⓌⒶⓉⒸⒽ

Like many Linux tools, RPM has short options with long option equivalents. For example, the -i option (a "short" option) can also be specified using the --install option (a "long" option). You can learn which options have "long" equivalents by checking the man pages for that command.

CERTIFICATION OBJECTIVE 4.05

Basic Networking

The network is where the power of Red Hat Linux really comes alive; however, getting there may not be trivial. As in all other things Linux, it's a learning experience.

The /etc/sysconfig/ Files Used in Network Setup

We'll start our tour in the /etc/sysconfig directory. This is where Red Hat Linux stores and retrieves its networking information. With linuxconf, you'll almost never have to touch these files, but it's good to know they're there (see Table 4-13).

/etc/sysconfig Files for Clock, Mouse, Static-routes, Keyboard, and PCMCIA

While we're in /etc/sysconfig, let's take a little detour and discuss some of the other things in here that make your system run (see Table 4-14).

Setting Up a Network Interface

Using linuxconf, you can modify your system name, as well as add, remove, and edit network interfaces.

TABLE 4-13	Files in the /etc/sysconfig Directory

Filename	Description
/etc/sysconfig/network	This file stores your system's host name, IPV4 forwarding information, your NIS domain, your gateway and gateway device, and whether or not your system uses any type of networking. Some of these values may not be present, depending on how your system is configured.
/etc/sysconfig/network-scripts/	This directory, as its name implies, stores the networking scripts necessary for your system to get itself up on the network.
/etc/sysconfig/network-scripts/ifcfg-lo	The loopback device configuration script. If you're running TCP/IP, you will almost always have a loopback device configured. The loopback isn't a real device, but a dummy interface designed to test your TCP/IP stack.
/etc/sysconfig/network-scripts/ifcfg-*	Each network interface on your machine will, if it is configured, have an associated ifcfg-* script. For example, the first Ethernet card on your system, eth0, will have a corresponding ifcfg-eth0 script. This file contains information about the interface's IP address, netmask, what network it's on, its broadcast address, and whether it should be brought up at boot time. Depending on the type of interface (such as PPP or SLIP), it may contain other information.
/sbin/ifup /sbin/ifdown	These scripts take a network interface as an argument. The ifup script brings the specified interface up; ifdown takes it down.
/etc/sysconfig/network-scripts/network-functions	This script contains functions used by other network scripts to bring network interfaces up and down. This script should never be called directly.
/etc/sysconfig/network-scripts/chat-*	Chat scripts for PPP and SLIP connections.
/etc/sysconfig/network-scripts/ifup-post	This script is called whenever a network device (SLIP excluded) comes up. This script calls the ifup-routes script for static routes, configures aliases for the given device, sets the host name if it's not already set (and if it can resolve a name to the IP address), and sends a SIGIO to programs that have requested notification of network events.

TABLE 4-13	Files in the /etc/sysconfig Directory *(continued)*

Filename	Description
/sbin/pump	pump is a command and a daemon process that manages network interfaces controlled by either DHCP or BOOTP protocol. It is normally started automatically by the /sbin/ifup script for devices configured by BOOTP or DHCP. To query the status of interface eth0, /sbin/pump -i eth0 --status
/etc/sysconfig/network-scripts/ifup-* and /etc/sysconfig/network-scripts/ifdown-*	These scripts bring up or take down, respectively, their assigned protocols. For example, ifup-ipx brings up the IPX protocol.
/sbin/ifconfig	This is the main network interface configurator utility used to set the network parameters on any specific interface.

EXERCISE 4-6

Changing Your System Name with linuxconf

1. From either a GUI or console terminal, run linuxconf.

2. Open Config | Networking | Client Tasks | Basic Host Information. You will see a display similar to Figure 4-5. The default host name is "localhost.localdomain."

3. Replace this with a new host name, (for example, rh7), followed by the domain name your server is in (if you are in *example.com* domain, then use rh7.example.com).

4. Select the Act/Changes button for your new host name to take effect. Note: The Act/Changes button runs scripts that take more than a nanosecond, so do NOT keep clicking if the prompt doesn't instantly disappear. It is working in the background and will remove the prompt when it is done. I know it is hard, but you just have to be patient at times, this being one of those times.

5. At the command line, enter the command **hostname**. You should see your new name.

6. Reboot the machine and you should see the login prompt reflect your new host name.

TABLE 4-14	File	Description
/etc/sysconfig Files for Clock, Mouse, Static-Routes, Keyboard, and PCMCIA	/etc/sysconfig/clock	Contains defaults for the system clock. There are currently only two entries: UTC=true|false—Indicates whether or not the clock is set to UTC (Universal Time Code). ARC=true|false—On alpha platforms, indicates the ARC console's 42-year time offset is in effect.
	/etc/sysconfig/mouse	Contains mouse configuration information. Entries include MOUSETYPE=*type*, where *type* is one of the following: microsoft, mouseman, mousesystems, ps/2, msbm, logibm, atibm, logitech, mmseries, and mmhittab. (See the Hardware- HOWTO in /usr/doc/HOWTO for information on supported mice.) XEMU3=yes|no—Indicates whether a three-button mouse should be emulated on two-button mice. If you have a two-button mouse, you'll want to select three-button emulation to run X, which uses the third button extensively. The third button is simulated by pressing the first and second buttons simultaneously.
	/etc/sysconfig/static-routes	Contains lines in this form: *device* net *network* netmask *mask* gw *gateway* These values correspond to arguments in the route(8) command.
	/etc/sysconfig/keyboard	Contains a single line, indicating which keyboard map to use: KEYTABLE="/usr/lib/kbd/keytables/us.map"
	/etc/sysconfig/pcmcia	Contains PCMCIA configuration information. The most relevant value in here is this: PCMCIA=yes|no—Indicates whether PCMCIA modules should be loaded on boot. Setting this to Yes would tell the kernel to load PCMCIA modules automatically at boot time. This setting is typically only needed for PCMCIA-enabled devices such as laptops.

EXERCISE 4-7

Modifying Network Interfaces with linuxconf

1. From a GUI or console terminal, start linuxconf.

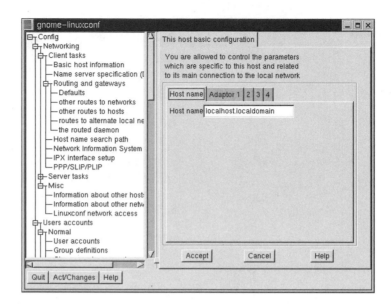

FIGURE 4-4

Changing the host name in linuxconf

2. Open Config | Networking | Client Tasks | Basic Host Information.

3. Select the Adaptor 1 tab (or the tab corresponding to the interface you wish to modify). You will see a form similar to the one shown in Figure 4-6.

   Note: record your current settings for this interface before proceeding.

4. Change the IP value to 192.168.1.11 and the network mask to 255.255.255.0.

   Note: This is a nonrouting IP address and will stop all access to the Internet if connected. It will also stop all access to your local network unless this is within the same network as your local network. The assumption is that this is not a valid local IP address and should isolate you from all other hosts on the local network. Test this by trying to ping any other host.

5. Select the Act/Changes button and wait for the process to complete.

6. At the command prompt, enter **ifconfig** and display your new IP settings.

7. Repeat steps 1–3 and then reset the values to your previous settings. Select the Act/Changes button and wait for the process to complete. Run ifconfig from a command line to check that the old values are being used.

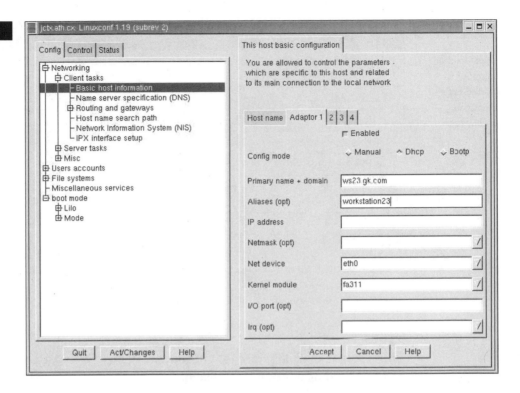

FIGURE 4-5

Modifying
network
interfaces with
linuxconf

There are many values associated with each network interface. The minimum you need is a valid and unique IP address and the corresponding network mask. linuxconf provides a convenient form for you to fill out for each device. You may enter or modify any of the values in this form. Table 4-15 lists each field and its description.

You may then select the Act/Changes button for your new interface edits to take effect.

ifup/ifdown

Recall that for each network interface present on your system, there is a corresponding ifcfg-* file in /etc/sysconfig/network-scripts. You can bring an interface up, or take it down, using the ifup and ifdown commands. You can also use the device name directly with the ifup and ifdown commands. The following two commands do the same thing:

```
ifup ifcfg-eth0
ifup eth0
```

TABLE 4-15	Field	Description
Fields on the linuxconf form for network interface modification	Primary Name + Domain	The host name and domain name that will be bound to this interface.
	Aliases	Any aliases you wish this interface to be known by.
	IP Address	The IP address assigned to this interface.
	Netmask	The netmask used by this subnet.
	Net Device	The device this interface uses.
	Kernel Module	If the driver for this module isn't loaded statically in the kernel, then the loadable module will need to be identified here.
	I/O Port	Only necessary if the driver requires you specify an I/O port.
	Irq	Only necessary if the driver requires you specify an IRQ setting.

Either one of the preceding commands will bring up the eth0 network interface.

ifconfig

The ifconfig command is used to configure and display network devices. Here is some sample output of an ifconfig command:

```
# ifconfig eth0
eth0      Link encap:Ethernet  HWaddr 08:00:20:74:17:33
          inet addr:207.174.142.141  Bcast:207.174.142.143  Mask:255.255.255.240
          UP BROADCAST RUNNING MULTICAST  MTU:1500  Metric:1
          RX packets:1426914 errors:0 dropped:0 overruns:0
          TX packets:1199517 errors:1 dropped:0 overruns:0
```

The preceding command is querying the first Ethernet device on the system, eth0. With only the device as an argument, ifconfig only displays information about the specified interface. When invoked with no parameters, ifconfig shows all interfaces. Table 4-16 lists what the significant fields in the ifconfig output mean.

As indicated, ifconfig is also used to configure network interfaces. The following command would be used to change the IP address of the eth0 interface:

```
# ifconfig eth0 207.174.142.142
```

The first parameter, eth0, tells us which interface is being configured. The next argument, 207.174.142.142, indicates the new IP address being assigned to this

TABLE 4-16	Field	Description
Significant Fields in the ifconfig	RX and TX	Indicates how many error-free packets have been received and transmitted, respectively. It also shows how many errors occurred, how many packets were dropped, and how many overruns occurred. An overrun usually happens when packets come in faster than the kernel can service the interrupt.
	Inet addr	The IP address assigned to this interface.
	Bcast	The network broadcast address.
	Mask	The netmask used by this subnet.

interface. If we want to make sure our change worked, we issue the ifconfig command again to view its current settings.

```
# ifconfig eth0
eth0      Link encap:Ethernet  HWaddr 08:00:20:74:17:33
          inet addr:207.174.142.142  Bcast:207.174.142.143  Mask:255.255.255.240
          UP BROADCAST RUNNING MULTICAST  MTU:1500  Metric:1
          RX packets:1426914 errors:0 dropped:0 overruns:0
          TX packets:1199517 errors:1 dropped:0 overruns:0
```

Looking at the output of our command, we successfully changed the IP address on the eth0 interface to 207.174.142.142. There are a number of other parameters used with ifconfig for modifying interface information (see Table 4-17).

netstat -r

The netstat command is used to display a plethora of network connectivity information. The most commonly used option to netstat, -r, is used to display the kernel routing tables. Here's a sample netstat -r output:

```
# netstat -n -r
Kernel routing table
Destination     Gateway        Genmask          Flags Metric Ref Use
127.0.0.1       *              255.255.255.255  UH    1      0
191.72.1.0      *              255.255.255.0    U     1      0
191.72.2.0      191.72.1.1     255.255.255.0    UGN   1      0
```

Did you notice we used a -n flag? -n tells netstat to display addresses as IP addresses, instead of as host names. This makes it a little easier for us to see what's going on.

TABLE 4-17	Parameter	Description
Parameters Used with ifconfig for Modifying Interface Information	Up	Marks the interface up to the IP stack.
	Down	Marks the interface down to the IP stack.
	netmask mask	Assigns a subnet mask to the interface. The mask can be entered as a 32-bit hexadecimal number preceded by the string 0x, as a dotted quad of decimal numbers, or as a string of hexadecimal numbers.
	Pointopoint	Used to configure PPP links that only involve two hosts.
	broadcast address	While ifconfig allows you to change the broadcast address, you'll almost never have to use this option, except in very old networking environments.
	metric number	Allows you to set a metric value for the routing table entry created for the interface. You will almost never need to set this.
	mtu bytes	Sets the maximum transmission unit.
	Arp	Allows ARP, the Address Resolution Protocol, to detect the physical addresses of hosts on the network. This is on by default.
	-arp	Turns ARP off.
	Promisc	Puts the interface in promiscuous mode. This allows the interface to receive all packets on the network, whether they were destined for this host or not. This is most commonly used for analyzing the network for problems or bottlenecks.
	-promisc	Turns off promiscuous mode.

The Destination column shows the different routes we set up for our network to access. The Gateway column indicates gateway addresses. A gateway, as its name implies, is a route a packet must take first to get to its destination. If no gateway is necessary, an asterisk is printed. The Genmask column shows the "generality" of the route. When attempting to determine a suitable route for an IP address, the kernel will go through the routing table and take a bitwise AND of the Genmask and the address, before comparing it to a route target. The Flags column describes the route. The values that may appear are listed in Table 4-18.

arp as a Diagnostic Tool

The arp command is used to view or modify the kernel's Address Resolution Protocol (ARP) table. Using arp, you can detect problems such as duplicate addresses on the

TABLE 4-18	Flag	Description
	G	The route uses a gateway.
The Ref column indicates how many other routes rely on this entry	U	The interface to be used is up.
	H	Only a single host can be reached via this route.
	D	This entry was created by an ICMP redirect message.
	M	This entry was modified by an ICMP redirect message.

network, or you can manually add arp entries when arp queries fail. Here's a sample arp command, showing all arp entries known to the kernel:

```
# arp -a
IP address        HW type              HW address
10.40.6.2         10Mbps Ethernet      00:00:C0:2C:33:CA
10.40.6.3         10Mbps Ethernet      00:00:C0:4A:B3:42
10.40.6.6         10Mbps Ethernet      00:00:C0:0C:A6:A2
```

The IP address column shows the IP addresses of the hosts it knows about. The HW Type column shows the hardware type of the host, while the HW Address column shows the Ethernet address of the device queried.

You can use the -H option to limit arp's output to the hardware specified. The hardware type can be ax25, ether, or pronet. The default is ether.

A common problem the arp command addresses is when a host on the network is configured with the IP address of a preexisting host on the network. Such cases happen by mistake, but may also happen under circumstances that are more nefarious. In any case, you'll want to remove the offending machine's arp entry from your arp table, and add the correct arp entry. To remove an arp entry, use the -d option.

```
# arp -d bugsy
```

This removes all arp information for the host "bugsy." To add an arp entry, use the -s option.

```
# arp -s bugsy 00:00:c0:cf:a1:33
```

This entry will add the host bugsy to the arp table. Note that an Ethernet, not an IP address, must be specified. The Ethernet address is a physical address associated with the network card.

CERTIFICATION OBJECTIVE 4.06

chkconfig and ntsysv

Red Hat Linux provides two utilities that assist the system's administrator in configuring and maintaining the startup and shutdown process. The ntsysv utility provides a screen-oriented interface, while chkconfig provides a command-line interface.

The Boot Process

Understanding how your system boots and shuts down will help you immensely as a Red Hat Systems administrator. Red Hat Linux uses a process called System V init. To understand the process better, let's go through the steps Red Hat Linux takes to boot itself up to a usable system.

The init program is called by the kernel when it starts up. The init process in turn runs /etc/rc.d/rc.sysinit. rc.sysinit performs a number of tasks, including configuring the network, setting up the default keymapping, starting up swapping, and setting the host name. The init process then determines which runlevel it should be in by looking at the initdefault entry in /etc/inittab. A runlevel is defined as a group of activities. For example, the entry:

```
id:5:initdefault:
```

indicates this system should start up in runlevel 5. After determining which runlevel it should be at, init runs the appropriate scripts to ensure that the activities intended for that runlevel are started. System V init scripts are stored in the directory /etc/rc.d. Within this directory are the following subdirectories:

```
init.d
rc0.d
rc1.d
rc2.d
rc3.d
rc4.d
rc5.d
```

If the default runlevel is 5, init will look in /etc/rc.d/rc5.d and run each "start" script it finds there. A start script is any file or symbolic link with a name beginning with the character S. However, if you run an ls -l command in this directory, you'll find that there are no real files here, only symbolic links to the actual scripts in /etc/rc.d/init.d.

```
# ls -l
[root@jctx init.d]# ls -l
total 182
-rwxr-xr-x   1 root      root         1535 Jul 15   2000 amd
-rwxr-xr-x   1 root      root          798 Aug  4   2000 anacron
-rwxr-xr-x   1 root      root         1289 Aug 17   2000 apmd
-rwxr-xr-x   1 root      root          908 Aug 11   2000 arpwatch
-rwxr-xr-x   1 root      root         1171 Aug 23   2000 atd
-rwxr-xr-x   1 root      root         8385 Aug 23   2000 autofs
-rwxr-xr-x   1 root      root         1177 Aug  5   2000 bootparamd
-rwxr-xr-x   1 root      root         1678 Aug 23   2000 ciped
-rwxr-xr-x   1 root      root         1304 Aug 24   2000 crond
-rwxr-xr-x   1 root      root         1189 Aug 30   2000 dhcpd
-rwxr-xr-x   1 root      root         7663 Aug 21   2000 functions
-rwxr-xr-x   1 root      root         1598 Jul 15   2000 gated
-rwxr-xr-x   1 root      root         1390 Jul 28   2000 gpm
-rwxr-xr-x   1 root      root         3388 Aug  2   2000 halt
-rwxr-xr-x   1 root      root         1625 Aug 23   2000 httpd
-rwxr-xr-x   1 root      root         1382 Jul 20   2000 identd
-rwxr-xr-x   1 news      news         2538 Jul 24   2000 innd
-rwxr-xr-x   1 root      root         2737 Aug 17   2000 ipchains
-rwxr-xr-x   1 root      root         1130 Aug  2   2000 irda
-rwxr-xr-x   1 root      root        14837 Aug 24   2000 isdn
-rwxr-xr-x   1 root      root         1605 Aug 16   2000 kadmin
-rwxr-xr-x   1 root      root         1084 Aug 16   2000 kdcrotate
-rwxr-xr-x   1 root      root         1298 Aug 27   2000 keytable
-rwxr-xr-x   1 root      root          434 Jul 24   2000 killall
-rwxr-xr-x   1 root      root         1316 Aug 16   2000 kprop
-rwxr-xr-x   1 root      root         1235 Aug 16   2000 krb524
-rwxr-xr-x   1 root      root         1235 Aug 16   2000 krb5kdc
-rwxr-xr-x   1 root      root         1427 Aug 30   2000 kudzu
-rwxr-xr-x   1 root      root         2098 Aug 22   2000 ldap
-rwxr-xr-x   1 root      root          609 Aug 23   2000 linuxconf
-rwxr-xr-x   1 root      root         2277 Sep 25   2000 lpd
-rwxr-xr-x   1 root      root         1282 Aug  5   2000 mars-nwe
-rwxr-xr-x   1 root      root         1326 Aug 21   2000 mcserv
-rwxr-xr-x   1 root      root         1798 Aug 30   2000 mysqld
-rwxr-xr-x   1 root      root         1573 Jan 27 02:11 named
-rwxr-xr-x   1 root      root         3360 Aug 22   2000 netfs
-rwxr-xr-x   1 root      root         5812 Aug  6   2000 network
-rwxr-xr-x   1 root      root         2257 Aug  2   2000 nfs
-rwxr-xr-x   1 root      root         1722 Aug  2   2000 nfslock
-rwxr-xr-x   1 root      root         2077 Aug 30   2000 nscd
-rwxr-xr-x   1 root      root         1347 Aug 23   2000 ntpd
```

```
-r-xr-xr-x    1 root      root      4077 Aug 22  2000 pcmcia
-rwxr-xr-x    1 root      root      1388 Aug 10  2000 portmap
-rwxr-xr-x    1 root      root      3081 Aug 24  2000 postgresql
-rwxr-xr-x    1 root      root      1492 Aug  8  2000 pppoe
-rwxr-xr-x    1 root      root      1066 Aug 18  2000 pvmd
-rwxr-xr-x    1 root      root      1071 Aug  5  2000 pxe
-rwxr-xr-x    1 root      root      1541 Aug  2  2000 random
-rwxr-xr-x    1 root      root      1068 Aug 17  2000 rarpd
-rwxr-xr-x    1 root      root      2264 Jul 24  2000 rawdevices
-rwxr-xr-x    1 root      root       907 Aug  4  2000 reconfig
-rwxr-xr-x    1 root      root      1734 Oct  6  2000 rhnsd
-rwxr-xr-x    1 root      root      1405 Aug  5  2000 routed
-rwxr-xr-x    1 root      root      1010 Aug  5  2000 rstatd
-rwxr-xr-x    1 root      root      1114 Aug  5  2000 rusersd
-rwxr-xr-x    1 root      root      1074 Aug  5  2000 rwalld
-rwxr-xr-x    1 root      root      1007 Aug 10  2000 rwhod
-rwxr-xr-x    1 root      root      1721 Aug 22  2000 sendmail
-rwxr-xr-x    1 root      root      1489 Jul 24  2000 single
-rwxr-xr-x    1 root      root      1502 Aug 14  2000 smb
-rwxr-xr-x    1 root      root       975 Jul 20  2000 snmpd
-rwxr-xr-x    1 root      root      2567 Jul 28  2000 squid
-rwxr-xr-x    1 root      root      1259 Jul 17  2000 sshd
-rwxr-xr-x    1 root      root       950 Dec  5  2000 sshd2
-rwxr-xr-x    1 root      root      1180 Aug  7  2000 syslog
-rwxr-xr-x    1 root      root      1515 Aug  1  2000 ups
-rwxr-xr-x    1 root      root       942 Aug  4  2000 vncserver
-rwxr-xr-x    1 root      root      2630 Aug 30  2000 xfs
-rwxr-xr-x    1 root      root      1716 Oct 17  2000 xinetd
-rwxr-xr-x    1 root      root      1797 Aug 20  2000 ypbind
-rwxr-xr-x    1 root      root      1439 Aug 16  2000 yppasswdd
-rwxr-xr-x    1 root      root      1454 Aug 16  2000 ypserv
root]# cd /etc/rc3.d
[root]# ls -l *yp* *ssh*
lrwxrwxrwx    1 root    root    19 Aug 14 16:49 K34yppasswdd ->
../init.d/yppasswdd
lrwxrwxrwx    1 root    root    16 Aug 14 16:49 K74ypserv ->
../init.d/ypserv
lrwxrwxrwx    1 root    root    14 Aug 14 16:49 S55sshd -> ../init.d/sshd
[root]#
```

What's going on here? System V init knows that scripts starting with an S (startup) mean to run the script when entering the runlevel specified by the directory name. For example, /etc/rc3.d is the directory containing all the S scripts (or links) to be executed upon entering run level 3. Scripts that start with K (kill) are also run upon entering a runlevel; in fact, they are executed before the S scripts. These K scripts will stop any process that may already be running, but aren't intended to be in that runlevel. By using symbolic links, any changes that need to be done to the real init scripts only need to be implemented in one place: /etc/rc.d/init.d. In addition, the two numbers after the S or K indicate the order in which the script should be run.

System V init runs the scripts alphanumerically, so the order displayed by ls is the order in which they will be run.

Startup scripts can usually take one of a few arguments, that always include the words "start" and "stop," which mean exactly what they say. For example, the smb (Samba) and sshd (secure shell daemon) management scripts have these options:

```
# /etc/rc.d/init.d/smb
Usage: /etc/init.d/smb {start|stop|restart|status|condrestart}
# service smb    # service is a shortcut to the management scripts
Usage: /etc/init.d/smb {start|stop|restart|status|condrestart}
# service sshd
Usage: sshd {start|stop|restart|condrestart|status}
#
```

So, when entering any runlevel, all the K scripts in the specified runlevel directory will be run with a stop argument. Then, all the S scripts in the same directory will be run with the start argument. Red Hat Linux uses the definitions for System V init runlevels listed in Table 4-19.

It should go without saying that if you set your initdefault to 0, your system will immediately halt when it comes up. Likewise, if you set the initdefault to 6, your machine will exist in a perpetual state of rebooting. Neither of these situations is desirable.

exam
Ⓦatcⅾ **Make sure you go through the /etc/rc.d hierarchy and /etc/inittab, and /etc/rc.d/rc.sysinit files, and understand what's happening along the way. This is the key to understanding what's happening during the boot process.**

TABLE 4-19	Runlevel	Description
System V init Runlevels	0	Halt
	1	Single-user mode—maintenance (clean backups/restores), repairs
	2	Multiuser, without NFS
	3	Multiuser mode (standard text mode login assumed)
	4	Unused
	5	X11 (standard X mode login as well as text mode login)
	6	Reboot (never set the runlevel to this value!)

The chkconfig Utility

The chkconfig command gives you a simple way to maintain the /etc/rc.d directory structure. With chkconfig, you can add, remove, and change services, list startup information, and check the state of a particular service. If you want to see which runlevels the Sendmail service is configured for, you should run this:

```
# chkconfig --list sendmail
sendmail 0:off 1:off 2:on 3:on 4:on 5:on 6:off
```

which indicates that the sendmail service is configured to run only on runlevels 2-5. If you want to turn the Sendmail service off for runlevel 4, you run:

```
# chkconfig --level 4 sendmail off
```

Now Sendmail is configured to run only on runlevels 2, 3, and 5. To turn it back on, you run the same command, substituting **on** for **off**. With chkconfig, you can also add or delete services. Adding a service sets up the appropriate links within the /etc/rc.d/ hierarchy. Deleting a service removes any symbolic links in the /etc/rc.d hierarchy.

The ntsysv Utility

The ntsysv command takes the functionality of chkconfig and wraps it into an easy-to-use screen interface. By default, ntsysv configures the current runlevel. You can specify a different runlevel with the -level flag.

The ntsysv interface is extremely easy to use. Select the service you want to modify using the arrow keys. You then toggle the service on or off using the SPACEBAR. Selecting OK will commit the changes, while selecting Cancel will cancel any changes you made (see Figure 4-7).

ntsysv

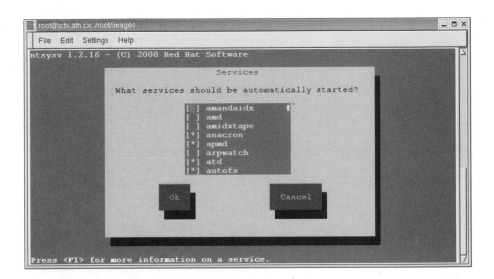

CERTIFICATION OBJECTIVE 4.07

Virtual Consoles

Because Red Hat Linux is a multitasking operating system, it allows you to have more than one login session on the system console at a time. It supports this behavior through the virtual console system.

You switch between virtual consoles using ALT-Function-key sequences. For instance, to switch to virtual console 2, hold down the ALT key and press F2. You can switch between adjacent virtual consoles by pressing ALT-RIGHT ARROW or ALT-LEFT ARROW. For example, to move to virtual console 2 while on virtual console 3, press ALT-LEFT ARROW (this does not work in X consoles). By default, Red Hat Linux comes with the first six virtual consoles configured. You can enable up to 12 virtual consoles by editing the appropriate /etc/inittab entries. Here are the default /etc/inittab entries for the first six virtual consoles:

```
1:2345:respawn:/sbin/mingetty tty1
2:2345:respawn:/sbin/mingetty tty2
3:2345:respawn:/sbin/mingetty tty3
4:2345:respawn:/sbin/mingetty tty4
```

```
5:2345:respawn:/sbin/mingetty tty5
6:2345:respawn:/sbin/mingetty tty6
```

Virtual consoles really bring the multiuser capabilities of Linux to life. You can be viewing a man page on one console, compiling a program in another, and editing a document in yet another virtual console.

Between X Display and Virtual Consoles

The X Display is also considered a virtual window and is assigned to the next numbered console after the text-based consoles. By default, there are six virtual consoles configured with Linux, so the X Display would be assigned to console 7. However, within the Gnome or KDE, if multiple virtual desktops are configured, you switch between these multiple desktops by pressing ALT-F*n*, where *n* is the number of the desktop. For four virtual desktops, you have ALT-F1 (=top-left), ALT-F2 (=top-right), ALT-F3 (bottom-left), and ALT-F4 (bottom-right) for quick access. The number of X Display desktops is configurable, but defaults to four.

To switch between X Display and virtual consoles, you are forced to use a CTRL-ALT-Function-key sequence to get back to the text based virtual modes, but you only need to switch back from text to X Display by using ALT-F7. You do not need the CTRL key as well when going from text console mode to X Display.

CERTIFICATION OBJECTIVE 4.08

kbdconfig, timeconfig, mouseconfig

Three screen-oriented programs included with Red Hat Linux make configuring your keyboard, system time, and mouse easier.

kbdconfig

The kbdconfig utility allows you to set the type of keyboard you have. Figure 4-8 shows the kbdconfig screen. You can use your RIGHT- and LEFT-ARROW, and PGUP and PGDN keys to traverse the list of keyboards. Highlight the proper keyboard and press the RETURN key to accept the new setting or the ESC key to exit without saving. Changes made here are saved to the /etc/sysconfig/keyboard file.

FIGURE 4-7

kbdconfig

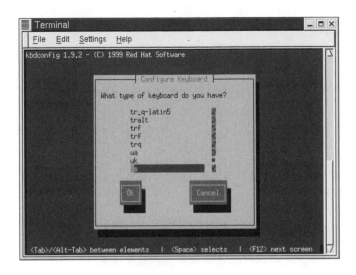

timeconfig

The timeconfig utility allows you to set your time zone. Figure 4-9 shows the timeconfig screen. If your system clock is set to Greenwich Mean Time (GMT), select the Hardware Clock Set To GMT entry. You can use your RIGHT- and LEFT-ARROW, and PGUP and PGDN keys to traverse the list of time zones. Highlight the proper time zone, then press the RETURN key to accept the new setting, or the ESC key to exit without saving. Changes made here are saved to the /etc/sysconfig/clock file.

FIGURE 4-8

timeconfig

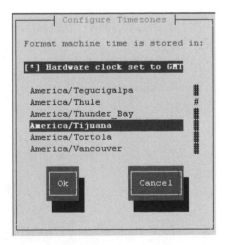

mouseconfig

The mouseconfig utility allows you to set your mouse setting to the correct type. Figure 4-10 shows the mouseconfig screen. You can use your RIGHT- and LEFT-ARROW, and PGUP and PGDN keys to traverse the list of mouse types. Highlight the proper mouse type and press the RETURN key to accept the new setting, or the ESC key to exit without saving. If you are using a two-button mouse and wish to emulate three buttons (by clicking both buttons at the same time), select the Emulate 3 Buttons entry. Changes made here are saved to the /etc/sysconfig/mouse file.

CERTIFICATION OBJECTIVE 4.09

Mounting Floppy Disks and Removable Media

To read floppy disks and other removable media with Red Hat Linux, you need to mount the device, just as you would any other file system. Red Hat has created mount points in the /mnt directory for just this purpose. The subdirectory, /mnt/floppy, is for mounting a single floppy disk at a time, while /mnt/cdrom is used to mount a single CD-ROM at a time. To mount an MS-DOS-formatted floppy, you would run:

```
# mount -t msdos /dev/fd0 /mnt/floppy
```

FIGURE 4-9

mouseconfig

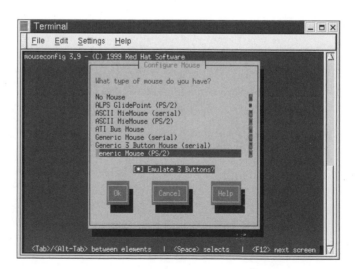

Recall that the -t option to the mount command specifies the type of file system we're mounting. The device, /dev/fd0, is the first floppy disk device. If you have a second floppy disk, the second device would be /dev/fd1. To mount both the first and second floppy at the same time would require another directory, such as /mnt/floppy2, as the mount point. The final argument tells mount which mount point to use. After you have mounted the floppy disk, any reads or writes you perform in /mnt/floppy happen on the floppy disk. The device for your CD-ROM is normally /dev/cdrom. To mount an IS09660 CD-ROM,

```
# mount -t iso9660 /dev/cdrom /mnt/cdrom
```

Now you can read the contents of /mnt/cdrom as if it were a normal file system on your system. To unmount a floppy or CD-ROM, use the unmount command with the mount point as an argument. The following commands unmount both our floppy and CD-ROM:

```
# umount /mnt/floppy
# umount /mnt/cdrom
```

It is important you unmount floppy disks before removing them. Because of the way UNIX caches information before writing to disk, there is a good chance you'll lose data by simply removing a floppy without unmounting it.

on the
Job *One system has a Zip drive of 100MB. The device is /dev/hdd and it was formatted as a Linux Native (Extended 2 File System) on the one partition /dev/hdd1. The directory /mnt/zip was created and a permanent entry in /etc/fstab was added to mount the device at every reboot. The command to manually mount the Zip drive is this:*

```
# mount /dev/hdd1 /mnt/zip
```

The command to manually unmount the Zip drive:

```
# umount /dev/hdd1
```

The command to eject the Zip drive (which automatically unmounts it):

```
# eject /dev/hdd1
```

CERTIFICATION OBJECTIVE 4.10

Sound Cards and the sndconfig Utility

Red Hat Linux provides a screen-oriented interface to make installing your sound card easier by setting up the necessary configuration files to run a sound card. If Plug-n-play (PnP) support is compiled in, (default for RH 7.*x*) sndconfig will probe for PnP sound cards. Sometimes, however, this probe causes the machine to lock up, so you can disable probing by running sndconfig with the -noprobe option.

If no cards are detected, or the -noprobe option was given, you'll be presented with a list of cards to choose from, shown in Figure 4-11. From there, you'll need to choose the I/O port, IRQ, and DMA settings for the sound card. These can be obtained by consulting your sound card documentation.

One other option, --noautoconfig, can be used when probing for PnP cards. Normally, sndconfig will determine the correct values to run the sound card. With --noautoconfig, you can set the settings yourself.

| FIGURE 4-10 |

sndconfig

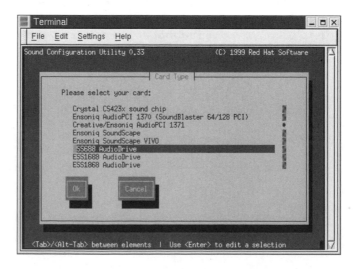

CERTIFICATION SUMMARY

This chapter covered basic configuration and administration of a Red Hat Linux system. We learned the steps necessary to create a basic user, how to populate a user's home directory with the templates in /etc/skel, and where window manager configuration files are located. We also covered the different types of file systems Linux uses, discussed how to mount them, and what mount options to use with them.

In the section Using RPM, we learned the steps necessary to validate a package signature, how to add, remove, and upgrade packages, and how to add updates. We also talked about verifying packages and how to see what package a file belongs to. We finished the topic with a discussion on installing SRPMs and building RPMs from SRPMs and tar archives.

In the Basic Networking section, we covered the configuration files in the /etc/sysconfig hierarchy, including files for the clock, mouse, static-routes, keyboard, network, and PCMCIA. We also discussed the ifup, ifdown, ifconfig, netstat, and arp commands.

We concluded the chapter by talking about virtual consoles, the kbdconfig, timeconfig, and mouseconfig screen utilities, how to mount floppy disks and removable media, and finally touched on the sndconfig utility.

TWO-MINUTE DRILL

Here are some of the key points from the certification objectives in Chapter 4.

Adding, Deleting, and Modifying User Accounts

❑ After installation, your system may have only a single login account: the root account. For most installations, you'll want to create more accounts. Even if you're going to be the only user on the system, it's a good idea to create a single, nonprivileged account to do your day-to-day work and use the root account only for administering the system.

❑ Accounts can be added to Red Hat Linux systems using the *linuxconf* utility.

❑ linuxconf can be run in graphical or character mode.

❑ linuxconf will let you get away with using invalid characters in usernames, such as %, &, *, and !. However, many Linux programs will fail to function with usernames containing these characters.

❑ If your installation doesn't require each user having their own unique group ID (GID), assign your users to the Users group. There's rarely a need for each user to have an individual GID, and having most users assigned to the Users group makes system administration easier.

The Basic User Environment

❑ Ask your users to use passwords that are difficult to guess. Spouses' and dogs' names make bad passwords. Several words strung together with numbers or symbols make better passwords, such as "toy+jobs" or "rule%key." These are easy to remember, yet difficult to guess.

❑ Discourage the use of shared accounts, where several people use a single account. Shared accounts are almost always unnecessary, and are easily compromised.

❑ If you'll be using Network File System (NFS), make user accounts with the same UID across systems.

File System Configuration

❑ Each user on your Red Hat Linux system has an *environment* when logged on to the system.

❑ The home directory for each login account is the initial directory in which users are placed when they first log on to a Red Hat Linux system.

❑ Window manager configuration files are stored in /etc/X11/*<windowmanager>*, where *<windowmanager>* is the name of the window manager.

❑ If you have the kernel source RPMs loaded on your system, you can see which file systems any version or distribution of Linux currently supports. Look at the file /usr/src/linux/fs/filesystems.c.

Using the Red Hat Package Manager

❑ The RPM database tracks where each file in a package is located, its version, and much more.

❑ The Install mode of RPM, as its name suggests, is used to install RPM packages on your system.

❑ The Upgrade mode of RPM will replace the old version of the package with the new one.

❑ The rpm -e command (erase) removes a package from your system.

❑ Verifying an installed package compares information about that package with information from the RPM database on your system or the original package.

❑ Using RPM's query mode, you can determine which packages are installed on your system or what file belongs to a particular package.

❑ Source RPMs are, as the name indicates, the source codes used to build architecture-specific packages.

❑ The spec file is stored in /usr/src/redhat/SPECS/*<packagename>*.spec. It controls the way a package is built, and what actions are performed when it is installed or removed from a system.

❑ Run # rpm -ba foo-2.2.spec to build your RPM and SRPM.

❑ Like many Linux tools, RPM has short options that have long option equivalents. For example, the -i option (a "short" option) can also be specified using the --install option (a "long" option). Learn which options have "long" equivalents by checking the man pages for that command.

Basic Networking

❑ To change your system name, run linuxconf.

❑ To manage network settings on each interface, use pump (dhcp/bootp client management), ifup, and ifdown

❑ The ifconfig command is used to configure and display network devices.

❑ Use ifup eth0 and ifdown eth0 to start and stop the eth0 interface.

❑ The netstat command is used to display a plethora of network connectivity information.

❑ The arp command is used to view or modify the kernel's Address Resolution Protocol (ARP) table.

chkconfig and ntsysv

❑ The ntsysv utility provides a screen-oriented interface, while chkconfig provides a command-line interface.

❑ Make sure you go through the /etc/rc.d hierarchy and /etc/inittab, and /etc/rc.d/rc.sysinit files, and understand what's happening along the way. This is the key to understanding what's happening during the boot process.

❑ The chkconfig command gives you a simple way to maintain the /etc/rc.d directory structure.

❑ The ntsysv command takes the functionality of chkconfig and wraps it into an easy-to-use screen interface. By default, ntsysv configures the current runlevel.

Virtual Consoles

❑ Because Red Hat Linux is a multitasking operating system, it allows you to have more than one login session on the system console at a time using virtual consoles.

❑ By default, six virtual consoles are started at boot time

❑ You can switch between virtual consoles by pressing ALT-F1 to ALT-F6. By default, you start on the first virtual (ALT-F1) console screen.

❑ You can get to console mode from your X Window session with CTRL-ALT-(F1 to F6). Return to X Window with ALT-F7.

kbdconfig, timeconfig, mouseconfig

❑ The kbdconfig utility allows you to change your keyboard settings.

❑ The timeconfig utility allows you to set your time zone.

❑ The mouseconfig utility lets you set your mouse to the correct type.

Mounting Floppy Disks and Removable Media

❑ To read floppy disks and other removable media with Red Hat Linux, you need to mount the device, just as you would any other file system.

❑ Red Hat has created mount points in the /mnt directory for just this purpose.

❑ Typically you use **mount /dev/fd0 /mnt/floppy** to access a Linux file system on a floppy disk inserted into the first diskette drive (A:).

Sound Cards and the sndconfig Utility

❑ Red Hat Linux provides a screen-oriented interface to make installing your sound card easier by setting up the necessary configuration files to run a sound card.

❑ Most modern sound cards should be easily set up by the probe; only very old or obscure chipsets may cause a problem

❑ You must run the sndconfig utility in a non-GUI interface.

SELF TEST

The following questions will help you measure your understanding of the material presented in this chapter. Read all the choices carefully, as there may be more than one correct answer. Choose all correct answers for each question.

Adding, Deleting, and Modifying User Accounts

1. When adding a user using linuxconf, what field is required to be filled in?
   A. Full Name
   B. Login Name
   C. Command Interpreter
   D. Home Directory

2. When deleting a user account using linuxconf, if Archive The Account's Data is selected, where is the deleted user's data archived?
   A. /home/oldaccounts
   B. /root/oldaccounts
   C. /home/oldusers
   D. /root/oldusers

The Basic User Environment

3. Window manager configuration files for the fvwm2 window manager are stored in which directory?
   A. /usr/lib/X11/fvwm2
   B. /etc/X11/wmconfig/fvwm2
   C. /etc/fvwm2/config
   D. /etc/X11/fvwm2

File System Configuration

4. To change the mount options for a local file system, you would edit which file?
   A. /etc/filesystems

B. /etc/fstab

C. /etc/group

D. /etc/mnttab

5. Which option would you mount a file system with so that binaries cannot be executed on that file system?

A. nouser

B. nosuid

C. noauto

D. noexec

Using the Red Hat Package Manager

6. Which of the following commands correctly installs the package penguin-3.26.i386.rpm?

A. rpm -I penguin-3.26.i386.rpm

B. rpm -i penguin

C. rpm -i penguin-3.26.i386.rpm

D. rpm --install penguin.rpm

7. Checking the Red Hat Corporation's Errata Web page, you find a package listed that is currently on your system. A good strategy to update your system would be what?

A. Check to see the ramifications of upgrading the affected package.

B. Watch for warnings when updating the package for config file replacements.

C. Test the new package to ensure it's been configured correctly.

D. All of the above.

8. Source RPMs are, by default, installed in which directory?

A. /usr/lib/rpm

B. /usr/src/rpm

C. /usr/src/redhat

D. /usr/src/redhat/rpm

9. What subdirectories are in the /usr/src/redhat directory?

A. SOURCES, SPECS, BUILD, RPMS, SRPMS

    B. SOURCES, SPECS, LIBS, RPMS, DESC

    C. SOURCES, SPECS, BINS, RPMS, DESC

    D. SOURCES, SPECS, ETC, RPMS, SRPMS

10. Which section of an RPM spec file is used to compile the source code?

    A. Clean

    B. Prep

    C. Build

    D. Install

11. The prep section of an RPM spec file serves what purpose?

    A. Describes what information users see when they request information about this package

    B. Contains commands to compile and build the binaries from source code

    C. Takes care of extra tasks to be performed when a verify command is issued

    D. Unpacks the source code and configures it for building

12. When building an RPM from a tar archive, the tar file should be placed in what directory?

    A. /usr/src/redhat

    B. /usr/src/redhat/SOURCES

    C. /usr/src/redhat/TAR

    D. /usr/src/redhat/SRPMS

13. Issuing the command `rpm -bc foo-2.2.spec` causes what to happen?

    A. A binary and source RPM is created based on the spec file.

    B. Only the SRPM is built.

    C. Only the install section of the spec file is executed.

    D. Only the build section of the spec file is executed.

Basic Networking

14. The /etc/sysconfig/network file contains information about what?

    A. Your system's host name

    B. The devices used for your network connections

C. Chat scripts for PPP and SLIP connections

D. The status of the network

15. What command is used to configure and display network devices?

A. netstat

B. arp

C. ifconfig

D. ifup

16. The netstat -r command is used to do what?

A. Display kernel routing tables.

B. Display gateway metrics.

C. Configure kernel routing tables.

D. Configure gateway metrics.

17. The command arp -d rhino causes which of the following to happen?

A. All ARP tables are removed on the host rhino.

B. All ARP information for the host rhino is removed.

C. All ARP tables on the host rhino are displayed.

D. All ARP information pertaining to the host rhino is displayed.

chkconfig and ntsysv

18. Upon boot, the kernel invokes init, which in turn runs what?

A. /etc/rc.d/init.d

B. /etc/inittab

C. /etc/rc.d/initdefault

D. /etc/rc.d/rc.sysinit

19. If you want to see what runlevels crond is configured to start in, which command should you issue?

A. chkconfig --list -crond

B. chkconfig --l crond

C. chkconfig --list crond

D. chkconfig crond

Virtual Consoles

20. To switch from the current virtual console to virtual console 4, you press which keys?

    A. ALT-4

    B. ALT-F4

    C. CTRL-4

    D. CTRL-F4

21. To switch from a text-based current virtual console to the X-Window display, press which keys?

    A. ALT-1

    B. ALT-F1

    C. ALT-7

    D. ALT-F7

22. To switch from the X Window display back to virtual console n, press which keys?

    A. ALT-n

    B. ALT-Fn

    C. CTRL-ALT-Fn

    D. CTRL-Fn

LAB QUESTION

Part 1

In this exercise, you are going to experiment with a few other neat utilities for system management, one for service control called tksysv and a set of user management utilities.

  1. From a XTerm in any X Window interface, start the graphical equivalent to chkconfig and ntsysv called tksysv. Run tksysv in the background so you can still use this terminal window.

```
[root]# tksysv &
```

    This will present a graphical tool for controlling which services are to be run at any level.

    These next questions assume that the autofs service is already running and installed; if not, pick another service to add and remove (it does not matter which as long as you put it back exactly as it was before).

  2. From within tksysv, edit the autofs record and record the current order number.

3. Remove the autofs service from level 3.

4. Switch back to the XTerm window and run chkconfig to see if it has been removed.

5. Add the autofs service back in with order number 29.

6. Switch back to the XTerm window and run chkconfig to verify that it is back.

   Although tksysv is a nice graphical interface, the chkconfig utility is probably faster and easier to remember, especially since X is not always available in an emergency or through remote login.

Part 2

Linuxconf is a large utility that does it all, but there are lots of small utilities that do certain tasks faster. For instance, for user accounts, there is useradd, usermod, and userdel utilities to add, modify, and delete user accounts.

1. Use the man pages for useradd (or just type useradd with no arguments for a simple usage statement) to find out which options are needed to add the following account with all these attributes:

   ```
   login: brianr
   name: brian rite
    UID: 5010
   GID: nobody
   shell: /bin/bash
   ```

2. Change the passwd for brianr to RvRg49().

3. Telnet into localhost and login as your new account brianr. What files are present in this new account? Exit from this login.

4. Remove the brianr account using the userdel command. Is the brianr home directory gone? What option would have done this for you?

   Now wasn't that simpler than using linuxconf?

SELF TEST ANSWERS

The following questions will help you measure your understanding of the material presented in this chapter. Read all the choices carefully as there may be more than one correct answer. Choose all correct answers for each question.

Adding, Deleting, and Modifying User Accounts

1. ☑ **B.** The only required field for a new user is the Login Name.

    ☒ **A, C, and D** are incorrect. linuxconf uses defaults for the rest of the fields, if required. Some options will use the default settings based on the username, specifically Home Directory (**D**) and Command Interpreter (**C**). **A**, the Full Name, is never required, just a good idea.

2. ☑ **A.** All files stored in a deleted user's account are archived to /home/oldaccounts when the Archive The Account's Data option is selected.

    ☒ **B, C, and D** are bogus filenames. Note: you should NEVER put any user data under the /root directory; this is the login directory for the superuser account and should be carefully guarded.

The Basic User Environment

3. ☑ **D.** /etc/X11/fvwm2. Window manager configuration files are stored in /etc/X11/<*windowmanager*>, where <*windowmanager*> is the name of the window manager.

    ☒ **A, B, and C** are bogus filenames.

File System Configuration

4. ☑ **B.** Information regarding local file systems, including mount options, is stored in /etc/fstab.

    ☒ **A, C, and D** are incorrect. Information about currently mounted file systems is stored in /etc/mtab. The list of system groups is maintained in /etc/group (**C**). /etc/mnttab (**D**) is an invalid filename. The file /etc/file systems (**A**) lists the valid types of file systems supported.

5. ☑ **D.** The noexec option does not allow binaries to be executed on the file system.

    ☒ **A, B, and C** are incorrect. The noauto option (**C**) stops automounting; nosuid (**B**) stops any program from asserting the SUID privilege bit; the nouser option (**A**) stops nonprivileged users from mounting this file system.

Using the Red Hat Package Manager

6. ☑ C, rpm -i penguin-3.26.i386.rpm. When installing a package, the -i option is used, followed by the name of the RPM file.
   ☒ D is almost correct. It has the wrong filename for the rpm, but it would work otherwise. B also does not use the full filename. An asterisk at the end would make it work (as in penguin*), but this would install every package starting with the name penguin, so it may install more than you want. The -I option is invalid with rpm (A).

7. ☑ D. All of the above. A, B, and C are all good strategies when updating an RPM on your system.
   ☒ There are no incorrect answer choices.

8. ☑ C. When installing SRPMs, they are, by default, extracted into the /usr/src/redhat directory structure.
   ☒ A, B, and D are nonexistent files and directories.

9. ☑ A. SOURCES, SPECS, BUILD, RPMS, SRPMS are the subdirectories within the /usr/src/redhat directory structure.
   ☒ B, C, and D are not subdirectories in the /usr/src/redhat directory.

10. ☑ C. Build. The build section of the spec file is used to compile the source code.
    ☒ A, B, and D are incorrect. The clean option removes unnecessary files, the prep section typically unpacks source and more, while the build section scripts the compilation step(s). The clean section may contain a script for any cleanup (A), the install section has commands to install the software on a system (D), and the prep section does preparation before the build, like unpacking the source code (B)

11. ☑ D. The prep section is performed just before the build section and usually is used to unpack the source code and run any configuration commands.
    ☒ A refers to the Preamble section of the spec file, B refers to the Build section of the spec file, and C refers to the Verify section of the spec file.

12. ☑ B. Tar files should be placed in /usr/src/redhat/SOURCES when building an SRPM from a tar archive, not the TAR subdirectory.
    ☒ A and D are not used. As mentioned earlier, tar files should be placed in /usr/src/redhat/SOURCES when building a SRPM from a tar archive, not the TAR subdirectory (C).

13. ☑ D. Only the build section of the spec file is executed. The c modifier to the build option (-b) causes only the build section to be executed.
☒ You would use -bs for **B**, -bi for **C**, and -ba for **A**.

Basic Networking

14. ☑ A. If networking is enabled, the file will contain your host name, and possibly configuration information for NIS and packet forwarding.
☒ It will not contain any status information nor any chat scripts (**B**, **C**, and **D**).

15. ☑ C. The ifconfig command is used to configure and display network devices.
☒ The ifup command (**D**) can be used to start|stop|status an interface, arp (**B**) manages the arp table in memory, and netstat (**A**) displays network statistics.

16. ☑ A. netstat -r is used to display the kernel's network routing tables.
☒ Gateway metrics are routing information and not a function of netstat (**B**). The route command can configure the routing table and any metrics associated with them (**C** and **D**).

17. ☑ B. The -d option to arp tells the kernel to remove all arp info regarding a specified host.
☒ The previous statement also means **D** is incorrect. **A** and **C** are incorrect because they are nonexistent uses of the arp command.

chkconfig and ntsysv

18. ☑ D. init runs /etc/rc.d/rc.sysinit, which performs a number of tasks, including configuring the network, setting up keymapping, the swapping, and the host name.
☒ **A** is a directory, while **B** is the init table file, /etc/inittab, which sets the runlevel at startup, but is not a script to be run. The runlevel setting within /etc/inittab is initdefault, so **C** is a bogus filename.

19. ☑ C. chkconfig --list crond. The output of this command is the following: crond 0:off 1:off 2:on 3:on 4:on 5:on 6:off.
☒ The --l option is not valid, nor is the -crod option (**A** and **B**). You must provide an option to chkconfig, therefore **D** is incorrect.

Virtual Consoles

20. ☑ **B.** Press ALT-F4. Each virtual console has an ALT-function key associated with it to move to that virtual console.
☒ **A, C,** and **D** denote unrecognized key combinations in terminal mode.

21. ☑ **D.** Press ALT-F7 to switch from a virtual console to the default X Window display.
☒ **A, B,** and **C** would be ignored when in a console terminal.

22. ☑ **C.** Press CTRL-ALT-F*n* to switch from the X-Window display to virtual console number *n*.
☒ If you press ALT-*n*, you will switch to that desktop area when in Gnome (**B**). **A** and **D** have no effect in X, and are incorrect.

LAB ANSWER

Part I

1. From a XTerm in any X Window interface, start the graphical equivalent to chkconfig and ntsysv called tksysv. Run tksysv in the background so you can still use this terminal window.

```
root]# tksysv &
```

This will present a graphical tool for controlling which services are to be run at any level. These next questions assume that the "autofs" service is already running and installed, if not, pick another service to add and remove, it does not matter which as long as you put it back exactly as it was before.

2. From within tksysv, edit the autofs record, record the current order number 28.

3. Remove the autofs service from Level 3.

4. Switch back to the XTerm window and run chkconfig:

```
root] # chkconfig --list autofs
```

This should show that the autofs is no longer started in runlevel 3.

5. Add the autofs service back in with order number 29.

6. Switch back to the XTerm window and run chkconfig:

```
root] # chkconfig --list autofs
```

This should show that the autofs is started in runlevel 3.

Part 2

1. To add the account, enter:

   ```
   [root]# useradd brianr -u 5010 -g nobody -c 'brian rite' -s /bin/bash
   ```

2. Change the password:

   ```
   [root]# passwd brianr
   ```

3. Check the new account:

   ```
   [root]# telnet localhost
   ```

   What files are there? Include all the hidden files to see the skeleton files copied over from the /etc/skel directory.

   ```
   [brianr]$ ls -a

   [brianr]$ exit
   ```

   Remove the brianr account using the userdel command. Is the brianr home directory gone? What option would have done this for you?

4. Remove the brianr account using the userdel command. Is the brianr home directory gone? What option would have done this for you?

   ```
   [root]# userdel brianr       # leaves the home directory

   [root]# userdel -r  brianr   # also removes home directory
   ```

5

Advanced Installation

I n this chapter, you will learn how to install and troubleshoot Linux in advanced scenarios. The installation topics cover booting multiple operating systems, troubleshooting and fixing hardware conflicts, and gaining a firm understanding of the boot scripts used. You will learn how to set up a Redundant Array of Inexpensive Disks (RAID), and master the intricate details of the rc.sysinit startup script and modules.

CERTIFICATION OBJECTIVE 5.01

Dual Boots: Linux and Windows NT

If your system was already configured with NT or Windows 9*x*, then, during any installation of Linux, you are given an option to dual-boot the system with the previous OS. The installation program defaults to using "dos" as the name for the other OS, no matter what it really is. You can change this default name to anything you want.

Dual Boot Configuration During Installation

Essentially, the LILO boot loader will cascade to the previous loader, whatever it was. The default is for Linux to load first. You can change this, if desired, by selecting the other OS and then clicking the Default Boot Image button.

Using the NT Loader Boot Manager

There are a few alternative solutions for setting up dual booting between Windows NT and Linux, and several different ways to accomplish dual booting itself. The first example uses NT's loader to load both Linux and NT.

NT's loader installs to the master boot record (MBR), and relies on three major files: ntdetect.com, ntldr, and boot.ini. All three files are hidden system files in the root directory of your boot drive. The only file that really concerns us, however, is the boot.ini file. Here is an example of a boot.ini file for an NT workstation install:

```
[boot loader]
timeout=30
default=multi(0)disk(0)rdisk(2)partition(1)\WINNT
[operating systems]
```

```
multi(0)disk(0)rdisk(2)partition(1)\WINNT="Windows NT Workstation
Version 4.00"
multi(0)disk(0)rdisk(2)partition(1)\WINNT="Windows NT Workstation
Version 4.00 [VGA mode]? /basevideo /sos
C:\="Microsoft Windows 98"
```

This example is a simple boot.ini on a system that has NT installed on the second hard drive and Windows 98 installed on the first. The timeout=## line shows how long the loader will wait for you to choose an OS before it boots the default OS. The next line is the default OS. Here it is pointing to NT. If you wanted it to boot Windows 98 you could change the default OS to: default=C:\.

We can see from this example that NT is capable of loading other operating systems, but note that it handles non-NT systems differently. It is not inherently obvious from this example how to load the second OS. There is a copy of the boot sector of the other OS in the C: drive, and as far as NT is concerned, the C: drive is the first drive (the boot drive). In the root of the C: drive, sits a file called bootsect.dos. This file contains the original bootsector of an alternative OS and is created for you if MS-DOS or Windows is installed before you install NT.

All we need to do is copy the Linux bootsector to the C: drive under a new name (ex: bootsect.ln1) and edit the boot.ini file. See Figure 5-1 for a graphical display of our physical disk layout.

If there isn't any space left on your disk and you have DOS, Windows 95, or Windows 98, then you can shrink the partition using FIPS. First, you must defrag the Windows partition, using the native Windows tools. This will force all your data to the beginning of the drive. Using the FIPS utility will allow you to shrink the C: drive partition size so it uses slightly more space than all the currently installed files require and frees up the remainder as a separate partition. Be careful not to make it smaller than the space you are using on your drive. For example: If you defrag a 2GB drive and have 1GB of space currently used, then you cannot shrink the partition less than 1GB. So, you need to add at least 200MB of additional free space to the total disk size for the C: driv. It does not matter if you are using NT (with NTFS), Windows 2000, or some other windows operating system, you can use a third-party utility, such as Partition Magic, that can repartition the disk.

FIGURE 5-1

Disk drive
partitions before
installing Linux

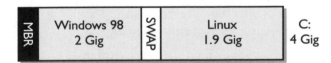

EXERCISE 5-1

Using FIPS to Shrink a Large Single Partition into Two Partitions

Warning: This example is for a system with a single partition holding a Windows OS like 95/98/NT4. Make a backup of anything important, as this may not work for you and you may damage the disk beyond repair. MAKE SURE you have READ the FIPS Documentation before proceeding. It can be found in the same directory as the utility: \dosutils\fips20:

1. Bring up Windows Explorer in a separate window. (It does not matter which —Windows 9x or NT.)

2. Put the Linux CD-ROM named Binary #1 into your CD-ROM drive. (The example assumes the CD-ROM to be D:)

3. Put a blank floppy into the A: drive.

4. Make the floppy a bootable DOS disk.

5. From the CD-ROM, D:\dosutils\fips20 directory, copy these files to the floppy drive:

   `FIPS.EXE, RESTORRB.EXE ERRORS.TXT`

   From Windows\command copy (9x):

   `FDISK.EXE`

6. Reboot this Windows machine with the new floppy.

7. When the A:> DOS prompt appears, type **FIPS** and press ENTER.

8. The FIPS utility will ask you to read a message; do so, then press ENTER at the first few prompts. Be aware, however, that if you are questioned whether to Continue or Redit (c/r)?, you have gone too far. If this happens, power down and back up again to restart this procedure from step 7; then proceed to the previous step.

   During the actual reconfiguration step, you will be presented with a line something like the following, assuming you have a 2080MB disk and each cylinder represents 16MB:

Old partition	New partition
912	1168

At this point, you have the new C: drive size on the left, while the right represents the new second partition. This 912MB represents files ONLY, with no extra space for the system. You should, however, add some space. Otherwise, the Windows OS may fail to start.

If you press the RIGHT-ARROW key once, the display will update to

Old partition   New partition
928   1152

You will have added 16MB to the new C: drive size; add about 200 more than the original size, in this case, 208MB. Each movement represents one more cylinder shifted from one partition to the other. 13 cylinders of 16MB equate to 208MB:

Old partition   New partition
1120   960

If you go past the point you want, simply press the LEFT-ARROW key to reduce the size by one cylinder and 16MB. You are now ready to press ENTER to continue.

FIPS will ask if you want to Continue or Re-edit (c/r)? Press C for continue.

You will then be asked to write the new disk partition table. If you accept, then the two partitions are actually created. If you decline, nothing will have changed.

9. Accept the change and reboot using the floppy one more time.

10. Run FDISK.EXE and delete the second partition.

11. Reboot the machine into Windows.

You are now ready to install Linux!

Installing Linux When Space Is Available

In this next example, you will install Linux at the end of the drive (after the now smaller C partition) from the example diagram. First, make a 32MB Linux Swap partition, then fill the rest of the drive with Linux. After the Linux installation, we will do the rest of the work from within Linux. Linux maps the layout as shown in following example.

```
    /dev/hda (C:Drive with free space)
/dev/hda1 (2 Gig VFAT - already existing)
/dev/hda2 (32 Meg Linux Swap - from free space)
/dev/hda3 (1.968 Gig Linux Native - free space)
    /dev/hdb (D:Drive)
/dev/hdb1 (4 Gig NTFS)
```

Figure 5-2 is a graphical look at the first disk.

Now we need to edit the /etc/lilo.conf file to set up our bootsector. There are many ways to do this, so make sure you have read Chapter 2 as well as studied the man pages for both lilo(8) and lilo.conf(5). Several different ways of placing your bootsector in the root of the boot drive are available. The quickest method is to install LILO to the SuperBlock of the Linux Native partition (hda3). This is the first sector of the partition and is used to boot when the partition is marked as active. Here is an example of the lilo.conf file:

```
boot=/dev/hda3
image=/boot/vmlinuz-2.2.5-15
label=linux
root=/dev/hda3
read-only
```

This is a very simplified lilo.conf file, but it should be sufficient to create a basic bootsector. To install this bootsector, type **lilo**.

Now we need to copy the bootsector from /dev/hda3. Issue the following command from linux:

```
dd if=/dev/hda3 of=/bootsect.ln1 bs=512 count=1
```

This command will dump the first 512 bytes from the beginning of /dev/hda3 to the file /bootsect.ln1. You can call the output file anything you like, but it must match what you add to the boot.ini file.

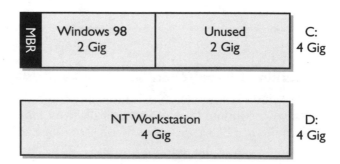

FIGURE 5-2

Graphical look
at the first disk

Next, copy the bootsect.ln1 to the C: drive. This can be accomplished by simply copying the file to a disk, rebooting, and then copying the file to the C: drive. Using this example, everything can be accomplished from within Linux. Next, you will create a directory to mount the Win98 partition:

```
mkdir /win98       # create a directory as the mount point
mount  /dev/hda1 /win98  # mount the device onto the new directory
```

Now copy /bootsect.ln1 to the mounted directory:

```
cp bootsect.ln1 /win98
```

and simply edit the boot.ini file on the mounted filesystem. Add the following line to the bottom of the file:

```
C:\bootsect.ln1="Linux 2.4"
```

Now once you reboot, Linux 2.4 should be the last option. Simply select it and Linux should load. You can also place development kernels under different names in the root directory, like bootsect.ln2. This is very useful for testing out new kernels. Be sure to keep your repair disk on hand that you made during setup, just in case you make any errors modifying the lilo.conf or boot.ini files.

If you are having problems, you should try to make a LILO boot disk. Just place a (DOS) formatted floppy disk in the floppy drive, and modify the /etc/lilo.conf file's boot option to read: boot=/dev/fd0.

Run LILO, and reboot with the floppy in the drive. You should be able to boot with this floppy disk.

```
# lilo
linux *
#  reboot
```

Once you have a working LILO boot disk, you can simply copy the bootsector from the disk instead of the hard drive. The following command will copy the bootsector from your floppy:

```
dd if=dev/fd0 of=/bootsect.ln1 bs=512 count=1
```

If you are still not booting, you should refer to the LILO man pages and check for updates to the LILO-HOWTO file on the Internet.

CERTIFICATION OBJECTIVE 5.02

RAID Configuration

Linux RAID has come a long way recently. There are lots of hardware RAID products now supporting Linux, especially with the big name brand PC manufacturers. Dedicated RAID hardware is definitely the best solution. The alternative is to use a software-based RAID service. Linux provides a RAID software RPM that you can use to configure multiple disk partitions to appear as one partition.

There are six RAID levels, representing different arrangements of redundancy, but only three are implemented in Linux software: Levels 0, 1, and 5, plus an additional mode known as Linear.

This text assumes you already have some knowledge of the differences in RAID levels, Table 5-1 gives a quick overview.

exam
ⓦatch   ***Both RAID0 and 1 require two or more drives, while RAID5 requires three or more drives.***

You can assign additional disks for failover called spare disks within the RAID set. When one disk fails it is marked as bad and the data is reconstructed on the first spare disk, which is used as a replacement, resulting in little or no downtime. The next example demonstrates both RAID1 and 5. Assuming your server has four drives, with the OS loaded on the first, it should look something like this:

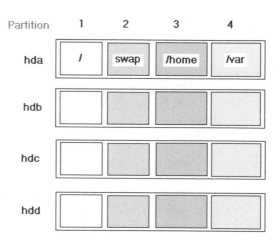

TABLE 5-1	RAID Level	Description
RAID Level Quick Overview	RAID Level 0: Striping	This is used primarily for increased disk access speed, but has no fault tolerance. Best cost factor; every byte available. NOT Recommended.
	RAID Level 1: Mirroring	This will keep a complete duplicate of one partition on another. Provides good single disk fault tolerance; has the best *read* performance; requires two or more disks. Worse cost factor.
	RAID Level 5: Data and Parity Striping	All data and (row) parity is striped across all disks. Using the local CPU, parity information can be used to rebuild information from any single failed disk. This method allows for good fault tolerance and potential read and write performance improvements. This setup requires 3 to 32 partitions/drives. Loss of one disk out of every set to parity. $((n-1)/n)*100$ percent.

This does not include three other drives (hdb, hdc, hdd) that are relatively the same size as Drive 1 (hda).

This first example shows how to mirror both the /home and the /var directories (RAID1) to Drive 2 and Drive 3, leaving Drive 4 as a spare.

You need to create nearly identically sized partitions on Drives 2 and 3. In this example, the assumption is that all disks will have been partitioned with the same sizes for each of the four partitions. Mark the last two partitions on all drives as type 0xFD (for autodetection) using the fdisk program, with the "t" option to toggle the drive ID type.

In the partition table of the first drive will be /dev/hda3 (currently mounted as /home) and /dev/hda4 (currently mounted as /var). The second drive will have /dev/hdb3 and /dev/hdb4. The third drive will be /dev/hdc3 and /dev/hdc4, while the last drive will have /dev/hdd3 and /dev/hdd4. All of these partitions have been marked with partition IDs of type 0xFD. Now, update the configuration file /etc/raidtab as follows:

```
raiddev /dev/md0
raid-level 1

nr-raid-disks 3
nr-spare-disks 1
persistent-superblock 1
chunk-size 4
```

```
device  /dev/hda3
raid-disk 0
device  /dev/hdb3
raid-disk 1
device  /dev/hdc3
raid-disk 2
device  /dev/hdd3
spare-disk 0


raiddev /dev/md1
raid-level 1
nr-raid-disks 3
nr-spare-disks 1
persistent-superblock 1
chunk-size 4
device  /dev/hda4
raid-disk 0
device  /dev/hdb4
raid-disk 1
device  /dev/hdc4
raid-disk 2
device  /dev/hdd4
spare-disk 0
```

Table 5-2 shows what some of the commands are, along with a brief description of what they do.

exam
Ⓦatch
Take special note that raid-disks and spare-disks start counting at 0; nr-raid-disks and nr-spare-disks are the correct number of drives. For example: If nr-raid-disks = 3, then the last raid-disk will be 2.

TABLE 5-2	Command	Description
RAID Commands	nr-raid-disks	Number of RAID disks to use
	nr-spare-disks	Number of spare disks to use
	persistent-superblock	Needed for autodetection
	chunk-size	Amount of data to read/write
	parity-algorithm	How RAID 5 should use parity

Now we have to initialize the md0 and md1 devices. To do this, run

```
mkraid /dev/md0; mkraid /dev/md1
```

The /proc/mdstat file will show you the status on your RAID configurations. You can now mount the device, format it, and continue with your project.

For a RAID5 example to be configured instead on the /var partition (in order to preserve mail, and so on), the /etc/raidtab should be modified to look as follows:

```
raiddev /dev/md0
raid-level 5
nr-raid-disks 3
nr-spare-disks 1
persistent-superblock 1
chunksize 32
parity-algorithm right-symmetric
device   /dev/hda4
raid-disk 0
device   /dev/hdb4
raid-disk 1
device   /dev/hdc4
raid-disk 2
device   /dev/hdd4
spare-disk 0
```

Again, run **mkraid /dev/md0** to initialize RAID5.

Formatting the RAID Partition

Before you run mke2fs to format the device, you should understand how to use the special mke2fs stripe option. For instance, if you have a chunk-size of 32KB, you should use 64 blocks per chunk to write 32KB consecutively. If you format using 4K block sizes, then use 8 blocks per chunk. If you specify the chunk size relative to the RAID read/write operations when you format the RAID5, device you will see a considerable increase in performance. For this latter example, type:

```
mke2fs -b 4096 -R stride=8 /dev/md0
```

For autodetection to work properly, you need to have the partitions set to type 0xFD, as described earlier. You also must have autodection turned on in the kernel, and you will need to use the persistent-superblock option. If all is well, when the kernel boots, it will automatically detect RAID and fix any errors from crashes during bootup.

Having a RAID level root device is a bit trickier. It may be in your best interest to manually copy the contents of your root partition to other drives. After doing so you should use LILO to write the kernel to the root devices of those drives as well. This will allow for a static copy of your root device in case of failures. To do a true root RAID is possible, but is beyond the scope of this text. For more information, read the Root-RAID-HOWTO documentation for a detailed explanation.

EXERCISE 5-2

Mirror the /home Partition Using Software RAID

Assuming the following two-drive partition schemes exist

```
Drive 1:
hda1     256      /
hda2      64      swap
hda3     500      /home
hda4     256      /var

Drive 2:
hdb1    1200      /usr
hdb2      64      swap
hdb3     100      /tmp
hdb4     500      (not allocated)
```

You will now create a mirror of hda3 to hdb4 partition (their exact sizes should be close, but do not have to be exactly the same).

Warning: If this is a running system, you first need to BACK UP the /home partition before proceeding. Otherwise, all data on the current /dev/hda3 will be LOST.

1. Mark the two partition IDs as type 0xFD using the fdisk utility in Linux.

```
[root]# fdisk /dev/hda
Command (m for help) : t
Partition number (1-4)
3
Partition ID (L to list options): FD
Command (m for help) : w
Command (m for help) : q
# fdisk /dev/hdb
```

```
Command (m for help) : t
Partition number (1-4)
4
Partition ID (L to list options): FD
Command (m for help) : w
Command (m for help) :q
```

2. Update the configuration file /etc/raidtab with these lines of code:

```
[root]# vi /etc/raidtab
raiddev /dev/md0
raid-level 1

nr-raid-disks 2
nr-spare-disks 0
persistent-superblock 1
chunk-size 4
device  /dev/hda3
raid-disk 0
device  /dev/hdb4
raid-disk 1
```

3. Now make the RAID device file md0 and format it this way:

```
[root]# mkraid /dev/md0
[root]# mke2fs -b 4096 -R stride=8 /dev/md0
```

All that's left is to restore the files to the device, mount it, and you are done!

Using Kickstart to Automate Installation

Kickstart is Red Hat's solution for an automated installation of Red Hat. All of the questions asked during setup can be automatically supplied with one text file. You can easily set up nearly identical systems very quickly. Kickstart files are very useful for quick deployment and distribution of Linux systems.

There are three methods for creating the required kickstart configuration file:

1. Copy and edit the sample.ks file from the RH-DOCS directory of the Red Hat Documentation CD.

2. Load the mkkickstart utility from the rpm file of the same name on the second Red Hat install CD.

3. Use the X-based ksconfig command.

If you choose option 1 from the preceding list, you will need to copy and modify the kickstart sample file on the CD. If you choose option 2, you can create your own configuration file from scratch based on your current installation with the mkkickstart command. Install the mkkickstart rpm package; then run mkkickstart and save the output to a template file. You can then modify this template file to create your own customized kickstart script:

```
# cd /mnt/cdrom/RedHat/RPMS
# rpm -ivh  mkkickstart*.rpm
# mkkickstart > /root/kickstart.template
# vi /root/kickstart.template
```

Copy this kickstart template file and make the appropriate changes suitable for each generic host (same disk partition scheme, same size of disk or bigger, same video card and monitor, same mouse, and so on). Place this file where the installation can read it; this is either the boot disk or on the DHCP/BOOTP server. If you plan to put it on the boot disk, just mount the disk as an MS-DOS disk and copy it over. Assuming you have the MTOOLS utilities loaded, you can copy the file to the boot diskette with the following command:

```
# mcopy /root/kickstart.template a:
```

If you want to put the file on a DHCP/BOOTP server, you must specify the kickstart file (usually done with the filename: option). You can also specify a directory for kickstart. In this case, the setup program will look in the directory for *client_ip*-kickstart (for example: 192.168.17.18-kickstart). By default, it will use the DHCP/BOOTP server as the NFS server for the install, but you may specify another server if you like. To do this, use the next-server option.

No matter where you choose to put the kickstart file, you will typically boot with a floppy. Use LILO's boot options to fire off the kickstart file. To boot, and do the install from a floppy, type

```
boot: linux ks=floppy
```

To boot from the network, type

```
boot: linux ks
```

Most of the options in the sample kickstart file are self-explanatory. Every option is in the sample file and is well commented. Here are some ground rules and guidelines to use when setting up a kickstart file:

- Do NOT change the order of the options.
- You do not need to use all the options.
- If you leave out a required option the user will be prompted for the answer.
- For upgrades, you MUST have the following options defined:

  - Language
  - Installation method
  - Device specification
  - Keyboard setup
  - The upgrade keyword
  - LILO configuration

on the **Job**

If you leave out an option, you will be prompted to complete it. This is an easy way to see if your kickstart is configured correctly. Remember that nothing gets installed until the end of all the options, so it is easy to test your setup without actually making any changes to your system.

There are a couple of key options that need further explanation, however.

Network   Most options are obvious, but static network configuration options (which require manually configuring the IP settings) need special attention. Here is an example of a static network configuration:

```
network —bootproto static —ip 172.16.16.5 —netmask 255.255.255.0
-gateway 172.16.15.254 —nameserver 172.16.16.1
```

Please note that all options MUST be on ONE line.

If there are SCSI, Ethernet, or non-ATAPI CD-ROM devices on the client, don't forget to specify them. For example:

```
device scsi aha154x
```

If you have modules that need special IRQ and io ports set, you can also specify those. For example:

```
device ethernet 3c509 --opts "io=0x330, irq=7"
```

Add the --continue option if you have more than one device, such as two different SCSI adapters or Ethernet cards.

You have full control of the partitioning options, too. You can clear all partitions with "clearpart --all," or just clear any Linux type partitions "clearpart --linux," or just add to the end of the current partitions (no clearpart option given). You can create partitions on more than one drive, but you need to identify each device specifically.

To add Linux partitions, use the "part" command with the following syntax:

```
part <mount dir> --size <size> [--grow] [--maxsize <size>]
```

The *<size>* is in Megabytes. You can use the --grow option to allow the partition to expand and fill all remaining disk space (or share it with any other partitions marked "grow" on the same disk). This will not expand on the fly, but rather, when all fixed size partitions are added, these "growable" partitions will use the rest of the space. If you specify multiple partitions with the --grow option, their space will be divided evenly. You can also specify a --maxsize, which will allow the partition only to grow to the size specified in megabytes.

Another important option: When setting the root password, consider setting it up in your kickstart file encrypted, instead of cleartext. To use an encrypted root password, use the following options:

```
rootpw --iscrypted <Your_encrypted_password>
```

You will need to copy your root password from /etc/shadow or /etc/passwd and paste it into this file before it will work.

You should review the sample.ks file to see all the different options and familiarize yourself with the setup before taking the certification test. Here is a small sample kickstart file. We will use this kickstart file to set up similar PCs with only Linux, and wipe out anything that was previously installed:

```
# Select your language
lang en

#We will boot our IP from a DHCP server
network --bootproto dhcp
# It will be a CD-ROM based install
cdrom
```

```
# We need to clear out the MBR just to be safe
zerombr yes
# Also wipe out all of the partitions
clearpart --all
# We want a minimum of 400 Meg root partition but it can grow to be
# the full size of the disk minus the 32 Megs used for swap space.
part / --size 400 --grow
part swap --size 32
# We need to do a fresh install (especially since we just wiped out
#the partitions)
Install
# The PCs have 2 button PS/2 Mice but we want to emulate 3 buttons
mouse genericps/2 --emulthree
# Set our timezone ?
timezone --utc US/Eastern
# We are just using a generic SVGA driver and we can specify the
# monitors here.
xconfig --server "SVGA" --monitor "tatung cm14uhe"
# Our root password does not have to be encrypted since it will
#install locally from the CD-ROM
rootpw cleartext
# This will enable shadow password and encryption algorithm of MD5
auth --useshadow --enablemd5
# LILO will need to be installed in the master boot record (MBR)
lilo --location mbr
# We plan on doing a typical Workstation install for our packages.
%packages
@ Workstation
```

EXERCISE 5-3

Creating a Sample Kickstart File from a Running System for a Second Similar System Installation

In this exercise, you will use the mkkickstart utility to duplicate the installation from one machine to a second machine with identical hardware. This exercise simply installs all the exact same packages as on the first machine. Both machines are assumed to be using DCHP for their IP setup values. You will just add one root partition of 1300MB with a 64MB swap file. (This means you must have at least 1364MB of space available. If you have more space, it will be left unused for now.) You want to install all the same packages as your current installation, so you do not need to make any package changes to the kickstart file that mkkickstart creates, ks.cfg.

1. Install the mkkickstart rpm file from the CD-ROM and create the kickstart file:

```
[root]# rpm  -ivh /mnt/cdrom/RedHat/RPMS/mkkick*
mkkickstart-x.y.z-a.rpm   ################
[root]#  mkkickstart  > ks.cfg
[root]# cat ks.cfg # this is just FYI, no changes needed
lang en

network --bootproto dhcp
cdrom
zerombr yes
part / --size 1300
part swap --size 64
Install
mouse genericps/2 --emulthree
timezone --utc US/Eastern
xconfig --server "SVGA" --monitor "Dell1500FP"
rootpw sweatwater
auth --useshadow --enablemd5
lilo --location mbr
%packages
..
```

(The remaining hundred plus lines containing package names has not been included here.)

2. Create the boot disk and add this ks.cfg file to it:

```
[root]# dd if=/mnt/cdrom/images/bootnet.img of=/dev/fd0
[root]# mcopy ks.cfg a:
```

3. Prepare the second machine so it has the same configuration of disk space as the first machine, same C: drive size if it was present, same amount of unused and unpartitioned space as the first machine. Reboot the second machine with this kickstart file in the floppy drive and the first binary CD in the CD-ROM.

   At the LILO prompt, enter the following startup command:

```
Lilo: Linux ks=floppy
```

You should now see the system installation creating the same setup as the first system. You may be asked to put the second binary CD into the CD-ROM drive, if required.
Optional Exercise 5-3: Modify the packages to be installed.
Edit the ks.cfg file on the floppy and remove all the game packages you can find.

Hardware Conflicts and Plug-and-Play

Hardware conflicts in previous versions of Red Hat like 6.*x* were common with newer equipment because there was limited support for Linux, but the Linux community has become very strong lately and has added a significant amount of effort to supporting hardware and getting manufacturers to support Linux with their products.

Just in case you have hardware conflicts with relatively old equipment, these are fairly simple to eliminate. There are three possible areas of conflict:

- A physical hardware jumper is conflicting with another card.

- You have ISA Plug-and-Play cards that are not properly configured.

- You are out of interrupts or resources to add to your new device.

Physical hardware jumpers need to be set to nonconflicting values in order for them to work; this is typically a little jumper setting on the card somewhere. To check what interrupts you are using, issue the following command:

```
# cat /proc/interrupts

          CPU0
   0:   86311180     XT-PIC   timer
   1:      25820     XT-PIC   keyboard
   2:          0     XT-PIC   cascade
   6:        507     XT-PIC   floppy
   7:          0     XT-PIC   soundblaster
   8:          2     XT-PIC   rtc
   9:     263584     XT-PIC   aic7xxx
  11:    4065120     XT-PIC   eth0
  12:     529582     XT-PIC   PS/2 Mouse
  13:          1     XT-PIC   fpu
  14:     352260     XT-PIC   ide0
 NMI:          0
```

This is a list of devices that ARE loaded by the kernel. You can quickly scan over the left side to see what interrupts are available. In our example, IRQ 5 is not used yet. To get a list of IO addresses and DMA channels used, issue the following commands:

```
# cat /proc/ioports

0000-001f : dma1
0020-003f : pic1
0040-005f : timer
0060-006f : keyboard
```

```
0070-007f : rtc
0080-008f : dma page reg
00a0-00bf : pic2
00c0-00df : dma2
00f0-00ff : fpu
01f0-01f7 : ide0
0220-022f : soundblaster
02f8-02ff : serial(auto)
0388-038b : Yamaha OPL3
03c0-03df : vga+
03f0-03f5 : floppy
03f6-03f6 : ide0
03f7-03f7 : floppy DIR
03f8-03ff : serial(auto)
f800-f8be : aic7xxx
fc90-fc97 : ide0
fcc0-fcff : eth0
```

For DMA resources:

```
# cat /proc/dma
```

```
1: SoundBlaster8
2: floppy
4: cascade
```

With a physical conflict, you can simply check what is available and change the jumper. For an ISA PnP card, it is a little bit harder. First, probe for PnP cards and dump the results to a file by typing

```
# pnpdump > isapnp.conf
```

Next, edit the isapnp.conf file. You should see all of your ISA Plug-and-Play devices and all possible settings. This file is a configuration file, and almost all values are commented out with the # symbol. You need to uncomment all the valid IRQ, IO, DMA ports that you want your card to work on and uncomment the ACT Y line at the bottom of your cards information. After you have set up your card to nonconflicting values, you can run isapnp. The following is an excerpt from a pnpdump output:

```
# $Id: pnpdump.c,v 1.18 1999/02/14 22:47:18 fox Exp $
# This is free software, see the sources for details.
# This software has NO WARRANTY, use at your OWN RISK
#
# For details of this file format, see isapnp.conf(5)
#
# For latest information and FAQ on isapnp and pnpdump see:
```

```
# http://www.roestock.demon.co.uk/isapnptools/
#
# Compiler flags: -DREALTIME -DNEEDSETSCHEDULER -DABORT_ONRESERR
#
# Trying port address 0203
# Board 1 has serial identifier 6d ff ff ff ff f0 00 8c 0e
# (DEBUG)
(READPORT 0x0203)
(ISOLATE PRESERVE)
(IDENTIFY *)
(VERBOSITY 2)
(CONFLICT (IO FATAL)(IRQ FATAL)(DMA FATAL)(MEM FATAL)) # or WARNING
# Card 1: (serial identifier 6d ff ff ff ff f0 00 8c 0e)
# Vendor Id CTL00f0, No Serial Number (-1), checksum 0x6D.
# Version 1.0, Vendor version 1.0
# ANSI string -->Creative ViBRA16X PnPD<--
#
# Logical device id CTL0043
#     Device supports vendor reserved register @ 0x38
#     Device supports vendor reserved register @ 0x3a
#     Device supports vendor reserved register @ 0x3c
#
(CONFIGURE CTL00f0/-1 (LD 0

#     ANSI string -->AudioD<--
# Multiple choice time, choose one only !
#     Start dependent functions: priority preferred
#       IRQ 5.
#             High true, edge sensitive interrupt (by default)
# (INT 0 (IRQ 5 (MODE +E)))
#     First DMA channel 1.
#             8 bit DMA only
#             Logical device is not a bus master
#             DMA may execute in count by byte mode
#             DMA may not execute in count by word mode
#             DMA channel speed in compatible mode
# (DMA 0 (CHANNEL 1))
#     Next DMA channel 3.
#             8 bit DMA only
#             Logical device is not a bus master
#             DMA may execute in count by byte mode
#             DMA may not execute in count by word mode
#             DMA channel speed in compatible mode
# (DMA 1 (CHANNEL 3))
#     Logical device decodes 16 bit IO address lines
#             Minimum IO base address 0x0220
#             Maximum IO base address 0x0220
#             IO base alignment 1 bytes
#             Number of IO addresses required: 16
```

```
# (IO 0 (SIZE 16) (BASE 0x0220))
#       Logical device decodes 16 bit IO address lines
#               Minimum IO base address 0x0330
#               Maximum IO base address 0x0330
#               IO base alignment 1 bytes
#               Number of IO addresses required: 2
# (IO 1 (SIZE 2) (BASE 0x0330))
#       Logical device decodes 16 bit IO address lines
#               Minimum IO base address 0x0388
#               Maximum IO base address 0x0388
#               IO base alignment 1 bytes
#               Number of IO addresses required: 4
# (IO 2 (SIZE 4) (BASE 0x0388))
#       Start dependent functions: priority acceptable
#       IRQ 5, 7, 9 or 10.
#               High true, edge sensitive interrupt (by default)
```
[Many lines have been removed for clarity]
```
#       End dependent functions
(NAME "CTL00f0/-1[0]{Audio                }")
# (ACT Y)
))
#
# Logical device id CTL7005
#       Device supports vendor reserved register @ 0x38
#       Device supports vendor reserved register @ 0x3a
#       Device supports vendor reserved register @ 0x3c
#
(CONFIGURE CTL00f0/-1 (LD 1
#       Compatible device id PNPb02f

#       ANS
I string —>GameD
# Multiple choice time, choose one only !
#       Start dependent functions: priority preferred
#           Logical device decodes 16 bit IO address lines
#               Minimum IO base address 0x0201
#               Maximum IO base address 0x0201
#               IO base alignment 1 bytes
#               Number of IO addresses required: 1
# (IO 0 (SIZE 1) (BASE 0x0201))
#       Start dependent functions: priority acceptable
#           Logical device decodes 16 bit IO address lines
#               Minimum IO base address 0x0200
#               Maximum IO base address 0x020f
#               IO base alignment 1 bytes
#               Number of IO addresses required: 1
# (IO 0 (SIZE 1) (BASE 0x0200))
#       End dependent functions
```

```
(NAME "CTL00f0/-1[1]{Game                    }")
#  (ACT Y)
))
#  End tag... Checksum 0x00 (OK)
#  Returns all cards to the "Wait for Key" state
(WAITFORKEY)
```

With this output, you can see there is a SoundBlaster 16 ISA PnP card installed. This output also shows that there is a game port on the card that can be configured separately. Note, also, that all of the lines are commented out. You would have to check the /proc/interrupts and /proc/ioports to find available resources to configure your sound card. We will assume that IRQ 5, IO 0x220, and DMA 0 are not in use. To specify this, we can simply uncomment the following lines:

```
#  $Id: pnpdump.c,v 1.18 1999/02/14 22:47:18 fox Exp $
#  This is free software, see the sources for details.
#  This software has NO WARRANTY, use at your OWN RISK
#
#  For details of this file format, see isapnp.conf(5)
#
#  For latest information and FAQ on isapnp and pnpdump see:
#  http://www.roestock.demon.co.uk/isapnptools/
#
#  Compiler flags: -DREALTIME -DNEEDSETSCHEDULER -DABORT_ONRESERR
#
#  Trying port address 0203
#  Board 1 has serial identifier 6d ff ff ff ff f0 00 8c 0e
#  Board 2 has serial identifier 31 a0 bc 8f b4 30 30 72 56
#  (DEBUG)
(READPORT 0x0203)
(ISOLATE PRESERVE)
(IDENTIFY *)
(VERBOSITY 2)
(CONFLICT (IO FATAL)(IRQ FATAL)(DMA FATAL)(MEM FATAL)) # or WARNING
#  Card 1: (serial identifier 6d ff ff ff ff f0 00 8c 0e)
#  Vendor Id CTL00f0, No Serial Number (-1), checksum 0x6D.
#  Version 1.0, Vendor version 1.0
#  ANSI string -->Creative ViBRA16X PnPD<--
#
#  Logical device id CTL0043
#      Device supports vendor reserved register @ 0x38
#      Device supports vendor reserved register @ 0x3a
#      Device supports vendor reserved register @ 0x3c
#
  (CONFIGURE CTL00f0/-1 (LD 0
#      ANSI string -->Audio<@151<--
```

```
# Multiple choice time, choose one only !
#     Start dependent functions: priority preferred
#        IRQ 5.
#              High true, edge sensitive interrupt (by default)
(INT 0 (IRQ 5 (MODE +E)))
#        First DMA channel 1.
#              8 bit DMA only
#              Logical device is not a bus master
#              DMA may execute in count by byte mode
#              DMA may not execute in count by word mode
#              DMA channel speed in compatible mode
(DMA 0 (CHANNEL 1))
#        Logical device decodes 16 bit IO address lines
#              Minimum IO base address 0x0220
#              Maximum IO base address 0x0220
#              IO base alignment 1 bytes
#              Number of IO addresses required: 16
(IO 0 (SIZE 16) (BASE 0x0220))
#     End dependent functions
(NAME "CTL00f0/-1[0]{Audio                }")
(ACT Y)
# Returns all cards to the "Wait for Key" state
(WAITFORKEY)
```

You have to uncomment the ACT Y for the card to actually be set. Once this card is properly set up you can load the Soundblaster module with the following command:

```
# modprobe sb irq=5 io=0x220 dma=0
```

If you don't have a joystick then there is no reason to enable it in the isapnp.conf file.

```
# isapnp isapnp.conf
```

This will set up your card, and the resources should show up in the appropriate /proc file. To have this setup whenever you boot, you will need to copy the isapnp.conf file to the /etc directory.

PCI Plug-and-Play cards should set themselves up appropriately. If you cannot see what your PCI cards are set to, you can type: **cat /proc/pci**; otherwise you may have run out of resources. Your resources can vary depending on your architecture, but on an i386 PC you typically have up to 15 usable interrupts out of 16; 0–15. If you run out of interrupts, you may want to look into alternatives such as combo cards, which have two devices on one card, or Universal Serial Bus (USB) devices.

PCMCIA

Another aspect of the growing support for Linux on hardware has been in the area of laptops. Laptops have a special peripheral interface bus called PCMCIA that requires a specific set of drivers and services to handle it. With Red Hat 7.*x*, PCMCIA services are now well established, and the various network, SCSI, and modem devices should not be a problem. With older equipment, however, there is always a possibility of problems.

Typically the problem is having newer devices than drivers, which can sometimes be fixed by merely downloading the newest PCMCIA drivers and compiling them. However, you need to be aware that with the advent of the 2.4 kernel, PCMCIA functionality is now included with the base kernel. This support is still less extensive and robust than the support provided by the external kernel modules available from http://pcmcia-cs.sourceforge.net. Therefore, if the default Red Hat 7.1 kernel fails to boot or work properly with PCMCIA devices, you should considering downloading the latest PCMCIA sources from sourceforge.net and rebuilding the kernel without the built-in PCMCIA support. There is extensive documentation on sourceforge.net that will provide explicit instructions for building the software for a 2.4 kernel. You should examine the hardware compatibility list on sourceforge.net for the latest support information, but the following is a partial list of supported PCMCIA controllers:

- Cirrus Logic PD6710, PD6720, PD6722, PD6729, PD6730, PD6732, PD6832

- Intel i82365sl B, C, and DF steps, 82092AA

- O2Micro OZ6729, OZ6730, OZ6832, OZ6833, OZ6836, OZ6860

- Omega Micro 82C092GRicoh RF5C296, RF5C396, RL5C465, RL5C466, RL5C475, RL5C476, RL5C478SMC 34C90Texas Instruments PCI1130, PCI1131, PCI1210, PCI1220, PCI1221, PCI1250A, PCI1251A, PCI1251B, PCI1450

- Toshiba ToPIC95, ToPIC97 (limited functionality)

- Vadem VG465, VG468, VG469

- VLSI Technologies 82C146, VCF94365

- VIA VT83C469

- Databook DB86082, DB86082A, DB86084, DB86084A, DB86072, DB86082B

The PCMCIA driver will automatically load the devices and set up the IO ports to nonconflicting ports. However, if you do not want certain ports scanned or used, then you may specify them in the /etc/pcmcia/config.opts file. You may need to edit the file /etc/sysconfig/pcmcia and set PCMCIA=yes.

The cardmgr daemon actually takes care of the PCMCIA device. Type **ps x** to see if it is running. Whenever a card is loaded, you can check the /var/run/stab file:

```
#cat /var/run/stab:
Socket 0: empty
Socket 1: 3Com 3c589D Ethernet
1         network 3c589_cs          0        eth0
```

Here we see that Socket 0 does not have a card while Socket 1 contains a network card. There are five columns displayed for loaded devices. The first is the socket number. Second is the device class. Third is the actual driver that was loaded. Fourth is the device number (some devices support multiple devices per Socket). Finally, the fifth column contains the actual device name.

When you insert a card, you should hear two equal high-pitched beeps; one for successfully identifying the card and another for properly configuring the card. If identification fails, you should hear a lower-pitched beep. You will also hear a beep if you remove a card.

To see what settings your card is set to, you can issue the **cardctl** command as follows:

```
cardctl config

Socket 0:
not configured
Socket 1:
Vce = 5.0, Vpp1 = 0.0, Vpp2 = 0.0
Interface type is memory and I/O
IRQ 9 is exclusive, level mode, enabled
Function 0:
Config register base = 0x10000
Option = 0x41, status = 0000
I/O window 1: 0x0300 to 0x030f, 16 bit
```

You can specify what ranges cardmgr will use to configure the card, as well as IO and IRQ settings it should avoid. These settings are stored in the /etc/pcmcia/config.opts file. You may need to include lines that limit the boundaries cardmgr is allowed to use and exclude lines for the settings it should avoid. For example:

```
# cat /etc/pcmcia/config.opts
include memory 0xc0000-0xfffff, memory 0xa0000000-0xa0ffffff
exclude irq 4
```

You may also specify extra PCMCIA options in the /etc/sysconfig/pcmcia file:

```
PCIC=i82365|tcic
PCIC_OPTS=<socket driver (i82365 or tcic) timing parameters>
CORE_OPTS=<pcmcia_core options>
CARDMGR_OPTS=<cardmgr options>
```

These options will be run at boot time.

on the **job** *Many of our classes are run in hotels around the country, and this requires the use of laptop computers. In the early days of PCMCIA support, only the big name brand equipment worked consistently, but over the past few years, the support for other cards has grown. This does not mean there haven't been any problems, but it is less of an issue now than before the year 2000.*

EXERCISE 5-4

Listening to the Network De-Install, then Installing a PCMCIA Card

In this exercise, you will need a laptop with a PCMCIA port and at least one functioning PCMCIA card, like a network card. If you can find an old card that does not work, or does not work well, you can try that one, too.

Warning: This is not a recommended procedure according to most laptop manufacturers, so proceed AT YOUR OWN RISK. It could very well damage the system. It has been tried on a few laptops in the classroom, so we know they work. But yours may not! If your laptop manual does not allow it specifically, DO NOT ATTEMPT THIS LAB! This is your last warning.

When you pull the network card out of some laptops, the system emits a high-pitched beep. If you put a PCMCIA card into a powered up laptop that is running Linux, it should beep twice, once for the cardmgr service recognizing the addition (high-pitched beep if recognized, low-pitched if not), and if this is successful, another for the card being either configured correctly (high-pitched beep) or failing to configure (low-pitched beep). TRY THIS AT YOUR OWN RISK.

Advanced Power Management (APM) BIOS

The Advanced Power Management (APM) BIOS primarily monitors and controls the system battery. It is an optional service typically used with laptops. You can also use it on workstations and servers if you want to implement the BIOS standby and suspend modes that are available on newer PCs.

The daemon that needs to be running is apmd. If the apmd daemon is running on your system, there will be a file created that contains the battery information in the proc directory:

```
# cat /proc/apm
1.9 1.2 0x07 0x01 0xff 0x80 -1% -1 ?
```

As you can see, this format is not very readable. To have this information printed in a more readable format, simply issue the apm command:

```
# apm
AC on-line, battery status high: 100% (2:31)
```

This command reads the information created by apmd in the /proc/apm file and prints it in a much easier to read format.

The apmd daemon can be configured to do a variety of different things based on what BIOS reports back regarding the status of the battery. You can set apmd to log error messages to syslog when the battery life drops below a certain percentage level. You can also have it send a system-wide message to all logged-in users when this warning level is reached. All changes in battery information are logged via syslog. To set up options for apmd, you will need to edit the /etc/sysconfig/ampd file.

```
# cat /etc/sysconfig/apmd
APMD_OPTIONS="-p 10 -w 5 -W
```

In this example, apmd is instructed to log changes to the syslog file with every 10 percent of battery loss (-p 10). If the battery drops below 5 percent, apmd will send an alert to syslog (-w 5). Also, all logged-in users will be notified that the system is about to die (-W).

The apm log is broken down into four parts:

- Percentage of discharge (percentage/minute). This will be a negative amount if it is charging.

- Time since total charge, or time since last login, depending on whether the battery is fully charged or not.

- Estimate of battery time left.

- Percentage of battery life left.

When the BIOS tells the apmd daemon about a pending suspend or a standby call, it immediately calls sync (and writes all cached file system information to disk immediately). It will then sleep for two seconds and tell BIOS to continue.

EXERCISE 5-5

Pulling the Plug on a Laptop; Checking apmd

In this exercise, if you have a common laptop with Linux installed, you can run the apm command before you remove the power plug. Afterward, check to see how the system manages the transition. You can query the status of the battery at any time with apm.

Warning: While this is supposed to work for most any laptop, PROCEED AT YOUR OWN RISK. Make sure you know what you are doing before trying to remove the power cord from a running laptop. First and foremost, make sure a working battery is installed correctly.

```
$ apm
```

(Pull the plug on a laptop that has a working charged battery.)

```
$ apm
```

Do not forget to plug it back in before the battery runs out!

CERTIFICATION OBJECTIVE 5.05

Understanding /etc/inittab

The inittab describes what process should be started when booting, as well as what should be running at normal operations levels. Process init reads the /etc/inittab configuration file to determine what is to run at what runlevel. Valid runlevels exist in the ranges 0–6 and A–C. Runlevels A–C are considered ondemand runlevels. The format for inittab is as follows:

```
Id_number:runlevel:action:process
```

The *id_number* is a unique 1-4 alphanumeric character.

The *runlevel* is a list of runlevels that the action should occur on.

The *action* is what action should be taken.

The *process* is what process should be executed. If the process begins with a + then no accounting information will be done for that process.

To list multiple runlevels, list them without commas or spaces. For example, here is the comment and a sample line from /etc/inittab:

```
# Run gettys in standard runlevels
1: 2345:respawn:/sbin/mingetty tty1
```

This line will respawn the /sbin/mingetty utility on terminal port tty1 at runlevels 2–5, but not 1 and 6. For a complete description of runlevels, please refer to the following section. If init switches to a runlevel that is not associated with a process, then that process is killed.

The following is a list of the valid actions that can be used by inittab:

- **respawn** If the process is killed, it will be automatically restarted.
- **wait** Will wait for the process to terminate before continuing.
- **once** Only run the process once.
- **boot** Run when booting and ignore the runlevel field.
- **bootwait** A combination of both boot and wait.
- **ondemand** Execute when an ondemand runlevel is called (A–C).

- **initdefault**   This specifies the default runlevel after system boot. If this entry does not exist, then init will prompt the console for the runlevel. Process entries are ignored.

- **sysinit**   Executes during system boot, but before any boot or bootwait entries. The runlevel entries are ignored.

- **powerfail**   This will run when init receives a powerfailure message from the kernel (SIGPWR). This usually is generated from a UPS battery backup. The runlevel entries are ignored.

- **powerwait**   Same as powerfail, but it will wait for the process to finish.

- **powerokwait**   If init receives a SIGPWR signal and there is an "OK" in the /etc/powerstatus file, then this process will run.

- **ctrlaltdel**   This process is run when a user presses the CTRL-ALT-DEL keys. It is usually used to shut down the system into single user mode or to reboot the server.

- **kbrequest**   You can map specific keyboard combinations to fire a process. You have to specify these in your keymaps file and map them to KeyboardSignal.

Table 5-3 shows default runlevels for Red Hat.
The following code is an example of an inittab:

```
# Default runlevel
id:5:initdefault:
# System initialization.
si::sysinit:/etc/rc.d/rc.sysinit
l0:0:wait:/etc/rc.d/rc 0
```

TABLE 5-3		
	0	Halt the system
Default Runlevels for Red Hat	1	Single user mode
	2	Multiuser, without NFS
	3	Full multiuser mode
	4	Unused
	5	X11
	6	Reboot the system

```
l1:1:wait:/etc/rc.d/rc 1
l2:2:wait:/etc/rc.d/rc 2
l3:3:wait:/etc/rc.d/rc 3
l4:4:wait:/etc/rc.d/rc 4
l5:5:wait:/etc/rc.d/rc 5
l6:6:wait:/etc/rc.d/rc 6
# Things to run in every runlevel.
ud::once:/sbin/update
# Trap CTRL-ALT-DELETE
ca::ctrlaltdel:/sbin/shutdown -t3 -r now
# Power failures
pf::powerfail:/sbin/shutdown -f -h +2 "Power Failure; SystemShutting Down"
# Power restored
pr:12345:powerokwait:/sbin/shutdown -c "Power Restored;Shutdown Cancelled"
# Run gettys in standard runlevels
1:2345:respawn:/sbin/mingetty tty1
2:2345:respawn:/sbin/mingetty tty2
3:2345:respawn:/sbin/mingetty tty3
4:2345:respawn:/sbin/mingetty tty4
5:2345:respawn:/sbin/mingetty tty5
6:2345:respawn:/sbin/mingetty tty6
# Run X11 (xdm or other display manager)
# xdm is a separate service in Red Hat 6.0
x:5:respawn:/etc/X11/prefdm -nodaemon
```

The syntax is a SystemV syntax and appears difficult to read. Once you get used to it, however, you can read the entire file at a glance. Here is a breakdown of each line in the file.

```
id:5:initdefault
```

This command sets the default runlevel to 5 after the system has finished running its boot scripts. The implications of runlevel 5 are discussed later.

```
si::sysinit:/etc/rc.d/rc.sysinit
l0:0:wait:/etc/rc.d/rc 0
l1:1:wait:/etc/rc.d/rc 1
l2:2:wait:/etc/rc.d/rc 2
l3:3:wait:/etc/rc.d/rc 3
l4:4:wait:/etc/rc.d/rc 4
l5:5:wait:/etc/rc.d/rc 5
l6:6:wait:/etc/rc.d/rc 6
```

The first line (si) is the system initialization file. This is discussed in more detail in the next section. Lines l0–l6 are also initialization scripts that run at each runlevel.

More information on RC scripts is available in Chapter 5. Notice that init will not continue until each RC script has completed running.

```
ud::once:/sbin/update
```

This command gets run once every time we change runlevels. Notice that when you do not specify a runlevel, it will run for every runlevel.

```
ca::ctrlaltdel:/sbin/shutdown -t3 -r now
pf::powerfail:/sbin/shutdown -f -h +2 "Power Failure; SystemShutting Down"
pr:12345:powerokwait:/sbin/shutdown -c "Power Restored;Shutdown
Cancelled."
```

These are all special actions. The first (ca) will shut down the system in three seconds and then reboot. The second line (pf) will halt the system two minutes after receiving the SIGPWR signal (typically from a UPS that is about to expire). The third line (pr) states that if the power resumes (signal from the UPS) within two minutes (above line) and then cancel the shutdown. Notice the runlevels list all relevant runlevels in which a shutdown should be cancelled.

```
1:2345:respawn:/sbin/mingetty tty1
2:2345:respawn:/sbin/mingetty tty2
3:2345:respawn:/sbin/mingetty tty3
4:2345:respawn:/sbin/mingetty tty4
5:2345:respawn:/sbin/mingetty tty5
6:2345:respawn:/sbin/mingetty tty6
```

These lines configure six virtual consoles. Notice that no virtual consoles are loaded for runlevel 1 (Single user mode):

```
x:5:respawn:/etc/X11/prefdm -nodaemon
```

This line will run our X11 Display Manager (XDM). When the first line is called (id) it runs this line. This line in turn runs the preferred XDM, which presents the user with a graphical X11 login. Again, it is important to realize that initdefault does not actually run anything, it merely sets the runlevel. Later, in the inittab, you specify what you want that runlevel to do.

EXERCISE 5-6

Switch the Runlevels of Linux

In this exercise, it is assumed you have a Linux system that is configured to boot into the GUI interface (the default for a Workstation installation). This is runlevel 5.

1. Log in as root and start an xterm.

2. Within the xterm, at the prompt, type **init 3**

   This will cause your machine to stop any processes that are not supposed to be running in level 3, the most obvious to you should be that the X Window system is shut down.

3. Login at the console as root again and enter this command runlevel:

   ```
   # runlevel
   5 3
   #
   ```

   This indicates you were in level 5 last and are now in level 3. To go back to runlevel 5, simply enter the following:

   ```
   # init 5
   ```

   And your system will revert to the GUI interface (you will have to login again, however).

exam

ⓦatch

You need to be in runlevel 3 to run the Xconfigurator utility, not runlevel 1. If your system fails to run X, you might want to go to single user mode to change the runlevel value in /etc/inittab to 3 and then reboot to runlevel 3 before attempting to remedy the X Window configuration.

System Startup Script /etc/rc.d/rc.sysinit

This script does all of the major system setup and initialization. Here is a step-by-step rundown of the process that occurs when the script is run:

1. Checks for a /etc/sysconfig/network script. If it is there, the system runs it. Otherwise, it turns networking off and sets your hostname to localhost.

2. Executes /etc/rc.d/init.d/functions. This file sets up some basic functions that the rest of the scripts use. (Example: The boot daemon failure/success messages.)

3. Sets the loglevel.

4. Loads the keymap. If you have specified a default keyman file in /etc/sysconfig/console/default.kmap it will use that; otherwise it will use /etc/sysconfig/keyboard.

5. Loads the system fonts.

6. Activates all swap partitions specified in the /etc/fstab file.

7. Sets up your hostname and your NIS domain name.

8. Runs fsck to check your filesystem if necessary. If fsck fails, it will drop you to a shell and unmount the drives so you can work on repairing them.

9. Sets up ISA Plug-and-Play devices.

10. Remounts the root files system as read-write.

11. Checks quotas on the root partition.

12. All modules will now be loaded. Note that the sound and midi modules will be loaded if there is an alias listed as sound or midi in the /etc/modules.conf. If your system requires a different module, you may need to edit the /etc/modules.conf file.

13. Checks for a /etc/raidtab file and loads all RAID devices.

14. Checks your file systems with fsck again.

15. Mounts the rest of the file systems listed in the fstab.

16. Turns quota support on if /sbin/quotaon exists and is executable.

17. Sets the system clock. It will run /etc/sysconfig/clock if it exists.

18. Initializes swap space.

19. Initializes serial ports.

20. Loads SCSI tape module if a SCSI tape was detected.

21. Reads the /etc/sysconfig/desktop file for a preferred X11 Display Manager and sets a link file as /etc/X11/prefdm.

22. Finally it dumps the kernel ring buffer (Boot messages) to /var/log/dmesg.

This list is hard to remember. Once you familiarize yourself with the rc.sysinit bootup sequence, you can use the short summary cheat sheet that follows as a quick reference:

1. Runs network script

2. Loads script functions

3. Loglevel

4. Keymap

5. Fonts

6. Swap space

7. Hostname/NIS domain

8. Fsck root partition

9. ISA Plug-and-Play

10. Remounts root read-write

11. Checks root quotas

12. Loads modules

13. Initializes RAID

14. Fsck filesystem

15. Mounts all file systems

16. Turns on quotas

17. Sets clock

18. Reinitializes swap

19. Serial ports

20. SCSI tape drivers

21. Sets up XDM

22. Dumps dmesg

EXERCISE 5-7

Checking the Bootup Messages with dmesg

There is a log file named dmesg in /var/log, as well as a utility for displaying the content of that log file called dmesg. In this exercise, you will page through the output of the dmesg utility using the less utility and identify all the hardware captured.

```
# dmesg | less
Drives found : :
Network card driver loaded : :
RAID Tested Speed Setting : :
CD-ROM if found : :
Sound card if existant : :
Any other weird hardware : :
```

CERTIFICATION OBJECTIVE 5.07

Understanding Kernel Modules

When you compile your kernel, you have the option to have components compiled as modules. A kernel module is not compiled directly into the kernel, but instead operates as a plugable driver that can be loaded and unloaded into the kernel as needed. For the following reasons, it is a good idea to make modules, as opposed to directly compiling them into the kernel: 1) It makes the kernel size smaller; 2) With the kernel size smaller, the speed of the kernel increases; and 3) As modules become unnecessary, they can be dynamically unloaded to take up less memory.

To have the kernel dynamically load and unload kernel modules as needed, a special kernel thread, kmod, is called upon to control the loading and unloading of modules. For special parameters and options, you should edit the /etc/modules.conf.file.

To load modules on the command line, you should first issue

```
# depmod -a
```

This will scan through your modules and find out what the different dependencies for all your modules are and map them out to a file (modules.dep). This file has a Makefile-styled structure to list dependencies and is located under the /lib/modules/*x.x.x*/ directory, where *x.x.x* is your kernel version. This command is usually run during execution of the boot scripts. Once this command is completed, you can load a module. If it has dependencies, then all the needed modules will automatically load first. To load a module, use modprobe.

```
# modprobe 3c503
```

In this example, the Ethernet module for a 3com 503 network card requires the 8390 module to work properly. If depmod was run first then 8390 would have loaded automatically before the 3c503 driver. If a dependency in the list fails during loading, then all modules will be automatically unloaded.

You can do a lot of the tedious work with the /etc/modules.conf file.

The following commands are accepted in this file:

- **alias**   Allows you to bind a name to a module.
- **options**   Allows you to specify options for a module.
- **install module command**   Use command instead of insmod on this module.
- **pre-install module command**   Run command before install of this module.
- **post-install module command**   Run command after install of this module.
- **remove module command**   Use command instead of rmmod on this module.
- **pre-remove module command**   Run command before loading this module.
- **post-remove module command**   Run command after loading this module.

Here is an example of what a common modules.conf may look like:

```
alias eth0 3c59x
options sb irq=5 io=0x220 dma=1
alias midi awe_wave
alias parport_lowlevel parport_pc
```

Here the eth0 name is bound to the 3c59x module. To load the network card, you can simply type **modprobe eth0** without knowing what card is in the machine. The next two lines show that the Soundblaster module is desired for the default sound module. The Soundblaster module (sb) requires that you specify the IRQ, IO address and DMA on the command line when you load the module. The option line specifies these options and binds them to the alias' name of sound. The sound card happens to be an AWE 32, so the midi alias is bound to the awe_wave module. Finally, a parallel port module is bound to the parport_lowlevel alias.

The rc.sysinit script recognizes certain aliases and will load them if it finds them in this file. You need to specifically place the sound modules in modules.conf to have them automatically loaded. To have the sound modules automatically loaded during bootup without having to edit the /etc/rc.d/rc.sysinit file, you can simply create an alias to sound and or midi in the modules.conf file.

To see what modules are loaded you can either type

```
# cat /proc/modules
```

or

```
# lsmod
```

Both will reveal output similar to the following:

```
Module                 Size  Used by
awe_wave             157804   0  (unused)
3c59x                 18920   1  (autoclean)
nls_iso8859-1          2020   3  (autoclean)
nls_cp437              3548   3  (autoclean)
vfat                  11516   3  (autoclean)
fat                   25664   3  (autoclean)  [vfat]
sb                    33204   0
uart401                5968   0  [sb]
sound                 57208   0  [sb uart401]
soundlow                300   0  [sound]
soundcore              2372   5  [sb sound]
```

The module name is listed on the left and its size is in the following column. The "Used by" column shows more detail on how the module is being handled. An (autoclean) message means that the kernel (kmod thread) is taking care of the module and will handle removing it. If a module name is listed in brackets (Example: [vfat]), then the module is a dependant of the module in brackets. In our example, vfat is dependent on the fat module.

CERTIFICATION OBJECTIVE 5.08

The /lib/modules/*kernel_version*/ Directory Structure

All of your kernel modules are kept under /lib/modules/*kernel_version*/ directory, where *kernel_version* is your kernel version. For example, if you are running version 2.4.X.*yy* of a Linux kernel, then your modules will be kept under /lib/modules/2.4.X.*yy*/. If you have recently compiled a kernel and your modules are not loading properly, then you have probably forgotten to compile and install the modules. In the /usr/src/linux source directory, you will need to issue the following commands:

```
# make modules
# make modules_install
```

The first line compiles the modules, while the second places them under the proper directory tree. In this directory tree, there are different subdirectories that represent different groupings. The following is a sample of a module directory:

ls -l /lib/modules/2.2.5/

```
total 36

drwxr-xr-x   2 root       root        1024 May 15 14:54 block
drwxr-xr-x   2 root       root        1024 May 15 14:54 cdrom
drwxr-xr-x   2 root       root        1024 May 15 14:54 fs
drwxr-xr-x   2 root       root        1024 May 15 14:54 ipv4
drwxr-xr-x   2 root       root        3072 May 15 14:54 misc
-rw-r--r--   1 root       root       23312 May 30 10:04 modules.dep
drwxr-xr-x   2 root       root        2048 May 15 14:54 net
drwxr-xr-x   2 root       root        1024 May 15 14:54 pcmcia
drwxr-xr-x   2 root       root        1024 May 15 14:54 scsi
drwxr-xr-x   2 root       root        1024 May 15 14:54 video
```

Notice there is a modules.dep file that lists all the dependencies for all the modules within the directories. Inside of the directories are different kernel modules for each grouping. You might want to become familiar with where to find certain modules when needed. Here are some module types you will find under each directory:

- **block**   Block devices: ide-floppies, raid device levels
- **cdrom**   Non-ATAPI CD-ROM drivers: Mitshumi, Sony
- **fs**   Filesystem modules: vfat, ntfs,smbfs, minix
- **ipv4**   IP version 4 modules, masquerading modulesipv6 (Same as previous but for IP version 6misc); Misc. modules: joysticks, mouse, radio modules
- **net**   Network modules: drivers, ppp, slip
- **pcmcia**   Drivers used by the pcmcia cardmgr daemon
- **scsi**   SCSI tape and hard drive modules, video (Special video modules for Linux, MGA consoles)

All modules have .o for an extension (e.g., vfat.o). You do not need to specify the full name, just the first part (vfat). Once you know the directory structure you can have modprobe load all modules for a certain category. For instance, if you are on a PC and you don't know the network card, you can simply type

```
# modprobe -t net
```

This will try to load all modules in /lib/modules/*kernel_version*/net, stopping when a match is found. To remove a module and all its dependencies, you can type either

```
# modprobe -r 3c503
```

or

```
# rmmod -r 3c503
```

Both these commands will remove the modules and all its dependencies, provided they are not in use by another module. If you want to remove only the module and leave the dependencies loaded, you can omit the -r option for the rmmod command.

EXERCISE 5-8

Load Any Dependent Modules

In this exercise, you will use modprobe to attempt to load any currently uninstalled modules for the various groups (unless some module is missing, nothing should happen. Use rmmod "modulename" at the risk of rebooting):

```
# modprobe -t net
modprobe: Nothing to load ???
Specify at least a module or a wildcard like \*
```

(You will get the same result for all these if no module is missing.)

```
# modprobe -t fs
# modprobe -t pcmcia
# modprobe -t cdrom
# modprobe -t ipv4
# modprobe -t scsi
```

Remember, you can allow the kernel thread to maintain this area. You probably won't ever need to manage these modules manually with the current versions. Older versions, like RH6.*x*, required the odd manual intervention in this area.

CERTIFICATION SUMMARY

The Linux installation is extremely flexible. It can easily allow you to dual-boot multiple operating systems with LILO and incorporate them into NT's NTLDR boot program. You can also set up RAID level devices to mirror and stripe your drives. RAID levels 1 and 0 require that you have two or more drives, while RAID 5 needs three or more. You can automate your entire installation of Red Hat Linux by using kickstart.

Kickstart installation files can reside on the boot floppy or on a DHCP/BOOTP server. If the file resides on the floppy, you can initialize it by entering **linux ks=floppy** at the LILO boot prompt. To get the file from a BOOTP server, you can type **linux ks**. A kickstart installation can only install from a local CD-ROM or over NFS. When you are doing an upgrade, you must be sure to define the language, installation method, device specifications, keyboard setup, LILO configurations, and use the upgrade keyword.

When booting, the /etc/inittab file dictates the rest of the boot process, as well as everything that runs during each runlevel. You use the initdefault keyword to specify your default runlevel. Some common default runlevels are: runlevel 1: - single user; 3: Full multiuser; and 5: - X11 multiuser. The initial boot script is called by the sysinit keyword. This script is rc.sysinit, per the default.

The rc.sysinit script runs almost all crucial system-dependent bootup operations. This script will check your Linux partitions for filesystem errors. It will also load kernel modules and set up initial swap space. This script will initial RAID devices and set up all ISA Plug-and-Play devices, and if quotas are enabled on a partition, then those will be turned on at this time.

✓ TWO-MINUTE DRILL

The following are some of the key points from the certification objectives in Chapter 5.

Dual Boots: Linux and Windows NT

❑ A very common setup between Windows NT and Linux is dual-booting.

❑ There are several different ways to accomplish dual booting.

❑ You can use NT's loader to load both Linux and NT if NT's loader is already installed to the master boot record (MBR).

❑ You can let LILO install into the MBR on a previously built NT or Windows system and have it automatically dual-boot.

RAID Configuration

❑ There are two distinct types of RAID setups: software-based and hardware-based.

❑ There are lots of hardware RAID products now supporting Linux, especially with the big name brand PC manufacturers. Dedicated RAID hardware is definitely the best solution. The alternative is to use a software-based RAID service. Linux provides a RAID software RPM you can use to configure multiple disk partitions so they appear as one partition.

❑ There are six RAID "levels" representing different arrangements of redundancy but only three are useful: Levels 0, 1, and 5. With software-based solutions, there are three common choices, but only two (Levels 1 and 5) that offer true failover security.

❑ RAID 0 and 1 require two or more drives, while RAID 5 requires three or more drives.

❑ Take special note that raid-disks and spare-disks start counting at 0. Nr-raid-disks and nr-spare-disks represent the correct number of drives. For example, if nr-raid-disks = 3, then the last raid-disk will be 2.

Using Kickstart to Automate Installation

❑ Kickstart is Red Hat's solution for an automated installation of Red Hat.

❏ Kickstart installations can only be performed from a CD-ROM or NFS server. You CANNOT use FTP, HTTP, or SMB to do your install.

❏ The mkkickstart utility can be used to create a quick clone of an already installed host for other machines that have identical hardware (e.g., disks, video, and keyboard).

Hardware Conflicts and Plug-and-Play

❏ Linux 7.x has a very capable Plug-and-Play service that can configure most current hardware.

❏ Early PnP hardware might not "play" with Linux well.

❏ Early PnP hardware conflicts are fairly simple to eliminate. Three possible conflict areas exist:

    ❏ A physical hardware jumper is at odds with another card.

    ❏ Your ISA Plug-and-Play cards are not properly configured.

    ❏ You are out of interrupts or resources to add to your new device.

PCMCIA

❏ Linux support services for PCMCIA hardware has grown rapidly within the Linux community.

❏ Most major hardware vendors now provide supported chipsets that Linux can probe for and use.

❏ PCMCIA works on Intel and DecAlpha-based laptops.

Advanced Power Management (APM)

❏ Advanced Power Management (APM) primarily monitors and controls the system battery; typically for laptops.

❏ You can also use APM on workstations and servers if you want to implement the BIOS standby and suspend modes available on newer PCs.

❏ You can monitor the current apmd status with the apm utility.

Laptops

❑ Support for laptops of major system vendors has been extensive.

❑ Linux should install on most name brand laptop PCs and even most clone machines.

❑ When looking for the monitor, if you cannot find an FP (Flat Panel) type display name, some generic options will probably work as well.

Understanding /etc/inittab

❑ The file /etc/inittab describes what process should be started when booting, as well as what should be running at normal operation levels.

❑ Process init reads the inittab to determine what should run at what runlevel.

❑ Valid runlevels exist in the ranges 0–6 and A–C.

❑ Runlevels A–C are considered ondemand runlevels.

System Startup Script /etc/rc.d/rc.sysinit

❑ The first program called by the init process is rc.sysinit.

❑ Script /etc/rc.d/rc.sysinit does all of the major system setup and initialization.

❑ You should not make any changes to this file.

Understanding Kernel Modules

❑ When you compile your kernel, you have the option to compile components as modules. A kernel module is not compiled directly into the kernel, but instead as a plugable driver that can be loaded and unloaded into the kernel as needed.

❑ To have the kernel dynamically load and unload kernel modules as needed, a special kernel thread, kmod, is called upon to control the loading and unloading of modules. For special parameters and options, you should edit the /etc/modules.conf file.

❑ You can use lsmod to list the modules in memory and modprobe -t "group" to see all the modules for any of the following groups: net, pcmcia, fs, cdrom, ipv4, and scsi.

❑ All of your kernel modules are kept under /lib/modules/2.4.X.*yy*/ directory, where 2.4.X.*yy* is your kernel version.

SELF TEST

The following questions will help you measure your understanding of the material presented in this chapter. Read all the choices carefully, as there may be more than one correct answer. Choose all correct answers for each question.

Dual Boots: Linux and Windows NT

1. You are creating a dual-boot NT/Linux system. You already have NT installed and plan to use the NTLDR to load Linux on the second drive. Linux is installed, and you have made a bootdisk that properly boots Linux. What command would you issue from Linux to copy the bootsector from the floppy?

   A. dd if=bootsect.lnx of=/dev/fd0 bs=512 count=1

   B. dd if=/dev/fd0 of=bootsect.lnx bs=512 count=1

   C. dd if=bootsect.lnx of=/dev/fd0 bs=512

   D. dd if=/dev/fd0 of=bootsect.lnx count=512

2. You are dual-booting an NT/Linux system and have successfully copied a working bootsector to the NT boot partition, naming it bootsect.lnx. What do you need to do so that the NTLDR loads Linux as an operating system?

   A. Edit the NTLDR file with C:\bootsect.lnx="Linux".

   B. Edit the BOOT.INI file with "Linux"=C:\bootsect.lnx.

   C. Edit the BOOT.INI file with C:\bootsect.lnx="Linux".

   D. Do nothing. NTLDR will detect any bootsector file that has the bootsect.*xxx* syntax.

RAID Configuration

3. You have a mirrored RAID system with three drives. The first two are mirrored and the third is supposed to be a spare. When you look at the /etc/raidtab file, you see that it says spare-disks 0. What does this entry tell you?

   A. The raidtab entry is set up correctly.

   B. Spare-disks support is turned off. To turn it on, change spare-disks to 1.

   C. Currently no spare disks are loaded.

   D. The mirror failed and had to use the spare disk.

Using Kickstart to Automate Installation

4. You need to set up multiple Red Hat Linux systems over the network and decide to have a bootdisk connect to your DHCP/BOOTP server to load a kickstart file. The kickstart file resides on the DHCP/BOOTP server with the following syntax: *<client_ip-kickstart>*. You plan to have the kickstart install Linux from an FTP server that does not reside on the DHCP/BOOTP server. What is the problem with this plan?

   A. You cannot have the FTP server on a different server than your DHCP/BOOTP servers.

   B. The kickstart filename is incorrect.

   C. A BOOTP server can only be used to load kernels and will not load a kickstart file.

   D. You cannot install from an FTP server.

5. You need to install Linux on several similar computers at your site. You decide the best way to do this is to have all the installation answers preconfigured in a kickstart file, use a local DHCP server to obtain the required network configuration, and install using NFS. You are concerned that anyone sniffing on the network might possibly see the root password in the kickstart configuration. What can you do?

   A. Encrypt the kickstart file that resides on the DHCP/BOOTP server.

   B. Boot the disk by typing **linux ks=encrypted**.

   C. Use rootpw --iscrypted in the kickstart file.

   D. There is nothing you can do.

Hardware Conflicts and Plug-and-Play

6. When trying to load a sound module, you get a device busy error message. You think it is your ISA Plug-and-Play sound card and you'd like to view its Plug and Play configuration options so you can edit them to nonconflicting values. What command would you use to create a file of all your ISA Plug-and-Play device options?

   A. dumppnp > isapnp.conf

   B. pnpdump > isapnp.conf

   C. displaypnp > isapnp.conf

   D. showpnp > isapnp.conf

PCMCIA

7. You run Linux on a laptop. The cardmgr daemon for your PCMCIA cards is stomping on an IRQ that you want reserved. What file should you use to tell the cardmgr to exclude this IRQ from its list?

    A. /etc/pcmcia/config.opts

    B. /etc/sysconfig/pcmcia

    C. /etc/pcmcia/config.exclude

    D. /etc/rc.d/rc.sysinit

Advanced Power Management (APM) Laptops

8. You frequently use your laptop as a timesharing system during work hours, and many users log on to your laptop throughout the day. You are concerned, however, that there could be a loss of power and would like to warn the other users when the battery is about to run out. What would be the best way to handle this?

    A. Tell each user to run apm as often as possible to check battery life.

    B. Set up a user policy that instructs all users to save their files every five minutes.

    C. Use the wall option in the /etc/sysconfig/apmd file.

    D. Edit the shutdown script that runs at runlevel 0.

Understanding /etc/inittab

9. What runlevel should you switch to in order to run X11 as the default login service?

    A. 1

    B. 2

    C. 3

    D. 5

10. Which runlevel could you use to bring the system to single user mode?

    A. 1

    B. 2

    C. 3

    D. 5

11. What would happen if you modified the initdefault entry in the /etc/inittab file to look like this: id:5:initdefault:/usr/games/fortune?

    A. It would display a fortune every time you logged on.

    B. It would boot into X11 and display a fortune.

    C. It would display a fortune only when it booted.

    D. The fortune line would be ignored.

System Startup Script /etc/rc.d/rc.sysinit

12. What startup file loads the modules?

    A. /etc/rc.d/rc.modules

    B. /etc/init.d/S10modules

    C. /etc/rc.d/rc.sysinit

    D. None of the above

Understanding Kernel Modules

13. Which of the following does NOT describe kernel modules.

    A. They may make the kernel size smaller.

    B. They may increase the kernel speed.

    C. You can dynamically unload modules from a running kernel.

    D. Modules have .dll extensions.

The /lib/ modules /kernel_version/ Directory Structure

14. You have a network card that needs to have options specified at the command line when loading the module. You only need this network card occasionally, so you want to leave it as a module. What can you do to simplify loading of the module?

    A. Add a bind command to the modules.conf file.

    B. Add an options command to the modules.conf file.

    C. Add options to the end of the alias command in the modules.conf.file.

    D. None of the above.

15. When you type **lsmod** and see a list of running modules, you notice that some of them say (autoclean). What does this mean?

    A. The module will "automatically" remove its own files in the /tmp directory.

    B. The module is not in use and should be removed.

    C. The kernel will automatically take care of removing it from memory.

    D. The modprobe command has set the module to autoclean.

16. You are on a foreign computer and are not sure what network card is inside it. You have checked dmesg, but no network cards are listed, and even though you have a bunch of compiled network modules, none are currently loaded. What could you do to load the unknown network device quickly?

    A. Try loading each module manually.

    B. modprobe *

    C. Nothing. The kernel will load the module when the network card is accessed.

    D. modprobe -t net

17. You want to conserve as much memory as possible. While doing some checking you notice some modules that are loaded but unused. What command could you employ to remove these modules? (Choose all that apply.)

    A. rmmod

    B. rmmod -r

    C. modprobe -r

    D. modprobe -d

18. You notice that a module you want to load will not load because its dependencies fail. When you examine the /lib/modules/?/ directory closer you notice that the modules.dep file does not exist. What would be the easiest way to re-create this file?

    A. Add the dependencies by hand.

    B. In the /usr/src/linux directory type **make modules_install**

    C. depmod -a

    D. None of the above.

19. In a default Red Hat install, what is the name of the first script that runs on a system?

   A. /etc/rc.d/rc.sysinit

   B. /etc/init.d/rc.sysinit

   C. /etc/rc.d/rc.0

   D. /etc/rc.d/rc.1

20. If you wanted to change the initial boot script, what entry in the /etc/inittab file would you modify?

   A. boot

   B. bootwait

   C. sysinit

   D. initdefault

LAB QUESTION

You just got hold of ten new PCs for the Human Resources department from a name brand PC manufacturer and you want to install the Linux CD-ROM set that came with each one. You want Linux on all of them with an optimized set of packages, and you want to do it quickly.

Each of these machines has a standard 3COM network card that you know Linux has support for because you ordered the machines that way. They also each have one big 10GB disk that already contains Windows 98 and a CD-ROM. You do not have time to install each machine manually. What should you do?

SELF TEST ANSWERS

Dual Boots: Linux and Windows NT

1. ☑ **B**, dd if=/dev/fd0 of=bootsect.lnx bs=512 count=1 is the correct command.

   ☒ **A**, **C**, and **D** are incorrect. The options for the disk dump command need to be as follows: input file (if) needs to point to the floppy drive (which makes A incorrect), output file (of) needs to point to the file you want to create (which makes C incorrect), block size (bs) should be 512 (not count as in D), and count should be 1 because we only need the bootsector from the disk.

2. ☑ **C**. Edit the BOOT.INI file with C:\bootsect.lnx="Linux".

   ☒ **A**, **B**, and **D** are incorrect. The BOOT.INI file is loaded by NTLDR (which makes A incorrect) and parsed using the following syntax: <drive>:<filename>=<label> (which makes C and D incorrect).

RAID Configuration

3. ☑ **A**. Spare-disks start counting at 0, and we only have one spare disk so the raidtab entry is set up correctly.

   ☒ **B**, **C**, and **D** are incorrect. There is no way to know from this file the status of the raid disks, nor the current loading, as this is a configuration file not a log of the running service.

Using Kickstart to Automate Installation

4. ☑ **D**. Kickstart installs can only be done via CD-ROM or NFS servers.

   ☒ **A**, **B**, and **C** are incorrect. As of Linux 7.1, you can use kickstart to load from FTP, HTTP, or SMB, but the file has to be in a certain location so **A** is most likely incorrect. The name is correct assuming you used the actual client IP address in the name, as in 192.168.0.1-kickstart (so **B** is incorrect) and kernels are loaded by LILO, not kickstart (which makes **C** incorrect).

5. ☑ **C**. Use rootpw --iscrypted in the kickstart file. If you paste an encrypted password after this line, then the encrypted version of the password will be sent rather than the plain text version. Even network sniffers would only have access to the encrypted version of the password, which may be enough if they have access to a good crack program (sometimes you just have to take chances in life).

   ☒ **A**, **B**, and **D** are incorrect. **B** is not a proper option for LILO, and neither is **A**. Since there *is* something that can be done, **D** is incorrect.

Hardware Conflicts and Plug-and-Play

6. ☑ **B.** pnpdump > isapnp.conf. This command will dump all your Plug-and-Play devices with all their possible settings to a file called isapnp.conf. From here, you can edit the file and reset your Plug-and-Play cards.

☒ **A, C,** and **D** are incorrect because they represent invalid utility names.

PCMCIA

7. ☑ **A.** /etc/pcmcia/config.opts. This file is used to exclude any memory, IO addresses, and IRQs you want excluded.

☒ **B, C,** and **D** are incorrect. **D,** rc.sysinit, is the program called by init during bootup, so this is incorrect, as are the incorrect file names used in **B** and **C.**

Advanced Power Management (APM) Laptops

8. ☑ **C.** Configure the wall option in the /etc/sysconfig/apmd file. You can tell the apmd to notify the users before the battery runs out of power with the -W option.

☒ **A, B,** and **D** are incorrect. You can also have the other users run apm, but that means they have to remember to do so, and this is unlikely. Setting a policy of this nature is hard to enforce, so **A** and **B** are incorrect. It's too late to fix the shutdown script, so **D** is false too.

Understanding /etc/inittab

9. ☑ **D.** By default, runlevel 5 will load X11 as the default login service.

☒ **A** is incorrect because runlevel 1 is single user mode and will not run X. **B** is incorrect because runlevel 2 is not commonly used. **C** is incorrect because runlevel 3 is text-based multiuser mode.

10. ☑ **A.** By default, runlevel 1 specifies single user mode.

☒ **B** is incorrect because runlevel 2 is not commonly used. **C** is incorrect because runlevel 3 is text-based multiuser mode. **D** is incorrect because runlevel 5 is X Window and multiuser.

11. ☑ **D.** The fortune line would be ignored. The initdefault keyword ignores any process entries listed. All the initdefault line does is specify the default runlevel.

☒ **A, B,** and **C** are incorrect. The fortune program will print a random "fortune cookie" saying to the screen if run from a shell command line.

System Startup Script /etc/rc.d/rc.sysinit

12. ☑   C. The /etc/rc.d/rc.sysinit file checks for predefined aliases in the /etc/modules.conf
and loads them.
☒   A and B are incorrect filenames. D is incorrect because there *was* a correct answer.

Understanding Kernel Modules

13. ☑   D. Module files do NOT have .dll extensions (Microsoft Windows Dynamic Link Libraries),
they have .o (object libraries in Linux) extensions.
☒   A, B, and C are incorrect because they do not describe kernel modules.

The /lib/ modules /*kernel_version*/ Directory Structure

14. ☑   B. Add an options command to the modules.conf file. Once you have done this, simply
type **modprobe <*module*>** and the module will be added with the specified options.
☒   A, C, and D are incorrect. There is no such thing as the bind command for modules (which
makes A incorrect), nor is an option part of the alias command in modules.conf (which makes
C incorrect). D is incorrect because there *is* a correct answer.

15. ☑   C. The kernel will automatically take care of removing it from memory.
☒   A, B, and D are incorrect. This has nothing to do with the modprobe command (which
makes D incorrect), since it is controlled by the kernel thread managing modules. Since the
kernel thread handles modules automatically, you should not remove modules, hence B is
incorrect. Modules are stored in memory, not the /tmp directory as a file, therefore A is
incorrect.

16. ☑   D. The modprobe -t net command will run through your /lib/modules/?/net directory and
try each module. It will stop when a module successfully loads.
☒   A, B, and C are incorrect. The network will not load unless the card module is inserted,
so C is incorrect. You might try loading all modules manually, but that is not the quickest way, so
A is incorrect. The modprobe command can use the "*" wildcard character (needs to be * to work
on the command line) to invoke all options, so although B would work indirectly, and might
be considered fast, it would not be the best option.

17. ☑   A, B, and C, rmmod, rmmod -r, and modprobe -r will remove modules. Only rmmod -r
and modprobe -r will remove the module and all of its dependencies. rmmod will only remove
the module specified.
☒   D is incorrect because the -d option is incorrect.

18. ☑ C, depmod -a. This command will go through all your modules and find all dependencies. It then creates the modules.dep file for you.

☒ A, B, and D are incorrect. Writing this file by hand is not as easy as depmod -a, so A is false. The "make modules_install" command is part of building a kernel nothing to do with modules in memory yet, so **B** is false and since **C** is correct, **D** has to be false.

19. ☑ A. /etc/rc.d/rc.sysinit is the first script that is called. This script is specified in the /etc/inittab file.

☒ B, C, and D are incorrect. There is no /etc/init.d directory, so **B** is false. /etc/rc.d/rc.0 is the directory used by runlevel 0, therefore **C** is false, as is **D**, the directory for runlevel 1 service listings to be run.

20. ☑ C. Sysinit. This option runs during system boot but before any boot or bootwait entries.

☒ A, B, and D are incorrect. Sysinit runs during system boot but before any boot or bootwait entries. Initdefault merely sets the default runlevel, which is ignored at this level of booting.

LAB ANSWER

Simple, you install one machine, remove packages you do not want, and then use the mkkickstart utility to create a duplicate configuration file that you will then use on every machine. You modify the kickstart configuration to wipe out all the old partitions as they are not needed. Since you have a copy of Linux for each machine, you can just duplicate the diskette nine times and run each machine installation independently and quickly. No sweat!

6

Advanced User Administration

I n this chapter, you will learn how to create and implement policies for managing disk utilization on a per user or per group basis. Next, we'll look in detail at the steps Linux follows during bootup. Once you understand how bootup works, you'll be able to customize the process to enable the services you need and, more importantly, to disable the services you don't need.

Next, you will learn how to upgrade, configure, compile, and install your own custom kernels. You will know the difference between monolithic and modular kernels, and the benefits and disadvantages of using each style. You will see three different ways to customize and optimize your kernel configuration so it is as functional and small as possible. You will also learn the recommended techniques for configuring and installing the kernel.

This chapter will also discuss Pluggable Authentication Modules (PAMs) used by Red Hat to provide a consistent and powerful authentication package used to control accesses to many services. Finally, you will learn how to set up the system's various shell configuration scripts so users' sessions are configured according to your (and their) requirements, and how to schedule the periodic execution of jobs.

CERTIFICATION OBJECTIVE 6.01

Setting Up and Managing Disk Quotas

Quotas are used to limit a user's or a group of users' ability to consume disk space. This prevents a small group of users from monopolizing disk capacity and potentially interfering with other users or the entire system. Disk quotas are often used by ISPs, Web Hosting companies, on FTP sites, or on corporate file servers to ensure continued availability of their systems. Users can compromise availability by uploading files to the point of filling a file system (by default, there is nothing stopping this from happening). Once the file system is full, other users are effectively denied upload access to the disk (a denial of service). If the file system that fills is the root file system (/), this could also result in system instability or even a crash.

There are two limitations you can set up to manage disk consumption. You can limit the number of inodes a user may have, and you can also limit the number of disk blocks a user's files may consume. Linux uses one inode for each file a user has on a file system. Setting a maximum on the number of inodes a user may consume prevents a user from creating an excessive number of files. By limiting the number of disk blocks a user may consume, you limit the total amount of storage a user may have regardless of how many files they may have (i.e., either a small number of large files, or a large number of small files).

The quota system may be configured either by command line or through linuxconf. The command line method will be discussed first, followed by the linuxconf method.

exam
Ⓦatch

Quota support can only be installed on an ext2partition.

Kernel Configuration

Resource consumption while your system is running is maintained by the kernel. Consequently, it must be set up to support quotas before you can use this feature. On Red Hat, quota support is typically enabled. If not, you will need to either download a new kernel from Red Hat's FTP site or install the kernel's source and recompile it to include quota support. For more information, see the following section on Kernel Recompilation and Installation.

To verify quota support in any custom-built kernels you may have, issue the command:

```
# grep CONFIG_QUOTA /usr/src/linux/.config
```

You should see an output line like:

```
CONFIG_QUOTA=y
```

If you get:

```
CONFIG_QUOTA=n
```

Then quota support is not enabled in your kernel. If you get nothing, then you don't have a configured custom kernel source tree installed. This is not a problem because a stock Red Hat 7.x kernel does include quota support and is enabled in the kernel by default.

If you have a custom kernel, use either make menuconfig or make xconfig to enable quota support. The option is located under the file system section. Simply turn on quota support and rebuild and install your new kernel. (There will be more on building and installing kernels later in this chapter.) To complete the job, you will need to reboot to your new kernel and then install the quota rpms.

Installing the Quota rpm

First, check to see if you have the quota rpm installed on your system. You can check with the following command:

```
[root@notebook /]# rpm -qa | grep quota
quota-2.00pre3-7
```

There are several ways you can get the quota rpm file and install it. The most direct would be to mount your Red Hat CD-ROM and change to the rpms directory:

```
mount /dev/cdrom
cd /mnt/cdrom/RedHat/RPMS
```

Load the quota rpm with the following command:

```
rpm -Uvh quota-2.00pre3-7
```

This will tell rpm to -U update (or install if a previous version of the quota rpm is not present), to install verbosely (-v), and to use a series of hashes (-h) to indicate the current progress while installing the software. You may also get the package via FTP or HTTP, or use the Gnome rpm shipped with Red Hat 7.x and click Web Find. This will search the Internet for the quota package and install it.

The best choice for acquiring your rpm is the distribution CDs. The version of quota on the CDs is the one tested by Red Hat for your particular release. It should work flawlessly.

Once the package is installed, you can use the following commands and their associated man pages:

- **quotaon** */fs*   Enables quotas for the /fs file system.
- **quotaoff**   Disables quota tracking.
- **edquota** *name*   Edits the quota settings for user *name*. Can also be used to set defaults.
- **quota**   Allows users to see their current resource consumption and limits.

- **repquota** Generates a report of disk consumption by all users for a quota-enabled file system.
- **quotacheck** Scans a file system for quota usage. Initializes the quota databases.

You can get detailed information on any of these programs with either:

```
# man program
```

or:

```
# info program
```

The next step is to ensure the quotas are turned on and checked during bootup.

/etc/rc.d/rc.sysinit Quota Handling

The /etc/rc.d/init.d/rc.sysinit script as described in Chapter 4 is used to provide system initialization services for Linux when your system boots. Included in the script are commands to enable quota services. Specifically, this script runs both quotacheck (to ensure that disk consumption usage records are accurate) and quotaon (to enable quotas on all file systems indicated in /etc/fstab).

While you can run quotaon and quotaoff manually, there is usually little need. Red Hat 7.x's /etc/rc.d/init.d/rc.sysinit ensures quotas are enabled at boot time. When your machine shuts down, Red Hat performs an orderly umount of all file systems. When each quota-enabled file system is umounted, the kernel's latest information on resource consumption by users, groups, files, and inodes for that file system is written back to the partition.

Modifications to /etc/fstab

The file /etc/fstab is used to inform Linux about the file systems you wish to mount at boot time. The options column of this file is used to set file system mount options. These options are passed to the mount command for each file system as they are brought on line (mounted). To enable quotas for a file system, you have to update the options entry for the file system in /etc/fstab file to indicate that you want quotas enabled and that you wish to track quotas for either users, groups, or both. Quotas are enabled on a file system basis only. They cannot be set on directories.

Here is a sample fstab before editing:

```
Device      Mount point  Filesys Options    dump Fsck
LABEL=/     /            ext2    defaults      1 1
/dev/cdrom  /mnt/cdrom   iso9660 noauto,owner,ro 0 0
/dev/fd0    /mnt/floppy  auto    noauto,owner   0 0
none        /proc        proc    defaults       0 0
none        /dev/pts     devpts  gid=5,mode=620 0 0
/dev/hda5   swap         swap    defaults       0 0
/dev/hda1   /win         vfat    uid=500,gid=500,owner,rw  0 0
/dev/hda6   /home        ext2    defaults  0 0
```

In the previous example, we can only enable quotas on the root file system (LABEL=/)
and the /home file system (/dev/hda6). To enable user quota tracking on a file system,
add the keyword usrquota to the values listed in the options column. Similarly, you
enable group quota tracking with the grpquota option. Use vi or your favorite editor
to update /etc/fstab.

In our example, we will add both user and group quotas to the root file system:

```
Device      Mount point  Filesys Options       dump Fsck
LABEL=/     /            ext2    exec,dev,suid,rw,usrquota,grpquota   1 1
/dev/cdrom  /mnt/cdrom   iso9660 noauto,owner,ro 0 0
/dev/fd0    /mnt/floppy  auto    noauto,owner   0 0
none        /proc        proc    defaults       0 0
none        /dev/pts     devpts  gid=5,mode=620 0 0
/dev/hda5   swap         swap    defaults       0 0
/dev/hda1   /win         vfat    uid=500,gid=500,owner,rw  0 0
/dev/hda6   /home        ext2    defaults  0 0
```

If you edit the /etc/fstab file by hand, you'll need to ensure the line you are editing
does not wrap to the next line. If it does, the format for your /etc/fstab will be invalid
and you may not be able to successfully boot on the next power up.

Linuxconf can update /etc/fstab for you. You will need to enter the File systems
|Access local drive menu and edit the ext2 partitions you want to enable quotas on.
When editing, there is an Options section that has check boxes for both User and
Group quotas. Check these two boxes and activate changes. Linuxconf will then edit
the /etc/fstab file for you.

First, you will have to select an ext2 file system. This is shown in Figure 6-1.

To change the settings of a file system, highlight its entry and double-click. You
should see the screen shown in Figure 6-2.

Now, select the Options tab to bring up the file systems options settings (Figure 6-3).

Note that we have scrolled down to the bottom of the options list to bring the user
and group quota options into view.

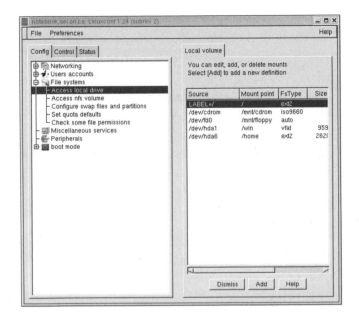

FIGURE 6-1

The Access local
drive menu

Finally, check both the User Quota Enabled and Group Quota Enabled check
boxes at the bottom of the tab. Then, Accept your changes and Dismiss the right-side
of the dialogue box. This should bring you back to linuxconf's main screen.

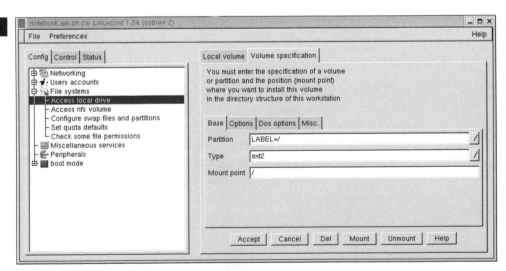

FIGURE 6-2

The Volume
Specification tab
of a selected file
system

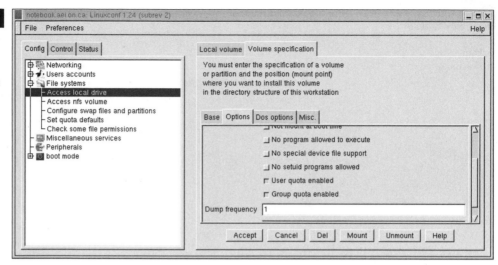

FIGURE 6-3

The Options tab
for the selected
(root) file system

Making the /quota.user and /quota.group Files

At this point, you'll need to jump to a terminal window (as root) and create the two
files that will be used to hold our quota information for the root file system. Enter
the commands:

```
# touch /quota.user
# touch /quota.group
# chmod 0600 /quota.user /quota.group
```

If these three commands are not run, you will not be able to complete your quota
configuration.

Preview Your Changes

You can preview your changes with File | Act/Changes option. Figure 6-4 is an
example of what linuxconf wants to do for us.

There is a potential error in the preceding dialogue relating to missing /quota.user
and /quota.group files. If you did not make these files by hand (as we discussed earlier)
you will not be able to start the quota system, even if you select the Do It button. If
you forgot to make these two files and you get a screen that resembles Figure 6-4,
select the Do Nothing button, start up a terminal window, and make /quota.user
and /quota.group.

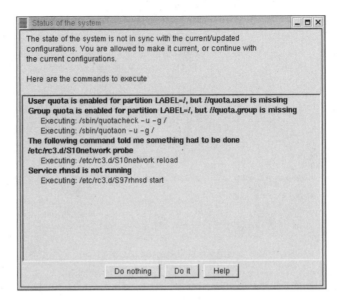

FIGURE 6-4

Our pending
changes

Note that linuxconf is very forthcoming with respect to the commands it intends to run. The advantage here is that you can learn from linuxconf and perform the commands yourself the next time you need to work with quotas.

Once you're ready, select Do It. Linuxconf is telling us it needs to remount root with our new file system options enabled. You must answer Yes here or quotas won't be turned on. Since we are turning on quotas for the first time, linuxconf needs to run quotacheck to inventory inode and disk space usage by user and group. Linuxconf asks for permission to do this, as shown in Figure 6-5.

You have just enabled quota checking for the root file system. However, we now need to specify which users will have quotas enforced. We will see how that is done in the next section.

Upgrader's Note

Red Hat has changed the way it manages quotas in Red Hat 7.1. It now uses the files aquota.user and aquota.group instead of quota.user and quota.group (in the root directory for the mounted file system). If you have a Red Hat 7.0 or earlier system, or if you have previously upgraded such a system to Red Hat 7.1, you may need to run the convertquota command to update these files. You'll know if this is the case, because quotaon will fail with a message about missing files (aquota.user and

FIGURE 6-5

Verifying it's OK
to run
quotacheck

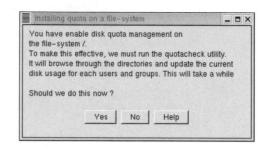

aquota.group). An example of the command I used on my system to update my quota files was:

```
# convertquota -u -g /
```

Now we can turn on quotas with:

```
# quotaon -u -g /
```

Managing Quotas by Hand

If you chose not to use the linuxconf utility to make your quotas, you will need to make /quota.user and /quota.group by hand. To do it by hand, create the empty files in the root of your partition and set the security so only root has read and write permissions. For example:

```
# touch /quota.user /quota.group      # RedHat 7.0 and earlier
# chmod 600 /quota.user /quota.group
```

or:

```
# touch /aquota.user /aquota.group      # RedHat 7.1
# chmod 600 /aquota.user /aquota.group
```

This step will be done automatically for you when you run quotacheck -avug. The options for quotacheck are:

- **-a**   Scans all file systems with quotas enabled by checking /etc/mnttab.
- **-v**   Performs a verbose scan. Otherwise quotacheck is silent.
- **-u**   Scans for user quotas.
- **-g**   Scans for group quotas.

This will check the current quota information for all users, groups, and partitions. It stores this information in the root of your quota partitions. If you did not create these files by hand, they will be created now and should have the appropriate security already set, but you should double-check just to be safe:

```
# ls -l /quota.usr /quota.group    # Red Hat 7.0 and earlier
```

or:

```
# ls -l /aquota.user /aquota.group  # for Red Hat 7.1
```

If you used linuxconf to enable quotas, when you activate changes it will ask if you want to run quotacheck. Simply say Yes and this step will be taken care of.

No matter how you create the files, you need to run quotacheck to collect initial information on your users. This can be accomplished either by rebooting or by issuing quotacheck if you haven't already. For example, to initialize your quota files on the root file system, use:

```
quotacheck /
```

Using edquota to Set Up Disk Quotas

To specify disk quotas, you need to run edquota. Edquota will edit the quota.user or quota.group file with the vi editor. You can change the editor by specifying a different one with the $EDITOR (i.e., EDITOR=/path/to/new/editor; export EDITOR) variable. In our example, we will pretend we have a user named craig, and we want to restrict how much disk space he is allowed to use. We type the following command to edit his quota record:

```
# edquota -u craig
```

This will launch vi and show us the following:

```
Edit block and inode quota for user craig:
Device /dev/hda2 (/):
Used 60KB, limits: soft=0 hard=0
Used 15 inodes, limits: soft=0 hard=0
```

exam
Watch

If you run this command and only see the first line, then you probably forgot to run quotacheck.

In this example, our soft and hard limits are set to 0 for both inodes and files. This is per default and it means we currently may consume as many inodes or as many disk blocks as we wish. We can see that craig is currently using 60K of disk space and has only 15 files (inodes) on this partition. We want to set a limit so he does not exceed the 20MB usage policy. First, we need to elaborate on the meaning of soft and hard limits.

- **Soft Limit** This is the maximum amount of space a user can have on that partition. If you have set a grace period, then this will act as the borderline threshold. The user will then be notified he is in quota violation. If you have set a grace period, you will also need to set a Hard Limit. A grace period is the number of days a user is allowed to be in quota violation before the system refuses to make new files or extend existing files on behalf of the user. Over time, users must stay under their soft limit.

- **Hard Limit** Hard Limits are only necessary when you are using grace periods. If grace periods are enabled, this will be the absolute limit a person can use. Any attempt to consume resources beyond this limit will be denied. If you are not using grace periods, the soft limit is the absolute space the user can use.

In our example, we will set our user an 18MB soft Limit and a 20MB hard Limit. We will also give craig a seven-day grace period to get his stuff cleaned up.

```
Edit block and inode quota for user craig:
Device /dev/hda2 (/):
Used 60KB, limits: soft=18000 hard=20000
Used 15 inodes, limits: soft=0 hard=0
```

Note that we have not limited craig's use of inodes. He is still able to use as many inodes as he likes.

Now we must save this file. To set the grace period, we use the edquota command, but provide a -t as an argument:

```
# edquota -t
```

vi will load and you will see something similar to the following:

```
Edit grace times for user quota:
Device /dev/hda2 (/):
Block grace: 7 days Inode grace: 7 days
```

Here, Linux has provided us with the default of seven days for both inodes and block usage. That is, a user may exceed his soft limit on either resource for up to seven days. After that, further requests to use inodes or disk blocks will be denied. Our user craig would have to delete files to get his total disk block consumption under 18MB before he could create new files or grow existing files.

To activate our grace period, we just save the file.

There is a quota quirk you should be aware of. When you use edquota and specify the grace period, you cannot have a space between the number and the unit. That is, the entry "7 days" will not work, but "7days" will. If you get an error message similar to:

```
Can't parse grace period time 7
```

You'll know you neglected to remove the blank. Oddly enough, Red Hat 7.1 inserts the blank when you invoke edquota -t.

Edquota allows you to use an already configured users quota as a template for new users. To use this feature, you need to type the -p <configured_user> arguments:

```
# edquota -u -p craig bob sue
```

This command will not provide any output, but it will take the configuration settings of craig and apply them to both bob and sue. You can list as many users as you want to edit or apply templates to.

You can also set up quotas on a per-group basis. To do this, simply run edquota with the -g <group_name> argument. <group name> would need to be a valid group as specified in the /etc/group file.

```
# edquota -g games
```

Edit block and inode quota for group games:

```
Device /dev/hda2 (/):
Used 0KB, limits: soft=0 hard=0
Used 0 inodes, limits: soft=0 hard=0
```

To use linuxconf, choose ?User accounts | Normal | User accounts,? and select the desired user. When editing the user's information, there is a section for quotas. You can add the hard and soft limits in this file.

First, select the user you wish to add a quota for; you'll see the screen shown in Figure 6-6. Next, you will need to choose the Disk Quotas tab to see the screen shown in Figure 6-7.

FIGURE 6-6

The User
Information menu

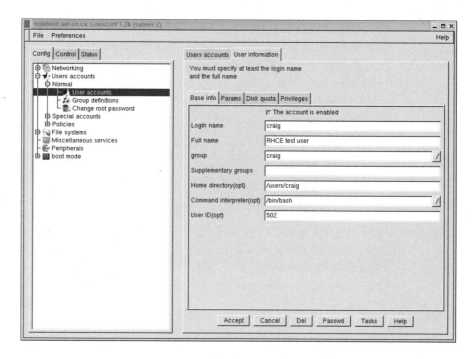

FIGURE 6-7

Disk quota
settings for user
craig

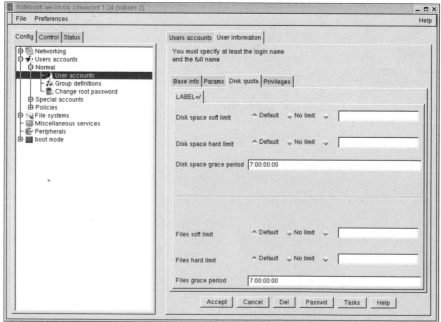

Select the desired user (in our case, craig) and click his account record. This brings up the User Information tab for our user. Select the Options tab.

You can now specify the disk and file hard and soft limits. You can also choose a grace period for this user. If you don't choose a grace period, your Hard Limits will be ignored. Once you are satisfied, click Accept. When you quit linuxconf, it will ask you to activate changes. As soon as the changes are activated, they will immediately go into effect.

Creating Default Quota Settings

You can set up system-wide defaults for your quotas, as shown in Figure 6-8. This is a nice feature that will save you some time if you have a system-wide policy. The easiest way to do this is with linuxconf. You need to access the Quota Defaults menu through File Systems | Set Quota Defaults. In this menu, you can add both soft and hard limits, as well as grace periods.

Here, our graphic displays the settings for user disk space and file consumption. Scrolling down, you can set group defaults. The format for the grace period is *days:hours:minutes:seconds.* To avoid excess overhead, simply set the grace period to days.

FIGURE 6-8

The Set Quota Defaults menu

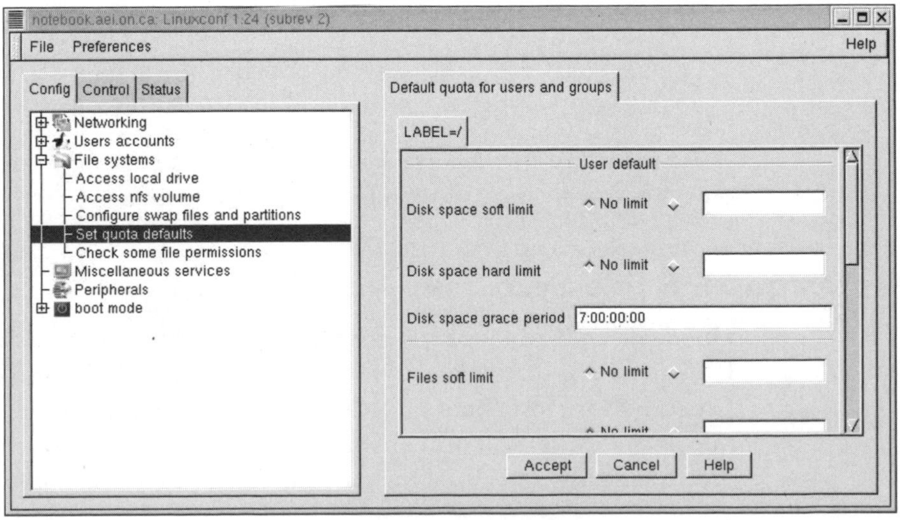

When you change this setting, all your other quota settings will be replaced with the system defaults. It's best to use this first and then set your users individually as needed.

Quota Reports

It is always nice to see reports on who is using the most disk space. You can generate reports on users, groups, or everybody on every partition. To view a report showing all the quota information, run the repquota -a command:

```
# repquota -a
*** Report for user quotas on device /dev/hda2 (/)
Block grace time: 7 days; Inode grace time: 7 days
Block limits                    File limits
User            used    soft    hard  grace    used  soft  hard  grace
                _____

root      —      24      0       0               2     0     0
craig     —      60      0       0              15     0     0
```

You can use repquota to show you specific reports on all the users on a particular file system with the command:

```
# repquota -u /
```

To see specific information on just one user, the following quota command can be used:

```
# quota -uv craig
Disk quotas for user craig(502):
Filesystem  blocks  quota  limit   grace   files  quota  limit  grace
/dev/hda2      60      0      0              15      0      0
```

An individual user can check his or her own usage with the quota command, but only root can use the -u option to look at other users.

Quotas on NFS File Systems

Quotas on an NFS file system are basically the same. NFS translates remote users to local users. You specify how this translation works with the nfsd configuration. See Chapter 7 for more about NFS drives and information. You need to set the disk quotas to the user you plan on mapping outside users to. So, if you create a local user called nfsuser, and you translate all remote requests to this user, then you need to set up quota restrictions for nfsuser on the mounted partition. This will limit the disk consumption of all incoming NFS users.

CERTIFICATION OBJECTIVE 6.02

System Initialization Scripts

Red Hat 7.x follows the standard UNIX System VR4 (System 5 Release 4) method for system startup and run state management. The init daemon is started as the very first process (it's process ID is 1). init reads it's configuration file; /etc/inittab and continues the initialization process based on what it sees in that file. Here's a listing of an /etc/inittab file for Red Hat 7.1:

Set the default run level here.

```
#    5 - X11
#    6 - reboot (Do NOT set initdefault to this)
#
id:3:initdefault:

# System initialization.
si::sysinit:/etc/rc.d/rc.sysinit

l0:0:wait:/etc/rc.d/rc 0
l1:1:wait:/etc/rc.d/rc 1
l2:2:wait:/etc/rc.d/rc 2
l3:3:wait:/etc/rc.d/rc 3
l4:4:wait:/etc/rc.d/rc 4
l5:5:wait:/etc/rc.d/rc 5
l6:6:wait:/etc/rc.d/rc 6

# Things to run in every runlevel.
ud::once:/sbin/update

# Trap CTRL-ALT-DELETE
ca::ctrlaltdel:/sbin/shutdown -t3 -r now

# When our UPS tells us power has failed, assume we have a few minutes

pf::powerfail:/sbin/shutdown -f -h +2 "Power Failure; System Shut Down"

# If power was restored before the shutdown kicked in, cancel it.
pr:12345:powerokwait:/sbin/shutdown -c "Power Restored"
```

```
# Run gettys in standard runlevels
1:2345:respawn:/sbin/mingetty tty1
2:2345:respawn:/sbin/mingetty tty2
3:2345:respawn:/sbin/mingetty tty3
4:2345:respawn:/sbin/mingetty tty4
5:2345:respawn:/sbin/mingetty tty5
6:2345:respawn:/sbin/mingetty tty6

# Run xdm in runlevel 5
# xdm is now a separate service
x:5:respawn:/etc/X11/prefdm -nodaemon
```

The /etc/rc.d/rc.sysinit script (described in Chapter 4) runs a few other scripts. If necessary, it runs /etc/rc.serial, which is used to initialize any serial ports. (That is, setserial commands to initialize serial ports to specific settings can be placed in this file.) This file was used in previous versions of Red Hat (e.g., RH 6.x) but it is no longer found on RH 7.x.

/etc/rc.d/rc.local is still present. It is used to perform local system initializations after all other system scripts have run (just before you get a login prompt). As a general configuration file, its use is deprecated. Currently, the only functionality it provides is to create a custom /etc/issue file that identifies both the version of Red Hat and the Linux kernel you are using. (This is the heading you get above your login prompt when you use a virtual terminal, or when you Telnet/ssh to your system.) As a final step, it also creates a file called /etc/issue.net by copying /etc/issue. If you wish to have different messages displayed for Telnet vs. serial or virtual console users, you can change the logic of /etc/rc.d/rc.local and place any content you like in /etc/issue and /etc/issue.net.

There is also an /etc/rc.d/rc. This script is used to manage runlevel changes. It should not be edited.

You should consider modifying the content of both the /etc/issue file and the /etc/issue.net file for security reasons. There are two issues:

■ Most people don't need to know the distribution and the kernel version of Linux you are using. Evil crackers crave this information because it allows them to quickly test your system for vulnerabilities. For this reason you may wish to change /etc/issue.net to provide disinformation to such individuals. By changing the kernel version or by fibbing about your Linux distribution (or even that you are using Linux at all) can send an evil cracker on a wild goose chase!

■ You need to specify that your system is for private use only. A failure to do so may significantly limit your ability to seek legal remedies against anyone who cracks your machine.

/etc/rc.d, /etc/rc0.d ... /etc/rc6.d

Linux, like most commercial UNIX spin-offs, manages the services it offers by using customizable runlevels. The runlevel command can be used to query the system for the current and previous runlevel.

```
# runlevel
N 3
```

The first letter (N) specifies that we had no previous runlevel. That is, we booted directly to runlevel 3. The 3 specifies our current runlevel. A word of advice to experienced UNIX users, the who -r command does not work in Linux.

In the /etc/inittab file, the /etc/rc.d/rc script is called and the desired runlevel is passed as an argument. Here is an excerpt from our /etc/inittab:

```
l0:0:wait:/etc/rc.d/rc 0
l1:1:wait:/etc/rc.d/rc 1
l2:2:wait:/etc/rc.d/rc 2
l3:3:wait:/etc/rc.d/rc 3
l4:4:wait:/etc/rc.d/rc 4
l5:5:wait:/etc/rc.d/rc 5
l6:6:wait:/etc/rc.d/rc 6
```

For more information on how /etc/inittab works, see Chapter 4. Here you can see that for each runlevel, /etc/rc.d/rc is called and the runlevel is passed.

/etc/rc.d/rc manages runlevel changes by changing to the specific directory that is appropriate for the runlevel. Once in the correct directory, it executes a series of scripts to stop services that are not appropriate and to start services that are required. There are unique runlevel directories for runlevels 0, 1, 2, 3, and 5. They are called /etc/rc.d/rc0.d, /etc/rc.d/rc1.d, /etc/rc.d/rc2.d, /etc/rc.d/rc3.d, and /etc/rc.d/rc5.d, respectively.

Typically, what you will find in these directories are symbolic links to scripts in the /etc/rc.d/init.d directory. These links will typically begin with either an S or a K, followed by a two-digit sequence number. Scripts that start with an S are referred to as start scripts. They indicate that a service is needed and must be started for this runlevel. Scripts whose name begins with a K are called kill scripts. They indicate services that are not appropriate for the new runlevel.

There is also a two-digit number after the first letter and then the service name. The two-digit sequence number is to ensure the scripts get executed in the desired order. Since Linux (like UNIX) sorts its filenames, using digits ensures our scripts get run in a predictable manner. That is, they are run in the order reported by ls.

Here is an example from an /etc/rc3.d directory:

```
K01kdcrotate    K25sshd       K92ipchains S20random    S90crond
K01pppoe        K30sendmail   K96irda     S25netfs     S90xfs
K14alsasound    K34yppasswdd  S05kudzu    S40atd       S91smb
K15httpd        K45arpwatch   S08iptables S45pcmcia    S95anacron
K20nfs          K45named      S10network  S50xinetd    S97rhnsd
K20rstatd       K60lpd        S12syslog   S56rawdevices S99linuxconf
K20rusersd      K65identd     S13portmap  S75keytable  S99local
K20rwalld       K83ypbind     S14nfslock  S77Win4Lin
K20rwhod        K84ypserv     S16apmd     S85gpm
```

These are not files but symbolic links to the actual program. The actual script sits in a file in the /etc/rc.d/init.d. If we take a closer look at one of the links, we will see it pointing to the init.d directory.

```
# ls -l S85gpm
lrwxrwxrwx    1 root root    13 May 15 15:05 S85gpm-> ../init.d/gpm
# ls -1L S90crond
-rwxr-xr-x    1 root      root        1316 Feb 12  2001 S90crond
```

Note: The -L option to ls tells ls to follow symbolic links and print the attributes of the file being pointed at rather than the link itself. It is useful for finding out more about the real target file. This program will start with a sequence of 85. That is, it executes after S77Win4Lin and before S90crond. The script that actually gets executed is ../init.d/gpm (up one directory, down the init.d directory to the gpm script), and because this link is in the rc3.d directory, it will start when runlevel 3 is activated. This method is fast and takes up very little disk space because almost all the files are links to the real files. It is also the easiest to customize. Scripts conform to a simple structure. They launch their service when they are provided a start argument and they terminate their service when they are given a stop argument.

Starting X-Window Automatically

Discussed briefly in Chapter 4, we'll now take a closer look at some of the other scripts that run. In Chapter 4, you noticed that runlevel 5 was the default level in the inittab file to load X-Window during bootup. Here are two lines that show how X boots:

```
l5:5:wait:/etc/rc.d/rc 5
x:5:respawn:/etc/X11/prefdm -nodaemon
```

Here, you can see the first thing that runs is the rc5.d links, then prefdm runs. If you look at the rc5.d links, you will see that most, if not all, of the daemons are the same and are not X-specific. The real magic happens when prefdm runs.

Prefdm is a link that points to the prefered display manager. This is typically xdm (the standard X Display Manager), kdm (the KDE display manager), or gdm (the GNOME display manager). Display managers are responsible for:

- Deciding whether you access the system graphically
- Authenticating you by accepting your username and password
- Starting the correct graphical environment based on your preferences

You may be thinking, "Wow. That is really fascinating, but I still don't know how to start X automatically." Well, to start X automatically, you simply change one number in the inittab file.

```
id:5:initdefault:
```

If this number isn't 5, change it to 5 and reboot. Alternatively, you can instruct Linux to change runlevels with the telinit command. To transition to runlevel 5, use:

```
# telinit 5
```

The graphics login screen should appear shortly.

If you choose to reboot, your system will switch to graphics mode and you will be able to sign on with your preferred window manager.

You can also change your default runlevel with linuxconf, as shown in Figure 6-9. You enable runlevel 5 indirectly by selecting Graphic & Network. (Note the path that we took to get to this window by looking at the selection tree on the left side of the linuxconf window.) You should set and test your X configuration before selecting this value (use Xconfigurator). If you set it and X-Window fails to start, you can switch to a text-based terminal by pressing CTRL-ALT-F1 through CTRL-ALT-F6.

FIGURE 6-9

The initial system
services menu

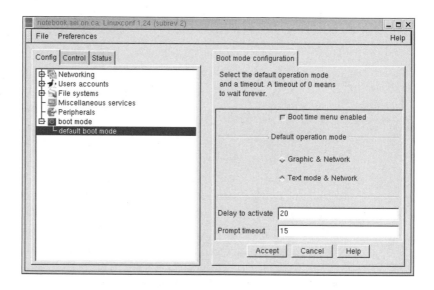

CERTIFICATION OBJECTIVE 6.03

Kernel Recompilation and Installation

One of Linux's strong features is the ability to rebuild your kernel to exactly meet your needs. The kernel is the heart of the whole operating system; it manages the hardware, decides which processes to run and provides processes with an isolated, virtual address space in which to run. The kernel is what the Linux loader (LILO) loads into memory. And it is the kernel that decides what device driver modules are required, as well as how hardware resources are allocated (i.e., interrupts, I/O ports, dual-ported memory, and direct memory access (DMA) channels). With the ability to recompile your kernel, you can:

■ Greatly improve the speed at which kernel services run by building in direct support for often-used drivers and dynamically loading less frequently needed drivers.

■ Lower the memory consumption of your kernel by removing unneeded components.

■ Configure support for high-end hardware, such as memory above 4GB, hardware array controllers, symmetric multiprocessing (multiple CPU) support, and more.

In essence, you can build a specific kernel for your architecture.

Best Practices

Your kernel should be compiled with only the things you need. The less stuff you add to the kernel that you probably won't use, the faster your whole system will run. For instance, if your server has no sound card, then there is probably no reason for you to compile sound support into your kernel. By removing devices that you don't need, you will:

■ Decrease the size of the kernel

■ Provide a modest increase in speed for the devices that are present

■ Make more hardware resources (i/o ports, interrupts, and so on) available for expansion cards, such as NICS, disk controllers, and others

■ Be less likely to run into PC hardware limitations (such as the size of the compressed kernel)

It is a good idea to have device drivers compiled as modules for any extra equipment you may have lying around. If you think you may wish to add a second network card, build the module for it in advance. Then, if you do add the card, your kernel will be ready to use it.

Modules are kernel extensions. They are not compiled directly into the kernel, but can be plugged in and removed as needed. They will be explained in more detail later in this chapter. The reason you would do this is so you do not have to recompile the kernel in the event of hardware failure. For example, if you have a 3COM 3c595 network card installed, but also have some 3COM 3c905 cards in storage, then it may be a good idea to make the 3c905 module. That way you will just have to swap in the new card and let the module load, causing minimum downtime.

Kernel Concepts

There are some basic kernel concepts you will need to understand before you can compile your own kernel. Most of these concepts were briefly discussed previously.

Monolithic versus Modular

A *monolithic* kernel is a kernel where all the device modules are built directly into the kernel. Modular kernels have many of their devices built as separate loadable modules. It can also talk directly to its devices faster than a module, while a kernel that uses modules must talk to the hardware indirectly through the module table.

Monolithic kernels, however, are large. Increasing the size of your kernel decreases your system-wide available memory, and some systems need to have the kernel smaller than a certain size in order to boot. You can add more than one device in a monolithic kernel, and it will load the right one for your architecture. Although this will slow down boot time (because the kernel is larger and each module must run its own initialization routine), there is a benefit. If you are working in an environment where others don't understand Linux, you could build in, say, network drivers that may eventually be used in the system. For example, if your network card failed and you only had a different brand available in storage but it was compiled into the kernel, then you could just swap the card in and turn the server back on. That's it! The server would boot up, load the different network card, and appropriately assign it the old IP.

A *modular* kernel has greater flexibility. You can compile almost all your drivers as modules, and then each module can be inserted into the kernel whenever you need it. Modules keep the initial kernel size low, which increases the boot time and overall performance. You can use modprobe or insmod to load modules as needed.

As you can imagine, most systems are a mix of both modular and monolithic kernels. Essential drivers may be built in directly, while other parts remain modules.

Updating the Kernel

Updating the kernel is a relatively easy process. You should always keep a copy of your old kernel around in case you make a mistake. New kernels are handled by installing the newly built kernel in /boot and then configuring the Linux boot loader (LILO) to point at the new kernel by adding another image= section in the /etc/lilo.conf file. If you do make a drastic mistake and the kernel doesn't boot, then you can simply reboot the server and select your old kernel at the LILO prompt. You should also save your kernel configuration files so you can easily copy to the newer kernels and use them as a guideline. This will be discussed in more detail a little later.

The /boot Partition

Before you can use it, you must copy your new kernel to the /boot directory. It is usually a good idea to make the /boot directory its own file system. This is done during installation and is used to ensure your kernel is addressable by your PC's BIOS. When you set up a Linux box, you can set the first partition to a small (20MB) size within the first 1024 cylinders and mount it as /boot. By doing this, you can then move your hard drive to a machine that has an older BIOS and still boot without any changes. Very old types of BIOS have a hard drive limitation of around 500MB and many machines built before 1998 cannot directly address more than 8GB of disk through the BIOS. If your /boot slice is out of the addressable range of the BIOS, then your kernel may fail to load. However, Linux does not suffer from disk addressing limitations. Once Linux is up, it can address disks of any size. So, if you take a bigger drive and set it up in the aforementioned way, Linux will boot on any system.

The /proc File System

/proc is a file system that is virtual; it doesn't actually exist on the hard drive. The kernel maintains all its information. This is a great source of information of what your kernel is doing. There are even kernel variables that you can adjust to instantly change your kernel's behavior. You should spend some time looking at the files in /proc to become familiar with the wealth of information it contains. Here's what you'll find in a typical Red Hat 7.1 system:

```
# ls /proc
1     1967  2058  2125  2446  430  bus          interrupts  misc       sys
1837  1968  2061  2127  2448  445  cmdline      iomem       modules    sysvipc
1865  1980  2064  2155  2449  5    cpuinfo      ioports     mounts     tty
1877  2     2066  2412  2471  501  devices      irq         mtrr       uptime
1909  2012  2070  2413  2475  531  dma          kcore       net        version
1921  2017  2072  2414  2493  543  driver       kmsg        partitions
1926  2018  2075  2432  3     6    execdomains  ksyms       pci
1963  2022  2076  2433  393   64   fb           loadavg     self
1964  2038  2077  2435  398   7    filesystems  locks       slabinfo
1965  2044  2078  2436  4     8    fs           mdstat      stat
1966  2055  2122  2438  410   apm  ide          meminfo     swaps
```

The numbered items are the address space of processes, by process ID, presented as directories. Within each directory are the memory segments that make up the active process. If you were to examine the contents of one of these files, you would be reading the active memory for that process (something that only programmers are likely to do). The other items in the listing are files and directories that correspond to configuration information for components or whole subsystems.

The following are some examples of the types of information files present. First, lets look at the memory we have installed in our system and how Linux is using it.

```
# cat /proc/meminfo
total:      used:      free:   shared: buffers:   cached:
Mem:     195674112 151814144 43859968      0    6709248   101732352
Swap:    232202240          0 232202240
MemTotal:        191088 kB
MemFree:          42832 kB
MemShared:            0 kB
Buffers:           6552 kB
Cached:           99348 kB
Active:          103632 kB
Inact_dirty:       2268 kB
Inact_clean:          0 kB
Inact_target:      2284 kB
HighTotal:            0 kB
HighFree:             0 kB
LowTotal:        191088 kB
LowFree:          42832 kB
SwapTotal:       226760 kB
SwapFree:        226760 kB
```

Now, let's see about our CPU:

```
# cat /proc/cpuinfo
processor      : 0
vendor_id      : GenuineIntel
cpu family     : 6
model          : 5
model name     : Pentium II (Deschutes)
stepping       : 2
cpu MHz        : 300.016
cache size     : 512 KB
fdiv_bug       : no
hlt_bug        : no
f00f_bug       : no
coma_bug       : no
fpu            : yes
fpu_exception: yes
cpuid level    : 2
```

```
wp             : yes
flags          : fpu vme de pse tsc msr pae mce cx8 sep mtrr pge mca cmov pat
pse36 … bogomips : 598.01
```

We can even see what hardware resources are used by examining files like
/proc/ioports, /proc/iomem, and /proc/dma. Here's the /proc/ioports file:

```
# cat /proc/ioports
0000-001f : dma1
0020-003f : pic1
0040-005f : timer
0060-006f : keyboard
0070-007f : rtc
0080-008f : dma page reg
00a0-00bf : pic2
00c0-00df : dma2
00f0-00ff : fpu
01f0-01f7 : ide0
0220-022f : soundblaster
02f8-02ff : serial(auto)
0310-031f : 3c589_cs
03c0-03df : vga+
03f6-03f6 : ide0
03f8-03ff : serial(auto)
0cf8-0cff : PCI conf1
1000-100f : Compaq Computer Corporation Triflex Dual EIDE Controller
1000-1007 : ide0
1008-100f : ide1
1400-14ff : PCI CardBus #02
1800-18ff : PCI CardBus #02
1c00-1cff : PCI CardBus #03
2000-20ff : PCI CardBus #03
```

There are many programs that simply look at the information stored in /proc and
report it in a more readable format. Top is a perfect example. It reads the process
table, queries used memory and swap as well as CPU utilization and presents it all
on one screen. A GUI version of top (gtop) is also available (see Figure 6-10).

More importantly, there are kernel variables you can alter to change the way the
kernel behaves while it's running. Here are some examples:

```
# cat /proc/sys/net/ipv4/ip_forward
0
# echo 1 > /proc/sys/net/ipv4/ip_forward
# cat /proc/sys/net/ipv4/ip_forward
1
```

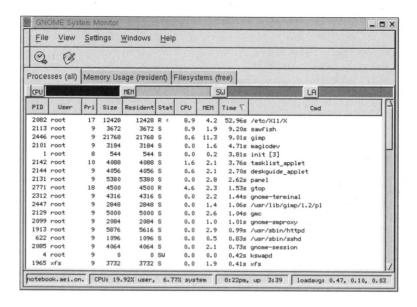

Congratulations, your system is now a router. It will now forward IP packets destined for a different network.

```
# echo 1 > /proc/sys/net/ipv4/tcp_syncookies
```

This will enable the use of TCP SYN packet cookies, which prevents SYN flood attacks on your system.

The Kernel Source Tree and Documentation

The source code for the kernel is kept in the /usr/src/linux directory. The /usr/src directory usually looks as follows:

```
# ls -l /usr/src/
total 12
lrwxrwxrwx    1 root      root          11 Jul 15 18:14 linux -> linux-2.4.4
lrwxrwxrwx    1 root      root          11 Jul 19 20:42 linux-2.4 -> linux-2.4.2
drwxr-xr-x   16 root      root        4096 Jul 19 20:41 linux-2.4.2
drwxr-xr-x   14 1046      101         4096 Jul 30 20:30 linux-2.4.4
drwxr-xr-x    7 root      root        4096 Jul 19 20:38 redhat
```

The physical directory is linux-2.4.4, and there is a soft link called linux that points to this directory. Using this method, you can create a directory for a new kernel, change the link to point to the new directory, and still keep your old source for reference.

Note that Red Hat 7.1 uses the new Linux 2.4 kernel. When installing a new set of kernel sources, you should make a link named linux-2.4 and symbolically link it to the real name of the new kernel (e.g., sym-link it to linux-2.4.4). You could do this with:

```
# ln linux-2.4.4 linux-2.4
```

The /usr/src/linux directory is laid out as follows:

```
arch         CREDITS       include   lib          net         scripts
config       Documentation init      MAINTAINERS  README      System.map
Config.Good  drivers       ipc       Makefile     REPORTING-BUGS
COPYING      fs            kernel    mm  Rules.make
```

It's best to read the README file. Also, check out the Documentation directory. It contains everything you need, from information on setting up symmetrical multiprocessors to serial consoles. The other directories are mainly source and you probably won't need to spend time in those (unless you *really* want to see how TCP/IP works). There is also a hidden file named .config that may be present in this directory. It will be described in more detail later in this chapter.

The Kernel rpms and the Linux Kernel Tar File

If you don't see the directories mentioned in the preceding section, then you haven't installed the kernel's source code. To install the source provided with your Red Hat installation, simply mount the CD-ROM drive and install the kernel rpm:

```
# mount /dev/cdrom
# cd /mnt/cdrom/redhat/RPMS/
# rpm -ivh kernel-2.4.2-2src.rpm
```

Or, you can download the newest kernel from http://www.kernel.org. The version numbers are discussed in the next section. Once you have downloaded the kernel source, you will need to properly install it. For our example, we will assume you downloaded linux-2.4.2.tar.gz into the /usr/src/ directory.

```
# cd /usr/src
# mkdir linux-2.4.2
# rm linux
# ln -s linux-2.4.2 linux
```

```
# ln -s linux-2.4.2 linux-2.4
# tar xvfz linux-2.4.2.tar.gz
```

Here we manually created a new directory for the kernel. Then we removed the old link and made a new one that pointed to the new directory. When we uncompress the tar.gz file, it will uncompress to the Linux link.

Required rpms

In order to build a kernel from sources, you need to ensure you have all the rpms necessary, not only for the kernel, but also for the tools needed to build the kernel. Check your system to ensure you have all the following rpms. Look at Figure 6-11 to ensure all the needed rpms are present. If not, mount the Red Hat 7.1 CD 1 and install the needed packages (use rpm -Uvh).

exam
ⓦatch

It is much easier to ensure you have all the tools needed when you install RedHat Linux than it is to try to remember the list of rpms needed. When you do any install, always ensure you do two things:

■ *Pick a Custom install. (This way you can pick the package sets that you wish to install.)*

■ *Ensure you always select kernel development and software development packages.*

By taking these two steps, you will save yourself a great deal of time and aggravation.

FIGURE 6-11

Checking for needed rpms when doing a kernel build

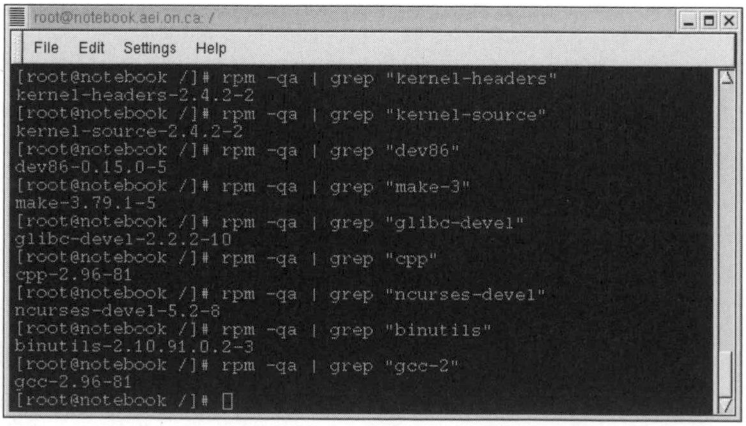

Understanding Kernel Version Numbers

The version number may look a little confusing, but it is actually very useful. For our example, we will use kernel version 2.4.2.

The first number (2) is the major version number. These are drastic changes to the kernel. Typically, older version stuff will *not* work in the newer version when this number changes. Kernel major version numbers are reserved for completely new kernel designs.

The second number (4) actually has two meanings. Firstly, it indicates this is the fourth major revision of major version 2 of the kernel. If this number is an even number, then the kernel release is believed to be a stable release. If it is an odd number, it is a developmental version.

The third number (2) is the minor version number for the kernel. These changes are typically small changes, bug fixes, security fixes, and enhancements.

Usually, software that has kernel version requirements will only refer to the first two major numbers. For example, you may install software that will only work with version 2.2 and later kernels. This would mean that all 2.2.*x* and later kernels would be required for this software. Older 2.0.x kernels would not likely be able to run this software (i.e., a third-party application such as a database).

Finally, it is common practice for Red Hat to tag an extra version number onto the kernel. This is used by Red Hat to indicate the revision level of the kernel (i.e., which revision of a 2.4.2 kernel) they have released. Red Hat extra version numbers always start with a dash.

The Kernel Configuration Scripts

There is a hidden file that contains all the kernel configuration information, /usr/src/linux/.config. It is structured as a listing of variables. Here are some entries from the .config file:

```
CONFIG_IP_MASQUERADE=y
CONFIG_IP_MASQUERADE_IPAUTOFW=m
# CONFIG_IP_ROUTER is not set
```

Here are the three main types of variables you'll see in this file. The first will compile in direct support (because of the "y"), the second entry will compile in support as a module (the "m"), and the third is commented out so this feature will be left out of the kernel we are building. You should never have to edit this file directly; there are many nicer ways to configure your kernel.

The bare minimum script used to configure a new kernel can be executed by running:

```
# cd /usr/src/linux
# make config
```

This script will prompt you through your different options. Here is a snippet of some output:

```
Processor family (386, 486/Cx486, 586/K5/5x86/6x86, Pentium/K6/TSC,
PPro/6x86MX) [386] 686
defined CONFIG_M586
Math emulation (CONFIG_MATH_EMULATION) [Y/n/?] n
MTRR (Memory Type Range Register) support (CONFIG_MTRR) [Y/n/?] n
Symmetric multi-processing support (CONFIG_SMP) [N/y/?] n
*
* Loadable module support
*
Enable loadable module support (CONFIG_MODULES) [Y/n/?] y
```

Here your variables are listed in parentheses and your answers are in brackets. The default answer is in capital letters. If you answer by hitting ?, then you will see a help page explaining what this option does. If you just press ENTER, the defaults will be accepted. Note that in Red Hat 7.1, there are 743 distinct settings and, consequently, you will be asked a question for each. This method of configuring a kernel is not used for this reason.

A nicer way to create the .config file is to use menuconfig. This requires you have ncurses installed. This is a text-based menu-driven system that makes changes to a kernel easier. To load this, simply type the following command:

```
# make menuconfig
```

Figure 6-12 shows what the screen will look like.

The nice thing about menuconfig is that it works very nicely over a Telnet connection. Also, there are options at the bottom of the menu to save the .config file to an alternate name as you exit the program.

The last way to make changes to the kernel is to use X-Window. You can generate a graphical menu system to configure your kernel by running make xconfig. Figure 6-13 shows the xconfig main menu.

Here you also have the ability to save to an alternate file. Screen shots in the following sections will show some of the options for the submenus.

FIGURE 6-12

The menuconfig main configuration menu

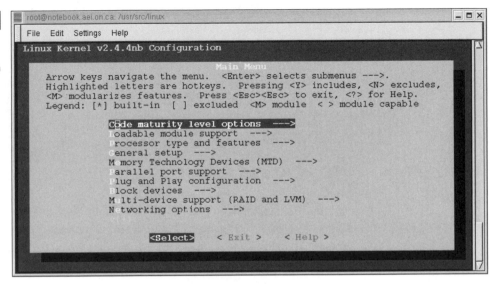

Understanding Kernel Configuration Options

You will need to understand some of the main kernel configuration options. To learn more, choose Help from one of the aforementioned configuration scripts for a more elaborate description on specific options.

FIGURE 6-13

The xconfig main menu

The Standard Red Hat Kernel Configuration

The standard distribution kernel supports just about everything. Almost every module that could be made is made. This is a big kernel and there are numerous modules that can be used for it with the standard installation. This is not a problem when installing, but it is highly recommended you streamline the distribution kernel and remove unwanted modules. All xconfig images displayed in this chapter are from the default Red Hat configuration.

Code Maturity Level Options

The Code maturity level option, shown in Figure 6-14, is used to enable prompting for kernel source code drivers not yet fully developed. These can be considered alpha-released drivers. These drivers are usually not ready for widespread use by uninformed administrators (in other words, the developers don't want e-mail saying there are still things that don't work).

Loadable Modules Support Options

The Loadable module support screen, shown in Figure 6-15, is where you enable the use of modules with your kernel. You also have the ability to enable the kernel to load modules for you. In such cases, the kernel will load a module when it is needed. Note: there is no reason to disable loadable module support. In fact, your kernel may not function properly if you disable this feature.

General Setup Options

Here are your general low-level options. Under General setup options, shown in Figure 6-16, you can turn support on or off for PCI, MicroChannel, and even SGI Visual Workstation. You can also specify your binary support. Linux comes preconfigured with support for most binary types (including old a.out format, the new ELF format, Java, and others). You should just accept the defaults here.

FIGURE 6-14

The Code maturity level submenu

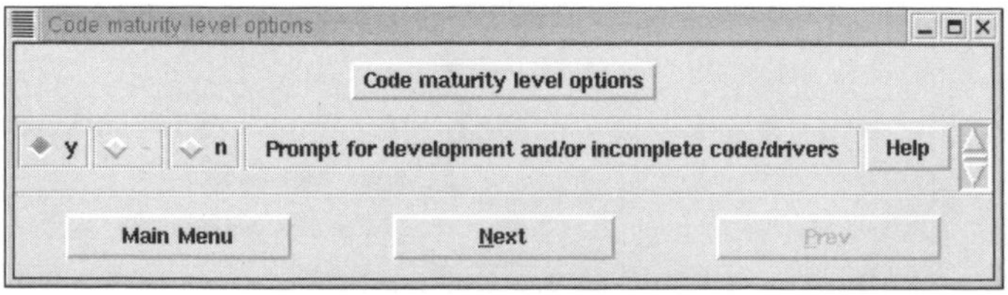

FIGURE 6-15

The Loadable
module support
submenu

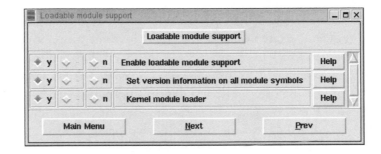

The MISC support allows the kernel to run a binary based on either a magic byte code at the beginning of the file (see /usr/src/linux/Documentation/binfmt_misc.txt), or based on the extension. For example, if you have the DOS emulator installed (DOSEMU), you could execute DOS programs from the command line. It will recognize the executable either by the magic number or the extension (e.g., .exe or .com).

Also in this section are the Advanced Power Management (APM) options. Here you can specify exactly how the BIOS APM will work with Linux. If you want the PC to turn off when booting, you can specify that here.

FIGURE 6-16

The General
setup submenu

ATA/IDE/MFM/RLL Support

These acronyms all relate to various implementations of PC style disk and CD-ROM interfaces. This menu, a new feature of Red Hat 7.1, is the primary configuration screen for enabling hard disk support and CD-ROM support. Previously, configuration for all mass storage devices was done using a single dialogue box.

Figure 6-17 shows the dialogue box for configuring disks.

The only reason you might disable support for these devices is if you were building a system that was entirely SCSI-based. Even then you would be well-advised to include support for these devices as modules.

Block Device Options

Here you specify your floppy devices and nonstandard hard disks, as shown in Figure 6-18. You can specify support for ATAPI CD-ROMs, tape drives, and even ATAPI floppy drives. You can also enable loopback support and network block support (which lets you use a physical disk on the network as if it is a local disk). If you have any parallel port devices such as external CD-ROMs or hard drives, you could enable support for those here. It should also be noted that RAM disk support is in this section.

Multi-device Support for RAID and LVM

This is a new section for 2.4 kernels. Here, you can configure logical volumes that span multiple disks. Note the support here for mirroring (RAID0), striping (RAID1), and striping with distributed parity (RAID5). Figure 6-19 shows the Multi-device support configuration screen.

Non-IDE/SCSI CD-ROM Support Options

If you have an older CD-ROM that is not an IDE or SCSI CD-ROM, then you need to enable special support for it, as shown in Figure 6-20. This section has many drivers

---

FIGURE 6-17

The ATA/IDE/MFM/R LL support dialog box

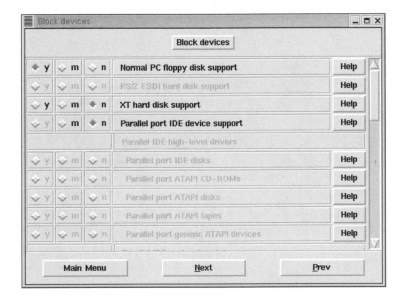

FIGURE 6-18

The Block devices submenu

for Mitsumi, Goldstar, Philips, Sony, SoundBlaster, and other old CD-ROM and disk types. All of these drivers can be loaded as modules. Note that this hardware was popular in the early and mid 1990s and was found typically on 486 class systems as well as early Pentium machines. These systems (because of their age) are not suitable for production work and should be configured only for experimentation (or pleasure).

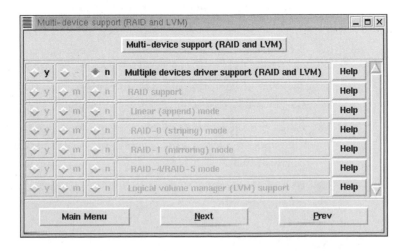

FIGURE 6-19

The Multi-device support configuration screen

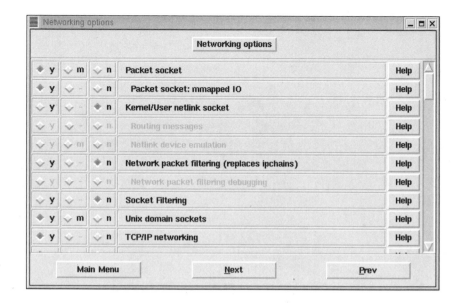

FIGURE 6-20

The old CD-ROM drivers submenu

Networking and Network Device Options

There are many options for networking in the Linux kernel, which we will now discuss in more detail. (Refer to Figures 6-21 through 6-23.)

■ **Packet Sockets and Kernel/User Netlinks** can be enabled to use low-level network programs. These programs typically do not use a network protocol and are usually packet sniffer applications, such as tcpdump and Ethereal. The Kernel/User netlink allows any user to read and write low-level packets to the network.

■ **Network Firewalls** allow you to set up a packet-level firewall. In addition, you will need to also enable IP Firewalling to use packet filtering. The IP Masquerading option also requires this to be enabled. It should be noted you cannot use fast switching with this option.

■ **Linux Socket Filtering** allows user programs to attach to a socket and filter their specific socket. This is based on the BSD-styled socket filtering, but is much simpler.

■ **IP Multicasting** allows you to set up a multicast server capable of participating on an MBONE. An MBONE is a high-bandwidth network that carries voice and video streams. You can also enable IP Multicast Routing if your server is a router.

■ **IP Kernel-Level Autoconfiguration** allows you to set up your IP address from either the command line when booting, or with BOOTP or RARP. You would also want this option if you want to boot your root file system with NFS.

■ **IP Firewalling** is used with the Network Firewalls option. You will need either ipchains(8) for version 2.2 and later, or ipfwadm(8) for older 2.0.x kernels. These programs usually come with the distribution of Linux.

■ **IP Firewall Packet Netlink Device** will create a user space device with rejected packets copied to it. By doing this, you could use a program to monitor this netlink device for attacks and appropriately respond.

■ **IP Transparent Proxy Support** allows for the router to secretly forward packets to a proxy server. This requires no additional setup for the clients since they just use the router as their gateway and the router forwards the packets. It also has a nice feature of using ipchains(8) to set up the forwarding rules. This would allow you to send only certain ports (port 80) to the proxy, and allow others without the proxy if you so desired.

■ **IP Masquerading** is very similar to the NAT routers. Masquerading allows one computer to masquerade as another. Typically, this is used by giving the router one valid IP address and using nonroutable internal IPs and masquerading the whole subnet out. This way, a private intranet could run with bogus IPs but appear to be fully connected to the Internet. You can also enable ICMP masquerading support, which will masquerade pings as well. You should likewise enable the special modules support. These additional modules allow for special communications to be masqueraded; for example, IRC, FTP passive connections, VDO live, and Quake.

■ **IP ipportfw masq support** allows you to redirect ports. For instance, say you have a masquerade server acting as a router for your company, but somebody wants to use their PC on the intranet side of the network for a Web server. You can redirect incoming packets on port 80 (Web port) transparently to the user's Web server. From the outside, it will appear as though the router is hosting the Web page instead of the internal user.

■ **IP optimize as router not host** should be enabled whenever you build a router. It will speed up routing by removing unnecessary packet checking.

■ **IP aliasing support** allows you to have multiple IPs on one network card. This can be used to host multiple Web servers on one PC, or to link two logical networks on your Ethernet. There is a mini-HOWTO on aliasing if you want to read more.

■ **IP TCP syncookie support** will protect you from SYN flooding attacks. These attacks are Denial-of-Service attacks that can severely slow down your server's network performance. Enabling syncookies will prevent this type of attack from occurring. After compiling this option, you will also need to issue the following command:

```
echo 1 >/proc/sys/net/ipv4/tcp_syncookies
```

■ **IP Reverse ARP** will allow your server to answer RARP requests from diskless workstations. These are typical Sun 3 machines and diskless Linux boxes. You can also use additional protocols such as IPv6, IPX, AppleTalk, X.25, and LAPD.

■ **Compile in WAN router support.** This will cut the cost of a typically high-priced WAN router in half. All you'll need is a WAN interface card, the WAN-tools package, and to enable this option to build a WAN router.

■ **Fast switching** is an option that allows you to connect two computers directly together with a network cable. This is an extremely fast way for two computers to communicate. This option is not compatible with IP FIREWALL, but it will work with the IP ADVANCED ROUTER options.

■ **QoS and/or fair queuing** allows you to set up decision rules for which packet to route. Enabling this option can give you many different ways of determining which packets you'll route and which you will queue or drop. This can allow for priority IPs to always get certain bandwidths, while at the same time forcing other IPs to use bandwidth consumption limits. QoS stands for Quality of Service and is currently being used, so people who pay more, get more. In the network device section, you can enable traffic shaping to limit outbound bandwidth.

■ **A wide range of network cards are supported.** You should typically only choose the network card that is in your machine, or network cards you are likely to use in the future.

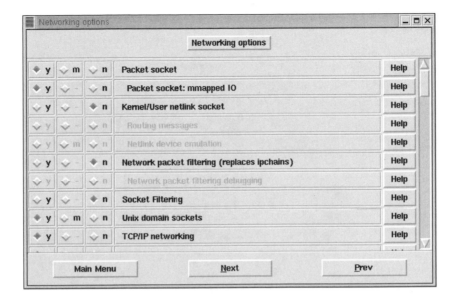

FIGURE 6-21

The Network
Options submenu

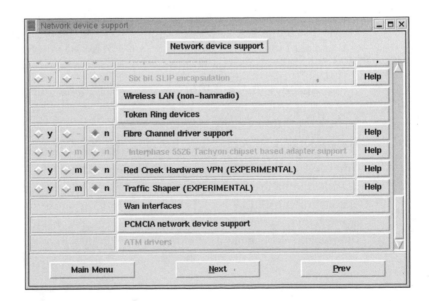

- **Other network devices are also supported,** such as T-1 cards, pocket network adapters, FDDI adapters, HIPPI adapters, Frame Relay DLCI, and wireless LAN cards.

FIGURE 6-22

The Network
device support
submenu

FIGURE 6-23

Another view of network device support showing submenus for PCMCIA network cards, WAN interfaces, and others

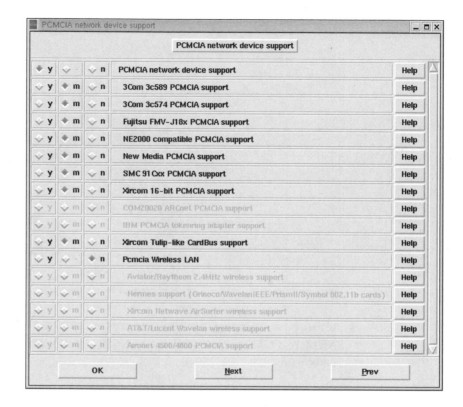

- **You can also encapsulate AppleTalk into IP, or vice versa.** This can allow your Linux box to be a gateway on a MAC-only network. Note: You can only choose one type of encapsulation.

- **SLIPP, PLIP, and PPP support** are all chosen under the network device support section.

SCSI Support Options and Low-level Drivers

You can enable SCSI hard disks, tape drivers, and CD-ROM support in this section, as shown in Figure 6-24. If you have a SCSI CD-ROM jukebox, you may have to enable probing all LUNs to force the controller to probe for multiple LUNs. There is a section for verbose SCSI error reporting. This section adds about 12K to the kernel, but it makes debugging SCSI errors easier. You may want to enable specific low-level SCSI support for your controller and disable all others, as shown in Figure 6-25.

FIGURE 6-24

The SCSI support
options submenu

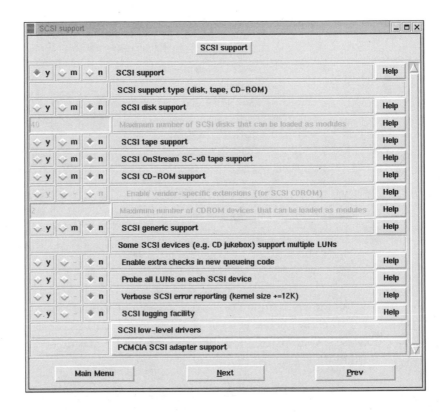

This will save a lot of room and improve your loading. If you have an ADAPTEC controller, you should disable all other controllers in your config file.

Note that Red Hat Linux 7.1 includes support for high-end hardware RAID-enabled SCSI host adapters, including 64-bit PCI adapters. Popular Adaptec adapters can be seen in the screen, but by scrolling down you can also find support for AMI, Mylex, and Compaq controllers, as well as controllers from other vendors.

ISDN Options

Integrated Services Digital Networks (ISDN) lines are fairly popular and inexpensive high-speed digital lines. Adding ISDN support will allow you to use an ISDN card for inbound or outbound dialing connections. The ISDN device has a built-in AT-compatible modem emulator, autodial, channel-bundling, callback, and caller-authentication without the need for an external daemon to be running.

FIGURE 6-25

The SCSI low-level drivers submenu

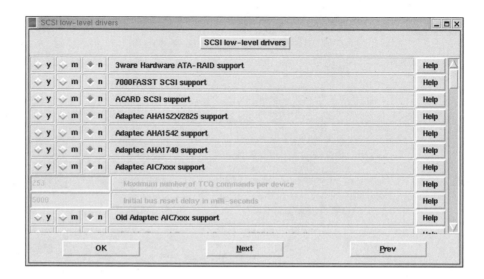

As shown in Figure 6-26, you can enable synchronous Point-to-Point Protocol (PPP) connections. You will need to download IPPPD to take advantage of this feature. With synchronous PPP and support for generic MP, you can bundle multiple ISDN lines together to increase your bandwidth.

FIGURE 6-26

The ISDN subsystem

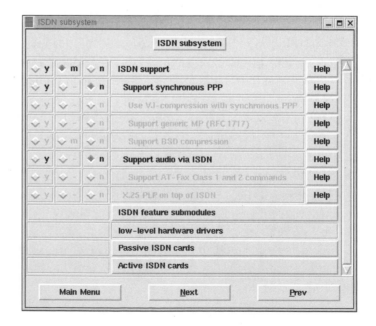

File System Options

The file system subsection is a list of all the different types of file systems Linux supports. Select the Quota option if you need to support quotas. You can also compile in the kernel automounter here. The menu for selecting supported file systems is presented in Figure 6-27.

Because Linux supports so many different hardware platforms, it includes support for most file system types. However, some vendors choose not to publish the specifications for their file systems and consequently the Linux implementers can never be sure they have faithfully implemented the file system. Please read the Help information associated with any file systems you feel you need. However, if you are using only Linux file system types (e.g., ext2 file systems) or foreign, but well-documented file systems (e.g., DOS FAT or VFAT) then you should have no problem reading and writing to these file systems. Table 6-1 lists some of the different file systems.

Character Device Options

Character devices are devices that work in a byte stream format. This includes real hardware devices (such as serial ports) or software only devices, such as virtual consoles or pseudo-ttys. The Character device submenu, shown in Figure 6-28, is where you can specify support for a wide variety of devices, including virtual terminals, serial ports, newer AGP video cards, mice, joysticks, non-SCSI tape drives, and many others. Support for parallel devices has its own submenu.

FIGURE 6-27

The file system submenu

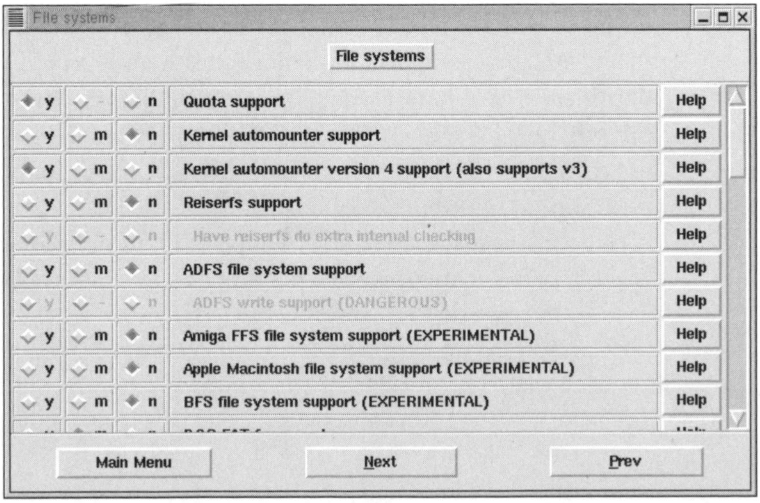

TABLE 6-1	File System	Description
Supported File System Reference	ADFS	(read-only) RiscOS file system
	Amiga FFS	AmigaOS
	Apple Macintosh	Macintosh file system
	MS-DOS	Old-style DOS file system
	VFAT	Windows 95/98 file system
	UMSDOS	UNIX file system on top of an MS-DOS file system
	ISO 9660/Microsoft Joliet CD-ROM	CD-ROM file system
	Minix	Old Linux file system, usually found on old floppies
	NTFS	(read-only or read/write) NT's file system. Because the implementation details of this file system are proprietary, Linux cannot guarantee to be able to write reliably to NTFS file systems. Best to mount these read-only.
	OS/2 HPFS	(read-only) OS/2s file system
	QNX	(read-only or read/write) QNX 4 file system
	ROM	(read-only) Small read-only file system
	Second extended file system	(Ext2) Linux standard file system
	UFS	(read-only or read/write) *BSD and NextStep file system

Many different types of standard or smart serial boards are supported. You can enable serial port support and reroute all system-level messages to it by disabling the console on virtual terminal support and enabling the console on serial port support. This will send all system-level messages to your serial port and your active terminal (use console=ttyS1 at bootup to turn this off). In addition, this section supports a wide range of multiport serial boards.

You can also enable Unix98 PTY support. This will allow you to leave the traditional pseudo terminal naming convention of ptyXX to a more elaborate naming convention. The Unix98 naming convention has a directory where all the devices are stored (/dev/pts/xxx). You will need to choose Yes to the /dev/pts file system for Unix98 option as well. The new pseudo terminals will now be created on-the-fly as pts/XXX; /dev/ttyp3 becomes pts/3. You can specify the maximum number of

FIGURE 6-28

The Character
device submenu

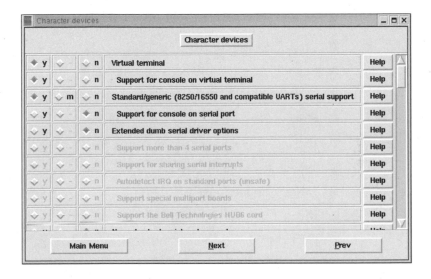

Unix98 (the default is 256). Each additional set of 256 will use around 8Kb of
kernel memory on a 32-bit architecture.

You can also enable Watchdog timer support. What this option will do is force the
kernel to write to the /dev/watchdog file. If it fails to do this every minute, the server
will reboot. You can enable either software support for Watchdog timers, or use a
Watchdog hardware card. Watchdog cards are much more reliable. This option could
be useful for a network server, such as a router, that needs to be online as much as
possible. This way, if a flood of packets or something has caused the kernel to lock
up, the router will simply reboot itself at the specified interval. In reality though, it
is unlikely you would need to set this option.

If you have a video card or a TV card, there is a whole section in the 2.4 kernels for
you. You can even directly compile in support for basic QuickCams and Mediavision
Pro Movie Studio cards.

If you have a floppy tape drive (QIC drive), then you will need to enable Ftape
support. If you forget to add this option, you will not be able to use your tape drive.

Sound System Support Options

Most popular sound cards are supported by Linux. These include:

- Ensoniq QudioPCI
- S3 SonicVibes

- Turtle Beach MultiSound Classic and Pinnacle
- ProAudioSpectrum 16
- SoundBlaster and 100 percent compatible
- Generic OPL2/OPL3 FM synthesizer
- Gravis Untrasound
- PSS
- Microsoft Sound System
- Ensoniq SoundScape
- MediaTrix AudioTrix Pro
- OPTi MAD16 (Mozart)
- Crystal CS4232-based PnP cards
- Yamaha OPL3-SAx-based PnP cards
- Aztech Sound Galaxy (non-PnP)
- Support for AD1816 cards
- Loopback MIDI
- 6850 UART
- ACI mixer
- AWE32 synch
- And many others

Cards that emulate any of those in the preceding list (in hardware only) can be used. Check the Sound submenu for the latest list of supported hardware for your kernel. If you have a card not named in the previous list, try to see if it emulates any card on the list. Many proprietary cards do emulate products from SoundBlaster or offer OPL/2 or OPL/3 compatibility. However, if your card was made for Windows and it needs to load a driver before it offers compatibility, chances are it won't work with Linux. When in doubt, purchase a quality, name brand card. Figure 6-29 shows the configuration screen for the Sound submenu.

FIGURE 6-29

The Sound
submenu

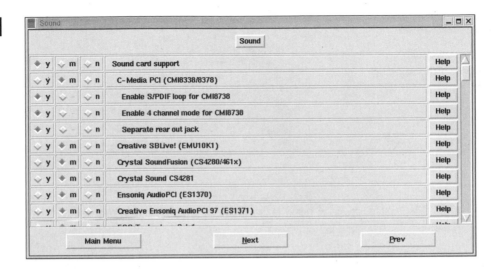

Parallel Ports

Parallel ports now have their own submenu (Figure 6-30). They were previously grouped
into the Character Devices submenu. In this dialogue box, you provide details on the
type of parallel port hardware you have, including the level of compatibility you wish
to support (e.g., standard port, EPP, or ECP). Multiple parallel port devices are
supported (i.e., LPT1, LPT2, and LPT3 can all be present at the same time). However,
parallel ports require kernel resources (i/o ports and interrupts), take up precious
card slots, and do not perform as fast as network attached printers. For this reason,
most Linux administrators typically go with just the standard parallel port that comes
built in to your system.

Compiling and Installing a Custom Kernel

After setting up all the options you want and saving your changes, you then need to
compile your kernel. The following is a list of things you should do to successfully
compile your kernel:

1. **cd /usr/src/linux**   This command will bring you to the proper directory. All
   of your commands should be issued from here. Note that in the procedures
   that follow, we will use /usr/src/linux as the base directory of your kernel.
   This implies that we have correctly set up this symbolic link to point to the
   correct kernel source tree.

FIGURE 6-30

The parallel port support dialogue box

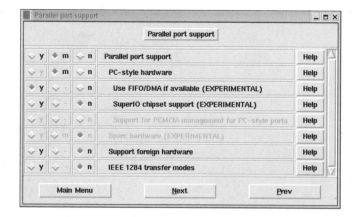

2. Edit line 4 of /usr/src/linux/Makefile. Change the definition for EXTRAVERSION=-2 to something that uniquely identifies your kernel. We'll use EXTRAVERSION=-2rh (for Red Hat) as an example. Use your initials, the month/day of your build, anything to uniquely define this kernel. Later on, we'll build a map of the kernel so modules can load, using the name you select here. Be sure to remember what you entered!

3. **make mrproper**   This command will ensure your source is in a consistent and clean state.

4. Save your old configuration file. Rebuilding the kernel involves making a new /usr/src/linux/.config. If you change your mind and choose to abandon your changes, it is nice to have a copy that is known to work. Red Hat ships with a standard config file located in configs/kernel-2.4.2-i686.config. Copy that to the default configuration file for your architecture. Use **cp configs/kernel-2.4.2-i686.config arch/i386/defconfig**.

5. Now, install the standard configuration into /usr/src/linux/.config. Use **make oldconfig**.

6. Customize your /usr/src/linux/.config file. Use the **make config** command, which will run the text-based configuration script. You can also issue **make menuconfig** for an ncurses menu configuration script, or run **make xconfig** to use the X-Window configuration tool.

7. **make dep**   This command will set up all your dependencies correctly. This takes the settings present in /usr/src/linux/.config and pushes them down into the correct source code sub-directory.

8. **make bzImage**   This command creates a gzip compressed kernel image file. There are a few other options besides bzImage you can use here that are discussed next. Note that this was called **make zImage** on 2.0.x kernels.

9. This is where kernel compilation actually takes place. This can be a fairly time-consuming process. On a 386 or 486, you will probably have to let it compile all night. On a Pentium 166, it will take approximately 30 to 45 minutes. If you have a Pentiun III or Pentium IV, it will probably take less than 15 minutes to compile your new kernel. Be patient, your system must recompile hundreds of megabytes of program code!

10. Now we need to build our modules (you did include kernel module support didn't you?). Use **make modules** to build all your modules.

11. With our kernel now built, we need to move it to /boot before we can boot from it. Use
    cp /usr/src/linux/arch/i386/boot/bzImage/boot/vmlinuz-2.4.2-2rh.

12. Now we need to install our newly made modules, which will install all your loadable modules into /lib/modules/2.4.2-2rh to correspond with the release and EXTRAVERSION setting of your kernel. If this name already exists, the new modules will overwrite your existing modules. This could render both your old kernel and your new kernel unbootable. Always be sure to set a unique EXTRAVERSION value for each kernel. Use **make modules_intall** to install your modules.

If you already have a kernel up and running, and you want to add support for another device but you didn't create the module for it, you can simply re-run the configurator. Start it (using make menuconfig or make xconfig), select your new module, and choose M for module support for the device. Next, run **make modules** then **make modules_install**. After that, you can immediately load the modules with modprobe or insmod. This will save a lot of time by just compiling the missing module. If the module fails, try modprobe * to load all modules with dependency checking.

Building a kernel is an involved process but it follows a standard pattern. It is very important you become familiar with kernel construction procedures and troubleshooting. Refer to the following Scenario & Solution for some common problems encountered and their recommended solutions.

SCENARIO & SOLUTION

You looked under /usr/src/ but did not see the Linux kernel source code. What did you do wrong?	You did not install the kernel source code. Install the kernel-source rpm or download a new kernel from www.kernel.org, or from ftp.redhat.com.
You configured the kernel as a monolithic kernel, but when you run make bzImage, it fails, saying the kernel is too big. What should you do?	You must reconfigure your kernel to use modules. There are limits on the size of a compressed kernel, so you should always build a modular kernel.
You can't find your new kernel.	Were you sure to use the kernel's extra version initials at every step of the process? If not, then you may not be able to correctly locate the kernel or it's modules.

Post-build Procedures

There are still some more steps that must be completed before you can use your new kernel. These include:

- Building support for an initial ram disk (to be used at boot time)
- Copying the remaining files to /boot

The mkinitrd command is used to create an initial RAM disk image for you. This image is reloaded when the kernel first boots. The initial RAM disk (initrd) is usually used to load essential block devices such as SCSI disk driver modules that are not part of a stock Red Hat kernel during boot time. For example, if you use a high-end, hardware RAID controller, you don't get automatic support for it in a stock kernel. While we can load the driver as a module, only stock kernel features are available during boot up. This would render the disks on our controller inaccessible. To solve the problem, we make a RAM disk, which is used to load our kernel image, a mini-root file system and all our kernel's loadable drivers (including our required SCSI driver). Then, when we boot, the initial RAM disk is loaded, our driver module is loaded, and the boot-up process can continue.

This command automatically loads all SCSI devices found in the /etc/conf.modules, as well as all other modules specified by /etc/conf.modules.

To make your initial RAM disk, use the command:

```
# mkinitrd /boot/initrd 2.4.2-2rh.img 2.4.2-2rh
```

This installs your initial RAM disk on the /boot file system.

Next, we need to copy the new kernel's symbol table to the /boot partition. Use:

```
# cp /usr/src/linux/System.map /boot/System.map-2.4.2-2rh
```

And finally, it is a good idea to keep a copy of your /usr/src/linux/.config file on the /boot partition as well (as new runs of menuconfig or xconfig could change your configuration significantly). Copy your config file with:

```
# cp /usr/src/linux/.config /boot/config-2.4.2-2rh
```

Updating LILO

The last step to perform is to configure the Linux boot manager, LILO, to use your new kernel. To do this, you first need to copy the kernel image to the /boot directory as shown in the previous section above. Next you edit the /etc/lilo.conf file and add a section that describes our new kernel. Warning: never delete your old kernel's configuration from either /boot or /etc/lilo.conf until you have tested your new kernel. Prematurely deleting your old kernel may give you an opportunity to test how well you know how to perform a recovery of a failed system!

Here is the original /etc/lilo.conf file before we edit it:

```
boot=/dev/had
map=/boot/map
install=/boot/boot.b
prompt
timeout=50
message=/boot/message
linear
default=linux

image=/boot/vmlinuz-2.4.2-2
      label=linux
      read-only
      root=/dev/hda2
other=/dev/hda1
      label=dos
```

From this information, you can see the original kernel is called vmlinuz-2.4.2-2 and reside on the second partition (hda2) of our primary disk (hda). Notice that we have a DOS file system on partition one. LILO resides on the MBR of the first disk and controls the boot process.

The default image to boot is the one whose label matches the default= setting at the top of the file. In this case, we boot the label linux, by default. You would now need to add another image section to point to the new kernel. The changes are in bold:

```
boot=/dev/hda
map=/boot/map
install=/boot/boot.b
prompt
timeout=50
message=/boot/message
linear
default=linux

image=/boot/vmlinuz-2.4.2-2
     label=linux
     read-only
     root=/dev/hda2

image=/boot/vmlinuz-2.4.2-2rh
     label=newLinux
     read-only
     root=/dev/hda2

other=/dev/hda1
     label=dos
```

Save this file, then run **/sbin/lilo -v.** The output should resemble the following:

```
LILO version 21.4-4, Copyright (C) 1992-1998 Werner Almesberger
'lba32' extensions Copyright (C) 1999,2000 John Coffman

Reading boot sector from /dev/hda
Merging with /boot/boot.b
Mapping message file /boot/message
Boot image: /boot/vmlinuz-2.4.2-2
Added linux
Boot image: /boot/vmlinuz-2.4.2-2rh
Added newLinux
Boot other: /dev/hda1, on /dev/hda, loader /boot/chain.b
Added dos
/boot/boot.0300 exists - no backup copy made.
Writing boot sector.
```

When you reboot, LILO will wait for you to enter a label. If you don't enter anything, or you just press ENTER, the image with the label linux will load. You would need to specifically select your new kernel (label newLinux) to get it to boot. This was done intentionally so your machine doesn't boot the new, untested kernel by default. If the new kernel doesn't work, then all you have to do is reboot the system and let LILO run the old kernel. Additionally, if your new kernel isn't entirely stable and reboots when you aren't present, you won't have to worry about it hanging on the boot.

mkbootdisk

mkbootdisk is a utility that can create a bootdisk for you. This is basically a rescue disk. After creating this disk, it can be used to simply boot your system, or you can type **rescue** at the LILO prompt. The only option you need to specify when using this command is the kernel version. Table 6-2 lists a few other options that may come in handy when creating a bootdisk with this command.

Here is an example of the mkbootdisk command:

mkbootdisk –device /dev/fd1 –verbose –noprompt 2.4.2-2rh

This will tell mkbootdisk to create a bootdisk on the second floppy drive. It will not suppress output and it will not prompt for a disk to be inserted. It will use kernel version 2.4.2-2rh. Note that mkbootdisk is not loaded as part of a standard Red Hat installation. To get it, you would have to use:

```
# mount /dev/cdrom /mnt
# cd /mnt/RedHat/RPMS
# rpm -Uvh mkbootdisk*
```

When using this disk, you can also type **rescue** at the LILO prompt to use the disk as a rescue disk.

TABLE 6-2	Command	Description
mkbootdisk options reference	–device <device file>	Specifies where to put the image.
	–mkinitrdargs <args>	Passes arguments to mkinitrd.
	–noprompt	Won't prompt to insert a disk.
	–verbose	Normally, mkbootdisk has no output. This command turns the output on.

exam
ⓦatch
A significant portion of the practical exam tests your ability to recover a system that has failed in some way. While I am sworn to secrecy on the exact nature of the problems you will encounter (this is the truth!), I can say that being able to make and use rescue disks is a very important Linux administration skill.

CERTIFICATION OBJECTIVE 6.04

PAM

PAM stands for Pluggable Authentication Modules. It provides a centralized authentication capability for most Linux services, and is used to create and enforce access restrictions. PAM is not very useful in a single-user environment or where the users are all on a trusted network. But PAM is perfect for a multiuser system, or for systems connected to untrusted networks (such as the Internet). PAM allows for more granularity in defining security. You can use PAM to manage access to certain resources with means that are not actually coded into the program. For example, you can have pppd authenticate users with a Novell or NT user database instead of the /etc/password or /etc/shadow file provided by Linux.

The PAM configuration files are kept in /etc/pam.d/. In older versions this was one file: /etc/pam.conf. Here is a sample /etc/pam.d directory listing for Red Hat 7.1:

```
adsl-config      kde              ppp             su
chfn             kppp             printconf-gui   system-auth
chsh             kscreensaver     reboot          system-auth.rpmnew
firewall-config  linuxconf        rexec           up2date
ftp              linuxconf-auth   rhn_register    up2date-config
gdm              linuxconf-pair   rlogin          up2date-nox
gnorpm-auth      login            rp3-config      xcdroast
halt             netcfg           rsh             xdm
internet-config  other            samba           xscreensaver
isdn-config      passwd           smtp            xserver
kbdrate          poweroff         sshd
```

These files are text configuration files telling PAM what authentication steps are required for the named applications. The syntax for these configuration files is as follows, using the FTP file as an example:

```
# cat ftp
#%PAM-1.0
```

```
auth        required   /lib/security/pam_listfile.so item=user
                       sense=deny file=/etc/ftpusers onerr=succeed
auth        required   /lib/security/pam_stack.so service=system-auth
auth        required   /lib/security/pam_shells.so
account     required   /lib/security/pam_stack.so service=system-auth
session     required   /lib/security/pam_stack.so service=system-auth
#
```

The older way of configuring the PAM modules was with the /etc/pam.conf file. The syntax of this file has the following form:

```
service-name   module-type control-flag   module-path arguments
```

As you can see, it is almost identical except that you need to specify a service name. This is because there is only one file that contains all the different services, while the directory system's filename tells the system which service the rules will apply to. Note that the /etc/pam.conf file is deprecated and no longer used in Red Hat 7.x.

Table 6-3 gives a brief description of the purpose of each column.

Table 6-4 contains PAM module type keywords with their respective meanings.

After selecting the module type, we must be able to determine how the test applies to the overall success of our authentication process. That is, is this one part of a larger test, is this test sufficient in and of itself, or is the test just optional. Table 6-5 contains a list of control flags with an explanation of their meaning.

PAM has many authentication tests. Each performs a unique authentication task and/or authorizes certain behavior. Again, PAM libraries are found in /lib/security. Table 6-6 is a quick reference list of the modules you can use with PAM and a brief description on how to use them.

TABLE 6-3	Column	Description
Column Definitions for PAM Configuration Files	Service-name	The name of the program for which the PAM configuration record applies. Not used in Red Hat 7.x
	Module-type	Must be either auth, account, session, or password
	Control-flag	Must be either required, requisite, sufficient, or optional
	Module-path	The absolute path to the PAM module responsible for managing this service. PAM modules usually live in /lib/security
	Arguments	The arguments for the PAM module. These are module-specific and can reference files, usernames, other PAM services, how to determine success or failure, and more.

TABLE 6-4	Keyword	Meaning
Module Type Keyword Reference	auth	The auth keyword instructs PAM to prompt for user identification.
	account	Account-based restrictions apply. The user must have an account on the system. User and Group IDs are tracked.
	session	Session-oriented limits are enforced (such as maximum file size, number of processes, and so on). Other session-based activities may be performed (such as logging).
	password	Sets tests for password management, including how validity is determined (e.g., are null passwords allowed), how passwords are hashed, is the /etc/shadow file used. This can also be used to test password strength by enforcing password lengths and randomness.

PAM services are designed to stack on top of each other. That way, a base policy can be set and then modified as needed by individual services. The base policy is set by the file /etc/pam.d/system-auth. Here is Red Hat 7.1's version of that file:

```
# cat /etc/pam.d/system-auth
#%PAM-1.0
# This file is auto-generated.
# User changes will be destroyed the next time authconfig is run.
auth        required      /lib/security/pam_env.so
auth        sufficient    /lib/security/pam_unix.so likeauth nullok
auth        required      /lib/security/pam_deny.so

account     required      /lib/security/pam_unix.so

password    required      /lib/security/pam_cracklib.so retry=3
password    sufficient    /lib/security/pam_unix.so nullok use_authtok
md5 shadow
password    required      /lib/security/pam_deny.so

session     required      /lib/security/pam_limits.so
session     required      /lib/security/pam_unix.so
```

The system-auth file sets the minimum tests required for each module type. For example, for the password module type (used for enforcing password update policies), we would need to pass the pam_cracklib.so test when changing our password. If our password is not strong enough (too close to our login name, a dictionary word, is too short, and so on) to be accepted after three tries, the password change operation fails. The next test performed would be the pam_unix.so test. This module is given the

TABLE 6-5	Control Flag	Meaning
Control Flag Reference	required	This test must succeed for the authentication process to complete successfully. There may be many required flags that must all succeed before a user is granted access.
	requisite	The test must succeed. Requisite is used when one test is sufficient.
	sufficient	This test is all that's needed to determine success or failure. Other tests may be present, but they will not be executed if this test passes.
	optional	This option plays no role in determining the overall success or failure of the authentication test. It is merely present as an additional test.

null_ok argument (allowing accounts with no passwords), use_authtok (to generate user authentication tokens), md5 (for stronger password hashing than traditional UNIX systems), and shadow (to update the user's account record in /etc/shadow with their new encrypted password).

Now, let's look at how a service might use these base settings. Here's the /etc/pam.d/rlogin file:

```
# cat /etc/pam.d/rlogin
#%PAM-1.0
# For root login to succeed here with pam_securetty, "rlogin" must be
# listed in /etc/securetty.
auth        required     /lib/security/pam_nologin.so
auth        required     /lib/security/pam_securetty.so
auth        required     /lib/security/pam_env.so
auth        sufficient   /lib/security/pam_rhosts_auth.so
auth        required     /lib/security/pam_stack.so service=system-auth
account     required     /lib/security/pam_stack.so service=system-auth
password    required     /lib/security/pam_stack.so service=system-auth
session     required     /lib/security/pam_stack.so service=system-auth
```

The only line for password management states that it is required that the /lib/security/pam_stack.so module pass. This module is used to indicate that we defer our tests to another configuration file. In this case, the service=system-auth tells us that passing the password tests in the /etc/pam.d/system-auth file are all that's needed for an rlogin user to change their password.

However, this is not the case for the auth module type. Our rlogin file states that we must pass the pam_nologin test, the pam_securetty test, and the pam_env test. Then it is sufficient for us to pass the pam_rhosts test (that is, if we are recognized

TABLE 6-6   PAM Library Reference

Module	Description
pam_chroot	Allows programs to change the root directory to somewhere under the real root directory. This is used by programs like anonymous FTP to ensure that unidentified users cannot go outside of /var/ftp.
pam_cracklib	This runs password strength tests found in cracklib. Tests include password length, randomness, use of special characters, dictionary tests, permutations on usernames, and so on.
pam_deny	Denies access to a service.
pam_env	Control a user's environmental variables.
pam_filter	Can invoke a terminal filter program.
pam_ftp	Allows for anonymous FTP mode access.
pam_group	Grants group access to the user by checking the /etc/group file.
pam_krb4	Authenticates using Kerberos 4.
pam_lastlog	Displays where the user lasted logged in from.
pam_limits	Limits the system resources that can be obtained.
pam_listfile	Allows access based on names in a file. FTP uses this to make sure that system accounts (such as root) cannot be attacked via the FTP service by listing all users who are denied FTP use in the /etc/ftpusers file. This mechanism is flexible enough so that any file of users can be created. This list can identify users who can (or cannot) use the service.
pam_mail	Checks for new mail.
pam_nologin	Denies Telnet or rlogin access if the /etc/nologin exists.
pam_permit	Always permits access.
pam_radius	Authenticates via a RADIUS server.
pam_rhost_auth	Authenticates via traditional rlogin styles by checking against the /etc/hosts.equiv file or the ~/.rhosts file.
pam_rootok	Permits root access without a password.
pam_securetty	Checks the /etc/securetty file to see if a privileged user (e.g., root) is permitted to log in from a terminal. This is used to enforce root logins only to physically trusted terminals such as the console.
pam_time	Restricts access based on time.
pam_warn	Logs information about the session.
pam_wheel	Provides root access if the user is a member of the wheel group.

by either /etc/hosts.equiv or ~/.rhosts). If we pass, we are in (because this test is sufficient). If we don't pass this test, then we must pass all additional auth tests found in the system-auth module (because of the pam_stack.so service=system-auth).

When validating a rule, PAM uses the following logic:

■ If a sufficient control flag is passed, the user is immediately granted access.

■ If a requisite control flag is passed, the user is also granted immediate access.

Otherwise, if any required or sufficient control flag fails a test, then PAM continues with all additional authentication checks. It is afterward that access is denied. The purpose for this is that some checks leave indications on the screen that they have run (e.g., a login prompt, a password prompt). If PAM were to stop at the first failure, then a clever user could deduce how they failed and possibly gain insight into how to attack your system.

The authconfig program sets basic system policies. Figure 6-31 is a shot of the second screen of this program.

Note that it gives us the option of using both shadow passwords (/etc/shadow) and MD5 hashing. (Both are strongly recommended.) Authconfig rewrites the /etc/pam.d/system-auth file each time it is run, so you should not make changes directly to that file.

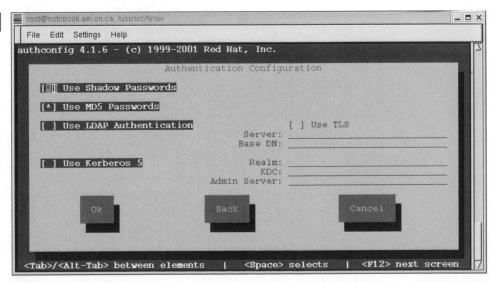

FIGURE 6-31

The second screen of authconfig, where password policies are set

PAM can be complex, but it can also greatly contribute to your system's security. For more information on configuring PAM, try this URL: http://www.sun.com/software/solaris/pam.

Also, you may want to install the HOW-TOs and check there as well.

exam
ⓦatch

Like most configuration Linux services, PAM is very sensitive to configuration file errors in spelling or format. Please edit these files carefully.

EXERCISE 6-1

Permitting Access to the FTP Service for Only a Limited List of Users

We want to permit access to the FTP service to only a limited list of users. Normally, FTP is available to anyone whose name is not in the /etc/ftpusers file. This is traditional UNIX behavior, but it assumes that most users will get access to FTP. By default, the /etc/ftpusers file contains only the account names of the system accounts created when Linux is installed.

Here is what our /etc/pam.d/ftp file looks like before we edit it:

```
# cat ftp
#%PAM-1.0
auth         required      /lib/security/pam_listfile.so item=user
                           sense=deny file=/etc/ftpusers onerr=succeed
auth         required      /lib/security/pam_stack.so service=system-auth
auth         required      /lib/security/pam_shells.so
account      required      /lib/security/pam_stack.so service=system-auth
session      required      /lib/security/pam_stack.so service=system-auth
```

We want to allow users tom, dick, and harriet access to FTP but no one else. To do this employ the following steps:

1. Make a new file called /etc/myftpusers. Put tom, dick, and harriet's name in the file.

2. The first line says that to gain access to FTP, we must pass the auth rule that requires a name to be in a list. The file is /etc/ftpusers. Since we want a custom list, we would need to change this filename to /etc/myftpusers.

3. The test sense is set to Deny. That means that if the username is in the file, they are denied access. We would need to change Deny to Allow to permit only users in our /etc/myftpusers file access.

4. The final edit needed is to remove the onerr=succeed directive. This says that users are allowed in if the test fails! Since we need our test to succeed at limiting users, we should remove this directive.

That's it! You should now be able to test your configuration and verify that our three users can use FTP, but no one else can.

CERTIFICATION OBJECTIVE 6.05

The cron System

The cron(8) system will allow the administrator or any user to schedule jobs to run at given intervals. A daemon runs named crond, which searches the /var/spool/cron directory under each user's name every minute to see if there is anything to do. Note that this behavior (in Linux's cron) is different from commercial UNIX's cron where the cron daemon only wakes up when it needs to launch a program.

crond also searches the /etc/crontab file as well as the files in /etc/cron.d. These files are not intended to be edited in the directory. You should use the crontab(1) command to edit (crontab -e), view (crontab -l), or delete (crontab -d) these files. You can allow users to utilize crontab or deny it from them. If the /etc/cron.allow file exists, then only users who are in this file may use crontab. If cron.allow does not exist, but cron.deny does, then the users listed in cron.deny *cannot* use crontab. If neither file exists, then anyone can use cron.

The cron daemon checks the crontab files every minute to see if they have been changed. If they have, it will reread all the cron entries.

exam
ⓦatch

Because cron always checks for changes, you do NOT have to restart cron every time you make a change.

The System crontab and Components

The crontab command is used to edit the cron files. Several options are available, including:

- **-u \<user\>**   Specifies a user's crontab to edit. If you are using su(8) to switch users, then you should always use the -u option.

- **-l**   Lists the current entries in the crontab file.

- **-r**   Removes the cron entries.

- **-e**   Edits an existing crontab entry using the editor specified in the VISUAL or EDITOR variables.

The crontab file has a certain format. Each line can be blank, a comment (#), a variable, or a command. Blank lines and comment lines (those that begin with #) are ignored. You cannot have a comment in a command line.

You can set environmental variables with the following syntax:

```
Variable=Value
```

Some variables are already set for you: HOME is your home directory, SHELL is the user's default shell, and LOGNAME is your username. HOME and SHELL can be overwritten; LOGNAME can't.

on the
Job

A handy variable to set is the MAILTO variable. If the MAILTO variable is set and is not a NULL value, then the cron daemon will send output via mail to the intended target. This can be useful if you are scheduling jobs for services such as UUCP or have another mail account you check more frequently. You could easily add the line: MAILTO=me@somewhere.com to reroute all cron messages for that user to another mail account. If this variable is not set, then mail will be sent to the user running the command.

Here is the format of a line in the crontab:

```
#minute, hour, day of month, month, day of week, command
*       *       *               *       *           command
```

Commands are the heart of what cron does. Table 6-7 provides a list of valid values for the specified fields.

TABLE 6-7	**Field**	**Value**

Field	Value
Minute	The minute of the hour from 0-59
Hour	The hour of the day in military time: 0-23
Day of month	In the range of 1-31
Month	The month of the year by number: 1-12
Day of week	0-6 with Sunday being day 0 and Saturday as day 6

cron
Configuration
Reference

For those fields we do not care about, use an asterisk (*). If you omit the value entirely, you would have too few fields on the line and your job would likely not be executed.

cron permits ranges of values and collections of discrete values as well. For example, if I wanted something to execute at 7:00 A.M., 8:00 A.M., 9:00 A.M., and 10:00 A.M., I could use the range 7-10 in the hour-of-day field. Comma-separated lists are also valid entries. I could execute a job every five minutes by using a list like: 0,5,10,15,20,25,30,35,40,45,50,55. Note that I don't use 60 here!

You can use names for both month and day-of-week fields, which are typically abbreviated as Jan, Mar, Sat, Sun, and so forth. You cannot have a list of names nor a specified range of names, however.

The actual command is the sixth field. This command will use up the rest of the line, or until it reaches a percent (%) symbol. If it reaches a % symbol, it will treat it as a new line, and all of the following text will be used as standard input. Here is an example cron file:

```
# crontab -l
# Sample crontab file
#
# Force /bin/sh to be my shell for all of my scripts.
SHELL=/bin/sh
# Run 15 minutes past Midnight every Saturday
15 0 * * sat   $HOME/scripts/scary.script
# Do routine cleanup on the first of every Month at 4:30 AM
30 4 1 * *     /usr/scripts/removecores > /tmp/core.tmp 2>&1
# Mail a message at 10:45 AM every Friday
45 10 * * fri  mail -s "Project Update employees%Can I have astatus
update on your project?%%Your Boss.%
# Every other hour check for alert messages
0 */2 * * * /usr/scripts/check.alerts
```

Create a cron Job

In this exercise, we will create a cron job that will update the locate database at 4:00 A.M. every night and mail a disk usage report every Friday. To do this, use the following steps:

1. Log in as root.

2. Run crontab -e.

3. Type in the following line to update the locate database:

   ```
   00 4 * * * updatedb &2>/dev/null
   ```

4. Add the following line to mail a disk usage report to your account. The remote admin account is admin@remote.site.com.

   ```
   00 9 * * 5 df | mail admin@remote.site.com -s DiskUsage &2>/dev/null
   ```

5. Save and exit.

CERTIFICATION OBJECTIVE 6.06

System-Wide Shell Configuration Files for Bourne and Bash Shells

All system-wide shell configuration files are kept in the /etc directory. These files are bashrc, profile, and the profile.d directory that contains special shell configuration scripts. Only a small amount of Bash shell programming will be discussed in this book, but the basics will be covered here. If you want more information, please read the man pages for bash(1).

/etc/bashrc

/etc/bashrc is used for system-wide aliases and functions. You can bypass this script with the -norc argument when invoking bash. Here is a short example of a /etc/bashrc file:

```
#/etc/bashrc
# System-wide aliases and functions
# Set up the prompt
PS1="[\u@\h \W]\\$ "
# This alias shows colors with ls(1)
alias ls='ls -color'
```

The /etc/bashrc file shipped with Red Hat 7.1 is about 30 lines long. Examine it now with:

```
# less /etc/bashrc
```

/etc/profile

/etc/profile is used for system-wide environments and startup files. This script can be bypassed by invoking bash with the -noprofile argument. The following is the profile script from Red Hat 7.1:

```
# /etc/profile

# System wide environment and startup programs
# Functions and aliases go in /etc/bashrc

if ! echo $PATH | /bin/grep -q "/usr/X11R6/bin" ; then
  PATH="$PATH:/usr/X11R6/bin"
fi

ulimit -S -c 1000000 > /dev/null 2>&1
if [ 'id -gn' = 'id -un' -a 'id -u' -gt 14 ]; then
   umask 002
else
   umask 022
fi

USER='id -un'
LOGNAME=$USER
MAIL="/var/spool/mail/$USER"

HOSTNAME='/bin/hostname'
HISTSIZE=1000

if [ -z "$INPUTRC" -a ! -f "$HOME/.inputrc" ]; then
   INPUTRC=/etc/inputrc
fi

export PATH USER LOGNAME MAIL HOSTNAME HISTSIZE INPUTRC
```

```
for i in /etc/profile.d/*.sh ; do
   if [ -x $i ]; then
. $i
   fi
done

unset i
```

Its primary job is to systematize basic system variables (HOSTNAME, LOGNAME, MAIL), account default permissions (with umask), and user maximum file sizes (with ulimit). It also runs the correct start-up script for your login shell.

/etc/profile.d/

Profile.d is not a script, but a directory of little scripts. You may have noticed that the /etc/profile script is actually the script in charge of handling this directory. Here is a partial directory listing:

```
-rwxr-xr-x   1 root      root          184 Apr 19 02:47 kde.csh
-rwxr-xr-x   1 root      root          149 Apr 19 02:47 kde.sh
-rwxr-xr-x   1 root      root         1444 Apr 19 15:39 lang.sh
-rwxr-xr-x   1 root      root           64 Apr 19 15:03 mc.csh
-rwxr-xr-x   1 root      root          107 Apr 19 15:03 mc.sh
```

By looking at the /etc/profile script, you can see that any script in this directory that ends with an "sh" and is set as an executable will be run when /etc/profile is executed. In this case, it will run kde.sh, lang.sh, and mc.sh. The .csh files do not actually match the *.sh requirement in the /etc/profile (these are called by /etc/csh.cshrc, which is used by other shells).

EXERCISE 6-3

Securing Our System

We want to keep our system as secure as possible. To do this, we must change the default permissions users have for new files and directories they make. We'll set all new files and directories to No Access to group or other members.

1. Edit the /etc/profile file. There are two lines in the file that set the umask. One of the two lines is selected depending on the if statement above them. See if you can determine which line gets executed for an average user.

2. The if statement tests to see if the user ID (uid) and group ID (gid) are the same, and that the uid is greater than 14. If this is true, then the first umask is executed, otherwise the second is executed. The second umask is for root and other key system accounts. The first is for users.

3. Change the first umask statement to exclude all permissions for groups and others. Use umask 077 to do the job.

4. Save and exit the file.

5. Log in as a nonprivileged user. Use the touch command to make a new empty file. Use ls -l to verify the permissions.

6. Log in as root. Again, use the touch command to make a new empty file and use ls -l to verify their permissions.

You have just changed the default umask for all shell users.

CERTIFICATION SUMMARY

You can have great control over how your Linux installation is set up and configured. You can control almost all aspects of user security, as well as the details of your kernel. You can set up quotas to limit the user's disk usage. You can set up one quota per partition, and set a soft and hard limit. If a grace period is set, then the soft limit will warn users they are over their limit and will not allow them to exceed their hard limit. If a grace period is not set, then the soft limit will be the users' maximum amount of storage space.

The /etc/rc.d directory controls what daemons load at which runlevel. Each /etc/rc.d/rc#.d/ directory contains a link to the daemon that is located in the /etc/rc.d/init.d/ directory. Links that begin with an S will start daemon links, and links that begin with a K will kill the daemon when exiting a runlevel.

The kernel can be optimized for your particular installation and hardware, and you have detailed control of every aspect of it. To make a monolithic kernel, you need to run six commands: make mrproper, make config, make dep, make clean, make modules, and make modules_install. If you are compiling a monolithic kernel, you will *not* need to run make modules or make modules_install.

System security and maintenance can be controlled with PAM and cron. The Pluggable Authentication Module (PAM) can give you extra security, as well as extra control on how applications work and authenticate. cron will allow you to schedule jobs to run at any given time. Any variables or system-wide functions you may need to run can be kept in the /etc/bashrc or /etc/profile script.

✓ TWO-MINUTE DRILL

Here are some of the key points from the certification objectives in Chapter 6.

Setting Up and Managing Disk Quotas

❑ Quotas are used to limit a user's or a group of users' ability to consume disk space.

❑ Quotas are set on a mountable file system basis.

❑ Quota support must be present in the kernel for this service to be available. Quotas are turned on, by default, in stock Red Hat kernels.

❑ Quotas have soft limits and hard limits. If both soft and hard limits are set, then a user can exceed their soft limit for a modest period of time.

❑ Users may never exceed their hard limits.

System Initialization Scripts

❑ The key configuration file for system initialization is /etc/inittab.

❑ The init process reads and acts on the contents of this file.

❑ Linux is configured to provide services in runlevels. You can query the runlevel the system is currently in by using the runlevel command.

❑ Runlevels can be changed using the init command. Just pass the new runlevel you want as an argument.

❑ Service scripts reside in the /etc/rc.d/init.d directory. The chkconfig, ntsysv, and tksysv programs are used to enable and disable services in appropriate run levels.

❑ You can start and stop services manually with the service command. Just use "service <serviceName> [start|stop]" to start or stop the named service.

Kernel Recompilation and Installation

❑ The kernel has to be set up to support quotas on your partitions. By default, this is typically enabled.

❑ A *monolithic* kernel is one where all the device modules are built directly into it.

❑ A monolithic kernel uses the most memory and will probably waste space with unused drivers. It also talks faster to devices than a modular kernel.

❑ A modular kernel offers support for loadable modules, which can be loaded with either insmod or modprobe, or removed with rmmod. Your current module list can be viewed with lsmod.

❑ Proc is a directory that is virtual; it doesn't actually exist on the hard drive. All of its information is maintained by the kernel, and obtained by formatting and displaying values actually present in the kernel.

❑ Changing the values of variables in the /proc directory can change the behavior of your running kernel. For example, setting ip_forward to 1 enables routing.

❑ The Code maturity level option is used to enable prompting for kernel source code drivers not yet fully developed.

❑ The Loadable module support screen is where you enable the use of modules with your kernel.

❑ If you have an older CD-ROM that is not an IDE or SCSI CD-ROM, you need to enable special support for it.

❑ mkbootdisk is a utility that can create a bootdisk. This may be needed to perform a system rescue after a crash. System rescues can also be done via your install CD (CD #1).

PAM

❑ PAM stands for Pluggable Authentication Modules. It is not very useful in a single-user environment, or where users are trusted, but is perfect for a multiuser system where users are not trusted.

❑ The simplest way to configure PAM is via the authconfig program.

❑ More fine-grained security can be set by editing the files in /etc/pam.d.

❑ The key configuration file for most PAM-controlled services is /etc/pam.d/system-auth. This sets the default security checks referenced by most other services.

The cron System

❑ The cron(8) system allows the administrator, or any user, to schedule jobs so they run at given intervals.

❑ The crontab command is used to work with cron files. Use crontab -e to edit, crontab -l to list, or crontab -d to delete cron files.

❑ The /etc/cron.allow and /etc/cron.deny files are used to control access to the cron job scheduler.

System-wide Shell Configuration Files for the Bourne and Bash Shells

❑ All system-wide shell configuration files are kept in the /etc directory.

❑ /etc/profile is the system-wide start up shell script for bash users.

❑ Changes made to this file are picked up by all Telnet and rlogin users.

SELF TEST

The following questions will help you measure your understanding of the material presented in this chapter. Read all the choices carefully, as there may be more than one correct answer. Choose all correct answers for each question.

Setting Up and Managing Disk Quotas

1. You have several users on your system. You want to restrict their disk space in their home directory, but because of the complexity of some of their programs, they need large temporary space. How could you restrict their disk usage in their home directories, but allow them unlimited access to the /tmp directory?

   A. Use edquota /home to edit the users' quota for their home directory.

   B. Use edquota and specify only the home directories in the text file.

   C. Mount the /tmp directory to a separate partition and use edquota on the partition that contains the /home directory.

   D. None of these options will work.

2. You are running an ISP service and provide space for users' Web pages. You only want them to use 40MB of space, but will allow up to 50MB until they can clean up their stuff. How could you use quotas to enforce this policy?

   A. Enable grace periods; set the hard limit to 40MB and the soft limit to 50MB.

   B. Enable grace periods; set the soft limit to 50MB, and the hard limit to 40MB.

   C. Enable grace periods; set the soft limit to 40MB, and the hard limit to 50MB.

   D. None of the above.

3. The CIO of your company wants to see a full report on how much disk space each user on the system is utilizing. What command would you use to display this information?

   A. repquota -a

   B. quotareport -a

   C. quotareport -all

   D. quotashow -a

System Initialization Scripts

4. You recently received a notice from your legal department. They want all servers to have a message to warn off unauthorized access at the login prompt. How would you go about doing this? (Choose all that apply.)

   A. Modify /etc/banner.net

   B. Modify /etc/issue

   C. Modify /etc/issue.net

   D. Modify /etc/login.msg

5. Your system currently boots into runlevel 3. After looking into the /etc/rc.d/rc3.d/ directory, you want to know what script will run first. Of the following links, what script will be the first to run when entering runlevel 3?

   A. K20rwhod

   B. S30syslog

   C. K96pcmcia

   D. S99linuxconf

6. How would you set the runlevel so your server boots into X-Window when you boot?

   A. Modify the /etc/inetd.conf file and uncomment startx.

   B. Modify the /etc/inittab file and set the initdefault to 5.

   C. Modify the /etc/inittab file and set the initdefault to 6.

   D. Modify the /etc/inittab.conf file and set the initdefault to 5.

Kernel Recompilation and Installation

7. Which commands would you NOT execute when building a monolithic kernel? (Choose all that apply.)

   A. make bzImage

   B. make lilo

   C. make modules

   D. make modules_install

8. You are compiling a new kernel for a machine with an older BIOS that does not support large hard drives. The hard drive you plan to use is 4GB. The following is a simple description of your partitions:

   /Boot   (15MB)

   /usr   (1GB)

   /home   (1.9GB)

   /   (1GB)

   Where could you place the kernel to avoid problems with the older BIOS?

   A. /usr/src/linux/arch/i386/boot

   B. /usr/src/linux

   C. /

   D. /boot

9. You are almost finished building a new router for your company. You have both network cards properly set up to two different networks. Each side can successfully ping its network card, but neither side can ping the other network. After checking your firewall and forwarding rules, you feel they are set up correctly. All the kernel configuration settings such as IP Firewalling are enabled. What is most likely the cause of this problem?

   A. You didn't load the router module.

   B. You need to enable the environmental variable, ENABLE_ROUTING=1.

   C. You need to add a "1" to the kernel variables file /proc/sys/net/ipv4/ip_forward.

   D. None of the above.

10. Which one of these kernels is a developers kernel?

    A. 2.0.0

    B. 1.2.25

    C. 2.3.4

    D. 3.0.13

11. When compiling a kernel, what are the valid configuration options used by make? (Choose all that apply.)

    A. config

    B. menuconfig

C. windowconfig

D. xconfig

12. After specifying all the options for your kernel, you type in your final command: make bzImage. The kernel goes through its final stages of compiling, but at the end complains the kernel is too large. What steps could you use to fix this problem? (Choose all that apply.)

A. Edit your kernel configurations and make as many options as you can.

B. Compile the kernel on a bigger system, then copy to your new system.

C. Remove some of the kernel source code.

D. Use make zImage -compress.

13. What does the command: mkinitrd /boot/initrd 2.4.2 do?

A. It creates a list of kernel modules for kernel 2.4.2.

B. It appends the system's /boot/initrd to kernel 2.4.2.

C. Nothing. The /boot directory is only referenced by the kernel during boot time.

D. It creates an initial RAM disk to load necessary modules during boot time.

14. You have just compiled a new kernel. You compiled the kernel with the command make bzImage. You need to copy the kernel to the /boot directory. Where is the kernel currently located at?

A. /usr/src/linux/

B. /boot/

C. /usr/src/linux/kernel/bzImage/

D. /usr/src/linux/arch/i386/boot/bzImage

15. You have just compiled a new kernel and want to set up LILO to boot your new kernel by default yet still have the option to boot the old kernel, if necessary. You have already copied your kernel to the /boot directory. What section do you need to add to the /etc/lilo.conf file?

A. boot=

B. image=

C. install=

D. map=

16. What command could you use to easily create a bootable recovery disk for your system?

A. fdrescue

    B. mkrescuedisk

    C. mkbootdisk

    D. None of the above.

PAM

17. Where could you look to find out how Pluggable Authentication Modules (PAM) are installed on your system? (Choose all that apply.)

    A. /etc/pamd.conf

    B. /etc/pam.conf

    C. /etc/pam.d/

    D. /etc/pamd.conf/

18. What is the difference between a required PAM module and a module that is a requisite?

    A. If a user fails to authenticate a required section, he will be immediately rejected.

    B. If a user fails to authenticate at a requisite section, he will be immediately rejected.

    C. Required sections are accumulated, and after all the required are checked, if one fails, access is denied.

    D. None of the above.

The cron System

19. You want to schedule a maintenance job to run on the first of every month at 4:00 A.M. Which of the following cron entries are correct?

    A. 0   4   1   *   *   ~/maintenance.pl

    B. 4   1   *   *   ~/maintenance.pl

    C. 0   4   31   *   *   ~/maintenance.pl

    D. 1   4   0   0   ~/maintenance.pl

System-wide Shell Configuration Files for the Bourne and Bash Shells

20. The system-wide shell startup file is:

    A. /etc/shells.conf

    B. /etc/startup.sh

C. /etc/profile

D. There is no system-wide shell startup file.

LAB QUESTION

Rather than a Lab, I want to take the reader through a detailed kernel-building exercise. The exercise will include concise steps on how to configure, install, and test a new kernel. Note that this is not only a good thing to know from the perspective of earning your RHCE certificate, it is also something you will need to do at some point in time as a Linux system administrator.

SELF TEST ANSWERS

Setting Up and Managing Disk Quotas

1. ☑ **C.** Mount the /tmp directory to a separate partition and use edquota on the partition that contains the /home directory. You can only specify one quota per user per partition. If you move /tmp to its own partition, you can control it separately.

☒ **A** is partially correct, but doesn't address the problem of unlimited file size and inode access for files in /tmp. **B** is incorrect because quotas are set on a file-system-by-file-system basis. Since there is an answer, **D** is therefore incorrect.

2. ☑ **C.** Enable grace periods; set the soft limit to 40MB, and the hard limit to 50MB. This will warn users they are over their limit after the grace period, but will make sure they do not exceed the 50MB true maximum barrier.

☒ **A** is incorrect because the soft limit must be less than the hard limit. **B** is incorrect because it is actually the same as **A**. **D** is incorrect because **C** does the job.

3. ☑ **A.** repquota will display a report of all users on your system. It shows the used space, as well as their soft and hard limits.

☒ **B, C,** and **D** refer to programs that don't exist on Red Hat Linux.

System Initialization Scripts

4. ☑ **B** and **C.** Modify /etc/issue and /etc/issue.net. The /etc/issue file is used to log in locally to the machine. The /etc/issue.net file is used when connecting remotely to a PC. Be careful you don't lose your changes on your next reboot. Look at /etc/rc.d/rc.local to see how Red Hat constructs a default /etc/issue file.

☒ **A** and **D** are incorrect because the login process does not reference either of these files.

5. ☑ **A.** Linux runs all kill scripts in number order before it runs any start scripts. Consequently, K20rwhod would run first, K96pcmcia next, S30syslog next, and S99linuxconf last.

☒ Since **B, C,** and **D** fall alphabetically after answer **A** (K20rwhod), they are incorrect.

6. ☑ **B.** Modify the /etc/inittab file and set the initdefault to 5. Runlevel 5 is used by Red Hat to load X-Window automatically.

☒ **A** is incorrect because there is no such requirement. **C** is REALLY BAD. This would cause your system to permanently reboot! However, if you wanted to test your system rescue skills, it might be a good choice. **D** is incorrect because there is no such file as /etc/inittab.conf

Kernel Recompilation and Installation

7. ☑ **C and D.** Make modules and make modules_install. These two commands are only necessary when building a modular kernel. A monolithic kernel contains all the drivers directly in the main kernel itself.

☒ **A** is done regardless of the type of kernel you are building. **B** is incorrect because there is no such argument to make.

8. ☑ **D.** /boot. Boot is a small partition placed at the front of the disk that the BIOS can recognize and boot from. Once the kernel has loaded, it can then use the rest of the large disk.

☒ **A** is incorrect because this is where bzImage is placed once it is built. It is not the spot LILO should look to find the kernel on bootup. **B** is incorrect because this is the base of the kernel source tree. **C** is incorrect because it is common to have LILO look for the kernel in the /boot directory. Note that by placing the /boot file system on the first disk partition, we ensure that our BIOS can read the partition even if it has a 2GB or 8GB addressing limit.

9. ☑ **C.** You need to add a "1" to the kernel variables file /proc/sys/net/ipv4/ip_forward. By default, routing is not enabled by the kernel. To enable it, you can simply add a "1" to this file with the following command: echo 1 > /proc/sys/net/ipv4/ip_forward. Note, to make the system a router permanently, you should edit the /etc/sysctl.conf file and set this variable in the file.

☒ **A** is incorrect because there is no such module. **B** is incorrect because there is no such variable. **D** is incorrect because performing the action in **C** will enable routing in your kernel.

10. ☑ **C.** The second number determines if it is a stable release or a developers kernel. If the second number is an odd number, it is a developers kernel. If it is an even number, it is a stable kernel release.

☒ **A, B,** and **D** all refer to "stable" kernel versions (in fact, **D** refers to a kernel architecture that doesn't even exist!).

11. ☑ **A, B,** and **D.** config, menuconfig, and xconfig. Config is a basic text-based utility. Menuconfig is a text-based menu utility, and xconfig is a graphical X-Window utility.

☒ **C** is incorrect because there is no such option.

12. ☑ **A.** Creating modules will greatly decrease the size of your kernel.

☒ **B** is incorrect because the problem concerns a 20-bit addressing limitation found in 8086 emulation (8086 emulation is the mode all Intel and compatible processors initialize to on power up). Moving to a bigger server won't solve the problem because the processor will still power up in 8086 mode. **C** is incorrect because if you remove some of the source code you need, your kernel won't compile, and if you try to remove source code you don't need, you'll find it isn't in the kernel to begin with. **D** is incorrect because the zImage kernel is actually bigger than the bzImage kernel due to the older compression method used when making the zImage kernel.

13. ☑ **D.** It creates an initial RAM disk. An initial RAM disk is a RAM-based file system that contains the kernel and all required kernel modules. It is used to load a kernel and initialize any special hardware drivers needed to access the disk-based kernel and its modules. In essence, it loads the necessary modules for our 2.4.2 kernel during boot time.
    ☒ **A** is incorrect because it doesn't mention that it actually makes a RAM disk image of our kernel with all the modules available. **B** is incorrect because there is no /boot/initrd file. **C** is just plain wrong!

14. ☑ **D.** /usr/src/linux/arch/i386/boot/bzImage. The kernels are always compiled to this directory and will have a name of bzImage.
    ☒ **A, B,** and **C** are all incorrect locations.

15. ☑ **B.** image=. You will need to add another image=<your_new_kernel>. The rest of the options can stay the same.
    ☒ **A** is incorrect because this specifies the boot device. **C** is incorrect because there is no such directive. **D** is incorrect because the map directive specifies the name of the system map file used for kernel module linkage at module load time.

16. ☑ **C,** mkbootdisk. This command will allow you to make a boot disk for your system that has the option of typing **rescue** at the LILO prompt.
    ☒ **A** and **B** are incorrect because there is no such command. **D** is incorrect because we can make boot floppy diskettes with mkbootdisk

PAM

17. ☑ **C.** All of PAM's configuration files are located in the /etc/pam.d/ directory.
    ☒ **A** and **D** are incorrect because Linux never had such files. **B** is incorrect because use of the file /etc/pam.conf is deprecated and no longer supported on Red Hat 7.x.

18. ☑ **B** and **C. B** is correct because requisite means we should fail immediately if a requisite rule fails. **C** is also correct because required sections are accumulated, and after all the required rules are checked, if one fails, access is denied.
    ☒ **A** is incorrect because all required sections are checked and the user is rejected if any required module fails. **D** is incorrect because there *are* correct answer choices.

The cron System

19. ☑   **A.** The syntax for cron is minute, hour, day of month, month of year, week day, and then the command.

   ☒   **B** executes at 4 minutes after 1 in the morning for every day. However, there are only 4 time fields, not five, so the entire line would be considered invalid. **C** is incorrect because it runs the job at 4 A.M. on the 31st of the month and then, only if the month has 31 days. **D** is incorrect because it executes the program at one minute after 4 A.M. But, there are only four time values and the day-of-month and month-of-year values start with a 1, not a 0.

System-wide Shell Configuration Files for the Bourne and Bash Shells

20. ☑   **C.** This is the system wide shell script executed whenever a user logs in.

   ☒   **A** and **B** are incorrect because there are no such files. **D** is incorrect because answer **C** is correct.

LAB ANSWER

Before we can build a new kernel, we have to ensure we have all the correct rpms.

1. Issue the following rpm commands to ensure your system is ready to build a new kernel:

```
rpm -Uvh —force ftp://server1/pub/RedHat/RPMS/kernel-headers*
rpm -Uvh —force ftp://server1/pub/RedHat/RPMS/kernel-source*
rpm -Uvh —force ftp://server1/pub/RedHat/RPMS/dev86*
rpm -Uvh —force ftp://server1/pub/RedHat/RPMS/make-*
rpm -Uvh —force ftp://server1/pub/RedHat/RPMS/glibc-devel*
rpm -Uvh —force ftp://server1/pub/RedHat/RPMS/kgcc*
rpm -Uvh —force ftp://server1/pub/RedHat/RPMS/cpp*
rpm -Uvh —force ftp://server1/pub/RedHat/RPMS/ncurses-devel*
rpm -Uvh —force ftp://server1/pub/RedHat/RPMS/binutils*
rpm -Uvh —force ftp://server1/pub/RedHat/RPMS/gcc-2*
```

It's necessary to make a new kernel configuration before we build our kernel. To do this, we need to give our new kernel a unique name, as well as identify what components will (and will not) be in the kernel.

2. Cd to /usr/src and do a long listing. Write down the name of the item that Linux is pointing to. If you were to install a newer kernel, you would need to make Linux symbolically link to the base directory of the new source tree. To do this, you would write-up something like this:

```
# rm linux
# ln -s linux-2.4.2-2 linux
```

3. Cd to linux and edit Makefile. Look for the line that starts with EXTRAVERSION. This is a suffix that Red Hat adds to the kernel included with Linux. Change the entry to add your initials after the existing suffix. Save and exit.

   Jot down your EXTRAVERSION value here: _____

4. Determine the correct CPU on your hardware. Use the command:

   ```
   # cat /proc/cpuinfo
   ```

   Jot down the CPU Model Name here: _____

   (Our classroom equipment uses Pentium IIIs, which are considered i686s)

5. Take the default configuration that Red Hat used for this kernel and save it as the default configuration. Use the command:

   ```
   # cp -p configs/kernel-*i686.config arch/i386/defconfig
   ```

6. Clean up from previous configurations by using:

   ```
   # make mrproper
   ```

7. Install the existing "old" configuration so we are ready to modify it to our requirements:

   ```
   # make oldconfig
   ```

   Ignore all the messages that blow by.

   Now you need to define what features (symmetric multiprocessing, memory size, modules, and so on) and customizations (processor level, drivers to include/exclude, and others) you want for your kernel.

8. There are three different ways to configure your kernel:

   - **1.1 make config**   Used for a line-by-line prompt
   - **1.2 make menuconfig**   A character cell configuration tool (full screen), or
   - **1.3 make xconfig**   An X graphics GUI interface to configure your kernel

   Each of the preceding methods invokes the kernel configuration tool after building the correct tool (option 1.2 and 1.3).

9. Set the processor type to match your hardware (e.g., Pentium, Pentium II, Pentium III, Pentium IV).

10. Kernel configuration makes a hidden file called .config. Copy that now to your /boot directory for safekeeping.

```
# cp .config /boot/Config.2.2.16-22Initials
```

11. Turn off all unnecessary devices. This includes devices such as:

- 1.1 ISDN subsystem
- 1.2 I2O
- 1.3 Old CD-ROMs
- 1.4 Amateur Radio
- 1.5 Telephony Support
- 1.6 Symmetric multiprocessing support
- 1.7 MTR Memory support

12. Be sure to turn on kernel loadable modules support.

13. Save your changes and exit.

14. Resolve all kernel dependencies (between sources). This will produce a lot of output (which is OK). Run:

```
# make dep
```

15. Once your dependencies are resolved, it's time to build a new compressed kernel image. The command to use is:

```
# make bzImage
```

This is the actual kernel build, and will take some time. You may want to run gtop to watch the load on the system as the kernel builds.

16. The easiest way to see if the kernel build worked is to issue this command immediately after make bzImage finishes:

```
# echo $?
0
```

If you got a 0, everything worked (success). Anything else indicates a failure. Go back and reconfigure your kernel to make a configuration that works.

17. Check for the existence of two new files. Run this command:

```
# ls -l System.map arch/i386/boot/bzImage
```

It should show you two files, a relatively small System.map and a much larger bzImage.

18. Make the loadable modules that will be used by this kernel.

```
# make modules
```

Install the new custom kernel files into their correct locations and update LILO so it knows about your new kernel.

19. Copy your new kernel onto the /boot file system:

```
# cp -p arch/i386/boot/bzImage /boot/vmlinuz-2.2.16-22Initials
# cp -p System.map /boot/System.map-Initials
# make modules_install
```

20. If your kernel includes any modules needed at boot time, you will need to make an initial RAM disk (initrd). To do this, use the command:

```
# mkinitrd /boot/initrd-2.2.16-22Initials.img 2.2.16-22Initials
```

Your kernel has just been properly installed.

The last step is to configure to LILO to make your new kernel available. Here is a default /etc/lilo.conf (with a DOS boot partition) with a new image= section for your new kernel.

```
boot=/dev/had
map=/boot/map
install=/boot/boot.b
prompt
timeout=50
message=/boot/message
linear
default=linux

image=/boot/vmlinuz-2.2.16-22lk
label=linux22lk
read-only
root=/dev/hda2

image=/boot/vmlinuz-2.2.16-22
label=linux
read-only
root=/dev/hda2

other=/dev/hda1
label=dos
```

The new image= section is in bold/italics. Note that we took the previous image= section, copied it and changed the image filename to match the kernel image we installed into /boot.

LILO will boot the kernel whose label matches the default= directive. Note that we have left it pointing at the old kernel (in case there are any errors in our new kernel).

Also note that we have NOT deleted our old kernel. Do not be too hasty to delete your old kernel. Your new configuration may not be reliable and you may not be aware of problems for days or even weeks after booting your new kernel. Always have a safe kernel you can boot should it become necessary.

21. Install your new LILO updates, using the command:

```
# lilo -v -v
```

This produces extra verbose output. Read over the output and look for any error messages. To test your new kernel, reboot your system. At the Red Hat splash screen, you should see your new kernel name on the list of images that can be booted. Select your kernel and press ENTER.

Congratulations, you have just installed a custom kernel on your new system.

RED HAT CERTIFIED ENGINEER

7

X-Windowing System

CERTIFICATION OBJECTIVES

O ne of the most important aspects of getting a Red Hat Linux system up and running is configuring the user interface. On most systems, this means configuring the *X-Window* interface. The *X-Window system* is the graphical user interface (GUI) for Linux. Unlike other operating systems in which the GUI interface is an integral part of the operating system itself, the X-Window system is not a part of Red Hat Linux, but is a layered application. Thus you can have a fully functioning Linux system without running the X-Window interface.

Although it is quite possible to run Linux without utilizing the X-Window GUI, most users using Linux for a workstation will benefit from the increased productivity provided by a graphical work environment and from the multitude of X-Window-based applications. If you are migrating users from Microsoft Windows to Linux, the X-Window system enables you to provide them with a familiar environment.

If you are running a dedicated system such as a DHCP server or a SAMBA server, you may elect not to configure the X-Window GUI, or you may be a dyed-in-the-wool command-line hacker and decide an X-Window interface isn't necessary. If this is the case, you may want to reconsider your decision; one of the strengths of Red Hat Linux is in the number of X-Window-based system configuration and administration tools provided.

Because the X-Window system is such an important part of almost any Red Hat Linux system you will encounter, it is essential that as a RHCE you are able to install, configure, and troubleshoot an X-Window system. This chapter will introduce you to the X-Window system and guide you through the process of installing and starting it on a Linux system. In addition, you'll also take a look at using X-Window applications.

CERTIFICATION OBJECTIVE 7.01

X-Server

The X-Window system is designed as a flexible and powerful, client-server based system. In order to configure and troubleshoot the X-Window interface, it is important you understand the client-server nature of the X-Window system.

As you might have guessed from the terms *client* and *server,* the X-Window system is designed to work in a networked environment. This does not mean your Linux system must be connected to a network in order to use X-Window applications; the

X-Window system will work on a *standalone* system as well as a networked system. If your system is part of a network, not only can you run X applications on your system, you can employ the powerful network capabilities of the X-Window system to run X applications on other computers on your network and have the graphical displays from those applications display on your monitor. In fact, X-Window applications handle this task so well that, providing the network doesn't go down, you really can't tell from a performance point of view which applications are running *locally* and which applications are running *remotely*.

Different Meanings for Client and Server

One small hurdle you must overcome when working with the X-Window system is coming to an understanding that, in the X-Window world, the meanings of the terms *client* and *server* have been somewhat reversed. If you have experience in the world of personal computer networking, the term *server* brings to mind a multiprocessor monster with multiple gigabytes of RAM and disk storage that sits behind glass walls in an air-conditioned machine room and holds all your company's vital data. A *client* is a computer, such as the workstation on your desk, that you use to access and process the information stored on the server.

In the X-Window environment, these roles have been reversed. The *X-server* is the component of the X-Window system you run on your desktop. The X-server is responsible for drawing images on your screen, getting input from your keyboard and mouse, and controlling access to your *display*. The X-Window applications you run make use of these services provided by the X-server to display their output; hence they are referred to as clients or X-clients.

Perhaps a better way of thinking about X-servers and X-clients is this: in a client/server environment, the server owns and manages a shared resource, while a client asks the server for access to the resource. A database is a perfect example of this. It sits on the central computer and the database server manages all the incoming requests. In the X world, the shared resource is your screen, keyboard, and mouse! Your X-server manages these resources and arbitrates access to many X-clients. These clients in return ask the server to update the screen and pass user keystroke and mouse event information back to the client. In this way, we can see that the X-server manages our graphics hardware in a manner similar to how a database server would manage a database.

X-clients can run *locally* or *remotely*. *Local* X-clients run on your workstation; *remote* X-clients run on other systems on the network. When you run an X-Window application remotely, you start the program on another system on the network and tell it to use the X-server running on your system for its console. The X-client sends its output to your X-server and gets keyboard and mouse input from your X-server. Figure 7-1 shows a local and a remote X-client accessing the X-server on a workstation. X-clients and X-servers communicate using the X protocol. We will look at running local and remote X-Window applications later in this chapter. Before we can talk about running client applications, we need to look first at getting an X-server running on our system.

Supported Hardware

Getting the X-Window system configured and working can be one of the most difficult tasks in setting up a Linux system. Fortunately, Red Hat Linux comes with tools and drivers that make this job relatively painless and easy.

One of the most important steps you can take to ensure that you wind up with a working X-Window configuration is selecting the proper hardware. Ironically, in the case of running the X-Window system under Linux, having the latest and greatest video card or monitor is not always the best situation to be in. When selecting video hardware, you should look for video cards and monitors that have been in production for a while (at least six months). The more popular a given type of card or a given type of monitor, the better your chances are that the chipset for your video card and

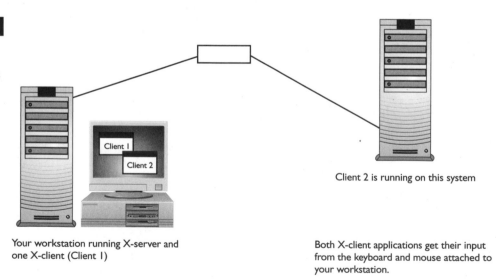

FIGURE 7-1

You can run X-Window client applications on more than one system

Your workstation running X-server and one X-client (Client 1)

Client 2 is running on this system

Both X-client applications get their input from the keyboard and mouse attached to your workstation.

monitor will be supported. Also, don't be tempted to spend a lot of money for your video card. A name brand 2D AGP video accelerator will probably perform quite well. The latest 3D games card may lack Linux drivers. If in doubt, visit Red Hat's Web site and find their hardware compatibility guide for your version of Linux.

As a footnote, more and more 3D action games are being released for Linux. If this is for you, then you may wish to acquire a supported 3D-accelerator card. Most Linux games require 3Dfx or nVidia TNT cards and cannot do software rendering. Check with your favorite games vendor for a list of supported cards.

Hardware: X-Server Selection

Red Hat Linux 7.x has support for hundreds of video cards and monitors. The best place to check to see whether your video card and monitor are supported is the Red Hat support site at http://www.Red Hat.com/corp/support/hardware/index.html.

If you don't find your video card or monitor among the list of Red Hat-supported hardware, you can also check http://www.XFree86.org/cardlist.html.

The X-Window server program shipped with Red Hat Linux is an open-source X-server program called *XFree86.* The version of XFree86 that you install depends on the type of video hardware and monitor you have. The latest version is either 4.0.x for accelerated video cards and 3.3.x for simple frame buffer (i.e., 2D) cards. If you have an older card, you'll likely need to install XFree86 version 3.3.6-35, as support for many older frame buffer cards was dropped from XFree86 v4. When you install the X-Window system, you need to install an X-server program that contains the correct video drivers and settings for your particular video card.

Different Servers of XFree86.org

The Red Hat Linux distribution includes precompiled versions of the XFree86 server for the most common types of video cards. These images are stored in Red Hat package files (RPMS). For example, if your video card uses the S3 video chipset and you are manually configuring the X-Window system, although I wouldn't recommend this, as you will see shortly, you need to install the XFree86-S3-3.3.6-35 package from the Red Hat/RPMS directory on your Red Hat distribution CD-ROM.

If you are using an unsupported video card, support is also included for simple SVGA and VGA devices. Most video cards and monitors will work with these X-servers.

Tools for X Configuration

The preferred Red Hat configuration tool for XFree86 is *Xconfigurator*.

The configuration tool that ships with XFree86 is XF86Config. Either tool can be used to configure your graphics environment, but you really need to be comfortable with Xconfigurator.

On earlier implementations of Linux, you had to edit this file manually to get the X-Window system working. This can be a time-consuming and frustrating process. One of the advantages of using Red Hat Linux is that it comes with tools that make it easy for you to configure the X-Window system and get it working. Although you can still edit the /etc/X11/XF86Config-4 file manually (using a text editor), utilizing these tools makes the task much easier. (Note: If you are using the older version of XFree86, v3.36, your configuration file is /etc/X11/XFree86Config.)

You can install the X-Window system at the same time you install Linux, or you can choose to install the X-Window system later. After the X-Window system is installed, you can reconfigure it at any time. Red Hat now installs in graphics mode if it can figure out what graphics driver to load. If not, you can perform a text-based install and configure your graphics hardware after the install completes. When configuring your graphics display, try to get accurate information on the make, model, and version of your graphics card. Also, try to find out how much display memory your card has. You will be asked to provide this information while using Red Hat's graphics configuration tools.

Xconfigurator

The first tool we're going to take a look at is the Red Hat *Xconfigurator* program. In addition to being a standalone program that you can run at any time from the command line, the Xconfigurator program is also called by the installation program when you choose to install and configure the X-Window system.

The Xconfigurator program is a character-based GUI that leads you through a series of menus that aid you in configuring your video hardware. The Xconfigurator program will automatically probe your video card and try to pick the appropriate X-server image for it. If Xconfigurator cannot determine what make of card you have, then you must select your video card from the list of supported video cards.

Running Xconfigurator

You start the Xconfigurator program by typing

```
# Xconfigurator
```

at a command prompt (note the leading capital X). You can do this from either a
console screen or from an X-terminal client.

You maneuver through the Xconfigurator screens using the TAB key, the UP- and
DOWN-ARROW keys, the SPACEBAR, and the ENTER key. When you start Xconfigurator,
the first screen you see is a welcome screen with an OK button and a Cancel button
at the bottom. The OK button is highlighted, which indicates the default action
that will happen when you press the ENTER key.

If Xconfigurator is successful at identifying your hardware, it displays a screen
telling you what it found. See Figure 7-2.

If it is unable to determine what type of video card you are using, pressing ENTER
from the startup screen places you in the video card selection screen. Use the UP- and
DOWN-ARROW KEYS to select the video card for your system. If you do not see your card
listed, it may not be supported. If this is the case, there are several options you can try:

■ Select a video card similar to your model. If in doubt, pick a model that is
older rather than newer than your hardware. Test, and if necessary edit the
/etc/X11/XF86Config file to complete your changes.

FIGURE 7-2

Xconfigurator
reporting on your
video hardware

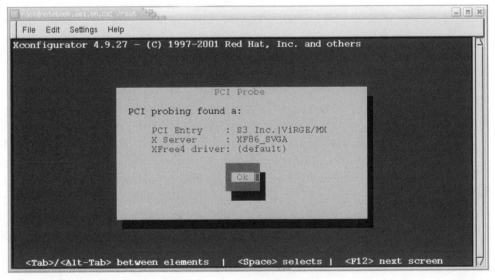

- Check the Web for others who are running the X-Window system with the same type of hardware.

- Use either the SVGA or VGA X-Window servers.

- Go to http://www.xfree86.org and download the latest drivers. Rebuild and reinstall this software. (Note that the author has done this, but in hindsight, it is easier, just not as much fun, to purchase a supported video card.)

After you have selected your monitor, you can either press TAB to move to the OK button and then press ENTER, or simply press ENTER, to move on to the monitor selection screen.

After you have selected a monitor, Xconfigurator will ask whether it can probe your video card to determine the resolutions it is capable of displaying. The default response is Don't Probe, and your configuration will generally work fine without a monitor probe. If you have newer hardware, probing for the monitor's settings is generally a safe thing to allow, so use the TAB key to highlight the Probe button and press ENTER.

During the probing process, your screen will blink several times and your monitor may click as different video modes and resolutions are tried. After the probing process finishes you may be asked to specify the amount of video RAM and the type of clockchip you have. If you are not sure, consult the documentation for your video card. The recommended setting for the clockchip is No Clockchip Setting.

At this point you are given a chance to select the video modes you wish to use. You should select multiple video modes so you control the resolution and *color depth* of your display by switching video modes. Configuring multiple video modes is a good way to ensure that your X-Window installation is successful. Your video card or monitor may have difficulty displaying at a higher resolution video mode such as 1024×768 pixels but may do fine at a lower resolution such as 800×600 pixels. If you have configured your X-server to support multiple video modes, you switch between different modes you have configured by pressing CTRL-ALT-+ (from the keypad) simultaneously until you find a mode that displays properly on your hardware. A higher resolution equates to being able to fit more on your screen. The price you pay is that the fonts in your application will be smaller. Another advantage to configuring multiple video modes is that you can toggle between different resolutions, depending on whether you're concentrating on one application, trying to fit as many windows as possible on your display, or just trying to find the setting that is easiest on your eyes!

Note that the key combination for switching modes includes the CTRL key, the ALT key and the keypad + or – keys. On notebooks, it may be impossible to achieve this key combination because the keypad is often integrated into the standard QWERTY keyboard layout and selected with a special function key that Linux does not recognize.

After you select the video modes you want to use, Xconfigurator will ask whether it can start the X-Window system to test your configuration. Select OK, and your display will go blank while the X-Window server starts. After a short interval, your X-server should start, and you should see a dialog box with a message asking whether you can read the display, which will show two buttons labeled Yes and No. If you can read the display and it looks like everything is working correctly, use your mouse to click Yes. If your display isn't working properly or you can't see the dialog box, don't worry. If you click the No button, or simply wait ten seconds, Xconfigurator switches back to the original video mode you were using and gives you the chance to retry your configuration or quit.

As the final step in configuring the X-Window system, you are asked whether you want to automatically start the X-server when the system boots. For most systems, the answer to this is Yes. If you decide not to configure the X-Window system for automatic startup, it is very easy to change this setting later.

If Xconfigurator is unable to determine what type of video card you have installed in your system and you are missing the documentation for your video card, you can use the XFree86 *SuperProbe* utility to obtain information about your video card. From a command prompt, type the following:

```
SuperProbe
```

The SuperProbe program issues a warning about possibly locking up your system and gives you a short time to cancel the program by pressing CTRL-C. As the program runs, you will see your screen flash, much as it does during the setup of the X-Window system. When SuperProbe finishes, it displays the information it found for your video card. Here is the output of the SuperProbe utility when run on a 1999 vintage notebook (Figure 7-3).

Laptops

Configuring the X-Window system to run on a laptop can be more challenging than configuring the X-Window system to run on a desktop system. If you are planning to install Red Hat Linux on a laptop, in addition to consulting the Red Hat support site, you should also check the Linux laptop page at www.linux-laptop.net.

```
root@notebook.ae1.on.ca: /root                                        _ □ x

 File   Edit   Settings   Help

        having been obtained.  Additional information obtained from
        'Programmer's Guide to the EGA and VGA, 2nd ed', by Richard
        Ferraro, and from manufacturer's data books

Bug reports are welcome, and should be sent to XFree86@XFree86.org.
In particular, reports of chipsets that this program fails to
correctly detect are appreciated.

Before submitting a report, please make sure that you have the
latest version of SuperProbe (see http://www.xfree86.org/FAQ).

WARNING - THIS SOFTWARE COULD HANG YOUR MACHINE.
          READ THE SuperProbe.1 MANUAL PAGE BEFORE
          RUNNING THIS PROGRAM.

          INTERRUPT WITHIN FIVE SECONDS TO ABORT!

First video: Super-VGA
          Chipset: S3 ViRGE/MX (Port Probed)
          Memory:  4096 Kbytes
          RAMDAC:  Generic 8-bit pseudo-color DAC
                   (with 6-bit wide lookup tables (or in 6-bit mode))
[root@notebook /root]# □
```

Drivers Shipped with Red Hat 7.1

Red Hat includes a number of prebuilt X-servers for use on most popular video
cards. The correct driver is loaded at installation time if you do a graphics-based
install. However, if you do a text install, you may need to load your drivers manually.
You can find the drivers along with most of the XFree86 software on CD 2 under
the Red Hat/RPMS directory. Here is a list of supported drivers:

```
XFree86-3DLabs-3.3.6-35.i386.rpm       # support for 3DFX cards
XFree86-8514-3.3.6-35.i386.rpm         # old IBM 8514 style cards
XFree86-AGX-3.3.6-35.i386.rpm
XFree86-I128-3.3.6-35.i386.rpm
XFree86-Mach32-3.3.6-35.i386.rpm       # Mach drivers are for ATI cards
XFree86-Mach64-3.3.6-35.i386.rpm
XFree86-Mach8-3.3.6-35.i386.rpm
XFree86-Mono-3.3.6-35.i386.rpm
XFree86-P9000-3.3.6-35.i386.rpm        # Older Weitech Power 9000 cards
XFree86-S3-3.3.6-35.i386.rpm           # Most S3 video cards
XFree86-S3V-3.3.6-35.i386.rpm          # S3 Virge cards
XFree86-SVGA-3.3.6-35.i386.rpm         # SVGA compatible driver
XFree86-V4L-4.0.3-5.i386.rpm
XFree86-VGA16-3.3.6-35.i386.rpm
XFree86-W32-3.3.6-35.i386.rpm
XFree86-xf86cfg-4.0.3-5.i386.rpm
XFree86-Xvfb-4.0.3-5.i386.rpm
```

FROM THE CLASSROOM

Configuring the X-Window System

Configuring the X-Window system is one of the few places in the process of setting up a Linux system in which the choices you make could potentially damage your hardware. The reason for this has to do with something called the *refresh rate* for your monitor. This is the rate at which the image you see on your screen is redrawn. The refresh rate is expressed in terms of Hertz (Hz). A refresh rate of 60Hz means that an image is redrawn 60 times in one second. Computer monitors have both a vertical and a horizontal refresh rate. Some monitors, known as multisync monitors, support multiple vertical and horizontal refresh rates. Whether fixed frequency or multisync, these refresh rates vary from one model of monitor to another. When you specify the type of monitor you are using, what you are really doing is telling the video card what frequencies it can use to *drive* the monitor.

If your monitor is a fixed-frequency monitor and the type of monitor you select does not match the type of hardware you actually have, it is possible for your video card to overtax your monitor, resulting in a blown monitor. Most modern monitors are of the multisync type, so this is less of a worry, but if you are installing Linux on older hardware you may want to make sure you have the specifications for the monitor's refresh frequencies available before you configure XFree86.

Most generic video cards from chip manufacturers like Cirrus Logic, Chips & Technologies, Trident, Tseng Labs, and so on are supported directly by the SVGA rpm. Note that there is also an older xf86cfg rpm for using xf86cfg to manage your X server configuration files. Experiment with this only if you are unsuccessful with Xconfigurator.

Using a Two-Button Mouse

The X-Window system was designed to work with a three-button mouse. Most personal computers, however, come with a two-button mouse. Although you might choose to purchase a three-button mouse, you don't need to do so in order to use the X-Window system. If you have a two-button mouse, the "missing" button is the middle button. You can emulate the middle button of a three-button mouse by simultaneously clicking both the left and right buttons on a two-button mouse.

Also, don't expect esoteric mice or "wheel" mice to work fully on Linux. On the author's system, the scroll button on the Microsoft scrolling mouse is not recognized.

The Red Hat Certified Engineer exam is primarily a performance-based exam. It is very important, therefore, that you try out the concepts presented in this chapter and experiment with them. Don't just read about them.

/etc/X11

Information about your X-Window configuration is stored in the *etc/X11* directory (Figure 7-4).

```
# ls -l /etc/X11
total 76
drwxr-xr-x    9 root      root          4096 Jul 19 20:00 applnk
drwxr-xr-x    2 root      root          4096 Jul 19 19:55 fs
drwxr-xr-x    6 root      root          4096 Jul 19 19:53 gdm
drwxr-xr-x    2 root      root          4096 Jul 19 19:51 lbxproxy
-rwxr-xr-x    1 root      root          1380 Apr  7 11:12 prefdm
drwxr-xr-x    2 root      root          4096 Jul 19 19:51 proxymngr
drwxr-xr-x    4 root      root          4096 Jul 19 19:51 rstart
drwxr-xr-x    2 root      root          4096 Jul 19 19:53 twm
lrwxrwxrwx    1 root      root            29 Jul 31 21:13 X ->
../../usr/X11R6/bin/XF86_SVGA
drwxr-xr-x    3 root      root          4096 Jul 19 19:59 xdm
-rw-r--r--    1 root      root         15562 Jul 19 22:40 XF86Config
-rw-r--r--    1 root      root          2205 Jul 19 22:40 XF86Config-4
-rw-r--r--    1 root      root          1055 Mar 30 21:52 XftConfig
drwxr-xr-x    3 root      root          4096 Jul 19 19:53 xinit
lrwxrwxrwx    1 root      root            27 Jul 19 19:51 xkb ->
./../usr/X11R6/lib/X11/xkb
lrwxrwxrwx    1 root      root            24 May  2 19:10 X.Linux ->
/usr/X11R6/bin/XF86_SVGA
-rw-r--r--    1 root      root           613 Mar 20 16:38 Xmodmap
drwxr-xr-x    2 root      root          4096 Jul 19 19:51 xserver
drwxr-xr-x    2 root      root          4096 Jul 19 19:51 xsm
```

Two of the most important of these files are *XF86Config* and *XF86Config-4*. XF86Config is used by the Version 3.*x* family of X-servers, while XF86Config-4 is used by XFree86 version 4. To determine which family of X-servers you are using, just ask rpm to display your installed XFree86 software:

```
# rpm -qa | grep XFree86
XFree86-libs-4.0.3-5
XFree86-4.0.3-5
```

```
XFree86-devel-4.0.3-5
XFree86-xfs-4.0.3-5
XFree86-twm-4.0.3-5
XFree86-SVGA-3.3.6-35
XFree86-75dpi-fonts-4.0.3-5
XFree86-tools-4.0.3-5
XFree86-xdm-4.0.3-5
XFree86-Xvfb-4.0.3-5
```

Next, identify the X-server you are using. /etc/X11/X is symbolically linked to it:

```
# ls -l /etc/X11/X
lrwxrwxrwx    1 root      root           29 Jul 31 21:13 /etc/X11/X ->
../../usr/X11R6/bin/XF86_SVGA
```

From the preceding examples, we can see that our system is running the XF86_SVGA server, and from our rpm list we can see that we have SVGA version 3.3.6-35 installed.

XF86Config(-4) is read by the XFree86 X-server when it starts. This file is where the X-server obtains its configuration information and is where the changes you make when you run Xconfigurator are written. Although normally you should use one of these utilities to modify XF86Config, it is a text file and can be edited with any standard text editor. If you plan to modify this file manually, consult the XF86Config manual page.

FIGURE 7-4

Configuration information for X-Windows is in /etc/X11 directory

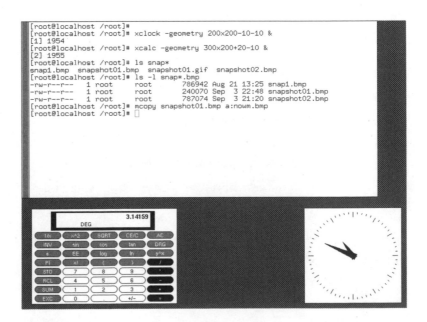

Another thing you should notice in the listing of the /etc/X11 directory is that there is an entry for a file called *X*. This file is actually a symbolic link that points to /usr/X11R6/bin/XF86_SVGA. This is the hardware-specific X-server that will be started when the X-Window system is started on this system. The file this link points to on your system will vary, depending on the display hardware you use.

You need to be familiar with both the /etc/X11 directory and the /usr/X11R6 directory. This is the directory where the X-Window software is stored. Of particular importance is the /usr/X11R6/bin directory, where the X-Window executable images are stored. This directory must be in your *PATH* environment variable if you want to use the X-Window system. If you have run Xconfigurator, your PATH should be set correctly. You can check the value of the PATH variable with this command:

```
echo $PATH
```

If your PATH environment variable isn't set correctly, you can add the X-Window image directory to your PATH with this command:

```
PATH=$PATH:/usr/X11R6/bin
```

EXERCISE 7-1

X-Server

In this exercise, we will start your X-server without running any window manager and start an xterm X-client application. Some of the commands used in this exercise are covered later in the chapter. If the X-Window system is not running, you can skip Steps 1 and 3.

1. If the X-Window system is running, change to a text console by pressing CTRL-ALT-F1.

2. Log in on the text console as root.

3. Stop the current X-Window server by typing this:

   ```
   init 3
   ```

4. Start the XFree86 X-server by typing the command:

   ```
   # X &
   ```

   Your X-server will start, but all you will see is a blank gray screen.

5. Switch back to your text console session by pressing CTRL-ALT-F1.

6. Type the following command:

   ```
   xterm  -display localhost:0.0  &.
   ```

   (Note: xterm starts with a lowercase x.)

7. Switch back to your X-Window display by pressing CTRL-ALT-F7.

You should now have an xterm terminal window. Select the window and try to enter commands from the xterm command line. Check out the contents of /usr/X11R6/bin. Try starting other X-client applications from the xterm command line. Reboot your system to return things to normal.

One last keystroke hint for X: pressing the CTRL-ALT-BACKSPACE keys sends the X server a signal that causes it to terminate instantly. Experiment with this to avoid having to reboot your machine.

CERTIFICATION OBJECTIVE 7.02

X-Clients

Once you have your X-server working, you are (almost) ready to start connecting to it with X-Window clients. X-Window clients, or *X-clients,* are the application programs you run that use the windowing services provided by your X-server to display their output. You run one X-server process to control your display. In contrast, you can run as many X-clients as your hardware resources, primarily RAM, will support. If your Linux system is part of a network, you may also start X-clients on other systems on the network and have those clients send their displays to your X-server.

X-clients exist for almost any application you wish to name. There are X-clients for word processing, spreadsheets, games, and more. Most command-line utilities, including many system administration utilities, come in an X-client version. There are even X-client versions of popular utilities such as the emacs program editor.

Starting X-Clients and Command-Line Options

Starting an X-client is very easy. When you start the X-Window system for the first time on Red Hat Linux, several X-clients will already be started for you. You can start additional X-clients by using the mouse and selecting a program to start from a menu, or you can start an X-client from a command line.

X-client applications are standard Linux applications. If you choose to start an X-client from a command line, you can follow the command name with any number of options. Most X-clients understand a common set of options. These options are used to control things such as the size and location of the X-client's window, the font the application uses to display the text, and even the display on which the application should display its output. Table 7-1 lists some of the more useful options you can supply when you start an X-client from the command-line.

The behavior of most of the command-line options in Table 7-1 is self-descriptive, but we need to take a more detailed look at how some of the options work. We will

TABLE 7-1	Option	Example	Result
	-display server:0.0	-display frodo:0.0	Send output to the X-server running on frodo.
Commonly Used X-Client Command-Line Options	-geometry XSIZExYSIZE+XOFF+YOFF	-geometry 100x100+10+20	Specify size and location of window. In this case, we want a window 100×100 pixels in size, offset from the upper-left corner by 10 pixels horizontally and down by 20 pixels.
	-font fontname	-font lucidasans-14	Display text for this client using a specified font.
	-background color	-background blue	Set window background to blue.
	-foreground color	-foreground white	Set window foreground to white.
	-title string	-title "My Window"	Place a title on the client window's title bar.
	-bordercolor color	-bordercolor green	Make the window border green.
	-borderwidth pixels	-borderwidth 5	Make the window border 5 pixels wide.

look at the *-display* option later on in this chapter when we look at running remote X-clients.

The *-geometry* option is used to specify both the size of the window that the X-client starts up in and the location of the window. Notice that the first two numbers, the XSIZE and YSIZE, are separated by a lowercase "x." These two numbers specify the size of the client window in either pixels or characters, depending on the application. If you are starting an *xterm* window, for example, the size represents a terminal screen with XSIZE columns and YSIZE lines. If you are starting an *xclock,* the size represents a window XSIZExYSIZE pixels in size. The next two numbers specify where you want the client window to appear on your display. The upper-left corner of your display is always +0+0. You can specify these two numbers using any combination of plus and minus signs. A specification of +10+10 says "position the client window so that the left edge is 10 pixels from the left edge of the screen and the *top* edge is 10 pixels from the top edge of the screen." A specification of −10−10 says "position the window so that the *right* edge of the window is 10 pixels from the right edge of the display and the bottom edge of the window is 10 pixels from the bottom of the screen."

The *-font* option specifies the font that the X-client should use to display text. The X-Window system comes with a wide variety of both fixed and proportionally spaced fonts and you can add to these. In order to use a specific font, the files that contain the font definition must either be installed on your system or be available from a network font server. The default path for X-Window fonts is /usr/X11R6/lib/X11/fonts. This directory contains a number of subdirectories, each of which contains font files for the various types of fonts installed on your system.

X-Window font names are usually very long. A typical font specification is: -b&h-lucida-medium-i-normal-sans-14-140-75-75-p-82-iso8859-l. This font specification contains all the information necessary to fully identify the font. Most fonts usually have an associated abbreviation. To use the font just listed, you can also use the abbreviated name: lucidasans-14.

Many of the X-client command-line options allow you to specify a color for different parts of the client window. You can specify a simple color such as red, green, white, black, and so on, or you can specify a color by indicating the red, green, and blue components of the color:

```
xclock -background RGB:FF/00/FF
```

xterm

One of the most useful X-clients is a program called *xterm*. As its name implies, xterm is an X-client application that creates a terminal window on your X-display. So, after all the hard work you've gone through to get a nice windowing display, you're right back where you started, with a command-line interface. The difference is that now you can start up as many of these command-line interfaces as you like, and you can switch between them with the click of a mouse. Since xterm is an X-client, you can even open up terminal windows on other computers on your network and have them display to your desktop. You can start *xterm* either from a menu or from a command-line prompt.

Window Managers

As mentioned earlier, once you have your X-server running you're almost ready to start running X-applications. Before you get to that point, however, we need to look at a special type of X-client known as a *window manager*.

When you start the XFree86 X-server, it turns your display into a blank electronic canvas. If you are running Linux on a slow machine, you may even glimpse this canvas as your system goes through the process of starting the X-Window system. What you are seeing is the default desktop display for XFree86, which is an uninteresting textured gray background. The default mouse pointer for the X-Window display is a graphic representation of an "X." Once XFree86 starts and you have this canvas on your screen, the X-server is ready to start serving X-clients. In fact, you can start X-clients up at this point, and your X-server will open up windows to display their output. You will notice, however, that the windows seem to be missing something. You don't have any of the useful features such as borders, title bars, menu bars, and minimize-maximize buttons that you've come to expect from a graphical user interface. To display your windows with all the standard features you've come to expect from a graphical user interface, you need the services of a *window manager*. A window manager is a special type of X-client, and cannot run on its own. Instead, it needs the services of an X-server to do its job. It is the job of the window manager to control how other X-clients appear on your display. This includes everything from placing title bars and drawing borders around the window for each X-client application you start, to determining the size of your desktop. In a nutshell, the window manager controls the look and feel of your window session.

As is usually the case with all things Linux, there are multiple ways to accomplish the same task. Red Hat Linux comes with several window managers for you to choose from. Your choice of window manager will determine how the X-Window system appears, and to some extent how it functions.

fvwm, WindowMaker

One of the most popular window managers available for Linux is the *fvwm* window manager. The *fvwm* window manager was developed specifically for Linux and can be configured to emulate other window environments such as the commercial Motif window manager or even Windows 95. This can make fvwm a good choice if you are migrating users from a Microsoft Windows platform to Linux.

When you are running the X-Window system, your display is referred to as the *desktop*. The desktop is a workspace into which the X-server places all of your windows and icons. The desktop itself is a special window called the *root window*. Some window managers limit the size of your desktop to be that of your actual hardware. If your hardware supports a video resolution of only 800×600 pixels, your desktop is limited to that size as well. Other window managers implement a *virtual desktop* that allows the area into which you can place windows to be larger than the area of your display hardware.

The fvwm window manager uses a virtual desktop; the *vwm* in the name stands for *virtual window manager*. With fvwm's virtual desktop, your desktop is many times larger than your display. What you see displayed is only a portion of your desktop. To move to another area of your desktop, you drag the mouse in the direction you want to move and your display scrolls so that a new portion of the desktop is visible. The advantage of a virtual desktop is that you can have many X-client windows open on your desktop without having to try to squeeze them into the tiny area bounded by your display. To help you navigate your desktop, fvwm starts a pager program that displays a small window with a miniature map of your virtual desktop showing what windows you have open. To move to a particular area of your desktop, you simply click that portion of your desktop with your mouse. The fvwm95 interface is shown in Figure 7-5.

WindowMaker is another very well done window manager that comes with Red Hat Linux. The WindowMaker interface is designed to resemble the commercial NEXTSTEP interface. We will see how to start the WindowMaker GUI later.

FIGURE 7-5

The fvwm95 interface (the pager applet is in the lower-right corner)

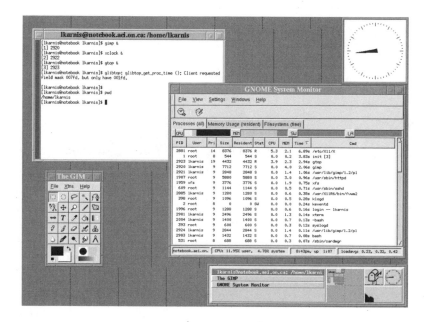

You can also use the switchdesk utility to switch to the other desktop environments not displayed. The switchdesk program creates two hidden files in your home directory *~/.Xclients* and *~/.Xclients-default* that are used to start your alternate desktop. If you have an existing *~.Xclients* file, it will be saved as *~.Xclients.switchdesk*. To switch to an alternate desktop, you simply need to modify ~/.Xclients-default.

As an example, suppose you want to use WindowMaker as your default desktop environment. Run switchdesk and select the KDE desktop environment, but do not log out after exiting switchdesk. Use your favorite text editor to edit the .Xclients-default file and change the line that reads like this:

```
exec startkde
```

to read:

```
exec wmaker
```

Save your changes and log out. On your next log in, you will be running the WindowMaker desktop. To revert back to your original desktop, simply delete the ~.Xclients and ~.Xclients-default files; then log out and log in again.

EXERCISE 7-3

Window Managers

Let's use switchdesk to explore the various window managers available to us with Linux.

1. Open a terminal window and run the command **switchdesk.**

2. Your current window manager (probably GNOME) is selected. Try one of the other window managers (such as KDE, the other popular window manager for Linux). Note that your configuration has been changed, but your current window manager is still running.

3. Log out of your current session. (GNOME Foot | Log out)

4. Log back in again. This time you should see KDE.

5. Try switching to fvwm or twm. You should see that fvwm and twm are much more basic window managers. You'll need to log out again for your changes to take effect.

6. Run switchdesk one last time. Select your favorite window manager. Log out and back in again to activate your favorite window manager.

on the
job
Commercial UNIX vendors like Sun Microsystems and Hewlett Packard have officially endorsed GNOME and are working to make their proprietary versions of UNIX (Solaris and HP-UX) fully GNOME-compliant. If you get comfortable with GNOME, you will find moving to Solaris or HP-UX much easier.

Desktops, GNOME, KDE

Two other powerful virtual desktop environments that come with Red Hat Linux are the GNOME (GNU Network Object Model Environment) desktop environment and the KDE (the Kool Desktop Environment). The GNOME desktop, shown in Figure 7-6, is the default desktop for Red Hat Linux 7 and is the desktop you first see after installing the X-Window system.

FIGURE 7-6

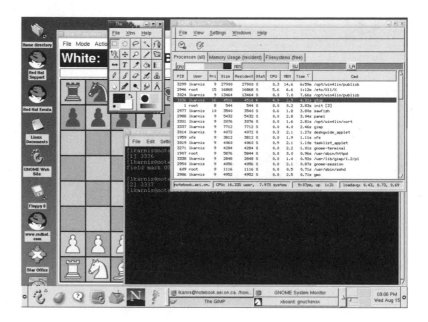

The GNOME desktop (the default desktop for Red Hat Linux 7.1)

GNOME Features

The GNOME desktop includes support for the Common Object Request Broker Architecture (CORBA), which allows GNOME software components written in any language and running on different systems to work together. In addition, the GNOME developer community is also working on an architecture similar to Microsoft's Object Linking and Embedding (OLE) architecture that will allow one GNOME application to call and control another GNOME application. One very nice feature of GNOME-compliant applications is that they are *session aware*; that is, when you quit an application, the application "remembers" the location in the document where you were last working and will reposition your cursor to that point when you restart the application.

Sawfish

Even though you may be using GNOME as your desktop environment, you still need the services of a window manager. The best way to think of the relationship between the window manager and GNOME is that they work together to control what you see on your display. The GNOME desktop will work with any window manager, but it works best with a GNOME-compliant window manager. Under Red Hat Linux, the default GNOME window manager is the Sawfish window manager. This is new to Red Hat 7.*x*. Previously, the Enlightenment window manager was used. IceWM is another GNOME-compliant window manager you can use. Work is under way to make fvwm and other window managers GNOME-compliant. You can find more information about GNOME at http://www.gnome.org.

Using GNOME

Many of the features of the GNOME interface will be familiar to you from other desktop environments. On the left side of the screen are icons representing files and applications that can be opened by double-clicking them with the mouse. The GNOME desktop environment also provides you with a virtual desktop. Next to the application buttons in the center of the panel is a pager you can use to move from one area of the desktop to another.

One of the key features of GNOME is the *panel,* which you can see at the bottom of the screen in Figure 7-6. The panel is the control center for most of your activities while you use GNOME. The button at the far left of the panel with the imprint of a foot is the *Main Menu* button. Use your mouse to click this button, and you will see a list of applications you can run. You can also launch applications from the panel by clicking the appropriate icon. In the center of the panel at the bottom of the screen in Figure 7-6 are buttons to launch the GNOME help utility, the GNOME configuration utility, a terminal emulator, and a Web browser. You can add applications and menus to the panel. You can also place additional panels on your desktop. Next to the main menu button is a narrow *Hide Panel* button. Click this button to store the panel out of sight. If a panel is hidden, click the Hide Panel button to make it reappear. Notice that there are Hide buttons on both ends of the panel.

CERTIFICATION OBJECTIVE 7.03

Startup

You can configure the X-Window interface to start automatically when your system boots, or you can choose to start the X-Window system manually. Recall that this is the last decision you make when running Xconfigurator. If your X-Window configuration appears to be working correctly, you will probably want to go ahead and tell Xconfigurator to make the changes necessary to boot your system directly into the X-Window system. You should answer No if your X-Window configuration doesn't appear to be working correctly, or if you are setting up your X-server to run with a new or nonstandard video card. If you choose not to boot into the X-Window system, Linux Red Hat will boot up with a text-based console screen, and you can start the X-Window system manually by using the startx command.

startx

You use the *startx* command to start the X-Window interface manually from a command-line prompt. Simply type the command

```
startx
```

at the Linux command prompt. This starts XFree86 and switches your display into graphics mode. If you run startx and the X-Window system is already started, you will receive an error message telling you that an X-server is already running on your display.

When you exit an X-Window session that was started by running startx, your display resets to text console mode, and you are placed back at the Linux command prompt level. You may decide to start the X-Window interface this way if you are debugging a new X-Window setup. Once you have your configuration working to your satisfaction, you can then configure Linux to boot into the X-Window system automatically.

on the **job** ***The startx command is actually a customizable shell script that serves as a front end to the xinit command. The default location for both the startx shell script and the xinit program is /usr/X11R6/bin.***

For a production system, especially a user's workstation, you will most likely want Linux to boot into the X-Window system. Fortunately, you don't have to rerun the Xconfigurator to change this. You can change the mode Red Hat Linux boots into by editing the /etc/inittab file and changing the default runlevel. In Red Hat Linux, the X-Window system is defined as runlevel 5. To make the X-Window system your default runlevel at boot time, use your favorite text editor and change the line in /etc/inittab that reads

```
id:3:initdefault:
```

to

```
id:5:initdefault:
```

Note that this change will not take effect until you reboot. If you are running as the root user, you can also use the init command to switch between X-Window runlevel 5 and non-X-Window runlevel 3. Running this command

```
init 3
```

switches your display from X-Window back to text terminal mode, whereas

```
init 5
```

switches you from text terminal mode to X-Window. You can find more information on changing runlevels in Chapter 5.

You can still use the virtual console feature of Red Hat Linux when you're running the X-Window system. You can switch between six text consoles and one GUI console. There are several key combinations you can use to control your X-Window session (Table 7-2).

xdm, gdm, kdm

In order to gain access to a Linux system, you must first pass an authentication check. On most systems, this consists of identifying yourself to the system by typing in a username and password combination. When you log in to Linux from a text terminal, you make use of the services of the *mingetty* (get tty) program. The mingetty program monitors the terminal waiting for someone to press a key indicating they wish to log in. When this happens, the mingetty program spawns the *login* program, which asks you for your username and password.

TABLE 7-2	Key Combinations	Description
Key Combinations to Control X-Window Sessions	CTRL-ALT-F1 through CTRL-ALT-F6	Switch from X-Window GUI to virtual console 1, 2, etc.
	CTRL-ALT-F7	Switch from text console to X-Window GUI.
	CTRL-ALT-+ or CTRL-ALT-– (minus sign)-ALT-–	Toggle forward or backward between X-Window video modes.
	CTRL-ALT-BACKSPACE	Terminate X-Window GUI.

When you log in from the X-Window GUI, the login and authentication task is handed over to another special type of X-client, the *display manager.* The display manager is a fairly simple program. Its primary purpose is to display a dialogue box on the screen asking for your username and password combination. You have a choice of display managers to use with Red Hat Linux. The default display manager is the GNOME display manager. To change your display manager, edit the *prefdm* shell script in the /etc/X11 directory (as shown in Figure 7-7).

Take the line that contains preferred= and add either kdm, gdm, or xdm for the KDE Display Manager, GNOME Display Manager, or X Display Manager, respectively.

How you start the X-Window system affects how it behaves. The most noticeable difference is that when you start the X-Window GUI using startx, exiting your X-Window session doesn't log you out but returns you to the command line from which you entered the startx command. Exiting an X-Window session that was started by logging in through a display manager is effectively the same as logging out of a command line login session. The startup process for an X-Window session launched by startx also differs slightly from one started through a display manager.

The default behavior for the gdm window manager is to launch a GNOME session for you. The kdm window manager launches a KDE session. As an alternative to using the switchdesk utility, both the gdm window manager and the kdm window

FIGURE 7-7

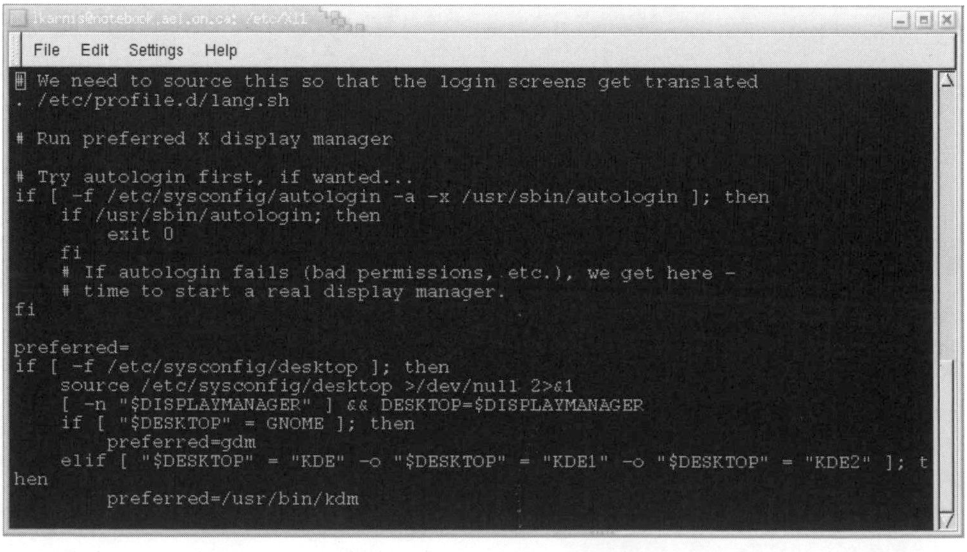

Set your preferred display manager by editing /etc/X11/prefdm

manager have option buttons to allow you to log in under a different desktop environment other than the default.

There are a number of configuration files you can use to customize the behavior of your X-Window session. These files are hidden files that reside in your home directory. Typically they are shell scripts, read and executed by the X-Window startup routines. If the X-Window startup program doesn't find a particular configuration file in your home directory, it will use a system-wide default version of the same file.

When you start the X-Window system with the startx command, the xinit program looks for a file to run named *.xinitrc* in your home directory. Using the shell's filename generation shorthand character for your home directory, the full pathname for this file is ~/.xinitrc. If the startx command cannot find ~/.xinitrc, it will run the file /etc/X11/xinit/xinitrc. This file, in turn, will run either the file ~/.Xclients or, if that file doesn't exist, /etc/X11/xinit/Xclients.

The ~/.xinitrc file usually contains a series of commands that start various X-clients. Figure 7-8 shows an example of a simple ~/.xinitrc file. The first line tells Linux which shell program to use to run the ~/.xinitrc script. The next two lines are comment lines. The first line after that starts up an xterm terminal client. The next line starts up the xclock application to display a clock on your screen. The line after that brings up an X-Window calculator. Notice that the three command lines end with an ampersand. This is important; it tells the shell to run each command line and return control to the calling program (~/.xinitrc) without waiting for the program started on the command line to finish running. The final line in the ~/.xinitrc file uses the exec command to start the fvwm window manager. This tells Linux to run the fvwm program and that fvwm should take control of the process that is running the .xinitrc shell script so that when the fvwm process exits—that is, when you choose to exit the X-Window system—the other programs started by the ~/.xinitrc process will be terminated.

You can create an *~/.xinitrc* file with any text editor. After you have saved the file and exited the editor, you should make sure the file is executable by issuing this command:

```
chmod a+x ~/.xinitrc
```

FIGURE 7-8

The .xinitrc file can be used to customize the behavior of startx

```
#!/bin/bash
#A simple ~/.xinitrc shell script
#/usr/X11R6/bin should also be in your PATH
xterm &
xclock -geometry 200x200-20+20 &
xcalc -geometry 300x300-20-20 &
exec fvwm
```

If you log in using a display manager, the initialization of your X-Window session takes place in a somewhat different manner than it does when you run startx. When you run startx, your X-Window session runs as a child process of your text-based login shell. You can verify this with the runlevel command. Even though the X-Window system is running, Linux is still at runlevel 3. After you exit the X-Window system, you still have to log out of this shell to terminate your login session.

When you log in from a display manager, Linux does not start an interactive shell. Instead, the display manager launches a program, called the session manager, that is the controlling process for your X-Window login session. If you are running the GNOME desktop, this program is */usr/bin/gnome-session*, if you are running KDE, it is */usr/bin/kwm*. The standard X-Window session manager is */usr/bin/xsession*. All X-clients that you run from your X-Window session are child processes of the session manager process. When you exit the session manager, all child processes of the session manager are terminated also. When you log in via a display manager, the session manager does not execute the contents of ~xinitrc.

Through the use of option buttons, both the GNOME and KDE display manager allow you to choose the desktop environment you wish to start. From the GNOME display manager, click the Options button and select the Sessions menu, then select the session manager you want to use. Both GNOME and the KDE environment use their own startup files.

If you start a window session using the default xsession program, you can customize your session using the ~/.xsession file or the ~/.Xclients file; xsession looks for ~/.xsession first and then looks for ~/.Xclients. If neither file exists, then it will use system defaults. The system defaults for most window managers and desktop environments are stored in directories under /etc/X11.

EXERCISE 7-3

startx

In this exercise, we will start the X-Window system using startx with a customized .xinitrc file.

1. If the X-Window system is running, stop it using the command:

   ```
   init 3
   ```

2. Log in to a text console.

3. Make sure you're in your home directory. Use your favorite text editor to create a .xinitrc file.

4. Make sure the .xinitrc file is executable by typing this:

   ```
   chmod  a+x  .xinitrc
   ```

5. Start the X-Window system by typing this:

   ```
   startx
   ```

   Your X-Window session should automatically start the applications in your .xinitrc file.

Remote Display of X Apps

One of the most powerful features of the X-Window system is the strength of its networking support. The X-Window system was designed from the beginning to run in a networked environment. If you are a system manager with a number of Red Hat Linux systems under your care, there's no need to leave your office and make a journey to the server room every time you want to run a GUI administration tool. With the X-Window system, you can connect to any number of systems and redirect the output from X-clients running on those systems back to the X-server running on your desktop.

X-Security

Before you can run remote clients and have them redirect their output back to your X-server, we need to take a look at some basic X-Window security. When working with remote X applications, you should also keep in mind that all other Linux security features are still in effect. You will still need a user account and password, or the equivalent, such as an entry in a .rhost file on the remote system, in order to connect to the remote system to start an X-client. Authorization problems or network problems at layers below the X-Window system can prevent your X-Window client applications from running.

Part of the job of the X-server running on your system is to listen for requests from X-clients that want to send their output to your display. Those requests can come from local client applications, those that are running on your system, or they can come from remote client applications running on another system. Without some form of access control, any X-client application on any system on your network can send its output to the display controlled by your X-server. This includes client applications started up by other users on other systems. Although on a small network you might want to allow indiscriminate network access to your display, in a larger network environment or a production network environment, you will want to limit who can send client output to your X-server.

The simplest way to control access to your display is with the *xhost* command. The *xhost* command controls access to your X-server display on a machine-by-machine basis. Table 7-3 shows how you use the *xhost* command to secure your X-server.

The xhost command provides you with a basic security mechanism. The X-Window system can also make use of more sophisticated methods to control access to X-servers. These methods use DES-encrypted authorization strings and other mechanisms to validate remote users trying to access a local X-server display. Some of these methods have the advantage over xhost-based access control of allowing you to restrict or allow access to your display to specific users from specific machines or network domains. Access information for these other validation methods is stored in the hidden file ~/.Xauthority. You use the xauth program to manipulate the information in this file.

Remote X-Clients

Running a remote X-client requires that you have access to the remote system on which the client will run. In turn, the remote system, and possibly the account you are using on the remote system, must have permission to connect to the X-server display that the X-client you start will use for its console. In the following example, we will take

TABLE 7-3	Command	Description
Using the xhost Command to Secure Your X-Server	xhost	Show current security settings.
	xhost +	Disable security; allow connections from any system.
	xhost −	Enable security.
	xhost +server1.xyz.com	Allow connection from server1.xyz.com.
	xhost −server1.xyz.com	Disable connections from server1.xyz.com.

a step-by-step look at running an X-client on a remote system, server1.xyz.com, and sending the output back to our local workstation, work1.xyz.com.

The first step in the process is to make sure we allow server1 access to the display on our local system:

```
xhost +server1.xyz.com
```

If we have already granted server1 access to our display, we can skip this step.

The next step in the process is to log in to server1. Here, we will use the telnet command, but this could be done using any program, such as rsh or rlogin, that allows us to establish a remote login session on server1:

```
[root@work1]$ telnet server1.xyz.com
Trying 192.168.1.2...
Connected to server1.xyz.com.
Escape character is '^]'.
Red Hat Linux release 7.1 (Seawolf)
Kernel 2.4.2 on an i686
login: root
[root@server1]$
```

Since we are going to be running X-Window client applications, we will probably want to make sure the X-Window binary directory is in our search path:

```
[root@server1]$ PATH=$PATH:/usr/X11R6/bin
```

The final step in the process is to start our remote X-client, or X-clients if we plan to start up more than one remote program. At this point, we can choose to start our X-client in one of two ways. For this example, we will start the same X-client application using each method. The X-client program we will run is *xclock*.

Since X-Window clients behave like Linux applications, all we need to do to run the xclock program is type the program name on the command line. Since this program is an X-Window client application, however, we need to provide it with one crucial piece of information; the name of the X-server it is going to use. We can provide this information on the command line when we start the application by specifying the -display option:

```
[root@server1]$ xclock -display work1.xyz.com:0.0
```

This starts the xclock application on server1, but the output from the program is displayed on work1. At this point, your telnet session on server1 appears to be locked up. This is because the xclock application is running as your foreground process. Unless you received an error message when you started the application, you won't see any indication that something is happening on server1 because the output from xclock is being sent to the X-server on work1. To regain control of your telnet session, you can either terminate xclock by pressing CTRL-C, or you can suspend it by pressing CTRL-Z. If you are going to be starting multiple-client applications, you should end each command line with an ampersand (&) to tell Linux to run the X-client as a background process.

The other method for starting an X-client from the command prompt uses a shell environment variable to pass the display information to the X-client. When you start an X-client without the -display option, the X-client looks for the DISPLAY environment variable in your current process. In fact, this is how X-clients you run on your local system determine where to send their output. When you log in to your workstation from the display manager, the DISPLAY variable is automatically set to point to the X-server running on your workstation. If you are connecting to a remote host and will be starting multiple X-clients, you should set this variable so you don't have to specify the -display option for every X-client you run. Having pressed CTRL-C to regain control of our telnet session, we can set the DISPLAY variable and rerun xclock:

```
[root@server1]$ export DISPLAY=work1.xyz.com:0.0    # works on
sh,ksh,bash
[root@server1]$ xclock
```

The first part of the display specification is the X-server the X-client should connect to. The second part of the display specification requires further explanation. A single X-server can control multiple GUI displays attached to a single system. Each GUI display has its own set of input and output devices (monitor, keyboard, and mouse). In addition, each GUI display can have multiple screens or monitors. When you are redirecting the output for an X-client, you must tell it not only which system to connect to but also which GUI display and which screen on that display to use. On most systems this will be display 0, console 0 (written as *host*:0.0*). *The server portion* of the display can be a hostname, a fully-qualified domain name, or an IP address. The following are all valid specifications for remote displays:

- work1:0.0
- work1.xyz.com:0.0
- 192.168.1.5:0.0

Troubleshooting

The X-Window system is very robust and stable, but occasionally problems can arise. There are several things you can try when you troubleshoot X-Window problems:

- Session managers create log files in your home directory such as ~/.xsession-errors. Check these log files as well as /var/log/messages and /var/log/Xerrors for error messages from your X-server.

- Problems with the .xinitrc or .Xclients shell scripts may cause problems. Try deleting or renaming these files.

- Check the DISPLAY environment variable to make sure it is set correctly. If you are running X-clients locally, they still use this variable. You can set it with this command:

  ```
  export DISPLAY=localhost:0.0
  ```

  or

  ```
  export DISPLAY=:0.0
  ```

- Make sure /usr/X11R6/bin is in your search path.

- Check for underlying system problems or network problems that could be causing problems with the X-Window system.

- Even if your X-server is not responding or you can't read the display, don't forget that you can switch to a text console to gain access to the system.

- If you are troubleshooting X-server problems on a remote system, try starting an X-client from your workstation using the remote X-server's display. Note that you will need appropriate X-security access to do this:

  ```
  xclock -display remotesys:0.0
  ```

EXERCISE 7-4

Troubleshooting DISPLAY Problems

In this exercise, we will see what happens if you unset the DISPLAY variable.

1. Log in to an X-Window session.

2. Bring up a terminal window from the panel or a menu.

3. Start the xclock application using this command:

```
xclock  &
```

4. Unset your DISPLAY variable:

```
unset DISPLAY
```

5. Start another xclock:

```
xclock  &
```

6. You should get an error message saying that the X-client can't find your display. Reset the DISPLAY variable with the command:

```
export DISPLAY=localhost:0.0
```

7. Try starting the xclock application again.

---

exam
Watch

The X-server and most X-clients have associated man pages. You should make a habit of reviewing man pages to learn more about commands, features, and options. Linux also includes an info command that may provide more detailed and accurate information about an item. For more information about the X-server itself, man **X** *is a good place to start. Note that you may have to install the RPMs for the man pages. There are also several helpful text documents in /usr/doc and /usr/doc/HOWTO that explain various aspects of configuring the X-Window system.*

Now that you have seen how X-Window clients and the X-Window server work together, refer to the following Scenario & Solution for some common situations you may encounter, along with their solutions.

SCENARIO & SOLUTION

I'm having problems getting XFree86 to run on my hardware.	Check the Red Hat hardware support site. Run SuperProbe. (Be sure to get the case correct!)
I want to use a different desktop environment.	Use the switchdesk utility to change your desktop environment.
I want to stop the X-Window system without halting Linux.	Use the init command to change the system runlevel to runlevel 3.
I'm having problems starting an X-client.	Check that the DISPLAY variable is set and exported. For example: # export DISPLAY=my.computer.com:0.0 Check for underlying network problems. Check X-security problems.
My X-Window display is acting strangely and I can't log in.	Switch to a virtual console.

CERTIFICATION SUMMARY

The X-Window system provides a state-of-the-art graphical user interface and offers features not found in other GUI environments. Although the X-Window system can be complicated, the Xconfigurator program simplifies the process of setting up the X-Window system. One of the most important steps you can take in setting up the X-Window system on Red Hat Linux is to select hardware that the XFree86 X-server supports.

The look and feel of the X-Window interface is determined by your choice of window manager. Red Hat Linux comes with several desktop environments, including GNOME, KDE, AfterStep, WindowMaker, and fvwm. The GNOME desktop interface is the default for Red Hat Linux 7.1.

The X-Window system is designed to run on networked systems. You run client applications, both locally and remotely, that use the X-server on your workstation for their console.

TWO-MINUTE DRILL

Here are some of the key points from the certification objectives in Chapter 7.

X-Server

❑ The X-server is the software that manages your graphics display, which includes your monitor/graphics adapter, keyboard, and mouse.

❑ X-servers work with X-clients to keep your display up-to-date. X-servers report on keyboard and mouse events to X-clients, and X-clients send instructions back to the server on how to update their window appropriately (draw a character, resize the window, drop down a menu, and so on).

❑ The X-server included with Red Hat 7.1 is XFree86 version 4 for the latest graphics cards or version 3.36 for older graphics cards.

❑ The correct X-server software will be installed for you if you select a Workstation, Notebook, or Custom install that includes graphics. Note that if you select a Server Install, no graphics capabilities are included in the installation.

X-Clients

❑ Red Hat Linux provides a great number of X-client programs for your use. Popular programs include terminal emulators, desktop accessories (such as the File Manager), games, and more.

❑ X-clients are organized into categories such as Programs, Favorites, and Applets under the GNOME Foot menu. Browse the available set of programs to see what you can find.

❑ The list of supplied X-clients includes graphics manipulation tools (GIMP, the GNU Image Manipulation Tool), CD players, and many high quality games. XChess is challenging, even for experienced chess players!

❑ You can send the display of an X-client program to a remote system by using the –display option followed by the remote system and display (–display my.machine.com:0.0).

Startup

❏ By default, Red Hat 7.1 selects GNOME with the Sawfish window manager as the default window manager.

❏ The switchdesk tool can be used to select alternative window managers. Not every window manager on the list is necessarily installed. You may have to insert the appropriate CD (1 or 2) and use the rpm command to update your system to include your favorite window manager.

❏ If you change window managers with switchdesk, you will have to log out and log in again for your changes to take effect

❏ You can customize your graphics session to start your favorite applications when your graphics session starts. Just edit the ~/.xinitrc file to include commands to start the program(s) you want.

Remote Display of X Apps

❏ By default, an X-client will send its display to the host it was run on.

❏ You can send a window for a client to any other display by using the –display command line option for the program.

❏ The remote system must be willing to accept your remote request. On the remote system, use the xhosts + command to accept all incoming windows. Add a system name immediately after the + to accept display requests only from the named system.

❏ You can set the DISPLAY environment variable to direct all displays for every X-client you start on a remote system.

SELF TEST

The following questions will help you measure your understanding of the material presented in this chapter. Read all the choices carefully, as there may be more than one correct answer. Choose all correct answers for each question.

X-Server

1. Which of the following is true about the X-Window system?

   A. The X-server runs on your workstation; X-clients run on your workstation or on other computers on the network.

   B. If an X-server is running on your workstation, then X-client applications running on your computer cannot send their output to an X-server running on another system on the network.

   C. An X-client application gets its input from the keyboard and mouse attached to the same X-server where the client is sending its output.

   D. Aside from the steps necessary to start the remote application, there is no difference between running an X-client locally and running one remotely.

2. Your supervisor comes to you and says he is thinking of purchasing some new workstations for the graphics department and that he has decided they will run Red Hat Linux. They must be purchased and installed as quickly as possible, however. He has found what appears to be a good deal on some brand-name systems and would like you to determine whether they will be suitable for the planned task. You follow up on his suggestion and discover that the video card for the systems is built around a completely new video chip design. What recommendation do you make regarding the purchase?

   A. Go ahead and purchase the systems as they are.

   B. Since the graphics department will use these systems, make sure they have plenty of disk space to store graphics files.

   C. Purchase the systems, but have the vendor replace the new video cards with a model that is listed on the Red Hat Linux support site.

   D. Make sure the systems have 100Mbps Ethernet cards so that graphics files can be shipped across the network as quickly as possible.

3. You performed a new install of Red Hat Linux 7.1 and ran into problems when you tried to install the X-Window system. Your system is now up and running, and you can get logged in to a command prompt. How do you go about reconfiguring the X-Window system?

    A. Use the vi editor and modify the /etc/X11/XF86Config file.

    B. Run the Xconfigurator utility from the command line.

    C. Restart the X-Window GUI and run XF86Setup.

    D. Reinstall Red Hat Linux.

4. When you run Xconfigurator, it is unable to determine the type of video card installed in your system. You, unfortunately, can't find the documentation for your system anywhere. What can you do to determine the type of video hardware installed on your system?

    A. Rerun the Xconfigurator program to see whether it will recognize your video card the second time around.

    B. Try running XF86Setup.

    C. Run linuxconf.

    D. Run the SuperProbe program.

5. A user who is new to the X-Window system calls you with a question about his mouse. He has been reading some documentation, and it keeps referring to his middle mouse button, but he only has a two-button mouse. What do you tell him?

    A. Hold down the CTRL key and click the left mouse button.

    B. He will have to purchase a three-button mouse to use the X-Window interface.

    C. Click the left and right mouse buttons simultaneously.

    D. He will have to run Xconfigurator and configure the X-Window system to use a two-button mouse.

6. Your X-Window configuration appears to be working, and you have an xterm terminal window open on your desktop. Whenever you try to start other X-clients from the command line, however, you keep getting the error message "command not found." What is the likely cause of the problem?

    A. You have too many X-clients running, and Linux is unable to start any additional applications.

    B. The /usr/X11R6/bin directory is missing from your PATH.

    C. The /etc/X11/XF86Config directory is missing from your PATH.

    D. You need to use the xhost command to allow X-clients to access your server.

7. You want to start an xterm X-client that is 80 columns wide by 30 lines high from the command line and position it in the upper-right corner of your display when it starts. What command would you use?

A. xterm -geometry +0-0 -font 80×30

B. xterm -geometry 80×30–0+0

C. xterm -geometry 80+30+0+0

D. xterm -display 80×30–0+0

X-Clients

8. Which of the following are valid X-client command line options? (Choose all that apply.)

A. –display

B. –windowsize

C. –background

D. –forecolor

E. –bordercolor

9. When you migrate a Windows 95 user to a Linux workstation, what steps can you take to minimize the learning curve for this person?

A. Install the full set of online documentation.

B. Install the KDE desktop environment.

C. Use the switchdesk utility and set the user's desktop environment to AnotherLevel.

D. Set Linux to boot to runlevel 3.

10. You are using the GNOME desktop environment. You know that you just started up the GNOME spreadsheet application, but now it seems to have disappeared from your screen. How can you get it back?

A. Look at the task bar at the bottom of the screen and see if you have accidentally switched virtual desktops.

B. Log out and log back in. GNOME will restart the application.

C. Use the Main Menu button to restart the application.

11. You are troubleshooting a system that appears not to have been set to boot into the X-Window system, but you know that the system has been configured to run an X-server. What is the first step you should try?

    A. Type X to start the X-server.

    B. Run the startx command to start the X-Window system.

    C. Edit /etc/X11/XF86Config and set the X-Window system to start on system boot.

    D. Run the file .xinitrc in your home directory.

12. When you installed Red Hat Linux, you configured the X-Window system but chose not to have Linux boot up with the X-Window system running. You have been starting the X-Window system with the startx command and everything is working without any problems. You would now like to make the X-Window GUI the default runlevel for your system. How would you do this?

    A. Edit /etc/inittab and look for the line that reads "id:3:initdefault" and replace with a line that reads "id:5:initdefault" and reboot.

    B. Run Xconfigurator.

    C. Change the /etc/X11/prefdm link.

    D. Execute the runlevel 5 command.

13. You are troubleshooting a Linux server that boots into runlevel 5 and need to temporarily shut down the X-Window system. How would you do this?

    A. Use the ps command to obtain the process of the XFree86 server and use the kill command to stop it.

    B. Edit /etc/inittab and look for the line that reads "id:3:initdefault", then replace it with a line that reads "id:5:initdefault" and reboot.

    C. Use the command init 3.

    D. Use the stopx command.

14. Your system is using the xdm display manager. You want to use the GNOME display manager (gdm). How can you do this?

    A. Change the /etc/X11/prefdm shell script and define the preferred= variable.

    B. Run Xconfigurator.

    C. Edit /etc/X11/XF86Config.

    D. Use the GNOME Control Panel to change the display manager.

Startup

15. You would like to automatically start up the xclock application whenever you start up an X-Window session with startx. How would you do this?

    A. Create or edit the file .Xdefault and add this command:

    ```
    xclock &
    ```

    B. Create or edit the file xinitrc in the system root directory with this command:

    ```
    xclock -geometry 200x200-0+0 &
    ```

    C. Edit /etc/X11/XF86Config and add this command:

    ```
    xclock -geometry 200x200-0+0 &
    ```

    D. Create or edit the file .xinitrc in your home directory and add this command:

    ```
    xclock &
    ```

16. How could you start a KDE session from a system running the gdm display manager?

    A. Relink /etc/X11/prefdm.
    B. Click the Options button on the gdm login message box and select Sessions -> KDE.
    C. Log in normally and use switchdesk to change your default desktop.
    D. You can't log in to the KDE environment from the gdm display manager.

17. What command would you issue to allow X-clients running on the system with an IP address of 172.16.200.99 to access your X-server?

    A. xauth +172.16.200.99
    B. xhost –172.16.200.99
    C. xhost +
    D. xhost +172.16.200.99

Remote Display of X Apps

18. You log in to a remote system via Telnet with the intention of starting up several remote X-clients that will send their output to your local display (admin1.xyz.com). What can you do to make this easier?

    A. Use the –display admin1.xyz.com option.

B. Create a DISPLAY variable with this command:

```
DISPLAY=admin1.xyz.com:0.0
```

C. Create a DISPLAY variable with this command:

```
export DISPLAY=admin1.xyz.com
```

D. Create a DISPLAY variable with this command:

```
export DISPLAY=admin1.xyz.com:0.0
```

19. A user calls up to report that she is having problems getting a remote molecular modeling application to display on her screen. Assuming she has disabled all security on her X-server, how could you use the display option to help troubleshoot the situation? Your workstation is admin1.xyz.com; her workstation is ws97.xyz.com.

A. Tell her to run the SuperProbe utility with the –display option so you know what kind of monitor she is using.

B. Have her try to start an X-client and direct its display to her X-server with this command:

```
xclock -display localhost:0.0
```

C. Have her try to start an X-client and direct its display to your X-server with this command:

```
xclock -display admin1.xyz.com:0.0
```

D. You start an X-client from the command line and direct its display to her X-server with this command:

```
xclock -display ws97.xyz.com:0.0
```

20. The X-server on your company's Web server appears to be locked up. How might you gain access to the console?

A. Press CTRL-ALT-+.

B. Press CTRL-ALT-F1.

C. Press ALT-F1.

D. Press CTRL-ALT-DEL to reboot the system.

LAB QUESTION

We want to upgrade the video card in our Linux system. Our old video card is slow and doesn't have enough display memory to provide us with the resolution and color depth we require. We have obtained a new ATI 32MB Radeon card (I'm using this product for example purposes only). What steps might we follow to replace our old card with our new card?

SELF TEST ANSWERS

X-Server

1. ☑ **A, C, and D. A** is correct because the X-server runs on the system that has the graphics hardware, while X-clients may run locally or remotely. **C** is correct because the X-server (either remote or local) provides the X-client with its keyboard and mouse events. **D** is also correct because X-clients interact with the X-server via the X application level protocol. This protocol is machine and operating system independent, ensuring that there are no distinctions between local and remote X displays.

   ☒ **B** is incorrect because there simply is no such restriction.

2. ☑ **C.** Since the workstations are going to be used by the graphics department, they are going to be running the X-Window system. Although you might be able to get the new video cards working given ample time for experimentation, the requirement to have the new workstations up as quickly as possible precludes this. To be sure you don't have any problems configuring the X-Window system, you choose to replace the newer video card with a supported video card.

   ☒ **A** would require you to find drivers for the new video hardware. Since they may not even exist, you might be forced to acquire and install supported cards yourself. This would add unnecessary costs and delays to your workstation roll out. **B** and **D** are incorrect because the size of the graphics files used is irrelevant to the project if you don't have the capability to manipulate them.

3. ☑ **B.** You should use the Xconfigurator program any time you need to make changes to your X-Window configuration.

   ☒ **C**, run XF86Setup, is incorrect because it is no longer installed by default on your system. Also, it wouldn't be necessary, nor would it be possible in this case, to try to start the X-Window system first. XF86Setup will start up a VGA X-server if the X-Window system isn't available. **A** is possibly correct assuming we understand enough about the XF86Config file to be able to make the corrections we require. From experience, I would suggest you only edit this file if you have an (almost) working configuration you only wish to fine-tune. **D** is extreme. The only justification for this might be if we performed a custom install and perhaps neglected to include all the components of the X-Window system. It would likely be better to just install the needed rpms by hand.

4. ☑ **D.** The SuperProbe program will probe your video card and report on the type of video chip it uses, as well as the modes it uses.

   ☒ **A** is incorrect because Xconfigurator will no more be able to identify your video hardware the second time it runs than it did the first time it ran. **B** is incorrect because XF86Setup is not installed by default, and even if it were installed, it suffers from the same limitations Xconfigurator does with respect to identifying video hardware. **C** is incorrect because linuxconf is a general purpose setup tool that acts as a front-end tool for Xconfigurator. It does not add any additional functionality with respect to identifying video hardware.

5. ☑ **C.** To emulate the missing middle button on a two-button mouse, click the left and right mouse buttons at the same time.

☒ **A** won't provide the effect of clicking the middle mouse button. **B** will work, but is unnecessary. Also, if the user does replace their mouse with a three-button mouse, they would have to run mouseconfig (as root) to update their mouse settings. **D** is incorrect because the X-Window system is designed to assume the presence of a three-button mouse. It is possible to make a two-button mouse emulate a three-button mouse, but it is not possible to get the X-Window system to override its three-button mouse assumption.

6. ☑ **B.** Any time you receive the message "command not found," it is an indication that your search path is set incorrectly. In order to run X-client applications without having to specify an absolute pathname, make sure the /usr/X11R6/bin directory is in your search path.

☒ **A** is incorrect because Linux should let you start as many applications as you desire. **C** is incorrect because this is a configuration file. Only executable files need to be located by the PATH variable. **D** is also incorrect because it is normally the case that local clients have access to the local X-server. Besides, if this were truly the case, the X-client would complain that it "cannot open display," rather than the shell saying the command was not found.

7. ☑ **B.** The correct option is -geometry 80×30-0+0. Since you are creating a terminal window, the size specification 80×30 refers to the number of columns and lines. The offset specification -0+0 specifies that the right border of the xterm window should be offset 0 pixels from the right edge of the display and that the top border of the xterm window should be offset 0 pixels from the top of the display.

☒ **A** is incorrect because the –font option is used to specify the default font for the window, not the window location. **C** is incorrect because the window size is specified by 80×30, not 80+30. **D** is incorrect because a position of –0+0 positions the window at the lower-left corner of the screen.

X-Clients

8. ☑ **A, C,** and **E** are valid command line options for X-clients. –display identifies the system that receives the display for this command. –background sets the background color, and –bordercolor sets the border color for the window.

⊠ **B** is incorrect because this would be set by the first two values of the –display option. **D** is incorrect because the foreground color is set with the –foreground option.

9. ☑ **C.** The AnotherLevel desktop (available as an option box) from switchdesk closely resembles the look and feel of Windows 95. This interface would be a good choice for someone migrating from that operating system.

⊠ **A** is likely incorrect because, while the Linux online documentation is (usually) useful, it is presented in a manner different from Windows 95. **B** is incorrect because the KDE environment is quite different from Windows 95. Besides, the default window manager for Red Hat 7.1 is GNOME. Just installing KDE would not guarantee that our user would see it! **D** is incorrect because at runlevel 3, the user would only see the command line. If they were only comfortable working with a GUI, the Linux command line would be very uncomfortable to them!

10. ☑ **A.** GNOME sets up four virtual desktops that you can switch between just by clicking the desired desktop. It is possible (if you aren't used to virtual desktops) that you could have accidentally switched to another virtual desktop. All you would need to do to find your application would be to click your other virtual desktops until you found your application.

⊠ **B** is incorrect because if you log out of GNOME, all your applications will be terminated. **C** is incorrect because restarting your application would give you a new instance of that application, but wouldn't necessarily provide you with the same information/updates you had in the application you misplaced.

11. ☑ **B.** The startx command is used to start the X-Window system if it is not already started.

⊠ **A** is incorrect because, by running X, you would get an X-server with no window managers and no client programs. The session would be unusable. **C** is incorrect because the file you edit to start X automatically on the next boot is /etc/inittab. **D** is incorrect because the .xinitrc command is used to launch X-clients automatically when the server starts. It is incapable of starting the server itself.

12. ☑ **A and B.** The easiest way to change the default runlevel for your Linux system is to edit the /etc/inittab file and change the initdefault setting to runlevel 5. You could then enter the command **init 5** to change to runlevel 5. A reboot would also do the job. **B** is correct because Xconfigurator could change your /etc/inittab for you, ensuring that your system boots into graphics mode.

⊠ **C** is incorrect because this just configures the preferred display manager. **D** is incorrect because the runlevel command is used to report on the previous and current runlevel, not to set the new default runlevel.

13. ☑ **C.** You use the init command to change from the X-Window runlevel to runlevel 3. This will shut down the X-server. You can restart the X-Window system by issuing an init 5.

   ☒ **A** is incorrect because, even if you did shut down the X-server this way, the init process would just detect the termination of the X-server and launch a new one. **B** is incorrect because the change recommended would permanently change the system to turn off graphics mode, and the question asked for a temporary change only. **D** is incorrect because there is no such command.

14. ☑ **A.** The file /etc/X11/prefdm is a script that starts your preferred display manager. By default, the preferred= variable is not set, so Red Hat launches gdm (the GNOME display manager). To force a different display manager, set the preferred= variable to either kdm (for the KDE display manager) or xdm (for the X display manager).

   ☒ **B** is incorrect because Xconfigurator does not set the preferred display manager. **C** is incorrect because the preferred display manager is not set in XF86Config. **D** is incorrect because there is no such option in the Control Panel.

Startup

15. ☑ **D.** The startx command can be run by any user, not just the root account. You should put any customization commands in the .xinitrc hidden file in your home directory.

   ☒ **A** is incorrect because .Xdefault is not used to launch applications when your X-server is started. **B** is incorrect because it says we need to make a .xinitrc file in the root directory. We actually need to make it in our account's home directory. **C** is incorrect because the XF86Config file is used to configure the X-server to the correct hardware settings, not launch a user's favorite applications.

16. ☑ **B and C** are both correct. The advantage to B, however, is that you do not have to log out and log back in.

   ☒ **A** is incorrect because the prefdm file is used to select the preferred display manager on startup. The question specifically states that we need to select a KDE session while running gdm. Clearly, **D** is incorrect.

17. ☑ **D.** The xhost command is used to grant other systems access to your X-server. The command xhost + 172.16.200.99 enables access only from this remote system.

   ☒ **A** is incorrect because xauth is the incorrect tool. **B** is incorrect because xhost – would disable access for the host whose name follows. **C** would do the job because it enables access to all remote hosts. While this includes our client system (with an IP of 172.16.200.99) it also includes every other system on the network and consequently does much more than the question asks.

Remote Display of X Apps

18. ☑ **D.** X-client applications use the DISPLAY environment variable to determine where to send their output. It must be an environment variable, so you must use the export command to create it.

    ☒ **A** suggests using the –display option to every remote X-client we wish to start. While this is not the easiest way to do it, it could work. To make the option effective though, we would have to write it as –display admin1.xyz.com:0. **B** is incorrect because it makes a variable called DISPLAY with the correct value, but neglects to export the variable. With the bash shell, (as with the original Bourne shell (sh) and the Korn shell (ksh)), all shell variables are private (unshared) unless they are explicitly exported. Since we neglected to export our DISPLAY variable, our shell would know about our intentions, but it would fail to pass this information on to any X-client programs we might start. **C** is not quite correct. While we do export DISPLAY, we have neglected to identify the X graphics display and the screen.

19. ☑ **B and D.** I would first try **B** to see if the problem lies with the user's X-server configuration, or with the program they are attempting to run. If xclock will run locally but the modeling application won't, then the fault probably lies with the modeling program. Next, I'd see if I could send a simple X-client from my workstation to my users. By trying **D**, I'd be able to determine if the users' X-server is correctly responding to remote X-client requests. A failure here could be indicative of a network configuration error on the user's computer.

    ☒ **A** is incorrect because, while useful, SuperProbe won't help determine why an X-server that is correctly configured for the local hardware is refusing to allow X-clients to use the display. **C** won't help because having the user send an X-client window to my workstation won't help determine the cause of a problem with the user's workstation.

20. ☑ **B.** Since your company Web server is running on the system, you want to try to avoid rebooting. If your X-Window display doesn't appear to be working, you can switch to a standard text console with CTRL-ALT-F1. An alternative would be to press the CTRL-ALT-BACKSPACE keys. This sends a signal to the local X-server asking it to immediately terminate. Assuming that the local X-server hasn't failed too badly, it should gracefully exit on this keystroke combination.

    ☒ **A** is incorrect because CTRL-ALT-+ is used to change resolutions to higher resolutions. **C** is incorrect because ALT-F1 is used within the X-server and won't help us gain control of our system. **D** isn't correct for a number of reasons. First, this isn't some toy desktop operating system we can reboot on a whim. Second, our kernel may be configured to ignore CTRL-ALT-DEL keys (my personal preference). Third, Red Hat Linux comes preconfigured with six virtual character cell consoles (CTRL-ALT-F1 through CTRL-ALT-F6). All of these are active at the same time as our X-server (which is accessed via CTRL-ALT-F7). So, switching to any of these screens, logging in and restarting our X-server is infinitely more acceptable than just rebooting the system.

LAB ANSWER

1. Before we bring down our machine, we should configure it so it no longer attempts to start the X-server on bootup. This is controlled by the initdefault record in the /etc/inittab file. Edit this file and change field two to the value of 3 (Multi-User With No X Support) from the value 5 (Multi-User With X Support). We could use vi, pico, or any other suitable editor to do this job.

2. Perform an orderly shutdown on our system at a safe time. Use the command **shutdown –h** now.

3. Swap our video card.

4. Power up our Linux system and let it come up in multiuser mode. During bootup, Red Hat automatically probes for new hardware. If this probe finds our new video card, we can configure it when prompted.

5. If kudzu (the new hardware probe tool) fails to find our new hardware, we should log in as root and run Xconfigurator

6. Xconfigurator should correctly identify our new hardware. We should select the correct amount of display memory (32MB) and the graphics resolutions and color depths we desire. Next, Xconfigurator will request to test our new configuration. Allow it to do so.

7. Finally, Xconfigurator will ask whether it should arrange to start the X-Window system automatically. Answer Yes. Note that this just ensures the system now boots to runlevel 5.

8. Change to runlevel 5 to start using our new, high performance card. Use the command **init 5**.

   You have just replaced your video card on Red Hat Linux.

8

Network Client Services

Linux was designed with networking in mind. The extensive network services available with Red Hat Linux are not only the tops in their field, they create one of the most powerful and useful Internet-ready platforms available today at any price.

Red Hat Linux includes the Apache Web Server, which is currently used by more Internet Web sites than all the other Web servers combined (check www.netcraft.com for a current survey). It is based on the NCSA server code, with so many "patches" it was referred to as "a patchy" server. The Apache Web Server continues to advance the art of the Web, and provides one of the most stable, secure, robust, and reliable Web servers available. The Apache Web server is developed and maintained by the Apache Group (www.apache.org). The latest versions (including new development versions) are always available from this site. Alternatively, look for updates on Red Hat's FTP site (ftp.redhat.com). The advantage of Red Hat-built updates is that they are configured to drop in and work without extensive configure/build/install procedures.

The anonymous FTP and the WU_FTP (Washington University FTP) packages provide both a general and real fortress of an FTP server service. With WU-FTP, you can lock down users, directories, subdirectories, and files with various levels of access control.

Other standard services in the UNIX/Linux world are e-mail services using the sendmail SMTP server and the POP and IMAP e-mail client services (both secure and unencrypted versions are available). These are the de-facto standards for e-mail on the Internet, for the world's largest distributed e-mail systems.

Along with the traditional network services already mentioned, Red Hat Linux also provides interoperability packages for all of the most popular operating systems, including Windows (Samba), Novell (MARS-NWE), and Macintosh (MacUtils) networking.

Windows-based operating systems use the SMB file and print sharing protocol on top of TCP/IP. Samba services provide a stable, reliable, fast, and highly compatible file and print sharing service that allows your machine to do the following:

- Participate in a Microsoft Workgroup or NT Domain as a client
- Act as a Master Browser for a network
- Act as a Primary or Backup Domain controller
- Authenticate users through the NT security system on an NT server
- Download print drivers to Microsoft clients

In fact, Samba is so transparent that Microsoft clients cannot tell your Linux server from a genuine Windows NT/2000 server, and with Samba there are no server, client, or client access licenses to purchase.

Additionally, you have a Novell set of client utilities, a Novell "look-alike" server service, a set of Mac client utilities, and a Mac "look-alike" server available. These are not discussed in this chapter.

Printing is a fundamental service with all operating systems. Linux provides the BSD utilities and daemon services for local and remote UNIX-style print services. Linux also provides connectivity to most other network print services via their native protocols.

The next section deals with the basic concepts surrounding the use of these services, and a basic level of configuration. In all cases, the assumption is that your network settings are correct and functioning properly. You can run either linuxconf or the netcfg/netconf/netconfig commands to reconfigure your network settings.

CERTIFICATION OBJECTIVE 8.01

HTTP/Apache

Web services are the easiest way to provide simple, secure access to documents of any type. In fact, this was the original reason Dr. Tim Berners-Lee wrote the first Web server and Web browser. The Apache Web Server provides both normal and secure Web services using the HTTP and HTTPS protocols, respectively. The Apache Web Server has extensive functionality and can be further extended using add-in modules and macros to provide additional services.

Installation

If you selected a Server installation, you already have the Apache Web Server installed. If you selected a Workstation installation or a Custom installation and did not select the Web Server optional package set, you will need to install it. You can use the packages from the installation CD-ROM or from any network service that shares these RPM (Red Hat Package Manager) installation files. Figure 8-1 shows how to install the Apache Web Server package from a local CD-ROM.

FIGURE 8-1

Installing and
enabling the
Apache Web
Server package
from a local
CD-ROM

```
[root@notebook /] mount /dev/cdrom
[root@notebook RPMS] cd /mnt/cdrom/redHat/RPMS
[root@notebook RPMS] ls apache*
apache-1.3.19-5.i386.rpm    apacheconf-0.7-2.noarch.rpm
[root@notebook RPMS] rpm -Uvh apache-1.3.19-5.i386.rpm
Preparing...
###########################################################################
[100%]
[root@notebook RPMS] cd /
[root@notebook /] umount /mnt/cdrom
[root@notebook /] chkconfig -list | grep httpd
httpd           0:off  1:off  2:off  3:off  4:off  5:off  6:off
[root@notebook /] chkconfig --level 35 httpd on
[root@notebook /] chkconfig -list | grep httpd
httpd           0:off  1:off  2:off  3:on  4:off  5:on  6:off
[root@notebook /] /etc/rc.d/httpd start
Starting httpd:           [ OK ]
[root@notebook /]
```

Once Apache is installed, we use the chkconfig program to enable it to start in runlevels 3 and 5 (network multiuser and network multiuser with graphics). chkconfig will ensure that Apache runs the next time your system boots, but it will not start Apache right now. Here is how to run chkconfig to enable Apachestart up at bootup:

```
[root@notebook /] chkconfig --level 35 httpd on
```

To start Apache now, run the Apache service management script that was installed in /etc/rc.d/init.d by the Apache rpm. That script is httpd (hypertext transfer protocol daemon). Run this command:

```
[root@notebook /] /etc/rc.d/init.d/httpd restart
```

Once you've got Apache running, start Netscape and give it a URL of http://localhost. You should see the screen in Figure 8-2.

When you read the screen, you will see that Red Hat is advising us that the directories used by Apache have changed since Red Hat 6.2. In Red Hat 6.2 and earlier, the DocumentRoot (your Web content) was stored in /home/httpd. Under Red Hat 7.x, it is now stored in /var/www. The base Apache configuration directory of /etc/httpd has not changed.

FIGURE 8-2

The default Web page installed by Red Hat 7

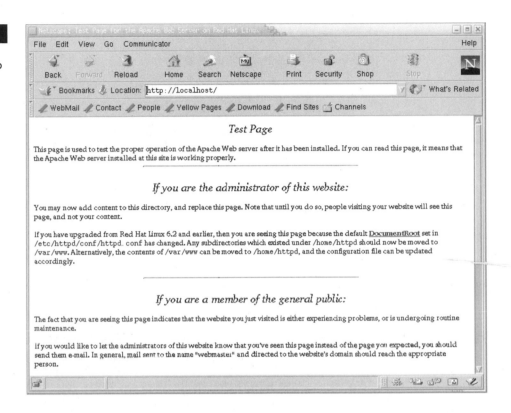

Setup Files

The files installed are maintained in these locations:

/var/www/httpd	Most of the HTTPD files
/etc/httpd	Much of the network-side setup information

EXERCISE 8-1

Installing Apache Server

1. Put the Red Hat Installation CD into the local CD-ROM reader.

2. Check to make sure /mnt/cdrom exists and is available.

3. Mount the CD on /mnt/cdrom.

4. Locate the Apache RPM package.

5. Load the Apache RPM package.

6. Unmount the CD-ROM device.

7. Use chkconfig to verify that Apache is not configured to start.

8. Now, use chkconfig to start Apache for runlevels 3 and 5.

9. Start Apache by hand by invoking the Apache management script in /etc/rc.d/init.d.

10. Start Netscape. Point it at http://localhost. You should see the default Web page for Red Hat Linux. Review this page for advice to people upgrading from Red Hat 6.*x*.

11. Close Netscape.

Basic Apache Configuration for a Simple Web Server

There are three main configuration files for your Web server. The installation creates a generic Web server service you can further customize and optimize, if so desired. As installed, it will function just fine for a basic Web service. You can fine-tune your Web server by making changes to the configuration files, as shown in Figure 8-3.

In Red Hat 6.2 and earlier, the version of Apache included references to all three files. Web administrators now believe that Apache is better managed if all the configuration information for a site is kept in one spot. Consequently srm.conf and access.conf are no longer used. It is instructive to view these files to read what Red Hat has to say about their use.

on the
Ü o b

You need all three Apache configuration files to exist, or the server will refuse to start.

FIGURE 8-3	

Apache Web
Server
configuration file
list and usage

```
/etc/httpd/conf/srm.conf
# Was used to define system resources - use now deprecated
/etc/httpd/conf/access.conf
# Was used to define access rules/limits - use also deprecated
/etc/httpd/conf/httpd.conf
# Main Apache configuration file. Everything now goes in here!
```

Here is /etc/htpd/conf/srm.conf:

```
##
## srm.conf -- Apache HTTP server configuration file
##
# This is the default file for the ResourceConfig directive in httpd.conf.
# It is processed after httpd.conf but before access.conf.
#
# To avoid confusion, it is recommended that you put all of your
# Apache server directives into the httpd.conf file and leave this
# one essentially empty.
#
```

The config files listed in Figure 8-3 are located under the directory /etc/httpd/conf. The main configuration for Apache is httpd.conf. Browse through this file now with less:

```
[ root@notebook conf] less /etc/httpd/conf/httpd.conf
```

Access Restrictions

The httpd.conf configuration file has directives that can be used to define which types of services are allowed on a directory-by-directory basis. These controls are for directories directly accessed by the server, not necessarily for the whole system.

These restrictions are recursive from the parent directory. The first directory to configure is the root, /. You should configure the default to be a very restrictive set of permissions. You can then adjust these permissions on other selected directory subtrees such as the DocumentRoot, and the cgi-bin directory if you plan to use cgi scripts. Figure 8-4 is a section from httpd.conf that sets default directory access permissions.

The next directory to put restrictions on is the one containing your HTML files. The example in Figure 8-5 uses the default /var/www/html directory and sets finer access controls on it. Just scroll down a little past the previous screen (Figure 8-4) to view this information for yourself.

Per Directory Control—.htaccess   There is a way to override these passed-down permission controls in any directory below a restricted path. You create a hidden file, called .htaccess, in the target directory. Directives in it can override the permission settings unless the AllowOverride option is set to None. You can put a .htaccess control file in every directory that may be accessed by your Web server and customize access differently from the primary DocumentRoot access.

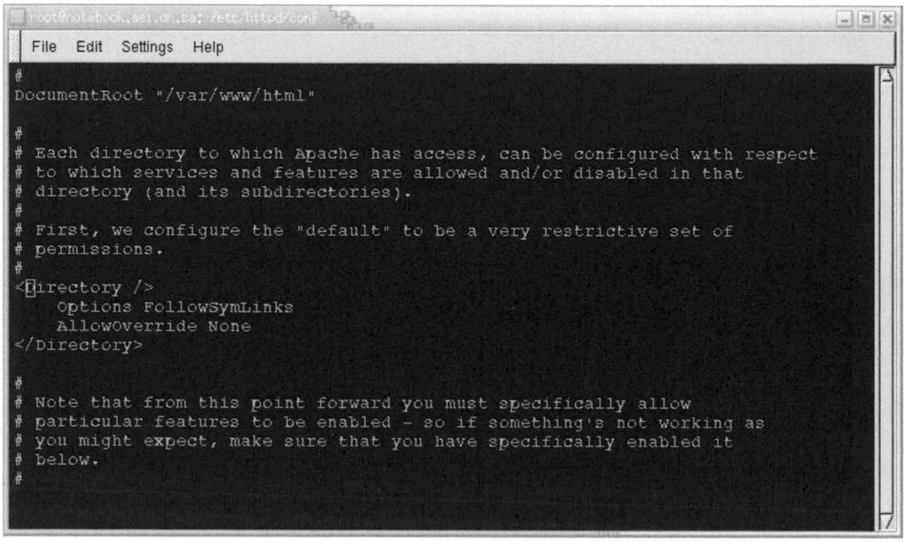

FIGURE 8-4

The default access settings for directories are controlled by the <Directory *path*> container

```
#
DocumentRoot "/var/www/html"
#
# Each directory to which Apache has access, can be configured with respect
# to which services and features are allowed and/or disabled in that
# directory (and its subdirectories).
#
# First, we configure the "default" to be a very restrictive set of
# permissions.
#
<Directory />
    Options FollowSymLinks
    AllowOverride None
</Directory>

#
# Note that from this point forward you must specifically allow
# particular features to be enabled - so if something's not working as
# you might expect, make sure that you have specifically enabled it
# below.
#
```

The Options line can have many choices, in many combinations. The most encompassing options for the AllowOverride directive are these:

None	For no custom options in force
All	To allow all overrides (see the following)

You can also use this:

Indexes	To permit FTP-style directory indexing

The Indexes directive controls directory indexing, which is the name for file lists that are generated automatically by Apache. Subdirectives for indexes include these:

- AddDescription
- AddIcon
- AddIconByEncoding
- AddIconByType
- DefaultIcon
- DirectoryIndex

FIGURE 8-5

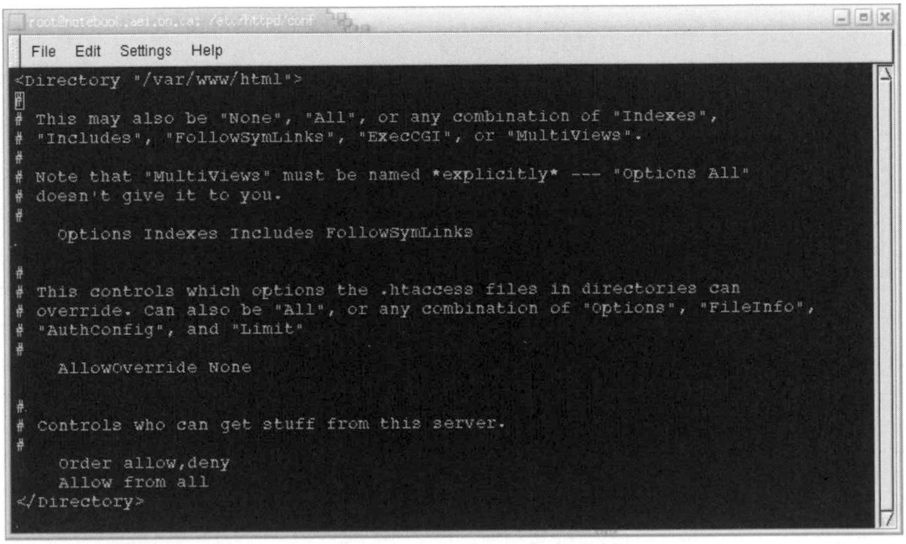

Access control
on the
/var/www/html
directory
as set by
/etc/httpd/conf/
httpd.conf

```
<Directory "/var/www/html">
#
# This may also be "None", "All", or any combination of "Indexes",
# "Includes", "FollowSymLinks", "ExecCGI", or "MultiViews".
#
# Note that "MultiViews" must be named *explicitly* --- "Options All"
# doesn't give it to you.
#
    Options Indexes Includes FollowSymLinks

#
# This controls which options the .htaccess files in directories can
# override. Can also be "All", or any combination of "Options", "FileInfo",
# "AuthConfig", and "Limit"
#
    AllowOverride None

#
# Controls who can get stuff from this server.
#
    Order allow,deny
    Allow from all
</Directory>
```

- FancyIndexing
- HeaderName
- IndexIgnore
- IndexOptions
- ReadmeName

Other Apache directives you can use include these:

Includes	The use of server-side include directives is permitted.
FollowSymLinks	Can follow symbolic links to other directories outside of DocumentRoot.
ExecCGI	CGI (common gateway interface) executable scripts are permitted.

A resource may be available in several different representations. For example, it might be available in different languages, different media types, or a combination of both. This allows the server to choose the best representation of a resource based on the browser-supplied preferences for media type, languages, character set, and encoding.

You should also control any ScriptAlias CGI directories if used. The default cgi-bin directory is /var/www/cgi-bin. If you configured another directory (which is common when you host virtual Web sites), you should change the directory reference to whatever your ScriptAlias points to:

```
<Directory /var/www/cgi-bin>
AllowOverride None    # .htaccess files ignored
Options ExecCGI        # allow execution of any CGI scripts
</Directory>
```

In this example code segment from /etc/httpd/conf/httpd.conf, we identify the directory for our cgi programs and specifically permit CGI access via the Options ExecCGI directive. Note that we do not allow overrides because we don't want people changing permissions/settings of our CGI directory. If we allow overrides, CGI programmers could inadvertently give away too much information about our system (by allowing users to cat any file) or could potentially allow users to name the CGI program they wish to run (and the arguments they want to supply).

The Server installation includes access to documentation, but through an alias name. The actual directory with the documentation has restricted access options. This is useful if you wish to map a directory out of the servers DocumentRoot directory into DocumentRoot. The default httpd.conf script does this to reference the /var/www/icons directory as the /icons directory inside the DocumentRoot directory (/var/www/html). See Figure 8-6 to see how an Alias directive is used to map /var/www/icons into the /var/www/html/icons.

Finally, you can add access control for any other directories available via your Web interface. Just wrap the directory you wish to control in a <Directory /*path/to/dir*>. . . </Directory> container and set the access restrictions you require.

```
====================================================================
<Directory /path/to/your/directory/goes/here/>
Options Indexes FollowSymLinks
order deny,allow                      # order of testing
deny from .evil.crackers.net          # This test is applied first
allow from .yourdomain.net            # Only we get access to the resource
</Directory>
====================================================================
```

For more information on any of these details, you can look at the HTML-based documentation included in the installation in /home/httpd/html/manual/core.html and the related links within this file.

Another important aspect of the httpd.conf file is the creation of virtual Web sites. Virtual Web sites allow this server to respond to more than one Web site name, such as www.corp1.net, www.company2.org, and so forth on a single IP address. The

FIGURE 8-6

Using aliases
to reference
directories
outside of
DocumentRoot

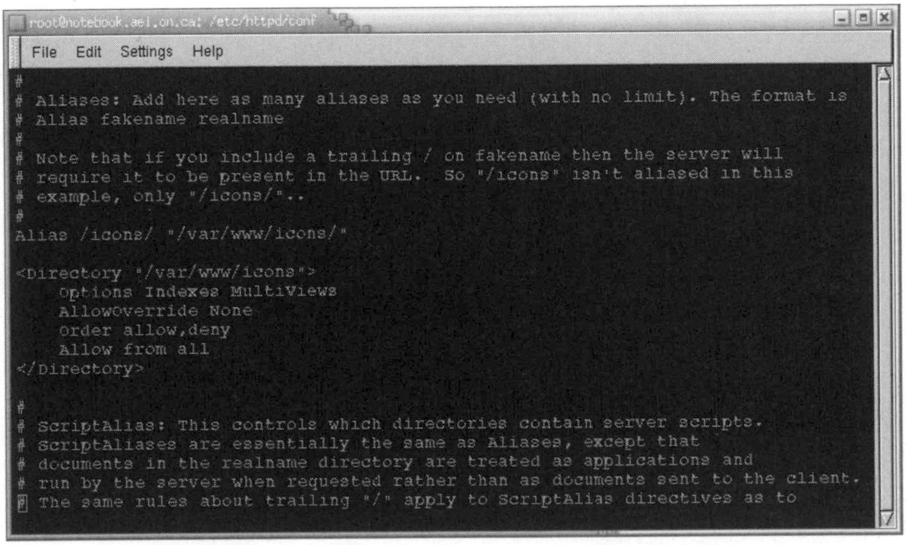

```
# Aliases: Add here as many aliases as you need (with no limit). The format is
# Alias fakename realname
#
# Note that if you include a trailing / on fakename then the server will
# require it to be present in the URL. So "/icons" isn't aliased in this
# example, only "/icons/"..
#
Alias /icons/ "/var/www/icons/"

<Directory "/var/www/icons">
    Options Indexes MultiViews
    AllowOverride None
    Order allow,deny
    Allow from all
</Directory>

#
# ScriptAlias: This controls which directories contain server scripts.
# ScriptAliases are essentially the same as Aliases, except that
# documents in the realname directory are treated as applications and
# run by the server when requested rather than as documents sent to the client.
# The same rules about trailing "/" apply to ScriptAlias directives as to
```

httpd.conf file is broken up into sections. Section 3 is used to define virtual hosts.
To enable a virtual host, you need to uncomment the NameVirtualHost directive
and set the IP address for your interface (Figure 8-7). You then need to make a
<VirtualHost> container with the IP address of your Linux server. Add the e-mail
address of the administrator for the site and the DocumentRoot for the site's content;
then set the server name by supplying the fully qualified domain name for your site.
If you like, customize the error logs and access (custom) log path. Then restart Apache,
and your new virtual site should be operational.

Web Server Log Files

The log files are listed as being in /etc/httpd, but they are linked to/var/logs/httpd.
You can change both their number and format. By default, there is only one log file
for all access events (access_log) and one log file for all errors (error_log). If you want
more detail about your Web site for tuning or statistical reasons, you can have the
Web server generate more information, generate separate log files for each virtual
Web site, and break the data up more granularly by month, week, day, or any other
period of time.

These are three lines in the default /etc/httpd/conf/httpd.conf file. There are
standard log file formats that can be used. First of all, the exact format of each type
of log file must be specified. The following shows four definitions of log file formats

---

FIGURE 8-7

The httpd.conf
supplied template
for creating
NameVirtualHosts

```
#
# If you want to use name-based virtual hosts you need to define at
# least one IP address (and port number) for them.
#
#NameVirtualHost 12.34.56.78:80
#NameVirtualHost 12.34.56.78

#
# VirtualHost example:
# Almost any Apache directive may go into a VirtualHost container.
#
#<VirtualHost ip.address.of.host.some_domain.com>
#    ServerAdmin webmaster@host.some_domain.com
#    DocumentRoot /www/docs/host.some_domain.com
#    ServerName host.some_domain.com
#    ErrorLog logs/host.some_domain.com-error_log
#    CustomLog logs/host.some_domain.com-access_log common
#</VirtualHost>

#<VirtualHost _default_:*>
#</VirtualHost>
```

(using the LogFormat directive). They are combined, common, referer (the link used to get to our site), and the agent (the users' Web browser).

We then use the CustomLog format to select where to put our log files and which log file format we wish to use.

on the
job

Some Web hit log analyzers have specific requirements for log file formats. For example, the popular Open Source tool awstats (advanced Web Stats) requires the combined log format. It will fail to run if you leave the default common format. Awstats is a great tool for graphically displaying site activity. Look for it at www.sourceforge.net.

Figure 8-8 shows the section of the /etc/httpd/conf/httpd.conf file that sets logging values.

FIGURE 8-8   Customizing Apache logs (as extracted from /etc/httpd/conf/httpd.conf)

```
# ErrorLog: The location of the error log file.
# If you do not specify an ErrorLog directive within a <VirtualHost>
# container, error messages relating to that virtual host will be
# logged here.  If you *do* define an error logfile for a <VirtualHost>
# container, that host's errors will be logged there and not here.
#
ErrorLog /var/log/httpd/error_log
#
```

FIGURE 8-8   Customizing Apache logs (as extracted from /etc/httpd/conf/httpd.conf) *(continued)*

```
# LogLevel: Control the number of messages logged to the error_log.
# Possible values include: debug, info, notice, warn, error, crit,
# alert, emerg.
#
LogLevel warn


#
# The following directives define some format nicknames for use with
# a CustomLog directive (see below).

LogFormat "%h %l %u %t \"%r\" %>s %b \"%{Referer}i\" \"%{User-Agent}i\""
combined
LogFormat "%h %l %u %t \"%r\" %>s %b" common
LogFormat "%{Referer}i -> %U" referer
LogFormat "%{User-agent}i" agent


#
# The location and format of the access logfile (Common Logfile Format).
# If you do not define any access logfiles within a <VirtualHost>
# container, they will be logged here.  Contrariwise, if you *do*
# define per-<VirtualHost> access logfiles, transactions will be
# logged therein and *not* in this file.
#
# CustomLog /var/log/httpd/access_log common
CustomLog /var/log/httpd/access_log combined


#
# If you would like to have agent and referer logfiles, uncomment the
# following directives.
#
#CustomLog /var/log/httpd/referer_log referer
#CustomLog /var/log/httpd/agent_log agent


#
# If you prefer a single logfile with access, agent, and referer information
# (Combined Logfile Format) you can use the following directive.
#
#CustomLog /var/log/httpd/access_log combined
```

Log Configuration Options   The log files have a very specific format for the information stored in them, per the HTTP RFC. You probably do not need to change these. Figure 8-9 is an excerpt from the /home/httpd/html/manual/mod/ mod_log_config.html help file supplied with your Apache Web server installation that explains the various macro reverence meanings.

FIGURE 8-9	Log format options

```
===================================================================
%...b:           Bytes sent, excluding HTTP headers.
%...f:           Filename.
%...{FOOBAR}e:   The contents of the environment variable FOOBAR
%...h:           Remote host.
%...a:           Remote IP-address.
%...{Foobar}i:   The contents of Foobar: header line(s) in the request
                 sent to the server.
%...l:           Remote logname (from identd, if supplied).
%...{Foobar}n:   The contents of note Foobar from another module.
%...{Foobar}o:   The contents of Foobar: header line(s) in the reply.
%...p:           The canonical Port of the server serving the request.
%...P:           The process ID of the child that serviced the request.
%...r:           First line of request.
%...s:           Status.  For requests that got internally redirected, this
                 is status of the *original* request --- %...>s for the last.
%...t:           Time, in common log format time format.
%...{format}t:   The time, in the form given by format, which should
                 be in strftime(3) format.
%...T:           The time taken to serve the request, in seconds.
%...u:           Remote user (from auth; may be bogus if return status (%s) is 401).
%...U:           The URL path requested.
%...v:           The canonical ServerName of the server serving the request.
%...V:           The server name according to the UseCanonicalName setting.
```

The . . . can be nothing at all (e.g., %h %u %r %s %b), or it can indicate conditions for inclusion of the item (which will cause it to be replaced with "-" if the condition is not met). Note that there is no escaping performed on the strings from %r, %. . .i, and %. . .o;.

The forms of condition are a list of HTTP status codes, which may or may not be preceded by "!". Thus, "%400,501{User-agent}"" logs User-agent: on 400 errors and 501 errors (Bad Request, Not Implemented) only; and "%!200,304,302{Referer}"" logs Referer: on all requests that did **NOT** return some sort of normal status.

Note that the common log format is defined by the string %h %l %u %t \"%r\" %s %b, which can be used as the basis for extending the format, if desired (e.g., to add extra fields at the end). NCSA's extended/combined log format would be:

"%h %l %u %t \"%r\" %s %b \"%{Referer}i\" \"%{User-agent}i\"".

The log format is consistent with the standard NCSA format and does not need to be changed in most cases.

Starting the Apache Web Server

The actual binary file is /usr/sbin/httpd. The binary file is normally started at system initialization. You can also stop and start the service using the httpd control script provided with the installation. With no arguments, a syntax usage statement is printed, as shown in Figure 8-10.

Requesting the status of the Web server simply shows the ten initial processes started by the server to handle requests. The output also indicates your server is running. The Stop option shuts down all server processes, while the Start option can be used to restart all functionality as indicated by the configuration files. The Restart option is equivalent to a stop-and-start request. A "reload" forces the main server to re-read the configuration files and update itself accordingly. This reload is normally only done if you do not want to kill a busy service.

Testing Your Configuration   You should perform a syntax check of your Apache configuration files before attempting to use a new configuration for the first time. Use the command

```
# httpd -t
```

to have Apache verify that you don't have any problems.

Assuming there were no problems, you should be able to start your Web server and connect to your local service with a browser request. Try these URLs (making substitutions as appropriate for your network and domain name):

```
http://localhost/            # even if no network hosts defined
http://206.195.1.222/   # if no hosts resolution, use IP address
http://www.yourweb.org/      # use DNS or hosts resolution of address
```

If you were to check your system processes, you would notice there are a number of child processes. These child processes are created by the parent httpd program and should not be terminated individually, because the httpd will just restart identical processes. Assuming you started the httpd server as root, these child processes will

FIGURE 8-10

Controlling the
Apache Web
Server daemon

```
==================================================================
[root@linux6 /root]# /etc/rc.d/init.d/httpd
Usage: /etc/rc.d/init.d/httpd {start|stop|restart|reload|status}
[root@linux6 /root]# /etc/rc.d/init.d/httpd  status
httpd (pid 535 534 533 532 531 530 529 528 527 526 525) is running...
[root@linux6 /root]#
```

be started under the user account specified in the configuration file. These extra processes handle the incoming requests to the server and are regenerated as needed, based on the parameters specified in the httpd.conf file as outlined earlier.

```
MinSpareServers 8          # Maximum number of
                           # potentially idle servers
MaxSpareServers 20         # kill off extras as necessary
StartServers 10            # initial processes
MaxClients 150             # all processes are renewed regularly
```

Some Possible Problems   The installation will normally create a running system. You should always make backups of the configuration files before introducing any changes. This is especially true for /etc/httpd/conf/httpd.conf. If you make changes to any of the configuration files and the resultant setup fails, here are a few suggested starting points to look at, per the documentation supplied with the server. If all else fails, go back to the originals and start over.

Here are some suggestions you might wish to try when troubleshooting your Web server configuration.

- If, when you run httpd, it complains about being unable to "bind" to an address, then either some other process is already using the port you have configured Apache to use, or you are running httpd as a normal user but are trying to use a port below 1024 (such as the default port 80).

- Double-check your network settings. Any problems with network addressing or routing should be fixed before you attempt to run Apache.

- If the server is not running, read the error message displayed when you run httpd. You should also check the server error_log for additional information (with the default configuration, this will be located in the file error_log in the logs directory).

- If you want your server to continue running after a system reboot, use chkconfig to enable httpd for the desired runlevels. For instance, use this:

  ```
  # chkconfig --level 35 httpd on
  ```

- To set Apache to start on every boot whenever the system enters either runlevel 3 or 5. Use

  ```
  # chkconfig --list httpd
  ```

  to verify your configuration changes.

■ To stop Apache, send the parent process a TERM signal. The PID of this process is written to the file httpd.pid in the logs directory (unless configured otherwise). Do not attempt to kill the child processes, because they will be renewed by the parent. A typical command to stop the server is this:

```
#kill -TERM `cat /usr/local/apache/logs/httpd.pid
```

Better yet, run the httpd management script with the stop option (service httpd stop).

Web Site Content

The actual HTML pages and pictures, CGI scripts, and the supplied documentation is in /home/httpd/html. Note that, by default, Linux uses .html, not .htm files. Also, be aware that Linux is case-sensitive so a file called Index.html will not read the same as a file called index.html.

These top directory files are supplied with the installation:

```
index.html       the default page returned by server
poweredby.gif    picture logo of Red Hat (in index.html)
manual/          manual pages and gifs
```

The Home Page Is index.html

Whenever a browser requests a site without a specific page, the Web server has a defined default page to send back. It can have any name. Common choices are home.html and index.html The file index.asp represents Active Server Pages from a Windows environment. So far, Linux does not have the capability to run ASP-encoded HTML documents. In Figure 8-11 that follows, we can see the files Apache will try to deliver (and the order in which Apache will look for files) whenever a URL without a filename is given.

In the previous example, we try the file index with either .html or .htm extensions. Then we try .shtml (for index.html with server-side includes). Next we try some variant of PHP (a very popular server side scripting language). Finally, if none of the other files match, we try to see if index is generated by a CGI script. If none of these options succeed, then Apache returns a Not Found error.

Your Web server has a default Web page that is included when you install the Web server. This page can be changed using any text- or HTML-specific editor. If you use a text editor, you need to know something about the basic tags used by a browser.

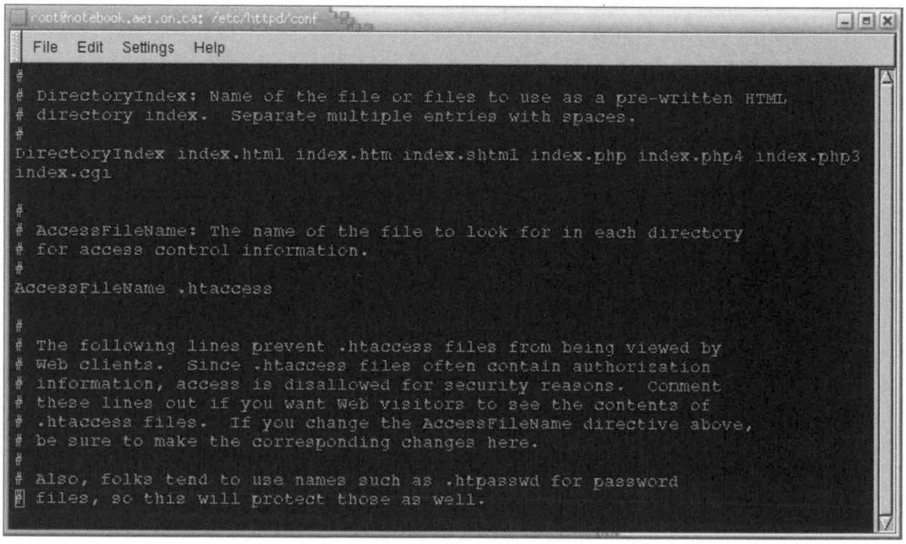

FIGURE 8-11

The DirectoryIndex directive tells Apache the files to look for whenever a URL doesn't provide a filename

```
root@notebook.ae1.on.ca: /etc/httpd/conf                              _ □ ⊠
 File  Edit  Settings  Help
#
# DirectoryIndex: Name of the file or files to use as a pre-written HTML
# directory index.  Separate multiple entries with spaces.
#
DirectoryIndex index.html index.htm index.shtml index.php index.php4 index.php3
index.cgi

#
# AccessFileName: The name of the file to look for in each directory
# for access control information.
#
AccessFileName .htaccess


#
# The following lines prevent .htaccess files from being viewed by
# Web clients.  Since .htaccess files often contain authorization
# information, access is disallowed for security reasons.  Comment
# these lines out if you want Web visitors to see the contents of
# .htaccess files.  If you change the AccessFileName directive above,
# be sure to make the corresponding changes here.
#
# Also, folks tend to use names such as .htpasswd for password
# files, so this will protect those as well.
```

Basics of HTML Coding   A basic Web page can be a simple text file. Tags represent requests to the client browser to display something a special way. The HTML coding came from a long line of markup languages that evolved on many platforms. An example of a simple Web page is provided in the text example in the following section.

Note: if you are not familiar with HTML tags, don't worry, you can just edit the supplied files and customize them your way. The HTML format is relatively straightforward. Most tags have a start-of-format and an end-of-format tag reference. For example, the title bar of the Web browser comes from the text between the tag <HEAD> and an end tag </HEAD>. Notice that the same tag name is used in both; the start-of-format-tag is just the name, while the end-of-format-tag has the tag name preceded by a slash.

A basic HTML document might look like Figure 8-12.

Browsing Your Homepage

You can use any browser from the network if your machine is reachable, or you can use a local browser to connect to the main Web page of your server. If you do not have X working, do not worry; there is a text-based browser installed that can be used quite effectively to browse the main Web page of your server.

FIGURE 8-12

An example of
a simple HTML
document

```
<HTML>
      <HEAD>
            <TITLE>My First HTML Document</TITLE>
      </HEAD>

      <!-- this is a comment. It is not displayed by your browser ->
      <BODY>
            <H1>Welcome</H1>
            <B>This site is under construction!</B><BR>
      This is my first Web page. Please check back later for
            something more interesting.
      </BODY>
</HTML>
```

Text-Based Browser lynx   You can connect to any Web site on your network, if accessible, using the lynx browser. This browser simply ignores all font and font size requests, as well as any directives to display graphics (wallpaper, images, and so on). lynx displays the HTML strings as single lines. URL tags, meanwhile, are shown in a different color or shade if your terminal supports this feature, and can be gotten to by using the UP- and DOWN-ARROW keys. To connect to the indicated URL, press the RIGHT-ARROW key; to go back, press the LEFT-ARROW key. To quit, press Q, as shown in Figure 8-13.

FIGURE 8-13

Browsing your
default Web page
with lynx

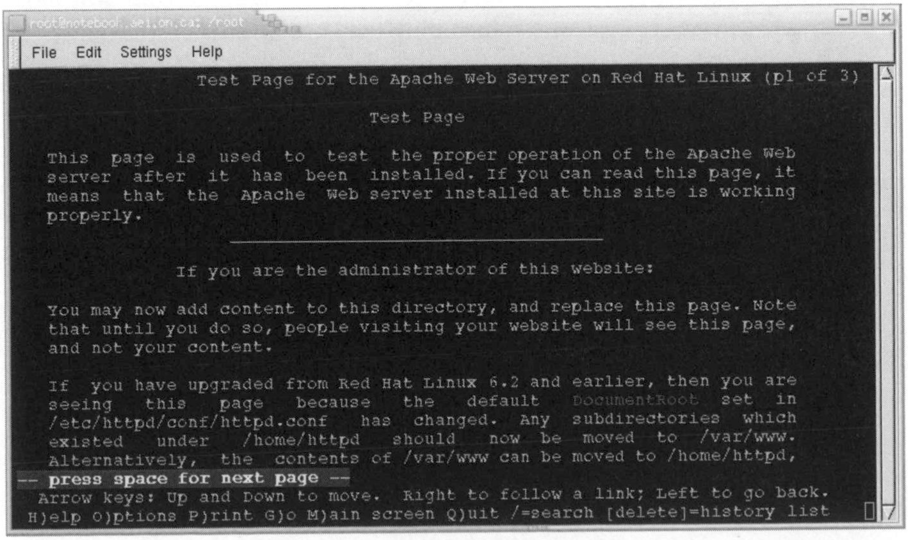

Using Netscape to Browse a Homepage You can connect to your new Web service using any browser. If you have your X-Window services running, you can use the supplied Netscape browser to connect to http://localhost, the fully qualified domain name, or use the IP address of your site.

EXERCISE 8-2

Update the Main Apache Web Page; Then Test It

1. Start the Apache Web server with the default configuration.

2. Copy the file /var/www/html/index.html to /home/httpd/html/index2.html.

3. Edit the file /var/www/html/index.html.

4. Change the title of the page to reflect your personal or corporate name.

5. Use the lynx text-based browser to connect to localhost (or 127.0.0.1).

Hosting a Virtual Web Site

You can add virtual hosts to /etc/httpd/conf/httpd.conf by adding a set of entries for each virtual host, including the local host itself:

Here is what the original configuration file contains:

```
#<VirtualHost host.some_domain.com>
#ServerAdmin webmaster@host.some_domain.com#DocumentRoot /www/docs/host.some_domain.com
#ServerName host.some_domain.com
#ErrorLog logs/host.some_domain.com-error_log
#TransferLog logs/host.some_domain.com-access_log
#</VirtualHost>
```

You can change this as follows. I have inserted an IP address that we used to arrive at our site. You would likely have to change your address to something different to get your site to work.

The pfr.net virtual Web site might look like this:

```
<VirtualHost  192.168.0.1>
ServerAdmin   {HYPERLINK "mailto:guru@pfr.net"}          # admin email
DocumentRoot  /pfr/html              # your choice, must have index.html
```

```
ServerName  www.pfr.net            # your fully qualified domain name
ErrorLog  /pfr/logs/error_log      # your choice
TransferLog  /pfr/logs/access_log  # transaction logs
ScriptAlias  /cgi/  /pfr/cgi-bin   # associates virtual with real dir.
<Directory /pfr/html>              # document root
Options  ExecCGI  Indexes  Includes # described above
</Directory>
</VirtualHost>
```

To test your new virtual host setup, you can restart the Apache Web Server with the following control script request:

```
[root@notebook /root]#  /etc/rc.d/init.d/httpd  restart
```

You should now be able to check the Web content page of all your virtual Web sites by using any browser. You should create an appropriately specific index.html page for each virtual host.

on the ! *Job*   **Once you create one virtual host, even the local host must be made virtual, or it disappears. Create another entry for localhost or your local Web name BEFORE all other virtual host entries, but AFTER the NameVirtualHost line, as shown in Figure 8-14.**

on the ! *Job*   **Apache administration is a necessary skill for any Linux system administrator. You should develop the ability to install, configure and troubleshoot Apache quickly. You should also be able to set up and customize virtual Web sites, which will make you a more effective Webmaster. You can test your skills using the exercise that follows.**

FIGURE 8-14

Sample virtual localhost setup

```
=================================================================
NameVirtualHost 127.0.0.1
<VirtualHost 127.0.0.1>
ServerName  localhost
ServerAdmin    root@localhost
DocumentRoot  /home/httpd/html/
ErrorLoglogs  /error_log
TransferLoglogs  /access_log
<Directory /home/httpd/html>
Options  ExecCGI Indexes Includes
</Directory>
</VirtualHost>
=================================================================
```

Patches, Upgrades, Need More Info

You can get the latest information, documentation, upgrades, options, patches, bug fixes, and more from the Apache Web site at http://www.apache.org/.

Create a Virtual Web Site; Then Test It

1. Add a virtual Web site for the fictional company SnoBard, called www.snobard.net.

2. Create a DocumentRoot directory called /snobard.

3. Copy the file /var/www/html/html/index.html to /snobard/index.html.

4. Edit the file /snobard/index.html.

5. Change the title of the page to reflect the SnoBard corporate name.

6. Test accessing the virtual Web site and the local Web site.

CERTIFICATION OBJECTIVE 8.02

FTP

The FTP, or File Transfer Protocol, is one of the two original applications developed with the initial TCP/IP protocol suite (the other is Telnet). There are two application-related sides to FTP: the client and the server. The client application is available and, usually, freely supplied on all other operating systems when they support the TCP/IP protocol suite. The server application is common on most Web hosting machines and predates the actual Web as the normal Internet method of transferring files between any type of system.

The FTP service is managed by the xinetd "superserver" service. Xinted is new to Red Hat 7.*x*. It is a replacement for the older inetd of Red Hat 6 and earlier. Like inetd, xinetd service listens for a list of services and launches them as needed for each subservice, such as Telnet, FTP, talk, finger, and so forth. The difference is that xinetd (the extended inetd) has more authentication capabilities (via Pluggable Authentication Modules) and more verification capabilities (via TCP wrappers). The configuration file, /etc/xinetd.conf, and /etc/xinetd.d/wu.ftpd indicates which services are listened for and how requests for those services are to be handled.

FTP Client

The original FTP client software was a basic command-line, text-oriented client application that offered a simple but efficient interface. Most Web browsers offer a more graphical interface and can be used as the interface, if desired.

The client allows you to access the directory tree and all files within it. The graphical client is optimized for download from the remote host. By simply clicking a file, you initiate a transfer download; by clicking a directory, you initiate a cd *targetdirectory* command, and the interface updates with the local files in the new director.

In the text-based interface, you must enter each command at the FTP prompt, one at a time. Almost all commands are run at the remote host, something like in a Telnet session. To run commands locally, you precede the command with an "!". Basic FTP client commands are shown in Figure 8-15.

This is only a subset of the commands available from the FTP client. Typing the command help will give you a full list of the available commands. The command help *<cmd>* yields a brief description of the command itself.

FIGURE 8-15

Basic FTP client commands

```
===================================================================
Remote Commands (Process on remote host)
cd      to change the current working directory at the remote host
ls      commands to list files at the remote host
get     to retrieve one file from the remote host
mget    to retrieve many files using wildcards or full filenames.
    (if logged in with a local login account, not anonymous)
put     to upload one file from your machine to the target host
mput    to upload many files to the target remote host
pwd     print working directory on remote host
quit    end the FTP session
   Local Commands (Process on your host)
!ls     list files on your host machine, current directory
lcd     change local host directory for upload/download
!pwd    print working directory on local host
===================================================================
```

For a more functional command-line-driven FTP client, check out the ncftp rpm. This FTP client adds these features:

- Recursive directory downloads
- Command-line recall and edit (in the style of bash)
- Command-line history
- Automatic anonymous logins
- Much easier command-line FTP use

The ultimate FTP client for Linux is the GNOME FTP client (called GFTP). It is part of the GFTP package. GNOME FTP provides an easy to use GUI interface to FTP. It also offers these features:

- Restartable transfers
- Multiple independent transfers
- Download file queuing
- Transferring whole directory trees (recursive transfers)
- Drag and drop transfer activation
- Session names and settings

all without requiring you to know a single FTP command. Figure 8-16 is a screen grab of the GNOME FTP client.

You can start the GFTP client from the command line with the gftp command.

FTP Installation

There are two key packages you can install to support FTP: anonftp and WU-FTP. Figure 8-17 is a listing of the FTP services provided by Red Hat for Red Hat 7.1.

To install any of these packages, use the Red Hat Package Manager. For example, to install the anonymous FTP service use this command:

```
# rpm -Uvh anonftp-4.0-4.i386.rpm
```

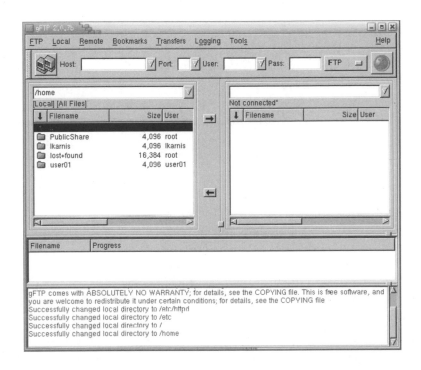

exam
ⓦatch

It usually doesn't hurt to install a package over itself. That is, if you try to install anonftp-4.0-4 on top of itself, the Red Hat Package Manager will just tell you that the package is already installed and then politely exit.

on the
ⓙob

An easy way to bring a package back to a known good state is to use the —force option to rpm. This tells rpm that the package should be installed, even if it is already present.

The anonftp package provides server-side anonymous access to anyone without the need for specific user accounts. You can install the anonftp rpm package if it is

```
# mount /mnt/cdrom
# cd /mnt/cdrom/RedHat/RPMS
# ls ftp
anonftp-4.0-4.i386.rpm
ftp-0.17-7.i386.rpm
gftp-2.0.7b-3.i386.rpm
ncftp-3.0.2-1.i386.rpm
wu-ftpd-2.6.1-16.i386.rpm
```

not already installed. The installation creates a /home/ftp tree and populates it with a minimal set of directories and files. One key aspect of the anonymous FTP package is that anyone using it will not be able to traverse above the /home/ftp directory. They are locked into this branch of the directory tree by having the FTP server execute a chroot system call. This system call tricks the FTP server into thinking that /home/ftp is really /. Since you can't go higher than /, you can't leave /home/ftp. Consequently, anonymous users cannot see files or run programs located outside of the /home/ftp directory. This is done as an extra security precaution so unknown users cannot probe your system. You should add files to the /home/ftp/pub directory that are to be made available to anonymous logins for download to their machines only.

The FTP server for authenticated (known) users is the WU-FTP package. The WU-FTP provides sophisticated features related to user management. With it, you can establish many more features and controls on many more objects. Additional features include control of transfer and command logs, on-the-fly compression and archiving (using gzip), user type and location classification, limits on a per-class (local, remote) basis, directory upload permissions, restricted guest accounts, messages per directory and system, and virtual name support.

One of the other excellent advanced features of WU-FTP is its ability to provide full user and group-specific authorization of FTP services. WU-FTP adds a third group of "guest" users. You can elect specific access for various users and groups in /etc/ftpaccess.

exam
ⓦatch
Workstation and Custom installations do not include any FTP servers. These packages can be installed at any time using the RPM package manager.

Configuring a Simple Anonymous FTP Server

The basic installation of the FTP packages creates an FTP service that allows for anonymous access. Before you test your installation from any host on the network. You should make sure that the FTP service is enabled by starting the associated service management script or by using chkconfig and rebooting.

The anonymous FTP service uses the /var/ftp/ directory as the only accessible tree. You should customize the content of this tree as the final step in configuration of this anonymous service. For example, you could put some RPM packages in the pub directory for all users to download to their Linux hosts, as shown in Figure 8-18. The default installation does not add any files to the pub directory.

FIGURE 8-18

Example listing
of /var/ftp with
RPM packages

```
==================================================================
[root@myhost ftp]# ls -R
bin    etc lib   pub
bin:
compress   cpio   gzip   ls   sh   tar   zcat
etc:
group   ld.so.cache   passwd
lib:
ld-2.1.1.so   libc-2.1.1.so      libnsl-2.1.1.so   libnss_files-2.1.1.so
ld-linux.so.2   libc.so.6        libnsl.so.1       libnss_files.so.2
pub:
206.195.1.hosts              vga_cardgames-1.3.1-7.i386.rpm
bsd-games-1.3-8.i386.rpm     vga_gamespack-1.3-7.i386.rpm
xv-3.10a-9.i386.rpm
[root@myhost ftp]#
==================================================================
```

Testing Your FTP Service   The last step is to test the anonymous login of the
FTP service. From any command line, you can use the client application to connect
to any host, including your own host machine. It does not matter what host your
FTP connects to, assuming it has an FTP service running. Windows 9*x* and NT
workstations, by default, do not have an FTP service, only the FTP client application.
NT Server 4.0/2000/XP requires the installation of IIS (Internet Information
Services) which includes an FTP service component.

Like any network connection, the FTP client needs a valid network address. If
you use a host name, the system must be able to resolve the name to an IP address.
The typical method is by a simple lookup of the /etc/hosts file. Every machine has
at least one entry in this file called localhost that points to the local machine. To test
your connection, without knowing the name of your host or its IP address, you can
use the name localhost.

Note that in Figure 8-19, the login name was anonymous, and the system complained
when the password used was root@localhost, even though this is the suggested e-mail-
based password. In fact, root@anydomain.anygroup would have been acceptable
instead of the suggested e-mail address.

on the
job

Never believe the e-mail address provided as a password by anonymous FTP
users. There is little that can be done to check the validity of the e-mail address
provided. Anonymous FTP will check to see the offered address fits the structure
of an e-mail address, but it will not attempt to verify the domain name, nor
will it try to verify the existence of a valid e-mail user at that domain. Even
if all of these checks passed, there would be no way to know if the e-mail
address used actually related to the person who was using it.

FIGURE 8-19

Test anonymous
login to FTP

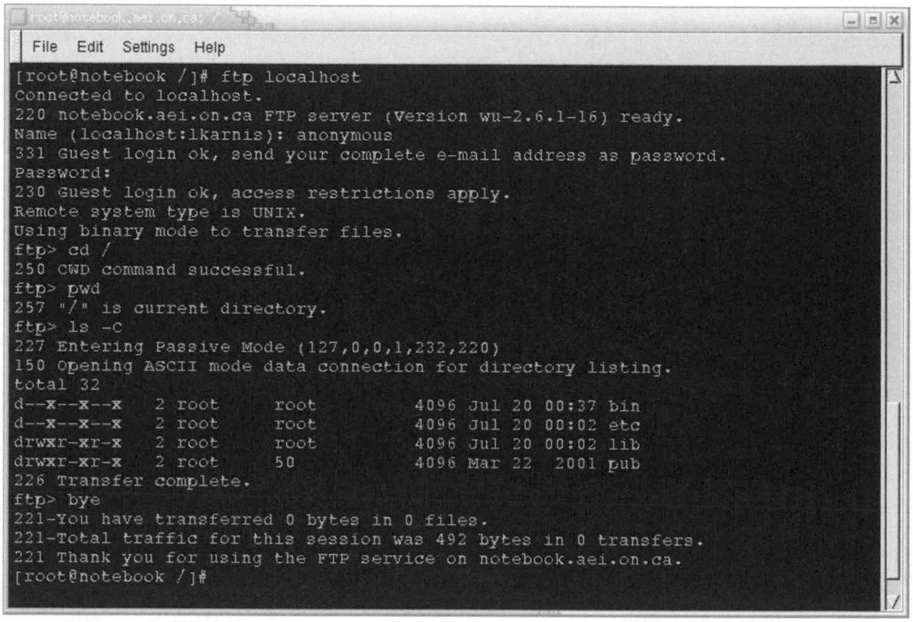

```
[root@notebook /]# ftp localhost
Connected to localhost.
220 notebook.aei.on.ca FTP server (Version wu-2.6.1-16) ready.
Name (localhost:lkarnis): anonymous
331 Guest login ok, send your complete e-mail address as password.
Password:
230 Guest login ok, access restrictions apply.
Remote system type is UNIX.
Using binary mode to transfer files.
ftp> cd /
250 CWD command successful.
ftp> pwd
257 "/" is current directory.
ftp> ls -C
227 Entering Passive Mode (127,0,0,1,232,220)
150 Opening ASCII mode data connection for directory listing.
total 32
d--x--x--x    2 root     root         4096 Jul 20 00:37 bin
d--x--x--x    2 root     root         4096 Jul 20 00:02 etc
drwxr-xr-x    2 root     root         4096 Jul 20 00:02 lib
drwxr-xr-x    2 root     50           4096 Mar 22  2001 pub
226 Transfer complete.
ftp> bye
221-You have transferred 0 bytes in 0 files.
221-Total traffic for this session was 492 bytes in 0 transfers.
221 Thank you for using the FTP service on notebook.aei.on.ca.
[root@notebook /]#
```

If the e-mail address is so unreliable, you might wonder why it is even requested. The answer is that, in the early days of the Internet (before evil crackers, viruses, and so on) everyone was expected to be polite and considerate. Consequently, leaving your e-mail address was just a polite way of saying "I was here—thanks." Sadly, in today's Internet world, this assumption about polite and considerate users remains only partially true.

By default, anonymous FTP sessions are logged to /var/log/messages. This includes the date and time of the session, as well as the e-mail name offered as the password.

Super Daemon Configuration

The FTP service daemon is actually started from the xinetd super daemon. The xinetd daemon listens for most incoming on-demand network connection requests (other than HTTP). Xinetd is configured by /etc/xinetd.conf and the individual service control files specified in /etc/xinetd.d/*service*. The xinetd daemon process launches the specific service whenever an incoming packet is received for that service. This is of course assuming that the service we wish to start has been turned on.

Note: Red Hat has made a significant shift in service management for Red Hat 7.1 from earlier releases. For security reasons, Red Hat 7.1 now comes configured with all unnecessary services turned off (so you must turn them on before using them). In the past, services were installed so that they were active by default. Leaving services turned on, however, encouraged evil crackers to exploit these services to possibly harm your system. Turning services off, by default, makes it much harder for evil crackers to exploit security flaws and gain access to your server.

Red Hat has many tools for managing services. Three popular tools are ntsysv (command line), tksysv (GUI), and chkconfig (command line). ntsysv and tksysv are tools for controlling standalone services in the service management script directory (/etc/rc.d/init.d), while chkconfig can be used for both standalone and xinetd-based services.

Figure 8-20 shows the /etc/xinetd.conf file. Note that it just defers individual service definitions to files found in /etc/xinetd.conf for Red Hat 7.1.

Note the includedir directive. You may wish to view the services that are under xinetd control. You can do this by doing a listing of the /etc/xinetd.d directory. Figure 8-21 is a sample from that directory; the swat file for controlling Samba's Samba Web Administration Tool.

When an xinetd managed service is installed, the disable keyword is set to Yes. When you use chkconfig to turn on the xinetd-managed service, chkconfig changes this value to No (that is, the service is not disabled).

FIGURE 8-20

The /etc/xinetd.conf file

```
[ root@notebook /] # cat /etc/xinetd.conf#
# Simple configuration file for xinetd
#
# Some defaults, and include /etc/xinetd.d/

defaults
{
instances            = 60
log_type             = SYSLOG authpriv
log_on_success   = HOST PID
log_on_failure   = HOST
}
includedir /etc/xinetd.d
```

FIGURE 8-21

The SWAT service configuration file from /etc/xinetd.d

```
[ root@notebook /] # cat /etc/xinetd.d/swat
# default: off
# description: SWAT is the Samba Web Admin Tool. Use swat \
#       to configure your Samba server. To use SWAT, \
#       connect to port 901 with your favorite Web browser.
service swat
{
disable      = no
port      = 901
socket_type      = stream
wait      = no
only_from = 127.0.0.1
user      = root
server    = /usr/sbin/swat
log_on_failure      += USERID
}
```

on the Job

Working from a home-based office and traveling the world can sometimes cause you to miss some important files. One way to counteract this is to install a basic anonymous FTP service on your Red Hat Linux server. Put any files for customer downloads under the anonymous public access directory (/home/ftp/pub). Use WU-FTP to manage access by privileged users to specific directories, and, if you wish, install the anonymous FTP package. With this setup, you can support you and your customers' needs with quick downloads of files from anywhere in the world. If you are not connected to the Internet, you could set up a PPP-type dial-in access connection to your machine. This would allow you, or your customers, to dial in to your machine to download files using FTP.

Configuring WU-FTPD

The anonymous FTP service only allows downloads from the public site. If you have users who want remote access to their home directory files or any generally accessible files on your system, the WU-FTP service provides a very secure control over what login names or groups can enter your system.

A few files control the many security aspects of the WU-FTP service. They can be used to restrict or control basic service access, allow additional groups, and permit guest users to access the site—all with different access privileges. These files are in the /etc directory. The most notable of these are /etc/ftpaccess and /etc/ftpusers.

The /etc/ftpaccess file controls the FTPD server's behavior. You can use it to restrict how a user uses the server (for example, disallow system accounts), you can identify programs for uncompressing files on demand during download, set login failure policies, and direct error and log messages to the appropriate place. Review the contents of the /etc/ftpaccess file now with this command:

```
# less /etc/ftpaccess
```

The /etc/ftpusers file was used in Red Hat 6.*x* and earlier to list usernames that are NOT allowed to use FTP. Typically every account that was created when you installed Red Hat has its name listed in this file. The intent is that only real users, and not system accounts should be using the FTP service. This is done to deter evil crackers from trying to break into your system by attacking known system accounts with a password guessing script. Figure 8-22 shows the contents of the /etc/ftpusers file from Red Hat 7.1. Note that as indicated in the file contents, use of this file is deprecated (obsolete). Its functionality is replaced by deny directives in the /etc/ftpaccess file.

The /etc/ftpconversions file is a special file that the FTP service uses to automatically compress and/or decompress files for transfer. The correct tool is selected based upon the file extension used by the file being transferred. By default, FTP will decompress files that are being downloaded. This feature allows FTP administrators to store files on the server in compressed format (so they take up less space). When an FTP client requests a file, the WU-FTPD server automatically decompresses the file and transfers it. That way, the users get the files they were expecting.

FIGURE 8-22	`# cat /etc/ftpusers`
	`# The ftpusers file is deprecated. Use deny-uid/deny-gid in ftpaccess.`
	`root`
	`bin`

The contents of
the deprecated
/etc/ftpusers file
from Red Hat 7.1
	`daemon`
	`adm`
	`lp`
	`sync`
	`shutdown`
	`halt`
	`mail`
	`news`
	`uucp`
	`operator`
	`games`
	`nobody`

The executables for these conversions are found in the /home/ftp/bin directory. Each line in /etc/ftpconversions represents a rule of action for specific filename extensions (Figure 8-23). More details are available from the user documentation files.

exam
ⓦatch

You need to install the anonftp package to provide an anonymous FTP service. You only need WU-FTP if you want to add security settings for various group and user login access.

EXERCISE 8-4

Configuring GFTPD

1. Insert your Red Hat CD 1.

2. Mount the CD.

3. Change directories to the CD mount point.

4. Descend further to the RedHat/RPMS directory.

5. Identify all files that provide FTP services. Use ls *ftp* to do this.

6. Use RPM to install all these packages.

7. Test anonymous FTP access. Where is your e-mail address logged?

8. What directories can you see?

9. Quit anonymous FTP.

10. Try GNOME FTP (GFTP). Log in as a "real" user. What limitations does GFTP place on you?

FIGURE 8-23

Support for decompressing various extensions

```
# cat /etc/ftpconversions
:.Z:  :  :/usr/bin/compress -d -c
%s:T_REG|T_ASCII:O_UNCOMPRESS:UNCOMPRESS
:   :   :.Z:/usr/bin/compress -c %s:T_REG:O_COMPRESS:COMPRESS
:.gz:  :  :/bin/gzip -cd %s:T_REG|T_ASCII:O_UNCOMPRESS:GUNZIP
:   :   :.gz:/bin/gzip -9 -c %s:T_REG:O_COMPRESS:GZIP
:   :   :.tar:/bin/tar -c -f - %s:T_REG|T_DIR:O_TAR:TAR
:   :   :.tar.Z:/bin/tar -c -Z -f -
%s:T_REG|T_DIR:O_COMPRESS|O_TAR:TAR+COMPRESS
:   :   :.tar.gz:/bin/tar -c -z -f -
%s:T_REG|T_DIR:O_COMPRESS|O_TAR:TAR+GZIP
```

11. If you have an Internet connection, try pointing GFTP at ftp.redhat.com. Look under the i386 binaries for your release of Red Hat. Are there any updates available for your FTP packages? If so, download and install them now.

12. Close your GFTP session.

CERTIFICATION OBJECTIVE 8.03

Samba

Starting with Windows for Workgroups, Microsoft clients could share their file systems and printers for other Windows clients to map to as remote resources. This sharing was provided through a facility called SMB, Server Message Block, a.k.a. NetBIOS requests over TCP/IP. Through the collective works of Andrew Tridgell and many others (in the Samba group), Linux systems provides transparent and reliable SMB support over TCP/IP via a package known as Samba.

There are four basic things one can do with Samba:

■ Share a Linux directory tree with Windows machines as a mapped drive letter.

■ Share a Windows drive with Linux machines as a Linux mount point.

■ Share a Linux printer with Windows machines.

■ Share a Windows printer with Linux machines.

Samba imitates many of the advanced network features and functions associated with the Win9x and NT/2000 operating systems via the use of the SMB protocol. Complete information can be found at the official Samba Web site: http://samba.org

Samba can be easily configured to do the following:

■ Share user home directory shares

■ Be the WINS server or a client of any WINS service

■ Link to or manage a workgroup browse service

- Be the master browser service if multiple workgroups exist
- Authenticate access from the local login security or from an NT PDC authority for all share access requests
- Provide local directory connections as mounted SMB file systems
- Provide domain logon validation services
- Provide synchronization of passwords between Windows and Linux systems

There are more aspects, but you get the idea. This is all done from one long file called smb.conf. The first time you see the file, you may be a little overwhelmed with detail. But there is no need to be. One of the enhancements provided by Red Hat 7.x is SWAT, the Samba Web Administration Tool. This is a mini-Web server with some CGI scripts that let you configure Samba's most popular features interactively through a Web browser.

Installing Samba Services

If you did a Server installation on your system, then the Samba package is already installed. If you did a Workstation or Notebook installation, Samba is not installed by default. If you did a Custom installation, you may or may not have selected Samba Services. You can query all packages installed by RPM and then grep for Samba to see if it is installed. Figure 8-24 is what you will see if Samba services are fully installed on a Red Hat 7.1 system.

Samba services are distributed between the two Red Hat binary CDs. Figure 8-25 is a screen grab of the first two Samba components being installed from CD 1.

FIGURE 8-24

RPM output on a system with Samba fully installed

```
[root@notebook log]# rpm -qa | grep -i samba
samba-common-2.0.7-36
samba-client-2.0.7-36
samba-swat-2.0.7-36
samba-2.0.7-36
[root@notebook log]#
```

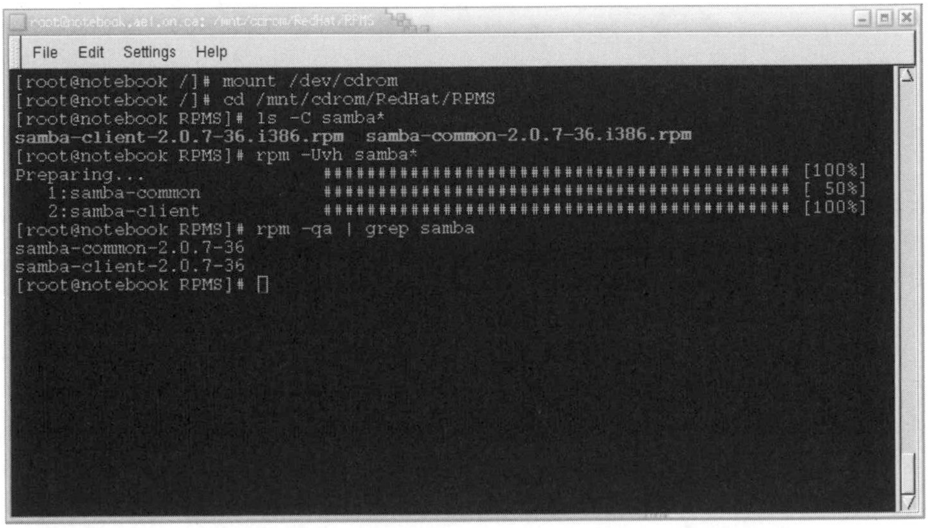

Installing Samba
services

```
[root@notebook /]# mount /dev/cdrom
[root@notebook /]# cd /mnt/cdrom/RedHat/RPMS
[root@notebook RPMS]# ls -C samba*
samba-client-2.0.7-36.i386.rpm   samba-common-2.0.7-36.i386.rpm
[root@notebook RPMS]# rpm -Uvh samba*
Preparing...                     ############################### [100%]
   1:samba-common                ############################### [ 50%]
   2:samba-client                ############################### [100%]
[root@notebook RPMS]# rpm -qa | grep samba
samba-common-2.0.7-36
samba-client-2.0.7-36
[root@notebook RPMS]# []
```

There are additional samba rpms on the second CD-ROM. Change CD-ROMs now to the Red Hat CD 2 and complete the installation (Figure 8-26).

Finally, be sure to enable SWAT. SWAT is initially disabled, which you can verify with

```
[root@notebook /] chkconfig --list | less
```

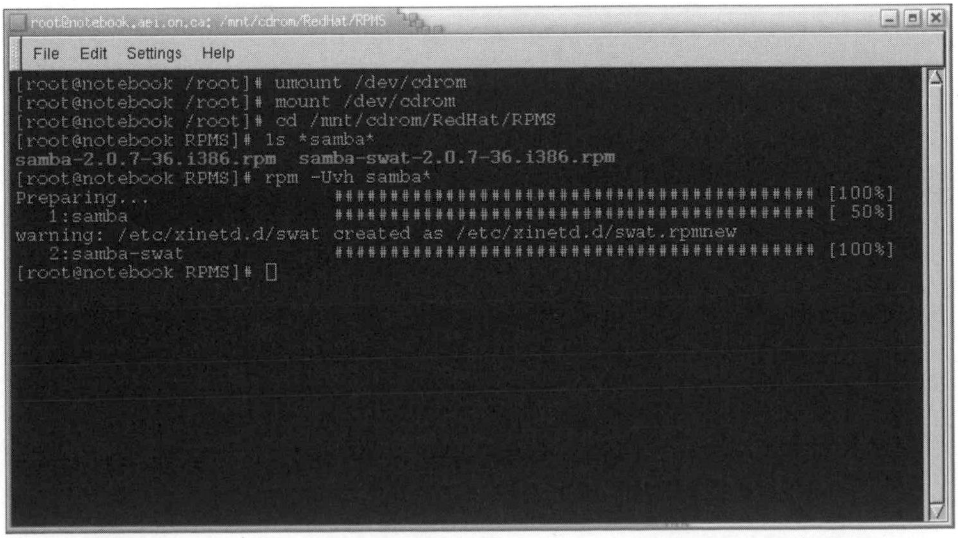

FIGURE 8-26

Continuing
with the Samba
installation
process

```
[root@notebook /root]# umount /dev/cdrom
[root@notebook /root]# mount /dev/cdrom
[root@notebook /root]# cd /mnt/cdrom/RedHat/RPMS
[root@notebook RPMS]# ls *samba*
samba-2.0.7-36.i386.rpm   samba-swat-2.0.7-36.i386.rpm
[root@notebook RPMS]# rpm -Uvh samba*
Preparing...                     ############################### [100%]
   1:samba                       ############################### [ 50%]
warning: /etc/xinetd.d/swat created as /etc/xinetd.d/swat.rpmnew
   2:samba-swat                  ############################### [100%]
[root@notebook RPMS]# []
```

SWAT is a service managed by xinetd. You should see it under the xinetd service list and it should be set to Off. Let's turn it On instead. To do this, use this:

```
[root@notebook /] chkconfig swat --list 35 on
```

Finally, let's verify SWAT is now running.

```
[root]# chkconfig swat on
[root]# chkconfig --list | grep swat
        swat: on
[root]#
```

Now, let's try launching SWAT. Samba runs on your localhost and listens on the privileged port 901. Let's start Netscape and take a look at SWAT. Use the URL http://localhost:901. SWAT should prompt you for the Samba administrator name and password. This is always **root** and **root's password**. Enter these now and select OK. Don't worry about others gaining access to SWAT and xinetd's SWAT configuration file. By default, only the root on localhost can administer SWAT.

Here is what SWAT's main configuration screen looks like (Figure 8-27).

on the
Job

SWAT runs with root level privileges and can be used to completely reconfigure your Samba service. Because username and password information travels across the network in cleartext, you should think carefully before you allow SWAT to run from any system other than localhost (via the /etc/xinetd.d/swat configuration file).

If you get an xinetd error about the connection being refused, you will need to have xinetd reload its configuration file. Run the xinetd management script with the reload option. To do this, use this command:

```
[ root@notebook /] # /etc/rc.d/init.d/xinetd reload
```

SWAT should now be recognized as a valid service. Try the preceding URL and supply root and root's password at the security prompt. You should see Figure 8-28.

Basics of Samba Services

Samba services provide interoperability between the Microsoft Windows network clients and Linux servers (or any UNIX server, for that matter). You need to have a basic understanding of how Microsoft Windows networking works in the TCP/IP realm.

Windows networking started with 15-characters or less NetBIOS hostnames. These unique hostnames provided a simple, flat hostnaming system for their

FIGURE 8-27

SWAT's main
screen

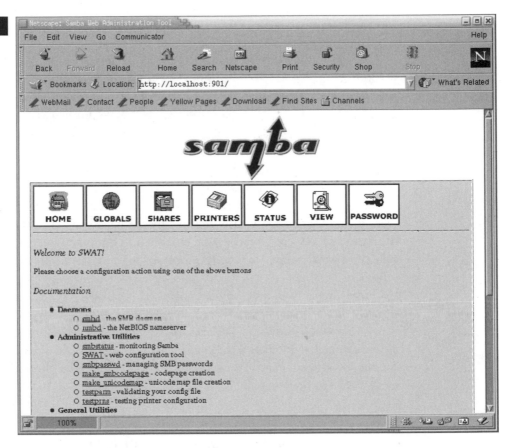

network identification. All identification requests were made through broadcast
packets. Windows defaulted to using NetBEUI as the protocol to transport packets
between hosts. NetBEUI is not "routeable," as it does not contain any network

FIGURE 8-28

The root
username and
password is
needed to gain
access to SWAT

segmentation information. For this reason, original PC networks were limited in size to small workgroups of up to 255 nodes.

Windows networks could also use IPX/SPX, which is routeable, but the widest support of services and WAN connectivity was with TCP/IP. Windows could not give up on their established design, so they added some features to TCP/IP via the usual RFC process whereby the entire protocol was published as a standard. This is the reason SAMBA exists. Because Microsoft's original SMB protocol was published, anyone could implement a compliant service by programming to that specification.

One of the nice features of Windows networks was the browser service. All machines register their NetBIOS names with one "elected" master browser, the keeper of the database of network wide services. In fact, a browse database is maintained by some "elected" host for every protocol running on the network. For instance, if NetBEUI, IPX/SPX, and TCP/IP protocols were installed on a host, then three duplicate browse databases were required—one per protocol as the services available may differ between protocols.

Originally, the Windows network only used NetBEUI for the Local Area Network (LAN). Current Windows networking uses TCP/IP as the primary protocol and may also use Novell's IPX/SPX. Connecting two or more LAN networks together creates an internetwork. The Internet is the world's largest internetwork. Trying to keep a single database of all hostnames across an internetwork proved to be impractical, so another solution had to be found.

Name Resolution—DNS   The Internet's naming service evolved a distributed service to provide hostname-to-IP resolution, called the Domain Name Service (DNS). The DNS design distributes the databases of known hosts across any number of servers organized by domain names. Each server runs a local DNS service with a static (text file) database of DNS records. A DNS record is simply a hostname and the related IP address. For example, in Table 8-1 there are two records from a DNS configuration file that identify the IP address associated with two hosts.

When a system queries DNS with a fully qualified domain name (FQDN) of www.foo.bar, DNS returns the IP address 10.1.1.1.

Each DNS service maintains a list of the local LAN hosts only. DNS is manually administered in most cases, each record being added by an administrator into a text configuration file.

Windows gurus decided to create their own centralized service that was dynamically updated by each host when it booted up. This dynamic Windows-only-based service

TABLE 8-1	DNS Name	Type	IP Address
DNS A=Address records	www.foo.bar	A	10.1.1.1
	ftp.foo.bar	A	10.1.1.2

was called the Windows Internet Naming Service (WINS). WINS is a database of IP addresses and the related NetBIOS names. The Internet does not use WINS; it only uses DNS.

For almost all network clients, there is an automatic IP configuration service, called the Dynamic Host Configuration Protocol (DHCP). When a DHCP client boots, it sends a request to a network service for IP configuration information. The DHCP server can supply all the network information for the client, plus the additional Windows IP parameters information, notably the WINS IP address, if the client is a Windows-based system.

Name Resolution—WINS   WINS was designed as a dynamic (records added by client at bootup), centralized (all records on one or more central servers), and robust service, an alternative to using DNS, that provided WAN "browsing" of Windows-based client LANs, if properly configured.

Each WINS server maintained a central database with multiple records for all machines. On a large network, this was a big data file. For each host, at least three, and as many as 10 records or more, could be added to WINS to satisfy all the Windows networking needs. Naturally, this multirecord-per-machine format became very cumbersome as the network's size grew. So, over the next few releases of Windows, WINS will be phased out.

UNIX systems also have their own authentication services for users and network access. Windows has the NT Domain or LAN Manager Domain authentication system designs. They are based on different strategic designs, and interoperability was not one of them originally.

What About Samba?   This is where Samba fits in. Samba on Linux provides all the Windows networking services available on any Windows TCP/IP client or server. You can configure Samba services so your Linux system does these things:

■ Looks like another Windows host

■ Participates in browse lists and WINS

- Is a look-alike NT Domain server

- Validates Windows logon authentication requests

- Is a WINS server itself

- Acts as a file and print server of Windows services

- Acts as the Master Browser for a Workgroup or Domain (and much, much more)

To configure Samba, you simply need to know what your NT Domain or workgroup is, and configure the parameters accordingly for your Linux workstation or server to match your local Microsoft network needs. The variations are too numerous to mention. Fortunately, Samba comes with extensive on-line documentation (with examples) available via the SWAT main screen. A basic workstation participating in a workgroup and a server acting as part of a domain are discussed here.

Figure 8-29 is a list of the key components installed when you installed Samba's rpms:

Samba Has Two Daemons

The actual running daemons that make up Samba services are the smbd and nmbd, both located in /usr/sbin. Their configuration comes from one file: /etc/samba/smb.conf. A simple test program, called testparm, checks the basic syntax of your /etc/samba/ smb.conf, looking at the format of smb.conf and producing error messages if any directives in that file are improperly formatted or unknown to Samba. testparm does not test the actual functionality of any shares.

FIGURE 8-29

Major Samba service "pieces"

```
===================================================================
/usr/sbin/smbd        - main SMB service daemon
/usr/sbin/nmbd        - NetBIOS name service daemon
/etc/samba/smb.conf   - SAMBA's primary configuration file
/usr/bin/smbclient    - connects to SMB shares, ftp-like syntax
/usr/bin/testparm     - tests validity of /etc/smb.conf file
/etc/rc.d/init.d/smb - daemon start and stop control script
/usr/bin/smbmount     - used to mount SMB share on local directory
smbfs                 - file system extension to mount SMB shares on
    directories
/usr/bin/smbprint     - a script to print to a printer on an SMB host
/usr/bin/smbstatus    - lists current SMB connections for the local host
===================================================================
```

Main Configuration File of Samba - /etc/samba/smb.conf

The main configuration file is rather long-winded and contains many parts that require a good understanding of the Windows world. There are some very helpful documents, mentioned in the home page for SWAT. The supplied smb.conf file is also well documented with suggestions and example configurations that you can uncomment, modify, and use. Finally, the Samba manual entries and supplied additional documentation files.

SWAT's job is to manage the creation of the /etc/samba/smb.conf file and update it for you. In the past, Samba administrators had to create and edit this file by hand. Considering the range of functionality and the number of options and settings available, this was no small task. With SWAT, Samba administrators can set up global server definitions, define and manage file and print shares, manage users and user authentication, and set up access restrictions to your shares.

We'll start by looking at the raw /etc/samba/smb.conf file. Once we see how the file is structured, we'll look at SWAT to assist us with our configuration. The Samba configuration file covers most of the major Windows-oriented global settings. Many more details about Samba services can be found in the documentation. Use either the man pages on Samba or look in /usr/doc for Samba HOW-TOs.

In Figure 8-30, a few options and a few example sections have been removed for brevity. Some of the comments have been shortened, and additional comments are shown in bold. You might want to browse your own /etc/samba/smb.conf file to see a complete Samba configuration (e.g., less /etc/samba/smb.conf).

The smb.conf file uses two types of comment symbols. The hash symbol (#) is used for a general text comment. This is typically verbiage that describes a feature. The second comment symbol is the semicolon (;), used to comment out Samba directives (that we may later wish to uncomment in order to enable the disabled feature).

FIGURE 8-30   The main Samba configuration file for Red Hat 7.1-/etc/samba/smb.conf
(the more interesting features are in bold)

```
# This is the main Samba configuration file. You should read the
# smb.conf(5) manual page in order to understand the options listed
# here. Samba has a huge number of configurable options (perhaps too
# many!) most of which are not shown in this example
#
# Any line that starts with a ; (semicolon) or a # (hash)
# is a comment and is ignored. In this example we will use a #
# for commentry and a ; for parts of the config file that you
# may wish to enable
```

FIGURE 8-30	The main Samba configuration file for Red Hat 7.1-/etc/samba/smb.conf (the more interesting features are in bold) *(continued)*

```
#
# NOTE: Whenever you modify this file you should run the command "testparm"
# to check that you have not made any basic syntactic errors.
#
#======================= Global Settings =====================================
[global]

# workgroup = NT-Domain-Name or Workgroup-Name
workgroup = MYGROUP

# server string is the equivalent of the NT Description field
server string = Samba Server

# This option is important for security. It allows you to restrict
# connections to machines which are on your local network. The
# following example restricts access to two C class networks and
# the "loopback" interface. For more examples of the syntax see
# the smb.conf man page
;    hosts allow = 192.168.1. 192.168.2. 127.

# if you want to automatically load your printer list rather
# than setting them up individually then you'll need this
printcap name = /etc/printcap
load printers = yes

# It should not be necessary to spell out the print system type unless
# yours is nonstandard. Currently supported print systems include these:
# bsd, sysv, plp, lprng, aix, hpux, qnx
printing = lprng

# Uncomment this if you want a guest account, you must add this to
# /etc/passwd
# otherwise the user "nobody" is used
;    guest account = pcguest

# this tells Samba to use a separate log file for each machine
# that connects
log file = /var/log/samba/%m.log

# Put a capping on the size of the log files (in Kb).
max log size = 0
```

FIGURE 8-30   The main Samba configuration file for Red Hat 7.1-/etc/samba/smb.conf
(the more interesting features are in bold) (continued)

```
# Security mode. Most people will want user level security. See
# security_level.txt for details.
security = user
# Use password server option only with security = server or
# security = domain
;    password server = <NT-Server-Name>

# Password Level allows matching of _n_ characters of the password for
# all combinations of upper and lower case.
;    password level = 8
;    username level = 8

# You may wish to use password encryption. Please read
# ENCRYPTION.txt, Win95.txt and WinNT.txt in the Samba documentation.
# Do not enable this option unless you have read those documents
;    encrypt passwords = yes
;    smb passwd file = /etc/samba/smbpasswd

# The following is needed to keep smbclient from spouting spurious errors
# when Samba is built with support for SSL.
ssl CA certFile = /usr/share/ssl/certs/ca-bundle.crt

# The following are needed to allow password changing from Windows to
# update the Linux system password also.
# NOTE: Use these with 'encrypt passwords' and 'smb passwd file' above.
# NOTE2: You do NOT need these to allow workstations to change only
#          the encrypted SMB passwords. They allow the UNIX password
#          to be kept in sync with the SMB password.
;    unix password sync = Yes
;    passwd program = /usr/bin/passwd %u
;    passwd chat = *New*UNIX*password* %n\n *ReType*new*UNIX*password* %n\n
*passwd:*all*authentication*tokens*updated*successfully*

# UNIX users can map to different SMB User names
;    username map = /etc/samba/smbusers

# Using the following line enables you to customize your configuration
# on a per machine basis. The %m gets replaced with the NetBIOS name
# of the machine that is connecting
;    include = /etc/samba/smb.conf.%m
```

FIGURE 8-30 The main Samba configuration file for Red Hat 7.1-/etc/samba/smb.conf (the more interesting features are in bold) *(continued)*

```
# Most people will find that this option gives better performance.
# See speed.txt and the manual pages for details
socket options = TCP_NODELAY SO_RCVBUF=8192 SO_SNDBUF=8192

# Configure Samba to use multiple interfaces
# If you have multiple network interfaces then you must list them
# here. See the man page for details.
;   interfaces = 192.168.12.2/24 192.168.13.2/24

# Configure remote browse list synchronization here
#  request announcement to, or browse list sync from:
#      a specific host or from / to a whole subnet (see below)
;   remote browse sync = 192.168.3.25 192.168.5.255
# Cause this host to announce itself to local subnets here
;     remote announce = 192.168.1.255 192.168.2.44

# Browser Control Options:
# set local master to no if you don't want Samba to become a master
# browser on your network. Otherwise the normal election rules apply
;    local master = no

# OS Level determines the precedence of this server in master browser
# elections. The default value should be reasonable
;    os level = 33

# Domain Master specifies Samba to be the Domain Master Browser. This
# allows Samba to collate browse lists between subnets. Don't use this
# if you already have a Windows NT domain controller doing this job
;    domain master = yes

# Preferred Master causes Samba to force a local browser election on startup
# and gives it a slightly higher chance of winning the election
;    preferred master = yes

# Enable this if you want Samba to be a domain logon server for
# Windows95 workstations.
;    domain logons = yes

# if you enable domain logons then you may want a per-machine or
# per-user logon script
# run a specific logon batch file per workstation (machine)
;    logon script = %m.bat
# run a specific logon batch file per username
;    logon script = %U.bat
```

FIGURE 8-30   The main Samba configuration file for Red Hat 7.1-/etc/samba/smb.conf
(the more interesting features are in bold) *(continued)*

```
# All NetBIOS names must be resolved to IP Addresses
# 'Name Resolve Order' allows the named resolution mechanism to be specified
# the default order is "host lmhosts wins bcast". "host" means use the UNIX
# system gethostbyname() function call that will use either /etc/hosts OR
# DNS or NIS depending on the settings of /etc/host.config, /etc/nsswitch.conf
# and the /etc/resolv.conf file. "host" therefore is system configuration
# dependant. This parameter is most often of use to prevent DNS lookups
# in order to resolve NetBIOS names to IP Addresses. Use with care!
# The example that follows excludes use of name resolution for machines
# that are NOT
# on the local network segment
# - OR - are not deliberately to be known via lmhosts or via WINS.
; name resolve order = wins lmhosts bcast

# Windows Internet Name Serving Support Section:
# WINS Support - Tells the NMBD component of Samba to enable its WINS Server
;     wins support = yes

# WINS Server - Tells the NMBD components of Samba to be a WINS Client
# Note: Samba can be either a WINS Server, or a WINS Client, but NOT both
;     wins server = w.x.y.z

# WINS Proxy - Tells Samba to answer name resolution queries on
# behalf of a non-WINS capable client, for this to work there must be
# at least one      WINS Server on the network. The default is NO.
;     wins proxy = yes

# DNS Proxy - tells Samba whether or not to try to resolve NetBIOS names
# via DNS nslookups. The built-in default for versions 1.9.17 is yes,
# this has been changed in version 1.9.18 to no.
dns proxy = no

# Case Preservation can be handy - system default is _no_
# NOTE: These can be set on a per-share basis
;   preserve case = no
;   short preserve case = no
# Default case is normally upper case for all DOS files
;   default case = lower
# Be very careful with case sensitivity - it can break things!
;   case sensitive = no
```

FIGURE 8-30 The main Samba configuration file for Red Hat 7.1-/etc/samba/smb.conf
(the more interesting features are in bold) *(continued)*

```
#============================ Share Definitions ===============================
[homes]
comment = Home Directories
browseable = no
writable = yes

# Uncomment the following and create the netlogon directory for Domain
# Logons
;  [netlogon]
;     comment = Network Logon Service
;     path = /home/netlogon
;     guest ok = yes
;     writable = no
;     share modes = no


# Uncomment the following to provide a specific roving profile share
# the default is to use the user's home directory
; [Profiles]
;     path = /home/profiles
;     browseable = no
;     guest ok = yes


# NOTE: If you have a BSD-style print system there is no need to
# specifically define each individual printer
[printers]
comment = All Printers
path = /var/spool/samba
browseable = no
# Set public = yes to allow user 'guest account' to print
guest ok = no
printable = yes

# This one is useful for people to share files
; [tmp]
;     comment = Temporary file space
;     path = /tmp
;     read only = no
;     public = yes
```

FIGURE 8-30 The main Samba configuration file for Red Hat 7.1-/etc/samba/smb.conf
(the more interesting features are in bold) *(continued)*

```
# A publicly accessible directory, but read only, except for people in
# the "staff" group
;[public]
;     comment = Public Stuff
;     path = /home/samba
;     public = yes
;     writable = yes
;     printable = no
;     write list = @staff

# Other examples.
#
# A private printer, usable only by fred. Spool data will be placed in
# fred's
# home directory. Note that fred must have write access to the spool
# directory,
# wherever it is.
;[fredsprn]
;     comment = Fred's Printer
;     valid users = fred
;     path = /homes/fred
;     printer = freds_printer
;     public = no
;     printable = yes

# A private directory, usable only by fred. Note that fred requires write
# access to the directory.
;[fredsdir]
;     comment = Fred's Service
;     path = /usr/somewhere/private
;     valid users = fred
;     public = no
;     writable = yes
;     printable = no

# a service which has a different directory for each machine that connects
# this allows you to tailor configurations to incoming machines. You could
# also use the %u option to tailor it by username.
# The %m gets replaced with the machine name that is connecting.
```

| **FIGURE 8-30** | The main Samba configuration file for Red Hat 7.1-/etc/samba/smb.conf (the more interesting features are in bold) *(continued)* |

```
; [pchome]
;    comment = PC Directories
;    path = /usr/pc/%m
;    public = no
;    writable = yes

# A publicly accessible directory, read/write to all users. Note that
# all files created in the directory by users will be owned by the default
# user, so any user with access can delete any other user's files. Obviously
# this directory must be writable by the default user. Another user could of
# course be specified, in which case all files would be owned by that user
# instead.
; [public]
;    path = /usr/somewhere/else/public
;    public = yes
;    only guest = yes
;    writable = yes
;    printable = no

# The following two entries demonstrate how to share a directory so that two
# users can place files there that will be owned by the specific users.
# In this setup, the directory should be writable by both users and
# should have the sticky bit set on it to prevent abuse. Obviously this could
# be extended to as many users as required.
; [myshare]
;    comment = Mary's and Fred's stuff
;    path = /usr/somewhere/shared
;    valid users = mary fred
;    public = no
;    writable = yes
;    printable = no
;    create mask = 0765
```

on the
job

The default /etc/samba/smb.conf file contains a wealth of hints to help guide you through Samba configuration. However, when you update your configuration with SWAT, all comments are removed! It is a good idea to save a copy of this file before you use SWAT to change it.

Global Settings   Global settings define the overall attributes of your server. In this section, you define the following:

- The server's WorkGroup name, NetBIOS name, and identification string
- User password management policies, such as how users are authenticated, which hosts (by domain on IP address) can use this service
- Browse options for acting as a master browser for your Domain or workgroup
- WINS support options

SWAT makes configuring Samba simple by doing the following:

- Offering help for every option, with text explanations just a click away
- Allowing you to select a reasonable default by using the Set Default button
- Making choices available via a drop-down box (wherever possible), rather than forcing the user to enter a setting
- Supporting two views of each configuration screen. The Basic View (default) provides minimal prompts sufficient for configuring your server, shares, or users. The Advanced View gives you complete control over your service definitions. Be prepared for long dialogues with many options.

Figure 8-31 shows the Samba Global Variables screen.

You should customize this screen to meet your local Microsoft network requirements. Note that you may have to select the Advanced View to gain access to some of the more specialized features for domain, access, and authentication settings.

Share Declarations   The remainder of the smb.conf file is used for share declarations. Each starts with a section name, such as [tmp]. This section name contains the name that will be seen by Microsoft clients only if the service is set to browseable (browseable = yes).

There are two reserved names for special sections that smb.conf uses. These special names are [homes], which automatically shares all user home directories as private, nonbrowseable shares with any user who connects with a Linux username, and [printers], which automatically shares out printers on this system to all users with the printers' NetBIOS names set to their primary queue name. As an example,

FIGURE 8-31

SWAT's global
settings screen—
the Basic View

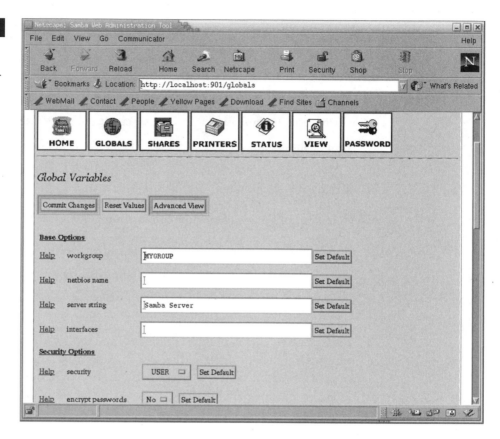

let's enable the home directories of a user as a private share for that user. Click the
Shares button on SWAT. You should see the screen in Figure 8-32.

Now, click the unlabeled button drop-down between the Choose Share and the
Delete Share buttons. You should see the Homes share as the only option available.
Select Homes, and the unnamed button should relabel itself as Homes. Now click
Choose Share to work with this share. You should see the screen in Figure 8-33.

The purpose of the Homes share is to share out the home directories of a user as
a user private share. We don't need to supply a home directory, because Samba will
read the user's account record in /etc/passwd and /etc/shadow to determine the
directory to be used. Scroll down through Samba's home share options. Notice that
we do not allow access to unknown users (guest ok = no) and that we can limit the
systems that can use this share (hosts allow = ?, and hosts deny = ?). Click the Help
button for these options for more instructions on how to set these values.

Creating a private
share of the
home directories
of a user—step 1

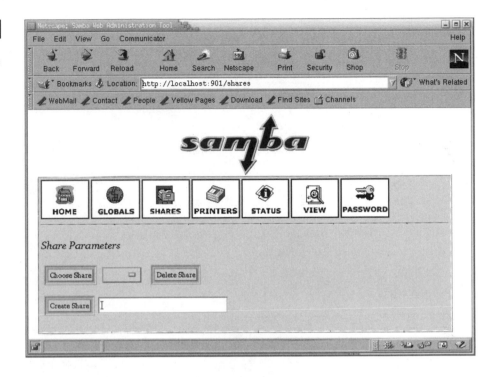

Once you are satisfied with your homes share definition, scroll back to the top of the screen and click Commit Changes to activate your share.

Now, let's look at what SWAT did with our changes. At the top of the Samba Web page, click the VIEW box to view your current /etc/samba/smb.conf file. It should look like Figure 8-34.

In Figure 8-34, we can see that we have home directory shares as well as print sharing enabled, but nothing more. Also notice that all the comments (except for the header comments) are gone! For the sake of simplicity, we have left all server configurations set to the default. Consequently, our Samba server will act as a WorkGroup server (as opposed to a domain server) and will service clients only in the MYGROUP work group. It would also make sense to change the Server String to something that identifies your Linux server from all the other Linux/Samba services you configure. (You may even want to change this string to respond in a manner consistent with certain, proprietary operating systems to avoid possible political problems you may encounter from deploying Linux technology instead of something with big licensing fees and restrictions!).

FIGURE 8-33

FIGURE 8-33

Verifying home share settings— step 2

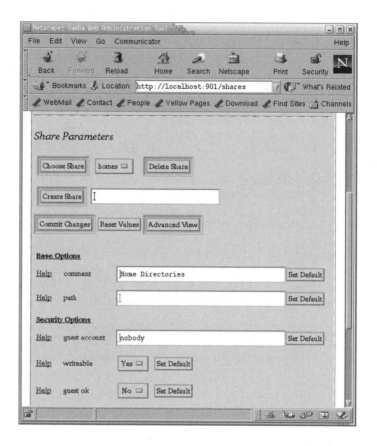

Adding Linux to an NT network can be smoothed over by configuring the Samba service to look like another Windows host on the network. You can configure Samba services to be a client of the WINS server, share out print services and file systems just like all the other Windows hosts, and participate in the browser service.

Creating a Public Share

Now, let's create a public access share for use with the entire network. Click the Shares box to get to the correct Web page. Now, enter the name of our new share, **PublicShare**, in the input field beside the Create Share button. You should see the screen in Figure 8-35.

We want our share to reside on the /home/PublicShare directory. It should be usable by all users who have a Linux account, but we will deny access to guest users and

FIGURE 8-34

A minimal
/etc/samba/smb.
conf file as
displayed by
SWAT's VIEW
button

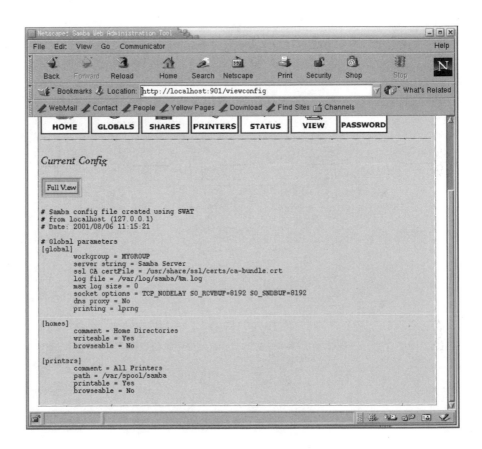

everyone else. We wish to provide access to anyone in our domain (.myCompany.com), and we wish to deny access to everyone in the suspect domain (which we'll call evil.crackers.com). Finally, your shares should be browseable to valid users. An example screen with these options set is presented in Figure 8-36.

Now, scroll back to the top of the page and select Commit Changes. Go to the VIEW box and examine the changes Samba has made to your /etc/samba/smb.conf file.

Finally, note that Samba will define the share attributes, but it will not make the directories needed by the share. Let's do that now. Issue these commands:

```
[ root@notebook /] # mkdir /home/PublicShare

[ root@notebook /] # chmod 1777 /home/PublicShare
```

FIGURE 8-35

Creating a new
Samba share
called PublicShare

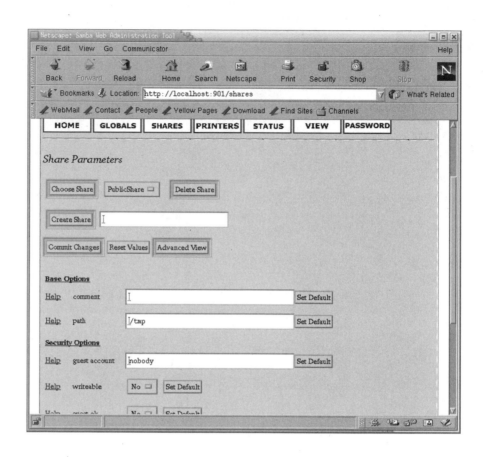

<u>exam</u>
ⓦatch

The digit 'I' in front of the 777 directory permission string is the sticky bit. By enabling the sticky bit, we are saying that anyone can do anything in the directory (because of the 777 permission value) but only to files they make! Otherwise, any user could delete or rename any file in our PublicShare, regardless of the file's owner.

Client Configuration for Print Services

There is a simple option line in the /etc/samba/smb.conf file that shares out all local printer systems as if this were another Windows host. The only difference is that it does not, by default, support the NT style of downloading the driver to the host. Any Windows client would have to have the correct driver locally installed to use the Linux-based printer. Note that this feature is available in the latest version of Samba from www.samba.org.

FIGURE 8-36

Defining your
PublicShare share

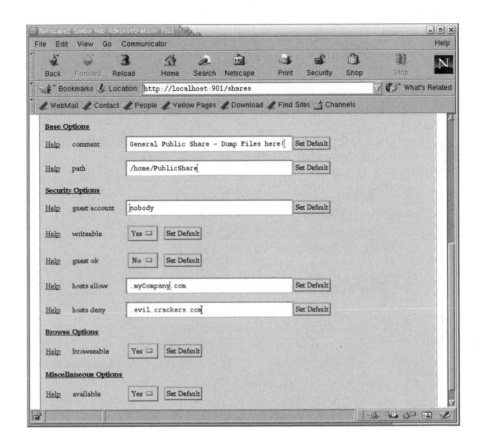

Printer definitions start with the section heading named [printers]. Using the same standard share options, Samba can create a shared print service for each installed print queue available through the local print control service. In the case of Linux, the local print service is based on the BSD LPD/LPRng (Line Print Daemon) service. These print shares are available to Microsoft clients when users install network printers.

There is a slight difference in configuration between a file and a print service. File services are writable but not printable, whereas print services are printable but not writable. Printable shares allow printer shares to upload spool files to print them (typically to /tmp). Once the print job is completed, the file is removed. Writeable shares permit users to upload their own files to the share for permanent storage. Since printer spooler files are no longer needed once the job is printed, it is common for the directory used to support printing to be /tmp.

Although this simple "share all" design is the easiest for printer options, you could selectively share out any printer instead by creating a section title for each printer to be shared. For more details, check the Samba documentation.

Testing Changes to /etc/samba/smb.conf

After making any changes to /etc/samba/smb.conf, it is always a good idea to test your system before putting it into production.

Testing a New smb.conf Configuration with testparm   You can do a simple syntax check using the supplied test utility, testparm, as shown in Figure 8-37. This does not actually check to see if the service is running or functioning correctly, it only checks basic text syntax and groupings.

Enabling Samba Services

We can control Samba service daemons from within SWAT. Go to the STATUS box and click it. You should see that both smbd and nmbd (the Samba service and NetBIOS name daemons) are disabled. Click Start smbd and Start nmbd to enable Samba. This will start Samba now, but will not arrange to start Samba after a reboot. Verify that the smb service is off, then turn it on (Figure 8-38).

Another available option is to control Samba via the smb management script that was loaded when Samba was installed. The script is called /etc/rc.d/init.d/smb.

/etc/rc.d/init.d/smb Utility   The script /etc/rc.d/init.d/smb is used to start, stop, and restart the Samba daemons, as shown in Figure 8-39. This utility may be used whenever the configuration file changes to force an instant update of the Samba services.

FIGURE 8-37
Running testparm

```
================================================================
[root@notebook /root]# testparm
Load smb config files from /etc/samba/smb.conf
Processing section "[homes]"
Processing section "[printers]"
Processing section "[public]"
Processing section "[PublicShare]"
Loaded services file OK.    # this is what to look for: 'OK'
Press enter to see a dump of your service definitions
CTRL+C       # you could press return to watch 10+ pages of output
[root@notebook /root]#
================================================================
```

```
[ root@notebook / ] # chkconfig --list | grep smb
smb              0:off  1:off  2:off  3:off  4:off  5:off  6:off
[ root@notebook / ] # chkconfig smb --level 35 on
[ root@notebook / ] # chkconfig --list | grep smb
smb              0:off  1:off  2:off  3:on  4:off  5:on  6:off
```

Checking Samba File and Print Services

You can test actual connectivity using the smbclient utility. Before testing actual connectivity, you should force the Samba daemons to restart.

Client Tool—smbclient   The last tool we'll discuss is the client access tool: smbclient. With this tool, you can test connectivity to any SMB host, whether it's Windows- or Samba-based. It even provides a familiar (to most Linux and UNIX users) FTP-like interface. You smbclient connect to an SMB share and authenticate yourself. Then, you get an SMB prompt, much like in FTP, and you use the same basic movement and file manipulation commands. The only difference is that the remote host is not running FTP services; this is all done through the SMB protocol service. This means you can connect to any Win9x/NT-based system and get or put any files from their shares (assuming you have a valid logon name and password).

You can use smbclient to verify your share list is correct. This is always a good first step before trying to use your new share (Figure 8-40).

There are two arguments you must use here: -L to specify the computer to query and -U to identify the user to connect as. (Note: you are prompted to supply that user's password.)

You can now connect via smbclient to your Samba server in order to use your PublicShare. (You should already have made the /home/PublicShare directory.) Connect to your share and then copy the /etc/passwd file to it. Look at Figure 8-41 to see an example session.

```
================================================================
[root@notebook /root]# /etc/rc.d/init.d/smb    # print syntax statement
Usage: smb {start|stop|restart|status|condrestart}
[root@unix34 /root]# /etc/rc.d/init.d/smb  restart
Shutting down SMB services:                            [  OK  ]
Shutting down NMB services:                            [  OK  ]
Starting SMB services:                                 [  OK  ]
Starting NMB services:                                 [  OK  ]
[root@notebook /root]#
================================================================
```

FIGURE 8-40

Viewing shares with smbclient

```
[ root@notebook / ] # smbclient -L notebook -U root
added interface ip=192.168.1.21 bcast=192.168.1.255 nmask=255.255.255.0
Password:
Domain=[MYGROUP] OS=[Unix] Server=[Samba 2.0.7]

        Sharename       Type        Comment
        ---------       ----        -------
        PublicShare     Disk        General Public Share - Dump Files here!
        IPC$            IPC         IPC Service (Samba Server)
        root            Disk        Home Directories

        Server                      Comment
        ---------                   -------
        NOTEBOOK                    Samba Server

        Workgroup                   Master
        ---------                   -------
        MYGROUP
[ root@notebook / ] #
```

To connect to our share, we use smbclient \\server\shareName. If the share is a restricted access share, we are prompted for a password. Once we successfully connect, we are prompted by an smb> prompt. Note in our session that some UNIX commands work (pwd) and some do not (ls -l). Smbclient prefers to use DOS- and FTP-style

FIGURE 8-41

Using smbclient to use our PublicShare

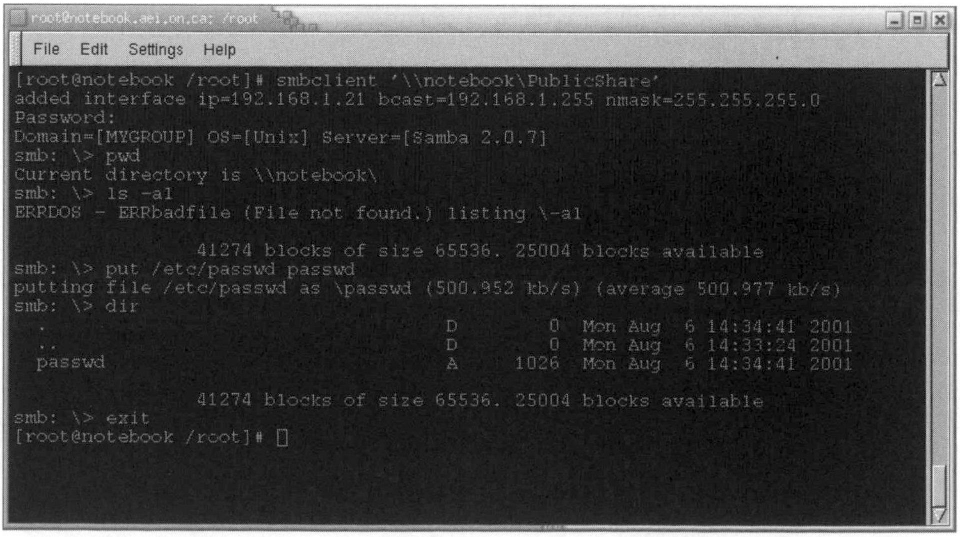

commands. We take a local Linux file (/etc/passwd) and copy it to our share as passwd. To get a complete list of smbclient built-in commands, enter **Help**.

exam
①atch

There are both client and server portions to Samba services. You should be familiar with the basic steps of how to configure the server characteristics and the shared services.

Managing Samba Users

Users for Samba services are often independent from users who have accounts on your Linux system. The Samba development team chose to do this because

- There is no reason to grant Samba access to all UNIX users (e.g., root).

- You may wish to grant Samba access to users who do not have a Linux account.

- You may wish to manage user access via NT, so Linux wouldn't necessarily even know about users.

- Samba user authentication may involve cleartext passwords (for compatibility with Windows 95 and Windows 3.1). This could potentially compromise your Linux system.

As a result, Samba may employ a user account database that's distinct from Linux's /etc/passwd user file. If it is, the user account file used by Samba would be /etc/samba/smbpasswd. This file may or may not be present, depending on how the Security value is set (on the SWAT Globals screen).

There are two steps required to make a new Samba user authenticated via the /etc/samba/smbpasswd file:

1. Create the user entry by name and add a password for the user.

2. Enable Samba access for the new user.

Users can be managed by command line or via SWAT. To manage users from the command line, use smbpasswd. To make the user and set the user's password, use this:

```
[ root@notebook / ] # smbpasswd -a newUser
New SMB password:
Retype SMB password:
[ root@notebook / ] #
```

To enable Samba access for this user, use this:

```
[ root@notebook / ] # smbpasswd -e newUser
Enabled user newUser
[ root@notebook / ] #
```

Changes made by smbpasswd are passed to the Samba server to be propagated to the system that responsible for user authentication (e.g., the local server, a remote server, or an NT Domain controller). The actual server updated is defined in the SWAT Globals Screen, Security Options section, under the Security option.

The default for user authentication is User, which refers to the local system account database. By setting the Security value to Server, we can name another server (running Samba) to act as an authentication server. And, by setting the Security value to Domain, we can authenticate our user against an NT Domain controller. In the case of Server and Domain security, we would set the remote server name by selecting the Advanced View for the Globals screen.

An alternative to command-line user configuration is SWAT. With SWAT, you can create, update, and enable users from an easy-to-use Web interface. Figure 8-42 is a screen grab of SWAT's PASSWORD screen.

Creating Local SMB Mounts to Remote File Services

The system reads the text file /etc/fstab at every reboot to mount all the file systems local to the machine. This file may also contain mounts of remote file systems using the NFS and SMB file systems.

You can update the /etc/fstab file with a permanent connection to each SMB share on the network you want to make available to local users. This is similar to a permanent NFS network connection. The main difference between SMB and NFS connections in the /etc/fstab file is that the type of file system for the SMB shares is the SMB file system, denoted as smbfs, instead of the NFS File Share, nfsfs, as with an NFS connection. You can get more details by reading the man page on smbmount and fstab.

The SMB File System   If you do not want a permanent connection, you can use the smbmount command to make a temporary smbfs connection to any network-accessible share. You can create a directory and then mount an SMB remote share service on it using the smbmount command. For Figure 8-43, let's assume we have a Microsoft system named w98laptop with a share called doc that we wish to connect to.

FIGURE 8-42

Using SWAT
to manage
Samba users

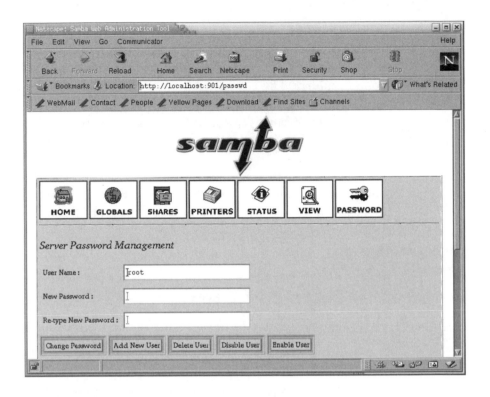

FIGURE 8-43

Sample
smbmount of
Windows-based
service

```
================================================================
[root@notebook /root]# mkdir  /mnt/docs  # make sure a directory exists
[root@notebook /root]# smbmount \\\\w98laptop\\docs -c 'mount /mnt/docs'
Added interface ip=206.195.1.222 bcast=206.195.1.255 nmask=255.255.255.0
Got a positive name query response from 206.195.1.23 ( 206.195.1.23 )
Server time is Sat May  6 16:34:56 2001
Timezone is UTC-5.0
security=share
[root@notebook /root]# ls  -l  /mnt/docs/*.zip
-rwxr-xr-x   1 root      root        115070 May 19 18:37
/mnt/docs/PERL4DAVE.zip
-rwxr-xr-x   1 root      root         56022 May  7 18:45 /mnt/docs/UNIX1IG.zip
[root@notebook /root]#
[root@notebook /root]# mount     # list all mounted file systems
/dev/hda8 on / type ext2 (rw)
none on /proc type proc (rw)
/dev/hda7 on /boot type ext2 (rw)
/dev/hda1 on /dosC type vfat (rw)
//W98LAPTOP/DOCS on /mnt/docs type smbfs (0)
[root@notebook /root]# umount /mnt/docs      # disconnect from share
[root@notebook /root]#
================================================================
```

In Figure 8-43, a directory is created to act as the mount point for the SMB share. The root user can then make a long-term connection (until reboot) of the service named DOCS on the (Win98) host named W98LAPTOP on the directory point /mnt/docs. This connection is then available to all users on the Linux host as a local directory, and will exist until the next reboot. To make this connection persist after a reboot, an entry such as the following should be added to the /etc/fstab file:

```
//W98LAPTOP/DOCS   /mnt/docs   smbfs   defaults   0  0
```

If your host connection is going to an NT Domain service, then a username and password may be necessary to make the connection in all cases. You can specify the username with the "-U username" optional string on all commands.

EXERCISE 8-5

Creating a Samba File and Print Shares

1. Install the Samba RPM from the Red Hat Installation CD.

2. If you have a WINS server configured, authorize Samba to participate as a WINS client. Use the IP of your WINS server.

3. Configure Samba to share as public, in read-only mode, the /home/ftp/pub directory tree.

4. Configure Samba to share all installed print queues to all users.

5. Allow guest access to all public shares, create a guest account with UID 500, GID 500, where the password is anonymous.

6. Share all user home directories.

7. Create separate log files for each host that connects.

8. Make all print and file shares browseable, but not home directories.

CERTIFICATION OBJECTIVE 8.04

Mail Services

If you have Linux, you have a powerful mail server. The Internet predominantly uses Sendmail, and Linux has a current version of it as well, not to mention other popular mail services. Out of the box, Red Hat 7.1 will act as a mail server for Internet mail. It will not relay mail (and thus is of no interest to spammers), nor will it honor POP or IMAP client requests (these have to be turned on explicitly). There is a huge configuration file associated with the Sendmail daemon, but there are only a few entries you are ever likely to have to change.

Three major independent but interrelated parts make up the mail service world. You need all of them to have a fully functional mail system (see Table 8-2).

On the hub server, you will need to configure the sendmail service for various outbound services related to mail, including forwarding, relaying, method of transport between systems, lists of hosts to exchange mail with, optional aliases for lists of names, and the spooling directories.

Mail depends on your network name resolution working correctly. This can be either through /etc/hosts for a small network or via DNS on a large network. Make sure that name resolution is functioning correctly before trying to configure mail.

Tech Note: Always get DNS working first. Mail relies heavily on DNS name resolution services in order to work with remote clients and servers. If DNS is not properly configured, your mail system will not function.

on the ⬥o b   *You can use linuxconf to create a specific POP mail user account.*

SMTP

SMTP, Simple Mail Transfer Protocol, has become one of the most important service protocols of the modern era. Much of the Internet-connected world lives and dies by their e-mail, and SMTP is the heart of it. SMTP is a *protocol*, a set of rules for transferring data used by some Mail Transfer Agents.

TABLE 8-2			
	MTA	Mail Transfer Agent	Sendmail, POP, IMAP
Mail System Components	MUA	Mail User Agents	mail, Netscape, elm
	MDA	Mail Delivery Agents	UUCP, TCP, SMTP

The Sendmail daemon is configured from a set of files in /etc and a directory of configuration files in /usr/lib/sendmail-cf. Refer to Table 8-3 that follows.

on the *Job*

You should be able to configure a basic POP mail account.

The Basic Sendmail Configuration

If you are going to set your system to act as a mail hub, you need to ensure both the sendmail and the sendmail-cf rpms are installed. It is common for the first rpm to be installed but not the second. The second rpm is found on CD 1. To install it, do the following:

1. Insert CD 1.

2. cd to the RPMS directory. Use: cd /mnt/cdrom/RedHat/RPMS.

3. Check the presence of the sendmail-cf rpm. Use **ls -l sendmail-cf***.

4. Add the new rpm. Use **rpm -Uvh sendmail-cf*rpm**.

There is also a sendmail-doc rpm on CD 2 you may wish to install. If so, just switch CDs (umount/mount) and install the sendmail-doc rpm according to the previous steps listed.

Configuring Sendmail

When sendmail starts, it reads the /etc/sendmail.cf file. This is a 1490-line file and nearly completely unintelligible to humans! This file provides detailed rules (organized into rulesets) on how sendmail should process mail addresses, filter spam, talk to other mail servers, and so on. This file is extremely complex and uses cryptic syntax. Most of the directives included in this file are for compliance with various RFCs (relating to processing e-mail addresses, working with Mail Transport Agents, and so on) and are not relevant to an administrator. That, plus the size and complexity of the file, make mail configuration very difficult. To address this problem, Red Hat uses a

TABLE 8-3	/etc/sendmail.cf	Main configuration file
Files needed by the SMTP service	/etc/aliases	E-mail alias definitions for users and groups
	/usr/share/sendmail-cf/cf	Various files that can be used to configure your mail service. These are only needed if you customize your mail setup
	/etc/mail	Configuration files used by various mail programs

condensed file that contains only the most relevant configuration directives. That file is /etc/mail/sendmail.mc. sendmail.mc is a much smaller file; about 54 lines including comments! It is composed entirely of macro definitions for key sendmail.cf settings. It is processed by the m4 macro processor and used to generate a new, custom sendmail.cf file.

Figure 8-44 shows what the /etc/mail/sendmail.mc looks like.

FIGURE 8-44   The /etc/mail/sendmail.mc file used for configuring Sendmail

```
divert(-1)
dnl This is the sendmail macro config file. If you make changes to this
 file,
dnl you need the sendmail-cf rpm installed and then have to generate a
dnl new /etc/sendmail.cf by running the following command:
dnl
dnl         m4 /etc/mail/sendmail.mc > /etc/sendmail.cf
dnl
include('/usr/share/sendmail-cf/m4/cf.m4')
VERSIONID('linux setup for Red Hat Linux')dnl
OSTYPE('linux')
define('confDEF_USER_ID',''8:12'')dnl
undefine('UUCP_RELAY')dnl
undefine('BITNET_RELAY')dnl
define('confAUTO_REBUILD')dnl
define('confTO_CONNECT', '1m')dnl
define('confTRY_NULL_MX_LIST',true)dnl
define('confDONT_PROBE_INTERFACES',true)dnl
define('PROCMAIL_MAILER_PATH','/usr/bin/procmail')dnl
define('ALIAS_FILE', '/etc/aliases')dnl
define('STATUS_FILE', '/var/log/sendmail.st')dnl
define('UUCP_MAILER_MAX', '2000000')dnl
define('confUSERDB_SPEC', '/etc/mail/userdb.db')dnl
define('confPRIVACY_FLAGS', 'authwarnings,novrfy,noexpn,restrictqrun')dnl
define('confAUTH_OPTIONS', 'A')dnl
dnl TRUST_AUTH_MECH('DIGEST-MD5 CRAM-MD5 LOGIN PLAIN')dnl
dnl define('confAUTH_MECHANISMS', 'DIGEST-MD5 CRAM-MD5 LOGIN PLAIN')dnl
dnl define('confTO_QUEUEWARN', '4h')dnl
dnl define('confTO_QUEUERETURN', '5d')dnl
dnl define('confQUEUE_LA', '12')dnl
dnl define('confREFUSE_LA', '18')dnl
dnl FEATURE(delay_checks)dnl
FEATURE('no_default_msa','dnl')dnl
FEATURE('smrsh','/usr/sbin/smrsh')dnl
FEATURE('mailertable','hash -o /etc/mail/mailertable')dnl
FEATURE('virtusertable','hash -o /etc/mail/virtusertable')dnl
FEATURE(redirect)dnl
FEATURE(always_add_domain)dnl
```

FIGURE 8-44   The /etc/mail/sendmail.mc file used for configuring Sendmail *(continued)*

```
FEATURE(use_cw_file)dnl
FEATURE(use_ct_file)dnl
FEATURE(local_procmail)dnl
FEATURE('access_db')dnl
FEATURE('blacklist_recipients')dnl
EXPOSED_USER('root')dnl
dnl This changes sendmail to only listen on the loopback device 127.0.0.1
dnl and not on any other network devices. Comment this out if you want
dnl to accept e-mail over the network.
DAEMON_OPTIONS('Port=smtp,Addr=127.0.0.1, Name=MTA')
dnl We strongly recommend to comment this one out if you want to protect
dnl yourself from spam. However, the laptop and users on computers that do
dnl not have 24x7 DNS do need this.
FEATURE('accept_unresolvable_domains')dnl
dnl FEATURE('relay_based_on_MX')dnl
MAILER(smtp)dnl
MAILER(procmail)dnl
```

Sendmail.mc Directives   The sendmail.mc file is made up of directives (macros) used to create content for sendmail.cf. These macros do the following:

- Add comments to aid in comprehension
- Define key variables and values
- Enable or disable features
- Create variables with specific settings

The most basic macro value is dnl. This macro tells m4 to delete from this point through to the end of the line. It is used to comment out descriptive text or disable a feature that would otherwise be included (when dnl occurs at the beginning of a directive).

The include directive instructs m4 to read the contents of the named file and insert it at the current spot in the output. This is how additional configuration information (needed by Sendmail but not relevant to mail configuration) is kept separately from settings we may wish to change.

The undefine directive deletes the named keyword. In the previous example, by undefining UUCP_RELAY and BITNET_RELAY, we disable mail relaying through these two network types.

The define directive is used to set files or enable features that we wish to use. In the preceding example, we set the path to our e-mail name user alias file (/etc/aliases), identify where procmail lives, and provide the path for the official database of e-mail users.

The FEATURE directive enables specific features. For example, we use FEATURE to set accept_unresolvable_domain. This allows us to accept mail where we cannot do a reverse IP address to domain name look up on the sender. While it would be nice to filter such mail (as this is often used by spammers to hide their true identity), it also filters out too much valid mail because many server administrators fail to implement reverse DNS (or do it incorrectly).

DAEMON_OPTIONS directly controls the SMTP daemon. In the default case, we do not accept any mail from outside our own system.

Configuring Your System for Internet Mail   There are just a couple of adjustments we need to make to get our system ready for use on the Internet. First, comment out (by adding dnl to the front of the) DAEMON_OPTIONS directive. This enables mail processing on all network interfaces.

Next, comment out the FEATURE directive that sets accept_unresolvable_domains. This prevents spammers who use just an IP address, or spammers who fake their domain name to hide themselves from sending us mail.

Now, generate a new sendmail.cf file and turn on Sendmail services:

```
[ root@notebook/ ] # mv /etc/sendmail.cf /etc/sendmail.cf.ORIG
[ {HYPERLINK "mailto:root@notebook"} / ] # m4 /etc/mail/sendmail.mc > /etc/sendmail.cf
[ root@notebook / ] # chkconfig sendmail --level 235 on
[ {HYPERLINK "mailto:root@notebook"} / ] # /etc/rc.d/init.d/sendmail restart
```

Your Sendmail (SMTP) service should now be up and running and ready to accept mail from any (valid) source.

Incorrect Mail Setup   When your name resolution is not working, your mail messages get stuck in a queue that will try to resend them at regular intervals. This is standard practice. If a host or network connection is down for some segment, then the mail forwarder or relay host will store the message and forward it at the next interval. The user need not do anything. The administrator needs to make sure this queue does not regularly fill up. If so, they may wish to reconfigure messages for that network to be sent at more irregular times (Figure 8-45).

FIGURE 8-45 If the system is unable to transport mail, root is notified

```
====================================================================
[root@notebook /]# mail
Mail version 8.1 6/6/93.  Type ? for help.
"/var/spool/mail/root" 1 messages 1 unread
>U  1 MAILER-DAEMON@linux6  Sun Oct  3 03:55  67/2221  "Warning: could not send"
&       # simply press <ENTER> key to see each message
Message 1:
From MAILER-DAEMON@linux7.4egans.com  Sun May  6 03:55:39 1999
Date: Sun, 6 May 2001 03:55:39 -0700
From: Mail Delivery Subsystem <MAILER-DAEMON@linux7.4egans.com>
To: root@linux7.4egans.com
MIME-Version: 1.0
Content-Type: multipart/report; report-type=delivery-status;
        boundary="DAA03153.938948139/linux7.4egans.com"
Subject: Warning: could not send message for past 4 hours
Auto-Submitted: auto-generated (warning-timeout)
This is a MIME-encapsulated message
--DAA03153.938948139/linux7.4egans.com
     **********************************************
     **       THIS IS A WARNING MESSAGE ONLY      **
     **   YOU DO NOT NEED TO RESEND YOUR MESSAGE  **
     **********************************************
The original message was received at Sat, 5 May 2001 23:55:21 -0700
from root@localhost
--- The following addresses had transient non-fatal errors ---
root@rh7laptop.4egans.com

   --- Transcript of session follows ---
root@rh7laptop.4egans.com... Deferred: Name server: rh7laptop.4egans.com.: host
name lookup failure
Warning: message still undelivered after 4 hours
Will keep trying until message is 5 days old

--DAA03153.938948139/linux7.4egans.com
...  # internal message format removed from here
--DAA03153.938948139/linux7.4egans.com-
& d      # delete current read buffer
& q      # quit mail
[root@notebook /]#
====================================================================
```

In the previous example, the local name server (rh7laptop.4egans.com) could not be resolved. Consequently the sender (root@localhost) is being advised that their mail could not be delivered.

Command-Line Mail

To test your mail system, you can use the built-in command-line mail utility, a simple text-based interface. The system keeps each user's mail in a system directory. Once users read a message, they can reply, forward, or delete it. If they do not delete the message before quitting the mail utility, the system stores the message in their home directory in a file called mbox. Any messages not read during a session remain in the system area.

To send mail to another user, you can use the mail command-line utility and either enter the body of the text as prompted by mail or redirect a file to the mail utility as the body of the text (shown next):

```
====================================================================
[root@notebook /root]# mail root      # assumes local host
Subject: First message
Sent to you by me
cheers.
Cc: user01@localhost
[root@notebook /root]# mail root@notebook -s 'hosts file' < /etc/hosts
[root@notebook /root]#
====================================================================
```

Reading Mail Messages   You must have mail messages pending in the system in order to read mail. The mail utility is only interactive when there is mail to be read. You can read pending messages by running mail with no arguments.

To read any message, enter the number of the message at the mail prompt and press ENTER. If you press ENTER with no argument, the mail utility assumes you want to read the next unread message. To delete a mail message, use the d command after reading the message, or use d# to delete the message numbered #. (See Figure 8-46.)

Mail Group "Alias" Lists:Aliases   The /etc/aliases is compiled by the newaliases command into a random access database for fast alias expansions during processing. The basic format is this:

```
groupname:  user01, user02, othergroupname, ?
```

Once a groupname has been created, it can be included in subsequent newgroupname entries, rather than having to add all the same usernames again.

FIGURE 8-46

Using
command-line
e-mail

```
=================================================================
[root@notebook /root]# mail     # start mail in interactive mode
Mail version 8.1 6/6/93.   Type ? for help.
"/var/spool/mail/root": 1 message 1 new     # system stores mail here
>N  1 root@rh6laptop.4egan  Sat May  5 16:43  15/418   "First message"
&              # press <RETURN> key to read current 'N' (not-read) message
Message 1:
From root  Sat May  5 16:43:26 2001
Date: Sat, 5 May 2001 16:43:25 -0700
From: root <root@localhost>
To: root@rh6laptop.4egans.com
Subject: First message
Cc: user01@rh6laptop.4egans.com
Sent to you by me
cheers.
& d              # delete current message
& q              # quit mail
[root@notebook /root]#
=================================================================
```

Workstation

If you installed as a Workstation, you got basic mail services installed. If you selected
Server or Custom install, you needed to select the Mail/News group packages option.
If you have not installed them yet, you can use RPM to install the mail and news
RPM packages.

POP

The POP, Point Of Presence, is a mail delivery protocol. It has very basic commands,
including retrieve and send messages. A mail service can be configured to be a central
depository (POP) for incoming mail messages from any other MTA service. Client
applications then download the mail messages off the POP server for processing at
the local host. The ipop3d daemon service handles all requests.

You can configure the ipop3d daemon service to listen for requests within the
/etc/xinetd.conf configuration file of the inetd service (see the code listing in the IMAP
section).

You can configure user accounts that are only designed to service POP user accounts, where users log in and receive mail only, and no interactive service is provided. The easiest method is to use linuxconf to configure the POP account.

IMAP

The IMAP daemon service provides another client access method: an imapd service (daemon) listens for all IMAP requests for mail. With IMAP, the server maintains all mail messages for the user locally, acting as the central repository of all IMAP account mail messages. This is the common service used by Web-based mail services. You do not need to have a client utility such as Netscape or Outlook. The mail user agent service is a browser-based Web interface. All user messages remain on the server. This makes it easy for someone traveling the world to access their mail without having to carry a laptop or hand-held computer. They can simply log in from any Internet terminal to retrieve their mail messages by way of any browser.

Configured POP and IMAP with xinetd

Both POP3 and IMAP servers are available with Red Hat. These servers are used to download mail-to-mail client programs such as Outlook, Eudora, Netscape, and more. By default, these programs are not enabled, and unless you did a server install, they are not even present on your system. Both are available on the IMAP rpm, however.

e x a m
Watch

Be warned that there is no corresponding POP3 rpm. All mail client services are installed from the IMAP rpm!

Check to see that the IMAP service is present under xinetd. Refer to Figure 8-47. If your output from chkconfig looks like Figure 47, you will need to find (on CD 1 or CD 2) the IMAP rpm and install it. Here is what you would do:

```
[ root@notebook / ] # mount /dev/cdrom
[ root@notebook / ] # rpm -Uvh /mnt/cdrom/RedHat/RPMS/imap*
Preparing...################################[100%]
   1:imap   ################################[100%]

[ root@notebook / ] # chkconfig imap on
[ root@notebook / ] # chkconfig ipop3 on
```

You should now be able to provide e-mail client services.

| FIGURE 8-47 | ```
[ root@notebook / ] chkconfig --list
...
xinetd based services:
finger:       off
linuxconf-web:        off
rexec:        off
rlogin:       off
rsh:        off
swat:       on
ntalk:        off
talk:        off
telnet:       on
tftp:        off
wu-ftpd:        on
chargen:        off
chargen-udp:        off
daytime:        off
daytime-udp:        off
echo:        off
echo-udp:        off
time:        off
time-udp:        off
rsync:        off
imap:  on
imaps:  off
ipop2:  off
ipop3:  on
pop3s:  off
``` |
|---|---|
| Verifying that POP3 and IMAP services are not present | |

CERTIFICATION OBJECTIVE 8.05

Printing

The Linux printing utilities are modeled after the BSD printing service and use the LPD service. LPD uses the /etc/printcap text file to define the printer queues, their characteristics, and destinations.

In general, a defined printer is a queued delivery system of data to a port or device. Most original UNIX hosts used serial ports for data connections. Printers were attached to serial ports, and print queues were fed the data at the prescribed baud rate to the print device.

Another key feature was the ability to create a local queue name that actually redirected the print request to a network printer on some other host.
```

The Printing Subsystem

The printing subsystem uses the LPRng (or LPR Next Generation) print service. This is a much improved version of the earlier printing service offered by Red Hat in 6.*x* and earlier. Improvements in printing include these:

- A significantly larger list of supported printers
- Easier GUI programs that reduce the need for command-line printer configuration
- The addition of some UNIX System V style print commands to make Linux printing easier for experienced UNIX users

As with most other services, the Linux printer service daemon listens for requests and spawns a child process to handle each event. It then continues to listen for more requests. The other thing that hasn't changed is the printer configuration file. It's still /etc/printcap.

Adding a Printer

The improved printconf-gui GUI is used to manage printers. It can configure local print queues to print to.

- Local UNIX ports
- Remote UNIX lpd print services
- Windows Print Shares
- Novell NCP Print Queues
- HP JetDirect print servers

Be aware that previous versions of Red Hat used the printtool GUI printer manager. This has been replaced by the command printconf-gui. For backward compatibility, printtool is symbolically linked to printconf-gui. You can still launch the printer manager with printtool but you'll see in the window title area that you are actually running printconf-gui.

You should be able to connect to just about any type of printer available on your network. You can start printconf-gui from linuxconf or directly from the command line. Figure 8-48 is the printconf-gui main screen.

FIGURE 8-48

The printtool
main screen

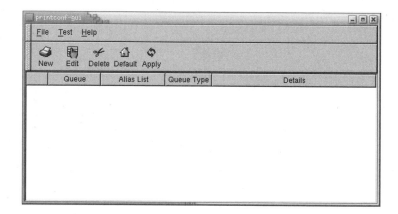

After installation, you do not have any print queues defined. As an example, you can add an Epson Stylus 800 color inkjet printer to your local parallel port. Click the New menu. You should see the Edit Queue dialogue box (Figure 8-49).

Next, select the Queue Type list item on the left. The Local Printer and default parallel port are selected for you. Select Print Driver. A list of printer manufacturers should appear. Scroll down until you see Epson. The diamond to the left of Epson is used to expand the list of supported Epson printers. Click the diamond and scroll down the list until you see Stylus Color 800 as depicted in Figure 8-50.

To complete the job, select OK and your print queue should appear in the printtool list of printers. To get the lpd print service to accept your new print queue, click the Apply button.

FIGURE 8-49

The Edit Queue
dialog box with
our epson800
queue name
already entered

FIGURE 8-50

Selecting the Epson Stylus Color 800 print driver

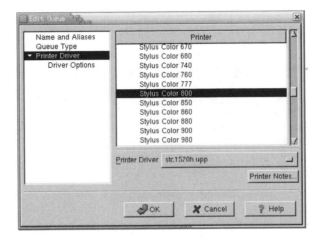

It is a good idea to test your new printer. Before you test it, however, you need to inform the print service about its presence. Under File, select Restart Lpd to have the print service reread and process your changes. Now, if everything is correct, you should be able to test. Select Test | Print ASCII Test Page to print to your new print queue.

One last step is advisable. Linux will use the printer with the alias lp as the default print queue. Since this is the only print queue we have, you should probably set it to be the default. Select Edit, and under Aliases in the Edit Queue dialogue box, click Add. Enter the name lp and click OK. Finally, close the Edit Queue dialogue by clicking OK. Notice that the lp alias is now present under the Aliases column of printtool.

The /etc/printcap file

All printer definitions are kept in the /etc/printcap file. This file has some odd syntax with format dependencies because it is edited by printtool. You can view it to verify your settings and even edit it (if you are careful) to correct minor problems. Figure 8-51 is what our /etc/printcap file looks like after adding our epson800 print queue:

The entry for your queue is made up of a number of colon-separated records. Because you typically put one setting per line, you can use the line continuation character (or the backslash (\)) at the end of all but the last line. Table 8-4 lists what these fields mean.

Each of these directives is needed to print correctly. If you set up a printer and get gibberish, you probably need to change the input filter (that is, select a different print driver).

The updated
/etc/printcap
file with our
epson800 queue
defined

```
[ root@notebook / ] # cat /etc/printcap
# /etc/printcap
#
# DO NOT EDIT! MANUAL CHANGES WILL BE LOST!
# This file is autogenerated by printconf-backend during lpd init.
#
# Hand edited changes can be put in /etc/printcap.local, and will
# be included.

epson800|lp:\
     :sh:\
     :ml=0:\
     :mx=0:\
     :sd=/var/spool/lpd/epson800:\
     :lp=/dev/lp0:\
     :lpd_bounce=true:\
     :if=/usr/share/printconf/mf_wrapper:

######################################################################
## Everything below here is included verbatim from /etc/printcap.local  ##
######################################################################
# printcap.local
#
# This file is included by printconf's generated printcap,
# and can be used to specify custom printcap entries.
```

Field Descriptions
for /etc/printcap

Field	Description
epson800llp	The queue name and alias. The lp alias defines this queue as the default.
sh	Suppress header pages. No banner is printed.
ml=0	The minimum number of characters that must be present in a print job (any #).
mx=0	The maximum number of pages allowed per print job. Zero means unlimited.
sd=	The spool directory. This is where spool files are placed before a job is printed.
lp=/dev/lp0	The device that gets the print stream.
lpd_bounce	This is a Boolean (true/false). True instructs the local lpd service to filter jobs. False tells a remote lpd service to do filtering.
if=<*program*>	The input filter. This is a program that processes our file in preparation for printing.

Access Control to Printing

By default, access to printing is open to all users. To restrict access, control is provided by two means:

1. Only from machines listed in the file /etc/hosts.lpd (if this file exist).

2. If the rs capability is specified in the printcap entry for the printer being accessed, lpr requests will only be honored for those users with accounts on the machine with the printer.

exam
ⓦatch

Installation of a printer is usually to the /dev/lp0, parallel port, on a PC.

/etc/hosts.lpd File

Access can be restricted by implementing the access control file list, /etc/hosts.lpd. For each host or network, put one line entry into this file. Once you create this file, only hosts or hosts on networks identified in this file will be able to use your printer.

Using lpc, lpq, and lprm

The lpd service includes three user utilities used to add print requests, list queued print requests, and remove print requests: lpr, lpq, and lprm. There is also a single administration control and management utility called lpc.

lpc—Line Print Control (of queues) Utility   You can use lpc to control, start, and stop all local queues if you have the privilege. The lpc utility is not commonly available to users, just superusers.

To view all known queues, use the status option to lpc. To see all of lpc's commands, use the Help option, as illustrated in Figure 8-52.

FIGURE 8-52   Using lpc

```
[ root@notebook / ] lpc status
 Printer  Printing Spooling Jobs Server Subserver Redirect Status/(Debug)
epson800@notebook   enabled  enabled    0    none     none

[ root@notebook / ] lpc help
usage: lpc [-a] [-Ddebuglevel] [-Pprinter] [-Shost] [-Uusername] [-V] [command]
 with no command, reads from STDIN
  -a            - alias for -Pall
  -Ddebuglevel - debug level
```

FIGURE 8-52   Using lpc *(continued)*

```
-Pprinter    - printer or printer@host
-Shost       - connect to lpd server on host
-Uuser       - identify command as coming from user
-V           - increase information verbosity
commands:
active    (printer[@host])         - check for active server
abort     (printer[@host] | all) - stop server
class     printer[@host] (class | off)      - show/set class printing
disable   (printer[@host] | all) - disable queueing
debug     (printer[@host] | all) debugparms - set debug level for printer
down      (printer[@host] | all) - disable printing and queueing
enable    (printer[@host] | all) - enable queueing
flush     (printer[@host] | all) - flush cached status
hold      (printer[@host] | all) (name[@host] | job | all)* - hold job
holdall   (printer[@host] | all) - hold all jobs on
kill      (printer[@host] | all) - stop and restart server
lpd       (printer[@host]) - get LPD PID
lpq       (printer[@host] | all) (name[@host] | job | all)*  - invoke LPQ
lprm      (printer[@host] | all) (name[@host]|host|job| all)* -
invoke LPRM
msg printer message text  - set status message
move printer (user|jobid)* target - move jobs to new queue
noholdall (printer[@host] | all) - hold all jobs off
printcap  (printer[@host] | all) - report printcap values
quit                             - exit LPC
redirect  (printer[@host] | all) (printer@host | off )*       -
redirect jobs
redo      (printer[@host] | all) (name[@host] | job | all)*   -
release job
release   (printer[@host] | all) (name[@host] | job | all)*   -
release job
reread    (printer[@host])         - LPD reread database information
start     (printer[@host] | all) - start printing
status    (printer[@host] | all) - status of printers
stop      (printer[@host] | all) - stop  printing
topq      (printer[@host] | all) (name[@host] | job | all)*   -
reorder job
up        (printer[@host] | all) - enable printing and queueing
  diagnostic:
     defaultq          - show default queue for LPD server
     defaults          - show default configuration values
     lang              - show current i18n (iNTERNATIONALIZATIONn)
     support
```

lpr—Line Print Request Utility   Any user can use the lpr utility to send print requests to any local queue name. You can lpr any files to a queue, or you can redirect any output via lpr. To print to any specific-named queue, precede the queue name with -P, with no space between this and the queue name. Figure 8-53 illustrates this feature.

lpq—Line Print Queue (Print Status) Utility   As we've seen, lpc has many commands. Some are extremely useful, such as these:

disable/enable [qucue]	Rejects or accepts jobs into the printer's queue or into all queues
stop/start [queue]	Dequeues jobs from the spooler, sending them to the printer.

So, if our epson800 printer were out of ink, we could issue this command:

```
[ root@notebook / ] # lpc stop epson800
```

To stop printing jobs but still allow new jobs to be queued against the printer. We can verify the status of our printer with this:

```
[ root@notebook / ] # lpc stop epson800
Printer             Printing Spooling Jobs  Server Subserver Redirect
Status/(Debug)
epson800@notebook  disabled enabled    0    none     none
```

Note that our printer is no longer printing requests. Now, let's queue up a new job. Issue these commands:

```
[ {HYPERLINK "mailto:root@notebook"} / ] # lpr -P epson800 /etc/printcap
[ {HYPERLINK "mailto:root@notebook"} / ] # lpq
Printer: epson800@notebook 'lp' (printing disabled)
 Queue: 1 printable job
 Server: no server active
 Rank    Owner/ID             Class Job Files           Size Time
1        root@notebook+849      A   849 /etc/printcap    729 21:32:40
```

We can release our job to the printer by reenabling it. To do this, use this command:

```
[ {HYPERLINK "mailto:root@notebook"} / ] # lpc start epson800
```

FIGURE 8-53

Using lpr

```
===================================================================
[root@notebook /root]# lpr /etc/hosts
[root@notebook /root]# lpr -Ptest /etc/printcap
[root@rh6laptop /root]#
===================================================================
```

If instead, we wished to delete all print jobs owned by root, we could have used this command:

```
[ {HYPERLINK "mailto:root@notebook"} / ] # lprm root
```

There are more options to most of these utilities. See the man pages for details.

Using Other Print Services

Linux can also connect to remote printer services such as any LPD service on any other host (UNIX, Linux, NT running LPD, and so on), any SMB type printers from Windows or Samba services, and any Novell-based print services. For Novell-based print services, you will not be able to print to a NetWare printer without ncpfs (Novell File System) installed. If you are not interested in Novell printers, you do not need to install ncpfs. If you are not interested in Windows-based printers, you do not need Samba services installed.

Selecting a Network Print Service

Other print services can also be attached to using the printtool utility, as illustrated in Figure 8-54.

When you add a network printer queue, you can use any name you want locally, as long as it is unique. You are not required to use the same name as the remote queue.

Remote LDP Service

To connect to any LPD type service, you will need the IP (or equivalent resolvable name for the host) and the name of the queue at the remote site. You may need to know the filter program if it is on a foreign operating system, such as NT.

Most network print devices can be accessed as though they were an LPD service, such as HP Jetdirect ports. These can also be reached via NetWare if configured that way.

FIGURE 8-54

Adding a network print service

Printing with Samba

To connect to an SMB service, you will need either the NetBIOS name or the IP address and the name of the shared print service. You will most likely need a print filter for the remote printer to be installed locally. This may vary, so test before using it.

Connecting to the Novell Print Service

If your network already contains a NetWare server providing print services, you can create a printer connection using the printtool interface.

You will need to have installed the ncpfs. You will then need to know the name of the preferred server and the printer name, and a valid username and related password. Add the print filter if needed.

Remember to always test your printers thoroughly before putting them into production. Now that you are more familiar with printers, let's look at some possible scenarios and their solutions.

SCENARIO & SOLUTION

Your boss has decided that everyone in the company should have easy access to the human resources information pertaining to all employees, such as their benefits and services.	Set up the Apache Web Server to share all the HR documents only to the local network. Let HR figure out how to create the HTML. Then fix it!
The benefits package for most new hires has two 50-page parts that Human Resources wants to be downloadable for users anywhere.	Set up the WU-FTP service with restricted access to the HR site documents for only logged-on users. Do not allow anonymous logins to access this site.
Human Resources would like all users to be able to post their ideas and complaints to a central service that they can easily deal with on a day-by-day basis	Set up interoffice mail services and create two specific accounts to handle ideas and complaints.
Naturally, everyone wants to be able to print to the latest and greatest color laser printer hanging off the newest PC on the network.	Depending on the host operating system of the new PC, you have several options: use Samba, if it is NT/Win9x; LPD, if it is Linux/UNIX; or NetWare (or Macintosh) services. Set up as appropriate. Be sure to set a limit on the number of pages they can send to the printer because color printing is expensive (on high-end printers), and a misdirected print job could cost $$$.

CERTIFICATION SUMMARY

Most of the services you would want as a basic user are configured during a Workstation installation. As an administrator, you would probably have to configure a few additional aspects for access or use of any centralized services like e-mail, DNS or hosts table, Web, print, and Samba services.

After a Server installation, you need to configure all centralized services that this, and every other, server will offer, such as e-mail, Web, Samba services, anonymous and/or controlled FTP services, and print services.

Most of these services have a main configuration file, as well as some security control files, commonly all found in /etc but this varies. These services use text-based configuration files that can be manipulated using any text editor, individually or all together via linuxconf.

All of the services discussed in this chapter are used in a typical Linux server environment. Not only will you be expected to be able to enable and configure these services at your site, but your ability to do so effectively and securely will have a major effect on how secure your system is and how happy your users are in using it.

Because RHCE is a performance-based exam, it is important to practice all the skills discussed in this chapter so you will be ready to apply them should the exam call for it.

✓ TWO-MINUTE DRILL

Here are some of the key points from the certification objectives in Chapter 8.

HTTP/Apache

❑ Red Hat Linux includes the Apache Web Server. The Apache Web Server is currently used by over twice as many Internet Web sites as all other Web servers combined.

❑ Web services are the easiest way to provide simple, secure access to documents of any type. The Apache Web Server provides both normal and secure Web services using the HTTP and HTTPS protocols, respectively. The Apache Web Server has extensive functionality and can be further extended using add-ins and macros to provide additional services.

❑ If you selected a Server installation, you already have the Apache Web Server installed. If you selected a Workstation installation or a Custom installation and did not select the Web Server optional package set, you will need to install it.

❑ You can get the latest information, documentation, upgrades, options, patches, bug fixes, and more from the Apache Web site at http://www.apache.org/.

FTP

❑ The FTP, or File Transfer Protocol, service has been around a long time. There are two application-related sides to FTP: the client and the server. The client application is available and, usually, freely supplied on all other operating systems when they support the TCP/IP protocol suite. The server application is common on most Web hosting machines and predates the actual Web as the normal Internet method of transferring files between any types of systems.

❑ There are two key packages you can install: anonftp and WU-FTP. The anonftp package provides anonymous access to anyone without the need for specific user accounts. You can install the anonftp rpm package if it is not already installed. The installation creates a /var/ftp tree and populates it with a minimal set of directories and files. You should add files to the /var/ftp/pub directory that is to be made available to anonymous logins for download to their machines only.

❑ The WU-FTP provides sophisticated features related to user management. With it, you can establish many more features and controls on many more objects. Additional features include control of transfer and command logs, on-the-fly compression and archiving (using gzip), user type and location classification, limits on a per-class (local, remote) basis, directory upload permissions, restricted guest accounts, messages per directory and system, and virtual name support.

❑ The FTP service daemon is actually started from the xinetd super daemon. The xinetd daemon listens for most configured protocols other than HTTP and NFS. Each service protocol to listen for is specified in /etc/xinetd.d/*. The xinetd, daemon process, launches the specific service whenever an incoming packet is received for that service.

Samba

❑ Starting with Windows 3.11, Windows clients could share their file systems and printers for other Windows clients to map to as remote resources. This sharing was provided through a facility called SMB, Server Message Block, a.k.a. NetBIOS. Through the collective works of Andrew Tridgell and many others, Linux systems provide SMB support over TCP/IP via a package known as Samba. Samba is one of the most widely used, best supported, and highest quality open source projects available. It easily ranks up there with Apache considering the size of its installed base.

❑ There are both client and server portions to Samba services. You should be familiar with the basic steps of how to configure the server characteristics and the shared services.

❑ Samba support is readily available from the main Samba Web site. Additionally, look for news groups and other Samba-oriented sites for answers to your questions.

❑ Samba is very transparent to Microsoft clients. It is readily accessible to any MS desktop without needing to download and install custom software. This makes Samba a great choice when it's necessary to offer file and print sharing services.

❏ In many cases, Linux machines aren't the primary file/print sharing servers on the network. When this is the case, Samba can authenticate users against a Microsoft SAM service.

❏ Because Samba is open source, there are no server, client, or client access licenses to acquire. This alone can add up to thousands of dollars of savings for your company when compared to commercial alternatives.

Mail Services

❏ If you have Linux, you have a powerful mail server. The Internet is predominantly using Sendmail, and Linux has a very current version of it and some of the other popular mail services.

❏ You can configure user accounts that are only designed to service POP user accounts, where users log in and receive mail only, and no interactive service is provided. The easiest method is to use linuxconf to configure the POP account.

❏ The base directory is /etc/mail. The sendmail.mc file is used (along with the m4 macro processor) to generate new sendmail.cf files needed to process your mail properly.

Printing

❏ The Linux printing utilities are modeled after the BSD printing service and use the LPRng service. LPD uses the /etc/printcap text file to define the printer queues, their characteristics, and destinations. Either linuxconf or printconf-cfg can be used to create and manage print queues.

❏ The printconf-gui program can be used to create queues for most popular printers.

❏ When purchasing a printer, it is a good idea to ensure that the printer you have in mind is supported by Linux. Note that printers that are Windows Only printers should be avoided.

❏ Linux supports local printers (connected via your system's parallel port), remote printing (to other Linux or UNIX servers), and network printing (to network-attached print devices).

SELF TEST

The following questions will help you measure your understanding of the material presented in this chapter. Read all the choices carefully, as there may be more than one correct answer. Choose all correct answers for each question.

HTTP/Apache

1. What service would you use to provide human resource documents to selected users on the network?

   A. Samba

   B. Apache

   C. X-Window

   D. FTP

2. The Human Resources wants to restrict access to its Web site. What features of the Apache Web Server could you incorporate?

   A. Virtual Host

   B. Port 4001

   C. Allow from mycompany.com

   D. All of the above

3. The sales department wants to amalgamate its Web service with the HR department to save money. What is the easiest way to do this?

   A. Virtual Host

   B. .htaccess

   C. DocumentRoot

   D. memory

4. The sales department wants to keep detailed and separate log files about page hits and error messages. Which options should it use?

   A. Virtual Host

   B. CustomLog

   C. DocumentRoot

   D. ErrorLog

5. When you view all system processes, you notice there are over 35 HTTP daemons running. You thought you configured 10. What has happened?

   A. It is spiraling out of control.

   B. Each virtual service can start additional daemons.

   C. There may be some FTP service requests.

   D. Apache is dynamically configuring for current load needs.

6. You copy over the Windows-based Web site to your site, set up the virtual host, and try to hit the homepage, but it fails. Which of these could be the problem if this was a straightforward Web site copy of existing files that worked?

   A. DocumentRoot

   B. Port Number

   C. index.html

   D. Wrong browser settings

7. Finally, you accessed your site, late at night, from your home office, but your site has a lot of graphical images and you have a slow modem connection. How can you test the Web site without a graphical interface?

   A. SWAT

   B. lynx

   C. linuxconf

   D. netscape -text

8. The sales department wants to make test results, FAQs, and new product data sheets available to resellers for their own sales literature. How would you make the material available to them for quick downloads?

   A. Samba

   B. Apache

   C. FTP

   D. Anonymous FTP

FTP

9. The Sales department wants to know if it can selectively give certain users access to specific directories. Which FTP options could be used to make their request a reality?

    A. .htaccess

    B. ftpaccess

    C. rpm

    D. hosts.allow

10. When a user logs in via FTP anonymously, she cannot access any of the sales documents. In fact, there are no documents available at all. Why might this be?

    A. Virtual host in pointing to the wrong system.

    B. DocumentRoot is set incorrectly.

    C. The ftpaccess file is not pointing to the correct directory.

    D. Anonymous FTP is separate from WU-FTP.

11. You notice no FTPD service running when you randomly check your system, but no complaints have been made. Why is there no daemon?

    A. It is started by xinetd as needed.

    B. It only runs at designated intervals during the day.

    C. Nobody uses it, and the system cleans house regularly.

    D. We ran out of memory.

12. The sales force complains occasionally that they are refused an FTP connection, even though their customers never see this. What may be set too low?

    A. Access times

    B. Local login limit

    C. Limited number of daemons

    D. System memory

Samba

13. There is a rogue set of users on the curriculum development team who insist on using their own equipment on their own network. Corporate wants to share information with their Windows-only network without having to retrain them. Which service should you install on Linux to "join" with theirs?

    A. Apache Web services.

    B. FTP GUI clients.

    C. Samba services.

    D. There is nothing you can do.

14. The rogue curriculum people have set up an NT server to handle their printing and file services. It uses WINS for name resolution, and all user logins are at the domain server. You want to make connections to some server-hidden shares and back up these files for them. What options would you configure in Samba?

    A. Browse Master

    B. WINS Server IP as Client

    C. NT Server for Authentication

    D. Connect to the special backup share service from Linux

15. Which is not a component of the Samba file-sharing service?

    A. /usr/bin/smbd

    B. /usr/bin/nmbd

    C. /usr/bin/smbclient

    D. /etc/samba/smb.conf

16. You made a couple of quick changes to your Samba configuration file and you need to test it quickly for syntax errors. Which utility should you run?

    A. smbmount

    B. smbclient

    C. smbfs

    D. testparm

17. You are asked to share the HR downloadable documents to Windows users who are not that familiar with FTP and want a shared drive connection. What can you use to force the Samba service to reread the configuration file immediately after you have made the configuration changes?

    A. testparm

    B. /etc/smb.conf

    C. /etc/rc.d/init.d/smb restart

    D. /etc/samba/restart

18. Windows users are complaining that they cannot see the HR document share in their Network Neighborhood diagram. What option is missing from smb.conf?

    A. Hidden = no

    B. Browseable = yes

    C. NetworkDisplay = on

    D. Viewable = no

19. One of your Linux workstation clients needs to get at a file from one of the curriculum developers who has a basic Win98 machine and has created a shared service to the files that are to be retrieved. Assuming our user was familiar with FTP, what utility would you introduce to the Linux user that she'd probably be able to use, even if you only showed it to her once?

    A. smbmount

    B. smbfs

    C. smbclient

    D. smb

20. Suddenly, many more users are requesting access to the curriculum development files because they need to make some technical changes on a regular basis. If they are all connecting to just one server host, how could you make the service local?

    A. smbclient-all

    B. smbmount

    C. smbfs

    D. /etc/rc.d/init.d/smbstatus

Mail

21. A few other departments have been using their own DOS-based mailing systems. The company wants to use a standard service so both employees and customers can all use the same system. What would be the best choice?

    A. Internet Explorer 53

    B. DaVinci Mail

    C. DaMail Mail

    D. Sendmail

22. Some of the salespeople are no longer local, and they need to be able to get their mail from any Web-based server in the world. What option would you configure for this?

    A. Sendmail-Web interface

    B. POP3 daemon

    C. IMAP daemon

    D. Apache Mail interface

Printing

23. You want to look at your current printer configuration in X-Window. What utility might you use?

    A. smbclient

    B. /etc/printcap

    C. printconf-gui

    D. lprsetup

24. The HR and Sales departments want to restrict users who can print to their printers. What file can be used to restrict access to print services?

    A. printconf-gui

    B. /etc/printcap

    C. /etc/lpraccess

    D. /Etc/hosts.lpd

LAB QUESTIONS

In our Lab, we will install and configure Samba services. This is typically necessary if you performed a Red Hat Workstation, Laptop, or Custom installation (and neglected to install Samba services).

Part 1 – Installing and Starting Samba

1. Ensure that all four components of the Samba service are correctly installed. What rpms did you install and where are they located (which CDs)?

2. Use one of the three service management tools available to us to ensure that the Samba services are configured to start correctly on boot up. What tool did you use?

3. Start Samba services now. You can use either the service management script located directly in /etc/rc.d/init.d, or you can use the "service" startup tool. How did you start your Samba service?

4. Verify that Samba services are now running. How did you do this?

Part 2 – Configuring Samba's Global Settings

1. We'll use SWAT to configure our Samba service. Start SWAT now and log in as the SWAT administrator. What ID/password did you use to do this?

2. Configure the Samba global settings. We will provide Workgroup services to our users. Set the Workgroup name to something appropriate for your company

3. Set the hosts allow string to your company's domain name (i.e., example.com)

4. Set the hosts deny string to evil.cracker.com.

5. Commit your changes.

Part 3 – Configuring File Shares

1. Activate the File Share screen.

2. Select the predefined homes share.

3. Ensure that the homes share is only available to hosts on our example.com network.

4. Ensure that the share is writable to authenticated users but not available to guest users.

5. Commit your changes.

6. Create a new share called public.

7. Change the path to the public share to /home/public.

8. Configure the public share so anyone in our domain can access the share.

9. Disallow authenticated users

10. Make the /home/public directory in a terminal window. Change the permissions to this directory to 1777.

11. Why do we set permissions to 1777?

12. Commit your changes.

Part 4 – Setting Up Printer Shares

1. Our Linux server has many printers defined. We want to offer access to them to our desktop client users. Enable access to the generic printers share now.

2. Surprisingly, printers are not browseable by default. Change that now.

3. Again, restrict access to our print shares to members of our example.com domain.

4. Commit your changes.

Part 5 – Verifying the Smb.conf file

1. We want to verify our changes. Click on the View button at the top of the SWAT Web page.

2. Review the /etc/samba/smb.conf file. Look over each section including the [globals] section. Ensure that all updates are correct and reflect the requirements previously stated. Go back and make changes, if necessary. Commit all changes.

3. Start a terminal window. Run the syntax tester tool on our Samba configuration tool. What program did you use?

4. Again, go back and make revisions if the test program indicates problems with the smb.conf file.

Part 6 – Starting the Samba Servers

1. Click on the Status button at the top of the SWAT Web page.

2. Start the smbd server.

3. Start the nmbd server.

4. Open a terminal window. Use the command line Samba client tool to connect to our Samba public share. What command line did you use?

5. Go back to the SWAT window. Refresh the list of connected users. Can you see your connection on the screen?

   Congratulations – you have just configured your Samba server to share files with your local workgroup.

Part 7 – Persistency Check

It is important for your server (and critical to pass the RHCE exam) that any changes you make to your server should be persistent. This means that changes should be reflected on the next reboot. Perform an orderly reboot of your server now and verify that Samba starts up at boot time.

1. What command did you use to perform an orderly shutdown?

SELF TEST ANSWERS

HTTP/Apache

1. ☑ **A, B, or D.** Samba can serve files to PC users, Apache can serve html documents, and FTP can serve any type of file to any type of client. You would need to select a method appropriate for your document type.
   ☒ **C** is incorrect because the X-Window system is a graphics server. It can give access to files via various X client programs, but it does not serve files directly.

2. ☑ **C.** By restricting access to a site to clients on a particular network, we can manage who is allowed to see our content. This is typically used inside a <Directory> container to limit access only to hosts in the mycompany.com domain.
   ☒ **A** is incorrect because Virtual Host directives are used to support multiple domain names on a single IP address. **B** is incorrect because the Port 4001 directive is used to have Apache listen on a nonstandard port. This hides the Web server, but not very well. Any port scanner (such as nmap or nessus) could easily find the hidden port. Once the port is found, a simple test could easily verify that a Web server is listening on that port.

3. ☑ **A.** We would set up a Virtual Host on our server and then host the Sales department's site under that name.
   ☒ **B** is incorrect because the .htaccess directive is used for overriding default permissions. **C** is incorrect because the DocumentRoot directive is used to say were HTML documents for a site live. **D** is incorrect because, while memory is a hardware component you can never have enough of, it is not a requirement for hosting the Sales site on our existing server.

4. ☑ **B and D.** CustomLog and ErrorLog. These directives specify where page hit logs (CustomLog) and error logs (ErrorLog) entries should be saved.
   ☒ **C** is incorrect because DocumentRoot is the HTML directory that contains our Web files. **A** is not correct because Virtual Host is used to define new Web sites that share our IP address.

5. ☑ **B.** Apache starts up to maxservers per virtual host. It does this so it can limit the number of servers that can respond to an individual host name. Consequently, you may see many more httpd servers running than you would have guessed.
   ☒ **A** is incorrect. If you think you are spiraling out of control, it is probably just because you aren't used to seeing so many servers. Apache will strictly control the number of servers it starts for each Virtual host. **C** is incorrect because FTP services are separate from http. Consequently FTP has no impact on the number of httpd sessions that run. Finally, **D** is incorrect because Apache does not

dynamically configure itself beyond specified limits (in /etc/httpd/conf/httpd.conf). If you have too many servers running, you can edit this file and restart Apache. However, if you have 35 servers running, it is usually because your system is getting a lot of Web traffic against many virtual hosts.

6. ☑ **C.** Assuming you copied over the content to the correct directory. Windows loves to use index.htm as its starting point, not index.html (because of the old 8.3 filename convention for Windows). The DirectoryIndex directive may not be configured to look for index.htm files. Also, check for Windows files in uppercase. Windows is case preserving but not case distinct. Linux is both case preserving and case distinct. Consequently the INDEX.HTM file that Windows uses would not be recognized by Linux as index.htm.

   ☒ **A, B,** and **D** are incorrect. While it is possible an incorrect document root or port number could be to blame, it is not as likely as a filename problem. Also, browser settings do not typically inhibit viewing of HTML documents.

7. ☑ **B.** lynx is a text-based Web browser that is extremely fast. It skips the downloading of any image files, ignores font requests, and renders your page in text mode. However, lynx can work with advanced HTML directives like forms.

   ☒ **A, C,** and **D** are incorrect. None of the other options would let you browse a site in text mode. Netscape has no such command option as -text.

8. ☑ **B, C,** or **D.** Each of these methods involves file transfers to remote networks.

   ☒ **A** is incorrect because Samba is typically configured to work only with known networks and/or local users.

FTP

9. ☑ **B.** The /etc/ftpaccess file is used to customize WU-FTP's configuration, including access rights.

   ☒ **A** is incorrect because it relates to the Apache Web Server (.htaccess). **C** is wrong because it is the Red Hat package manager (rpm). RPM is used to install, query, test, and delete packages, not limit access on FTP. **D** is incorrect because /etc/hosts.allow (and /etc/hosts.deny) are used by TCP wrappers to limit access to desired domains and networks, not users.

10. ☑ **D.** The anonymous FTP package is separate from WU-FTP. Users of anonymous FTP are placed in the /var/ftp directory and cannot move above this directory. Users of authenticated FTP are placed in the /home/ftp directory, which is likely to have much different content.

    ☒ **A** and **B** are incorrect because VirtualHost and Document root both relate to the Apache

Web server, not FTP. **C** is incorrect because the ftpaccess file is for users of the full FTP service (WU-FTP), not anonymous FTP.

11. ☑ **A.** The FTP service is controlled by xinetd. A new FTPD session is started for each incoming FTP request.

☒ While **B** is possible, it is not the default behavior. **C** and **D** are incorrect because the system does not deconfigure a service just because it hasn't been used in a while. Running out of memory shouldn't be an issue either, because all memory access is virtual, and swap storage is used when the system is low on main memory.

12. ☑ **B.** There is a facility within WU-FTP to set user counts and session counts. This directive is called limit. It may be possible that the FTP server has a limit on the number of sessions from the Sales department it will service at one time, while there are no such limits on customer access.

☒ **A** could not be correct or it would apply to all users. **C** is incorrect because there is no inherent limit on the number of FTP daemons, although daemons will not be started if other limits have been reached. **D** is incorrect because system memory, while always a factor is just as available to sales people as it is to everyone else.

Samba

13. ☑ **C.** Samba makes Linux look like a Windows NT or workgroup server. This would be the easiest and most transparent way to grant Windows-only users access to Linux files and directories.

☒ While we could install FTP GUI clients (FTP Explorer is excellent) as suggested in **B**, this wouldn't be a seamless solution. Meanwhile, Apache (**A**) would provide for a unidirectional file exchange. **D** is just wrong (because of Samba).

14. ☑ **C.** To gain access to files on the NT server, we would need an account that could be authenticated on NT. From there, we would use that account's permissions to gain access to the desired shares and back them up.

☒ **A** is incorrect because being a Browse Master does not give us inherent rights to access a local server's resources. It just gives us a record of those resources (that are browseable). **B** is incorrect because the WINS service is just a Microsoft naming service. **D** is incorrect because there is no such thing as a special backup share.

15. ☑ **C.** This is a tricky question. smbclient is a client program, it is not part of the service that provides Samba file shares.

☒ **A**, **B**, and **D** are all components that are either daemons (smbd and nmbd) that manage the service or are the server's configuration file (smb.conf).

16. ☑ D. testparm is the smb.conf configuration file syntax and semantics checker.
☒ A is wrong because smbmount is used to make remote SMB shares available to Linux. It wouldn't test your local configuration. B is wrong because smbclient is the Linux SMB client program for accessing Samba services anywhere on the network. C is incorrect because smbfs is the file system type used when smbmounts are performed automatically via /etc/fstab. Again, it is not a syntax error checker.

17. ☑ C. This is one way to tell Samba to restart itself (and thus reread its configuration file).
☒ A is incorrect because testparm is just a syntax checker. B is incorrect because smb.conf is just the Samba configuration file (albeit in the wrong location, it should be /etc/samba/smb.conf). Finally, D is incorrect because there is no such command.

18. ☑ B. A share must be marked as Browseable before it will show up in Network Neighborhood. Otherwise, the shares will be available but will be left unadvertised.
☒ A, B, and C are all invalid Samba directives.

19. ☑ C. Smbclient has a command-line format (# smbclient //serverName/ShareName) that will connect to a remote share. Once the user is authenticated, it offers a command prompt (smb>) that offers FTP client-like functionality.
☒ According to the letter of the question, A is incorrect. smbmount could be used to attach to the remote share, but it does not offer FTP-style functionality. Also, as a normal user, she may not have permission to use smbmount. B is incorrect as well. smbfs is the SMB file system type used by /etc/fstab. D is incorrect because smb by itself is not the name of any Samba component or service.

20. ☑ B. smbmount from the local system connects the remote SMB share as part of the local file system. These mounts can be made automatically by updating the /etc/fstab file.
☒ A is incorrect because there is no smbclient -all command. C is incorrect. We've already discussed smbfs (see question 19). Finally, D is incorrect because there is no /etc/rc.d/init.d/smbstatus command.

Mail

21. ☑ D. This is the only one of the named services that actually runs on Linux. Sendmail is also the Internet standard Mail Transfer Agent.
☒ DaVinci mail (B) and Internet Explorer (A) only run on PCs, and DaMail Mail (C) is is made up.

22. ☑ **B** and **C**. We don't so much configure POP and IMAP as we enable them (using chkconfig, ntsysv, tksysv, or chkconfig). Remember that POP services are part of the IMAP rpm.

    ☒ **A** and **D** are incorrect because there are no such services as the Apache Mail interface or Sendmail-Web interface. However, if you are interested in WebMail functionality, check out www.squirrelmail.org. This is an excellent PHP-based package that does the job quite nicely.

Printing

23. ☑ **C**. Printconf-gui is the X-Window GUI for configuring and managing printers.

    ☒ **A** is incorrect because smbclient is the Samba client access tool. **B** is wrong because /etc/printcap is the printer definition and configuration file. But it is not a program. **D** is wrong because there is no such file as lprsetup.

24. ☑ **D**. The /etc/hosts.lpd identifies the systems that can use the local lpd print service. Further access restrictions can be set up by editing the /etc/lpd.perms file.

    ☒ **A** is incorrect because printconf-gui is used for configuring printers, not printer access. **B** is incorrect because it doesn't contain system access information. **C** is incorrect because there is no such file as /etc/lpraccess.

LAB ANSWERS

Our end of chapter lab is designed to be easy to follow. However, there are some specific steps you'll need explicit Linux knowledge to complete. Answers to these steps can be found in the following:

Part I

Step 1 – Samba-Common and Samba-Client from the Red Hat CD 1. You'll also need to install the samba and samba-swat rpms from CD 2. Use mount /dev/cdrom to mount the Red Hat CDs. Use rpm –Uvh to install the packages. All RPMs are located in the /mnt/cdrom/RedHat/RPMS directory.

Step 2 – You could use either ntsysv, tksysv, or chkconfig to configure the Samba service to run. ntsysv is the easiest and doesn't require graphics mode.

Step 3 – Use the service smb start command to begin Samba.

Step 4 – One way to verify samba is to look for the existence of the smbd and nmbd processes in the process table. Use ps –fea | grep mbd to see if these processes are present. Another way is with the service command. Try **service smb status**.

Part 2

Step 1 – To configure Samba via SWAT, you need to log in with the root account name and password.

Part 3

Step 10 - To manually make the directory for our public share, use this:

```
# mkdir /home/public
# chmod 1777 /home/public
```

Step 11 – The 777 aspect of permissions grants read, write, and execute/search permissions to all users (root, root's group and everyone else). The 1 at the beginning of the permission value sets the sticky bit. This bit, when set on directories, restricts users from deleting or renaming files they don't own.

Part 5

Step 2 – Use the testparm command to verify the syntax of your smb.conf file. This is typically only necessary if you make hand edits to /etc/samba/smb.conf. Edits made by SWAT are always correct.

Part 6

Step 4 - smbclient \\localhost\public –U root

Part 7

Step 1 – The command you should always use to perform an orderly shutdown is shutdown –r now.

RED HAT CERTIFIED ENGINEER

9

Network Management

M

ore complex networking services in Red Hat Linux require more advanced administration methods. While graphical tools such as linuxconf are available to assist in configuring all aspects of Linux networking, a more concrete knowledge of the concepts is gained by appreciating the command-line environment of the network services.

The first section of this chapter discusses the Domain Name System (DNS). This service allows human-readable domain names (e.g., www.redhat.com) to be translated into machine-readable IP addresses (e.g., 206.132.41.202), and vice versa. The next section goes into the Squid proxy server, which serves as a mediator between an end user and a Web site. The caching server can make a user's performance while surfing the Internet increase considerably. The Network File System (NFS) is a large section that discusses a powerful and versatile way of sharing file systems between servers and workstations. The section on Internet News outlines the old familiar Usenet, and how to run a server on your network for local users. DHCP allows a Linux server to serve out dynamic IP addresses. The PPP section demonstrates how a Linux server can use a dial-up connection for individual or network Internet access.

CERTIFICATION OBJECTIVE 9.01

DNS/Bind

DNS is the Domain Name System, which converts between machine names and IP addresses. It maps from name to address and from address to name and provides other useful information to machines and their users.

In this section, two server configurations will be discussed: a caching-only server, and a primary DNS server for a domain. Files such as /etc/nsswitch.conf, /etc/resolv.conf and /etc/hosts should already be set up properly on the DNS server. This setup also assumes the server is not behind any kind of firewall that blocks name queries.

A program called named (name daemon) does name serving on Red Hat Linux. This is a part of the BIND (Berkeley Internet Name Daemon) package that is coordinated by Paul Vixie for the Internet Software Consortium. named is included in most Red Hat Linux installations and is usually installed as /usr/sbin/named. If named is not on the server, download the latest rpm from Red Hat or get the latest source from http://www.isc.org. There are two versions of BIND currently available: BIND 8 and

BIND 4. BIND 8 uses a configuration file known as /etc/named.conf, whereas
BIND 4 uses /etc/named.boot. Red Hat 7.1 ships with BIND 8, so only BIND 8
will be discussed here.

A Caching-Only Name Server

A caching-only name server will find the answer to name queries and remember the
answer the next time you need it. This will shorten the discovery time for all subsequent
requests to the same name significantly, especially for a slow or shared connection.
The first file to look at is /etc/named.conf. This is read when named starts. For now,
it should simply contain the listing in Figure 9-1.

The "directory" line tells named where to look for files. All files named subsequently
will be relative to this. For example, pz is a directory under /var/named; in other words,
/var/named/pz. /var/named is the right directory according to the Linux File Hierarchy
Standard. The file /var/named/root.hints is named in this. /var/named/root.hints should
contain the listing in Figure 9-2.

The file describes the root name servers in the world. This changes over time and
must be maintained. A shell script for maintaining this file can be found at the end
of this section.

The next section in named.conf is the last zone. A file named 127.0.0 in the
subdirectory pz should contain the listing in Figure 9-3.

Next, /etc/resolv.conf should look something like the listing in Figure 9-4.

FIGURE 9-1

The named.conf
file

```
// Config file for caching only name server
options {
        directory "/var/named";
        // Uncommenting this might help if you have to go
        // through a firewall and things are not working out:
        // query-source port 53;
};
zone "." {
        type hint;
        file "root.hints";
};
zone "0.0.127.in-addr.arpa" {
        type master;
        file "pz/127.0.0";
};
```

```
;
.                              6D IN NS        G.ROOT-SERVERS.NET.
.                              6D IN NS        J.ROOT-SERVERS.NET.
.                              6D IN NS        K.ROOT-SERVERS.NET.
.                              6D IN NS        L.ROOT-SERVERS.NET.
.                              6D IN NS        M.ROOT-SERVERS.NET.
.                              6D IN NS        A.ROOT-SERVERS.NET.
.                              6D IN NS        H.ROOT-SERVERS.NET.
.                              6D IN NS        B.ROOT-SERVERS.NET.
.                              6D IN NS        C.ROOT-SERVERS.NET.
.                              6D IN NS        D.ROOT-SERVERS.NET.
.                              6D IN NS        E.ROOT-SERVERS.NET.
.                              6D IN NS        I.ROOT-SERVERS.NET.
.                              6D IN NS        F.ROOT-SERVERS.NET.

G.ROOT-SERVERS.NET.            5w6d16h IN A    192.112.36.4
J.ROOT-SERVERS.NET.            5w6d16h IN A    198.41.0.10
K.ROOT-SERVERS.NET.            5w6d16h IN A    193.0.14.129
L.ROOT-SERVERS.NET.            5w6d16h IN A    198.32.64.12
M.ROOT-SERVERS.NET.            5w6d16h IN A    202.12.27.33
A.ROOT-SERVERS.NET.            5w6d16h IN A    198.41.0.4
H.ROOT-SERVERS.NET.            5w6d16h IN A    128.63.2.53
B.ROOT-SERVERS.NET.            5w6d16h IN A    128.9.0.107
C.ROOT-SERVERS.NET.            5w6d16h IN A    192.33.4.12
D.ROOT-SERVERS.NET.            5w6d16h IN A    128.8.10.90
E.ROOT-SERVERS.NET.            5w6d16h IN A    192.203.230.10
I.ROOT-SERVERS.NET.            5w6d16h IN A    192.36.148.17
F.ROOT-SERVERS.NET.            5w6d16h IN A    192.5.5.241
```

FIGURE 9-3

The pz/127.0.0
file

```
@            IN      SOA     ns.your-domain.com. hostmaster.your-domain.com. (
                                1       ; Serial
                                8H      ; Refresh
                                2H      ; Retry
                                1W      ; Expire
                                1D)     ; Minimum TTL
                     NS      ns.your-domain.com.
1                    PTR     localhost.
```

FIGURE 9-4

```
search subdomain.your-domain.com your-domain.com
nameserver 127.0.0.1
```

The resolv.conf
file

The "search" line specifies what domains should be searched for any hostnames that may be required. The "nameserver" line specifies the address of the local nameserver; in this case, the local server, since that is where named runs (127.0.0.1 is right, no matter if the machine has another address as well). If a list of several nameservers is required, put in one "nameserver" line for each. (Note: named never reads this file; the resolver that uses named does.)

To illustrate what this file does: If a client tries to look up a client named "host," then *host.subdomain.your-domain.com* is tried first, followed by *host.your-domain.com,* then finally host. If a client tries to look up ftp.redhat.com, ftp.redhat.com.*subdomain.your-domain.com* is tried first, then ftp.redhat.com.*your-domain.com,* and finally ftp.redhat.com. Do not put too many domains in the search line; it takes time to search them all.

The example assumes that the server belongs in the domain *subdomain.your-domain.com;* that server then is probably called *your-machine.subdomain.your-domain.com.* The search line should not contain a TLD (Top Level Domain, "com" in this case). If there is a frequent need to connect to hosts in another domain, that domain can be added to the search line like this:

```
search subdomain.your-domain.com your-domain.com other-domain.com
```

Obviously, real domain names should be used instead. Please note the lack of periods at the end of the domain names. This is important and will be explained momentarily.

Next, look at /etc/nsswitch.conf. This is a long file, specifying where to get different kinds of data types, from what file or database. It usually contains helpful comments at the top, which should be read. After that, find the line starting with "hosts:". It should read

```
hosts:      files dns
```

If there is no line starting with "hosts:", then put in the previous one. It says that programs should first look in the /etc/hosts file and then check DNS according to resolv.conf.

Starting named

After all this, it's time to start named. The server should be connected to the Internet before starting named. Type **service named start**, and press ENTER, no options. If that does not work, try **/etc/rc.d/init.d/named start** instead. If you view the syslog message file (usually called /var/log/messages) while starting named (do tail -f /var/log/messages), you should see something like the listing in Figure 9-5.

If there are any messages about errors, then there is a mistake. named will display the file with the error (one of named.conf and root.hints). Stop named, go back, and check the files.

Now test the setup. Start nslookup to examine the work.

```
$ nslookup
Default Server:  localhost
Address:  127.0.0.1
>
```

If something other than that appears, go back and check everything. Each time the named.conf file is changed, restart named using either "/etc/rc.d/init.d/named restart" or the "service named restart" command. Now, enter a query:

```
> mail.redhat.com
Server:  localhost
Address:  127.0.0.1

Name:    mail.redhat.com
Address:  199.183.24.239
```

nslookup now asks named to look for the machine mail.redhat.com. It then contacts one of the nameserver machines named in the root.hints file and asks

---

FIGURE 9-5

The messages file

```
Oct 10 12:23:34 ns named[2795]: starting.  named 8.1.1 Sun Oct 10 12:23:34
EDT 1999 root@ns:/var/tmp/bind-8.1.1/src/bin/named
        Oct 10 12:23:34 ns named[2795]: cache zone "" (IN) loaded (serial 0)
        Oct 10 12:23:34 ns named[2795]: master zone "0.0.127.in-addr.arpa"
        (IN) loaded (serial 1)
        Oct 10 12:23:34 ns named[2795]: listening [127.0.0.1].53 (lo)
        Oct 10 12:23:34 ns named[2795]: listening [10.0.0.1].53 (eth0)
        Oct 10 12:23:34 ns named[2795]: Forwarding source address is
        [0.0.0.0].1040
        Oct 10 12:23:34 ns named[2795]: Ready to answer queries.
```

its way from there. It might take a little while before the result comes back, as nslookup may need to search all the domains in /etc/resolv.conf.

If the same query is made again:

```
> mail.redhat.com
Server:   localhost
Address:  127.0.0.1

Non-authoritative answer:
Name:    mail.redhat.com
Address: 199.183.24.239
```

Note the "Non-authoritative answer:" line that appears this time around. That means that named did not go out on the network to ask this time; the information is in the cache now. However, the cached information might be out of date (stale). So nslookup announces this (very slight) possibility by saying "Non-authoritative answer:". When nslookup says this the second time a host is queried, it's a sure sign that named cached the information and that it's working. Exit nslookup by giving the command "exit".

A Simple Domain

Now, a simple domain can be defined. The domain will be your-domain.com, and it will define the machines in it. Not all characters are allowed in hostnames. DNS is restricted to the characters of the English alphabet A–Z, and numbers 0–9, and the character - (dash). Upper and lowercase characters are the same for DNS, so Mail.Your-Domain.Com is equivalent to mail.your-domain.com. (named.conf has already been set up in Figure 9-1.) Note the lack of a period (.) at the end of the domain names in this file. This says that the zone 0.0.127.in-addr.arpa will be defined, that the localhost is the master server for it, and that it is stored in a file called pz/127.0.0. That file has already been set up in Figure 9-3.

Please note the period (.) at the end of all the full domain names in pz/127.0.0, in contrast to the named.conf file. Some like to start each zone file with a $ORIGIN directive, but this is superfluous. The origin (where in the DNS hierarchy it belongs) of a zone file is specified in the zone section of the named.conf file; in this case, it's 0.0.127.in-addr.arpa.

This zone file contains three resource records (RRs): an SOA RR, an NS RR, and a PTR RR. SOA is short for Start of Authority. The @ is a special notation meaning the origin, and since the "domain" column for this file says 0.0.127.in-addr.arpa, the first line really means:

```
0.0.127.in-addr.arpa.    IN     SOA ...
```

NS is the Name Server RR. There is no @ at the start of this line; it is implicit since the last line started with a @. So, the NS line could also be written:

```
0.0.127.in-addr.arpa.    IN     NS    ns.your-domain.com.
```

It tells DNS that ns.your-domain.com is the nameserver of the domain 0.0.127.in-addr.arpa. "ns" is a customary name for nameservers, but as with Web servers, which are customarily named www.*something*.com, the name may be anything. Finally, the PTR record says that the host at address 1 in the subnet 0.0.127.in-addr.arpa (i.e., 127.0.0.1) is named localhost.

The SOA record is the preamble to all zone files, and there should be exactly one in each zone file. It describes the zone, where it comes from (a machine called ns.your-domain.com), who is responsible for its contents (hostmaster@your-domain.com, insert the proper e-mail address here), what version of the zone file this is (serial: 1), and other things having to do with caching and secondary DNS servers. For the rest of the fields (refresh, retry, expire, and minimum), the numbers described here are safe, but the files should be individualized for each network. Insert a new zone section in named.conf:

```
zone "your-domain.com" {
    type master;
    file "pz/your-domain.com";
};
```

Note again the lack of an ending period (.) on the domain name in the named.conf file. Now, populate the your-domain.com zone file with the listing in Figure 9-6.

Two things must be noted about the SOA record. ns.your-domain.com must be an actual machine with an A record. It is not legal to have a CNAME (Canonical NAME) record for the machine mentioned in the SOA record. Its name need not be ns; it could be any legal hostname. Next, hostmaster.your-domain.com should be read as hostmaster@your-domain.com—this should be a mail alias, or a mailbox, where the person(s) maintaining DNS should read mail frequently. Any mail regarding the domain will be sent to the address listed here. The name need not be hostmaster; it can be a normal e-mail address, but the e-mail address of hostmaster is often expected to work as well.

FIGURE 9-6

The your-
domain.com
zone file

```
;
; Zone file for your-domain.com
;
; The full zone file
;
@       IN      SOA  ns.your-domain.com. hostmaster.your-domain.com. (
                     200110101       ; serial, todays date + todays serial
#
                     8H              ; refresh, seconds
                     2H              ; retry, seconds
                     1W              ; expire, seconds
                     1D )            ; minimum, seconds
;
                TXT   "your-domain.com, your domain"
                NS    ns.your-domain.com. ; Internet Address of name server
                NS    ns2.your-domain.com.
                MX    10 mail.your-domain.com. ; Primary Mail Exchanger
                MX    20 mail2.your-domain.com. ; Secondary Mail Exchanger

localhost       A     127.0.0.1

gw              A     192.168.196.1
                HINFO "Cisco" "IOS"
                TXT   "The router"

ns              A     192.168.196.2
                MX    10 mail.your-domain.com.
                MX    20 mail2.your-domain.com.
                HINFO "Pentium" "Linux 2.2"
www             CNAME ns

ns2             A     192.168.196.3
                MX    10 mail.your-domain.com.
                MX    20 mail2.your-domain.com.
                HINFO "i486"      "Linux 2.0"
                TXT   "DEK"

mail            A     192.168.196.4
       MX    10 mail.your-domain.com.
                MX    20 mail2.your-domain.com.
                HINFO "386sx" "Linux 2.4"

mail2           A     192.168.196.5
       MX    10 mail.your-domain.com.
                MX    20 mail2.your-domain.com.
                HINFO "P6" "Linux 2.4"

ftp             CNAME mail2
```

There are a number of new RRs here: HINFO (Host INFOrmation) has two parts; it's a good habit to quote each. The first part is the hardware or CPU on the machine, and the second part is the software or OS on the machine. The machine called ns has a Pentium CPU and runs Linux 2.2.

CNAME is a way to give each machine several names. For example, www is an alias for ns. CNAME record usage is a bit controversial; however, it's safe to follow the rule that an MX, CNAME, or SOA record should never refer to a CNAME record; they should only refer to something with an A record. It's also safe to assume that a CNAME is not a legal hostname for an e-mail address: webmaster@www.your-domain.com is an illegal e-mail address given the setup shown previously (that is what MX (Mail eXchanger) records are for). Expect many mail administrators to enforce this rule, even if it works for some. The way to avoid this is to use A records (and perhaps some others too, like an MX record) instead. Many DNS administrators recommend not using CNAME at all.

The MX RR, tells mail systems where to send mail that is addressed to someone@your-domain.com; namely, to mail.your-domain.com or mail2.your-domain.com. The number before each machine name is that MX RR's priority. The RR with the lowest number (10) is the one mail should be sent to if possible. If that fails, the mail can be sent to one with a higher number, a secondary mail handler (i.e., mail2.your-domain.com, which has priority 20 here). Restart named by running "service named restart". Examine the results with nslookup:

```
$ nslookup
Default Server:  localhost
Address:  127.0.0.1

> ls -d your-domain.com
```

This means that all records should be listed. The results ought to look very similar to the zone file itself.

The Reverse Zone

Now programs can convert the names in your-domain.com to addresses that they can connect to. Also required is a *reverse* (or *inverse*) *zone*, one making DNS able to convert from an address to a name. This name is used by many servers of different kinds (FTP, IRC, WWW, and others) to decide if they want to talk to a given server or not, and if so, maybe even how much priority it should be given. For full access to all services on the Internet, a reverse zone is required. Add another zone to named.conf:

```
zone "196.168.192.in-addr.arpa" {
type master;
        file "pz/192.168.196";
  };
```

This is similar to the 0.0.127.in-addr.arpa, and the contents resemble the listing in Figure 9-7.

Once again, restart named and examine the output of nslookup. If the results do not look similar to the actual zone file, look for error messages in the syslog.

Common DNS Pitfalls

DNS is a net-wide database. Make sure the information that goes into the database is up to date and well formatted. Many network outages can be traced to poorly administered DNS servers. A few examples of common DNS errors can be found in the following sections.

The Serial Number Wasn't Incremented

The single most common DNS error occurs when an administrator makes updates to a zone file, restarts DNS, and notices that no one else on the Internet knows about the updates. If a DNS server doesn't detect a new serial number on a zone file, it assumes the file is the same, and sticks with its cache. The serial number is the first

FIGURE 9-7	@	IN	SOA	ns.your-domain.com. hostmaster.your-domain.com.(
				199910101 ; Serial, todays date + todays serial
The 196.168.192.				8H ; Refresh
in-addr.arpa zone				2H ; Retry
file				1W ; Expire
				1D) ; Minimum TTL
			NS	ns.your-domain.com.
	1		PTR	gw.your-domain.com.
	2		PTR	ns.your-domain.com.
	3		PTR	ns2.your-domain.com.
	4		PTR	mail.your-domain.com.
	5		PTR	mail2.your-domain.com.

thing that should be edited when updating a zone file. Be sure to put the current date (with a four-digit year!) on it, and increment the last number, if necessary.

The Reverse Zone Isn't Delegated

When a service provider assigns a network-address range and a domain name, the domain name is normally delegated as a matter of course. A *delegation* is the "glue" NS record that helps you get from one nameserver to another. The reverse zone also needs to be delegated. If the 192.168.196 net with the your-domain.com domain came from a provider, they need to put NS records in for the reverse zone and the forward zone. If the chain is followed from in-addr.arpa and up to the assigned net, a break in the chain will be discovered at the service provider. If you find the break in the chain, contact the service provider and ask them to correct the error.

exam
⬙atch

From an end-user perspective, DNS might be considered the glue that holds the Internet together. Pay special attention to the nuances of the configuration files, so that network-wide problems are avoided.

Keep It Working

There is one maintenance task to do on DNS other than keeping it running: making sure the root.hints file is updated. The easiest way to do this is by using *dig*. First, run dig with no arguments. You will get the root.hints according to the local server. Then ask one of the listed root servers with dig @rootserver. Note that the output looks like a root.hints file. Save it to a file (dig @e.root-servers.net.ns >root.hints.new) and replace the old root.hints with it. Remember to reload named after replacing the cache file.

The following script can be run automatically to update root.hints. Install a crontab entry to run it once a month, and forget it. The script assumes mail is working and that the mail-alias "hostmaster" is defined.

```
#!/bin/sh
 #
 # Update the nameserver cache information file once per month.
 # This is run automatically by a cron entry.
 #
 # Original by Al Longyear
 # Updated for bind 8 by Nicolai Langfeldt
 # Miscellaneous error-conditions reported by David A. Ranch
 # Ping test suggested by Martin Foster
 #
 (
```

```
echo "To: hostmaster <hostmaster>"
echo "From: system <root>"
echo "Subject: Automatic update of the root.hints file"
echo

PATH=/sbin:/usr/sbin:/bin:/usr/bin:
export PATH
cd /var/named

# Are we online?  Ping a server on the Internet
case 'ping -qnc 1 www.redhat.com' in
  *'100% packet loss'*)
        echo "The network is DOWN. root.hints NOT updated"
        echo
        exit 0
        ;;
esac

dig @A.ROOT-SERVERS.NET . ns >root.hints.new 2>&1

case 'cat root.hints.new' in
  *Got answer*)
        # It worked
        :;;
  *)
        echo "The root.hints file update has FAILED."
        echo "This is the dig output reported:"
        echo

        cat root.hints.new
        exit 0
        ;;
esac

echo "The root.hints file has been updated to contain the following
  information:"
echo
cat root.hints.new

chown root.root root.hints.new
chmod 444 root.hints.new
rm -f root.hints.old
mv root.hints root.hints.old
mv root.hints.new root.hints
/etc/rc.d/init.d/named restart
echo
echo "The nameserver has been restarted to ensure that the update
  is complete."
echo "The previous root.hints file is now called
```

```
/var/named/root.hints.old."
) 2>&1 | /usr/lib/sendmail -t
exit 0
```

EXERCISE 9-1

DNS/Bind

Following the example files shown previously, set up your own DNS server. Serve the domain called rhce.test.

1. Edit the /etc/named.conf file to reflect the new information. Name the zone file pz/rhce.test and set it to be a master domain.

2. Edit the file /var/named/pz/rhce.test and place the proper zone information in it. Start by adding in the header with the serial number and expiration information.

3. Add the SOA RR with a proper hostmaster contact to the zone file.

4. Add NS and MX RRs for the domain. Use the 192.168.*.* address range.

5. Add several hosts with A, HINFO, and TXT RRs. Use WWW, FTP, and mail for a few.

6. Save the zone file and then restart named with the *service named restart* command.

7. Use dig to check the rhce.test domain.

CERTIFICATION OBJECTIVE 9.02

Squid Proxy Server

Squid is a high-performance HTTP and FTP caching proxy server. It conforms to the Harvest Cache architecture and uses the Inter-Cache Protocol (ICP) for transfers between participating peer and parent/child cache servers. It can be used either as a traditional caching proxy or as a front-end accelerator for a traditional Web server. Squid accepts only HTTP requests, but speaks FTP on the server side when FTP objects are requested.

Squid is most useful for reducing bandwidth utilization (via cache hits) and load-leveling (via having better-connected parents request objects and then feed them back to bandwidth-limited downstream clients). Extremely large studies have shown bandwidth reduction of 10–20 percent for all HTTP and FTP traffic, which is economically compelling for large installations. A worldwide hierarchy of Harvest Cache sites can be joined by those so inclined (see http://www.ircache.net/ for more details).

Required Packages for Squid

The following files associated with the squid package should already be installed on your Linux server. Squid will not operate without them all, so check the list now:

- **/etc/rc.d/init.d/squid**   Start/stop script
- **/etc/squid/**   Configuration directory
- **/usr/doc/squid-version**   Documentation, mostly in HTML format
- **/usr/lib/squid/**   Support files and internationalized error messages
- **/usr/sbin/client**   Command-line diagnostic client program
- **/usr/sbin/squid**   Main daemon program
- **/var/log/squid/**   Log directory
- **/var/spool/squid/**   Cache directory (100MB or more in hundreds of hashed directories)

Initialization of Squid

When started for the first time from the Red Hat Squid package, /etc/rc.d/init.d/squid automatically runs squid -z to create the cache directories under /var/spool/squid/, and then proceeds to actually start Squid. Squid will then be running as a caching proxy server listening on port 3128. Afterward, Web clients can point to it at port 3128 as their explicit Web proxy.

Starting and Stopping Squid on a Linux Server

On Red Hat systems, Squid is started and stopped via */etc/rc.d/init.d/squid start* and */etc/rc.d/init.d/squid stop*. It may take a while to start as it inspects its many hashed directories.

Configuration Options

Advanced configuration features are adjusted via the /etc/squid/squid.conf configuration file. This allows many tuning and security parameters to be adjusted. A key configuration section contains *cache_host* lines, which specify parent and sibling Squid cache servers and should be consulted before fetching a new object. The following example sets specify one parent and three sibling cache hosts:

```
# squid.conf - On the host: childcache.example.com
#
# Format is: hostname  type  http_port  udp_port
#
cache_host parentcache.example.com   parent  3128 3130
cache_host childcache2.example.com   sibling 3128 3130
cache_host childcache3.example.com   sibling 3128 3130
```

Squid first checks its own cache, then queries its siblings and parents for the object. If neither the cache host nor its siblings have the object, it asks one of its parents to fetch it from the source (or fetches it itself if it has no parents that responded to its request).

on the

Ob

Squid can greatly improve the performance of a corporate intranet. If your company has many employees who surf the Net, a Squid server will decrease the bandwidth usage of your Internet connection.

EXERCISE 9-2

Configuring Squid to Act as a Proxy for Web and FTP Service from Your Intranet

You will need a client machine and a server connected to the Internet and your intranet. Configure Squid to act as a proxy for Web and FTP service from your intranet.

1. Configure one parent and one child cache site.

2. Start and stop the Squid service.

3. Configure a test client to use your Squid service. Test your client by using both HTTP and FTP to retrieve a file from a large site on the Internet, like sunsite.unc.edu.

<hr>

CERTIFICATION OBJECTIVE 9.03

NFS

NFS is a file-sharing protocol originally developed by Sun Microsystems in the mid-1980s. It is based on Sun's XDR (external data representation, a byte-order-independent data formatting standard) and RPC (remote procedure call) technologies. Sun provided working reference source code, which enabled NFS to quickly become the preferred file-sharing protocol in nearly all versions of UNIX, as well as other multiuser operating systems such as VMS. Linux has supported NFS (both as a client and a server) since quite early on, and NFS continues to be popular in organizations with UNIX- or Linux-based networks.

Variants of NFS

Like most other server protocols, NFS has several common variants that prove useful in different circumstances. A general familiarity with the most common variants will lead to more stable systems that can be configured on a case-by-case basis.

Universal NFS Daemon (UNFSD)

The UNFSD NFS server runs as a user-mode process, as opposed to the kernel. This provides some advantages in terms of flexibility, but tremendous disadvantages in performance and scalability. A UNFSD can only effectively handle one to two clients on a strong server, and even with a single client, throughput is a fraction of what it would be on the same server using a kernel-mode NFS daemon. Bottlenecks in UNFSD include the filename lookups, extra copies between kernel and user address space, and a single-threaded NFS daemon.

One of the "flexibility" advantages of UNFSD (over kernel-mode NFS daemons) is that it can export any number of mount points in the same file system, which are subsets or supersets of each other. This is a minor point, however, and administrators who learned NFS on commercial UNIX variants will generally find UNFSD a bit alien. Also, the daemon processes in UNFSD only read their configuration file when they start; the entire NFS service must be stopped and started again (potentially disrupting clients) to change the list of exported file systems.

All major Linux distributors shipped UNFSD through 1998. With the advent of the 2.2 kernel series, UNFSD is being quickly phased out, and is no longer being maintained as actively as KNFSD.

Kernel-Mode NFS Daemon (KNFSD)

The Linux kernel-mode NFS server, like the NFS server implementations in most commercial UNIX implementations, runs kernel processes to serve the NFS requests from clients. This means that the NFS daemon processes use kernel data structures (dentries, inodes, and devices) rather than their user-mode equivalents (filenames, file descriptors). This eliminates some serious bottlenecks present in UNFSD, enabling an inexpensive server to achieve full 100 Mbps throughput and to efficiently serve dozens of simultaneous, active clients (limited more by disk and network I/O than by CPU usage or protocol bottlenecks).

The Linux KNFSD implementation started as a patch to the 2.0.x kernels, and was worked on heavily in the 2.1 development series. It became a standard kernel feature as of the 2.2 kernels, and has quickly become the default NFS implementation in most Linux distributions.

NFS Version 3 (NFS v3)

Version 2 of the NFS protocol has been in use since the late 1980s. By the early 1990s, higher-bandwidth networks and demands for better performance prompted Sun Microsystems to revise the protocol. NFS v3's key features include support for client-side caching of data, use of larger block sizes for more efficient transfers, the capability to have multiple outstanding write requests, and the capability to run over TCP instead of UDP. Taken together, NFS v3 greatly improves write performance and scalability on large busy networks and makes modest improvements to read performance on low-traffic networks.

NFS v3 requires changes to both client and server implementations. Some NFS v3 features are implemented in the Linux 2.4 kernel, both on the client side and in KNFSD, with the important exception that knfsd does not yet support TCP. Servers and clients automatically negotiate whether to use v3 or v2, and whether to use TCP or UDP, so compatibility between newer and older implementations is rarely an issue.

PC-NFS

In the late 1980s, Sun and several third parties developed an NFS client for single-user, single-tasking operating systems such as MS-DOS and Microsoft Windows. Unfortunately, the NFS authentication model is best suited for secure, multiuser client machines, and PC-NFS has always been a difficult protocol to support reliably. Typically, PC-NFS servers must run one or more extra "helper" processes (called something like rpc.pcnfsd) that handle logins from the single-user client machines, act like rpc.mountd to process mount requests, and handle printing. The helper processes are generally specific to a particular implementation of the PC-NFS clients they will be working with, and the vendor often provides source to the pcnfsd. A world-writeable spool directory is generally needed in /var to handle print requests (typically, /var/spool/pcnfs).

Due to the flaws in the PC-NFS concept, most organizations today prefer to use *Samba* to serve files to the single-user clients (like Windows 9x) using the clients' own native file- and print-sharing protocols. Samba is a very strong implementation, and should be used instead of PC-NFS given the choice.

WebNFS

WebNFS, another Sun-designed variant of NFS, is intended for Internet use. It differs from ordinary NFS in that clients do not have to "mount" the file systems, and they receive read-only access solely. It may be suitable for publishing data to the public in a transparent manner, but it is rarely used.

Secure NFS

Since about 1990, Sun and other vendors have supported versions of NFS using public key-based strong authentication. Secure NFS has proven itself extremely tedious and complex to administer, and is still not sufficient to keep data safe in hostile environments. As a result, Secure NFS is rarely used outside of specialized government installations.

NFS Server Configuration and Operation

NFS servers are relatively easy to configure. All that is required is to export a file system, either generally or to a specific host, and then mount that file system remotely.

Required Packages

Most of the NFS package should have been installed already if either a Server installation was performed or a custom installation with the NFS Server package was installed, but double-check the required file list provided next just to be sure.

    # **rpm -qf nfs**
    knfsd (server daemons and control programs)

- /etc/rc.d/init.d/nfs   (start/stop script)
- /usr/doc/knfsd-<*version*>   (documentation, mostly in HTML format)
- Server daemons in /usr/sbin: rpc.mountd, rpc.nfsd, rpc.rquotad
- Control programs in /usr/sbin: exportfs, nfsstat, nhfsstone (a benchmark)
- Status files in /var/lib/nfs: etab, rmtab, xtab

    knfsd-clients (client daemons and control programs)

- /etc/rc.d/init.d/nfslock   (start/stop script for lockd and statd)
- Server daemons in /sbin: rpc.lockd, rpc.statd
- Control program in /usr/sbin: showmount

    portmap (Sun RPC portmapper, a prerequisite to both NFS client and server)

- /etc/rc.d/init.d/portmap   (start/stop script)
- /usr/doc/portmap-<*version*>   (documentation)
- Server daemon in /sbin: portmap
- Control programs in /usr/sbin: pmap_dump, pmap_set

Starting and Stopping NFS on a Linux Server

NFS is normally started at boot time, and in the case of knfsd it is not normally stopped or restarted during configuration (the exportfs command is typically used instead). However, if NFS or its main configuration file, /etc/exports, was not installed when the machine booted, it may be necessary to start it using the command /etc/rc.d/init.d/nfs start. In cases where NFS must be shut down (perhaps for testing or upgrades), use the command /etc/rc.d/init.d/nfs stop. Generally, the portmapper (controlled via the /etc/rc.d/ init.d/portmap start/stop script) should be started before NFS, and shut down after NFS, because NFS depends on it to function and may timeout if portmapper is not running.

exam
Watch | *Be aware that multiple daemons are required for NFS services to work; portmapper, as well as nfsd.*

This script starts the following processes:

- ■ **rpc.mountd**   Handles mount requests
- ■ **rpc.nfsd**   Spawns the specified number of nfsd kernel processes and exits
- ■ **rpc.rquotad**   Reports disk quota statistics to clients

The /etc/exports File

/etc/exports is the only major configuration file for NFS on Linux. It explicitly lists which parts of which file systems are to be exported to clients via the exportfs command. The file format is similar to that used in SunOS 4.*x*, except that some additional options are permitted. Each line lists one directory that may be exported, the hosts it will be exported to, and the options that apply to this export. A given directory may only be exported once. With knfsd, there are additional restrictions: directories that are parents or children of each other cannot both be exported unless they are in different file systems, and only directories in the same file system are exported (knfsd will not traverse mount points).

```
/pub                    (ro) someone.mylocaldomain.com(rw)
/home                   *.mylocaldomain.com(rw)
/opt/diskless-root      diskless.mylocaldomain.com(rw,no_root_squash)
```

In the preceding example, /pub is exported to everyone as read-only and to just one specific machine as read-write; /home is exported to any host whose inverse DNS pointer (IN PTR) is for a hostname ending in .mylocaldomain.com; and /opt/diskless-root is exported with full read-write (even for the root account) to just one specific machine.

Changing the List of Exports

Simply changing /etc/exports does not automatically change anything right away. This file is simply the default set of exported directories for the *exportfs -a* command, which is typically run at boot time or by hand whenever /etc/exports has been changed. File systems can also be exported directly (and temporarily) via the exportfs command without modifying /etc/exports.

If exports are only being added to, running *exportfs -a* is sufficient to add them. However, if any exports are being modified, moved, or deleted, it is safest to first do *exportfs -ua* to temporarily unexport all file systems (potentially inconveniencing users) followed by *exportfs -a*. If many different directories are being exported and actively used and only one is being changed, the exportfs command can explicitly unexport just the one being modified.

NFS Client Configuration and Operation

Now the client side mounts can be done. This is accomplished in a manner similar to mounting local file systems.

Configuration Files

NFS clients normally mount their remote file systems at boot time, based on entries in /etc/fstab. For example:

```
## Server Directory     Mount Point   Type   Mount Options      Dump Fsckorder
nfsserv:/homenfs        /nfs/home     nfs    soft,timeout=100    0     0
```

Alternatively, an automounter, such as autofs or amd, can be used to dynamically mount NFS filesystems as they are referenced on the client and later unmount them when they have not been recently accessed.

Starting/Stopping

The startup script for remote NFS file systems is specified in /etc/fstab. This script also manages remote SMB and NetWare file systems specified in /etc/fstab.

Client-Side Helper Processes

You may notice a few new system processes in the main process status (*ps aux*). These are required for proper client-side NFS mounts. They include

■ **rpc.statd**   Tracks the state of servers, for use by *rpc.lockd* in recovering locks after a server crash.

■ **rpc.lockd**   Manages the client side of file locking. It is usually not required to start rpc.lockd, since the NFS lock manager is now started automatically by the kernel.

Diskless Clients

NFS supports diskless clients, which use either a boot floppy or a boot PROM to get started and then mount their root file system, swap space, a shared read-only /usr file system, and other shared read-write file systems such as /home. If "net-booting" from a boot PROM is used, the client will need *bootp* (or DHCP) and *tftp* services to obtain its network information and then download its kernel. See the Diskless-HOWTO for details on setting up diskless clients.

Quirks and Limitations of NFS

NFS does have its problems. An administrator who controls NFS mounts would be wise to take note of these limitations.

Statelessness

Unlike most other file-sharing protocols, NFS is designed to be (at least theoretically) completely "stateless." Thus, there is not a separate login phase prior to gaining access to NFS resources. Instead, the NFS client normally contacts rpc.mountd on the server, which checks the request against currently exported file systems and provides an *NFS file handle* (a "magic cookie" that is generally hard to guess), which is then used for subsequent I/O. The advantage of this stateless protocol is that if the server must be rebooted, the client can simply wait for it to come back up without any of its software failing. The stateless concept, however, does not work well when insecure single-user clients are involved, makes file-locking very complex, and is counterintuitive to most people trained on other file-sharing technologies.

Superset/Subset Exports and Mount Points

As mentioned earlier, knfsd processes NFS requests from a kernel internal data structure perspective, not from a user perspective. This has two important implications for exported directories. First, any mount points that are under an exported directory are not automatically exported, with the interesting side effect that the real contents of the directory that is the mount point are seen instead. Second, it is impossible to export two directories in the same file system if one is inside the other. For example, /usr and /usr/local cannot both be exported unless /usr/local is a separate file system partition from /usr.

Absolute and Relative Symbolic Links

Symbolic links over NFS are interpreted by the client, not the server. Thus, any absolute symbolic links are evaluated starting at the root directory of the client, usually leading to somewhere else on the client, which is often not what is expected or desired. This problem should generally be worked around via the thoughtful use of relative symbolic links inside exported file systems. There is also a server-side export option (*link_relative*) that automatically converts absolute symbolic links to relative; this can have nonintuitive results if the client mounts a subdirectory of the exported directory.

Root Squash

For security reasons, NFS servers normally translate access by the root account (UID 0) on clients to an unprivileged account (on Red Hat, user and group *nobody*). This behavior can be disabled (via the no_root_squash server export option) or modified in various ways; see the exports(5) man page.

NFS Hangs

Because NFS is stateless, clients normally wait for a server for up to several minutes or, in some cases, even indefinitely if the server stops responding. While this is occurring, any reference to the file system(s) on the unresponsive server will cause a process to hang, and it is generally difficult or impossible to unmount the offending file systems once the problem starts. Several steps can be taken to reduce the impact of this problem:

- Take great care to ensure the reliability of NFS servers and the network.
- Avoid mounting many different NFS servers at once, especially in a circular fashion.
- Clients should mount infrequently used NFS file systems only when needed and unmount them after use.
- Mission-critical systems should avoid doing any NFS mounts at all, if possible.

- Keep NFS mounted directories out of the search path for users, especially that of *root*.

- Keep NFS mounted directories out of the root (/) directory; instead, segregate them to somewhere else not accessed as often, (e.g., /nfs/home, /nfs/share).

- Consider using the *soft* option when mounting NFS file systems. This causes accesses to file systems mounted from unresponsive NFS servers to fail rather than hang; however, this risks making long-running processes fail due to temporary network outages. The timeout interval before requests are made to fail, in tenths of seconds, is set with the additional option *timeo*. The following example sets the timeout to 30 seconds:

```
mount -o soft,timeo=300 myserver:/home /nfs/home
```

Inverse DNS Pointers

When knfsd checks a mount request against the current list of exports, it looks up the client's IP address in DNS to find the hostname associated with that client. This hostname is then finally checked against the list of exports. If the IP address to hostname lookup fails (because that IP address does not have an IN PTR record listed with whoever is the authority for its IP address range), rpc.mountd will deny access to that client. It leaves a message in /var/log/messages reporting a "request from unknown host." Another way to detect this problem is to directly look up the client's IP address, which must be turned backward and must have .in-addr.arpa. appended. For example, this command would look up the inverse DNS pointer for 192.168.1.2:

```
nslookup -type=ptr 2.1.168.192.in-addr.arpa.
```

If there is no inverse DNS pointer, you'll get a message like this:

```
***ns1.tux.org can't find 2.1.168.192.in-addr.arpa.: Non-existent host/domain
```

File Locking

Since an NFS shared file system may be present on more than one client, if two or more clients want to open the same file, the File Locking daemon service takes care of checking for any preexisting request(s) that may already have that file "locked" for their use. Most NFS implementations have historically had serious problems making file locking work reliably and correctly, particularly between the implementations of different vendors. Any applications depending on file locking over NFS should be tested thoroughly before depending on their use.

Performance Tips

There are several suggestions to follow that will keep NFS running in a stable and reliable manner. Make sure you are aware of these pointers:

- Do not even consider employing the user-mode NFS daemon if performance is an issue or if you will have more than one or two simultaneously active clients.

- Eight kernel NFS daemons (the default) are sufficient for good performance, even under fairly heavy loads. For extremely busy NFS servers, it may be worth increasing the number of NFS daemons beyond eight, keeping in mind that the extra kernel processes consume valuable kernel resources.

- In any network in which packet retransmissions are common, it is more efficient to use NFS over TCP than UDP, if available.

- NFS write performance can be extremely slow, particularly with NFS v2 clients, as the client waits for each block of data to be written to disk. Specialized hardware with nonvolatile RAM for holding writes pending their being physically written to disk is the best solution to this problem. In applications where data loss is not a big concern, the filesystem can be mounted by the client with the *async* option, which effectively removes this bottleneck as well.

- Hostname lookups are performed frequently by the NFS server; run the Name Switch Cache Daemon (nscd) to improve performance here.

exam
ⓦatch

Understand the implications of NFS. It is a powerful file-sharing system, but should not be used lightly, nor should it be used on the Internet. NFS is primarily utilized on secure LAN/WAN networks.

NFS Security

The NFS introduces a number of serious security problems and should never be used in hostile environments (such as on a server directly exposed to the Internet) without taking extreme precautions.

Shortcomings and Risks

NFS is an easy-to-use yet powerful file-sharing system. However, it is not without its problems. A few security risks to keep in the forefront of your mind include

■ **Authentication** NFS normally relies on the client host to accurately report the client's credentials (user ID and group IDs). This model breaks down if there is a possibility of users with root access to their own boxes, or even with the capability to add a computer to the network or to boot an existing computer off a boot floppy of their choice. The implications are that any data that is accessible via NFS to *any user* can potentially be accessed by *any other* user.

■ **Privacy** Not even Secure NFS encrypts its network traffic.

■ **SunRPC Infrastructure** Both client and server parts of NFS depend on the RPC portmapper daemon. Portmapper has in the past had a number of serious security holes, and is not recommended for use on machines directly exposed to the Internet or other potentially hostile networks.

Security Tips

If NFS *must* be used in or near a hostile environment, here are some approaches that can reduce the corresponding security risks.

■ Educate yourself in detail about NFS security. If you do not clearly understand the risks, you should restrict your NFS use to friendly, internal networks behind a good firewall.

■ If an Internet-exposed server needs to access internal files via NFS, use separate network interfaces on the server for the Internet (untrusted) network and the internal (trusted) network. Use ipchains to prevent the untrusted network from accessing the TCP and UDP ports that portmapper, mountd, and nfsd use.

■ Export as little data as possible, and export filesystems as read-only if possible.

■ Use root squash to prevent clients from having root access to exported file systems.

■ Use ipchains to deny access to the portmapper, mountd, and nfsd ports, except from explicitly trusted hosts or networks. The ports are

```
111     TCP/UDP     portmapper     (server and client)
745     UDP         mountd         (server)
747     TCP         mountd         (server)
2049    TCP/UDP     nfsd           (server)
```

Use a port scanner to verify that these ports are not accessible from untrusted network(s).

NFS

On the NFS server:

1. Create a directory called /MIS that is owned by the MIS group (create this group first).

2. Set the SGID bit to enforce group ownership.

3. Update the exports file to allow read and write for your local network.

4. Restart the NFS services.

On a client:

1. Create a directory for the server share called /mnt/MIS.

2. Mount the share from the server on this new directory /mnt/MIS.

3. List all exported shares from the server and save this output as /mnt/MIS/thishost.shares.list.

4. Make this service a permanent connection in the /etc/fstab file. Assume that the connection might be flaky and add the appropriate options.

5. Test that the service is restored with a reboot.

6. Test the flaky options by stopping the service on the server, then trying to copy a file to the /mnt/MIS directory. It should fail but recover.

7. Restart the server service.

8. Change the options to non-flaky settings.

9. Remount the service with the new settings.

Now test what happens when you shut down the server. Your system should be hung when you try to access the service.

Restart the server service and see if your client service resumes.

CERTIFICATION OBJECTIVE 9.04

Internet News

Network News Transport Protocol (NNTP) uses TCP port 119, as documented in RFC 977. It is a high-performance, low-latency message transfer protocol based on SMTP. A collection of NNTP servers accept posts and distribute them worldwide, moving billions of characters daily. Newsgroups are the organizational unit, with hierarchies existing for almost any subject area one can imagine. The major groups are alt, comp, gnu, misc, news, rec, sci, soc, and talk. Other newsgroups include commercial feeds and local distributions.

INND

INND was written in 1991 by Rich Salz to replace Cnews, as the volume of NNTP traffic had risen to the point where Cnews was not able to keep up due to architectural limitations.

INND is now maintained by ISC at www.isc.org. Red Hat supplies INND 2.3 in rpm format. Release 2.3 supports circular message buffers as well as file system-based spooling. This is a performance advantage if a large number of newsgroups are being carried. Alternative news servers include Cnews and Cyclone.

Doc's Open News Servers, a list of unsecured NNTP servers updated weekly, is found at http://home1.gte.net/docthomp/servers.htm.

Configuring INND (Leafnode Services)

Red Hat keeps the INND configuration files in /etc/news. The minimal leafnode setup requires that you edit inn.conf, incoming.conf, and newsfeeds. Edit readers.conf if you want to allow readers on other computers. It is good to edit motd.news and put a banner for your readers with any policies you may have.

You should set the organization directive in inn.conf. The defaults for the remainder are okay, but can be set as desired:

```
organization: Your Organization Here
```

Your ISP typically supplies NNTP services. Put their e-mail and telephone number in your incoming.conf file. This can be handy if you are troubleshooting.

You will need a peer definition for your ISP in incoming.conf, such as

```
# A peer definition.
# Myisp.net (800) 555 1212 joenews@myisp.net
peer myisp {
      hostname: news.myisp.net
    }
```

If you want to post articles, you need an entry in *newsfeeds*. This example will use nntpsend to transmit your outbound traffic. nntpsend is run hourly from /etc/cron.hourly/inn-cron-nntpsend:

```
# Myisp.net (800) 555 1212 joenews@myisp.net
news.myisp.net:!junk/!foo:Tf,Wnm:news.myisp.net
```

Articles will be kept in /var/spool/news, so make sure there is enough space available. Your newsfeed will determine how quickly that fills and what expire policies will be required. If possible, make /var a separate file system and allocate plenty of inodes with -i 1024.

If you find that performance is an issue and file systems are slowing you down, investigate cycbuffs. Enabled in inn.conf with the storageapi: true directive, you will have to set up cycbuff.conf and allocate some space for circular buffers.

- Run inncheck and correct any permissions problems or other conditions detected before starting INND.

- Start INND with /etc/rc.d/init.d/innd start.

- Stop INND with ctlinnd shutdown "Some Reason or Other."

- Check status with innstat.

Most of the INND files have man pages.

Troubleshooting

Here are a few common news errors and their solutions.

News Won't Start

If INND won't start at all, check the following:

- Try inncheck.

- If INND starts manually, but not at reboot, then confirm that INND is in /etc/rc.d/rc?.d/S95innd or similar, and that the runlevel is appropriate.

- See /var/log/news/news.err.

Readers Can't Read

Innd is running, but no one can read any news articles. Points to check:

- Check nnrp.access and confirm that the desired reader is allowed.

- Confirm INND is running by typing **ps ax | grep innd**.

- Telnet to port 119 and see if the banner comes up.

- See /var/log/news/news.err.

Posters Can't Post

If posters can't post:

- Check nnrp.access and confirm that the desired poster is allowed.

- Telnet to port 119 from the problem host and see if the banner comes up with (posting allowed).

- See /var/log/news/news.err.

News logs are in /var/log/news. Read them when there is a problem, especially /var/log/news/news.err. News databases are in /var/lib/news and can get very large. Keep an eye on /var disk space.

Telneting to port 119 on the INND server is always helpful and gives an indication of responsiveness. The banner should come up immediately. Typing **mode reader** in INNP will switch to NNRP. Type **help** for syntax, and **quit** to exit. Figure 9-8 is an example of a debugging session.

FIGURE 9-8

Debugging news
through Telnet
to port 119

```
telnet localhost 119
Trying 127.0.0.1...
Connected to localhost.
Escape character is '^]'.
200 localhost InterNetNews server INN 2.2 21-Jan-1999
    ready mode reader
200 localhost InterNetNews NNRP server INN 2.2 21-Jan-1999
    ready (posting ok).
503 Timeout after 10 seconds, closing connection.
Connection closed by foreign host.
```

EXERCISE 9-4

INND

Following the preceding files listed, create a new news service for your company
(for example, mycorp.com).

1. Put your company name as the organization.

2. Use your ISP service as your peer definition.

3. Update nntpsend to transmit your outbound traffic. Make sure it is updated
   hourly.

4. Configure your banner to indicate "only corporate data is allowed, all feeds
   are moderated."

5. Restart your news service. Check the status and ensure it is configured for
   runlevels 3, 4, and 5.

6. Test the service by Telneting into the NNTP port and changing to mode
   reader.

7. Test with a client posting, and another client reading the post and replying to it.

DHCP/Bootp

DHCP (Dynamic Host Configuration Protocol) and bootp are protocols that allow a client machine to obtain network information (such as an IP number) from a server. Many organizations are starting to use dynamic host control because it simplifies and centralizes network administration, especially in large networks or networks that have a significant number of mobile users. DHCP is backward-compatible with bootp. Therefore, this section will only cover the configuration of DHCP.

DHCP Operational Overview

As with most network services, there is a server side and a client side to DHCP. Both configurations will be explained. The examples use the DHCPd daemon on the server side, and the pump executable on the client side. There are other packages available, but these binaries are the ones installed with Red Hat.

Server Configuration

First, make sure that multicast is running on the server's network interface. Type **/sbin/ifconfig -a**. The output for the eth0 (first NIC) should look something like the listing in Figure 9-9.

If MULTICAST doesn't appear, the kernel will need to be recompiled to add multicast support. On most systems, this will not be necessary.

In order for DHCPd to work correctly with picky DHCP clients (e.g., Windows 95), it must be able to send packets with an IP destination address of 255.255.255.255. Unfortunately, Linux insists on changing 255.255.255.255 into the local subnet broadcast address. This results in a DHCP protocol violation, and while many DHCP

FIGURE 9-9

ifconfig output
to check for
MULTICAST
capability

```
eth0      Link encap:10Mbps Ethernet  HWaddr 00:B0:5F:D2:C4:34
          inet addr:192.168.248.45  Bcast:192.168.248.255
          Mask:255.255.255.0
            UP BROADCAST RUNNING MULTICAST  MTU:1500  Metric:1
            RX packets:43557 errors:0 dropped:0 overruns:0
            TX packets:52646 errors:0 dropped:0 overruns:0
            Interrupt:10 Base address:0x300
```

clients don't notice the problem, some (e.g., all Microsoft DHCP clients) do. Clients that have this problem will appear not to see DHCPOFFER messages from the server. In this case, issue the command:

```
route add -host 255.255.255.255 dev eth0
```

eth0 is the name of the network interface card (NIC) that connects the server to the network. If the name on your server differs, make the appropriate change.

Now configure DHCPd by creating or editing /etc/dhcpd.conf. Most commonly, IP addresses are assigned randomly. Figure 9-10 illustrates the configuration.

This will result in the DHCP server giving a client an IP address from the range 192.168.1.10–192.168.1.100 or 192.168.1.150–192.168.1.200. It will lease an IP address for 600 seconds if the client doesn't ask for a specific timeframe. Otherwise, the maximum (allowed) lease will be 7200 seconds. The server will also "advise" the client that it should use 255.255.255.0 as its subnet mask, 192.168.1.255 as its broadcast address, 192.168.1.254 as the router/gateway, and 192.168.1.1 and 192.168.1.2 as its DNS servers.

If you need to specify a WINS server for your Windows clients, include the netbios-name-servers option:

```
option netbios-name-servers 192.168.1.1;
```

FIGURE 9-10

A sample
dhcpd.conf file

```
# Sample /etc/dhcpd.conf
default-lease-time 600;
max-lease-time 7200;
option subnet-mask 255.255.255.0;
option broadcast-address 192.168.1.255;
option routers 192.168.1.254;
option domain-name-servers 192.168.1.1, 192.168.1.2;
option domain-name "mydomain.org";

subnet 192.168.1.0 netmask 255.255.255.0 {
    range 192.168.1.10 192.168.1.100;
    range 192.168.1.150 192.168.1.200;
}
```

You can also assign specific IP addresses based on a client's Ethernet address:

```
host dragonfire {
    hardware ethernet 08:00:12:23:4d:3f;
    fixed-address 192.168.1.201;
}
```

This will assign the IP address 192.168.1.201 to a client with the Ethernet address 08:00:12:23:4d:3f.

on the Job

To preassign an address to a specific client, you need the NIC hardware address. If you want to obtain the hardware address (MAC) without taking the machine apart, simply let each host obtain a random DHCP IP address; then look up the IP address of each MAC address in the leases file and reconfigure the dhcp configuration file with a reservation. Make sure the client releases and renews using the pump command.

DHCP can be customized to the individual machine's needs. Machines such as servers can get static IP addresses, and mobile users with laptops can be allotted dynamic IPs. There are a number of other options, such as NIS server addresses, timeserver addresses, and so on. The *dhcpd.conf* man page goes into detail on these options.

In most cases, DHCP installation doesn't create a dhcpd.leases files. This file is used by DHCPd to store information about current leases. The file is in plain text form, so you can view it during the operation of DHCPd. To create an empty dhcpd.leases file (required before DHCP will work), type

```
touch /var/state/dhcp/dhcpd.leases
```

on the command line. This will create an empty file for DHCPd to write its information into. Some of the older versions of DHCPd 2.0 placed the file in /etc/dhcpd.leases. If you get a message saying that the file exists, simply ignore it. Start up DHCPd by typing

```
/etc/rc.d/init.d/dhcpd start
```

This will invoke DHCPd on the eth0 device. If you want to invoke it on another device, supply it on the command line:

```
/etc/rc.d/init.d/dhcpd start eth1
```

To verify that everything is working, turn on debugging mode and put the server in the foreground by typing:

```
/usr/sbin/dhcpd -d -f
```

Bring up one of the clients and watch the console of the server. A number of debugging messages will come up to indicate that a client has been leased an IP address.

on the

Ⓙob

Another easy way to get the MAC address for a given client is to watch the debugging messages.

Client Configuration

Configuring DHCPd under Red Hat is done from the Control Panel and via utilities netconf, netcfg, and linuxconf. Simply type **control-panel**, or any of the other utilities, as root from a terminal window. Note that the root user will need permission to display the Control Panel on the X-Window screen. Display permissions are covered in the XWindow-User-HOWTO.

In the Control Panel:

1. Select Network Configuration.

2. Click Interfaces.

3. Click Add.

4. Select Ethernet.

5. In the Edit Ethernet/Bus Interface, select Activate Interface At Boot Time, and choose DHCP as the Interface configuration protocol.

For the new configuration to take effect, reboot the machine if you changed other important information, such as the hostname and primary domain information, or, to request a new IP address for the eth0 interface, type as root:

```
# /sbin/ifup eth0
```

You can also use the following pump utility to request IP addresses for all DHCP-enabled interfaces:

```
# pump
```

Client Issues

If the configuration according to the preceding steps does not work, there may be a problem with the setup. A few possibilities:

- The NIC is not configured properly. Consult the Ethernet-HOWTO to double-check the functionality of the NIC.

- If the network works for a few minutes and then stops responding, check to see if *gated* (gateway daemon) is running. There are some reports of gated breaking routes on Linux boxes, which results in this type of problem.

- If the machine is still not able to connect, you may have firewall rules (ipfwadm or ipchains rules) that disallow port 67/68 traffic used by DHCP to distribute configuration info. Check your firewall rules carefully.

EXERCISE 9-5

DHCP

You will need a server and a client that are on the same LAN segment for this exercise.

1. Configure the server with a range of 192.168.11.11 to 192.168.11.15 with mask 255.255.255.0.

2. Configure your client to use DHCP. Restart the network interface on the client and see which client gets which IP address.

3. Add a Gateway and DNS server option with IP addresses of 192.168.11.254 and 12.34.45.56, respectively. Restart the DHCP service and then force the client to renew the lease.

4. Make sure the client has all the right information by using the status output of the pump command "pump -s eth0."

CERTIFICATION OBJECTIVE 9.06

Other File-Sharing Methods

There are many other methods of file sharing on a Red Hat Linux system. The most popular ones, like NFS and Samba, have already been covered. Several minor ones, such as Coda and Andrew, fall outside the detail level of this text. Linux can also speak IPX, the language of Novell NetWare. Configuring a simple Linux-based NetWare server will be covered briefly.

IPX (mars_nwe)

There are two packages available that allow Linux to provide the functions of a Novell Fileserver, lwared and mars_nwe. This section will only briefly explain how to configure mars_nwe. Using mars_nwe, files can be shared on a Linux machine with users using Novell NetWare client software. Users can attach and map file systems to appear as local drives on their machines just as they would to a real Novell fileserver. Martin Stover <mstover@freeway.de> developed mars_nwe to enable Linux to provide both file and print services for NetWare clients. The name stands for Martin Stovers NetWare Emulator (mars_nwe).

Configuring the Server

Edit the /etc/nwserv.conf file. The format of this file may at first look a little cryptic, but it is actually fairly straightforward. The file itself contains a number of single-line configuration items. Each line is whitespace delimited and begins with a number that indicates the contents of the line. All characters following a # character are considered a comment and are ignored. A thorough example is listed in Figure 9-11.

If the server is configured to expect external programs to configure the network and/or provide the routing function, then start those before starting the server. If the server is configured so that it will configure the interfaces itself and provide the routing services, then type the command **nwserv**. To test the server, try to log in from a NetWare client on the network. Set a CAPTURE from the client and attempt a print. If both the login and print are successful, then the server is working.

FIGURE 9-11   /etc/nwserv.conf

```
# Sample /etc/nwserv.conf file by Kevin Thorpe.
# VOLUMES (max. 5)
# Only the SYS volume is compulsory. The directory containing the SYS
# volume must contain the directories: LOGIN, PUBLIC, SYSTEM, MAIL.
# The 'i' option ignores case.
# The 'k' option converts all filenames in NCP requests to lowercase.
# The 'm' option marks the volume as removable (useful for cdroms etc.)
# The 'r' option set the volume to read-only.
# The 'o' option indicates the volume is a single mounted filesystem.
# The 'P' option allows commands to be used as files.
# The 'O' option allows use of the OS/2 namespace
# The 'N' option allows use of the NFS namespace
# The default is upper case.
# Syntax:
#    1 <Volumename> <Volumepath>    <Options>

   1   SYS        /home/netware/SYS/               # SYS
   1   DATA       /home/netware/DATA/      k       # DATA
   1   CDROM      /cdrom                   kmr     # CDROM

# SERVER NAME
# If not set then the linux hostname will be converted to upper case
# and used. This is optional, the hostname will be used if this is not
# configured.
# Syntax:
#    2 <Servername>

   2    LINUX_FS01

# INTERNAL NETWORK ADDRESS
# The Internal IPX Network Address is a feature that simplifies IPX routing
# for multihomed hosts (hosts that have ports on more than one IPX
# network).
# Syntax:
#    3 <Internal Network Address> [<Node Number>]
# or:
#    3 auto
#
# If you use 'auto' then your host IP address will be used. NOTE: this may
# be dangerous, please be sure you pick a number unique to your network.
# Addresses are 4byte hexadecimal (the leading 0x is required).

   3    0x49a01010  1
```

FIGURE 9-11   /etc/nwserv.conf *(continued)*

```
# NETWORK DEVICE(S)
# This entry configures your IPX network. If you already have your
# IPX network configured then you do not need this. This is
# the same as using ipx_configure/ipx_interface before you start
# the server.
# Syntax:
#    4 <IPX Network Number> <device_name> <frametype> [<ticks>]
#                            Frame types: ethernet_ii, 802.2, 802.3, SNAP

   4   0x39a01010   eth0   802.3   1

# SAVE IPX ROUTES AFTER SERVER IS DOWNED
# Syntax:
#    5 <flag>
#        0 = don't save routes, 1 = do save routes

  5 0

# NETWARE VERSION
# Syntax:
#    6 <version>
#        0 = 2.15, 1 = 3.11

   6 1
# PASSWORD HANDLING
# Real Novell DOS clients support a feature that encypts your
# password when changing it. You can select whether you want your
# mars server to support this feature or not.
# Syntax
#    7 <flag>
#    <flag> is:
#        0 to force password encryption. (Clients can't change password)
#        1 force password encryption, allow unencrypted password change.
#        7 allow non-encrypted password but no empty passwords.
#        8 allow non-encrypted password including empty passwords.
#        9 completely unencrypted passwords (doesn't work with OS/2)

   7 1


# MINIMAL GID UID rights
# permissions used for attachments with no login. These permissions
# will be used for the files in your primary server attachment.
```

FIGURE 9-11   /etc/nwserv.conf *(continued)*

```
# Syntax:
#    10 <gid>
#    11 <uid>
#    <gid> <uid> are from /etc/passwd, /etc/groups


   10  200
   11  201


# SUPERVISOR password
# May be removed after the server is started once. The server will
# encrypt this information into the bindery file after it is run.
# You should avoid using the 'root' user and instead use another
# account to administer the mars fileserver.
#
# This entry is read and encrypted into the server bindery files, so
# it only needs to exist the first time you start the server to ensure
# that the password isn't stolen.
#
# Syntax:
#    12 <Supervisor-Login> <Unix username> [<password>]


   12  SUPERVISOR  chris  secretpassword


# USER ACCOUNTS
# This associates NetWare logins with unix accounts. Password are optional.
# Syntax:
#       13 <User Login> <Unix Username> [<password>]


   13   CHRIS chris
   13   DAVE  dave


# LAZY SYSTEM ADMIN CONFIGURATION
# If you have a large numbers of users and could not be bothered using
# type 13 individual user mappings, you can automatically map mars_nwe
# logins to linux user names. BUT, there is currently no means of making
# use of the linux login password so all users configured this way are
# will use the single password supplied here. My recommendation is not
# to do this unless security is absolutely no concern to you.
# Syntax:
#    15 <flag> <common-password>
#    <flag> is: 0 - don't automatically map users.
#               1 - do automatically map users not configured above.
#               99 - automatically map every user in this way.
```

FIGURE 9-11	/etc/nwserv.conf (continued)

```
    15  0   password

# SANITY CHECKING
# mars_nwe will automatically ensure that certain directories exist if
# you set this flag.
# Syntax:
#    16 <flag>
#    <flag> is 0 for no, don't, or 1 for yes, do.

    16  0


# PRINT QUEUES
# This associates NetWare printers with unix printers. The queue
# directories must be created manually before printing is attempted.
# The queue directories are NOT lpd queues.
# Syntax:
#    21 <queue_name> <queue_directory> <unix_print_cmd>

    21  EPSON  SYS:/PRINT/EPSON lpr -h
    21  LASER  SYS:/PRINT/LASER lpr -Plaser

# DEBUG FLAGS
# These are not normally needed, but may be useful if are you debugging
# a problem.
# Syntax:
#    <debug_item> <debug_flag>
#
#    100 = IPX KERNEL
#    101 = NWSERV
#    102 = NCPSERV
#    103 = NWCONN
#    104 = start NWCLIENT
#    105 = NWBIND
#    106 = NWROUTED
#                    0 = disable debug, 1 = enable debug

  100 0
  101 0
  102 0
  103 0
  104 0
  105 0
  106 0
```

FIGURE 9-11   /etc/nwserv.conf *(continued)*

```
# RUN NWSERV IN BACKGROUND AND USE LOGFILE
# Syntax:
#    200 <flag>
#         0 = run NWSERV in foreground and don't use logfile
#         1 = run NWSERV in background and use logfile

  200  1

# LOGFILE NAME
# Syntax:
#     201 <logfile>

  201   /tmp/nw.log

# APPEND LOG OR OVERWRITE
# Syntax:
#    202 <flag>
#         0 = append to existing logfile
#         1 = overwrite existing logfile

  202   1

# SERVER DOWN TIME
# This item sets the time after a SERVER DOWN is issued that the
# server really goes down.
# Syntax:
#    210 <time>
#         in seconds. (defaults 10)

  210   10

# ROUTING BROADCAST INTERVAL
# The time is seconds between server broadcasts
# Syntax:
#    211 <time>
#         in seconds. (defaults 60)

  211   60

# ROUTING LOGGING INTERVAL
# Set how many broadcasts take place before logging of routing
# information occurs.
```

FIGURE 9-11 /etc/nwserv.conf *(continued)*

```
# Syntax:
#    300  <number>

  300  5


# ROUTING LOGFILE
# Set the name of the routing logfile
# Syntax:
#    301 <filename>

  301  /tmp/nw.routes


# ROUTING APPEND/OVERWRITE
# Set whether you want to append to an existing log file or
# overwrite it.
# Syntax:
#    302 <flag>
#        <flag> is 0 for append, 1 for create/overwrite

  302  1


# WATCHDOG TIMING
# Set the timing for watchdog messages that ensure the network is
# still alive.
# Syntax:
#    310 <value>
#        <value> =   0 - always send watchdogs
#                  < 0 - (-ve) for disable watchdogs
#                  > 0 - send watchdogs when network traffic
#                        drops below 'n' ticks

  310  7


# STATIONS FILE
# Set the filename for the stations file, which determines which
# machines this fileserver will act as the primary fileserver for.
# The syntax of this file is described in the 'examples' directory
# of the source code.
# Syntax:
#    400 <filename>

  400  /etc/nwserv.stations
```

FIGURE 9-11	/etc/nwserv.conf *(continued)*

```
# GET NEAREST FILESERVER HANDLING
# Set how SAP Get Nearest Fileserver Requests are handled.
# Syntax:
#    401 <flag>
#         <flag> is: 0 - disable 'Get Nearest Fileserver' requests.
#                    1 - The 'stations' file lists stations to be excluded.
#                    2 - The 'stations' file lists stations to be included.

   401 2
```

EXERCISE 9-6

IPX/SPX

You will need a Novell Client machine for this exercise.

1. Install the MARS-NWE rpm if it is not already installed.

2. Configure your server to share out all your printers and the /usr/share/doc directory as read-only to all clients. Add a user account called *nwetest*. Give this user access to the share.

3. Set your network number to DAD1DEAD and use 802.2 as the protocol type.

4. Configure your client to connect to the share and copy a file to test that the share is working.

CERTIFICATION OBJECTIVE 9.07

Time Synchronization

Several applications that may be run on a Linux server require accurate timestamps, such as logging, system accounting, and many other operations. Time synchronization with a centralized server is available through two protocols: NTP and rdate.

XNTP

XNTPd is a complete implementation of the NTP (Network Time Protocol) Version 3 specification, as defined in RFC 1305. The approach used by NTP to achieve reliable time synchronization from a set of possibly unreliable remote timeservers is somewhat different from other protocols. In particular, NTP does not attempt to synchronize clocks to each other. Rather, each server attempts to synchronize to Universal Coordinated Time (UTC) using the best available source and available transmission paths to that source.

Time is distributed through a hierarchy of NTP servers, with each server adopting a stratum that indicates how far away from an external source of UTC it is operating at. Stratum-1 servers, which are at the top of the hierarchy, have access to some external time source, usually a radio clock synchronized to time signal broadcasts from radio stations that explicitly provide a standard time service. A stratum-2 server is one that is currently obtaining time from a stratum-1 server, a stratum-3 server gets its time from a stratum-2 server, and so on. To avoid long-lived synchronization loops, the number of strata is limited to 15.

Each client in the synchronization subnet (which may also be a server for other, higher stratum clients) chooses exactly one of the available servers to synchronize to, usually from among the lowest stratum servers it has access to. NTP prefers to have access to at least three sources of lower stratum time. It then applies an agreement algorithm to detect discrepancies on the part of any one of the lower stratum servers. Normally, when all servers are in agreement, NTP will choose the best one in terms of lowest stratum, shortest network delay, claimed precision, and several other considerations. Synchronization takes place over TCP or UDP port 123.

NTP has the distinct advantage over other time protocols in its accuracy. However, one point worth noting is that NTP will never run a system clock backward. If NTP detects that a client's clock is running faster than a lower stratum server, it will slow the clock down to allow it to catch up with UTC. This provides a more stable system clock for time-dependent applications.

NTP Configuration

The configuration file for NTP is */etc/ntp.conf.* A good example configuration file would contain the listing in Figure 9-12.

This particular host is expected to operate as a client at stratum-2 by virtue of the *server* keyword and the fact that all of the servers declared run at stratum-1. When configured using the *server* keyword, this host can receive synchronization from any of the listed servers, but can never provide synchronization to them. Unless restricted, this host can offer synchronization to dependent clients, which do not have to be listed in the configuration file.

A timeserver that is expected to receive synchronization from another server, as well as to provide synchronization to it, is declared using the *peer* keyword instead of the *server* keyword. It is usually considered unwise to use the *peer* keyword excessively.

One of the things the NTP daemon does when it is first started is to compute the error in the intrinsic frequency of the clock on the computer it is running on. It usually takes about a day or so after the daemon is started to compute a good estimate of this drift. Once the initial value is computed, it will change only by relatively small amounts during the course of continued operation. The *driftfile* keyword indicates to the daemon the name of the file where it may store the current value of the frequency error. If the daemon is stopped and restarted, it can reinitialize itself to the previous estimate and avoid the day's worth of time it will take to recompute the frequency estimate.

FIGURE 9-12

A sample ntp.conf file

```
# peer configuration for host www
# (expected to operate at stratum 2)

server clock.llnl.gov
server norad.arc.nasa.gov
server tock.usno.navy.mil

driftfile /etc/ntp.drift
```

rdate

A much more simplistic way of setting the date from a network server is rdate. rdate uses TCP to retrieve the current time of another machine using port 13, as described in RFC 868. The time for each system is returned in ctime format (Sun Oct 17 20:36:19 1999). The default mode for rdate simply prints the time as taken from the requested server. The command rdate www will return the date from the server on the local subnet named www. Adding the -s option to the command line and running rdate as root will set the local system clock to the time retrieved from the server. rdate is not as accurate as NTP and has the disadvantage of setting the system clock backward if the reported time is earlier than the current system time. Some applications such as databases may suffer serious consequences if they perceive "negative time." NTP is therefore recommended for general use.

EXERCISE 9-7

Time Synchronization

You will need two machines running Linux for this exercise:

1. Configure one machine, referred to as client, with its clock set five minutes ahead of the other machine, referred to hereafter as time-source.

2. Use rdate on the client to synchronize the local time to the time-server host time.

3. Make sure you have access to the Internet.

4. Using the information provided previously (test that the server names can be pinged first), configure your time-server host to synchronize with the servers listed within this section for the /etc/ntp.conf file, as a stratum-2 service, and the driftfile as /etc/ntp.drift.

5. Force time-server to synchronize with the central time server host.

6. Force the client host to synchronize with the local time-server host.

CERTIFICATION OBJECTIVE 9.08

PPP Configuration (as a Client) Using netcfg and the Files Generated

A working hardware communication link is a prerequisite for a network connection. Such links include residential phone lines, ISDN and xDSL lines, leased communication links, or more exotic media like radio, laser, or fiber optic connections, as well as traditional networking systems like Ethernet.

Each such raw physical data link must have a protocol that defines atomic data units (packets), specifies packet addressing and checksums, and so forth. Ethernet hardware provides this protocol transparently; other communication links require explicit protocol, handled in software.

For simplicity, this section will refer to all point-to-point communication devices as "modems." The official specification of the link protocol for modems is provided by RFC 1171, "The Point-to-Point Protocol for the Transmission of Multi-Protocol Datagrams Over Point-to-Point Links." The PPP protocol is designed to be reliable on a variety of communication links; it achieves that by including data checksums, and negotiating optimum link parameters. These features introduce slight overhead into PPP, but they also make it into a reliable protocol that is widely deployed on most existing computing platforms; it practically displaced SLIP, the simple point-to-point protocol that was a precursor to PPP.

The daemon pppd is the most common implementation of the PPP protocol. When started, pppd sequences through several stages to make a working network connection. First, the link has to be brought up—in the case of a modem, by dialing out to the ISP's number. Next, the existing raw connection is authenticated, so that the ISP can identify its customer. Finally, the PPP protocol negotiates the link parameters such as MTU, IP addresses/masks, and protocol compression mode.

It should be noted that the PPP protocol is symmetric; in other words, both nodes connected by PPP can originate all the protocol phases. In practice, however, usually the ISP runs a dial-in server that satisfies the requests from remote clients.

The Link Setup

The method to open up the link is very device specific. The simplest point-to-point link is a direct hardware connection: a simple serial port cable linking two computers, or a leased communication circuit that is always connected.

If the link is not always up, we need to send appropriate commands to the communication device when we need to open it. There is enough variety in the details of this process that pppd uses a general-purpose program, called "chat." This program will attempt to send the appropriate commands and data, such as telephone numbers, to the communication device—as specified in the configuration file for chat, called a *dialup script*. It also captures and reacts in response to various return codes that may be received from the server.

In some cases, chat might actually also be involved in setting up the simple authentication of the login:/password: kind, since this dialog looks very similar to the question/response scenario that chat is handling while setting up the communication device.

The Authentication

Some communication links implicitly authenticate their participants. A dedicated line is a trivial example—there is no doubt which computers are on both ends. A non-obvious example might be a radio modem such as Ricochet: the identity of the calling station is implicitly defined to be "the owner of the Metricom's proprietary radio modem." On the public telephone network, however, anyone can call the ISP's number; therefore, callers have to authenticate themselves before they are allowed to connect to the ISP's network.

Such authentication can be a simple userid/password query, issued after the telephone connection is made. Such simplistic methods are being replaced by authentication methods that are part of PPP specification, namely Password Authentication Protocol (PAP) and Challenge Handshake Authentication Protocol (CHAP, and its illegitimate cousin, MS-CHAP). Strictly speaking, these methods are part of the next phase: the negotiation.

The Negotiation

The next step in setting up the PPP link is the negotiation of protocol parameters. This is done by exchanging messages of the Link Control Protocol (LCP). It is mostly transparent to the user, unless there are protocol version problems. This is rather unlikely at this point, since the PPP protocol is quite mature.

The Link

After completing the negotiation, the pppd program creates a network device in the kernel, and starts accepting IP (and other network protocols) packets to be shipped via the PPP interface to the server.

It should be noted that, while Linux uses the routing information from PPP, it does not obtain the DNS server information this way, but instead uses the information from /etc/resolv.conf.

Setup the Easy Way

Modern Linux environments have fairly sophisticated tools to set up the PPP; KDE ships the kppp program, and Red Hat Linux provides

- **modemtool**   For setting up modems
- **netcfg**   For setting up network parameters, and the dial-up scripts
- **usernetctl**   For starting up and shutting down the PPP link

The first two tools are used once, to configure PPPD. The last one allows nonprivileged users to turn the PPP device on and off.

The modemtool program helps discover existing serial ports and sets up the /dev/modem link mentioned earlier. netcfg is a general-purpose network configuration tool for setting network names, host lists, interface properties, and routing. The network interface properties for the ppp0 device include the dial-up script setup and in particular, the phone number and the name/password combination.

Setting up the ppp0 interface creates the shell script /etc/sysconfig/network-scripts/ifup-ppp, containing the instructions to start up the interface. This script requires root privileges to run successfully, which is inconvenient if we want to be able to control networking from a regular account. The SUID-root usernetctl program helps here—it will run the startup/shutdown scripts from any account on the system.

Detailed Setup and Debugging Instructions

Obviously, a prerequisite for a PPP connection is a working point-to-point hardware, normally a modem/serial COM port. The Linux naming scheme for such devices is /dev/ttyS0 (and ttyS1, ttyS2, and so on), which correspond to DOS names of COM1, COM2, COM3, and so on, respectively. Such a COM port has to have its own address, and it shouldn't share interrupts with other devices. By convention, there should be a symbolic link /dev/modem pointing to a port that has the modem associated with it; if that is not the case, the command ln -s /dev/ttyS1 /dev/modem will create it, assuming that the modem is connected to the second serial port /dev/ttyS1. This is basically what the graphical shell modem tool does.

Another prerequisite is the information from the ISP about their setup:

- Phone numbers to their modem bank, with all the appropriate prefixes (area codes, PABX codes, and so on)
- Whether they use Dynamic IP or Static IP address assignment
- DNS hosts used by the ISP
- Authentication method, and the username and password
- Commands to start PPPD on the server, if needed

A useful program, minicom, can be used to test the serial port and the modem. After starting it up, type **ATH**, and a working modem should respond with the string "OK." Minicom can even be used to check serial ports without modems: all it takes is shorting pins 2 and 3 of the serial port connector, and all characters typed and sent out will come back and appear in the minicom window.

If the serial port works correctly, we may try to dial up the remote host by typing the ATDT command followed by the phone number:

ATDT 1-800-2MODEMS

This should be followed by the sound of modem dialing tones emanating from the modem's speaker, and by the screeching sound of an opening modem connection.

The remote system might simply start up with the PPP protocol right away, in which case we will see gibberish text in the minicom window. It could also ask us for name/password, and/or show a command-line prompt, requiring us to run PPPD on the remote end.

Having established the method to get to the stage where the remote system is sending PPPD traffic to our computer, we have to configure the dial-up script to automate this process. An extremely useful feature here is the verbose debugging option: chat -v and pppd -d. The debugging messages will appear in the syslog file /var/log/messages; a convenient method of watching this file is to open another window (or another text console) and run the command tail -f /var/log/messages in it.

Setting the PPP Server

Setting the PPP server for dial-in connections is only slightly more complicated. Most commonly, the server will forward traffic coming via the modem connections to the Internet via the Internet-connected second interface. Therefore, the kernel must have IP forwarding built into it.

Additional Information

A very good source of detailed information about PPP is the Linux PPP HOWTO by Robert Hart. This file is provided as /usr/doc/HOWTO/PPP-HOWTO and is available on the Documentation CD.

EXERCISE 9-8

PPP

You will need a machine with a common modem that is known to be working and a number for an ISP that you have an account name and password.

1. Disconnect the client machine from any other network.

2. Configure your PPP connection to use DHCP.

3. Configure your modem to dial the ISP; supply the username and password.

4. Display your network configuration information with ifconfig and your PPP configuration information with pump -s.

5. Ping www.redhat.com via a terminal session if using X or from any logged-in console prompt.

6. Disconnect your PPP connection. Display your network and PPP connection information again to verify that the connection has been dropped.

CERTIFICATION SUMMARY

Networking services are an integral part of Red Hat Linux. DNS, Squid, NFS, News, NTP, and PPP are a few of the services that can be configured.

DNS serves as the name resolution standard of the Internet. The service runs as a network-wide database with many administrators, where each administrator has the responsibility to keep the zone files that he or she supervises in working order. The diagnostic tool for DNS is now dig. You can use nslookup, but it has been deprecated and should not be used.

Squid is a proxy server that allows a network to filter its HTTP and FTP traffic through a single caching server. This has the distinct advantage of reducing the load on the main Internet connection of the network.

NFS shares file systems across networks. This is a powerful method of controlling data, and distributing I/O load, but there are many security concerns involved with its use. Care should be taken when setting up an NFS share on an unprotected network.

News services provide users with an open forum of information exchange with other users on the Internet. Internet news is easy to set up and maintain. A watchful eye should be kept out for full disk volumes or a lack of inodes.

DHCP allows a network administrator to easily manage the IP addresses and network information of many clients from a centralized server. DHCP requires some specialized setup on both the client and server sides, but is easy to maintain once it is configured.

NTP enables each machine on a network to be synchronized to a central time standard. This standard is not a single machine, but rather several machines that serve out UTC. The algorithms included with NTP allow for a highly accurate representation of time to an individual machine or a whole network.

PPP connects a machine to the Internet through a dial-up connection to an ISP. The daemon can be run as a single user on a single workstation, or it can be run on a network server with IP forwarding to allow the entire network to connect to the Internet.

✓ TWO-MINUTE DRILL

Here are some of the key points from the certification objectives in Chapter 9.

DNS/Bind

❏ DNS is the Domain Name System, and it converts between machine names and IP addresses.

❏ The SOA record is the preamble to all zone files, and there should be exactly one in each zone file.

❏ CNAME is a way to give each machine several names.

❏ DNS is a net-wide database.

❏ The single most common DNS error occurs when an administrator makes updates to a zone file, restarts DNS, and notices that no one else on the Internet knows about the updates. This is most likely due to a failure to update the zone file serial number.

❏ A *delegation* is the glue NS record that helps you get from one nameserver to another.

Squid Proxy Server

❏ Squid is a high-performance HTTP and FTP caching proxy server. It conforms to the Harvest Cache architecture and uses the Inter-Cache Protocol (ICP) for transfers between participating peer and parent/child cache servers.

❏ On Red Hat systems, Squid is started and stopped via /etc/rc.d/init.d/squid start and /etc/rc.d/init.d/squid stop.

NFS

❏ NFS is a file-sharing protocol originally developed by Sun Microsystems in the mid-1980s. It is based on Sun's XDR (external data representation, a byte-order-independent data formatting standard) and RPC (remote procedure call) technologies.

❏ The startup script for remote NFS file systems specified in /etc/fstab is /etc/rc.d/init.d/netfs.

❑ Put all shared directory resource information in /etc/exports.

❑ Clients can make permanent connections for shares mounted locally in /etc/fstab.

Internet News

Red Hat keeps the INND configuration files in /etc/news.

❑ The minimal leafnode setup requires that you edit inn.conf, incoming.conf, and newsfeeds.

❑ Edit readers.conf if you want to allow readers on other computers.

❑ It is good to edit motd.news and put a banner for your readers with any policies you may have.

❑ You should set the organization directive in inn.conf.

❑ Your ISP typically supplies NNTP services. Put their e-mail and telephone number in your incoming.conf file. You need a peer definition for your ISP in incoming.conf.

❑ If you want to post articles, you need an entry in newsfeeds.

❑ Update nntpsend to transmit your outbound traffic and make sure it runs hourly from /etc/cron.hourly/inn-cron-nntpsend.

DHCP/Bootp

❑ DHCP (Dynamic Host Configuration Protocol) and bootp are protocols that allow a client machine to obtain network information (such as an IP number) from a server.

❑ eth0 is the name of the first network interface card (NIC) that connects the server to the network.

❑ You must supply a range of available addresses along with the network mask and any optional parameters for each network interface being served.

Other File-Sharing Methods

❑ There are two packages available that allow Linux to provide the functions of a Novell Fileserver, lwared and mars_nwe.

❑ The mars_nwe server only emulates 2.15 or 3.11 services.

❑ Using mars_nwe, files can be shared on a Linux machine with users using Novell NetWare client software.

❑ Users can attach and map file systems to appear as local drives on their machines, just as they would to a real Novell fileserver.

❑ Edit the /etc/nwserv.conf file for all configuration information.

Time Synchronization

❑ Time synchronization with a centralized server is available through two protocols: NTP and rdate. (NOTE: This book replaces references to XNTP partly because the "protocol" is NTP, and partly because the current release of NTP has dropped the 'X'.

❑ The configuration file for NTP is /etc/ntp.conf.

❑ The rdate command can be used for simple synchronization of time between local hosts.

PPP Configuration (as a Client) Using netcfg and the Files Generated

❑ A working hardware communication link is a prerequisite for a network connection.

❑ modemtool is for setting up modems.

❑ netcfg is for setting up network parameters and the dial-up scripts.

❑ usernetctl is for starting up and shutting down the PPP link.

❑ Setting up the ppp0 interface creates the shell script /etc/sysconfig/network-scripts/ifup-ppp, which contains the instructions for starting up the interface.

❑ A useful program, minicom, can be used to test both the serial port and the modem.

SELF TEST

The following questions will help you measure your understanding of the material presented in this chapter. Read all the choices carefully, as there may be more than one correct answer. Choose all correct answers for each question.

DNS/Bind

1. Which program checks the DNS setup?

   A. dnscheck

   B. BIND

   C. nslookup

   D. resolve

2. You have added several new servers into your primary DNS server. The zone files are formatted properly, and you've restarted named. You advertise the new servers, and your help desk immediately starts getting calls that no one outside your domain can see the new servers. What is the most likely cause?

   A. Your servers are not connected to the network.

   B. The serial number was not incremented in the zone file.

   C. Someone has changed the zone files without your knowledge.

   D. The users at the other end are having ISP problems.

3. Which is an example of a properly formatted MX record?

   A. MX 10.mail.domain.com.

   B. MX mail.domain.com.

   C. MX 10 mail.domain.com

   D. MX 10 mail.domain.com.

Squid Proxy Server

4. Squid serves as a caching server for which Internet protocols?

   A. FTP

   B. News

C. HTTP

D. DNS

NFS

5. Which is not a variant of NFS?

A. KNFSd

B. PCNFS

C. MacNFS

D. UNFSd

6. In the /etc/exports file, if we want to export /data as read-only to all hosts and grant read and write permission to the host superv in domain.com, the proper line is

A. /data (rw) superv.domain.com(ro)

B. /data (ro) superv.domain.com(rw)

C. /data (ro) *.domain.com(rw)

D. /data superv.domain.com(rw)

7. On bootup, the system will check what file for NFS shares to mount?

A. /etc/exports

B. /etc/nfs.conf

C. /etc/fstab

D. /nfs/conf

Internet News

8. Assume that /var fills up. What will restore the operation of your News service?

A. Remove /var/spool/news/articles/alt/binaries.

B. Remove /var/lib/news/history.pag.

C. Expire aging news articles.

D. Make more inodes.

9. A message pops up that News is out of space, but df -k shows plenty remaining on /var. What's wrong?

   A. You are out of inodes on the filesystem.

   B. There be hackers afoot! Yaaar!

   C. Invisible files on the filesystem.

   D. df is broken.

10. No news traffic has come in, but innd is running. How could this be?

    A. Your ISP has dropped you.

    B. The TCP/IP link is down.

    C. The Internet has vanished and no one is posting.

    D. innd is overloaded.

DHCP/Bootp

11. DHCP has been installed and configured properly, and the network is responding. There are no firewalls or extraneous server processes, and yet the clients are not getting their network information. What could be the cause?

    A. Not enough disk space.

    B. The dhcpd.leases file was not created.

    C. DHCP is in loopback mode.

    D. DHCP has phased the multicast server array.

Other File-Sharing Methods

12. You wish to configure a new IPX user to share a printer. What line should be inserted into the nwserv.conf file?

    A. User roger Pass changeme

    B. 100 roger changeme

    C. roger changeme

    D. 13 roger changeme

Time Synchronization

13. Which are proper keywords that can be used in a ntp.conf file?

   A. server

   B. client

   C. peer

   D. child

14. The driftfile in NTP serves as

   A. A calculation of the average drift from true UTC of the local system clock

   B. A random constant used to synchronize the clock with itself

   C. A measure of the Earth's rotational drift

   D. The "zero" from which system time is determined

PPP Configuration (as a Client) Using netcfg and the Files Generated

15. What naming scheme describes a serial port on a Linux system?

   A. /modem

   B. /dev/modem

   C. /dev/ttyS0

   D. COM1

Squid

16. You work at a large company. Every day at about noon, the network slows to a crawl. The CEO just noticed he has trouble reading and sending e-mail at that time and wants answers. What should you do?

   A. Reconfigure your DNS servers to increase their local cache.

   B. Upgrade your network.

   C. Route all Web surfing through a Squid server.

   D. Route the CEO's mail over a different subnet.

NFS

17. Your company has just suffered an external security breach. As a result, the security department has tightened the screws on all the servers, routers, and firewalls. Up until this point, all user data had been mounted over NFS, but now, nothing works. What happened?

    A. The hackers erased the NFS data, and they got the backups, too.

    B. The NFS ports are no longer allowed through the necessary firewalls.

    C. The two are unrelated. Check your disk space.

    D. The filesystem is no longer shared from the server.

DHCP

18. You add a new workstation to your dhcpd.conf file. You're in a hurry to finish, so you save and go to lunch. When you return, your phone mail is full of user complaints that they can't access the Internet, but the local network is fine. You surmise that you accidentally changed something in the dhcpd.conf file that you shouldn't have. What is the most likely cause?

    A. The absence of a "routers" line.

    B. The subnet mask was changed.

    C. The IP range was thrown off.

    D. The broadcast address was changed.

PPP Configuration (as a Client) Using netcfg and the Files Generated

19. You've set up a PPP dialup for your small company's Internet connection. The dial-up server is connected to the network so that all may share the connection. You can see the Internet from the dial-up server, and you can see your internal network as well. However, the users are unable to access the Internet. What's wrong?

    A. The users each need their own modems.

    B. Be sure routed or gated is running on the dial-up server.

    C. Check to see that the network card knows about the modem.

    D. Make sure IP forwarding is turned on.

Other File-Sharing Methods

20. You have the printer in your office set up as a NetWare printer for all to share. Your hard drive crashes and you have to restore from backup. Everything works from your console, and all the users employ a default password, but no one can print except you. What is the fix?

    A. Hook the printer directly to the network.

    B. Have everyone reboot his or her machine to reestablish the connection.

    C. Make sure the last backup caught the "21" directive in the nwserv.conf file.

    D. Add in each individual user instead of using a default password.

LAB QUESTION

Your network has over 500 hosts with users in three major groups wanting to share their files with each other only. There are also 30 Novell 3.11 clients in the publishing department that cannot use the Linux OS for their proprietary software needs. Everything is time-critical, as the outputs are stock quote-related and need to be synchronized to the same clock. What should you do?

SELF TEST ANSWERS

1. ☑ **C.** nslookup checks the configuration of the nameserver based on the resolv.conf file.
   ☒ **A, B,** and **D** are incorrect. Neither dsncheck nor resolve are valid utilities. BIND refers to the Berkeley Internet Naming Domain service.

2. ☑ **B.** Make absolutely sure that the serial number at the top of the zone file is incremented each time you change a zone file. If it is not changed, external DNS servers will think that nothing changed in your domain, and they will not bother to pull new RRs.
   ☒ **A** might be correct if something strange happened to your server, but the original server name still works internally, so your service is still connected to the network. **C** and **D** are also not likely scenarios, as root access is needed locally and your ISP may or may not be between your servers and all your clients.

3. ☑ **D.** Make sure the preference is defined, and the trailing "." is included at the end of the record.
   ☒ **A, B,** and **C** are incorrectly formatted.

Squid Proxy Server

4. ☑ **A** and **C.** HTTP and FTP sessions are cached by Squid.
   ☒ **B** and **D** are incorrect. There is no need to cache News services. There is something called a DNS caching server, but this is part of the DNS (named) service, not Squid.

NFS

5. ☑ **C.** There was no such thing as NFS for the Mac.
   ☒ **A, B,** and **D** are incorrect. Since the new Mac OS is Unix/Linux-based, it uses the same NFS services, not a hybrid service specific to the Mac.

6. ☑ **B.** Export the file system as a general read-only; then specify the machines that have read-write permission.
   ☒ **A** provides read/write to all general hosts and gives superv host read-only access. **C** provides read-only to all, but allows any resolvable hostname that is in the domain.com domain to have read/write access. **D** gives read/write access only to the superv host in domain.com.

7. ☑ **C.** /etc/fstab contains all the necessary information for NFS to mount its file shares.
   ☒ **A** is the exported file systems configuration file for nfs, /etc/exports. **B** and **D** are bogus files.

Internet News

8. ☑ **C.** Run /usr/bin/news.daily delayrm as the news user. This should be run daily by /etc/cron.daily/inn-cron-expire.

☒ **D** is a possible alternative solution that might need to be implemented if the error log indicates you are out of inodes. You would need to either replace the current partition, use another bigger partition with more inodes, or back up this partition, reformat with more inodes and then restore the data. A and B refer to nonexistant files.

9. ☑ **A.** No more inodes. Run mkfs with a smaller -i (bytes-per-nodes) option or use cycbuffs. Confirm this diagnosis with df -i.

☒ **B** is always a possibility (but likely not the cause this time), and **C** is not possible. There are no invisible files, just hidden filenames. The df command may be broken (thanks to hackers) but it's not very likely, so **D** is also bogus.

10. ☑ **D.** Use ctlinnd mode to confirm this. The reason can then be traced through the error logs.

☒ **A** and **B** are possible and lead to **C**, but you can always confirm that all three of these possibilities are not true with a ping of a remote host.

DHCP/Bootp

11. ☑ **B.** Make sure the dhcp.leases file is created before DHCP is started.

☒ **A** may also be true if you are out of disk space and cannot add to the dhcp.leases file, but you can check file system usage first with the df command. C and D are bogus, since DHCP is not related to loopback or the multicast server array.

Other File-Sharing Methods

12. ☑ **D.** The "13" directive should be followed by the username and password.

☒ **A, B,** and **C** are all incorrectly formatted.

Time Synchronization

13. ☑ **A** and **C** server denotes a lower stratum server and peer denotes an equal stratum machine.

☒ **B** and **D** are incorrect. Client and child refer to the ntp stratum order and are not relevant in the ntp.conf file.

14. ☑ **A.** NTP takes about a day to calculate the contents of the driftfile. This assures accurate restart if the daemon is shut down for some reason.

☒ **B, C,** and **D** are all incorrect definitions.

PPP Configuration (as a Client) Using netcfg and the Files Generated

15. ☑ **B and C.** /dev/modem can be a symbolic link to /dev/ttys0 (or ttyS1 and so forth), which is the main hardware designator for a serial port.

☒ **A and D** are incorrect. COM1 is the Microsoft OS way of referring to a port, not UNIX/Linux, and /modem might be correct but typically all device files are maintained in /dev directory.

Squid

16. ☑ **C.** The users are most likely surfing the Web on their lunch hour. All 500 of them just hit their favorite stock quote site. The fix: a great deal of bandwidth can be recovered by routing Web traffic through a Squid server.

☒ **A** may help somewhat if there are mostly redundant lookups for the same DNS names being made every day, but Squid is a better solution. **B** is an expensive and lengthy possibility. **D** is possible, but you might need to update your LAN networking with switches instead of routers to get this alternate subnet to actually be more efficient, otherwise the packets are still on the same LAN and will suffer the same congestion locally.

NFS

17. ☑ **B.** Ports 111, 745, 747, and 2049 must be allowed through the network security to function. Consider the possibility that NFS may have been to blame for the break-in, and restrict its use to isolated or protected subnets.

☒ **A, C,** and **D** are all possibilities you should check for, but the most likely culprit is B.

DHCP

18. ☑ **A.** The lack of a router declaration would cause an Internet outage.

☒ **B, C,** and **D** would probably cause a general network outage.

PPP Configuration (as a Client) Using netcfg and the Files Generated

19. ☑ **D.** IP forwarding passes packets from one network to another. You need to have the server set up as a router, and it needs to know that it can forward packets from the network to the modem and vice versa.

☒ **A, B,** and **C** are possible and should be checked if IP forwarding is already turned on.

Other File-Sharing Methods

20. ☑ **C.** Double-check the print queue (21) in the nwserv.conf file. You may have added the printer after your last backup.

☒ **A** would require additional configuration, as well as the 21 directive being revised. **B** and **D** are bogus choices.

LAB ANSWER

You need to configure a few services on your central host. NIS can be used to manage all the users so that all hosts use the same user IDs. Then configure a central server with IPX/SPX and NFS and sufficient disk space for the four groups, restricting each service to members of each group only. Use NTP to synchronize the NFS server to an Internet time server, if available, and then have all the other hosts synchronize their time to the NFS server host on an hourly basis.

10

Systems Administration and Security

A s a Red Hat Linux systems manager, you probably wear several hats, one of which is that of security manager. This is especially true if you work for a small company. Even if you work for a large organization that has a dedicated network or systems security staff as a systems administrator, you will probably be the person responsible for implementing the security policies on the Linux systems you manage.

You may spend very little time worrying about Linux security, or it may turn out to be a full-time job. For most Linux systems administrators, the amount of time spent on securing systems falls somewhere between these two extremes. The level of security you decide to impose on systems under your care depends on many factors, including what the system is used for and the security policies your company or organization has in place. If you are using your Red Hat Linux system for a home computer, you probably have much lower security requirements than for a system that is being used to process credit card orders for a Web site.

Red Hat Linux comes with a large and varied assortment of tools for handling security. This includes tools for managing the security on individual Linux hosts and tools for managing security for an entire network of systems, both Linux and otherwise. In this chapter, we look at some of the tools Red Hat Linux provides for managing security. We start out by looking at tools for controlling access to individual Linux host systems; then we look at tools for securing networks.

CERTIFICATION OBJECTIVE 10.01

Configuring NIS Client

In order to access a system running Red Hat Linux, you usually must identify yourself by providing a valid username and password. One of the potential problems with managing a large network of Linux systems is that in order to allow a user access to any system on the network, you must provide that user with an account on every individual system.

The Network Information System, or NIS, provides you with a way to handle this. NIS allows you to share one centrally managed authorization database with other Linux systems in the network. With NIS, you maintain one password database on an *NIS server* and configure the other systems on the network to be *NIS clients*. When a user initiates a login session on the NIS client, that system consults its authorization file (usually */etc/passwd*). If the username entered doesn't exist there, the system will look up the authorization information on the NIS server.

NIS clients and NIS servers participate in *NIS domains.* You can have multiple NIS domains on a single network, but clients and servers can only participate in one domain. Note that an NIS domain is not the same as a BIND domain; in fact, for security reasons, your NIS domain name should be different from your BIND domain name. If you are coming from the Microsoft Windows NT world, NIS domains are analogous to LAN manager domains. If you are using NIS, you can find out the name of your NIS domain by using this command:

```
domainname
```

NIS provides you with more than a shared authorization database. With NIS, you can provide shared access to any kind of information. By default, NIS under Red Hat Linux shares the following files:

- /etc/passwd
- /etc/group
- /etc/hosts
- /etc/networks
- /etc/services
- /etc/protocols
- /etc/netgroup
- /etc/rpc

You can configure NIS to share other files as well.

To provide NIS services, you must have at least one system that serves as the *NIS master server.* The *NIS master server* is where the centralized NIS database files, referred to as *maps,* are stored. To make a change to an NIS database, you must update the appropriate map on the master server. You can only have one NIS master server per NIS domain. (NIS maps are stored in /var/yp/*DOMAIN*, where *DOMAIN* is the name of your NIS domain.)

In order to reduce the load on the NIS master server and provide some redundancy in case the master server goes down, you can also have Linux systems that serve as *NIS slave servers.* Slave servers receive copies of the NIS maps from the master server.

NIS clients that need to validate a user can then validate against either the master server or a slave server. You can have multiple NIS slave servers on a network. If your network is subnetted, a recommendation is to have one slave server per subnet.

NIS clients are systems that use information from an NIS server. NIS clients don't store any information that is contained in the NIS databases; whenever that information is needed, it is retrieved from a server.

exam
Ⓦatch

You will notice that most NIS commands start with yp. This is a holdover from the previous name of NIS when it was known as the Yellow Pages service.

NIS Components on Red Hat Linux

The directory */usr/lib/yp* contains utilities used to configure and manage NIS services. You use the *ypinit* program in this directory to configure an NIS server. Table 10-1 lists the files needed to configure an NIS server.

Although NIS was designed to allow you to manage security by controlling who has access to your systems, NIS is not a very secure product. One thing you need to be aware of if you use NIS is that anyone who knows your NIS domain name and can connect to your network has access to all the information stored in your NIS databases. There are a couple of mechanisms you can employ to limit this vulnerability.

TABLE 10-1	File	Description
NIS Configuration Files and Commands	/usr/lib/yp/ypinit	Shell script to build initial database maps in /var/yp; ypinit -m builds the databases for a master server.
	/var/yp/Makefile	Configuration file. Edit this file to control which maps are shared via NIS. You should edit this file and run *make* from the /var/yp directory.
	/usr/lib/yp/makedbm	Convert text database files to NIS maps. Called by /var/yp/Makefile.
	/usr/sbin/ypserv	NIS server daemon, usually started at boot time in /etc/rc.d/rc?.d.
	/usr/sbin/yppasswdd	NIS password change daemon. You must run this in order for users to be able to change their NIS passwords with the yppass command. Usually started in /etc/rc.d/rc?.d.
	/etc/ypserv.conf	ypserv daemon configuration file.
	/var/yp/securenets	Controls which systems can access NIS databases.

You can use the file */var/yp/securenets* to control who can connect to your NIS server. If your system is configured to use *tcp_wrappers*, the NIS software will detect this when it is installed, and you can use this method to limit access to your NIS domain. tcp_wrappers is covered later in this chapter. There is a variant of NIS, called NIS+ (or NIS plus), that uses encryption and performs secure RPC authentication. Red Hat Linux has support for NIS+ clients, but cannot be an NIS+ server.

To configure your workstation as an NIS client, use the *authconfig* utility or the *linuxconf* utility. Figure 10-1 shows the authconfig screen used to configure NIS. This will configure your system to use the *ypbind* daemon. The ypbind daemon queries the NIS server whenever an NIS lookup is needed. The authconfig window will require you to enter some information for the NIS domain you want to join. After selecting the box Use NIS, you should specify the NIS domain name and NIS server name. Authconfig will then complete the configuration.

The other command you need to know about when running an NIS client is *yppasswd*. This command is necessary to change your NIS password.

on the **Job**

One security risk to keep in mind if you use NIS is that anyone with access to the root account on any system that uses NIS can use the su command to switch user to any account in your NIS database.

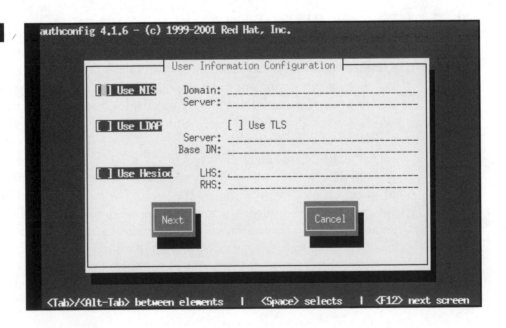

FIGURE 10-1

The authconfig utility is used to configure an NIS client

/etc/nsswitch.conf

The Name Service Switch file (*/etc/nsswitch.conf*) is used to control the order in which the various configuration databases available to the system are searched when information is requested. For example, consider the following entry from /etc/nsswitch.conf:

```
hosts: files nisplus nis dns
```

When an application requests a host name lookup (perhaps something as simple as ping host22), this entry tells the system it should resolve the host name as follows:

1. Check the local host table */etc/hosts*.

2. If not found, try to locate the host name in a shared hosts map using NIS+.

3. If not found, try to locate the host name in a shared hosts map using NIS.

4. If not found, do a DNS lookup for the host name.

CERTIFICATION OBJECTIVE 10.02

Basic Host Security

A network is only as secure as the most open system in that network. Although no system can be 100 percent secure, you can follow certain basic host measures to enhance the security on any given system and, consequently, your network. When devising security measures, you have to plan for two types of security violations: accidental security violations and intentional security violations.

Accidental security violations occur because users lack adequate training or because someone tries to speed up completion of a task by not following procedures. In fact, an important consideration to make when devising security measures is how much of an extra burden they place on the end users of your system. Tighter security usually equates to more difficulty in getting productive work done. If security procedures are too stringent, they may backfire because users try to avoid them due to the fact that they complicate their job. The amount of security you impose on a system should be directly proportional to the importance of what you are protecting.

Intentional security violations are deliberate attempts by someone to either gain access to information or deny the legitimate users of information access to that information.

These types of attacks can range from someone who is simply "browsing around," to someone trying to destroy or bring down your system for revenge or notoriety, to a competitor trying to access trade secrets or confidential financial information.

Several things should become habit to ensure that your host is secure. The first is practicing good password security. Good password security consists of requiring your users to employ passwords that aren't easily guessed and requiring that they change their passwords on a regular basis. This also means closely guarding your root password.

Another step you can take to minimize security breaches is to keep your password database current. Unused accounts lying around can make good springboards for crackers trying to access your system.

You should also check system log files and accounting files and look for any unusual patterns or occurrences. Knowledge of your users' work patterns can also aid you in detecting security violations. If you notice that someone who normally works nine to five has been logging in for long periods after midnight, you should consider finding out why. It could simply be that he is trying to meet a deadline on an important project, or it could be that a cracker has been logging on using his username and password after hours.

Another step you can take to keep your Red Hat Linux system secure is to install the latest errata releases from Red Hat. These contain patches or fixes for problems in applications or the operating system that could result in security violations.

Red Hat provides a built-in service to check for updates called up2date that you can configure if your machine is directly connected to the Internet. The up2date service can be found on the GNOME desktop, as well as in the menu of programs.

Pluggable Authentication Modules (PAM) and the /etc/pam.d/. . .Files

Red Hat Linux comes with an authentication mechanism called Pluggable Authentication Modules, or PAM. PAM consists of a set of dynamically loadable library modules that allow you, as the system administrator, to determine how applications perform user authentication. The idea behind PAM is to separate the process of authenticating users from the development of an application. For example, the login program uses PAM to perform authentication of each user. One specific authentication requirement performed by PAM is that every root login must be on a terminal listed as secure in /etc/securetty.

In traditionally written applications, the authentication mechanism is usually written into the code and compiled as part of the application. If you want to change authentication mechanisms, you have to modify the application source code and recompile. Programs that use PAM function calls to perform authentication tasks are said to be "PAM aware." With PAM-aware applications, you can change the authentication mechanism an application uses without rewriting the application. All that's required to change the authentication mechanism an application uses is to simply modify a configuration file. Another advantage to using PAM is that you can use modules to extend the capabilities of your software. As an example, suppose you have an application that is only capable of using /etc/passwd for authentication. If you rewrite the application to use PAM modules for authentication, then the application can authenticate against any database you have a PAM module for, such as a Novell password database or an NT password database.

PAM breaks the process of authenticating a user into four separate tasks. Modules are provided to handle these tasks. In addition to the provided modules, you can also develop your own modules. The PAM authentication tasks are these:

- **Authentication management** Establish the identity of a user (by prompting for a username/password combination, for example).

- **Account management** Allow or deny access based on the account policies, such as no access at a certain time of day, no access when too many users are on the system, and no root access from a network terminal.

- **Session management** Apply settings for a user before he is given access to a service.

- **Password management** These modules are required to update the user's associated authentication token. There is usually one of these for each challenge/response authentication module.

You can require PAM to use any combination of these four authentication steps when authorizing a user. When you use multiple modules to authenticate access to an application, the modules are said to be *stacked*.

You configure PAM using files in */etc/pam.d*. Each file in this directory controls one service. Every line in the authorization file has the following format:

```
module_type  control_flag  module_path  [arguments]
```

The next section of code shows an example PAM configuration file for configuring the login program. The # character indicates the start of a comment; for long command lines that need to be on one line within a file, use the backslash character (\) at the end of one line to continue the command onto the next line of the file.

```
#%PAM-1.0
auth          required    /lib/security/pam_securetty.so
auth          required    /lib/security/pam_pwdb.so service=system-auth
auth          required    /lib/security/pam_nologin.so
account       required    /lib/security/pam_stack.so service=system-
authpassword  required    /lib/security/pam_stack.so  service=system-auth
session       required    /lib/security/pam_stack.so  service=system-auth
session       optional    /lib/security/pam_console.so
```

When a user logs in, the authentication process proceeds through each step in the *etc/pam.d/login* file in the order they are listed. The control flag in the second field determines whether the authentication process skips some steps or terminates immediately if one of the modules returns with a failure. When a step in the authentication process fails, the application doesn't know which module failed; it only knows that the authentication process, as a whole, failed. Table 10-2 explains each of the fields in a PAM configuration file.

You use the control flag field to determine how the authentication process reacts when a module returns a failure code. A value of *required* means that this module must return a success code for the authentication to succeed; however, if a particular module fails, other modules of the same type will still execute. A value of *requisite* indicates that the entire authentication process should terminate and fail immediately if the module returns a failure code. A value of *sufficient* indicates that if no other module of this type has failed, then the success of this module is sufficient enough to guarantee that the security requirements have been met. If the control flag for a module is marked as *optional*, the module is not considered crucial to granting a user access to a service, and PAM ignores the success or failure code from that module.

As an example of how the control flags work, the code that follows shows the *etc/pam.d/shutdown* configuration file that controls access to the shutdown command. Notice that the first *auth* module checked is the *root_ok* module. If you invoke this

TABLE 10-2	**Field**	**Description**
The PAM Configuration File Fields	module type	The type of authentication task being performed as outlined previously. Can be *auth, account, password,* or *session.*
	control_flag	How PAM should handle module success or failure. Can be *required, requisite, sufficient, optional.*
	module_path	The path of the module. Most modules will be in */lib/security.*
	arguments	Optional arguments used by the module being invoked.

command from the root account, PAM will skip the other *auth* module and proceed to the *account* module on the last line of the file. The other possible criteria acceptable for shutdown if the user is not root is that the user is logged into a secure console. The second line tests this option before proceeding to the account module on the last line. In both cases, a valid user has successfully logged in and can shut down the system if they are on the console.

on the job

Allowing just any user to shut down a server system is NOT normal for corporate servers, but it is a commonly accepted practice on workstations. This way users can shut down their own laptop or desktop without having to change to the root account.

```
#%PAM-1.0
auth        sufficient      /lib/security/pam_rootok.so
auth        required        /lib/security/pam_console.so
account     required        /lib/security/pam_permit.so
```

/etc/securetty and PAM

Looking at the code that follows, you will notice that the first module in the PAM configuration file for the login program is *pam_securetty.so*.

```
#%PAM-1.0
auth          required      /lib/security/pam_securetty.so
auth          required      /lib/security/pam_pwdb.so service=system-auth
auth          required      /lib/security/pam_nologin.so
account       required      /lib/security/pam_stack.so service=system-
authpassword  required      /lib/security/pam_stack.so  service=system-auth
session       required      /lib/security/pam_stack.so  service=system-auth
session       optional      /lib/security/pam_console.so
```

This module is used to control which terminals the root account may log in from. Whenever the root account initiates a login, this module reads the file */etc/securetty*. This file contains a list of the terminals permissible for root login and fails if the terminal being used to log in is not in this list. By default, the Red Hat Linux virtual consoles are listed in this file. You should be careful which terminals you add to this file. Restricting root access to terminals physically connected to your Linux system makes it that much more difficult for someone to attack your system via the Internet or a dial-up line.

EXERCISE 10-1

Configuring PAM

In this exercise, we experiment with some of the PAM security features of Red Hat Linux.

1. Make a backup copy of /etc/securetty cp /etc/securetty /etc/securetty.sav.

2. Edit /etc/securetty and remove the lines for tty3 through tty8. Save the changes and exit.

3. Use ALT-F3 (CTRL-ALT-F3 if you're running X-Window) to switch to virtual console number 3. Try to log in as *root*. What happens?

4. Use ALT-F2 to switch to virtual console number 2 and try to log in as root.

5. Restore your original /etc/securetty file: mv /etc/securetty.sav /etc/securetty.

---

exam
Ⓦatⱺh

Make sure you understand how Red Hat Linux handles user authorization. Make sure you create a backup of EVERYTHING in PAM before making any changes, because any error introduced to PAM can disable your system completely (it is that secure).

Buffer Overruns and Security Problems

One method of attacking systems that has been successful is that of making use of *buffer overruns* in improperly written applications. Some server applications don't check the size of the input data stream they are receiving and allow the input to overwrite other areas of the program's memory. When this happens, the server program behaves unpredictably and will often allow the user of the client application to obtain access to the system on which the server program is running. The best way to combat buffer overruns is to monitor Red Hat security advisories and install security patches as soon as they are posted.

on the

The most common early buffer overrun exploits were in the early Web sites that used simple CGI scripts for data forms that ran on the server and not the client. This exploit is well documented and can still occur but is not all that common. Most Web sites are aware of this type of exploit and test their applications for it.

System Logging

An important part of maintaining a secure system is keeping track of the activities that take place on the system. Knowing the normal patterns of use on your system can help you spot unusual activity. Red Hat Linux comes with several utilities you can use to monitor activity on a system and can help you identify the responsible party if security violations do occur.

Red Hat Linux comes with two daemons that perform logging. The kernel log daemon service, klogd, logs kernel messages and events. The syslog daemon, syslogd, logs all other process activity. You can use the log files that syslogd generates to track activities on your system. If you are managing multiple Red Hat Linux systems, you can configure the syslogd daemon on each system to log messages to a central host system. Typically, you configure syslogd to start up at boot time by placing a symbolic link in the appropriate runlevel directory under /etc/rc.d. Once invoked, syslog examines /etc/syslog.conf to determine its configuration options.

/etc/syslog.conf

You choose the events that syslogd will log using the file */etc/syslog.conf.* This file is a text file that consists of lines of rules. Each rule has two fields separated by one or more spaces: a *selector* field and an *action* field. The selector field is a two-part field that tells syslogd which events (facilities) to log and the severity level (priority) at which events should be logged. The action field tells syslogd whether to write the message to a file or send it to someone immediately. The format of a rule in syslogd is this:

```
facility.priority      action
```

Table 10-3 lists the valid entries for each field in /etc/syslog.conf.

You can use the asterisk as a wildcard in both the facility and priority subfields. For example, a specification of *.* indicates you want to log everything. A specification of auth.* means you want to log all messages from the auth facility. You can modify the priority subfield with the ! and = characters. The default behavior for syslog is to log any message from a facility that has a priority equal to or higher than the one you specify. If you only want to see error messages from a facility, use the = modifier to specify only messages of that severity; auth.=err means only log error messages from the auth facility. The ! character negates a priority, so auth.!err means ignore any message coming from the auth facility with a priority of err or higher; auth.!=err means log all messages from the auth facility except messages with a priority of err.

Most messages from syslogd are written to files in the /var/log directory. You should scan these logs on a regular basis and look for changes in activity patterns that could indicate a break-in, or attempts at breaking in to your system. If you are logging the activity on many systems, or if your system is very busy, wading through the log files and maintaining them can become a time-consuming process. Red Hat Linux 7 comes with utilities that you can use to leverage the effectiveness of your log files.

Managing Logs (logrotate)

The *logrotate* utility allows you to set up automatic management tasks for log files. These tasks include rotating log files, compressing log files, mailing log files, and removing log files. The logrotate utility is run via cron, and you can specify the frequency at which any given log file is modified. You configure the logrotate utility using the /etc/logrotate.conf file.

TABLE 10-3	Facility	Priority	Action
Entries in /etc/syslog.conf Are Used to Configure System Logging	auth, auth-priv, cron, daemon, kern, lpr, mail, news, syslog, user, uucp, local0 - local7, *	Lowest to highest: debug, info, notice, warning, err, crit, alert, emerg, * modifiers of a priority: !, = Examples of use: **=debug** only this priority **!debug** ignore debug or higher **!=debug** all except debug	**absolute path** log event to specified file **/dev/console, /dev/ttyN** log event to specified terminal **@host** log event to remote host *user1, user2,*?-send message to specified users *-do a write-all (wall) to all users

CERTIFICATION OBJECTIVE 10.04

xinetd

On a TCP/IP network, communication occurs between clients and servers. For example, when you use the Telnet application to establish a login session on a remote system, Telnet communicates with the *Telnet server daemon* on the remote system. A client application needs two pieces of information to establish a connection to a remote system: the address of that system, and the *port number* (or *socket number*) of the server process running on the remote system. Every commonly used TCP/IP application has a standard defined port number. For example, the standard port number for the Telnet server daemon is always 23. The reason you don't normally have to specify the port number when Telnetting to another system is that the Telnet client application assumes you are connecting to port number 23 on the remote system. The file /etc/services lists port numbers and the services they address.

For a client to connect to a service on a remote system, the corresponding server program for that service must be running on the remote system. The port number for that application is the address of the *running* server application. If you are using a Telnet client, you will connect to the Telnet daemon at port 23; if you are using a Web browser, you will connect to the httpd daemon at port 80. If you look at the list of defined port numbers, you will see there are potentially dozens of services that client applications could request connections to. If you are managing a server, it appears that in order to allow connections to these services, you will have to start the dozens of different server applications at system boot.

The x*inetd* (which stands for *Extended Internet services daemon*) program provides a way around this problem. xinetd is a special server program usually started at boot time. The startup script is /etc/rc.d/init.d/xinetd (there should be links to this program in the appropriate /etc/rc.d/rc?.d directories). The xinetd program listens for connection requests from client applications to these socket addresses. When it receives a connection request, xinetd starts up the server program for that port, hands the port over to the server application, and then goes back to waiting for another connection request. Once the client finishes with the service, the server application terminates until another client requires that service. The advantage this mechanism provides is that you don't have to have a server daemon running for every possible type of client request you might wish to satisfy; the xinetd server will start up servers as they are needed.

exam
ⓦatch

Previous to Red Hat 7.0, this superdaemon service was called inetd and had a configuration file called /etc/inetd.conf, which contained one line per service that inetd was to manage. This new version, xinetd, provides more management control over the services on an individual basis. You configure which services xinetd manages from within the /etc/xinetd.conf file, and each individual service has its own management script in the /etc/xinetd.d directory. Each file in the /etc/xinetd.d directory specifies a particular service you want to allow xinetd to manage. xinetd will listen for connection requests coming to the ports for those services. As a security measure, you should disable services you don't want to run. The following code shows a sample of the /etc/xinetd.d/ntalk configuration file, with this service disabled:

```
# Example /etc/xinetd.d/ntalk file
#Lines beginning with a '#' are comments
service ntalk

{
disable     = yes
socket_type = dgram
wait                = yes
user                = nobody
group               = tty
server              = /usr/sbin/in.ntalkd
}
```

The ntalk example file contains fields listed in Table 10-4; other fields are described in the man pages for xinetd.conf.

TABLE 10-4	Field	Description of Field Entry
Description of xinetd.d Configuration Files	disable	Either Yes or No. Yes will cause the service not to be started.
	socket_type	Either stream, dgram, raw, rdm, or seqpacket
	wait	Set to Yes for single-threaded applications, or No for multithreaded applications. Multithreaded applications start up multiple copies, such as httpd and nfs services.
	user	Account under which the server should run. NEVER use account root.
	group	Group under which the server should run.
	server	The program to execute.

You should only use xinetd to start infrequently used services. Daemons for services such as a busy Web server, which receives constant connection requests, should NOT be managed by xinetd. Only if you are providing Web services very intermittently, such as when the server connects to the Internet specifically, would you allow xinetd to handle the httpd service. Any full-time service should be started by the system at boot time to avoid the overhead involved in starting them through xinetd.

on the
Job

Most large client installations are not supporting httpd on every desktop due to the inherent risks and policing required. Instead they run full service, full time Web site servers. (These sites would never use xinetd to manage httpd services.)

When you modify xinetd configuration files, you must use the kill command to tell xinetd to reread its configuration files. The PID for the xinetd daemon is stored in /var/run/xinetd.pid, so one way to kill the current xinetd process would be to use this sequence:

```
[root]# kill -SIGUSR1 `cat /var/run/xinetd.pid`
```

Alternatively, you can use the service management script with either stop and then start or with the restart option as follows:

```
[root]# /etc/rc.d/init.d/xinetd stop
[root]# /etc/rc.d/init.d/xinetd start
```

or you can do both of the preceding steps through the use of one request. Either

```
[root]# /etc/rc.d/init.d/xinetd restart
```

or

```
[root]# service xinetd restart
```

EXERCISE 10-2

Configuring xinetd

In this exercise, we will enable the Telnet service using xinetd. Attempt to establish a Telnet session using the command **telnet localhost**. Telnet is disabled by default in Red Hat Linux, so your attempt should fail, unless you have already enabled Telnet.

1. Edit /etc/xinetd.d/telnet and change the value of Disable from Yes to No.

2. Tell xinetd to reread its configuration file using the command:

   ```
   kill -SIGUSR1 `cat /var/run/xinetd.pid`
   ```

3. Try to establish a Telnet session now. You should be able to.

4. Restore the value of Disable in the Telnet configuration file, and send SIGUSR1 to xinetd again. Attempt to use Telnet again; assuming you had restored the Yes setting, you should not be able to use Telnet.

tcp_wrappers, /etc/hosts.allow, and /etc/hosts.deny

Although you can achieve some measure of security by commenting or removing unused services in /etc/xinetd.conf, there is still the possibility of someone mounting an attack against the services you left enabled. xinetd provides the capability to restrict access to services to specified hosts or networks through optional fields in its configuration files or configurations specified in the /etc/hosts.allow or /etc/hosts.deny files. Red Hat Linux implements these host or network-based restrictions through a mechanism known as tcp_wrappers, which is enabled by default. tcp_wrappers fits between xinetd and the applications it starts up. With tcp_wrappers enabled, when xinetd receives a network request for a service, it passes the request on to tcp_wrappers. tcp_wrappers logs the request, then checks its access rules. If the request is from a client that is allowed to access your server, then tcp_wrappers starts the requested server program and exits.

tcp_wrappers is invisible to the client. It is application independent, and the only time it is active is when xinetd is establishing a session—it doesn't impose any overhead on the running application. Other applications can also be built using the tcp_wrappers library routines. Network access to these applications can then be controlled through the tcp_wrappers configuration files.

You configure the access rules for tcp_wrappers using two files: */etc/hosts.allow* and */etc/hosts.deny*. Clients listed in *hosts.allow* are allowed access; clients listed in *hosts.deny* are denied access. An important point to remember is that if a client is not listed in either file, then the client is automatically granted access. When tcp_wrappers searches its access files, the search stops on the first match found for a client. If either file is missing, it is treated as an empty file; you can turn off access control by deleting *hosts.allow* and *hosts.deny*.

The search order is this:

1. hosts.allow

2. hosts.deny

3. no match = access granted

You use the same access control language in both /etc/hosts.allow and /etc/hosts.deny to tell tcp_wrappers which clients to allow or deny. The basic format of the lines in both files is this:

```
daemon_list : client_list
```

For example, this line:

```
in.telnetd : 192.168.1.5
```

in the file /etc/hosts.allow tells tcp_wrappers that a client with the IP address 192.168.1.5 is allowed to Telnet in to your system. The same line in /etc/hosts.deny tells tcp_wrappers that the client is *not* allowed to Telnet in to your system. You can specify clients a number of different ways, as shown in Table 10-5.

The *ALL* wildcard listed in the table can be used to represent any client or service. Multiple lists can be separated by commas. Restrictions or exceptions can be applied to both daemon lists and client lists using the *EXCEPT* operator. The following code contains a sample hosts.allow file to see how lists can be built to control access.

```
#hosts.allow
ALL : LOCAL, .asafe.dom.com
in.ftpd : 192.168.25.0/255.255.255.0 EXCEPT 192.168.25.73
in.fingerd, in.ftpd : 192.168.1.10
```

TABLE 10-5 Ways to Specify Clients in /etc/hosts.allow and /etc/hosts.deny	.xyz.com	Note: Begins with a dot. Matches any client where the last part of the host name contains xyz.com. Matches both *ws1.xyz.com* and *server1.engr.xyz.com.*
	172.16.	Note: ends with a dot. Matches any client with an IP of 172.16.*x.y.*
	172.16.72.0/255.255.254.0	IP network with subnet mask. Matches any client with an IP of 172.16.72.0 through 172.16.73.255.
	ALL	Match any client, match any daemon.
	LOCAL	Match any client host name that doesn't contain a dot.

The first line in the hosts.allow file is simply a comment. The next line specifies that any client in the same domain as this system or any client from the .asafe.dom.com can connect to any service. The third line specifies that any client on the 192.168.25 subnet (except for the client with an IP of 192.168.25.73) can FTP to this system. The last line specifies that the client with an IP of 192.168.1.10 can finger this host or use FTP. The code that follows contains a hosts.deny file to see how lists can be built to control access.

```
#hosts.deny
ALL EXCEPT in.fingerd : .xyz.com
in.telnetd : ALL EXCEPT 192.168.1.10
ALL:ALL
```

The first line in the hosts.deny file is a comment. Comment lines begin with a number sign (#) and can appear anywhere in either file. The second line specifies that any client in the .xyz.com domain can't do anything other than run finger on our host. The third line specifies that no one other than the client with an IP of 192.168.1.10 is allowed to Telnet to our host. The last line specifies that any other client that doesn't match a single rule will be denied access to all services controlled by tcp_wrappers.

The tcp_wrappers access control language also allows you to specify a shell command to execute for a given client list. The format for a rule like this is as follows:

```
daemon_list : client_list : shell_command
```

There are a number of expansion patterns you can use with these rules. When you include these as part of a shell command to be run, they will be expanded before the command is run. Some of the patterns you can use are listed in Table 10-6.

tcp_wrappers also comes with some optional extensions that you enable when you build tcp_wrappers. The most interesting of these is the *twist* operator. An example of using this operator in hosts.deny is shown next:

```
in.telnetd : .hack.org : twist /bin/echo Sorry %c, access denied
```

TABLE 10-6	%a	Client address	%h	Client host name
	%A	Host address	%H	Server host name
Possible tcp_wrappers Expansion Patterns	%c	Client information	%p	Daemon process ID
	%d	Daemon process name	%s	Server information

The twist operator replaces the current process with the shell command and connects stdin, stdout, and stderr to the client process. In the preceding example, if someone from the hack.org domain tries to Telnet to your system, he will receive a customized error message.

EXERCISE 10-3

Configuring tcp_wrappers

In this exercise, we will use tcp_wrappers to control access to network resources. Since Red Hat Linux ships with tcp_wrappers enabled, you shouldn't have to make any modifications to /etc/xinetd.conf.

1. Verify that you can Telnet to the system using the address localhost.

2. Edit /etc/hosts.deny and add the following line:

   ```
   ALL : ALL
   ```

3. What happens when you try to Telnet to the address localhost?

4. Edit /etc/hosts.allow and add the following line:

   ```
   in.telnetd : localhost
   ```

5. Now what happens when you try to Telnet to the address localhost?

6. If you have other systems available to you, try restricting access to the Telnet service using some of the other tcp_wrappers rules.

7. Undo your changes when finished.

CERTIFICATION OBJECTIVE 10.05

IP Aliasing and Virtual Hosts

If you have more than one network interface card (NIC) in your Red Hat Linux system, you can attach your system to multiple networks and use it as a router between two or more physical subnets. At times, you may find it necessary or useful to use a Linux system as a router between logical subnets; that is, if you wish to route packets between two different IP subnets that exist on the same physical network.

This is actually a quite useful capability, and one used very often. As an example, suppose you have two official Class-C IP network addresses for your company. All of the systems in your company are on the same LAN, but half of the systems have IP addresses in one subnet, while the other half have IP addresses in the second subnet. In order for a system on one subnet to communicate with a system on the other by way of IP, a router is required, even though both systems are on the same physical network.

To enable this capability, known as IP aliasing, you must assign IP addresses to your network interfaces using the ifconfig command. When you specify an Ethernet interface, the interface name for the first Ethernet card in your system is eth0. The first IP address you assign to this interface will be the primary address for that interface. Subsequently assigned IP addresses will be aliases. To specify the interface for the alias addresses, you should specify the interface name followed by a colon and the alias number. As an example, here is how to assign three IP addresses to an Ethernet card:

```
ifconfig eth0 192.168.10.5
ifconfig eth0:0 192.168.200.5
ifconfig eth0:1 10.20.15.80
```

The final step in the process is to set up the appropriate routing information for the networks you have defined. We will look at setting up static routes later in this chapter.

Another use for IP aliases is when setting up virtual host services. When you assign multiple IP addresses to an interface, that system can participate in multiple DNS domains. Virtual host services essentially allow a single physical server to appear to be multiple different servers when viewed from different clients, depending upon the services (such as FTPD or httpd) configured for those clients.

The ftpservers file is used to tell which set of virtual domain configuration files the FTPD (WU-FTPD package) server should use. The WU-FTPD can be configured to use separate configuration files for each virtual domain. Essentially, configuration files for each site are placed into a separate virtual domain directory dedicated to that site. The directory path and the IP address for each virtual site is listed in the ftpservers file. The actual configuration files put into the virtual domain directory must be named

■ **ftpaccess** Virtual domain's access file.

- **ftpusers**   Restrict accounts that can use the Web server.
- **ftpgroups**   SITE GROUP and SITE GPASS support.

An example configuration file for the FTP service shown next has two fields per row: the IP Address (or any name that can be resolved) and the directory containing the files.

```
192.168.10.5 /virtual/xyz.com
192.168.200.5 /virtual/netzine.org
10.20.50.80 /virtual/widgetsrus.com
```

If you are providing virtual host services for Web services, you should use the virtual domain mechanism built in to the Apache Web Server. This will provide faster response for your users and allow Apache to use its built-in mechanisms for controlling traffic. You also do not need to duplicate your entire system into each virtual host using Apache virtual hosts. You simply create a directory structure for each host that contains all the associated HTML files and any associated CGI scripts and programs.

CERTIFICATION OBJECTIVE 10.06

Firewall Policies—Elements

If your organization's network is connected to the Internet or another external network, you should consider putting a firewall in place between your network and the external network (or have at least considered putting one in). A system running Red Hat Linux can make a very good firewall system, even if the other systems on your network are running another operating system such as Windows NT or the Macintosh OS. Firewalls are used to secure an internal network by controlling who can connect to systems on the internal network, and by controlling what kind of information is allowed out of the internal network.

A firewall sits between your company's internal LAN and an outside network. It is the job of the firewall to examine every network packet that passes in to or out of your LAN and to filter out those packets that you, as the security administrator, have deemed a security risk. To understand this *packet filtering* process, you have to understand a little bit about how information is sent across networks.

When you send a message over a network, it isn't sent as a single unit. Instead, the message is first broken down into smaller-sized units called *packets,* and it is these packets that are sent. When the packets reach their final destination, they are reassembled into the complete message. In addition to holding a portion of your message, each packet also contains some administrative information, including the source address of the packet (where it came from), the destination address of the packet (where it's going), and the type of information contained in the packet. A firewall examines these administrative fields in each packet to determine whether to allow the packet to pass.

Red Hat Linux comes with everything you need to configure a system to be a firewall. On earlier versions of Red Hat Linux, *ipfw* was used to configure a Linux firewall configuration, while *ipfwadm* was the utility used to manage the firewall configuration. ipfw has since been replaced by *ipchains*, which contains several improvements over ipfw. ipchains, in turn, is in the process of being replaced by *iptables/NetFilter;* however, the ipchains interface will remain available for some time due to backward compatibility reasons, and it is the interface that will be discussed here.

Packet filtering has to be compiled into the kernel to use Linux as a firewall system. By default, as of Red Hat Version 7.0 and later, packet filtering is compiled into the kernel. To check that packet filtering is present, look for the file /proc/net/ip_fwchains. If it isn't present, you will probably need to rebuild the kernel (see the section on rebuilding a kernel) and make sure that the CONFIG_IP_NF_COMPAT_IPCHAINS option is set to "m".

Configuring ipchains

The "chains" in ipchains are sets of rules applied to each network packet that passes through your Linux firewall system. Each rule does two things: it specifies the conditions a packet must meet to match the rule, and it specifies the action or *target* to take if the packet matches. ipchains has seven chains total but only three chains can be modified. You can, however, add your own new chain. The three modifiable chains are these:

- **input**   All incoming packets are checked against the rules in this chain.
- **output**   All outgoing packets are checked against the rules in this chain.
- **forward**   All packets being sent to another machine are checked against the rules in this chain.

These default chains cannot be deleted. You configure your firewall by modifying these default chains and adding your own rules. You can also add and delete your own chains.

If you are running X on the console, you can also use the firewall_config utility as shown in Figure 10-2.

Use the ipchains command with the appropriate command options to manage rules and chains.

Table 10-7 lists some of the commands you can use with the ipchains command-line utility.

You can be very specific when telling ipchains which packets to match for a given rule. Some of the criteria you can use to filter packets include the packet's source address, its destination address, and the protocol type of the packet. Table 10-8 summarizes some of the parameters you can use to specify packets to filter.

The target you specify with the *-j* parameter is the action the firewall should take if the packet matches the criteria for that rule. In addition to your own user-defined targets, you can employ one of the following predefined targets:

■ **ACCEPT**   Allow packet to pass.

■ **DENY**   Drop packet; client doesn't receive any indication of packet's fate.

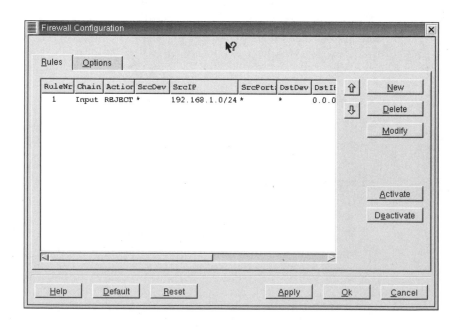

FIGURE 10-2

GUI-based
firewall_config
utility

Command	Purpose
-N	Create a new chain
-X	Delete an empty chain
-L -v -n	List rules in a chain print counters no address lookups, use IP only
-F	Flush rules for a chain
-P	Change policy for a chain
-Z	Zero counters for all rules in a chain
-A	Append new rule to a chain
-I	Insert new rule in a chain
-R	Replace a rule in a chain
-D	Delete a rule in a chain

Parameter	Argument	Explanation
-s	source address	Can be specified four ways: full name: *host1.xyz.com* IP address: *192.168.1.1* group of IP addresses: *192.168.1.0/24* or *192.168.1.0/255.255.255.0* match any address: *0/0*
-d	destination address	Same as for source address
-p	protocol	TPC, UDP, or ICMP
-i	interface	
-j	*<target>*	Action to perform on packet if it matches, can be one of ACCEPT, DENY, REJECT, MASQ, REDIRECT, RETURN, or user defined
-y		Block TCP SYN packet
!	can precede any parameter argument	Inversion operator -p TCP—match any TCP packet -p ! TCP—match any non-TCP packet

- **REJECT** Drop packet; send client an ICMP "destination unreachable" message.
- **MASQ** Used for network address translation.
- **REDIRECT** Send a TCP or UDP packet to a local port on the firewall system.
- **RETURN** Return to previous calling chain or jump to chain's policy target.

We will look at some examples of defining ipchains to see how you can use them to configure firewall services. To list all the rules in all the chains defined on the system, use this command:

```
ipchains -L
```

To define a rule that would prohibit any access from the 192.168.75.0 subnet and send a "destination unreachable" message back to any client that tried to connect, use this command:

```
ipchains -A input -s 192.168.75.0/24 -j REJECT
```

To define a rule that would prohibit users on the host 192.168.25.200 from "pinging" our system (remember that ping uses the ICMP protocol), use this command:

```
ipchains -A input -s 192.168.25.200 -p icmp -j DENY
```

To guard against TCP SYN attacks, from outside our network, (assuming our network address is 192.168.190.0), use this command:

```
ipchains -A input -s !192.168.190.0/24 -p tcp -y
```

To delete the first rule we added, use this command:

```
ipchains -D input -s 192.168.25.200 -p icmp -j DENY
```

The policy for a chain is the default action or target to apply if no rule matches. By default, the policies for all three built-in chains are ACCEPT. To change the policy for the *forward* chain to be more secure, use this command:

```
ipchains -P forward DENY
```

You can save your firewall configuration to a file using the ipchains-save command:

```
ipchains-save >firewall.conf
```

To restore the configuration, use the ipchains-restore command:

```
ipchains-restore <firewall.conf
```

The ipchains service can be configured to run at all times. It uses the /etc/sysconfig/ipchains configuration file at startup. During installation, you have the option to configure a firewall, which is actually configuring ipchains for your system. You can manage the firewall service so it runs in all runlevels, using the chkconfig command so it is always started at bootup in all runlevels providing network services:

```
[root]# chkconfig —level 2345 ipchains on
[root]# chkconfig —list ipchains
ipchains        0:off   1:off   2:on    3:on    4:on    5:on    6:off
[root]#
```

You can use the graphical utility to add a blockage for a specific network, as depicted in Figure 10-2, and you can get help on most aspects of setting firewall rules with the help service provided, as depicted in Figure 10-3.

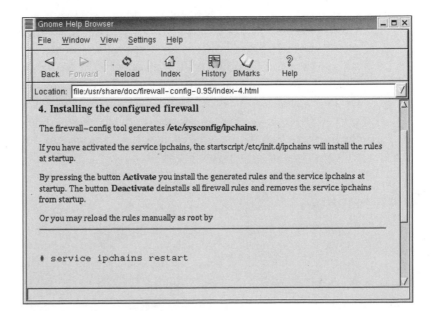

FIGURE 10-3

firewall_config utility Help

CERTIFICATION OBJECTIVE 10.07

Network Address Translation

Network address translation (NAT) is a firewall feature that allows you to connect systems to the Internet and disguise their true IP addresses. NAT works by modifying the header information in IP packets as they pass through the firewall. As each packet crosses through, the internal source address in the header is replaced with a public address. When the firewall receives incoming packets destined for a host on the internal network, the process unfolds in reverse. As the packets pass through the firewall, the header of each packet is modified so the public address in the packet's destination field is replaced with the internal address of the system it is destined for.

There are several reasons why this is useful. The most obvious is the fact that disguising your internal IP addresses makes it harder for someone to attempt a break in on your network. One of the major uses for NAT is that it allows you to connect systems to the Internet without having an officially assigned IP address for each system you want to have access to the Internet. Many organizations use the RFC1597 free IP network addresses to set up their internal IP networks. RFC1597 sets aside the networks 10.0.0.0, 172.16.0.0, and 192.168.0.0 for private use. Systems using these addresses will find that the Internet will not "be there" as these addresses are not routed (forwarded to any other networks). If using any one of these network ranges, you should not directly connect to the Internet. With the aid of NAT, however, these systems can access the Internet as if they had an officially assigned IP address.

IP Masquerading

Red Hat Linux supports a variation of NAT called *IP masquerading*. IP masquerading allows you to provide Internet access to multiple computers with a single officially assigned IP address. Like NAT, the masquerade process is invisible to both your internal systems and systems on the Internet. Unlike NAT, which is basically a one-to-one mapping of an internal IP address to a valid external IP address, IP masquerading lets you map multiple internal IP addresses to a single valid external IP address.

Connecting multiple systems to the Internet using IP masquerading is a fairly straightforward process. Your firewall will need one NIC to connect to your LAN, and another NIC or PPP connection for the Internet. If you have a cable modem or xDSL service, you can connect it to the second NIC. If you have a modem to dial out with as your second NIC, you will configure it as a PPP interface to connect to the Internet. The basic outline of the process can be seen in the following:

- Assign your official IP address to the interface connected to the Internet.

- Assign your LAN systems addresses from one of the RFC1597 networks.

- Reserve one address for the NIC on your firewall.

- Assign this reserved address to the NIC on your firewall.

- Use ipchains to set up IP masquerading.

- Configure the systems on your LAN to use your firewall for their Internet gateway.

When an internal client system on your LAN sends a packet addressed to a host on the Internet, the packet will be handed off to the firewall. The firewall will modify the packet's header by replacing the source address with the firewall's official IP address, then assigning a new port number to the packet. The firewall will remember the original packet header information. When a packet comes in from the Internet to the firewall addressed to the port number assigned to the outgoing packets from the internal client, the process is reversed. The firewall will replace the destination field and port with the internal client's private IP address and original port number, and then forward the packet back on to the LAN.

In order to use IP masquerading, IP forwarding must be enabled, as outlined in the next section. The next step in the process is using the ipchains command to enable masquerading. In this example, we will assume your internal LAN is using the RFC1597 address of 192.168.80.0. The commands necessary to enable masquerading are these:

```
ipchains -P forward DENY  # Turn OFF forwarding for everybody
ipchains -A forward -s 192.168.80.0/24 -j MASQ
```

IP Forwarding

IP forwarding is more commonly referred to as *routing*. Routing is critical to the operation of the Internet or any IP network. To be a router, a system must have multiple network connections. A router is not usually the final destination for a network packet; instead, it is simply a waypoint for that packet en route to its final destination. A router works by examining the destination address of each packet it receives from a network interface. It then decides which network interface to send the packet back out on in order to get it to its final destination. To use a Red Hat Linux system as a router, you must enable the built-in routing support, as well as enable routing to support IP masquerading.

To enable IP forwarding, edit /etc/sysconfig/network and change the line that reads

```
FORWARD_IPV4=false
```

to

```
FORWARD_IPV4=true
```

and reboot.

exam
ⓦatch

Work is underway to build a complete Linux router that will fit on a single floppy. Visit <http://www.linuxrouter.org> to find out more.

CERTIFICATION OBJECTIVE 10.08

Routing and Static Routes

Even systems that don't serve as routers must know how to route packets in order to reach systems outside their subnet. Any system that uses IP keeps a list of rules, called a *routing table*, that it uses to determine where to send packets. Each entry in the routing table contains at least three fields. The first field is a destination address. If a packet's destination address matches this field, then this rule will be used to forward the packet. The second field is the interface to which the packet will be sent. The third field is optional and contains the address of a router that will route the packet further along its journey across the network. Keeping routing tables current and accurate on all the systems on a network is crucial to keeping the network running. There are many methods for doing this automatically, but that discussion is beyond the scope of this study guide.

The simplest method for managing routing tables is through the use of *static routes*. Static routes are entries you input to the routing tables manually. If your network is small, your configuration doesn't change very frequently, or your system is an end system, static routes can be adequate for managing routing configuration. You manage static routes using the *route* command. Table 10-9 shows the route commands you can use to manage your routing table.

The following code shows the routing table that results when the commands in Table 10-9 are issued.

```
[root@localhost HOWTO]# route -n
Kernel IP routing table
Destination    Gateway      Genmask         Flags Metric Ref Use Iface
192.168.1.80   0.0.0.0      255.255.255.255 UH    0      0   0 eth0
192.168.50.10  192.168.1.1  255.255.255.255 UGH   0      0   0 eth0
192.168.1.0    0.0.0.0      255.255.255.0   U     0      0   0 eth0
172.16.64.0    192.168.1.1  255.255.224.0   UG    0      0   0 eth0
127.0.0.0      0.0.0.0      255.0.0.0       U     0      0   0 lo
0.0.0.0        192.168.1.1  0.0.0.0         UG    0      0   0 eth0
```

Now that you have seen some of the security capabilities of Red Hat Linux, refer to the following Scenario & Solution for some possible scenario questions and their answers.

TABLE 10-9	Routing Command	Description
Commands for Managing Your System's Routing Table	route −n	Display the current routing table.
	route add -net 192.168.1.0 netmask 255.255.255.0 eth0	Add a route to the 192.168.1.0 subnet via interface eth0.
	route add -host 192.168.50.10 gw 192.168.1.1	Add a route to the host 192.168.50.10 via the gateway (gw) or router 192.168.1.1. The gateway must be reachable (you should be able to ping it) in order to specify it in the route.
	route add default gw 192.168.1.1 eth0	Set default gateway. Every system should have a default gateway. If the destination address for a packet doesn't match any of the other entries in the routing table, it will be sent to this system. The default gateway will show up with a destination address of 0.0.0.0 when you display the routing table with *route -n*.
	route add -net 172.16.64.0 netmask 255.255.224.0 gw 192.168.1.1	Add a route to the 172.16.64.0 subnet via the router 192.168.1.1.

SCENARIO & SOLUTION

You have installed an FTP server on your company network, but you would like to restrict access to certain departments. Each department has its own subnet.	Use tcp_wrappers to block access to the FTP service for unwanted subnets.
You only have one official IP address, but you need to provide Web access to the Internet for five systems.	Use ipchains to implement IP masquerading.
You are having trouble connecting to network services from your workstation.	Use the *route -n* command to make sure your default gateway is set.

CERTIFICATION SUMMARY

Being able to ensure that a Red Hat Linux system and the information it contains is adequately protected from attack from both inside and outside sources is a normal responsibility for most Red Hat Linux system administrators. Red Hat Linux comes with a variety of utilities that can be used to establish a secure computing environment. You must select the tools and determine the level of security appropriate for your environment.

Red Hat Linux can be a powerful tool for securing networks from outside attack. You can use centralized account management with an NIS service, and provide multiple aliases for IP addresses to support multiple FTP and Web services. With tcp_wrappers and ipchains, you can turn your Red Hat Linux system into a nearly impenetrable firewall. To be a firewall, your system needs at least two Network Interface Cards (NICs). You must enable routing when two NICs are configured to be a router or a firewall. You can also use Red Hat Linux as a secure portal to the Internet for your LAN using the IP masquerading features built in to the kernel.

✔ TWO-MINUTE DRILL

The following are some of the key points from the certification objectives in Chapter 10.

Configuring NIS Client

❏ NIS allows you to share one centrally managed authorization database with other Linux systems in the network.

❏ With NIS, you maintain one password database on an *NIS server* and configure the other systems on the network to be *NIS clients.*

❏ You can configure NIS to share other files as well.

❏ To provide NIS services, you must have at least one system that serves as the *NIS master server.*

❏ The NIS master server is where the centralized NIS database files, referred to as *maps,* are stored.

❏ To make a change to an NIS database, you must update the appropriate map on the master server.

❏ You can only have one NIS master server per NIS domain.

❏ The NIS maps are stored in /var/yp/*DOMAIN*, where *DOMAIN* is the name of your NIS domain.

Basic Host Security

❏ Red Hat Linux comes with an authentication mechanism called Pluggable Authentication Modules, or PAM.

❏ PAM consists of a set of dynamically loadable library modules that allow you, as the system administrator, to determine how applications perform user authentication.

❏ The first module in the PAM configuration file for the login program is *pam_securetty.so.* This module is used to control which terminals the root account may log in from. Whenever the root account initiates a login, this module reads the file */etc/securetty.*

❏ Red Hat Linux comes with two daemons that perform logging.

❏ The kernel log daemon service, klogd, logs kernel messages and events.

❑ The syslog daemon, syslogd, logs all other process activity.

❑ You can use the log files that syslogd generates to track activities on your system

❑ You choose the events that syslogd will log using the file */etc/syslog.conf.*

xinetd

❑ xinetd is a special "superserver" program usually started at boot time.

❑ The startup script is */etc/rc.d/init.d/xinetd*; there should be links to this program in the appropriate */etc/rc.d/rc?.d* directories.

❑ The xinetd program listens for connection requests from client applications.

❑ When xinetd receives a connection request, it starts up the server program for that port, hands the port over to the server application, then goes back to waiting for another connection request.

❑ From within the */etc/xinetd.conf* file, you configure which services xinetd manages. Each individual service has its' own management script in the /etc/xinetd.d directory.

❑ You should only use xinetd to start infrequently used services.

❑ Daemons for services such as a busy Web server, which receives constant connection requests, should NOT be managed by xinetd.

❑ Red Hat Linux comes with a package called tcp_wrappers, enabled by default, that allows you to limit access to the services you offer via xinetd.

❑ You configure the access rules for tcp_wrappers using two files: */etc/hosts.allow* and */etc/hosts.deny*.

❑ Clients listed in *hosts.allow* are allowed access; clients listed in *hosts.deny* are denied access.

IP Aliasing and Virtual Hosts

❑ If you have more than one network interface card (NIC) in your Red Hat Linux system, you can attach your system to multiple networks and use it as a router between two physical subnets.

❑ With virtual host services, you can use one system as a server for multiple virtual domains.

❑ The ftpservers file is used to tell which set of virtual domain configuration files the FTPD (WU-FTPD package) server should use.

❑ If you are providing virtual host services for Web services, you should use the virtual domain mechanism built in to the Apache Web Server.

Firewall Policies—Elements

❑ A system running Red Hat Linux can make a very good *firewall* system, even if the other systems on your network are running another operating system, such as Windows NT or the Macintosh OS.

❑ Firewalls are used to secure an internal network by controlling who can connect to systems on the internal network, and by controlling what kind of information is allowed out of the internal network.

❑ As of versions 6.*x*/7.*x*, ipfw has been replaced by ipchains, which is an improvement over ipfw in several ways.

❑ The "chains" in ipchains are sets of rules applied to each network packet that passes through a Linux firewall system.

❑ Each rule does two things: it outlines the conditions a packet must meet to match the rule, and it specifies the action or *target* to take if the packet matches.

❑ You can use the firewall_config utility to configure ipchains.

Network Address Translation

❑ NAT works by modifying the header information in IP packets as they cross the firewall. As each packet passes through, the internal source address in the header is replaced with a public address.

❑ Red Hat Linux supports a variation of NAT called *IP masquerading*.

❑ IP masquerading allows you to provide Internet access to multiple computers with a single officially assigned IP address.

❑ Your firewall will need one NIC to connect to your LAN and another NIC or PPP connection for the Internet. If you have a cable modem or xDSL service, you can connect it to the second NIC.

Routing and Static Routes

❑ IP forwarding is more commonly referred to as *routing*.

❑ Routing is critical to the operation of the Internet or any IP network.

❑ To be a router, a system must have multiple network connections.

❑ A router is not usually the final destination for a network packet; instead, it is simply a waypoint for that packet en route to its final destination.

❑ A router works by examining the destination address of each packet it receives from a network interface. It then decides which network interface to send the packet back out on in order to get it to its final destination.

❑ To use a Red Hat Linux system as a router, you must enable the built-in routing support.

❑ To enable IP forwarding, edit */etc/sysconfig/network* and change the line to FORWARD_IPV4=true.

❑ The simplest method for managing routing tables is through the use of *static routes*. Static routes are entries you enter to the routing tables manually.

❑ You manage static routes using the *route* command.

SELF TEST

The following questions will help you measure your understanding of the material presented in this chapter. Read all the choices carefully, as there may be more than one correct answer. Choose all correct answers for each question.

Configuring NIS Client

1. You have a network consisting of 50 Linux workstations and five Linux servers. Most of the workstations are in public areas, and your users need to be able to log in from any workstation on the network. How might you satisfy this requirement?

   A. Keep a master copy of /etc/passwd on one of the servers, and do a backup and restore of that copy to all the workstations every evening.

   B. Set one of the servers up to be an NIS server. Arrange another server to be a NIS slave server. Make the workstations NIS clients.

   C. Set the workstations up to be NIS clients.

   D. Create a common account on every workstation and give each person the password to this account.

2. How would you set up the workstations to be NIS clients?

   A. Edit /etc/passwd and add the line USE_NIS at the end of the file.

   B. Start the ypbind daemon.

   C. Add a line to start ypbind to /etc/xinetd.conf.

   D. Run authconfig and enable NIS.

3. A user on one of the NIS workstations calls you and tells you she is having trouble changing her password using the passwd command. What should you tell her?

   A. You'll change her password for her.

   B. Try picking a more secure password.

   C. Make sure the caps lock key isn't on.

   D. She must use the yppasswd to change her NIS password.

Basic Host Security

4. Which of the following are *not* good basic host security measures?

    A. Jotting down the root password on your desk blotter.

    B. Checking system log files regularly for unusual activity.

    C. Hanging on to unused accounts in case their original users want to reactivate them.

    D. Providing users with adequate training so they know how to properly use the tools at their disposal.

xinetd

5. What are the four steps that PAM breaks the authentication process into?

    A. Authentication management, account management, session management, and password management

    B. Authentication management, account management, network management, and password management

    C. Authentication management, account logging, session management, and password management

    D. Authentication management, account management, session management, and firewall management

6. You are editing the PAM configuration file by adding a module. How would you indicate the authentication process should immediately terminate and fail if the module fails?

    A. Make sure the module is either an auth module or a password module, since these must always succeed.

    B. Use the required control flag.

    C. Use the requisite control flag.

    D. It doesn't matter; the authentication process always stops as soon as a module fails.

7. You experience a moment of forgetfulness and try to log in to the root account of your server via Telnet from your Internet connection at home. Why doesn't this work?

    A. You are using ipchains to filter out Telnet access to the root account.

    B. You miskeyed your password.

C. Login to the root account is never allowed from any terminal other than the console.

D. The network terminal device you are trying to log in from is not listed in /etc/securettys; therefore, the root account will not be allowed to log in from that terminal.

8. Assume you normally work from a user account called sysadm. How might you configure your Red Hat Linux System to notify you whenever there is a serious problem with the kernel?

A. Edit /etc/syslog.conf and add an entry such as this:

```
kern.err          root,sysadm
```

B. Recompile the kernel to include error notification and specify sysadm as the user to be notified.

C. Write a C program to monitor the /proc/err directory and send any messages that appear there to sysadm.

D. Edit /etc/syslog.conf and add an entry such as this:

```
*.*          root,sysadm
```

9. You have a server application that is only used about once a day. How would you configure this service to start so it doesn't have to run continuously?

A. Add an entry in the system cron table to start the service at about the time you think the service will be needed. Add another entry to stop the service a few minutes later.

B. Write a shell script to start the service at boot time with a file in /ect/rc.d, but use a sleep command to put the process to sleep until it's needed.

C. Start the service by adding an entry for it in /etc/services.

D. Add an entry for the application in /etc/xinetd.d.

IP Aliasing and Virtual Hosts

10. You would like to restrict access to your FTP site to clients in a particular subnet. How can you do this?

A. Use ipchains to filter out FTP requests for all but the given subnet.

B. Remove the configuration for FTPD in the /etc/xinetd.d directory.

C. Edit /etc/ftp.conf and add a reject line for all networks other than the given subnet.

D. Use tcp_wrappers and add the appropriate lines to /etc/hosts.allow and /etc/hosts.deny.

11. You are using the xinetd program to start services. How could you restrict Telnet access to be available only to clients on the 192.168.170.0 network? (Assume no other configuration has been done for tcpd.)

    A. Edit /etc/xinetd.conf and add DENY EXCEPT 192.168.170.0 to the entry for the telnet daemon.

    B. Edit /etc/hosts.allow and add this line:

```
in.telnetd : 192.168.170.0/255.255.255.0
```

    C. Edit /etc/hosts.deny and add this line:

```
in.telnetd : 192.168.170.0/255.255.255.0
```

    D. Edit /etc/hosts.deny and add this line:

```
in.telnetd : ALL EXCEPT 192.168.170.0/255.255.255.0
```

12. You work at the headquarters of a company that has several divisions. Each division is part of the headquarters LAN, but each division has its own logical subnet and its own domain. You would like to set up an internal FTP server for each division, but you don't want to have to configure and manage multiple systems. What solution can you devise?

    A. Set up a user's workstation in each division to be the FTP server and delegate the management of that server to the user of that workstation.

    B. Use NIS and set up shared virtual FTP directories.

    C. Use IP aliasing and set up virtual host services for each division.

    D. Edit /etc/xinetd.conf and change all occurrences of tcpd to virtuald.

Firewall Policies

13. You have just recently connected your organization's network to the Internet, and you are a little worried because there is nothing other than your router standing between your network and the Internet. You have a spare 200MHz PC lying around that just happens to have two Ethernet cards. You also have a mixture of systems on your network that includes Macintosh, Windows 95, and Linux. What might you do to ease your mind?

    A. Nothing, you're not advertising the systems on your LAN via DNS, so no one will ever find them.

    B. Install Red Hat Linux on the 200MHz PC and use ipchains to set it up as a firewall.

    C. Install Red Hat Linux on the 200MHz PC and use tcp_wrappers to set it up as a firewall.

    D. Install Linux on all systems on your network.

14. Consider the following command:

```
ipchains -A input -s 192.168.77.77 -j REJECT
```

What effect will this have when the client with an IP of 192.168.77.77 tries to connect to your system?

- A. No effect at all.
- B. Access will be denied, and the client application will not receive any indication of what happened.
- C. Access will be denied, and the client application will receive a message about the target destination being unreachable.
- D. You will receive a notification message on the system console.

Network Address Translation

15. You are setting up a small office and would like to provide Internet access to a small number of users, but you don't want to pay for a dedicated IP address for each system on the network. How could Linux help with the problem?

- A. Assign the official IP address to a Linux system and create accounts on that system for all of the office personnel.
- B. Install Linux and configure it for IP forwarding.
- C. Install a Linux router.
- D. Use the Linux system to connect to the Internet; then use ipchains to set up IP masquerading.

Routing and Static Routes

16. Which of the following are correct?

- A. Only routers need to maintain route tables.
- B. You must enter static routes manually.
- C. The system bases its decision on where to route a packet by looking at the packet's destination address.
- D. You don't need to worry about changing your routing tables when your network changes.

17. You are trying to connect to a remote system, but can't get through. While using the ping command to troubleshoot, you notice you can ping your own system as well as others on the same subnet as you. When you try to ping a system outside your subnet, however, you get no response. What steps can you take to resolve the problem?

    A. Contact the system administrator for the remote system and tell him to remove the ipchains DENY rule he has placed on your system.

    B. Disable tcp_wrappers for on your system.

    C. Use the route -n command and check to see you have a default gateway set. Reconfigure your network setup.

LAB QUESTION

You want to set up a secure Web server on your corporate LAN that supports inbound requests from your LAN and the Internet, but you do not want any of these requests from the Internet to get into your intranet. What can you do?

SELF TEST ANSWERS

1. ☑ **B.** This would be an ideal situation for NIS.
   ☒ **A** is incorrect because it is labor intensive and would lead to many password and database inconsistencies. **C** is incorrect because you need at least one NIS server. **D** is incorrect because this is obviously an insecure way to run a network.

2. ☑ **D.** Although you can configure NIS clients manually, the easier way is to use either the authconfig utility or the linuxconf utility.
   ☒ **A** is incorrect because this is invalid syntax. **B** is incorrect because you need to do more than start ypbind. **C** is incorrect because ypbind should be started from /etc/rc.d/init.d.

3. ☑ **D.** She must use the NIS yppasswd command to change her NIS password.
   ☒ **A, B,** and **C** are all incorrect because the user's account is a NIS account; therefore, the only valid choice is **D.**

Basic Host Security

4. ☑ **A** and **C** are both not recommended.
   ☒ **B** and **D,** on the other hand, are both good security practices.

xinetd

5. ☑ **A.** PAM breaks the authentication process into these four steps.
   ☒ **B, C,** and **D** are not the four steps that PAM breaks the authentication process into.

6. ☑ **C.** The *requisite* flag is used to indicate the authentication process should end immediately if the module fails.
   ☒ **A** is incorrect because any PAM module can fail and the authorization process will continue. **B** is incorrect because failure would be delayed until any other modules of the same type have been checked. **D** is incorrect because the control flag determines when the authorization process terminates.

7. ☑ **D.** The root account is only allowed to log in from terminals listed in /etc/securettys.
   ☒ **A** is incorrect because this is not a typical firewall function. **B** is obviously incorrect. **C** is incorrect because answer **D** explains how access can be granted.

8. ☑ **A.** Although **D** might seem like a good choice, this would also show you all messages from every facility. It would be very difficult to pick out just the kernel messages from everything else that would be coming to your screen.
   ☒ **B** and **C** are obviously incorrect because there is too much effort involved.

9. ☑ **D.** xinetd is used to start services on an as-needed basis. You tell xinetd which services to start by placing an appropriate control file in /etc/xinetd.d.

☒ **A** and **B** obviously won't work very well. **C** is incorrect because the /etc/services file is used to associate a service name with a port number.

IP Aliasing and Virtual Hosts

10. ☑ **D.** This is a good situation for tcp_wrappers.

☒ **A** is incorrect because ipchains is better used to filter entire protocols. **B** is incorrect because this would disable FTP completely. **C** is incorrect because there is no ftp.conf file.

11. ☑ **D.** Although **B** would allow the requested access, since no other configuration has been done for tcp_wrappers, /etc/hosts.deny will be empty, so other clients will be allowed access by default. The best choice is to restrict all access to the Telnet daemon and then make an exception for clients in the requested subnet.

☒ **A** is incorrect because the syntax is wrong. **C** is incorrect because it would result in Telnet access being denied to the 192.168.170.0 network.

12. ☑ **C.** Since each network has its own domain and subnet, this is the perfect situation for IP aliasing. With IP aliasing, you can use one system as the server for multiple domains.

☒ **A** is incorrect because this is an insecure way to accomplish this and would require knowledgeable users. **B** is incorrect because this isn't what NIS is used for. **D** is incorrect because you should only need to virtualize the FTP daemon.

Firewall Policies

13. ☑ **B.** Your best choice would be to take the unused PC and turn it into a firewall using Linux and IP chains. If you use a router to connect to the Internet, then your firewall system sits between your LAN and the router. This results in a two-node network consisting of the router and one of the network interfaces in your firewall that serves as a buffer zone between the Internet and your LAN. You assume that any traffic on this side of the firewall is potentially unsafe. This buffer network is sometimes referred to as the "demilitarized zone," or DMZ.

☒ **A** is incorrect because this is a poor way to secure a network. **C** is incorrect because although you might also want to use tcp_wrappers as part of your security strategy, it is designed to secure individual machines, not an entire network. Although **D** might be a good option in general, it won't necessarily make your network more secure.

14. ☑ **C.** Because of the REJECT target, the client will receive an ICMP error message. If the target was DENY, the client would receive no indication of what happened to the packet.

☒ **A, B,** and **D** describe incorrect effects when the client with an IP of 192.168.77.77 tries to connect to your system.

Network Address Translation

15. ☑ **D.** If you need to connect several systems to the Internet but only have one official IP address to use, IP masquerading is the perfect solution.

☒ **A** is incorrect unless your users want to Telnet to a single system and use a command-line interface. **B** and **C** are essentially the same answer and are both incorrect because a router will not help in this situation.

Routing and Static Routes

16. ☑ **B** and **C** are correct statements.

☒ **A** is incorrect because every system must maintain some routing information. **D** is incorrect because when your network changes, you really need to make sure your routing tables are correct.

17. ☑ **C.** In this situation, the first thing you should check is that you have a default route (or default gateway) set and that the system is up. Any packet you send that is addressed to a network other than your system's subnet must go through the router to get to its destination. If the router is down, or your system doesn't have an entry for it in its routing table, then your packets aren't going anywhere.

☒ **A, B,** and **D** are all less likely to resolve the problem.

LAB ANSWER

Scenario 1: Cost is not an object. This means you can build a DMZ, DeMilitarized Zone, using two firewalls and a separate Web server, all running Linux. You should have the Web server dedicated only to Web. You configure two more Linux hosts each with two network cards and essentially isolate the intranet behind one firewall. You then put the Web server in the middle, placing the second firewall between the Web server and the Internet. You configure the firewall on the intranet with IP Masquerading to ensure anonymity for all your intranet hosts.

Scenario 2: You have one old machine available, and the Web server is a separate machine. Use your one machine as the firewall between you and the Internet and only forward HTTP packets to the Web server IP address directly, use NAT for all intranet requests going out to the Internet for HTTP and FTP. Disallow all other services.

11

Operational Administration Recovery and Security

This final chapter of the Red Hat Linux certified study guide continues the discussion of system security started in the last chapter. This will include taking a look at secure ways to run certain network services, a Red Hat Linux-specific way of specifying file security, and installing security packages.

Also discussed is one of the most fundamental and important topics of concern to any systems administrator: what to do when a system will not boot. When the inevitable happens, knowing the right things to look for and having some tricks up your sleeve may possibly help you avoid a potential nightmare and a major loss of service for your users.

CERTIFICATION OBJECTIVE 11.01

Services Should Run as Users or nobody, Not root

When a Red Hat Linux system boots, a special process, *init*, is the first process started. The init process is responsible for starting all the other processes that comprise a working Linux system, including your own interactive shell process or X-Window session. Since the init process is responsible for keeping things going, it runs with the user ID of the root account.

If you are a new systems administrator, or are new to the UNIX or Linux world, and are configuring your first Linux system, you might make the logical assumption that any network services you install should also be run under the user ID of the root account since they are "system-wide" services. However, this is not the case if you are at all concerned about network security.

Suppose you have configured a system to start several network services running under the root user ID. Although you did your homework and made sure to load the latest security patches, a daemon for one of the services you configured has a security hole that slipped your attention. A cracker stumbles upon your system on the Internet and starts plying his craft. He soon discovers the hole in the service and, using information published on the Internet, quickly has root access to your system through the service daemon. Using this access, he is able to run a remote program on your system that gives him login access to a little-used user account.

To circumvent problems like this, services should run under their own user accounts whenever possible. That way, if a cracker does succeed in exploiting a security hole in a particular application, the damage he can do is limited because the service he has broken into is running as a normal, unprivileged user. If you do not want to create an account for every single network service you start, there is an account called *nobody* that is often used to run services. The following code listing shows a typical /etc/passwd file. Notice that most common network services have their own user accounts under which to run.

```
root:x:0:0:root:/root:/bin/bash
bin:x:1:1:bin:/bin:
daemon:x:2:2:daemon:/sbin:
adm:x:3:4:adm:/var/adm:
lp:x:4:7:lp:/var/spool/lpd:
sync:x:5:0:sync:/sbin:/bin/sync
shutdown:x:6:0:shutdown:/sbin:/sbin/shutdown
halt:x:7:0:halt:/sbin:/sbin/halt
mail:x:8:12:mail:/var/spool/mail:
news:x:9:13:news:/var/spool/news:
uucp:x:10:14:uucp:/var/spool/uucp:
operator:x:11:0:operator:/root:
games:x:12:100:games:/usr/games:
gopher:x:13:30:gopher:/usr/lib/gopher-data:
ftp:x:14:50:FTP User:/home/ftp:
nobody:x:99:99:Nobody:/:
gdm:x:42:42::/home/gdm:/bin/bash
xfs:x:100:233:X Font Server:/etc/X11/fs:/bin/false
```

EXERCISE 11-1

Verifying That Services Have Their Own Accounts

In this exercise, you will verify that certain system and network services run with their own accounts. You should try this exercise on a system that is configured to offer various network services.

At a shell prompt, issue this command:

```
[root]# ps -aux --headers | less
```

What account is the Web server (httpd) running under? What account is the identd service running under?

You should get as much hands-on experience as you can before taking the exam.

CERTIFICATION OBJECTIVE 11.02

SGID Red Hat Scheme

One major difference between Red Hat Linux and other versions of UNIX or UNIX-like operating systems that you should be aware of is how new users are assigned to groups. Using the traditional way of generating user accounts, you create one or more groups in /etc/group and then assign one of these groups to be the *primary group* for each new user account that is added. For example, you might create one group for the accounting department and a group for the information systems department in your organization. When you create accounts for new hires in the accounting department, each user account receives a unique identifier but receives the same group identifier as the other accounts that are in the accounting group. Note that user accounts can belong to more than one group; the primary group for an account is simply the default group for that account.

The user and primary group identifiers for a user are stored in the third and fourth fields, respectively, in /etc/passwd. When you look through this file on a traditional UNIX system, you will usually notice several user accounts that share a common group identifier. If you use the supplied user administration tools (useradd, linuxconf) to add users to your system and then examine the /etc/passwd file on a Red Hat Linux system, you will notice that each new user account has been assigned to its own group. This *user private group* scheme is the default behavior for creating accounts under Red Hat Linux.

The purpose for having groups in the first place is to allow users who are members of a particular group to share files. But, this also means everyone in the same group has access to the home directories of all other group members. This may not be desirable in some situations (for instance, at an ISP where no users are associated with each other).

Instead of having access to everyone else's home directories to share files, a specific shared directory is created for everyone to use. This is done by creating a directory and changing the group ownership of the directory to that of the group that is going to share files in the directory. All users who must share this resource are then added to the group entry for that group ID. Finally, you must set the Group ID bit (setgid) on this directory so that any object created in this directory will inherit the group ID associated with the directory.

For example, suppose you have a group set up for the users in the accounting department called accgrp, and you would like to create a shared directory called accshared under /home:

```
[root]# mkdir   /home/accshared
[root]# chown   nobody:accgrp  /home/accshared
[root]# chmod   2770  /home/accshared
```

Any user who is a member of the accgrp group can now create files in the /home/accshared directory. Any files generated will then be associated with the accgrp group ID, and all users listed on the accgrp line in the /etc/group file will have read, write, and execute access to the accshared directory.

```
[root]# grep accgrp /etc/group
accgrp:x:1212:stewardh,jamiec,davidw,debl,callend,vanessar
```

Normally, when a user who happens to be a member of accgrp but whose primary group is something other than accgrp creates a file in the /home/accshared directory, the user who created the file would be the owner of the file and the group ownership of the file would be the user's primary group. Unless the user who created the file remembers to issue a chgrp command on the file to set the group ownership of the file to the accgrp group, other users in that group may not have the necessary permissions to access the file.

The solution to this particular problem is to use something called the *set group id bit*, or *setgid bit*. The setgid bit is applied to a directory with the chmod command. When the setgid bit is set for a directory, any files created in that directory automatically have their group ownership set to be that of the group owner of the directory. The command to set the setgid bit for the /home/accshared directory is as follows:

```
chmod  g+s  /home/accshared
```

or, alternatively:

```
chmod  2775 /home/accshared
```

Setting the setgid bit solves the problem of making sure all files created in a shared directory belong to the correct group. The other problem that can arise has to do with permission settings. Typically, most users run with a umask setting of 022, which specifies that any files they create are not modifiable by any account that is a member of the user's group or by anyone else on the system. If the user is creating a file in a shared directory and he wishes to allow others update access to the file, he will have to remember to issue a chmod command to make the file group writeable. The way around this problem is to set the default umask (usually in /etc/profile) to be 002. With this umask, any files a user creates will be modifiable by the user and any member of the group that owns the file.

At this point, especially if you are coming from a traditional UNIX environment, you may be saying to yourself, "Wait a minute, with a umask of 002, anyone who is a member of that user's primary group will automatically have write access to any file that the user creates in his home directory!" This is the advantage behind the user private group scheme. Since every user account is the only member in its own private group, having the umask set to 002 has no detrimental effect on file security.

EXERCISE 11-2

Controlling Group Ownership with the setgid Bit

In this exercise, you will verify the effect the setgid bit has on file creation.

1. Add users called *test1*, *test2*, and *test3*. Check the /etc/passwd and /etc/group files to verify that each user's private group was created:

```
[root]# useradd test1; passwd test1
[root]# useradd test2; passwd test2
[root]# useradd test3; passwd test3
```

2. Edit the */etc/group* file and add a group called *tg1*. Make the *test1* and *test2* accounts a member of this group. The line you add should look like this:

```
[root]#  echo 'tg1::9999:test1,test2' >> /etc/group
```

Make sure the gid you assign to the group is not already in use.

3. Create a shared director for the *tg1* group:

```
[root]# mkdir  /home/testshared
```

4. Change the ownership of the shared directory:

```
[root]# chown  nobody:tg1  /home/testshared
```

5. Log in as *test1* and *test2* separately. Change the directory to the *testshared* directory and create a file. Check the ownership on the file:

```
[test1]$ date  >test.txt
[test1]$ ls  -l  test.txt
```

6. From the *root* account, set the setgid bit on the directory:

```
[root]# chmod  g+s  /home/testshared
```

7. Switch back to the *test1* account and create another file. Check the ownership on this file:

```
[test1]$ date  >testb.txt
[test1]$ ls  -l
```

8. Repeat the last step for the test2 account.

9. Switch to the test3 account and check whether they can or cannot create files in this directory, and whether they can view or not view the files in this directory.

CERTIFICATION OBJECTIVE 11.03

COPS

Properly securing any computer system, whether Red Hat Linux or otherwise, requires attention to many details. Even the most experienced system administrator can occasionally overlook something when it comes to system security. One of the tools you may wish to employ if you are securing your system from network attacks is the Computer Oracle and Password System, or COPS.

COPS is actually a suite of programs that perform a variety of security checks. If COPS finds a potential problem, it will warn you. COPS does not fix any problems it finds, although it does have an option that will generate a shell command file that can be run manually. Among the types of things COPS will check for are these:

- Permission settings on files, directories, and devices
- Bad passwords (i.e., those that are easily guessed)
- Files that are owned by root and have the SUID bit set
- Important binary files that have changed
- Holes in network service configurations

COPS is available from http://www.linux-firewall-tools.com/ftp/cops/ as a GNU-zipped tar file. You must perform some minor manual configurations to run the program (clearly explained in the README* files). You can configure COPS to mail its output to you, or you can have it leave its reports in a directory. A very effective way to use COPS is to put an entry for it in your system crontab, so that you get periodic updates on the security status of your system. The following code shows a sample report generated by COPS.

```
ATTENTION:
Security Report for Thu Oct 14 05:28:30 EDT 1999
from host localhost.localdomain

Warning!  /etc/security is _World_readable!
```

CERTIFICATION OBJECTIVE 11.04

Interaction of CMOS Clock Time and Linux System Time

Most personal computers have provisions in hardware for keeping track of the date and time. Among other purposes, the date and time values are used to record the time a file was created or modified. This date and time value is also used by the various logging utilities to timestamp events.

Knowing when something happened or when a given file was changed or accessed can be a vital tool if you are tracking down a security breach or debugging system problems. If your system time is more than a few minutes out of synch with real time, then the information in your log files and any other information that is marked with a timestamp may be nearly worthless if you are trying to determine the chronological order in which something happened.

One of the places you can change your system time is from the BIOS setup routine that is usually invoked by pressing a function key or the DEL key as the system is loading in the BIOS prior to booting into Linux. The time that you see here is the time that is actually stored in hardware. On many systems, this time will be the same as the local time. Other systems may have a requirement to keep this time in Greenwich Mean Time (GMT). If your system's hardware clock is set for GMT, then you will need to tell Linux to compensate by adding or subtracting the appropriate number of hours depending on how far east or west of the prime meridian you are.

Fortunately, this is easy to do; in fact, if you'll recall, you were asked to supply this information when you installed Red Hat Linux. If you need to change this information later, simply use the timeconfig command from a shell prompt. This will bring up the Configure Timezones screen, shown in Figure 11-1. Use the SPACEBAR to check the Hardware Clock Set To GMT box, and then TAB down to the timezone list and select your timezone using your arrow keys. TAB to OK, press ENTER, and you're done. The next time you reboot, your system time will be offset from the GMT time stored in your hardware clock.

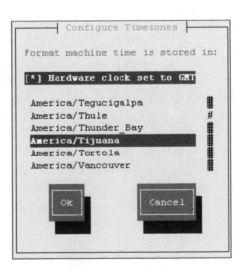

FIGURE 11-1

Use the timezone configuration screen to adjust your timezone offset

---

EXERCISE 11-3

Adjusting Your Timezone

In this exercise, you will use the timeconfig command to reconfigure your system's time offset.

1. On a test system, run the timeconfig command. Set or unset the Hardware Clock Set To GMT check box accordingly, TAB down to OK, and press ENTER.

2. Use the date command to check the current system time.

3. Reboot your system.

4. Use the date command to check the current system time. It should have changed by however many timezones away from Greenwich, England you are.

CERTIFICATION OBJECTIVE 11.05

User Process Accounting

One resource that you may not immediately think about when planning security for your site is the information that can be obtained by keeping track of user processes. The original intent behind user process accounting tools was to provide a mechanism for IS departments to keep track of the resources each account on a system used, so charges could be billed back to the account owner. With the accounting utilities, you can track such useful information as when your system was last rebooted, the last time a particular user account logged in, and the specific commands a user executed.

Support for accounting is built into the Red Hat Linux kernel, but you will need to install the psacct RPM to use some of the tools mentioned here. In Red Hat Linux 7.1, the specific RPM to install (from the second binary disk) is psacct-6.3.2-4.i386.rpm.

After you have installed the process accounting rpm, you will need to turn on process accounting using the accton command, along with the specification for the process accounting log file. The default file used for storing accounting information is /var/log/pacct, so the command to enable accounting is this:

```
[root]# /sbin/accton  /var/log/pacct
```

If you plan on running process accounting as part of your normal system configuration, you will want to add the accounting command to your /etc/rc.d/rc.local system initialization script.

There is some small overhead associated with running process accounting, but the wealth of information it provides can easily offset any small loss in performance. You can disable process accounting at any time by using the accton command without any arguments.

The information in /var/log/pacct file is written in binary, so you must use the process accounting utilities to view this information. The two commands you have for viewing the information in this file are ac and sa.

The ac command is used to print out a report of connect time. This type of information could be useful in pinpointing suspicious activity. For example, if you know that one of your users left last week for a two-week vacation in Hawaii, but notice that his account has accumulated 30-plus hours of connect time since the last time you checked, it might be a tip-off that some sort of illicit activity is occurring on your system. Of course, it could also be an indication that the user in question was so excited about his upcoming vacation that he forgot to log out, which in itself is a potential security breach.

The default action for the ac command is to print a summary of the total connect time for the system. You use options to control what information is displayed. Two of the most useful are the -d option, which provides a day-by-day summary of connect time, and the -p option, which breaks down the connect time by user. The following code shows an example of using the ac command to obtain a report of connect times for users on a system.

```
[root]# ac  -dp
        root                              2.61
Oct 12  total         2.61
        root                             14.32
        zippy                             1.01
Oct 13  total        15.33
        zippy                             2.83
        hank                              5.47
        root                             27.03
```

```
Oct 14    total              35.34
          zippy                                        1.02
          hank                                         2.50
          root                                         5.70
Today     total               9.22
```

The sa command is provided with the psacct rpm. You can use it to summarize information contained in the /var/log/pacct file. In terms of security, however, a more useful command is the lastcomm command. You can use the lastcomm command to display which commands have been executed on your system. You can restrict the information that lastcomm returns by specifying arguments for the username, command name, or a specific terminal. For example, to view a list of users who have used the su command, you would type:

```
[root]# lastcomm su.
```

In addition to the process accounting utilities, you can also glean useful information from two other files on Red Hat Linux, whether accounting is enabled or not. The files are /var/run/utmp and /var/log/wtmp. Both files store information in binary format, so you must use special utilities to access the information they contain.

The /var/run/utmp file must always exist on Red Hat Linux systems. This file is used to store information about currently running processes. It is used by utilities, such as the who command. In fact, if you feel that the who command represents a security risk, you can disable it by removing world read access from this file. Note that this file should never be writeable by any account other than root.

The /var/log/wtmp file is used by the init process and the login command to create a historical record of logins and logouts. Neither init nor login create the file, so if you want a record of logins and logouts, you should make sure the file exists. If it doesn't exist, create it using the touch command:

```
[root]# touch /var/log/wtmp; chown root:utmp /var/log/wtmp
[root]# chmod 664 /var/log/wtmp
```

If you want to disable recording of logins and logouts, simply remove /var/log/wtmp. To view the information in this file, use the *last* command. Simply issuing the command without any arguments displays the entire contents of the login database to your screen. You can limit the information that is returned by specifying a list of usernames or terminals as arguments to the *last* command. The following code shows an example of using the *last* command:

```
[root]$ last hank
hank     pts/0     192.168.1.1     Fri Jul 5 10:35    still logged in
```

```
hank     tty4                        Thu Jul 4 21:09    still logged in
hank     tty5                        Thu Jul 4 12:51 - down   (00:21)
hank     tty3                   .    Thu Jul 4 12:51 - down   (00:21)
hank     pts/0    localhost          Thu Jul 4 01:59 - 03:55  (01:55)
wtmp begins Sun Jul 1 22:02:56 2001
```

Reading from left to right, the information that is displayed in the output from the last command is the username of the account, the terminal at which this user logged in (tty terminal means either a console terminal or possibly a serial terminal; pts is a network terminal), the location the user logged in from if the terminal is a network terminal, the login time for the session, and how long the user stayed logged in. The word "down" in some of the entries indicates the session was terminated by a system shutdown. You can use the command *last reboot* to list when your system has been booted.

Another useful command for detecting suspicious activity is the lastb command. If you create the file /var/log/btmp (using the touch command), Linux will record failed login attempts in this file. You use the lastb command to display the records in this file. If you notice an unusually large number of failed login attempts for a user, it may be an indication that somcone is trying to break into your system via that account.

EXERCISE 11-4

User Process Accounting

In this exercise, you will try some of the user accounting tools.

1. Use the *last* command to view the record of logins on your system.

2. Create the file /var/log/btmp if it does not exist:

   ```
   # touch /var/log/btmp
   ```

3. Try to log in to an account on the system, but supply a bad password:

   ```
   # telnet  -l  someuser  localhost
   ```

4. Use the lastb command to view your bad login history file.

CERTIFICATION OBJECTIVE 11.06

tmpwatch

The tmpwatch command (/usr/sbin/tmpwatch) is used to remove files that have not been accessed in a specified number of hours. As its name implies, you normally run it on directories such as /tmp and /var/tmp. The tmpwatch command works recursively, so if you specify the top-level directory in a tree, tmpwatch will search through the entire directory tree looking for files to remove. To use tmpwatch to delete all files in the /tmp directory that haven't been accessed within a week (7×24=168 hours), you would use this command:

```
/usr/sbin/tmpwatch  168  /tmp
```

Although you can run the tmpwatch command interactively, you can automate this kind of housekeeping task with cron. If you do a standard install of Red Hat Linux, the /etc/cron.daily directory will contain an entry to run tmpwatch on the /tmp, /var/tmp, and /var/catman directories.

EXERCISE 11-5

Clearing Imaginary /db Directory

In a bizarre twist of fate, a runaway process has just created 200 temporary files in /db that it did not remove. You could remove them manually, or you can let tmpwatch delete all the files that are more than one hour old. Note that this removes all files over an hour old, not just these imaginary files, so this should NOT be done on a production server directory, use an example directory. If you have /db, do NOT use it.

```
[root]# CNT=1;MAX=200; # next line is the runaway process
[root]# while ( "$CNT" -ne "$MAX" );do touch /db/bad$CNT; done
[root# ls /db | wc -w  # how may files need to be removed
200
[root]# wait 3690 # wait 1 hour and 1.5 minutes
[root]# tmpwatch 1 /db # remove everything in /db that is over 1 hr old
[root]# ls /db/bad*  # files should be gone
```

As an alternative to this, if you have a backup of any files, or a tar archive that is more than an hour old, then you can extract some files into a dummy directory, like /db, and have tmpwatch delete them. If they are all more than seven days old, then use 168 as the criteria. You could even try various times to see which files are deleted. This may not be practical if you do not have current files, because you would have to calculate the number of hours between now and the backup date to selectively delete files.

CERTIFICATION OBJECTIVE 11.07

Emergency Boot Procedures

At some point in your career as a Red Hat Linux systems administrator, you're going to be faced with a system that will not boot. It will be up to you to determine the cause of the problem and implement a fix. Sometimes, the problem may be due to hardware failure: the system in question has a bad power supply or has experienced a hard disk crash. Quite often, however, the failure of a system to boot can be traced back to the actions of a user: you, the system administrator! When you are editing certain system configuration files, leaving off a character or adding a character in the wrong place can render your system unbootable. Improperly configured system files probably cause more boot failures than actual hardware problems. A corollary to this bit of knowledge is that any time you plan to make any substantial modifications to your system or change certain configuration files (we'll discuss which ones later), make a backup of the configuration file(s) first. Then, after making changes, you should actually reboot your system rather than assume that it will boot up the next time you need a reboot. It's much better to encounter problems while you can still remember exactly which changes you made. It is even better if you can go back to a working configuration file.

Alternative Methods for Booting a System

To prepare for boot failures, you should make sure you have a valid boot floppy for your system and knowledge regarding how to get to rescue mode using a floppy and the CD-ROM (or just the CD-ROM if your system will boot from it).

If you want to save some time and trouble, there was a single floppy-based "rescue" diskette that you could use to recover your system, which came with Red Hat 6.0 and before. If you go to any Linux archive, you can probably get a copy of it. It will be a file like Rescue.img, similar to the Boot.img and Bootnet.img disk files. Use the same method to create this rescue floppy, use dd in Linux or the supplied Rawrite.exe on the first binary CD.

To create a rescue disk, you need to mount your Red Hat Linux distribution CD and dump the rescue disk image to a floppy. Assuming you mounted your distribution CD to /mnt/cdrom, the easiest way to do this is with this command:

```
[root]# cat /mnt/cdrom/images/rescue.img >/dev/fd0
```

Or if you have copied the rescue.img file into /download, use this:

```
[root]# cd /download; dd if=rescue.img of=/dev/fd0
```

Using mkbootdisk

When you installed Red Hat Linux, one of the last things you were asked was whether to make a boot disk. If you answered No to this prompt, you can use the mkbootdisk command to create a valid (specifically knows which partition on this system has /boot and / in them) boot floppy. The mkbootdisk command reads your /etc/lilo.conf file to create a boot image that can be used to boot your system from the floppy. To use the mkbootdisk command, you must specify which version of the kernel (in /boot) to store on the floppy disk. For example, to make a boot disk for the standard Red Hat Linux 7.1 kernel, use this command:

```
[root]# mkbootdisk 2.4.2-2
```

Alternatively, you can generate the kernel ID using uname:

```
[root]# mkbootdisk 'uname -r'
```

You may be able to fix some problems that arise, such as accidentally deleting your master boot record, by simply booting from your boot disk. Other problems may require the use of rescue mode. If the kernel can't locate the root file system, or if the root file system is damaged, the Linux kernel will issue a kernel panic and halt as shown in the following code:

```
.
.
.
.Partition check:
had: hda1 hda2 < hda5 hda6 hda7 >
autodetecting RAID arrays
autorun ?
? autorun DONE.
VFS: Cannot open root device 00:30
Kernel panic: VFS: Unable to mount root fs on 00:30
```

Although this may look very bad the first time you encounter it, often the problem can easily be fixed from rescue mode with a little bit of work.

The boot disk and rescue mode from the CD install a compact version of a root file system that has a minimal set of utilities that will allow you to mount a disk and either repair the problem with the disk or pull files off the disk. If you do not have a functioning Linux system from which to make a rescue disk, you can also create a rescue disk from DOS, using the rawrite.exe program located in the dosutils directory on your Linux distribution CD. You can also use this program to make a copy of the generic boot disk, boot.img, if you did not make a specific boot floppy for your system.

To boot into rescue mode, first boot your system either using your boot floppy or directly with the first binary CD in a bootable CD-ROM drive (Figure 11-2).

At the boot: prompt, type **linux rescue** and press ENTER.

After the kernel is loaded from this boot floppy, you will be prompted to enter your rescue disk.

The minimal root image from this rescue mode (or on the rescue disk) will be loaded into the RAM disk created by the kernel, and you will be placed at a root shell prompt (#). At this point, you have access to a basic set of commands. You can mount file systems, create directories, move and edit files using the pico editor, and perform other functions. The file doc/rescue.txt on your documentation CD has a complete list of the commands available to you.

The great difficulty in operating from the rescue environment is that you are working with a minimal version of the Linux operating system. Many of the commands you are used to having at your disposal are not available at this level. If your root partition has not been completely destroyed, you may be able to mount this partition to your temporary root directory in memory and access commands from there.

Enter rescue
mode from the
Linux boot
screen.

```
                      Welcome to Red Hat Linux 7.1!
   -  To install or upgrade Red Hat Linux in graphical mode,
      press the <ENTER> key.

   -  To install or upgrade Red Hat Linux in text mode, type: text <ENTER>.

   -  To enable low resolution mode, type: lowres <ENTER>.
      Press <F2> for more information about low resolution mode.

   -  To disable framebuffer mode, type: nofb <ENTER>.
      Press <F2> for more information about disabling framebuffer mode.

   -  To enable expert mode, type: expert <ENTER>.
      Press <F3> for more information about expert mode.

   -  To enable rescue mode, type: linux rescue <ENTER>.
      Press <F5> for more information about rescue mode.

   -  If you have a driver disk, type: linux dd <ENTER>.

   -  Use the function keys listed below for more information.

   [F1-Main] [F2-General] [F3-Expert] [F4-Kernel] [F5-Rescue]
   boot:
```

exam
Ⓦatch

One important thing to make note of is that if you mount partitions from your hard drive from rescue mode and then make changes to files on those partitions, you will need to use the sync command to manually flush changes you make to files from memory to the disk drive. As a precaution, run the sync command three times before exiting from rescue mode just in case. Remember to perform an unmount on any partitions you had mounted. When you have finished working in rescue mode, you must use the exit command to halt the system and then restart the system to reboot.

Single-User Mode

One other option that is available to you if you are experiencing system problems is to boot into *single-user mode*. Your system may not have problems finding its root partition and starting the boot process, but may encounter problems when changing into one of the higher runlevels. If this is the case, you can still use the boot partition and root partition on your hard drive, but you want to tell Linux to perform a minimal boot process. To boot into single-user mode, issue this command:

```
lilo: linux  s
```

Actually, linux [s | 1 | single] are all valid. Linux will boot into a minimal runtime environment, and you will receive a bash shell prompt (*bash#*). Note that when you boot into single-user mode, no password is required to access the system. Running your system in single-user mode is somewhat similar to running a system booted into rescue mode. Many of the commands and utilities you normally use are unavailable. You may have to mount additional drives or partitions and specify the full pathname when running some commands. When you have corrected the problem, you can reboot the system or use the init or telinit commands to bring the system up to its normal runlevel.

What to Look for When Things Go Wrong

Although there are potentially many things that will cause a system not to boot, they can roughly be categorized as either hardware problems or software and configuration problems. The most common hardware-related problem you will probably encounter is a bad hard disk drive; like all mechanical devices with moving parts, these have a finite lifetime and will eventually fail. Hardware problems can sometimes be fairly easy to diagnose; you turn the power switch on and nothing happens. Software and configuration problems, however, can be a little more difficult. They can sometimes appear to be hardware problems at first glance. Often, the hardest part of fixing a system that won't boot is figuring out what the cause of the problem is.

on the *job*

After being away from the office for a week, you come back to notice the main Web server was powered off. This seems very odd. All the other servers are running so that means the UPS is fine. The power on switch does not respond after the first few attempts, but then it finally starts up. After stepping away for a few minutes, then returning, the machine is again in a powered off state. The system was in the process of starting, so that means the disks are probably fine. The culprit turns out to be the power supply on the machine. The power supply is quickly replaced and the machine starts immediately. What a relief!

One place you can look for information when diagnosing problems with a system is the LILO boot loader. When you see the LILO prompt on your screen before your system boots, LILO is actually conveying the information to you that it was able to successfully load its components into memory. If you do not see the LILO prompt, or only see part of the LILO prompt, this indicates that LILO had problems finding everything it needed to do its job. Table 11-1 summarizes how to interpret the *LILO* boot prompt for error information.

In addition to knowing how to mount disk partitions, edit files, and manipulate files, there are several other commands you will need to know how to use in order to be able to fix problems from rescue mode or single-user mode. Three of the most useful are the fdisk command, the e2fsck command, and the lilo command. Unfortunately, the commands you don't have access to at this level include the man pages and the info utility. So, in the event that you do not have a hardcopy manual nearby or another working Linux system at your disposal, it helps to know how to use these commands at a rudimentary level at least.

fdisk

You may have already encountered the fdisk utility when you installed Red Hat Linux. It is one of the choices you are given when setting up disk partitions during the install process. You can invoke fdisk at any time from a command prompt, but you must indicate, with a single argument, which disk you want fdisk to work with. One of the first things you will want to know, if you are trying to rescue a system, is what partitions you have available for mounting. You can use the fdisk -l (list option) command to obtain this information. The following code shows an example of using the fdisk command to display the partition information for a system.

TABLE 11-1	Error	Description
The LILO Boot Prompt Can Provide Useful Debugging Information	Nothing	LILO not loaded.
	L	First stage loaded but not second stage; usually indicates disk problems or invalid parameters in /etc/lilo.conf.
	LI	Second stage loaded but invalid parameters in /etc/lilo.conf, or /boot/boot.b was moved without running /sbin/lilo.
	LIL	Second stage started, but can't load descriptor table because of a bad disk or invalid parameters in /etc/lilo.conf.
	LIL?	Second stage loaded at wrong address, caused by invalid parameters in /etc/lilo.conf, or /boot/boot.b was moved without running /sbin/lilo.
	LIL-	Invalid parameters in /etc/lilo.conf, or /boot/boot.b moved without running /sbin/lilo.
	LILO	LILO successfully loaded.

```
[root]# fdisk
Usage: fdisk [-l] [-b SSZ] [-u] device
E.g.: fdisk /dev/hda  (for the first IDE disk)
or: fdisk /dev/sdc  (for the third SCSI disk
or: fdisk /dev/eda  (for the first PS/2 ESDI drive)
or: fdisk /dev/rd/c0d0  or: fdisk /dev/ida/c0d0  (for RAID devices)
...


[root]# fdisk -l /dev/hda

Disk /dev/hda: 240 heads, 63 sectors, 559 cylinders
Units = cylinders of 15120 * 512 bytes

Device     Boot   Start      End    Blocks  Id  System
/dev/hda1    *        1       41   309928+   6  FAT16
/dev/hda2            42      559  3916080    5  Extended
/dev/hda5            42       44    22648+  83  Linux
/dev/hda6            45       53    68000+  82  Linux swap
/dev/hda7            54      192  1050808+  83  Linux
```

Looking at the output from the fdisk command just shown, you can immediately see that if you were searching for the appropriate partitions to mount in rescue mode, /dev/hda5 and /dev/hda7 look like the most logical choices. Furthermore, you could probably conclude that, based on the size of the partitions, /dev/hda5 is the partition that is normally mounted to /boot, and /dev/hda7 is the root partition.

For simple partitioning schemes, this is easy. It gets far more complicated when you have lots of partitions, as in this next example. You should always have some documentation available that clearly identifies your partition layout within your file system:

```
[root]# fdisk -l /dev/had
Disk /dev/hda: 255 heads, 63 sectors, 2495 cylinders
Units = cylinders of 16065 * 512 bytes

Device     Boot   Start      End    Blocks   Id  System
/dev/hda1    *        1      255   2048256    c  Win95 FAT32 (LBA)
/dev/hda2           256      257     16065   83  Linux
/dev/hda3           258     2495  17976735    5  Extended
/dev/hda5           258      576   2562336   83  Linux
/dev/hda6           577      608    257008+  83  Linux
/dev/hda7           609      634    208813+  83  Linux
/dev/hda8           635      660    208813+  83  Linux
/dev/hda9           661      673    104391   83  Linux
/dev/hda10          674      686    104391   83  Linux
/dev/hda11          687      699    104391   83  Linux
/dev/hda12          700      712    104391   83  Linux
/dev/hda13          713      723     88326   82  Linux swap
```

```
/dev/hda14       724      978    2048256    83   Linux
/dev/hda15       979     1900    7405933+   83   Linux
/dev/hda16      1901     2495    4779306    83   Linux
```

In the previous code example, you can see the swap and can probably guess at the /boot partition, but after that, you have no real idea without a proper file system "map."

There is a possible answer, however. Added to version 7.*x* of Red Hat is the ability to mark disks with labels. So, you might be able to check the label to find out what the disk was mounted as, using the e2label command as follows:

```
[root]# e2label
Usage: e2label device [newlabel]
[root]# e2label /dev/hda5
/usr
[root]#
```

File System Check—e2fsck

You should also know how to use the e2fsck command. The e2fsck command performs the same function on the Linux second extended file system as the fsck command does on a standard UNIX file system: it is used to check the file system on a partition for consistency. In order to effectively use the e2fsck command, you need to understand something about how file systems are laid out on disk partitions.

When you format a disk partition under Linux, using the mke2fs command, the mke2fs command sets aside a certain portion of the disk to use for storing *inodes*, which are data structures that contain the actual disk block addresses that point to file data on a disk. The mke2fs command also stores information about the size of the file system, the file system label, and the number of inodes in a special location at the start of the partition called the *superblock*. If the superblock is corrupted or destroyed, the remaining information on the disk is unreadable. Because the superblock is so vital to the integrity of the data on a partition, the mke2fs command makes duplicate copies of the superblock at fixed intervals on the partition. The locations of the copies are dependent upon the block size of the filesystem (examples are provided in the e2fsck(8) manual page).

The e2fsck command checks for, and corrects problems with, file system consistency by looking for things such as disk blocks that are marked as free but are actually in use (and vice versa), inodes that don't have a corresponding directory entry, inodes with incorrect link counts, and a number of other problems. The e2fsck command will also fix a corrupted superblock. If fsck fails due to a corrupt superblock, you can use the e2fsck command with the -b option to specify an alternative superblock. For example, the command:

```
# e2fsck  -b  -n  8193  /dev/hda5
```

tells e2fsck to perform a consistency check on the file system on disk partition /dev/hda5. The -n option is used to tell e2fsck to automatically assume you answered no to all questions and prompts. It's common to use the -n option to determine the extent of file system damage that may have to be repaired, without actually performing the repairs. You can then run e2fsck again, replacing the -n with a -y to actually perform all the repairs specified during the previous -n run.

exam
ⓦatch

Get to know e2fsck and these options.

lilo

You should run lilo whenever you rebuild your Linux kernel, change disk partitions, or do anything else that might affect the physical location of the files in /boot. If you make changes and forget to do this, you will have to boot into rescue mode and fix the problem. Although you may be familiar with using the lilo command when your system is running normally, you will have to make some adjustments when running lilo from rescue mode.

As an example, suppose you have a Linux system and have configured a separate */boot* and a separate root partition. The /boot partition is on /dev/hda1, and the root partition is on /dev/hda5. You forgot to run lilo or make an emergency boot disk after rebuilding your kernel, so you have had to boot into rescue mode to fix the problem. Since you are running in the rescue environment, the rescue RAM disk is mounted as your root file system. Rescue mode will typically be able to locate and mount your filesystems under /mnt/sysimage; if your filesystems aren't mounted automatically, you should be able to mount them yourself, as in this example:

```
# mkdir  /tmpmnt

# mount  /dev/hda5  /tmpmnt
# mount  /dev/hda1  /tmpmnt/boot
```

At this point, if necessary, you could edit the lilo.conf file and make changes:

```
# cd  /tmpmnt/etc
# pico  lilo.conf
(make changes to lilo.conf if necessary)
```

Now you're ready to run lilo. Since you're in rescue mode, you will have to specify the path for the lilo command. The other thing you will need to do is use the -r option to tell lilo to use an alternative root (remember, your current root is the RAM disk file system). This will enable lilo to locate its configuration file and the /boot directory:

```
..      # /sbin/lilo  -r  /tmpmnt
```

You should receive confirmation from lilo that the boot block was written. The only thing left to do is to flush your changes from memory to the disk drive, unmount the partitions, and reboot:

```
# sync     #repeat,, or just wait a few seconds#
# sync
# sync
# cd  /
# umount  /dev/hda1
# umount  /dev/hda5
# exit
```

Places to Look First

Two places where you are likely to make errors that result in a nonbootable system are in the files /etc/lilo.conf and /etc/fstab. In both of these files, identifying the wrong partition as the root partition (specifying /dev/hda when you meant /dev/hda1, for example) can result in a kernel panic. Other configuration errors in /etc/lilo.conf will also cause a kernel panic at boot time. Any time you make changes to these files, you should reboot your system if at all possible, and test that things work as you intended.

exam
⦿atch

As a Red Hat Linux administrator, you will be expected to know how to fix systems when things break. For this reason, a substantial portion of the exam is devoted to testing your troubleshooting and analysis skills.

Summary of the Rescue Process

To summarize, here are the basic steps to follow when you are trying to restore a system from a rescue disk:

■ Boot using your system's boot floppy.

■ Insert your rescue disk when prompted.

- At the rescue shell prompt, use fdisk -l to identify your partitions if necessary.

- If file system problems are suspected or indicated, run e2fsck on the afflicted partitions.

- If the problem is with a configuration file:

    1. Create (a) temporary mountpoint(s), if necessary

    2. Mount the appropriate partition(s), if necessary.

    3. Use the pico editor to fix the problem.

    4. Run lilo if you are making changes to lilo.conf or the /boot partition.

- Sync your changes to the drive.

- Unmount any mounted partitions.

- *Exit* and restart the system.

on the
Job
Whenever you're working in rescue mode or single-user mode, always remember to sync your drives before halting.

EXERCISE 11-5

Performing an Emergency Boot Procedure

To do this exercise, you should have a test system at your disposal. Do not try this exercise on any system on which you are not prepared to lose all of the data on the system.

In this exercise, you will "break" your system by purposely misconfiguring a file and then reboot into rescue mode to fix the problem. You will have to replace the partitions used in the commands for the /boot and root partitions with the actual partitions that are used for the /boot and root partitions on your system.

1. Make sure you have the Red Hat Linux distribution cd mounted:

   ```
   # mount /dev/cdrom /mnt/cdrom
   ```

2. If the mkbootdisk RPM is not installed, install it:

   ```
   # rpm -i /mnt/cdrom/RedHat/RPMS/mkbootdisk*
   ```

3. If you do not have a boot disk and a rescue disk, make them. Insert a floppy into the disk drive and type the following:

```
# mkbootdisk 'uname -r'
```

4. Edit the file /etc/lilo.conf and make a copy of your boot stanza. Label this stanza badboot. Change the location of the root device to point to an invalid partition. For example, if your original lilo.conf looks like this:

```
boot=/dev/hda
map=/boot/map
install=/boot/boot.b
prompt
timeout=50
image=/boot/vmlinuz-2.2.5-15
        label=linux
        root=/dev/hda7
        read-only
other=/dev/hda1
        label=dos
        table=/dev/hda
```

5. Your new version should look like this:

```
boot=/dev/hda
map=/boot/map
install=/boot/boot.b
prompt
timeout=50
image=/boot/vmlinuz-2.4.2-2
        label=linux
        root=/dev/hda7
        read-only
image=/boot/vmlinuz-2.4.2-2
        label=badboot
        root=/dev/hda
        read-only
other=/dev/hda1
        label=dos
        table=/dev/hda
```

6. Run lilo to update your boot mappings:

```
# lilo
```

7. You should see a message similar to this:

```
Added linux *
Added badboot
Added dos
```

8. Reboot your system. At the LILO prompt, select badboot. You should see the boot process start, then receive a kernel panic message.

9. Since you left a valid boot stanza, your system isn't really broken. To fix the problem, however, we're going to boot into rescue mode. Insert your CD-ROM (or boot disk and CD-ROM), and reboot the system. At the boot prompt type linux rescue.

10. Although you know the source of the problem, once you boot into rescue mode, you should familiarize yourself with some of the repair utilities:

```
# fdisk  -l
   Device  Boot     Start        End    Blocks   Id  System
/dev/hda1    *          1         41   309928+    6  FAT16
/dev/hda2              42        559  3916080     5  Extended
/dev/hda5              42         44    22648+   83  Linux
/dev/hda6              45         53    68000+   82  Linux swap
/dev/hda7              54        192  1050808+   83  Linux

e2fsck  -y  /dev/hda5   # your output will vary
e2fsck 1.19, 13-Jul-2000 for EXT2 FS 0.5b, 95/08/09
/dev/hda5: clean, 23/5664 files, 3008/22648 blocks
```

11. Create (a) temporary mount point(s) for your /boot and root partitions, and mount those partitions (if not already mounted).

```
# mkdir  /tmpmnt
# mount  /dev/hda7  /tmpmnt
# mount  /dev/hda5  /tmpmnt/boot
```

12. Edit the bad stanza in lilo.conf and fix the problems:

```
# pico  /tmpmnt/etc/lilo.conf
```

13. Your new version should look like this:

```
image=/boot/vmlinuz-2.4.2-2
      label=badboot
      root=/dev/hda7
      read-only
```

14. Save your changes to the lilo.conf file. Now you must run lilo to update your boot block:

```
# /tmpmnt/sbin/lilo  -r  tmpmnt
```

15. Sync your changes and unmount any mounted partitions:

```
# sync
# sync
# cd
# unmount  /dev/hda5
# unmount  /dev/hda7
```

16. Remove any boot media from your disk drives. Type **exit** to halt the system; then restart the system. You should now be able to boot from the badboot stanza.

Using the Secure Shell Package—OpenSSH

Red Hat Linux now includes the OpenSSH Secure Shell package. This package is also available from the Internet. The Secure Shell (ssh) and secure copy program (scp) are secure replacements for the rsh, telnet, and rcp programs. The secure daemon, sshd, listens for all inbound traffic on port 22.

OpenSSH is a refinement of the original (free) ssh 1.2.12 release, with bugs removed and new features added. After the 1.2.12 release of ssh, more restrictive license requirements were added to each new release. The OpenSSH version has removed and/or replaced all restrictive component coding. It is also important to point out that this OpenSSH version supports ssh protocol versions 1.3, 1.5, and 2.0, but defaults to 2.0.

Matched Keys for the Encryption Algorithm

When using a standard mathematical formula (algorithm) that has unpredictable output, if you have a big enough number, the chance of stumbling onto this number is infinitesimal, and so is the output from this formula when using this number. There are quite a few known algorithms that are used, one such is SHA and is very commonly used. The way it all works is that you must create a pair of numbers for this formula that are then unique for you. The numbers are so large, typically at least 512 bits, that the chance of duplicates is very small. These 2 numbers are referred to as your private key (a value) and your public key (also a value). You encrypt the data with some lesser but equally strong standard, like DES (56 bit) or Triple DES (168 bit) (or blowfish, and so on). Then you checksum this data and finally you digitally "sign" (use your big fancy key and formula to encrypt this checksum) the data (which is to say that you add your final "signature" value). A third part of the keys used to encrypt the data is the target. Only the target (an e-mail or SSL site) can decrypt this package. You use your private key and the target to encrypt; the target can use your public key.

Private Keys

Your private key (essentially a file containing your special number) must be maintained as your secret. You, or your applications, "attach it" to your program(s) and these programs use it on your behalf. Anything you send, say from your e-mail account, can then be digitally signed (data encrypted, checksum thereof encrypted with your public key and added to the end as your signature), and ONLY the recipient will be able to decrypt the message.

Public Keys

Your public key value is just that, publicly available. A central authority, (CA), like Verisign, Thawte, and so on, provides public access to public keys they have created. They would also keep a copy of the private key securely on their system if they were the ones who generated it. You can just attach your public key to the e-mail, or the end users can publicly retrieve it from some the CA site, it matters not. Only with their e-mail account and this public key can they decrypt the message.

The following example shows the directories and files associated with SSH usage as well as a public key that has been "added" to your "keyring":

```
[dreg]$ ls .ss* -d
.ssh   .ssh2
[dreg]$ ls .ssh2
AdminKey.pub   authorization
[dreg]$ cat .ssh2/AdminKey.pub
— BEGIN SSH2 PUBLIC KEY —
Subject: AdminKey
Comment: "Administrator@ji7j8bn6"
AAAAB3NzaC1yc2EAAAABJQAAAIEAkuxZwxs7gxdZu1kP+3IwCR/AEXlK/piPRQ8PuF19rj
cSX57L97G9QA+3NryI14mKDZ4TtOwjYCY2/zUOXy87HsHXLXnb/3PgTwrAzH4pdvoBOGlh
iPkwn+pSDXW65hJ5r/xGBjEseAdL8S9OJ+SR6G7r4TVrgaUb3Z6zw1iFuW8=
```

```
— END SSH2 PUBLIC KEY —
[dreg]$
```

These terms "keyring" and "added to your keyring" are used within the SSH applications to denote the location, and the adding of one of these huge numbers (public key) to your system in some format conducive to the application wanting to use it (your "keyring" in this case is just files in the .ssh and .ssh2 directories). Specifically, the .ssh2 (an alternative, and also free, version that uses a newer encoding standard, found at www.ssh.org) directory is used by the ssh2 client applications (secure versions of Telnet, ftp, rcp). This is where they look for public keys or deposit them after usage.

In the case of an e-mail application, it would internally keep the key, as shown in Figure 11-3.

The Hash Algorithm is SHA1 or MD5, the encryption algorithms for the data part are 3DES (Triple DES: - Data Encryption Standard set by the US Government), RC2 in either 128-bit (fairly secure), 40-bit (not very secure anymore), or just (single) DES (56-bit) encryption.

This key is like a password used to encrypt your data. Imagine trying to remember the 1024-bit number expressed in hexadecimal value (Figure 11-4)! That is why the applications save this value for you, on a "public keyring." You can add as many public keys from other users, sites, and services that you wish.

FIGURE 11-3

Sample e-mail key

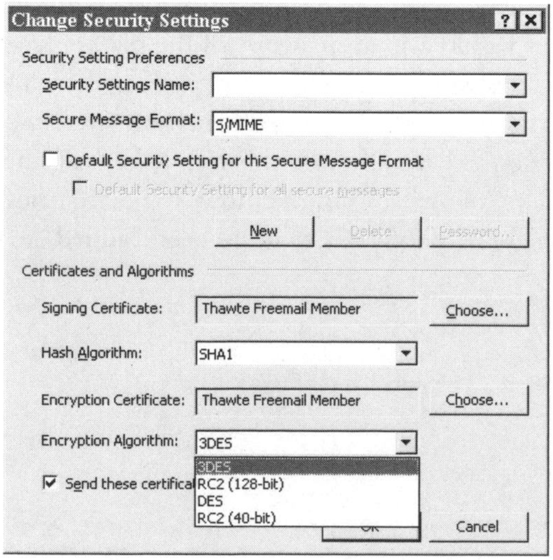

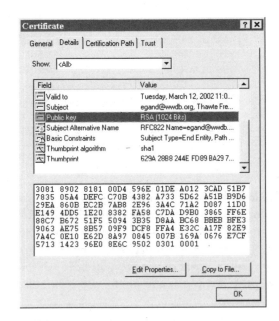

A sample
Certificate
showing the
1024-bit public
key value

Your private key is similar, BUT YOU MUST KEEP IT PRIVATE, or this
whole system does not work. Keeping it private means no one should have access to
your PC, or if they do, you put a passphrase (password) in order to use this key.
Anyone that knows the passphrase can essentially "sign" your name onto a
document:

```
[dreg]$ ls .ssh2
AdminKey.pub  authorization
[dreg]$ cat .ssh2/AdminKey.pub
— BEGIN SSH2 PUBLIC KEY —
Subject: AdminKey
Comment: "Administrator@ji7j8bn6"
AAAAB3NzaC1yc2EAAAABJQAAAIEAkuxZwxs7gxdZu1kP+3IwCR/AEX1K/piPRQ8PuF19rj
cSX57L97G9QA+3NryI14mKDZ4TtOwjYCY2/zUOXy87HsHXLXnb/3PgTwrAzH4pdvoBOGlh
iPkwn+pSDXW65hJ5r/xGBjEseAdL8S9OJ+SR6G7r4TVrgaUb3Z6zw1iFuW8=
— END SSH2 PUBLIC KEY —
[dreg]$ cat .ssh2/authorization
Key AdminKey.pub
[dreg]$ ls .ssh
known_hosts2
[dreg]$ cat .ssh/known_hosts2
iel.ath.cx,24.207.33.19 ssh-dss
AAAAB3NzaC1kc3MAAACBAPLYZR13Ny1D4tMjEDZi5KKHb30fpzfUS6bNWv4N2TYJenMsCSnxIkkh7
npasu/zlGIne4Rvs55qsbeB8EoEb+/XsWKft9Hj72s5Uvy1+ErN9XmdoazNG4/BPGlw31T3BL4TIr
```

```
QvGfE07lxf7Cn1dWst9UzL71r1E914KR1kMeH1AAAAFQDz4sNW5a+4ou6Tycq+PvtqNRO8JQAAAIE
A1KPCUSVCiCroPc3PIpVEozYBVZ3cCoYkqJI0xixQ1myLYYdWGFiO9i4h2oTQFb1TnDPF5PFKxqVA
38ARmZpx6Iw/xpftj7pWgw6q6R0ve/dvObx7F/Tdoq+yqrKisCfxSdniQLjf8YdwQVBuP1RfthNB6
QUKcv+nfIey3fBxZ1QAAACBANKaKUwcCNoHZbPJ39uYOjnyS0P/66OmGBf/PU4y8avEACSxG+/pXd
gs06zA/sbtH/2yDTU15O77RSJFpGZDYyhUjp+1J0I+ynIdW73PsXuBypgMTgTk/7YpWjS/PukKke8
kvYwf4H6gVtpzjxtOrZg9yyq66/vc9OATN/OebiMB
```

In the previous listing, the files and directories created by and for ssh are shown, as well as some public keys on the local users' "keyring." The keyring is the .ssh/known_hosts2 file, which contains the public key of a host and its IP address.

on the !ob

The known hosts file maintains the name and its IP address, plus the public key of hosts visited. If this client uses DHCP to get its IP address, then whenever it changes, your login is no longer valid, as these numbers do not all jive. The system response, however, may not indicate that it is because of the IP address. To get around it, you have to remove this entry and let your system rebuild the entry at the next valid connection.

Digital Signatures Legalized in USA

In the summer of 2000, the U.S. Government digitally and physically "signed" an act of congress making your "digital signature" as valid as your handwriting. For businesses that want to transact over the Internet, this was a major hurdle that has now been overcome and should spur electronic commerce even more.

How to Generate Your Keys

There are a few ssh-oriented utilities you need to know about:

- **sshd** The daemon service; this must be running for inbound ssh client requests.

- **ssh-agent** A program to hold private keys used for RSA authentication. The idea is that ssh-agent is started in the beginning of an X-session or a login session, and all other windows or programs are started as clients to the ssh-agent program.

- **ssh-add** Adds RSA identities to the authentication agent, ssh-agent.

- **ssh** ssh (Secure Shell) is a secure Telnet/rlogin into a remote machine, and can also replace rcp for executing commands on a remote machine. The authentication method is two-fold, the rhosts or hosts.equiv method combined with RSA-based host authentication means that if the login would be permitted by $HOME/.rhosts, $HOME/.shosts, /etc/hosts.equiv, or /etc/ssh/shosts.equiv, and if additionally the server can verify the client's host key (looks in /etc/ssh_known_hosts and then $HOME/.ssh/known_hosts), only then is login permitted. This two-fold authentication method closes security holes due to IP, DNS, and routing types of spoofing.

■ **ssh-keygen** A utility that will create your keys for you. You can let it prompt you or you can enter some or all of the requested information as shown in the following listing. (The sample inputs entered are in **boldface** type.)

```
[dreg]$ ls /usr/bin/ssh*
ssh          ssh-add      ssh-agent    ssh-keygen   sshd
[dreg]$ ssh-keygen -?
ssh-keygen: invalid option -- ?
Usage: ssh-keygen [-lpqxXydc] [-b bits] [-f file] [-C comment] [-N new-pass]
[-P pass]
[dreg]$ ssh-keygen   # with no arguments, prompts user
Generating RSA keys:
.........................................oooooooO...............
Key generation complete.
Enter file in which to save the key (/home/davidw/.ssh/identity): dw.main.key
Enter passphrase (empty for no passphrase):
Enter same passphrase again:
Your identification has been saved in dw.main.key.
Your public key has been saved in dw.main.key.pub.
The key fingerprint is:
8a:51:fe:3a:8d:a1:7d:7e:8b:cc:8c:7e:27:c3:92:34 davidw@jctx.ath.cx
[dreg]$
[dreg]$ ssh-keygen -b 1024 -f dreg.private -C "Private key for Dreg"
Generating RSA keys: ..........................oooooooO.........oooooooO
Key generation complete.
Enter passphrase (empty for no passphrase):
Enter same passphrase again:
Your identification has been saved in dreg.private.
Your public key has been saved in dreg.private.pub.
The key fingerprint is:
b9:58:b5:e0:ab:ca:e4:e5:a2:78:8b:ec:72:ad:23:38 Private key for Dreg
[dreg]$ ls dreg*
dreg.private  dreg.private.pub
[dreg]$ cat dreg.private
SSH PRIVATE KEY FILE FORMAT 1.1
```

```
³AvD'-?<yÚCâÉ?Ê´WÌôL¼?Uê =?|DZîeúôg,L?ý&°d¬"à-§JiU='\ 1ñ®TÄ¡ûlTÜ²d&-¹Dö _Ñ5-
TÕ<<Unicode: 90>>%þöÜ½iVùÁÎ?ãú³*Ñ'{$,ArÓ h,SÌ¾EG¡#Private key for
Dregw<~"Å,6b Òw1"øÝãÀ)cz¥ XíÖ'?g<<Unicode:
90>>"m¨Õa_Ëï¶pøs¨4G7>dÒlöMeÇßYå8È,#Ä'ÇKf-
```

```
[dreg]$ cat dreg.private.pub
1024 35
125877640929260329473583693396328213581674683925240666434953239109144700218895
844000098600157780873157857246207414026621121984426895911631809164480145959528
242513335728238609966626392893880645779963619555947513430562133011867544583923
809080447344109015934844362623969262140371702674173901591088172837847223337
Private key for Dreg
[dreg]$
```

The previous listing shows the various ssh utility names, then displays sample usage of the ssh-keygen program, with and without arguments, and ends with a display of the actual private and public key files that were generated (edited here for brevity).

Why Use SSH?

The Internet is a public network, that means anyone in the world can access this public network; like a public library, anyone can enter to use it. Private networks are used for security within an organization, like the VISA or Mastercard networks that merchants dial into to get authorization. These are dedicated private networks that users have to pay for in order to use the service.

The Internet is open to all. This is good for access, but bad from a security point of view. In the UNIX world that evolved the Internet, the common tools for remote management were not designed with security in mind, they were originally on private networks. The tools used were Telnet and ftp, then the "r" (remote) commands :rlogin, rcp (remote copy), and rsh (remote shell). These utilities would pass all information, including login names and the passwords you typed in, across the network in cleartext format. All of this is fine on a secure private network, but bad on a public network.

The Secure Shell utilities were an answer to this problem, using high encryption standards, these tools replaced their insecure brethren and provided full encryption of all data between the hosts that is very hard to break, even by the "brute force" method.

Brute Force Method Decryption

Your password, whatever you used, is just a bit pattern. A bit pattern is just a number to a computer. Say you had 6 characters in a password. Assuming 7 of the 8 possible bits are used for each character, you have 48 bits total with 42 that are significant.

Essentially, if you start at 0 and increment by one each time up to the value 2^{48} (4,398,046,511,104), one of those values is your password "value." With an XT, that could take many years, with a 486, maybe a year, but a quad PIII (or equivalent) CPU system at 1200 MHz and 1GB of RAM can crunch through this in minutes! The old 40-bit encryption standard used for years is now too easy to break with modern computers. 48 bits is not much either, but get to 56 bits (DES) and you raise the bar significantly. The value (2^{56}) is 72,057,594,037,927,936, 10,000 times larger, and 10,000 times longer to break. Now, just imagine what 128-bit encryption means, or the mind-boggling 512-bit encryption. Essentially, with modern computers, you could do it eventually, but not within the next millennium at least. Although, as computer power continues to climb, these numbers will just keep on increasing to make the calculation possibility, known as the "brute force method," essentially remain near zero.

Lost Passphrase on Private Keys

Sorry, there is no recovery from a lost passphrase on private keys; that is true security and the best solution. You must start over, which means you need to create a new set of keys and send your public key to all concerned for them to replace your old public key with.

PGP—Pretty Good Privacy

E-mail has become a standard fixture in everyday business, much like the telephone and fax. As a result, the security of e-mail in now an issue. The answer was PGP, which provided this private and public key system for your e-mail client. GPG is Gnu Privacy Guard, an implementation of the OpenPGP standard, now included with Red Hat Linux. Many companies use PGP or GPG regularly to send their correspondence. The public key is usually attached to the end of the data:

```
**************************************************************************
To:   Dreg (SD444466)
From: The SANS NewsBites service


*************************

---BEGIN PGP SIGNED MESSAGE---
Hash: SHA1
... (text removed)

Please feel free to share this with interested parties via e-mail (not
```

```
on bulletin boards).  For a free subscription, (and for free posters)
e-mail sans@sans.org with the subject: Subscribe NewsBites

...

-----BEGIN PGP SIGNATURE-----
Version: GnuPG v1.0.4 (BSD/OS)
Comment: For info see http://www.gnupg.org

iD8DBQE63beV+LUG5KFpTkYRAu/WAJ0fUwoQFUOETTd+wAbe1L784S3PDwCfULr0
DXDk20qZotKDLMfjLz1Gty4=
=K1Av
-----END PGP SIGNATURE-----
```

Notice in the previous listing that the BSD/OS (Berkeley Software Distribution/ Operating System) is using the GNU Foundation GnuPG. Linux also uses the GnuPG programs for signatures.

Validating RPMs with pgp

If you download an RPM from some location on the Internet and would like to verify that it is an official Red Hat RPM and has not been tampered with, you can verify the package's PGP-encrypted checksum using the *rpm -K* command. To obtain Red Hat's public key, point your browser to: http://www.redhat.com/about/contact.html.

CERTIFICATION OBJECTIVE 11.09

linuxconf

The linuxconf utility is a graphical utility that ties together most system administration tasks under a common interface. You can use linuxconf to do everything from adding user accounts to rebuilding the kernel. You start linuxconf from the Start menu, or you can start it from the command line by typing **linuxconf**.

System administration tasks in linuxconf are grouped by hierarchy. Items listed with a plus sign (+) next to them have subtasks. You view these subtasks by clicking the plus sign to expand the higher-level item. Expanded items have a minus sign next to them. Clicking the minus sign collapses the subtasks so that only the higher level item is visible. Clicking a subtask that doesn't have a plus sign next to it will bring up a configuration window for that particular task. Figure 11-5 shows the linuxconf utility being used to add user accounts.

Now that you have a better idea of the steps you can take to make your system more secure and reliable, as well as the process to go through when problems arise, refer to the Scenario & Solution on the next page for some possible scenario questions and their answers.

CERTIFICATION SUMMARY

As you've seen in this chapter and the last, there are many facets to system security. Making sure that network services run under nonprivileged accounts is one of the most important things you can do to ensure that your system remains secure from outside attack. If connected to the Internet or any insecure network service, you should convert all users to the secure shell utilities for all remote access services. The standard process accounting tools that come with Red Hat Linux can also be used to monitor your system for security problems.

FIGURE 11-5

linuxconf provides an integrated interface for system administration.

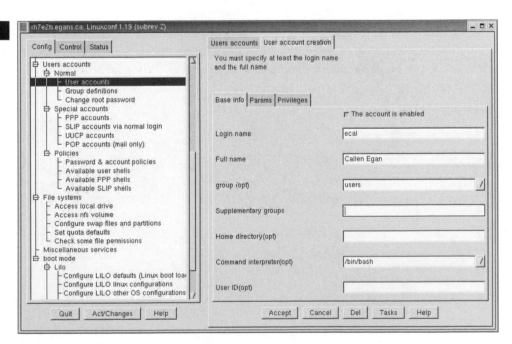

SCENARIO & SOLUTION

You come into work one morning and find that an extended power failure caused your Web server to shutdown even though it was on a UPS. When you try to reboot the system, you get a "kernel panic" message on the console. What is the first thing you should try?	In this situation, the first thing you would try should be to see if you can boot the system from a boot floppy. If the boot floppy fails, then you will have to boot into rescue mode to repair whatever problem is causing the kernel panic.
You suspect that someone from outside your organization has gained access to one of your accounts and is using the account for cracking purposes late at night. What could you do to help verify your suspicions?	Use the command last *<username>* to obtain a record of the login times and session duration for the username in question.

One of the most valuable skills you can have as A Red Hat Linux systems administrator is knowing how to fix configuration problems that may prevent a system from booting. When systems break, you are often placed in a highly visible position in your organization as the person expected to fix the problem. Compounding the stress and difficulty of being "under the gun" to solve a problem is the fact that you are lacking a complete system when you are working in repair mode. Taking a test system and experimenting with the various ways to break and repair things is good practice for the time when things go wrong for real.

TWO-MINUTE DRILL

Here are some of the key points from the certification objectives in Chapter 11.

Services Should Run as Users or Nobody, Not Root

❑ When a Red Hat Linux system boots, a special process, init, is the first started. All other processes are started afterward by init. All major network services should use a process that has no privileges by using a specific dummy account or the nobody account as the process ID.

❑ The user and primary group identifiers for a user are stored in the third and fourth fields, respectively, in /etc/passwd.

❑ Most processes that need a special user ID will create a user record in /etc/passwd and in /etc/group, if required.

❑ No one should be able to log in as these accounts; they just need to be there. They should never have a UID of 0 as that is for privileged accounts only.

SGID Red Hat Scheme

❑ Setting the setgid bit solves the problem of making sure all files created in a shared directory belong to the correct group.

❑ If you need to create a directory that is owned by a specific group, you use chmod 2770 on this shared directory, and afterward, all files created there by any group member become owned by the directory.

COPS

❑ COPS is a suite of programs that performs a variety of security checks and is freely available from the Internet. Although it is not necessarily current, it is still valid.

❑ You can configure COPS to mail its output to you, or you can have it leave its reports in a directory. A very effective way to use COPS is to put an entry for it in your system crontab, so you get periodic updates on the security status of your system.

Interaction of CMOS Clock Time and Linux System Time

❑ Most personal computers have provisions in hardware for keeping track of the date and time. Among other purposes, the date and time values are used to record the time a file was created or modified. This date and time value is also used by the various logging utilities to timestamp events.

User Process Accounting

❑ Support for accounting is built into the Red Hat Linux kernel, but you will need to install the psacct RPM to use some of the tools mentioned here.

❑ The ac command is used to print out a report of connect time.

❑ The /var/run/utmp file must always exist on Red Hat Linux systems. This file is used to store information about currently running processes.

❑ The /var/log/wtmp file is used by the init process and the login command to record logins and logouts.

tmpwatch

❑ The tmpwatch command (/usr/sbin/tmpwatch) is used to remove files that have not been accessed in a specified number of hours.

❑ Current versions of Linux have a cron job that runs regularly to cleanup the /tmp directory.

❑ You can configure tmpwatch to clean application directories, as well as the /tmp directory.

❑ You can use the tmpwatch command whenever necessary to clean up any directory with files older than one hour.

❑ The e2fsck command performs the same function on the Linux second extended file system as the fsck command does on a standard UNIX file system; it is used to check the file system on a partition for consistency.

Emergency Boot Procedures

❑ To prepare for boot failures, you should make sure you have a valid boot floppy for your system and knowledge on how to get to rescue mode using a floppy and the CD-ROM (or just the CD-ROM if your system can boot from it).

Using the Secure Shell Package—OpenSSH

❑ The standard remote management utilities supplied—Telnet, ftp, rlogin, rcp, and rsh—are NOT secure and should never be used on the Internet.

❑ The OpenSSH utilities—sshd, ssh, ssh-keygen, ssh-add, and ssh-agent—provide secure remote services over any network connections.

❑ You can even encrypt an X Window session using ssh-agent.

❑ You can validate the signature of any RPM using the gpg utility.

Linuxconf

❑ The linuxconf utility is a graphical utility that ties together most system administration tasks under a common interface.

❑ You can use linuxconf to do everything from adding user accounts to rebuilding the kernel. You begin linuxconf from the Start menu, or you can start it from the command line by typing **linuxconf**.

❑ System administration tasks in linuxconf are grouped by hierarchy.

SELF TEST

The following questions will help you measure your understanding of the material presented in this chapter. Read all the choices carefully, as there may be more than one correct answer. Choose all correct answers for each question.

Services Should Run as Users or nobody, Not root

1. You are setting up a Red Hat Linux system and are configuring several network services. What can you do to make sure your system is more secure from outside attack?

   A. Set up individual user accounts to run the services under.

   B. Pick a really secure password for the root account.

   C. Run the services under the user nobody account.

   D. Make sure the system is locked away in a machine room somewhere.

SGID Red Hat Scheme

2. What should you do to a shared directory to ensure that all user accounts that are members of the group that owns the directory will have access to files created in that directory?

   A. Make sure the root account owns the directory.

   B. Make sure the nobody account owns the directory.

   C. Make sure directory is in every user's PATH.

   D. Make sure the setgid bit is set on the directory.

3. How would you set the setgid bit on the /home/developer directory? (Assume that you have already issued the command: chown nobody.developgrp /home/developer.)

   A. chmod 2775 /home/developer

   B. chgrp 2775 /home/developer

   C. chmod 775 /home/developer

   D. chmod g+s /home/developer

4. How would you ensure that all files created by your users are automatically created with full access for the owner and group owner of the file?

   A. Have your users type the command **umask 002** *<filename>* whenever they create a file.

B. Place the command umask 002 in /etc/profile.

C. Have your users type the command **chmod 002** *<filename>* whenever they create a file.

D. Place the command umask in /etc/profile.

COPS

5. You are concerned about the security of your system and would like some way to ensure that you haven't overlooked some minor configuration setting that could result in a potential toehold for a cracker. What could you do to check the security of your system?

A. Publish an invitation on the Internet for crackers to attempt to break into your system as a test of your security measures.

B. Hire a security consultant.

C. Download and install the Computer Oracle and Password System.

D. Assume your system was secure enough and hope for the best.

User Process Accounting

6. You installed the psacct process accounting RPM and issued the command /sbin/accton, but nothing shows up when you issue the ac command or the sa command. You've checked and you have a /var/log/pacct file, but its size is 0 bytes. What is wrong?

A. You will have to reboot to start the accounting process.

B. Nothing is happening on your system, so nothing is being logged.

C. You turned accounting off.

D. The /var/log/pacct file is corrupt.

7. Your manager has asked you for a report of all the system reboots in the past week. How will you obtain this information?

A. By checking the /var/log/messages file

B. By issuing the command last reboot >reboot.rpt

C. By checking the /var/log/reboot file

D. By issuing the command lastb >reboot.rpt

8. You suspect someone has been trying to break into several accounts on your system. How could you check on this?

   A. Configure system logging to notify you whenever a failed login attempt occurs.

   B. Use the sa command to get a summary of failed login attempts.

   C. Use the command cat /var/log/btmp.

   D. Use the lastb command to display failed login attempts.

tmpwatch

9. What would you use the tmpwatch command for?

   A. To monitor the system for break-in attempts.

   B. To clean up unused user account directories.

   C. To scan system-wide temporary directories and clean up old temporary files.

   D. To monitor the /tmp directory for the appearance of certain files.

Emergency Boot Procedures

10. The junior system administrator at your site has just come to you to report a suspected bad hard drive on the system he was working on. Whenever he tries to boot the system, he gets a kernel panic with a message saying the root partition cannot be found. What is the most likely cause of this?

   A. The hard drive has crashed.

   B. The I/O bus is going bad.

   C. Intermittent RAM problems are masquerading as disk problems.

   D. The junior system administrator was modifying a system configuration file and has managed to configure the system so it will not boot.

11. What emergency repair items should you always have on hand?

   A. A custom boot floppy for your system

   B. A repair boot disk and/or Red Hat installation CD #1 (for version 7.1)

   C. Documentation on the partition layouts for the disk drives on your system

   D. Documentation on using the repair utilities

12. How would you obtain a rescue disk if you don't have one?

   A. Order one from Red Hat.

   B. Run the mkrescuedisk utility.

   C. Place a floppy in the floppy drive, mount the Red Hat distribution CD-ROM v6.0, and issue the command cp /mnt/cdrom/images/rescue.img /dev/fd0.

   D. Place a floppy in the floppy drive, mount the Red Hat distribution CD-ROM v6.0, and issue the command cat /mnt/cdrom/images/rescue.image >/dev/fd0.

13. How can you boot a damaged Linux system in order to perform repairs?

   A. Boot from your systems custom boot floppy

   B. Boot into rescue mode

   C. Boot into single-user mode using the command linux s

   D. Boot into runlevel 4

14. When you boot your Linux system, the boot process gets as far as displaying the word LIL on the screen. What should you do?

   A. Boot into rescue mode and run e2fsck

   B. Boot into rescue mode and check /etc/fstab for errors

   C. Boot into rescue mode and check /etc/lilo.conf for errors

   D. Reinstall Linux

15. You are a consultant and are helping a client who has managed to render his system unbootable. You have booted into rescue mode, but the client doesn't have any documentation on the partition layout on his disk drive. What can you do?

   A. Use the fdisk -l /dev/devicename command to display the partition table for the drive

   B. Reinstall Linux

   C. Use the e2fsck command and look for the superblock

   D. Use the fdisk command in interactive mode

16. You are trying to boot a system and keep receiving a message about a corrupted partition. You manage to boot into rescue mode. From this point, what might you do to fix the problem?

   A. Use fdisk and delete the partition; then add it back

   B. Use the fdisk -l command

    C. Run lilo to rebuild the boot block

    D. Run the command e2fsck -b 8193

17. What should you remember to do when running lilo from rescue mode?

    A. Use the -r option to tell lilo to use an alternative root location.

    B. Use the correct path to locate the lilo utility.

    C. Use the sync command to flush changes you make to disk.

    D. All of the above.

18. Where are some likely places for configuration errors that can prevent your system from booting? (Choose all that apply.)

    A. /etc/lilo.conf

    B. /etc/fstab

    C. /etc/passwd

    D. /boot

linuxconf

19. You have trouble remembering all the dozens of different commands and options required to administer a system. What can you do?

    A. Become adept at using the man pages and info utility.

    B. Make copious notes to remind you how things work.

    C. Use linuxconf to manage your system.

    D. Write a shell script menu program for the tasks you most commonly perform.

LAB QUESTION

Your company bought another competitor on the opposite coast recently, just as the new corporate application was being deployed everywhere, so you sent the app to them, too. They use a UNIX host for this application on their network. You need to be able to connect to this host for maintenance purposes on the new system-wide application you deployed. You do have Internet access with each other, but the main system application is core-dumping and you need to fix it now.

SELF TEST ANSWERS

Services Should Run as Users or nobody, Not root

1. ☑ **A and C.** You should run network services under their own accounts or the nobody account. If someone does succeed in exploiting a security hole in the server application, his actions will be limited to those of a normal user.

   ☒ **B and D are incorrect. B** is a good idea, but most crackers get root account privilege through program loopholes that they exploit. Rarely do they "brute force" the password. **D** is always a good idea, but physical security may be a bigger problem in larger organizations than network crackers.

SGID Red Hat Scheme

2. ☑ **D.** When the setgid bit is enabled for a directory, all files that are created in that directory are created with the same group owner as that of the directory.

   ☒ **A, B, and C are incorrect.** Anything owned by root is considered privileged use only (**A**); ownership of the directory is not important here, group ownership is (**B**); and the PATH variable is where the system looks for binary commands, which has nothing to do with setgid (**C**).

3. ☑ **A and D.** Both commands will set the setgid bit. The advantage to **D** is that you don't have to worry about affecting the other permission settings.

   ☒ **B** is incorrect as chgrp does not modify setgid bits, and **C** is incorrect because it does not include the proper value for setgid bit (2*xxx*).

4. ☑ **B.** Placing the command umask 002 will set the default umask for all users.

   ☒ **A, C, and D are incorrect.** Typing the umask command without any arguments displays the current umask setting for your process (**D**). The umask command does not change file permissions, chmod does that (**A**). The chmod 002 <*filename*> command would set the file to world write, nothing else(**C**).

COPS

5. ☑ **C.** The COPS package will perform a scan of your system and look for configuration settings that could potentially compromise your system's security.

   ☒ **A, B, and D are incorrect.** Publishing an invitation to crackers (**A**) is essentially what you do when you climb on board the Internet anyway; you are now just another target. Hiring a security consultant (**B**) may be a starting point, and they may even have their own replacement for COPS or equivalent. Hoping for the best luck (**D**) is what the Windows world does unless you add a private firewall.

User Process Accounting

6. ☑ **C.** By default, when you issue the accton command without any arguments, accounting is disabled. To enable accounting, you need to specify the accounting log file to use, as in /sbin/accton /var/log/pacct.

☒ **A, B,** and **D** are incorrect. There may well be nothing happening on your system (**B**), but it is unlikely unless your system has been accidentally removed from the network. The log file may be corrupt (**D**), but that's only a remote possibility if it has no characters in it yet.

7. ☑ **B.** The last reboot command will list the times your system has been rebooted. Edit the file reboot.rpt and remove all but the last week's entries.

☒ **A, C,** and **D** are incorrect. There may be reboot information in /var/log/messages (**A**) buried under lots of other messages, but there is no /var/log/reboot (**C**) file, and lastb is for bad login attempts (**D**).

8. ☑ **D.** The lastb command is used to display failed login attempts. You must have a /var/log/btmp file in order to record failed login attempts.

☒ **A, B,** and **C** are incorrect. By creating the /var/log/btmp file, the system will log failed logins (**A**). sa does the logging (**B**) of this information to /var/log/btmp (**C**), which is not a readable format file, so you cannot just "cat" the contents.

tmpwatch

9. ☑ **C.** The tmpwatch command is usually run as a cron job. It is used to recursively search through temporary directories and remove files that have not been accessed within a specified time frame.

☒ **A, B,** and **D** are incorrect. You may want to clean up any unused account directories (**B**), but you would have to script this yourself. You may want to monitor the system for break-ins (**A**) by creating /var/log/btmp and letting the system logging service do this for you. The tmpwatch utility (**D**) just clears out "old" files based on access times and usage.

Emergency Boot Procedures

10. ☑ **D.** In a situation like this, the cause is most likely human error.
☒ **A, B,** and **C** are incorrect. If the system panics, then this is after it has started, hence the hard disk is not bad (**A**), nor is the bus bad (**B**), or RAM (**C**).

11. ☑ **A, B, C,** and **D** are all good to have on hand if you have to perform a system rescue.
☒ There are no incorrect answer choices.

12. ☑ **D.** is the correct way to make a rescue disk from the RH v6.0 CD-ROM distribution.
☒ **A, B,** and **C** are incorrect. There is no mkrescuedisk utility (**B**) and you cannot order it from Red Hat (**A**). The copy command, cp, is not the correct way to transfer the image to a floppy (**C**); only dd or cat imagefile > fd0 will work.

13. ☑ **B** and **C** are correct procedures to boot a damaged Linux system in order to perform repairs.
☒ **A** and **D** are incorrect. The Custom boot floppy (**A**) might get you up and running if the MBR on the local hard disk is bad and runlevel 4 (**D**) is not really used for anything, by default.

14. ☑ **C** and possibly **A**. LILO is telling you that it got part of the way through the boot process, but couldn't continue because of errors in lilo.conf or because of possible disk errors. If you suspect disk problems, you might run e2fsck on the /boot partition. If your disk isn't having problems, then you should investigate lilo.conf for errors.
☒ **B** and **D** are incorrect. The boot process has not gotten far enough at this point for /etc/fstab to have anything to do with the problem (**B**). Reinstallation (**D**) is a pretty drastic step.

15. ☑ **A** is a good starting point, and **D** will give you some clues as to partition sizes but nothing about mount points. You could also try e2label to get the old labels OR you could just mount each partition, look at the file contents, and deduce what file system it represents.
☒ **C** and **D** are incorrect. The e2fsck might tell you the name (**C**), but you may end up waiting a long time. A reinstall (**B**) would be a drastic measure.

16. ☑ **D.** Try running a file system check using an alternative superblock.
☒ **A** might fix the problem, but would have the unfortunate side effect of deleting all the data on the partition. **B** would just list the partitions, and **C** you are not ready for until you have checked all the disks and tested them by mounting them.

17. ☑ **D.** You should keep all of these in mind when using lilo in rescue mode. You should always remember to use the sync command when you are running in rescue mode or single-user mode to make sure your changes are written to disk.
☒ There are no incorrect answer choices.

18. ☑ **A, B,** and **D.** The omission of a single character in /etc/lilo.conf or /etc/fstab can mean the difference between a bootable system and one that will not boot. Any time you make changes that affect the files in /boot, you should rerun lilo to ensure that the boot loader can locate the files in the directory it needs.

  ☒ **C** is incorrect. The /etc/passwd file contains user authentication information and is not relevant to system booting.

linuxconf

19. ☑ **C.** The linuxconf utility provides you with an easy-to-use interface for system management.

  ☒ **A, B,** and **D** are incorrect. Writing your own script (**D**) is not a bad idea, then you would know what you were doing more closely, and this would be easier than looking through notes (**B**), or the man and info utilities (**A**).

LAB ANSWER

If you need access now, and you have to use the Internet as your connection media, you need to use SSH. If the other host does not already have it, you can have them download it from the Internet, install it, and then create an account for you to log in with. You could probably be connected in less than ten minutes with this scenario and have a competent UNIX administrator at the other end.

There are a few steps outlined here, nothing specific, as it will depend on the version of UNIX used at the other end.

Get the OpenSSH utility source from the net and put it into a specific directory. Untar it and then compile and configure it (create system public and private keys) before using it:

```
# mkdir /opt/ssh; cd /opt/ssh

ftp://xxxsource4rpms.org/ssh.tar.gz

# tar xvzf ssh.tar.gz

# make  all  install

# ssh-configure  # there is some script like this to configure it

# ssh your-other-host
```

As an alternative, if you have the luxury of an overnite service, send them a preconfigured Linux host with the application running and with SSH ready to go. Have them add it to their network, and you can check the problem from your site securely with less pressure. The application is running on the Linux box you sent.

You could use a kickstart script if you already have one to customize a PC with, the right application mix for Red Hat, and then test the application on it before sending it. This might even be one of your development machines that's available for a few days. Send it. You know it works. It can be configured for the short run to handle the application until you get the main server out there working.

A

About the CD

This CD-ROM contains the CertTrainer software. CertTrainer comes complete with ExamSim, Skill Assessment tests, and the e-book(electronic version of the book). CertTrainer is easy to install on any Windows 98/NT/2000 computer and must be installed to access these features. You may, however, browse the e-book directly from the CD without installation.

Installing CertTrainer

If your computer CD-ROM drive is configured to autorun, the CD-ROM will automatically start up upon inserting the disk. From the opening screen you may either browse the e-book or install CertTrainer by pressing the *Install Now* button. This will begin the installation process and create a program group named CertTrainer. To run CertTrainer use START | PROGRAMS | CERTTRAINER.

System Requirements

CertTrainer requires Windows 98 or higher and Internet Explorer 4.0 or above and 600 MB of hard disk space for full installation. A version of CertTrainer for Linux is also found on the CD, with the files being optimized for Netscape Navigator. The Linux version must be run directly from the CD and is not installable.

CertTrainer

CertTrainer provides a complete review of each exam objective, organized by chapter. You should read each objective summary and make certain that you understand it before proceeding to the SkillAssessor. If you still need more practice on the concepts of any objective, use the In Depth button to link to the corresponding section from the Study Guide.

Once you have completed the review(s) and feel comfortable with the material, launch the SkillAssessor quiz to test your grasp of each objective. Once you complete the quiz, you will be presented with your score for that chapter.

ExamSim

As its name implies, ExamSim provides you with a simulation of the actual exam. The number of questions, the type of questions, and the time allowed are intended to be an accurate representation of the exam environment. You will see the screen shown in Figure A-1 when you are ready to begin ExamSim.

When you launch ExamSim, a digital clock display will appear in the upper-left corner of your screen. The clock will continue to count down to zero unless you choose to end the exam before the time expires.

Saving Scores as Cookies

Your ExamSim score is stored as a browser cookie. If you've configured your browser to accept cookies, your score will be stored in a file named *History*. If your browser is not configured to accept cookies, you cannot permanently save your scores. If you delete this History cookie, the scores will be deleted permanently.

E-Book

The entire contents of the Study Guide are provided in HTML form, as shown in the following screen. Although the files are optimized for Internet Explorer, they can also be viewed with other browsers including Netscape as shown in Figure A-2.

FIGURE A-1

The ExamSim opening page

Help

A help file is provided through a help button on the main CertTrainer screen in the lower-right corner.

Upgrading

A button is provided on the main ExamSim screen for upgrades. This button will take you to www.syngress.com, where you can download any available upgrades.

Linux

A limited version of CertTrainer for Linux is included on the CD. In order to access CertTrainer, browse to the CD-ROM drive, and open the folder named Linux. setup.html will open the HTML version of CertTrainer. These files are optimized for Netscape Navigator. The Linux version includes CertTrainer and E-Books (Figure A-2).

FIGURE A-2

Study Guide
contents in
HTML format

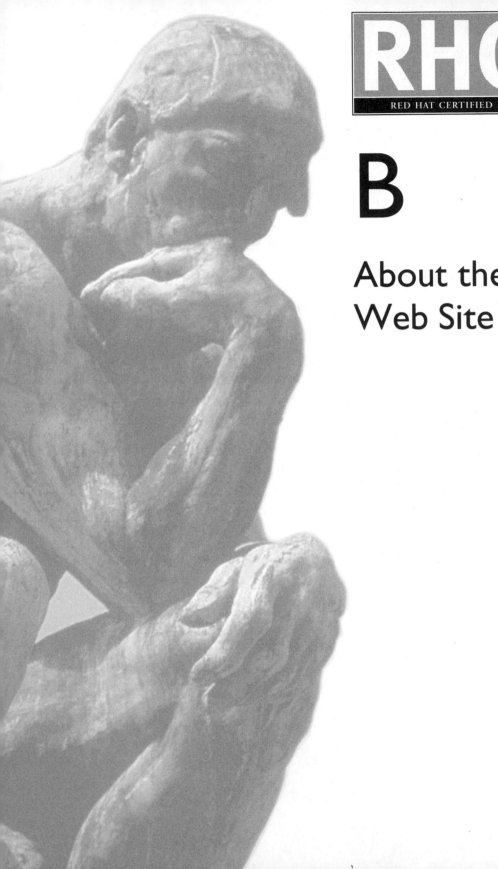

B

About the
Web Site

A t Access.Globalknowledge, the premier online information source for IT professionals (http://access.globalknowledge.com), you'll enter a Global Knowledge information portal designed to inform, educate, and update visitors on issues regarding IT and IT education.

Get *What* You Want *When* You Want It

At the Access.Globalknowledge site, you can do the following:

- Choose personalized technology articles related to your interests. Access a news article, a review, or a tutorial, customized to what you want to see, regularly throughout the week.

- Continue your education, in between Global courses, by taking advantage of chat sessions with other users or instructors. Get the tips, tricks, and advice that you need today!

- Make your point in the Access.Globalknowledge community by participating in threaded discussion groups related to technologies and certification.

- Get instant course information at your fingertips. Customized course calendars show you the courses you want, and when and where you want them.

- Obtain the resources you need with online tools, trivia, skills assessment, and more!

All this and more is available now on the Web at http://access.globalknowledge.com. Visit today!

RED HAT CERTIFIED ENGINEER

Glossary

Access configuration file   The access configuration file, access.conf, defines control modes and allowed types of services on a directory by directory basis. These controls are for directories directly accessed by the server, not for the whole system necessarily.

Accidental security violation   Accidental security violations occur because users lack adequate training, or because someone tries to speed up completion of a task by not following procedures. In fact, an important consideration to make in any security measures you devise is how much of an extra burden they place on the end users of your system.

Acorn Disc Filing System (ADFS)   The standard filesystem of the Acorn's RISC-PC systems and the Archimedes line of machines. Currently, Linux supports ADFS as read-only.

Acorn Econet/AUN   An older protocol, used by Acorn computers to access file and print servers.

Address Resolution Protocol (ARP)   An IP that maps Internet addresses dynamically to the actual addresses on a LAN.

Address Resolution Protocol (arp) command   The arp command is used to view or modify the kernel's ARP table. Using arp, you can detect problems such as duplicate addresses on the network, or manually add arp entries when arp queries fail.

ADFS   See Acorn Disc Filing System

Advanced Power Management (APM)   The APM BIOS primarily monitors and controls the system battery. It is an optional service typically used with laptops. You can also use it on workstations and servers if you want to implement the BIOS standby and suspend modes that are available on newer PCs. The daemon that needs to be running is apmd. If the apmd daemon is running on your system there will be a file created that contains the battery information in the proc directory. This API regulates the speed of programs in battery-powered computers.

Advanced Technology Attachment Packet Interface (ATAPI) The specification and standards for IDE and CD-ROM drives.

Aliasing support Aliasing support allows you to have multiple IPs on one network card.

Apache web server The Apache web server provides both normal and secure web services using the http and https protocols respectively. The Apache web server has extensive functionality and can be further extended using add-ins and macros to provide additional services.

APM See Advanced Power Management

Apple Hierarchical File System (HFS) This system is used by the Apple Mac Plus and all later Macintosh computers.

AppleTalk The protocol used for Apple computers to communicate with each other. AppleTalk is a LAN standard developed by Apple Computer capable of linking as many as 32 Macintosh computers, IBM PC-compatible computers, and peripherals.

ARP See Address Resolution Protocol

ATAPI See Advanced Technology Attachment Packet Interface

Authentication The process by which a user or an incoming message is identified

Basic Input/Output System (BIOS) The BIOS is a set of programs (encoded in ROM on IBM PC-compatible computer programs) that handle startup operations such as POST and low-level controls. Some system components have a separate BIOS.

Berkeley Internet Name Daemon (BIND) BIND is a free implementation of the Domain Name System that runs the Internet. Two versions of BIND are currently available: BIND 8 and BIND 9. BIND 8 uses a configuration file known as */etc/named.conf*, and BIND 4 uses */etc/named.boot*. Red Hat 7.1 ships with BIND 9.

Berkeley Software Distribution (BSD)   A version of the Unix operating system that was developed and formerly maintained by the University of California at Berkeley. BSD helped to establish the Internet in colleges and universities because the distributed software included TCP/IP.

BIND   See Berkeley Internet Name Daemon

BIOS   See Basic Input/Output System

BOOTP   See BOOTstrap Protocol

BOOTstrap Protocol (BOOTP)   A TCP/IP for network and diskless computers used to obtain IP addresses and miscellaneous network information.

Buffer   A temporary storage space for data. A buffer is ordinarily used as a timing coordination device to compensate for the difference in the speeds of two or more processes.

Buffer cache   See Write-back buffer cache; Write-through buffer cache

Build section   Like the prep section, the build section is also a shell script. This script will handle building binary programs out of the source code. Depending on the software, this step may be very easy or quite involved.

Busmouse   You can usually identify a busmouse from its round nine-pin connector. The mice usually plug into a card, which might have jumper settings or some with software (for DOS) to set IRQs and base I/O addresses. While most busmice use the BusMouse protocol, there are some older mice that use other protocols such as MouseSystems or Logitech. The device files for Inport, Logitech, and ATI-XL busmice are /dev/inportbm, /dev/logibm, and /dev/atibm, respectively.

Caching-only name server   A caching-only name server will find the answer to name queries and remember the answer the next time you need it. This will shorten the discovery time for all subsequent requests to the same name significantly, especially for a slow or shared connection. The first file to look at is */etc/named.conf.* This is read when named starts.

Canonical Name (CNAME)   The CNAME is a way to give each machine several names. For example, www is an alias for ns. CNAME record usage is a bit controversial; however, it's safe to follow the rule that an MX, CNAME, or SOA record should never refer to a CNAME record. Any of them should refer to something with an A record. It's also safe to assume that a CNAME is not a legal hostname for an e-mail address; webmaster@www.your-domain.com is an illegal e-mail address given the setup shown previously; that is what MX (Mail eXchanger) records are for.

CCITT   See Consultative Committee for International Telephony and Telegraphy

CDE   See Common Desktop Environment

CGI   See Common Gateway Interface

Chains   Chains in ipchains are sets of rules that are applied to each network packet that passes through your Linux firewall system. Each rule does two things: it specifies the conditions that a packet must meet to match the rule, and it specifies the action or target to take if the packet matches.

Challenge Handshake Authentication Protocol (CHAP)   A protocol (e.g., PPP) in which a password is required to begin a connection as well as during the connection. If the password fails any of these requirements, the system breaks the connection.

CHAP   See Challenge Handshake Authentication Protocol

Character devices   Character devices are where to specify support for a variety of things. These things include Virtual terminals, serial ports, parallel ports, mice, joysticks, Non-SCSI tape drives, etc.

Checksum   A checksum is a field created by adding bits or characters for a result that claims for error checking. Checksums are used to determine whether a file has been modified, which comes in handy if you need to verify the integrity of one or more packages.

Chkconf   The chkconfig command gives you a simple way to maintain the /etc/rc.d directory structure. With chkconfig, you can add, remove, and change services, list startup information, and check the state of a particular service.

Client   A client is a computer, such as the workstation on your desk, that you use to access and process the information that is stored on the server.

Coda   Coda is a networked filesystem similar to NFS. Currently Linux supports Coda clients only.

Common Desktop Environment (CDE)   A GUI for open systems.

Common Gateway Interface (CGI)   How HTTPD-compatible WWW servers accesses external programs. If this process is followed, data will be returned to the user as a generated Web page. CGI programs or scripts are commonly employed as a user fills out an on-screen form. The form generation or search process then brings other programs into play.

Common Object Request Broker Architecture (CORBA)   A distributed object communication standard suited for multiple-tier client/server applications

Computer Oracle and Password System (COPS)   This is a suite of programs that perform a variety of security checks. If COPS finds a potential problem, it will warn you. COPS does not fix any problems it finds, although it does have an option that will generate a shell command file that can be run manually. COPS will check for the following: permission settings on files, directories, and devices; bad passwords; files owned by the root; changed binary files; and holes in network service configuration.

Consultative Committee for International Telephony and Telegraphy (CCITT)   The CCITT is a defunct international organization that designed analog and digital communication standards involving modems, computer networks, and fax machines, such as V.21, V.22, V.32bis, and V.34.

Consultative Committee for International Telephony and Telegraphy (CCITT) X.25 Packet Layer   The X.25 networking protocol.

COPS   See Computer Oracle and Password System

Copyleft   See GNU Public License

CORBA   See Common Object Request Broker Architecture

Custom installation   The custom install gives you the most flexibility to choose how you want your system installed, at some loss of ease and speed. You determine how the disk is laid out, what size each partition is, and which packages will be installed. The custom install is recommended for veteran Linux users only.

Custom-class installation   A custom-class installation requires 300MB for a minimal installation and at least 2.4GB of free space if every package is selected.

Daemon   A Unix process designed to handle a specialized function (such as handling Internet server requests) and requiring a limited user interface.

Data Encryption Standard (DES)   See also Triple DES.

DES   See Data Encryption Standard

Desktop   The desktop is a workspace where the X server places all of your windows and icons.

/dev/pts   The /dev/pts filesystem is the Linux implementation of the Open Group's Unix98 PTY support.

DHCP   See Dynamic Host Control Protocol

Direct Memory Access (DMA) channels   A channel used to transfer data from the RAM memory to peripheral devices such as hard disk controllers, network adapters, and tape backup equipment. Requests for data are handled by a special chip called a DMA controller, which operates at half the microprocessor's speed.

Dirty buffer   A buffer in which the data have changed.

Disk buffering   Disk buffering is what happens when information from a disk is stored in memory until it is no longer needed. The memory that is used for disk buffering is called the buffer cache.

Disk Druid   One of the excellent additional programs supplied with the Red Hat Linux installation is the Disk Druid program that provides a more intuitive interface than Fdisk. The actions are similar, but the interface hides the need to know about the partition ID (just uses a text name ID) and has an option called Growable. This option allows the system to determine how much disk space a partition will take based on available free space. However, Disk Druid is available only at initial installation time.

Diskless clients   Diskless clients use either a boot floppy or a boot PROM to get started and then mount their root file system, swap space, a shared read-only /usr file system, and other shared read-write file systems such as /home. If "net-booting" from a boot PROM is used, the client will need *bootp* (or DHCP) and *tftp* services to obtain its network information and then download its kernel.

Display manager   The display manager displays a dialogue box on the screen that asks you for your username and password combination. You have a choice of display managers to use with Red Hat Linux. The default display manager is the GNOME display manager.

DMA See Direct Memory Access

DNS See Domain Name System

Domain Name System (DNS) This service allows human-readable domain names (e.g., www.redhat.com) to be translated into machine-readable IP addresses (e.g., 206.132.41.202), and vice versa. The DNS converts between machine names and IP addresses. It maps from name to address and from address to name, and provides other useful information to machines and their users.

DMA See Direct Memory Access

Dynamic Host Configuration Protocol (DHCP) This protocol allows a client machine to obtain network information (e.g., an IP number) from a server. Many organizations are starting to use dynamic host control because it simplifies and centralizes network administration, especially in large networks or networks that have a significant number of mobile users. DHCP is backward compatible with bootp. Therefore, this section will only cover the configuration of DHCP.

e2fsck The *e2fsck* command performs the same function on the Linux second extended file system as the *fsck* command does on a standard UNIX file system; it is used to check the file system on a partition for consistency. In order to use the *e2fsck* command, you need to understand something about how file systems are laid out on disk partitions.

edquota To specify disk quotas you need to run edquota. Edquota will edit the quota.user or quota.group file with the vi editor.

EIDE See Enhanced Integrated Drive Electronics

EISA See Enhanced Industry Standard Architecture

Enhanced Industry Standard Architecture (EISA) A bus architecture supportive of 32-bit peripherals compatible with 16-bit peripherals, transferring data at 33 Mb/s.

Enhanced Integrated Drive Electronics (EIDE)   As well as being able to support hard disks larger that 504MB, EIDE also improved access speeds to hard drives. Support was added for additional hard disks and DMA and ATAPI, such as CD-ROMs and tape drives. ANSI adopted EIDE as a standard in 1994 as Advanced Technology Attachment-2 (ATA-2 or Fast ATA).

Environment   The environment defines where a user looks for programs to be executed, what the login prompt looks like, what terminal type is being used, and more. This section explains how default environments are set up.

/etc/exports   /etc/exports is the only major configuration file for NFS on Linux. It explicitly lists which parts of which file systems are to be exported to clients via the *exportfs* command. The file format is similar to that used in SunOS 4.*x*, except that some additional options are permitted. Each line lists one directory that may be exported, the hosts it will be exported to, and the options that apply to this export. Simply changing /etc/exports does not automatically change anything right away. This file is simply the default set of exported directories for the *exportfs -a* command, which is typically run at boot time or by hand whenever /etc/exports has been changed. File systems can also be exported directly (and temporarily) via the exportfs command without modifying /etc/exports.

/etc/ftpconversions file   The /etc/ftpconversions file is a special file that the ftp service uses to automatically compress files and or decompress files for transfer. The executables for these conversions are found in the /home/ftp/bin directory. Each line in /etc/ftpconversions represents a rule of action for specific file name extensions.

Ethernet   The networking protocol linking up to 1204 nodes in a bus topology.

Extended partition   You are limited to making only four primary partitions on each hard disk. To work around this, the extended partition was developed. Within an extended partition, logical partitions can be created.

eXternal Data Representation (XDR)   A networking standard used for interchange formats in networking by employing certain data formats.

Fast switching   Fast switching is an option that allows you to connect two computers directly together with a network cable. This is an extremely fast way for two computers to communicate.

FAT   See File Allocation Table

FDDI   See Fiber Distributed Data Interface

fdisk   The fdisk utility is universally available and should be considered one of the first tools you should get familiar with. You can modify the physical disk partition layout using many programs. FDISK.EXE from DOS has the same name and is used for creating partitions but doesn't incorporate any Linux-compatible features. A simple rule to follow is to use whichever fdisk is supplied with an operating system when you are creating partitions for that operating system. You can invoke fdisk at any time from a command prompt. You must indicate, with a single argument, which disk you want fdisk to work with.

Fiber Distributed Data Interface (FDDI)   Fiber-optic networks running at 100 Megabits per second, utilizing wiring hubs as prime servers for network monitoring and control devices.

File Allocation Table (FAT)   An area on a disk indicating the arrangement of files in the sectors.

File locking daemon   Since an NFS shared file system may be present on more than one client, if two or more clients want to open the same file, the File Locking daemon service takes care of checking for any preexisting request(s) that may already have that file locked for their use. Most NFS implementations have historically had serious problems making file locking work reliably and correctly, particularly between the implementations of different vendors. Any applications depending on file locking over NFS should be tested thoroughly before depending on their use.

File server   A computer within a LAN allowing access to a main system of files for all computers on the network.

File Transfer Protocol (FTP)   An Internet protocol allowing the exchange of files. A program enables the user to contact another computer on the Internet and exchange files.

File Transfer Protocol (FTP) client   The client allows you to access the directory tree and all files within it. The graphical client is optimized for download from the remote host. By simply clicking on a file, you initiate a transfer download, by clicking on a directory, you initiate a cd targetdirectory command and the interface updates with the local files in the new director.

Files section   This is a list of files that will become part of the package. Any files that you want to distribute in the package must be listed here.

FIPS   Using the FIPS utility will allow you to shrink the C drive partition size such that it uses slightly more space than all the currently installed files require and frees up the remainder as a separate partition. Be careful not to make it smaller than the space you are using on your drive.

Firewall   A utility preventing unauthorized users from entering a restricted database or server via a LAN and/or the Internet for security reasons.

Free software   Free software is the term typically used to refer to software that has been released under the GNU Public License, or GPL. The idea of free software is not new. In fact, back when mainframes ruled the data centers and universities, most software was free, and end users were free to modify it to suit their needs.

FTP   See File Transfer Protocol

fvwm window manager   The fvwm window manager was developed specifically for Linux and can be configured to emulate other window environments such as the commercial Motif window manager or even Windows 95. This can make fvwm a good choice if you are migrating users from a Microsoft Windows platform to Linux.

Gateway   A gateway, as its name implies, is a route a packet must take first to get to its destination. If no gateway is necessary, an asterisk is printed. The Genmask column shows the "generality" of the route.

Geometry   The size of a hard drive is determined by its geometry. The geometry includes the number of cylinders, heads, and sectors available on the hard disk. Together, these numbers make up an address on the hard disk. Normally, the geometry that your BIOS will support is limited to 1024 cylinders, 256 heads, and 63 sectors. All modern disk drives use 512 bytes per sector. So, 1024 cylinders times 256 heads times 63 sectors times 512 bytes equals about 8GB or 8000MB. If your hard disk is larger than 504MB, and you have an old BIOS that reports this disk has just 1024 cylinders, your computer will not be able to address the entire hard disk. Most modern day PCs bypass this problem by using LBA for your hard disks.

geometry option   The -geometry option is used to specify both the size of the window that the X client starts up in and the location of the window.

Getty program   The getty program monitors the terminal waiting for someone to press a key indicating that they wish to log in. When this happens, the getty program spawns the login program, which asks you for your username and password.

GNOME   See GNU Network Object Model Environment

GNU is Not Unix (GNU)   This is a self-recursive definition meant to imply that GNU software, unlike UNIX software, is open and free. Today, most of the software and utilities used in most Linux distributions, including Red Hat, are GNU utilities. In 1984, Richard Stallman began work on the GNU project.

GNU Network Object Model Environment (GNOME)   GNOME is the default desktop for Red Hat Linux 6.0 and is the desktop you first see after you install the X Window system.

Gnu Privacy Guard (GPG)   GPG is an implementation of the OpenPGP standard, now included with Red Hat Linux. Many companies use PGP or GPG regularly to send their correspondence. The public key is usually attached to the end of the data. GPG is used to establish the authenticity of the file; it can be used to confirm, for example, that an RPM file is indeed an official Red Hat RPM. Red Hat provides a GPG public key for its RPM files; the key is located in the RPM-GPG-KEY file on your distribution CD, or it can be downloaded.

GNU Public License (GPL)   GNU Public License, or GPL (also called Copyleft) has the philosophy that all software should be free. Not free as in zero price, but free as in open.

GPG   See Gnu Privacy Guard

GPL   See GNU Public License

Graphical User Interface (GUI)   An overall and consistent for the interactive and visual program that interacts (or interfaces) with the user. GUI can involve pull-down menus, dialog boxes, on-screen graphics, and a variety of icons.

GUI   See Graphical User Interface

HFS   See Apple Hierarchical File System

High Performance File System (HPFS)   A large-disk file and filename handling system able to coexist with FAT systems.

High Sierra File System (HSFS)   See ISO9660 CD-ROM

Home directory   The home directory is the initial directory in which users are placed when they first log on to a Red Hat Linux system. For most normal users this will be /home/*username*, where *username* is the user's login name. Users typically have write permission in their own home directory, so they're free to read and write their own files there.

HPFS   See High Performance File System

HSFS   See ISO9660 CD-ROM

HTML   See HyperText Markup Language

HTTP   See HyperText Transfer Protocol

HTTPD   See HyperText Transfer Protocol Daemon

HURD   The Free Software Foundation, headed by Richard M. Stallman, announced a kernel called The HURD. Unfortunately, efforts on this new kernel faltered, and it wasn't until 1996 that a stable version of The HURD was available.

HyperText Markup Language (HTML)   The language used for Web documents on the Web that defines the tags, codes, etc., for that particular Web page.

HyperText Transfer Protocol (HTTP)   An Internet standard supporting Web exchanges. By creating the definitions for URLs and their retrieval usage throughout the Internet, HTTP allows Web authors the ability to embed hyperlinks and also allows for transparent access to an Internet site.

HyperText Transfer Protocol Daemon (HTTPD)   A web server developed at the CERN and called CERN HTTPD. HTTPD was also developed at the NCSA. Unlike the CERN version, the NCSA version allowed for authentication, clickable imagemaps, forms, and word searches.

ICMP   See Internet Control Message Protocol

ICP   See Internet Cache Protocol

IDE   See Enhanced Integrated Drive Electronics; Integrated Drive Electronics

Ifconfig   The ifconfig command is used to configure and display network devices.

IMAP   With IMAP, the server maintains all mail messages for the user locally, acting as the central repository of all IMAP account mail messages. This is the common service used by web-based mail services.

Inetd program   The Inetd server program is usually started at boot time. The startup script is */etc/rc.d/init.d/inet*; there should be links to this program in the appropriate */etc/rc.d/rc?.d* directories. The inetd program listens for connection requests from client applications to these socket addresses. When it receives a connection request, inetd starts up the server program for that port, hands the port over to the server application, and then goes back to waiting for another connection request.

Init process   The init program is called by the kernel when it starts up. The init process in turn runs /etc/rc.d/rc.sysinit. rc.sysinit performs a number of tasks, including configuring the network, setting up the default keymapping, starting up swapping, and setting the host name. The init process then determines which runlevel it should be in by looking at the "initdefault" entry in /etc/inittab. The init process is responsible for starting all the other processes that comprise a working Linux system, including your own interactive shell process or X Window session. Since the init process is responsible for keeping things going, it runs with the user ID of the root account.

Inittab   The inittab describes what process should be started when booting, as well as what should be running at normal operations levels. Process init reads in the /etc/inittab configuration file to determine what is to run at what runlevel. The valid runlevels range from 0–6 and A–C. Runlevels A–C are considered ondemand runlevels.

INND   INND was written in 1991 by Rich Salz to replace Cnews, as the volume of NNTP traffic had risen to the point that Cnews was not able to keep up, due to architectural limitations. INND is now maintained by ISC at www.isc.org. Red Hat supplies INND 2.3in rpm format. Release 2.3 supports circular message buffers, as well as file system-based spooling. This is a performance advantage if a large number of newsgroups are being carried. Alternative news servers include Cnews and Cyclone.

Install section   Yet another shell script, the install section allows you to build install targets within the source distribution.

Integrated Drive Electronics (IDE)   IDE is on the IBM PC ISA 16-bit bus standard, and it was adopted as a standard by ANSI in 1990 as ATA. A setback to IDE was that it could only access 504MB of disk space. To work around this, EIDE was created.

Integrated Drive Electronics (IDE) drive   An IDE drive is a hard disk drive for 80286, 80386, and 80486 processors containing most controller circuitry within the drive. IDE drives combine ESDI speed with SCSI hard drive interface intelligence. It is on the IBM PC ISA 16-bit bus standard, and it was adopted as a standard by ANSI in 1990 as ATA. A setback to IDE was that it could only access 504MB of disk space.

Integrated Services Digital Network (ISDN)   ISDN is a set of standards still evolving for a digital public telephone network. ISDN lines are a fairly popular and inexpensive high speed digital line. Adding ISDN support will allow you to use an ISDN card for inbound or outbound dialing connections. The ISDN device has a built in AT compatible modem emulator, autodial, channel bundling, callback and caller authentication without the need for an external daemon to be running.

Intentional security violation   Intentional security violations are deliberate attempts by someone to either gain access to information or deny the legitimate users of information access to that information. These types of attack can range from someone who is simply "browsing around," to someone trying to destroy or bring down your system for revenge or notoriety, to a competitor trying to access trade secrets or confidential financial information.

Internet Cache Protocol (ICP)   When proxy server queries another about an incoming Web page, this is the protocol used enabling the server to avoid going to the Internet to get the page.

Internet Control Message Protocol (ICMP)   A protocol for sending error/control messages. ICMP employs TCP/IP.

Internet Packet eXchange (IPX)   IPX is Novell NetWare's built-in networking protocol for LAN communication and was derived from the Xerox

Network System protocol. IPX moves data between a server and/or workstation programs from different network nodes.

Internet Protocol (IP)   The IP was originally developed by the U.S. Department of Defense (DoD) for internetworking of dissimilar computers across a single network. This connectionless protocol aids in providing a best-effort delivery of datagrams across a network.

Internet Protocol (IP) masquerading   IP masquerading allows you to provide Internet access to multiple computers with a single officially assigned IP address. Like NAT, the masquerade process is invisible to both your internal systems and systems on the Internet. Unlike NAT, which is basically a one-to-one mapping of an internal IP address to an valid external IP address, IP masquerading lets you map multiple internal IP addresses to a single valid external IP address.

Internet Relay Chat (IRC)   A process enabling to computers to communicate (chat) with one another similar to a telephone conference call.

Internetwork Protocol eXchange (IPX)   The Novell networking protocol used to access Novell file and print servers.

Interrupt ReQuest (IRQ)   An IRQ is a signal that is sent by a peripheral device (e.g., NIC, Video, Mouse, Modem, or Serial Port) to the CPU to request some processing time. Each device that you attach to a computer may need its own IRQ value. This value is unique to each device so as not to confuse the computer, except for possibly PCI devices (explained later). The Intel architecture is limited to using only 16 IRQs (0–15) of which usually IRQs 5,7,9,10,11, and 12 are available with a bare-bones system.

Inverse zone   See Reverse zone

IP   See Internet Protocol

IPX   See Internet Packet eXchange; Internetwork Protocol eXchange

IRQ   See Interrupt ReQuest

ISDN   See Integrated Services Digital Network

ISO9660 CD-ROM   The standard filesystem used on CD-ROMs. It is also known as the High Sierra filesystem (HSFS) on other UNIX systems.

Jolitz, William and Lynne   William and Lynne Jolitz, in 1991, ported Berkeley UNIX, BSD, to the Intel platform.

Jumperless cards   Some cards have no jumpers; instead, information on which port, IRQ, and the I/O address it uses is stored in a ROM chip on the card. These cards are usually shipped with a program that will allow you to change these settings. Alas, it is a Microsoft world, and these utilities usually need DOS to run. If you have a card that works like this, you'll need a DOS boot disk or partition to be able to configure them.

K Desktop Environment (KDE)   A GUI for Unix computers.

kbdconfig   The kbdconfig utility allows you to set the type of keyboard you have. You can use your arrow, PGUP, and PGDN keys to traverse the list of keyboards. Highlight the proper keyboard, then press the RETURN key to accept the new setting, or the ESC key to exit without saving. Changes made here are saved to the /etc/sysconfig/keyboard file.

KDE   See K Desktop Environment

Kernel   The kernel is the heart of the whole operating system. This is what boots and loads up your different system level device drivers. With the ability to recompile your kernel you can greatly improve the speed and lower the memory consumption of your kernel. In essence you can build a specific kernel for your architecture. Increasing the size of your kernel decreases your system-wide available memory, plus some systems need to have the kernel smaller than a certain size in order to boot.

Kernel module   When you compile your kernel, you have the option to have components compiled as modules. A kernel module is not compiled directly into the kernel but in a pluggable driver that can be loaded and unloaded into the kernel as needed. It is a good idea to make modules instead of directly compiling them into the kernel.

Kernel-mode NFS Daemon (KNFSD)   This Linux kernel-mode NFS server, like the NFS server implementations in most commercial UNIX implementations, runs kernel processes to serve the NFS requests from clients. This means that the NFS daemon processes use kernel data structures (dentries, inodes, and devices) rather than their user-mode equivalents (filenames, file descriptors). This eliminates some serious bottlenecks present in UNFSD, enabling an inexpensive server to achieve full 100Mb/sec throughput and to efficiently serve dozens of simultaneous, active clients (limited more by disk and network I/O than by CPU usage or protocol bottlenecks).

Kickstart   Kickstart is RedHat's solution for an automated installation of RedHat. All of the questions that are asked during setup can be automatically supplied with one text file. You can easily setup nearly identical systems very quickly. Kickstart files are useful for quick deployment and distribution of Linux systems. If the file resides on the floppy, you can initialize it with *linux ks = floppy*. Kickstart installations can only be performed from a CD-ROM or NFS server.

KNFSD   See Kernel-mode NFS Daemon

Laptop-class installation   A laptop-class installation provides a workstation-class installation but allows some customization for the laptop environment. A laptop-class installation, when you choose to install GNOME or KDE, requires at least 1.2GB of free space. If you choose both GNOME and KDE, and the Games, you will need at least 1.5GB of freedisk space.

Last In Last Out (LILO)   After assigning LILO, you can enter in the hostname for your machine. Hostnames do not have to be unique unless you are connecting to the Internet or some other established network. When you restart the system, after the internal POST, Power On Self Test, the LILO boot block, MBR, is loaded. To pass a parameter to LILO, type the parameter after the label name. You should run *lilo* whenever you rebuild your Linux kernel, change disk partitions, or do anything else that might affect the physical location of the files in */boot*.

LBA   See Logical Block Addressing

LDP   See Linux Documentation Project

LILO   See Last In Last Out

Line Print Control (LPC)   You can use LPC to control, start and stop all local queues if you have the privilege. The LPC utility is not commonly available to users, just superusers.

Line Print Queue (LPQ)   To view jobs that have not already printed or are currently being printed, you can use the LPQ command.

Line Print Remove (LPRM)   This utility is used to remove currently nonprinting jobs.

Line Print Request (LPR)   Any user can use the LPR utility to send print requests to any local queue name.

Linear mode   Linear mode is the combining of one or more disks to work as one larger device. No redundancy exists in linear mode; the disks are filled in the order they appear (e.g., disk 1, disk 2). The only performance gain linear mode will experience is when several users access data that reside on different disks.

Linux   Linux is a preemptive multitasking operating system allowing symmetrical multiprocessing, networking, multiple users, advanced memory management, POSIX support, and multiple filesystems.

Linux Documentation Project (LDP)   The LDP is a global effort to produce reliable documentation for all aspects of the Linux operating system, including hardware compatibility. Within the LDP, you can find the Linux Hardware HOWTO.

Linux Hardware HOWTO   The Linux Hardware HOWTO is a document that lists most of the hardware components supported by Linux. The list is updated regularly with added hardware support, so it is an up-to-date source of information. The latest version of the Linux Hardware HOWTO can be found at http://users.bart.nl/~patrickr/hardware-howto/Hardware-HOWTO.html, or within the LDP, which can be found at Sun Microsystems' Sunsite at http://metalab.unc.edu/LDP/HOWTO/Hardware-HOWTO.html or any mirror sites of Sunsite.

Linuxconf   The *linuxconf* utility is a graphical utility that ties together most system administration tasks under a common interface. You can use *linuxconf* to do everything from adding user accounts to rebuilding the kernel. You start *linuxconf* from the Start menu, or you can start it from the command line by typing **linuxconf**.

Loadin program   The loadlin program is also MS-DOS based and requires a copy of the Linux kernel, and possibly an initial RAM disk if your drives are SCSI types, to be MS-DOS available.

Logical Block Addressing   Most modern PCs manufactured after 1995 have built in a fix called Logical Block Addressing, or LBA. LBA involves a special way of addressing sectors. Instead of referring to a cylinder, head, and sector for a location on the hard disk, each sector is assigned a unique number from 0 to $N-1$, where N is the number of sectors on the disk. LBA mode allows geometry translation, which means that the BIOS can be fooled into believing that the hard disk's geometry is acceptable. A system that can report LBA will adjust the cylinder, head, and sector numbers so that the entire disk is available using these logical addresses. In general, only on relatively old machines would this ever occur. If your computer was manufactured after 1994, then you will likely be able to select LBA mode for your hard disks in your computer's CMOS.

logrotate utility   The logrotate utility allows you to set up automatic management tasks for log files. These include rotating log files, compressing log files, mailing log files, and removing log files. The logrotate utility is run via cron, and you can specify the frequency at which any given log file is modified. You configure the logrotate utility using the /etc/logrotate.conf file. The package file for the logrotate utility is logrotate-3.2-1.i386.rpm.

Logical partition   Within an extended partition, logical partitions can be created. IDE disks can have up to 16 total partitions (three primary and one extended containing up to 12 logical partitions), and SCSI disks are limited to fifteen. All logical partitions created within the extended partition have device names that range from 5 to 16 (or 15 for SCSI) no matter how many primary partitions are configured.

Login name   The user logs in with this name. The Login name should only contain alphanumeric characters, and the - and _ characters. In almost all cases, the Login name should not contain uppercase letters. Although a login name can be up to 256 characters, you typically want to keep it to ten or fewer, for ease of account maintenance.

LPC   See Line Print Control

LPQ   See Line Print Queue

LPR   See Line Print Request

LPRM   See Line Print Remove

Master Boot Record (MBR)   The original Intel motherboard design provided a mechanism to start any operating system. It would load a bootup program, located in the first sector of the first disk starting with A:, then C:. This program is located in an area most often called the Master Boot Record. This is the first program loaded by the BIOS. This program then loads the real operating system boot control program(s), which in turn starts the operating system.

MBR   See Master Boot Record

MD5   See Message Digest 5

Message Digest 5 (MD5)   A one-way hash function designed to create message digests. MD5 is fast but less secure than SHA-1. MD5 is adequate for verifying that the file is intact (no data were lost or corrupted while copying or downloading the file).

Minix   This is the original default Linux filesystem, although the ext2 filesystem has since superceded it. Minix is another UNIX-like operating system. It is a microkernel-based teaching operating system. Minix had many limitations, and Torvalds set about writing a new operating system that did not suffer the limitations of MS-DOS and Minix.

Mkbootdisk   Mkbootdisk is a utility that can create a bootdisk. This is basically a rescue disk. After creating this disk it can be used to simply boot your system, or you can specify the word **rescue** at the LILO prompt.

Modular kernel   A modular kernel has greater flexibility than a monolithic kernel. You can compile almost all of your drivers as modules. A module can be inserted into the kernel whenever you need it. Modules keep the initial kernel size low, which increases the boot time and overall performance.

Monolithic kernel   A monolithic kernel is a kernel that has all of the device modules built directly into the kernel. The modular kernels have all of there devices as separate loadable modules. A monolithic kernel can talk directly to its devices faster than a module, but it will increase the size of your kernel.

Mouseconfig   The mouseconfig utility allows you to set your mouse to the correct type. You can use your arrow, PGUP, and PGDN keys to traverse the list of mouse types. Highlight the proper mouse type; then press the RETURN key to accept the new setting or the ESC key to exit without saving. If you are using a two-button mouse, and wish to emulate three buttons (by clicking both buttons at the same time), select "Emulate 3 Buttons?" Changes made here are saved to the /etc/sysconfig/mouse file.

NAT   See Network Address Translation

NCP   See Netware Core Protocol

NETBEUI   See NETwork Basic Input/Output System Extended User Interface

NETBIOS   See NETwork Basic Input/Output System

Netstat   The netstat command is used to display a plethora of network connectivity information. The most commonly used option to netstat, -r, is used to display the kernel routing tables.

Netsysv   The ntsysv command takes the functionality of chkconfig and wraps it into an easy-to-use screen interface. By default, ntsysv configures the current runlevel. You can specify a different runlevel with the -level flag. The ntsysv interface is extremely easy to use. Select the service you want to modify using the arrow keys.

Netware Core Protocol (NCP)   This is the network filesystem used by Novell, over the IPX protocol. NCP allows Linux to use NCP as a client.

Network Address Translation (NAT)   NAT is a firewall feature that allows you to connect systems to the Internet and disguise their true IP addresses. NAT works by modifying the header information in IP packets as they pass through the firewall. As each packet passes through the firewall, the internal source address in the header is replaced with a public address. When the firewall receives incoming packets destined for a host on the internal network, the process happens in reverse. As the packets pass through the firewall, the header of each packet is modified so that the public address in the packet's destination field is replaced with the internal address of the system it is destined for.

NETwork Basic Input/Output System (NETBIOS)   A program included in the MS-DOS versions 3.1 and later for linking personal computers to a LAN. NETBIOS was originally developed by IBM and Sytek; a version of NETBIOS is now offered by many hardware vendors so that their products can be networked.

NETwork Basic Input/Output System Extended User Interface (NETBEUI)   The transport layer for NETBIOS.

Network block support   Network block support lets you use a physical disk on the network as if it is a local disk.

Network File System (NFS)   NFS is a file-sharing protocol originally developed by Sun Microsystems in the mid-1980s. It is based on Sun's XDR and RPC technologies. This is the networked file system most commonly used among Linux and UNIX computers. The NFS is a powerful and versatile way of sharing file systems between servers and workstations. *See also* Kernel-mode NFS Daemon; PC-NFS; Secure NFS; Universal NFS Daemon; WebNFS.

Network File System (NFS, version 3)   Version 2 of the NFS protocol has been in use since the late 1980s. By the early 1990s, higher-bandwidth networks and demands for better performance prompted Sun Microsystems to revise the protocol. NFS v3's key features include support for client-side caching of data, use of larger block sizes for more efficient transfers, the ability to have multiple outstanding write requests, and the ability to run over TCP instead of UDP. Taken together, NFS v3 greatly improves write performance and scalability on large busy networks and makes modest improvements to read performance on low-traffic networks.

Network Information System (NIS)   NIS allows you to share one centrally managed authorization database with other Linux systems in the network. With NIS, you maintain one password database on a NIS server, and you configure the other systems on the network to be NIS clients. When a user initiates a login session on the NIS client, that system consults its authorization file (usually /etc/passwd), and if the username that was entered doesn't exist there, the system will look up the authorization information on the NIS server.

Network Interface Card (NIC)   A NIC is a board with encoding and decoding circuitry and a receptacle for a network cable connection that, bypassing the serial ports and operating through the internal bus, allows computers to be connected at higher speeds to media for communications between stations.

Network News Transport Protocol (NNTP)   This uses TCP port 119, as documented in RFC 977. It is a high-performance, low-latency message transfer protocol based on SMTP. A collection of NNTP servers accept posts and distribute them worldwide, moving billions of characters daily. Newsgroups are the organizational unit, with hierarchies existing for almost any subject area one can imagine. The major groups are alt, comp, gnu, misc, news, rec, sci, soc, and talk. Other newsgroups include commercial feeds and local distributions.

NFS   See Network File System

NIC   See Network Interface Card

NIS   See Network Information System

NNTP   See Network News Transport Protocol

NT File System (NTFS)   A Windows file system using the Unicode character set. NTFS allows file names up to 255 characters in length. NTFS has the advantage of supposedly being able to recover from disk crashes, especially hard disk crashes.

NTFS   See NT File System

ntsysv utility   The ntsysv command takes the functionality of chkconfig and wraps it into an easy-to-use screen interface. By default, ntsysv configures the current runlevel. You can specify a different runlevel with the -level flag.

Object Linking and Embedding (OLE)   A set of standards, developed by Microsoft and incorporated into Microsoft Windows and Apple Macintosh System software, for creating dynamic automatically updated links between documents and for embedding documents created by another. With OLE, changes made in a source document can be automatically reflected in a destination document.

Open source software   Open Source software, like free software, requires that software source code be provided and readable. What Open Source does not promote, however, are the philosophical reasons behind free software. Where the GPL makes freedom a central point, Open Source sidesteps the philosophy and sets only the guidelines for software to fit the Open Source definition.

Operating System/2 (OS/2)   A multitasking operating system for IBM PC and compatible computers that uses flat memory to emulated separate DOS machines; it can run DOS, Windows, and OS/2 programs concurrently, protecting the others if one program crashes and allowing dynamic exchange of data between applications.

OS/2   See Operating System/2

Package   A package is a container. It includes the files needed to accomplish a certain task, such as the binaries, configuration, and documentation files in a software application. It also includes instructions on how and where these files should be installed and how the installation should be accomplished. A package also includes instructions on how to uninstall itself.

PAM   See Pluggable Authentic Module

PAP   See Password Authentication Protocol

Partition   A partition on a disk is a logical set of cylinders that represent all or part of the entire disk. Each disk can be one big partition or can be separated into many. *See also* Extended partition; Logical partition; Primary partition

Partitioning   You should make several partitions when preparing your hard drive to install Linux. Red Hat Linux uses two filesystems to run, a Linux native filesystem and Linux swap space. If you want to install Red Hat Linux and another operating system on the same computer, you will have to create separate partitions for each. Partitioning the hard drive in this manner keeps system, application, and user files isolated from each other. This aids in protecting the file space that the Linux kernel and the rest of your applications use. Files cannot grow across partitions. Therefore, an application that uses huge amounts of disk space, such as a newsgroup server, will not be able to use up all of the disk space needed by the Linux kernel.

Partitioning naming conventions   UNIX has been notorious for weird file names for hardware, and no one standard has been used by all the UNIX versions. Still, Linux has been using a simple standard for disk drives. The disk device names have three letters then a number. The first letter identifies the controller type: h is for IDE/EIDE and s is for SCSI. The second letter uses d for disk, and the third letter represents the sequential disk controller starting with the letter a.

Password Authentication Protocol (PAP)   The protocol used when logging onto a network.

PCI   See Peripheral Component Interconnect

PC-NFS   In the late 1980s, Sun and several third parties developed an NFS client for single-user, single-tasking operating systems such as MS-DOS and Microsoft Windows. Unfortunately, the NFS authentication model is best suited for secure, multiuser client machines, and PC-NFS has always been a difficult protocol to support reliably. Typically, PC-NFS servers must run one or more extra "helper" processes (called something like *rpc.pcnfsd)* that handle logins from the single-user client machines, act like *rpc.mountd* to process mount requests and handle printing.

PCMCIA   See Personal Computer Memory Card Interface Adapter

Peripheral Component Interconnect (PCI) bus   A common problem with PCs today is having more devices than available interrupts. PCI devices can get around this predicament by sharing an IRQ. This is accomplished using the PCI bus. The PCI bus is independent of the processor, so PCI devices can have their own internal interrupts that determine which device will send an IRQ to the processor. However, your BIOS must support PCI sharing for it to work. If it does, you should be able to turn it on through your computers CMOS. Most modern PC's manufactured after 1998 contain PCI buses.

Personal Computer Memory Card Interface Adapter (PCMCIA)   A special style of expansion port designed primarily for laptops and sometimes used in small devices like digital cameras. Laptops have a special peripheral interface bus called PCMCIA that requires a special set of drivers and services to handle it. With Red Hat 7.*x,* PCMCIA services are now very well established and the various network, SCSI and modem devices should not be a problem. With older equipment, there is always a possibility of problems. If the default Red Hat 7.1 kernel fails to boot or work properly with PCMCIA devices, you should considering downloading the latest PCMCIA sources from sourceforge.net and rebuilding the kernel without the built-in PCMCIA support.

PGP   See Pretty Good Privacy

PID   See Process IDentifier

Plug and Play (PnP)   With plug-and-play devices, computer users do not have to tell the computer that the device is there. The operating system should be able to recognize the device and set it up automatically. Plug and play has been available for Macintosh computers for quite some time, and has been incorporated into Microsoft's Windows operating systems. Linux is a little behind on this technology. Linux is able to configure ISA PnP devices (isapnp utility) and PCI PnP. The unfortunate truth is that Linux doesn't handle plug and play well.

Pluggable Authentic Module (PAM)   PAM is not very useful on a single user environment or where the users are trusted, but it is perfect to a multiuser system where users are not trusted. PAM allows for more granularity in defining security. You can use PAM to control access to certain resources with means that are not actually coded into the program. PAM consists of a set of dynamically loadable library modules that allow you, as the system administrator, use to determine how applications perform user authentication. The idea behind PAM is to separate the process of authenticating users from the development of an application.

PnP   See Plug and Play

Point Of Presence (POP)   The point in a WAN where the local phone call provides access to the network. It has very basic commands including retrieve and send messages. A mail service can be configured to be a central depository (POP) for incoming mail messages from any other MTA service. Client applications then download the mail messages off the POP server for processing at the local host. The ipop3d daemon service handles all requests.

Point-to-Point Protocol (PPP)   One of two standards for dial-up telephone connection of computers to the Internet. PPP has better data negotiation, compression, and error corrections than SLIP but costs more to transmit data. PPP is unnecessary when both sending and receiving modems can handle some of the procedures.

POP   See Point Of Presence

POSIX   POSIX defines a minimum interface for UNIX-type operating systems. Linux currently supports POSIX 1003.1. This ensures that POSIX-compliant UNIX programs will port easily to Linux.

PPP   See Point-to-Point Protocol

Preamble entries   Preamble entries consist of a tag, followed by a colon, followed by information. Some entries are language specific; these are denoted by a two-letter country code in parentheses just before the colon. The order of the lines is unimportant.

Prefdm   Prefdm is a link that points to the proffered display manager. This is typically xdm, kdm, or gdm. Xdm is X Windows default window manager, Kdm is KDE's window manager and gdm is Gnome's window manager.

Prep section   The prep section prepares the source files for packaging. Usually the prep section starts out by removing the leftovers from any previous builds and unarchives the source files.

Pretty Good Privacy (PGP)   A cryptographic software package designed by Phil Zimmerman that uses RSA cryptographic methods. PGP provides a user-friendly, secure private and public key system for your e-mail client.

Primary partition   Due to a design in the early stages of the PC and the DOS operating system, you are restricted to a maximum of four primary partitions, (a special type of primary partition). Each of the other three primary partitions can represent one logical drive.

Private key   Your private key (essentially a file containing your special number) must be maintained as your secret. You, or your applications, "attach it" to your program(s), and these programs use it on your behalf. Anything you send, say from your e-mail account, can then be digitally signed (data encrypted, checksum thereof encrypted with your public key and added to the end as your signature), and ONLY the recipient will be able to decrypt the message.

/proc The /proc filesystem is the Linux *virtual* filesystem. *Virtual* means that it doesn't occupy real disk space. Instead, files are created on the fly when you access them. /proc is used to provide information on kernel configuration and device status.

proc Proc is a directory that is virtual. It doesn't actually exist on the hard drive. All of its information is maintained by the kernel. This is a great source of information of what your kernel is doing. It also has many kernel variables that you can change to instantly change how the kernel is acting.

Process IDentifier (PID) A nonpermanent number created by a computer's operating system for a variety of internal purposes.

PS/2 mice A PS/2 mouse (used on newer PCs and on most laptops) has its own port and uses IRQ 12. A PS/2 mouse uses a 6-pin mini DIN connector and communicates using the PS/2 protocol. The device file for PS/2 mice is /dev/psaux.

Public key Your public key value is just that, publicly available. A certificate authority, like Verisign or Thawte, provides public access to public keys they have created. The authority keeps a copy of the private key securely on its system if it generated it. You can just attach your public key to the e-mail, or the end users can publicly retrieve it from some CA site; it does not matter. They can only decrypt the message with their e-mail account and this public key.

QNX An operating system from QNX Software Systems which uses less memory with quicker response times.

Query mode One of the strengths of RPM is that, ideally, every system or application file on your system is accounted for. Using RPM's query mode, you can determine which packages are installed on your system, or what file belongs to a particular package. This can be a big help if you want to locate a file that belongs to a certain package. Query mode can also be used to identify what files are in an RPM file before you install it. This lets you see what files are going to be installed on your system before they're actually written.

RAID See Redundant Array of Independent Disks

rc.sysinit script   The rc.sysinit script runs almost all crucial system-dependent bootup operations.

rdate   A much more simplistic way of setting the date from a network server is rdate. rdate uses TCP to retrieve the current time of another machine using port 13, as described in RFC 868. The time for each system is returned in ctime format (Sun Oct 17 20:36:19 1999). The default mode for rdate simply prints the time as taken from the requested server. The command rdate www will return the date from the server on the local subnet named www. Adding the -s option to the command line and running rdate as root will set the local system clock to the time retrieved from the server. rdate is not as accurate as NTP and has the disadvantage of setting the system clock backward if the reported time is earlier than the current system time. Some applications such as databases may suffer serious consequences if they perceive "negative time." NTP is therefore recommended for general use.

Red Hat Hardware List   The Red Hat Hardware List is specific to all hardware that has been tested on systems running Red Hat Linux. Red Hat will provide installation support for any hardware that is listed as "supported." There is also an "unsupported" list. This list does not necessarily mean that the specified hardware will not run on Linux; it just means that Red Hat will not provide installation support for that hardware.

Red Hat Package Manager (RPM)   With RPM, software is managed in discrete packages, a collection of the files that make up the software, and instructions for adding, removing, and upgrading those files. RPM also makes sure that you never lose configuration files by backing up existing files before overwriting. RPM also tracks which version of an application is currently installed on your system. A key feature of RPM is that filenames can be specified in URL format. RPM packages are often identified by filenames that usually consist of the package name, the version, the release, and the architecture for which they were built. RPM also maintains an MD5 checksum of each file. *See also* Source RPM.

Redundant Array of Independent Disks (RAID)   RAID can be set up in Linux using either hardware or software. The tradeoffs between them are performance versus price. Hardware implementations are more expensive than software implementations but typically provide higher performance. The hardware implementation of RAID uses a RAID controller connected to an array of several hard disks. You must install a driver to be able to use the controller. Linux offers a software solution to RAID with the md kernel patch. You should use Linux kernel 2.0.36 or a recent 2.2.*x* version. Once you have configured RAID on your system, Linux can use it just as it would any other block device.

Redundant Array of Independent Disks 0 (RAID-0)   Reads and writes to the hard disks are done in parallel, increasing performance, but filling up all hard drives equally. There is no redundancy in this level, a failure of any one of the drives will result in total data loss. This level is used for speed increases. The limit to the speed of a RAID-0 system is the bus speed that connects to the disks. RAID-0 is also called Striping without parity. RAID level 0 provides access to 100 percent of all disks used and offers better performance with no recovery.

Redundant Array of Independent Disks 1 (RAID-1)   In a process known as mirroring, this level mirrors information to two or more other disks. If one disk is damaged/removed, all data will still be intact and accessible from the other disk(s) available. Also, if any spare disks exist in the system, they can be used as another mirror to replace a missing or damaged drive. While performance may actually be decreased in this level (writes), reliability is greatly increased. RAID level 1 provides the least usable space as all disks participating in the mirror contain a complete copy of the data. However, recovery is as good as read performance.

Redundant Array of Independent Disks 4 (RAID-4)   This level requires three or more disks. Like RAID-0, data reads and writes are done in parallel to all disks. One of the disks in the set maintains only parity information on all the data. If one drive fails, then the parity information can be used to reconstruct the data. Reliability is improved, but since parity information is updated with every write operation, the parity disk can be a bottleneck on the system.

Redundant Array of Independent Disks 5 (RAID-5)   RAID-5 works on three or more disks, with optional spare disks. With this level, several disks can be combined with both performance and reliability increases. Unlike RAID-4, parity information is striped across all the disks. Instead of dedicating one disk to store the parity information, it is distributed evenly across all disks. If one disk fails, the data can be reconstructed onto a spare disk or from the parity information. In either case, there is no stoppage of the RAID system, all data are still available, even with one disk failed. RAID level 5 is the preferred choice in most cases, the performance is good, the recovery is high and the cost is second best. You lose one disk out of the set essentially to parity, so with 5 disks in RAID level 5, you get 80 percent utilization for data, 20 percent for parity (recovery) information. With 32 disks, you get 31 of 32 disks for about 96 percent utilization.

Refresh rate   This is the rate at which the image you see on your screen is redrawn. The refresh rate is expressed in terms of Hertz (Hz). A refresh rate of 60 Hz means that an image is redrawn 60 times in one second. Computer monitors have both a vertical and a horizontal refresh rate. Some monitors, known as multisync monitors, support multiple vertical and horizontal refresh rates.

Remote Procedure Call (RPC)   Software tool developed by a consortium of manufacturers for developers who created distributed applications that automatically generates code for both client and server.

Reverse (inverse) zone   A reverse (inverse) zone is used by many servers of different kinds (FTP, IRC, WWW, and others) to decide if they want to talk to a given server or not, and if so, maybe even how much priority it should be given. It makes the DNS able to convert from an address to a name. For full access to all services on the Internet, a reverse zone is required.

Ritchie, Dennis   Around 1969, he was working on a new computer language called C. By 1974, he and Ken Thompson had rewritten UNIX in the C language, and ported it to several different machines. Linux owes its heritage to this combination of UNIX and C.

Router   The node that determines how best to transfer a message from one station to another, based on the address provided by the sending station. Unlike a bridge, the router services packets or frames containing certain protocols and can handle multiple protocol stacks simultaneously. Routers can connect networks that use different topologies and protocols.

Routing table   A list of rules used by any system using Internet protocols. The routing table uses to determine where to send packets. Each entry in the routing table contains at least three fields. The first field is a destination address. If a packet's destination address matches this field, then this rule will be used to forward the packet. The second field is the interface to which the packet will be sent. The third field is optional and contains the address of a router that will route the packet further along its journey across the network. Keeping routing tables current and accurate on all the systems on a network is crucial to keeping the network running.

RPC   See Remote Procedure Call

RPM   See Red Hat Package Manager

Runlevel   A runlevel is defined as a group of activities.

Samba   Starting with Windows Version 3.11, Windows clients could "share" their file systems and printers for other Windows clients to "map to" as remote resources. This sharing was provided through a facility called SMB. Linux systems provide SMB support over TCP/IP via a package known as Samba. Samba services provide interoperability between the Microsoft Windows network clients and Linux (or any Unix, for that matter) clients. You need to have a basic understanding of how Microsoft Windows Networking works in the TCP/IP realm.

SCSI   See Small Computer System Interface

Secure NFS   Since about 1990, Sun and other vendors have supported versions of NFS using public-key–based strong authentication. Secure NFS has proven itself extremely tedious and complex to administer, and is still not sufficient to keep data safe in hostile environments. As a result, Secure NFS is rarely used outside of specialized government installations.

Sendmail   Most of your e-mail is passed across the Internet using Sendmail, a free program written by Eric Allman in 1979.

Sequenced Packet eXchange (SPX)   The NetWare communications protocol controlling network message transport.

Serial Line Internet Protocol (SLIP)   This is the standard for how a workstation or personal computer can dial up a link to the Internet. It defines the transport of data packets through an asynchronous telephone line, allowing computers not part of a LAN to be fully connected to the Internet.

Serial mice   To use a serial mouse, you might need to assign it an IRQ if you are using more than three serial devices. Otherwise, it's just a matter of selecting the correct protocol for the mouse to use. Common protocols are Microsoft for Microsoft mice; and Logitech for Logitech mice.

Server   A computer that makes printer and communication services available to other network stations.

Server installation   The server installation will give you a fast and easy way (with some loss of flexibility in configuration) to set up a Web, FTP, or other type of server-class system.

Server Message Block (SMB)   The SMB is a protocol used by Windows for Workgroups, Windows 95, Windows NT, and OS/2 LAN Manager to share printers and files remotely.

Server-class installation   A server-class installation requires 650MB for a minimal installation and at least 1.2GB of free space if every package is selected.

Session aware   The ability for the application to remember the location in the document where you were last working and, thus, reposition your cursor to that point when you restart the application.

Simple Internet Protocol Plus (SIPP)   An SMDS interface protocol, one of three Internet Protocol ng (Ipng) candidates.

Simple Mail Transfer Protocol (SMTP)   A U.S. Department of Defense (DoD) standard for electronic mail systems that have both host and user selections. User software is often included in TCP/IP packages; host software is available for exchanging SMTP mail with mail from proprietary systems.

Single-user mode   The single-user mode option is available to you if you are experiencing system problems. Your system may not have problems finding its root partition and starting the boot process but may encounter problems when changing into one of the higher runlevels. If this is the case, you can still use the boot partition and root partition on your hard drive, but you want to tell Linux to perform a minimal boot process.

SIPP   See Simple Internet Protocol Plus

SLIP   See Serial Line Internet Protocol

Small Computer System Interface (SCSI)   SCSI, developed by Apple Computer, allows your computer to interface to disk drives, CD-ROMs, tape drives, printers, and scanners. SCSI is faster and more flexible than (E)IDE, with support for up to 7, 15, or even 32 devices, depending on the SCSI bus width. Data transfer speeds for SCSI range from 5 to 160 or 320MB per second. SCSI controllers are not common on most modern day desktop PCs, as SCSI disks are usually more expensive. The major PC vendors will almost always provide SCSI disks and controllers for their high-end server products, as the larger number of devices and faster bus speeds make them a better choice.

SMB   See Server Message Block

SMTP   See Simple Mail Transfer Protocol

SOA   See Start of Authority

Soft limit   This is the maximum amount of space a user can have on that partition. If you have set a grace period then this will act as the borderline threshold. The user will then be notified that they are in quota violation.

Source RPM (SRPM)　SRPMs are, as the name indicates, the source codes used to build architecture-specific packages. SRPMs are identified with the string "src" appearing where the architecture indicator normally appears. The SRPM contains the source code and specifications necessary to create the binary RPM. Like normal RPMs, an SRPM is installed using the - i option. This will place the contents of the SRPM within the /usr/src/redhat directory structure.

Spec file　To change the compile options in an SRPM, you must understand spec files. The spec file controls the way a package is built, and what actions are performed when it is installed or removed from a system. There are eight different sections in a spec file.

SPX　See Sequenced Packet eXchange

Squid　Squid is a high-performance HTTP and FTP caching proxy server. It conforms to the Harvest Cache architecture and uses the ICP for transfers between participating peer and parent/child cache servers. It can be used either as a traditional caching proxy, or as a front-end accelerator for a traditional Web server. Squid accepts only HTTP requests, but speaks FTP on the server side when FTP objects are requested. Squid is most useful for reducing bandwidth utilization (via cache hits) and load-leveling (via having better-connected parents request objects and then feed them back to bandwidth-limited downstream clients).

Stallman, Richard M.　See HURD

Start of Authority (SOA)　The SOA record is the preamble to all zone files, and there should be exactly one in each zone file. It describes the zone, where it comes from (a machine called ns.your-domain.com), who is responsible for its contents (hostmaster@your-domain.com, insert the proper e-mail address here), what version of the zone file this is (serial: 1), and other things having to do with caching and secondary DNS servers. For the rest of the fields (refresh, retry, expire, and minimum), the numbers described here are safe, but the files should be individualized for each network.

startx The startx command to start the X Window interface manually from a command-line prompt.

Statelessness Unlike most other file-sharing protocols, NFS is designed to be (at least theoretically) completely "stateless." Thus, there is not a separate login phase prior to gaining access to NFS resources. Instead, the NFS client contacts rpc.mountd on the server, which checks the request against currently exported file systems and provides an *NFS file handle* (a hard-to-guess magic cookie) used for subsequent I/O. The advantage of this stateless protocol is that if the server must be rebooted, the client can simply wait for it to come back up without any of its software failing. The stateless concept, however, does not work well when insecure single-user clients are involved, makes file locking very complex and is counterintuitive to most people trained on other file-sharing technologies.

Static routes Static routes are entries that you enter to the routing tables manually. If your network is small, if your network configuration doesn't change very frequently, or if your system is an end system, static routes can be adequate for managing your routing configuration. You manage static routes using the route command.

Stripe mode Also called Redundant Array of Inexpensive Disks Level One (RAID-0).

Super Video Graphics Array VGA (SVGA) An enhancement of the VGA display standard for IBM personal computers that can display at least 800 pixels horizontally and 600 lines vertically, and up to 1,024 pixels by 768 lines with 16 or 256 colors; it can use as much as 1MB of video memory.

Swap file A file used to store instructions and data that do not fit in RAM.

Swatch utility The swatch utility monitors log files for certain types of messages and takes action when certain events occur. You configure the events to monitor and the type of action to take. The action can be as simple as sending a message to your terminal, or something more involved such as calling a pager number. By default, swatch looks for its configuration information in the hidden file .swatchrc in your home directory. The package file for the swatch utility is swatch-2.2-7.noarch.rpm.

Switchdesk   A utility which easily switches your default desktop from one environment to another.

Symbolic links   Symbolic links over NFS are interpreted by the client, not the server. Thus, any absolute symbolic links are evaluated starting at the root directory of the client, usually leading to somewhere else on the client, which is often not what is expected or desired. This problem should generally be worked around via the thoughtful use of relative symbolic links inside exported file systems. There is also a server-side export option (*link_relative*) that automatically converts absolute symbolic links to relative; this can have nonintuitive results if the client mounts a subdirectory of the exported directory.

Syslinux   During installation, you will see another loader called Syslinux.n.m-x. This is an MS-DOS based loader and is used on all the installation images because it is small enough to fit on a floppy and boot a basic Linux kernel.

Tape ARchive (TAR)   A Unix utility for archiving files most often in conjunction with the compress utility.

TCP/IP   See Transmission Control Protocol/Internet Protocol

TELNET   A virtual terminal protocol from the U.S. Department of Defense (DoD) that interfaces terminal devices and terminal-oriented processes (MIL-STD-1782).

Thompson, Ken   In 1969, a Bell Labs programmer named Ken Thompson invented the UNIX operating system. By 1974, he and Dennis Ritchie had rewritten UNIX in the C language, and ported it to several different machines. It is this combination of UNIX and C to which Linux owes its heritage.

timeconfig   The timeconfig utility allows you to set your time zone. If your system clock is set to Greenwich Mean Time (GMT), select the Hardware Clock Set To GMT entry. You can use your arrow, PGUP, and PGDN keys to traverse the list of time zones. Highlight the proper time zone and press the RETURN key to accept the new setting or the ESC key to exit without saving. Changes made here are saved to the /etc/sysconfig/clock file.

tmpwatch   The *tmpwatch* command (*/usr/sbin/tmpwatch*) is used to remove files that have not been accessed in a specified number of hours. As its name implies, you normally run it on directories such as */tmp* and */var/tmp*. The *tmpwatch* command works recursively, so if you specify the top-level directory in a tree, *tmpwatch* will search through the entire directory tree looking for files to remove.

Token Ring   LAN technology that circulates a special message (the token) among network nodes, giving them permission to transmit.

Transmission Control Protocol/Internet Protocol (TCP/IP)   TCP/IP is a set of communcations standards created by the U.S. Department of Defense (DoD) in the 1970s that has now become an accepted way to connect different types of computers in networks.

Transparent proxy support   Transparent proxy support allows for the router to secretly forward packets to a proxy server.

UDP   See User Datagram Protocol

UFS   The standard filesystem for BSD and BSD derivatives, SunOS, and NeXTstep.

UMSDOS   UMSDOS allows you to run Linux from a DOS partition (not currently supported by Red Hat).

UNFSD   See Universal NFS Daemon

Uniform Resource Locator (URL)   A string of characters precisely identifying the type and location of an Internet resource, one of two basic kinds of URIs and the standard way to find a resource.

Uninterruptible Power Supply (UPS)   The UPS is a battery that can supply continuous power to a computer system if the power fails; it charges while the computer is on and if the power fails, it provides power allowing the user to shut down the computer properly to preserve crucial data.

Universal NFS Daemon (UNFSD)   UNFSD NFS server runs as a user-mode process, as opposed to the kernel. This provides some advantages in terms of flexibility, but tremendous disadvantages in performance and scalability. A UNFSD can effectively handle only one or two clients even on a strong server; even with a single client, throughput is a fraction of what it would be on the same server using a kernel-mode NFS daemon. Bottlenecks in UNFSD include the filename lookups, extra copies between kernel and user address space, and a single-threaded NFS daemon.

Universal Time Coordinated (UTC)   Formerly GMT, which is the international time standard.

Unix-to-Unix Copy Program (UUCP)   A standard utility for exchanging information between two Unix nodes, allowing Unix users to exchange files, electronic mail, and UseNet articles via long-distance telephone uploads and downloads.

UPS   See Uninterruptible Power Supply

URL   See Uniform Resource Locator

UseNet   UseNet is the news distribution and bulletin board channel of the UUCP, the international WAN that links Unix computers.

User Datagram Protocol (UDP)   A TCP/IP normally bundled with an Internet Protocol layer software that describes how messages received reach application programs within the destination computer.

User process accounting   The original intent behind user process accounting tools was to provide a mechanism for IS departments to keep track of the resources each account on a system used so charges could be billed back to the account owner.

With the accounting utilities you can track such useful information as when your system was last rebooted, the last time a particular user account logged in, and the specific commands a user executed.

UTC   See Universal Time Coordinated

UUCP   See Unix-to-Unix Copy Program

VFAT   VFAT allows you to read Windows 95 partitions

Virtual desktop   The virtual desktop allows the area where you can place windows to be larger than the area of your display hardware.

Virtual Memory System (VMS)   An operating system for VAX computers with multiusers and multitasking requirements.

VMS   See Virtual Memory System

VMWare   To have Windows and Linux running simultaneously, you need a virtual memory management system that allows the first booted OS (host OS) to provide a separate virtual memory space that the other OS (guest OS) can run simultaneously. One excellent product is VMWare for providing guest OS support as just another Windows application in NT or NT2000. You install the VMWare application into your Windows system, and then you install Linux into this virtual site. It will even create virtual disk space out of unused disk space so you do not have to have free partition space. This also works with Linux as the Host and NT as the guest OS, in case you want to try it that way as well.

WebNFS   WebNFS, another Sun-designed variant of NFS, is intended for Internet use. It differs from ordinary NFS in that clients do not have to "mount" the file systems, and they receive only read-only access. It may be suitable for publishing data to the public in a transparent manner, but is rarely used.

Window manager   The window manager is a special type of X client. A window manager cannot run on its own; it needs the services of an X server to do its job. It is the job of the window manager to control how other X clients appear on your display. This includes everything from placing title bars and drawing borders around the window for each X client application you start to determining the size of your desktop.

Winmodem   Winmodems are modems that handle processing on the system through proprietary interfaces. Because these interfaces are generally not published, Linux has little or no support for these devices.

Write-back buffer cache   Write-back buffer cache is used by most multiuser operating systems such as Linux, UNIX, NT and VMS to name a few. This second type is also referred to as lazy write. The system maintains the file changes in memory and when some CPU cycles free up, writes all file changes to the disk. The actual writes to the disk are done at a later time, usually in the background, so as not to slow down other programs. Though write-through cache is less efficient in terms of CPU cycles, write-back cache is more susceptible to errors.

Write-through buffer cache   With write-through buffer cache, any changes to blocks of data in the cache are written to the disk at once. Early MS-DOS OS versions used this immediate write of data to disk style of memory management. Though write-through cache is less efficient in terms of CPU cycles, write-back cache is more susceptible to errors.

X Display   The X Display is also considered a virtual window and is assigned to the next numbered console after the text based consoles. By default, there are six virtual consoles configured with Linux, and so the X Display would be assigned to console seven. However, within the Gnome or KDE, if multiple virtual desktops are configured, you switch between these multiple desktops by pressing ALT-Fn, where n is the number of the desktop. For four virtual desktops, you have ALT-F1 (=top left), ALT-F2 (=top right), ALT-F3 (bottom left) and ALT-F4 (bottom right) for quick access. The number of X Display desktops is configurable but defaults to four.

X.25   A CCITT standard for computer access to and data handling in a packet switched network.

Xconfigurator program   The Xconfigurator program is a character-based GUI that leads you through a series of menus aiding you in configuring your video hardware. The Xconfigurator program will automatically probe your video card and try to pick the appropriate X server image for it. If Xconfigurator cannot determine what make of card you have, then you must select your video card from the list of video cards supported under Red Hat Linux 6.0.

XDR   See eXternal Data Representation

XNTP   XNTP is a complete implementation of the NTP Version 3 specification, as defined in RFC 1305. The approach used by NTP to achieve reliable time synchronization from a set of possibly unreliable remote timeservers is somewhat different from other protocols. In particular, NTP does not attempt to synchronize clocks to each other. Rather, each server attempts to synchronize to UTC using the best available source and available transmission paths to that source.

X server   The X server is the component of the X Window system that you run on your desktop. The X server is responsible for drawing images on your screen, getting input from your keyboard and mouse, and controlling access to your display.

xterm application   xterm is an X client application that creates a terminal window on your X display. So, after all the hard work you've gone through to get a nice windowing display, you're right back where you started, with a command-line interface.

X window clients   X Window clients, or X clients, are the application programs you run that use the windowing services provided by your X server to display their output. You run one X server process to control your display. In contrast, you can run as many X clients as your hardware resources, primarily RAM, will support.

X Window system   X Window system is the GUI for Linux. Unlike other operating systems in which the GUI interface is an integral part of the operating system itself, the X Window system is not a part of Red Hat Linux but is a layered application. Thus, you can have a fully functioning Linux system without running the X Window interface.

INDEX

G

S

INTERNATIONAL CONTACT INFORMATION

AUSTRALIA
McGraw-Hill Book Company Australia Pty. Ltd.
TEL +61-2-9417-9899
FAX +61-2-9417-5687
http://www.mcgraw-hill.com.au
books-it_sydney@mcgraw-hill.com

CANADA
McGraw-Hill Ryerson Ltd.
TEL +905-430-5000
FAX +905-430-5020
http://www.mcgrawhill.ca

**GREECE, MIDDLE EAST,
NORTHERN AFRICA**
McGraw-Hill Hellas
TEL +30-1-656-0990-3-4
FAX +30-1-654-5525

MEXICO (Also serving Latin America)
McGraw-Hill Interamericana Editores S.A. de C.V.
TEL +525-117-1583
FAX +525-117-1589
http://www.mcgraw-hill.com.mx
fernando_castellanos@mcgraw-hill.com

SINGAPORE (Serving Asia)
McGraw-Hill Book Company
TEL +65-863-1580
FAX +65-862-3354
http://www.mcgraw-hill.com.sg
mghasia@mcgraw-hill.com

SOUTH AFRICA
McGraw-Hill South Africa
TEL +27-11-622-7512
FAX +27-11-622-9045
robyn_swanepoel@mcgraw-hill.com

**UNITED KINGDOM & EUROPE
(Excluding Southern Europe)**
McGraw-Hill Education Europe
TEL +44-1-628-502500
FAX +44-1-628-770224
http://www.mcgraw-hill.co.uk
computing_neurope@mcgraw-hill.com

ALL OTHER INQUIRIES Contact:
Osborne/McGraw-Hill
TEL +1-510-549-6600
FAX +1-510-883-7600
http://www.osborne.com
omg_international@mcgraw-hill.com

Custom Corporate Network Training

Train on Cutting Edge Technology
We can bring the best in skill-based training to your facility to create a real-world hands-on training experience. Global Knowledge has invested millions of dollars in network hardware and software to train our students on the same equipment they will work with on the job. Our relationships with vendors allow us to incorporate the latest equipment and platforms into your on-site labs.

Maximize Your Training Budget
Global Knowledge provides experienced instructors, comprehensive course materials, and all the networking equipment needed to deliver high quality training. You provide the students; we provide the knowledge.

Avoid Travel Expenses
On-site courses allow you to schedule technical training at your convenience, saving time, expense, and the opportunity cost of travel away from the workplace.

Discuss Confidential Topics
Private on-site training permits the open discussion of sensitive issues such as security, access, and network design. We can work with your existing network's proprietary files while demonstrating the latest technologies.

Customize Course Content
Global Knowledge can tailor your courses to include the technologies and the topics which have the greatest impact on your business. We can complement your internal training efforts or provide a total solution to your training needs.

Corporate Pass
The Corporate Pass Discount Program rewards our best network training customers with preferred pricing on public courses, discounts on multimedia training packages, and an array of career planning services.

Global Knowledge Training Lifecycle
Supporting the Dynamic and Specialized Training Requirements of Information Technology Professionals

- Define Profile
- Assess Skills
- Design Training
- Deliver Training
- Test Knowledge
- Update Profile
- Use New Skills

College Credit Recommendation Program
The American Council on Education's CREDIT program recommends 53 Global Knowledge courses for college credit. Now our network training can help you earn your college degree while you learn the technical skills needed for your job. When you attend an ACE-certified Global Knowledge course and pass the associated exam, you earn college credit recommendations for that course. Global Knowledge can establish a transcript record for you with ACE, which you can use to gain credit at a college or as a written record of your professional training that you can attach to your resume.

Registration Information

COURSE FEE: The fee covers course tuition, refreshments, and all course materials. Any parking expenses that may be incurred are not included. Payment or government training form must be received six business days prior to the course date. We will also accept Visa/MasterCard and American Express. For non-U.S. credit card users, charges will be in U.S. funds and will be converted by your credit card company. Checks drawn on Canadian banks in Canadian funds are acceptable.

COURSE SCHEDULE: Registration is at 8:00 a.m. on the first day. The program begins at 8:30 a.m. and concludes at 4:30 p.m. each day.

CANCELLATION POLICY: Cancellation and full refund will be allowed if written cancellation is received in our office at least six business days prior to the course start date. Registrants who do not attend the course or do not cancel more than six business days in advance are responsible for the full registration fee; you may transfer to a later date provided the course fee has been paid in full. Substitutions may be made at any time. If Global Knowledge must cancel a course for any reason, liability is limited to the registration fee only.

GLOBAL KNOWLEDGE: Global Knowledge programs are developed and presented by industry professionals with "real-world" experience. Designed to help professionals meet today's interconnectivity and interoperability challenges, most of our programs feature hands-on labs that incorporate state-of-the-art communication components and equipment.

ON-SITE TEAM TRAINING: Bring Global Knowledge's powerful training programs to your company. At Global Knowledge, we will custom design courses to meet your specific network requirements. Call 1 (919) 461-8686 for more information.

YOUR GUARANTEE: Global Knowledge believes its courses offer the best possible training in this field. If during the first day you are not satisfied and wish to withdraw from the course, simply notify the instructor, return all course materials, and receive a 100% refund.

In the US:

CALL: 1 (888) 762-4442

FAX: 1 (919) 469-7070

VISIT OUR WEBSITE:

www.globalknowledge.com

MAIL CHECK AND THIS FORM TO:

Global Knowledge

Suite 200

114 Edinburgh South

P.O. Box 1187

Cary, NC 27512

In Canada:

CALL: 1 (800) 465-2226

FAX: 1 (613) 567-3899

VISIT OUR WEBSITE:

www.globalknowledge.com.ca

MAIL CHECK AND THIS FORM TO:

Global Knowledge

Suite 1601

393 University Ave.

Toronto, ON M5G 1E6

REGISTRATION INFORMATION:

Course title _____

Course location _____ Course date _____

Name/title _____ Company _____

Name/title _____ Company _____

Name/title _____ Company _____

Address _____ Telephone _____ Fax _____

City _____ State/Province _____ Zip/Postal Code _____

Credit card _____ Card # _____ Expiration date _____

Signature _____